A & AS

Chemistry

The Complete Course for OCR A

Let's face it, Chemistry is a tough subject. You'll need to get to grips with a lot of difficult concepts, and have plenty of practical skills up your lab-coat sleeve.

But don't worry — this brilliant CGP book covers everything you'll need for the new OCR A courses. It's packed with clear explanations, exam practice, advice on maths skills and practical investigations... and much more!

It even includes a free Online Edition to read on your PC, Mac or tablet.

How to get your free Online Edition

Go to **cgpbooks.co.uk/extras** and enter this code...

1243 1377 5148 8734

This code will only work once. If someone has used this book before you, they may have already claimed the Online Edition.

Contents

How to use this book

Learning Objectives

- These tell you exactly what you need to learn, or be able to do, for the exam.
- There's a specification reference at the bottom that links to the OCR A specification.

Exam Tips

There are tips throughout the book to help with all sorts of things to do with answering exam questions.

Tips

These are here to help you understand the theory.

---

4. Structural Isomers

You can put the same atoms together in different ways to make completely different molecules. Two molecules are isomers if they have the same molecular formula but the atoms are arranged differently.

What are structural isomers?

In structural isomers, the molecular formula is the same, but the structural formula is different. There are three different types of structural isomer.

1. Chain isomers

The carbon skeleton can be arranged differently — for example, as a straight chain, or branched in different ways. Molecules that have different arrangements of the carbon skeleton are called **chain isomers**.

Examples — Maths Skills

There are different chain isomers of C_4H_{10}. The diagrams below show the straight chain isomer butane and a branched chain isomer methylpropane.

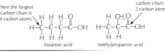

Here the longest carbon chain is 4 carbon atoms. butane   methylpropane *Here the longest carbon chain is 3 carbon atoms.*

There are different chain isomers of $C_4H_8O_2$. The diagrams below show the straight chain isomer butanoic acid and a branched chain isomer methylpropanoic acid.

Here the longest carbon chain is 4 carbon atoms. butanoic acid   methylpropanoic acid *Here the longest carbon chain is 3 carbon atoms.*

Chain isomers have similar chemical properties — but their physical properties, like boiling point, will be different because of the change in shape of the molecule.

2. Positional isomers

The skeleton and the functional group could be the same, only with the functional group attached to a different carbon atom. These are called **positional isomers**.

Example — Maths Skills

There are two positional isomers of C_4H_9Cl. The chlorine atom is attached to different carbon atoms in each isomer.

1-chlorobutane   *The Cl is attached to the first carbon atom.*

Figure 1: Molecular models showing two chain isomers of C_4H_{10} — butane (left) and methylpropane (right).

Exam Tip
You don't always have to draw all of the bonds when you're drawing a molecule — writing CH_3 next to a bond is just as good as drawing out the carbon atom, three bonds and three hydrogen atoms. But if you're asked for a displayed formula you <u>must</u> draw out all of the bonds to get the marks.

Tip: If the chlorine atom was attached to the carbon atom on the left, it would still be the <u>same molecule</u> — just drawn the other way round. It would still be 1-chlorobutane.

196   Module 4: Section 1 Basic Concepts and Hydrocarbons

---

10. Tests for Ions

PRACTICAL ACTIVITY GROUP **4**

If you're given something and asked to find out what's in it, there are loads of different tests that you can do — here are just a few...

False positives

When you're carrying out tests to identify an unknown substance you need to be wary of creating false positive results. A false positive is a result that suggests that a particular ion is present when it actually isn't. This can happen if there are ions present that will interfere with the test you are carrying out. To prevent false positive you can sometimes add a substance to your sample to remove problematic ions. You also need to be careful about what substances you add during the test — it's important not to add any ions that will lead to false positives. To help prevent false positives, you should do the three tests below in the following order:

Test for carbonates ⟶ Test for sulfates ⟶ Test for halides

Test for carbonates

If you have an unknown solution and you want to test it for carbonates (CO_3^{2-}), add a dilute strong acid (e.g. dilute nitric acid or dilute hydrochloric acid). If carbonates are present then carbon dioxide will be released. The ionic equation for the reaction of a carbonate and an acid is:

$$CO_3^{2-}{}_{(s)} + 2H^+{}_{(aq)} \rightarrow CO_2{}_{(g)} + H_2O_{(l)}$$
carbonate + acid → carbon dioxide + water

Example

Calcium carbonate reacts with hydrochloric acid to produce carbon dioxide, water and calcium chloride. The equation for this reaction is:

$$CaCO_3{}_{(s)} + 2HCl_{(aq)} \rightarrow CO_2{}_{(g)} + H_2O_{(l)} + CaCl_2{}_{(aq)}$$

You can test to see if the gas produced is carbon dioxide using limewater. Figure 1 shows the apparatus needed for this test.

A bung to seal the test tube — this stops any gas escaping
Delivery tube takes any gas released into a test-tube of limewater.
Dilute hydrochloric acid and unknown solution.
Limewater.

Figure 1: Apparatus for carrying out a test for carbonate ions.

Any gas created by the reaction is delivered into limewater — if it's CO_2, then it'll react and turn the limewater cloudy (see Figure 2).

Tip: Think about any safety precautions you might need to consider before doing these tests.

Tip: Carrying out experiments and investigations correctly is an important part of scientific enquiry.

Figure 2: Limewater turns cloudy when carbon dioxide is added to it.

Module 3: Section 1 The Periodic Table   147

Practical Activity Groups

If you're doing the A-level Chemistry course you'll need to show you've mastered some key practical skills in your Practical Endorsement. Information on the skills you need and opportunities to apply them are marked up throughout the book.

Examples

These are here to help you understand the theory.

How Science Works

- You need to know about How Science Works. There's a section on it at the front of the book.
- How Science Works is also covered throughout the book wherever you see this symbol.

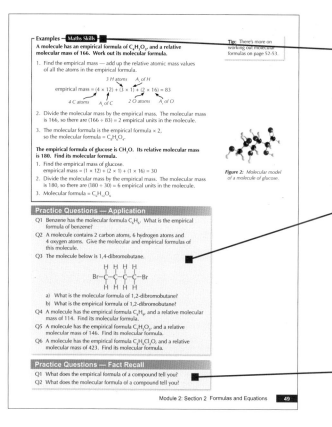

Maths Skills

There's a range of maths skills you could be expected to apply in your exams. Examples that show these maths skills in action are marked up like this. There's also a maths skills section at the back of the book.

Practice Questions — Application

- Annoyingly, the examiners expect you to be able to apply your knowledge to new situations — these questions are here to give you plenty of practice at doing this.

- All the answers are in the back of the book (including any calculation workings).

Practice Questions — Fact Recall

- There are a lot of facts you need to learn — these questions are here to test that you know them.

- All the answers are in the back of the book.

Exam-style Questions

- Practising exam-style questions is really important — you'll find some at the end of each section.

- They're the same style as the ones you'll get in the real exams — some will test your knowledge and understanding and some will test that you can apply your knowledge.

- All the answers are in the back of the book, along with a mark scheme to show you how you get the marks.

Exam Help

There's a section at the back of the book stuffed full of things to help with your exams.

Glossary

There's a glossary at the back of the book full of useful words — perfect for looking up key words and their meanings.

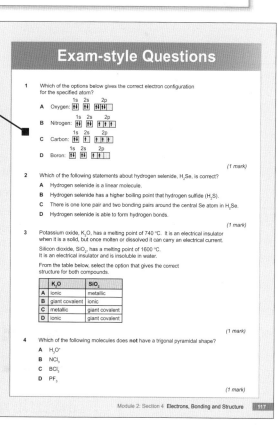

Published by CGP

Editors:
Katie Braid, Katherine Faudemer, Gordon Henderson, Emily Howe, Paul Jordin, Sophie Scott, Ben Train.

Contributors:
Vicky Cunningham, Ian H. Davis, John Duffy, Max Fishel, Lucy Muncaster, Derek Swain,
Paul Warren, Christopher Workman.

ISBN: 978 1 78294 322 8

With thanks to Barrie Crowther and Glenn Rogers for the proofreading.
With thanks to Jan Greenway for the copyright research.

OCR Specification reference points are adapted and reproduced by permission of OCR.

Graph to show trend in atmospheric CO_2 concentration and global temperature on page 250 based on data
by EPICA Community Members 2004 and Siegenthaler et al 2005.

Printed by Elanders Ltd, Newcastle upon Tyne.
Clipart from Corel®

The Scientific Process

Science tries to explain how and why things happen. It's all about seeking and gaining knowledge about the world around us. Scientists do this by asking questions and suggesting answers and then testing them, to see if they're correct — this is the scientific process.

Developing and testing theories

A **theory** is a possible explanation for something. Theories usually come about when scientists observe something and wonder why or how it happens. (Scientists also sometimes form a **model** too — a simplified picture or representation of a real physical situation.) Scientific theories and models are developed and tested in the following way:

Tip: A theory is only scientific if it can be tested.

- Ask a question — make an observation and ask why or how whatever you've observed happens.
- Suggest an answer, or part of an answer, by forming a theory or a model.
- Make a prediction or **hypothesis** — a specific testable statement, based on the theory, about what will happen in a test situation.
- Carry out tests — to provide evidence that will support the prediction or refute it.

⌐ Examples

Question: Why does sodium chloride dissolve in water?

Theory: Sodium chloride is made up of charged particles which are pulled apart by the polar water molecules.

Hypothesis: A solution of sodium chloride will conduct electricity much better than water does.

Test: Measure the conductivity of water and of sodium chloride solution.

Question: Why does changing the temperature affect the yield of a reversible reaction?

Theory: The equilibrium moves to counteract the change, favouring either the forward or reverse reaction, which increases the yield of this reaction and reduces the yield of the other.

Hypothesis: Increasing the temperature of an exothermic reversible reaction at equilibrium will decrease the yield, but for an endothermic reaction it will increase the yield.

Test: Measure the yield from exothermic and endothermic reversible reactions carried out at different temperatures. If the yield from the exothermic reactions decreases with increasing temperature, but the yield from the endothermic reactions increases with increasing temperature, then this evidence supports the hypothesis.

Figure 1: *Sodium chloride dissolving in water.*

Tip: The results of one test can't prove that a theory is true — they can only suggest that it's true. They can however disprove a theory — show that it's wrong.

PHILOSOPHICAL
TRANSACTIONS:
GIVING SOME
ACCOMP1
OF THE PRESENT
Undertakings , Studies , and Labours
OF THE
INGENIOUS
IN MANY
CONSIDERABLE PARTS
OF THE
WORLD·

Vol I.
For *Anno* 1665, and 1666.

In the *SAVOT* , ,
Printed by *T. N.* for *John Martyn* at the Bell, a little with-
out *Temple-Bar* , and *James Allestry* in *Duck-Lane* ;
Printers to the *Royal Society*.

***Figure 2:** The first British scientific journal, 'Philosophical Transactions of the Royal Society', published in 1665.*

Tip: Scientific research is often funded by companies who have a vested interest in its outcomes. Scientists are ethically obliged to make sure that this does not bias their results.

Tip: Once an experimental method is found to give good evidence it becomes a protocol — an accepted method to test that particular thing that all scientists can use.

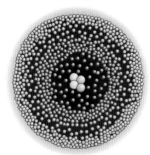

***Figure 3:** The quantum model of an atom — one of the current theories of atomic structure.*

Communicating results

The results of testing a scientific theory are published — scientists need to let others know about their work. Scientists publish their results in scientific journals. These are just like normal magazines, only they contain scientific reports (called papers) instead of the latest celebrity gossip.

Scientists use standard terminology when writing their reports. This way they know that other scientists will understand them. For instance, there are internationally agreed rules for naming organic compounds, so that scientists across the world will know exactly what substance is being referred to (see pages 199-200).

Scientific reports are similar to the lab write-ups you do in school. And just as a lab write-up is reviewed (marked) by your teacher, reports in scientific journals undergo **peer review** before they're published. The report is sent out to peers — other scientists who are experts in the same area. They go through it bit by bit, examining the methods and data, and checking it's all clear and logical. Thorough evaluation allows decisions to be made about what makes a good methodology or experimental technique. Individual scientists may have their own ethical codes (based on their humanistic, moral and religious beliefs), but having their work scrutinised by other scientists helps to reduce the effect of personal bias on the conclusions drawn from the results.

When the report is approved, it's published. This makes sure that work published in scientific journals is of a good standard. But peer review can't guarantee the science is correct — other scientists still need to reproduce it. Sometimes mistakes are made and bad work is published. Peer review isn't perfect but it's probably the best way for scientists to self-regulate their work and to publish quality reports.

Validating theories

Other scientists read the published theories and results, and try to test the theory themselves. This involves repeating the exact same experiments, using the theory to make new predictions, and then testing them with new experiments. This is known as **validation**. If all the experiments in the world provide evidence to back it up, the theory is thought of as scientific 'fact' (for now). If new evidence comes to light that conflicts with the current evidence the theory is questioned all over again. More rounds of testing will be carried out to try to find out where the theory falls down. This is how the scientific process works — evidence supports a theory, loads of other scientists read it and test it for themselves, eventually all the scientists in the world agree with it and then bingo, you get to learn it.

Example

The structure of the atom

It took years and years for the current model of the atom to be developed and accepted — this is often the case with the scientific process.

Dalton's theory in the early 1800s, that atoms were solid spheres, was disputed by the results of Thomson's experiments at the end of that century. As a result, Thomson developed the 'plum pudding' model of the atom, which was proven wrong by Rutherford's alpha scattering experiments in 1909. Rutherford's 'nuclear model' has since been developed and modified further to create the currently accepted model of the atom we use today — but scientists are still searching for more accurate models (see pages 30-32).

How do theories evolve?

Our currently accepted theories have survived this 'trial by evidence'. They've been tested over and over again and each time the results have backed them up. But they never become totally indisputable fact. Scientific breakthroughs or advances could provide new ways to question and test the theory, which could lead to changes and challenges to it. Then the testing starts all over again. This is the tentative nature of scientific knowledge — it's always changing and evolving.

Tip: Sometimes data from one experiment can be the starting point for developing a new theory.

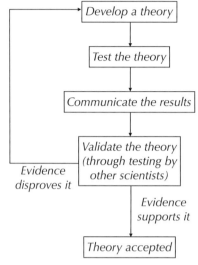

Figure 4: *Flow diagram summarising the scientific process.*

Example

CFCs and the ozone layer

When CFCs were first used in fridges in the 1930s, scientists thought they were problem-free — well, why not? There was no evidence to say otherwise. It was decades before anyone found out that CFCs were actually making a whopping great hole in the ozone layer (see page 247).

A couple of scientists developed a theory that CFCs were destroying ozone in the stratosphere, and this was tested, shared and validated by other scientists worldwide. The rigour of the scientific process meant that there was strong enough evidence against CFCs that governments could impose bans and restrictions in order to protect the ozone layer.

Figure 5: *Dumped fridges containing CFCs.*

Collecting evidence

1. Evidence from lab experiments

Results from controlled experiments in laboratories are great. A lab is the easiest place to control **variables** so that they're all kept constant (except for the one you're investigating). This means you can draw meaningful conclusions.

Tip: There's more about variables and drawing conclusions from lab experiments on pages 5 and 20 in the Development of Practical Skills section.

Example

Reaction rates

If you're investigating how temperature affects the rate of a reaction you need to keep everything but the temperature constant. This means controlling things like the pH of the solution, the concentration of the solution, etc. Otherwise there's no way of knowing if it's the change in temperature that's affecting the rate, or some other changing variable.

---

2. Investigations outside the lab

There are things you can't study in a lab. And outside the lab controlling the variables is tricky, if not impossible.

┌─ **Examples** ─────────────────────────

Are increasing CO_2 emissions causing climate change?

There are other variables which may have an effect, such as changes in solar activity. You can't easily rule out every possibility. Also, climate change is a very gradual process. Scientists won't be able to tell if their predictions are correct for donkey's years.

Does drinking chlorinated tap water increase the risk of developing certain cancers?

There are always differences between groups of people. The best you can do is to have a well-designed study using matched groups — choose two groups of people (those who drink tap water and those who don't) which are as similar as possible (same mix of ages, same mix of diets etc.). But you still can't rule out every possibility. Taking newborn identical twins and treating them identically, except for making one drink gallons of tap water and the other only pure water, might be a fairer test, but it would present huge ethical problems.

Figure 6: *Tap water can be chlorinated, but it's hard to design a fair and ethical test to measure its true effects.*

Tip: Don't get mixed up — it's not the scientists who make the decisions, it's society. Scientists just produce evidence to help society make the decisions.

Science and decision-making

Lots of scientific work eventually leads to important discoveries that could benefit humankind and improve everyone's quality of life. But there are often risks attached (and almost always financial costs). Society (that's you, me and everyone else) must weigh up the information in order to make decisions — about the way we live, what we eat, what we drive, and so on. Information can also be used by politicians to devise policies and laws. However, there is not always enough information available for society and politicians to be certain about the decisions made. The scientific evidence we do have can also be overshadowed by other influences such as personal bias and beliefs, public opinion, and the media. Decisions are also affected by social, ethical and economic factors.

┌─ **Examples** ─────────────────────────

Disinfecting water

Chlorine is added to water in small quantities to disinfect it (see page 145). Some studies link drinking chlorinated water with certain types of cancer. But the risks from drinking water contaminated by nasty bacteria are far, far greater. There are other ways to get rid of bacteria in water, but they're heaps more expensive.

Fuels for cars

Scientific advances mean that non-polluting hydrogen-fuelled cars can be made. They're better for the environment, but are really expensive. Also, it'd cost a fortune to adapt the existing filling stations to store hydrogen.

Developing drugs

Pharmaceutical drugs are really expensive to develop, and drug companies want to make money. So they put most of their efforts into developing drugs that they can sell for a good price. Society has to consider the cost of buying new drugs — the NHS can't afford the most expensive drugs without sacrificing something else.

Figure 7: *A hydrogen powered car being refuelled as part of a study into the use of hydrogen fuels.*

Practical Skills in Chemistry

Practicals and experiments crop up in every area of Chemistry and they can't be studied in isolation from the rest of your course. So this module draws on Chemistry knowledge that you'll learn in later modules. You should use it as a resource to help you apply the things you'll learn throughout the course in order to solve problems in a practical context.

1. Planning Experiments

You'll get to do loads of practicals in class during this course, which is great. Unfortunately, you can also get tested on how to carry out experiments in your exam. The first thing you need is a good plan...

Initial planning

It's really important to plan an experiment well if you want to get accurate and precise results. Before you even touch a piece of glassware, there are a few things you need to think about.

First, you have to identify what it is that you're trying to work out. This is the aim of your experiment. It could be something like 'how does the rate of this reaction change at different temperatures', or 'what is the concentration of this solution'. Once you know your aim, you can identify the independent, dependent and other **variables** (see below for more on variables). You can then decide what data you need to collect and how to collect it. This includes working out what equipment you'll need to use — it needs to be the right size and sensitivity so that your results are accurate.

Before you get going, there are two more things to do. The first is to make a risk assessment and plan any safety precautions. This ensures that you minimise the risk from any hazards there might be in your experiment, such as harmful chemicals. You should then write your whole plan down in a detailed method.

Variables

You probably know this all off by heart but it's easy to get mixed up sometimes. So here's a quick recap. A variable is a quantity that has the potential to change, e.g. mass. There are two types of variable commonly referred to in experiments:

> **Independent variable** — the thing that you change in an experiment.

> **Dependent variable** — the thing that you measure in an experiment.

As well as the independent and dependent variables, you need to think of all the other variables in your experiment and plan ways to keep each of those the same. This is to make sure that your test is fair, and any changes in your dependent variable are only due to changes in the independent variable.

Learning Objectives:

- Know how to design experiments, including to solve problems set in a practical context.
- Be able to identify variables that must be controlled, where appropriate.
- Be able to evaluate whether an experimental method is appropriate to meet the expected outcomes.

Specification Reference 1.1.1

Tip: Accurate results are close to the true answer. See page 21 for more on accurate and precise results.

Figure 2: Different coloured solutions. Colour is a type of categoric data.

─── Example ───

You could investigate the effect of temperature on rate of reaction using the apparatus in Figure 1 below:

Delivery tube — the gas produced travels through this from the conical flask into the gas syringe.

Gas syringe — to measure the volume of gas given off over time.

Thermometer — to check the temperature of the reaction mixture.

Figure 1: *Apparatus for measuring the rate of a reaction.*

- The independent variable will be temperature.
- The dependent variable will be the amount of gas produced.
- All the other variables must be kept the same. These include the concentration and volume of solutions, mass of solid, pressure, the presence of a catalyst and the surface area of any solid reactants.

Types of data

Experiments often involve some sort of measurement to provide data. There are different types of data — and you need to know what they are.

1. Discrete data

You get discrete data by counting. E.g. the number of bubbles produced in a reaction would be discrete. You can't have 1.25 bubbles. That'd be daft.

2. Continuous data

A continuous variable can have any value on a scale. For example, the volume of gas produced or the mass of products from a reaction. You can never measure the exact value of a continuous variable.

3. Categoric data

A categoric variable has values that can be sorted into categories. For example, the colours of solutions might be blue, red and yellow (see Figure 2). Or types of material might be wood, steel and glass.

4. Ordered (ordinal) data

Ordered data is similar to categoric, but the categories can be put in order. For example, if you classify reactions as 'slow', 'fairly fast' and 'very fast' you'd have ordered data.

Choosing the right data to collect

HOW SCIENCE WORKS

The data you choose to collect should be something that changes and can be easily measured or observed over the course of your experiment.

─── Example ───

You might want to measure the rate of the following reaction:

$$NaOH_{(aq)} + CH_3CH_2Br_{(l)} \rightarrow CH_3CH_2OH_{(l)} + NaBr_{(aq)}$$

There wouldn't be any point in collecting data about how the conductivity changes over the course of the reaction, for example, because there are salts in both the reactants and the products. But you could use a pH meter to measure how the pH changes from basic (due to sodium hydroxide) to almost neutral.

The data you collect also has to provide evidence that addresses the aim of your experiment and gives the right level of detail — there's no point collecting data that doesn't help answer your question.

Example

You might want to measure the enthalpy change of a reaction. It's no good just feeling whether the reaction vessel heats up or cools down — this tells you whether the reaction uses energy or gives out energy, but not what the enthalpy change actually is.

You also need to be careful about how often and how long you measure the temperature for. If you just measure the change over the first 30 seconds of the reaction then you'll only get the enthalpy change over that period of time, which isn't necessarily the total change. Instead, you should keep measuring the temperature until it stops changing. At this point, all the reactants should have been used up, and the reaction is complete. You can then work out the total change in temperature, and so the total enthalpy change.

Tip: The enthalpy change of a reaction is just the amount of energy taken in or given out by the reactants when they react to form the products. There's a whole section about enthalpy changes on pages 154-166.

Selecting equipment

Selecting the right apparatus may sound easy but it's something you need to think carefully about. Your equipment has to be appropriate for the specific experiment. It should be the right size and scale for whatever you're measuring, and it should have the right level of sensitivity to keep any errors in your measurement to a minimum.

(HOW SCIENCE WORKS)

Tip: You can find out how to calculate errors in your measurements on pages 21 and 22.

Example

In an experiment where you're measuring the volume of gas produced, you should think about the following things when choosing your equipment:

- The apparatus you use has to collect the gas, without letting any escape. For example, a gas syringe connected to a sealed vessel where the reaction is taking place (see Figure 3).

- The gas syringe needs to be big enough to collect all the gas produced during the experiment, or the plunger will just fall out the end. You might need to do some calculations to estimate how much gas will be produced, to work out what size of syringe to use.

- The gas syringe needs to measure to the right level of sensitivity. If you predict that about 10 cm³ will be produced, it will be more accurate to use a syringe that is graduated to the nearest 0.5 cm³ than to the nearest 1 cm³.

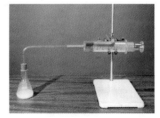

Figure 3: *Apparatus used to measure the volume of gas produced in a reaction.*

Drawing equipment

When you're writing out a method for your experiment, it's always a good idea to draw a labelled diagram showing how your apparatus will be set up. The easiest way to do this is to use a scientific drawing, where each piece of apparatus is drawn as if you're looking at its cross-section. Some basic pieces of equipment that you're likely to need to draw are shown in Figure 4.

Tip: There's more information about writing methods for experiments on page 8.

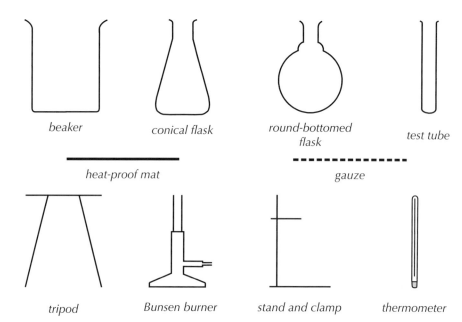

beaker   *conical flask*   *round-bottomed flask*   *test tube*

heat-proof mat   *gauze*

tripod   *Bunsen burner*   *stand and clamp*   *thermometer*

Figure 4: *Scientific diagrams of some basic laboratory equipment.*

Figure 5: *A student wearing gloves, goggles and a lab coat to protect his skin, eyes and clothes from any hazardous substances.*

Risk assessments

In order to work safely, you need to carry out a risk assessment for your experiment. To do this, you need to identify:

- All the dangers in the experiment, for example any hazardous compounds or naked flames.
- Who is at risk from these dangers — this could be you and your lab partner, but it could also be anyone who is in the same room or building.
- What can be done to reduce the risk. You should wear a lab coat and goggles as a standard precaution, but you may need to take other safety precautions, such as carrying out your experiment in a fume-hood, only using low concentrations or dilute solutions of reactive substances and preventing anything that can react with oxygen or water from coming into contact with them.

Writing a method

When writing a method, you need to make sure it's clear and detailed enough for anyone to follow — it's important that other people can recreate your experiment and get the same results. Make sure your method includes:

1. All substances and quantities to be used. You need to include the concentrations of any solutions, any catalysts that are needed and the conditions (such as temperature and pressure) that the experiment will be carried out at.
2. What variables you need to control and how to control them.
3. The exact apparatus needed, including sizes. A labelled diagram is usually helpful to show the set-up.
4. What data to collect and step-by-step instructions on how to collect it.
5. How to minimise any errors at each step. For example, how to reduce transfer errors (see pages 11 and 12).
6. Any safety precautions that should be taken.

Example

Copper(II) sulfate is an ionic compound with the formula $CuSO_4$. Sometimes, water molecules can be incorporated into the ionic lattice. When this happens, the crystal is hydrated and has the formula $CuSO_4.xH_2O$. You can carry out an experiment with the aim of finding the value of x. To do this, you need to find the difference in mass between a sample of copper(II) sulfate when it is hydrated and anhydrous. Here's a method for the experiment:

Tip: There's loads more about hydrated salts and calculating their molecular formulas on pages 69-70.

Equipment and substances:

PRACTICAL ACTIVITY GROUP **1**

- A mass balance
- A 30 cm³ crucible
- A spatula
- A Bunsen burner on a heat-proof mat
- A tripod and gauze
- About 2 g hydrated copper(II) sulfate

Tip: If something's anhydrous then it's got no water in it.

Safety Precautions:

This experiment uses a naked flame, so care should be taken when nearby. The Bunsen burner should be placed on a heat-proof mat, and shouldn't be near any flammable substances. Care should be taken when heating the copper sulfate as, if it is overheated, toxic gas can be given off. If the sample begins to go black, you should stop heating it immediately. Allow all your apparatus to cool before touching it. Copper sulfate is harmful if swallowed and can irritate skin and eyes, so a lab coat, gloves and goggles should be worn.

Tip: You should be able to explain why each step in a method is necessary.

Method:

1. Zero the mass balance, and then use it to weigh the empty crucible. Record the mass of the empty crucible.

2. Weigh out approximately 2 g of hydrated copper sulfate into the crucible and record their combined mass.

3. Gently heat the crucible containing the hydrated copper sulfate using the set-up in Figure 6.

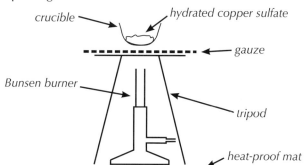

crucible — hydrated copper sulfate

gauze

Bunsen burner

tripod

heat-proof mat

Figure 6: The set-up for an experiment to find the formula of hydrated copper sulfate.

4. Heating the hydrated copper sulfate causes the water in the crystals to evaporate, leaving anhydrous copper sulfate in the crucible. Once all the copper sulfate has changed from blue to white, turn off the Bunsen burner and leave the crucible to cool.

5. When the crucible is cool, reweigh it and record the combined weight of the crucible and the anhydrous copper sulfate.

Figure 7: An experiment to find the formula of hydrated copper(II) sulfate.

Tip: Once you've calculated the difference in mass between the hydrated and anhydrous sample you need to do some more calculations to find the value of x in the formula. You can find out how to do this on pages 69-70.

Once you've got your three recorded masses, you can then work out:

- The original mass of hydrated copper sulfate, which you calculate by subtracting the mass of the empty crucible from the combined mass of the crucible and the hydrated copper sulfate.

- The final mass of anhydrous copper sulfate, which you calculate by subtracting the mass of the empty crucible from the combined mass of the crucible and the anhydrous copper sulfate.

- The difference in mass between the sample when it is hydrated and anhydrous, by subtracting the final mass from the initial mass.

Figure 8: *The apparatus used to determine whether the gas given off by a reaction is carbon dioxide.*

Figure 9: *Apparatus for collecting the gas given off in a reaction.*

Tip: A haloalkane is an organic molecule that contains carbon atoms, hydrogen atoms and halogen (fluorine, chlorine, bromine or iodine) atoms (see page 241).

Practice Questions — Application

Q1 A student wants to find out whether the gas given off when hydrochloric acid reacts with calcium carbonate is carbon dioxide. She does this by setting up a reaction between the two compounds in a sealed conical flask and bubbling the gas that is produced through a solution of limewater in a test tube. If the gas is carbon dioxide, then the solution of limewater should turn cloudy. The apparatus she uses is shown in Figure 8.

a) Draw a labelled scientific diagram of the apparatus used in this experiment.

b) Describe two hazards that might be associated with this experiment, and what you could do to reduce the risk.

Q2 A student wishes to determine the volume of gas given off in the first minute of an experiment. He suggests collecting the gas using test tubes inverted in a water bath (see Figure 9).
Explain why this is not an appropriate method of measuring how much gas has been given off, and suggest a better piece of equipment for carrying out this experiment.

Q3 Chloroalkanes and bromoalkanes react with water in the presence of silver nitrate and ethanol to form insoluble silver halide precipitates. The time taken for the precipitate to form depends on the rate of the reaction. A student wants to find out whether the rate of the reaction is affected by whether the haloalkane is a chloroalkane or a bromoalkane.

a) Identify the independent variable in this experiment.

b) What data could you collect to address the aim of the experiment?

c) Suggest two other variables in this experiment that would need to be kept constant.

Practice Questions — Fact Recall

Q1 What is an independent variable?

Q2 Is the colour of a solution categoric or continuous data?

Q3 Give three things you should consider when carrying out a risk assessment.

2. Practical Techniques

The way you carry out your experiment is important. You'll meet lots of specific techniques throughout this course, but there are some things you'll be doing all the time. You've probably met some of them before.

Precise results

The results of any experiment you carry out should be **precise**. This means that they are **repeatable** and **reproducible**. Repeatable means that if the same person does the experiment again using the same methods and equipment, they'll get the same results. Reproducible means that if someone else does the experiment, or a different method or piece of equipment is used, the results will still be the same.

To make sure your results are precise, you need to minimise any errors that might sneak into your data. This includes using apparatus and techniques correctly, taking measurements correctly and repeating your experiments and calculating a mean.

Measuring the mass of solids

PRACTICAL ACTIVITY GROUP **1**

You weigh solids using a balance. To do this you should put the container you are weighing your substance into on the balance, and make sure the balance is set to exactly zero before you start weighing out your substance. Once you've measured a quantity of a substance you need to be careful you don't lose any. In particular, think about how to minimise losses as you transfer the solid from the measuring equipment into another container. For example, if you're making up a standard solution, you could wash any remaining solid into the new container using the solvent. Or you could reweigh the weighing container after you've transferred the solid so you can work out exactly how much you added to your experiment.

Measuring the volumes of liquids

PRACTICAL ACTIVITY GROUP **2**

There are a few methods you might use to measure the volume of a liquid. Whichever method you use, always read the volume from the bottom of the meniscus (the curved upper surface of the liquid) when it's at eye level (see Figure 1).

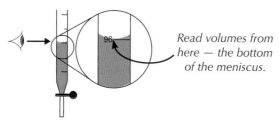

Read volumes from here — the bottom of the meniscus.

Figure 1: *The technique for correctly measuring the volume of a liquid.*

Pipettes

Pipettes are long, narrow tubes that are used to suck up an accurate volume of liquid and transfer it to another container. They are often calibrated to allow for the fact that the last drop of liquid stays in the pipette when the liquid is ejected. This reduces transfer errors.

Learning Objectives:

- Know how to use a wide range of practical apparatus and techniques correctly.
- Be able to measure the mass of a solid (PAG 1).
- Be able to measure the volume of a liquid (PAG 2).
- Be able to measure the volume of a gas (PAG 1).
- Be able to measure temperature (PAG 3).
- Be able to make and record qualitative observations (PAG 4).
- Be able to use reflux in the synthesis of an organic liquid (PAG 5).
- Be able to use distillation in the synthesis of an organic liquid (PAG 5).
- Be able to use a separating funnel to purify an organic liquid (PAG 5).

Specification Reference 1.1.2

Figure 2: *A scientist using a pipette to measure out an accurate volume of liquid.*

Burettes

Burettes measure from top to bottom (so when they are full, the scale reads zero). They have a tap at the bottom which you can use to release the liquid into another container (you can even release it drop by drop). To use a burette, take an initial reading, and once you've released as much liquid as you want, take a final reading. The difference between the readings tells you how much liquid you used.

Volumetric flasks

Volumetric flasks allow you to accurately measure a very specific volume of liquid. They come in various sizes (e.g. 100 ml, 250 ml) and there's a line on the neck that marks the volume that they measure. They're used to make accurate dilutions and standard solutions (solutions with a precisely known concentration). To use them, first measure out the liquid or solid that's being diluted or dissolved into a separate measuring vessel. Add this substance to the volumetric flask and rinse out the measuring vessel into the volumetric flask with some solvent to make sure everything's been transferred. Then fill the flask with solvent to the bottom of the neck. Fill the neck drop by drop until the bottom of the meniscus is level with the line. Stopper the flask and invert it a couple of times to make sure that the solution is properly mixed.

Figure 3: *A student using a burette.*

Figure 4: *Using a volumetric flask to prepare a solution.*

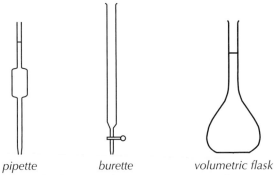

pipette   burette   volumetric flask

Figure 5: *Scientific diagrams of some equipment used to measure liquids.*

Tip: Burettes and volumetric flasks are both used in <u>titration</u> experiments — see page 71 for more about titrations. Gas syringes can be used to follow the <u>rate of a reaction</u> (see pages 173-175), and in <u>moles determination experiments</u> (see page 42).

Measuring the volumes of gases

PRACTICAL ACTIVITY GROUP **1**

Gases can be measured with a gas syringe. They should be measured at room temperature and pressure as the volume of a gas changes with temperature and pressure. Before you use the syringe, you should make sure it's completely sealed and that the plunger moves smoothly.

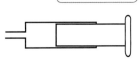

Figure 6: *A scientific diagram of a gas syringe.*

Measuring temperature

PRACTICAL ACTIVITY GROUP **3**

You can use a thermometer or a temperature probe to measure the temperature of a substance (a temperature probe is like a thermometer but it will always have a digital display). Think about where you need to take your measurement from — if you're measuring the temperature of a liquid, the bulb of the thermometer or probe should be submerged in the substance you're measuring. If you're measuring the temperature of a gas as it's distilled from a liquid, then the bulb of your thermometer or temperature probe should be at the outlet of the distillation apparatus. This is so you know the temperature being measured is the same as the temperature of the substance that is being distilled. Always wait for the temperature to stabilise before taking an initial reading and if you're using a thermometer with a scale, read off your measurement at eye level to make sure it's accurate.

Tip: Measuring temperature accurately is really important in <u>enthalpy determination</u>. See page 159 for more on experiments to determine enthalpy changes.

Making qualitative observations

Qualitative tests measure physical qualities (e.g. colour) while **quantitative** tests measure numerical data, (e.g. mass). Qualitative tests can be harder to reproduce because they're often subjective (based on opinion), such as describing the colour or cloudiness of a solution.

Tip: See pages 147-149 for examples of qualitative tests for ions.

Example

In an experiment to test whether a reaction is exothermic (gives out heat) or endothermic (takes in heat), one person might say that the reaction vessel 'warms up slightly', whilst someone else might say that the same vessel gets 'very hot'. These are qualitative observations and it's hard to make them reproducible because the observation is based on the opinion of the person carrying out the experiment.

If a thermometer was used to measure the change in temperature over the reaction, then the reading on the thermometer would be the same no matter who took the measurement. This is a quantitative observation.

There are ways to reduce the subjectivity of qualitative observations. E.g.:

- If you're looking for a colour change, put a white background behind your reaction container.

  PRACTICAL ACTIVITY GROUP **4**

- If you're looking for a precipitate to form, mark an X on a piece of paper and place it under the reaction container. Your solution is 'cloudy' when you can no longer see the X (see Figure 7).

Figure 7: *An experiment to time how long it takes for a solution to go cloudy.*

Organic techniques

PRACTICAL ACTIVITY GROUP **5**

Synthesis is used to make one organic compound from another. There are a number of techniques that chemists use to make and purify products:

Reflux

Reflux is used when making a volatile organic product (one that evaporates easily) from compounds that need to be heated in order to react. The reaction mixture is heated in a flask fitted with a condenser so that any materials that evaporate will condense and drip back into the mixture. This stops you losing any of the reactants or products from the mixture during the reaction.

Tip: Always carry out a full risk assessment before using any of the organic techniques on these pages.

Tip: There's more about using <u>reflux</u> to synthesise organic compounds on page 267.

Tip: Organic compounds are just molecules that contain carbon.

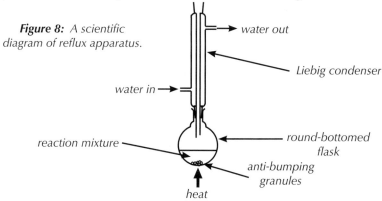

Figure 8: *A scientific diagram of reflux apparatus.*

water out

Liebig condenser

water in

reaction mixture

round-bottomed flask

anti-bumping granules

heat

Tip: Organic compounds are often flammable, so it's best to heat them with a hot plate or a water bath instead of a Bunsen burner.

Distillation

Distillation involves gently heating a mixture so that the compounds evaporate off in order of increasing boiling point. This allows the different compounds to be collected separately as they will evaporate out of the mixture at different temperatures. Distillation can be done during a reaction to collect a product as it forms, or after the reaction is finished to purify the mixture.

Tip: Anti-bumping granules help the mixture to boil evenly, and stop it suddenly bubbling up.

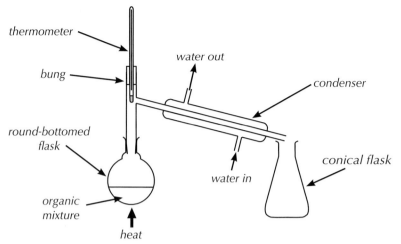

Figure 9: A scientific diagram of distillation apparatus.

Tip: There's more about using <u>distillation</u> to synthesise and purify organic compounds on pages 267-268.

Tip: If you need to draw a distillation diagram, make sure that the bulb of the thermometer is level with the outlet.

Tip: The flow of water in a condenser always goes <u>in</u> at the <u>bottom</u> and <u>out</u> at the <u>top</u>, stopping any air getting trapped which would heat up and disrupt how the water cools the condenser.

Tip: There's more about using <u>separation</u> to purify an organic liquid on pages 268-269.

Tip: Organic liquids are normally less dense than water so the organic layer will be the top layer in the separating funnel.

Removing water soluble impurities

You can use a separating apparatus to purify organic substances from any impurities that are soluble in water. You add water to an organic mixture in a separating funnel, any water soluble impurities move out of the organic layer and dissolve in the aqueous layer. The layers have different densities so are easy to separate.

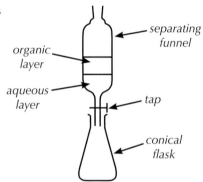

Figure 10: A scientific diagram of separating apparatus.

Practice Questions — Application

Q1 Two students carry out an experiment to see how long it takes a reaction mixture to turn cloudy. Despite carrying out identical experiments, there is a difference of 30 seconds between their results. Suggest what they could do to improve the agreement of their results.

Q2 A student is making up a standard solution.

a) Suggest what piece of apparatus the student should use to make up his solution in.

b) How could the student minimise transfer errors when moving the solid from the weighing vessel into the apparatus in part a)?

Practice Questions — Fact Recall

Q1 Suggest how you could reduce transfer errors when transferring a solid from a weighing vessel into a container containing a solution of known volume and concentration.

Q2 Name three pieces of apparatus you could use to measure the volume of a liquid.

Q3 Describe the process of distillation.

3. Tables and Data

When you're carrying out experiments, you usually need to collect your data in a table — it makes it easier to analyse. You'll then need to check your data's consistent and do a bit of maths before you get your final results.

Tables of data

Before you start your experiment, make a table to write your results in. When you draw a table, make sure you include enough rows and columns to record all of the data you need. You might also need to include a column for processing your data (e.g. working out an average). Make sure each column and row has a heading so you know what's going to be recorded where. It's usually a good idea to include the units of your measurements in the column heading, not the table itself.

You'll need to repeat each test at least three times. If your results are consistent it's a good indication that they're precise. Figure 1 (below) is the sort of table you might use when you investigate the effect of temperature on reaction rate. (You'd then have to add rows for different temperatures.)

Temperature (°C)	Time (s)	Volume of gas evolved (cm³)			Average volume of gas evolved (cm³)
		Run 1	Run 2	Run 3	
20.0	10	8.1	7.6	8.5	
	20	17.7	19.0	20.1	
	30	28.5	20.1	30.0	

Figure 1: Table of results showing the effect of temperature on the rate of reaction.

Anomalous results

Watch out for **anomalous results**. These are ones that don't fit in with the other values and are likely to be wrong. They're usually due to random errors, such as making a mistake when measuring. You should ignore anomalous results when you calculate averages or draw lines of best fit.

> **Example**
>
> Look at Figure 1 again — the volume of gas evolved after 30 s in Run 2 looks like it might be an anomalous result. It's much lower than the values in the other two runs. One reason it could be lower is that the syringe plunger could have got stuck during the experiment.

Calculating means

A mean is just an **average** of your repeated results. It's normally more **precise** than an individual result because it helps to balance out any random errors in your data (see page 22). To calculate the mean result, first remove any anomalous results. Then add up all the other measurements from each repeat and divide by the number of (non-anomalous) measurements.

> **Example** — **Maths Skills**
>
> The average volume of gas evolved at each time point in Figure 1 is:
>
> After 10 seconds: $(8.1 + 7.6 + 8.5) \div 3 = 8.1$ cm³
>
> After 20 seconds: $(17.7 + 19.0 + 20.1 \div 3) = 18.9$ cm³
>
> After 30 seconds: The result at 30 seconds in Run 2 is anomalously low, so ignore it when calculating the mean. $(28.5 + 30.0) \div 2 = 29.3$ cm³.

Learning Objectives:

- Know how to present observations and data in an appropriate format.
- Be able to identify anomalies in experimental measurements.
- Be able to use appropriate mathematical skills for analysis of quantitative data.
- Know how to use significant figures appropriately and use appropriate units for measurement.
- Know how to process qualitative and quantitative experimental results.

Specification Reference 1.1.2, 1.1.3, 1.1.4

Tip: Scientists need to be able to present and communicate their results clearly so that other people can understand what they've discovered.

Tip: A fancy way of saying a result is anomalous is to say that it 'isn't concordant' with the other results.

Units and significant figures

Units are really important — 10 g is a bit different from 10 kg, so don't forget to add them to your tables and graphs. It's often a good idea to write down the units on each line of any calculations you do — it makes things less confusing, particularly if you need to convert between two different units.

It's also important to keep track of significant figures when working with data. The first significant figure is the first number of a measurement that isn't zero. The second, third and fourth significant figures (and so on) are the numbers that come directly after the first significant figure, whether or not they are zero. The general rule is that the answer to any calculation should be rounded to the lowest number of significant figures (s.f.) given in the question. If there are lots of steps in your calculation before you reach the final answer, you don't need to round your intermediate answers. Rounding too early could make your final answer less accurate.

Tip: There are loads of useful unit conversions on pages 282-283.

Exam Tip
Always write down the number of significant figures you've rounded to after your answer — it shows you really know what you're talking about.

Tip: When using the ideal gas equation, temperature should be in K, pressure should be in Pa and volume should be in m^3. There's more about the ideal gas equation on page 40.

Tip: R, the gas constant, is 8.31 J K^{-1} $mol^{-1.}$

Example — Maths Skills

Given that the experiment in Figure 1 was carried out at a pressure of 1.0×10^5 Pa, calculate how many moles of gas were evolved after 20 seconds using the ideal gas equation, $pV = nRT$.
(At 20 °C, an average of 18.9 cm^3 of gas was evolved after 20 seconds.)

- First you have to convert all the values into standard units:

  To convert from °C to K, add 273: 20.0 + 273 = 293 K

  To convert from cm^3 to m^3, divide by 1 000 000:
  $$18.9 \div 1\,000\,000 = 1.89 \times 10^{-5} \, m^3$$

- Rearrange the equation to make n (the number of moles) the subject:
  $$n = (pV) \div (RT)$$
  $n = ((1.0 \times 10^5 \, Pa) \times (1.89 \times 10^{-5} \, m^3)) \div (8.31 \, J \, K^{-1} \, mol^{-1} \times 293 \, K)$
  $= 7.7623489... \times 10^{-4} \, mol$

- From the original values, temperature and volume were both given to three significant figures, and pressure was given to two significant figures. So the final answer should be rounded to two significant figures: $n = 7.8 \times 10^{-4} \, mol$ (2 s.f.)

Practice Questions — Application

Q1 The table below shows an extract from the results of an experiment investigating the rates at which different substances increase in temperature when heated in the same way. Calculate the mean for each of the data points when the experiment is carried out for water.

Substance	Time (s)	Temperature (°C)		
		Repeat 1	Repeat 2	Repeat 3
Water	0	18.7	18.4	19.0
	20	22.0	21.7	21.8
	40	24.6	25.0	24.8

Q2 An experiment to measure the change in mass when 1.0 g of hydrated zinc chloride is heated until it is anhydrous (has lost all its water) is repeated three times. The change in mass of the sample for each repeat is: 0.36 g, 0.35 g, 0.33 g. Given that the molar mass of water is 18.0, calculate the average number of moles of water lost from the sample in the experiment.

Tip: The formula moles = mass ÷ molar mass will be useful in Question 2.

4. Graphs and Charts

Once you've identified any anomalous results, and calculated your mean results, the next step is normally to put all your data into a graph.

Types of graphs and charts

You'll usually be expected to make a graph of your results. Graphs make your data easier to understand — so long as you choose the right type.

Bar charts

You should use a bar chart when one of your data sets is categoric or ordered data, like in Figure 1.

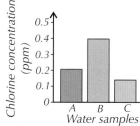

Figure 1: *Bar chart to show chlorine concentration in water samples.*

Pie charts

Pie charts are normally used to display categoric data, like in Figure 2.

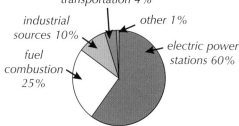

Figure 2: *Pie chart to show sources of a country's sulfur dioxide emissions.*

Scatter graphs

Scatter graphs, like Figures 3 and 4, are great for showing how two sets of continuous data are related (or correlated — see below). Don't try to join all the points — draw a line of best fit to show the trend.

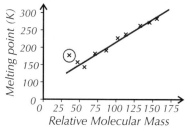

Figure 3: *Scatter graph showing the relationship between M_r and melting point of some alcohols.*

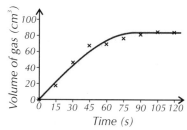

Figure 4: *Scatter graph to show volume of gas evolved against time.*

Scatter graphs and correlation

Correlation describes the relationship between two variables — usually the independent one and the dependent one. Data can show positive correlation, negative correlation or no correlation (see Figure 5).

Learning Objective:

- Be able to plot and interpret suitable graphs from experimental results, including selecting and labelling axes with appropriate scales, quantities and units and measuring gradients.

Specification Reference 1.1.3

Exam Tip
Whatever type of graph you make, you'll only get full marks if you:

1. Choose a sensible <u>scale</u> — don't do a tiny graph in the corner of the paper. Instead, make sure it takes up at least half the space you're given.

2. <u>Label</u> both axes — including units.

3. Plot your points <u>accurately</u> — using a sharp pencil.

Tip: Use simple scales when you draw graphs — this'll make it easier to plot points.

Tip: A line of best fit should have about half of the points above it and half of the points below. You can ignore any anomalous points, like the one circled in Figure 3.

Tip: Lines of best fit can be curves as well as straight lines — like the example in Figure 4.

Exam Tip
Always check that
you've drawn your
axes the right way
round. The thing you've
been changing (the
independent variable)
goes on the x-axis
and the thing you've
been measuring (the
dependent variable) is
on the y-axis.

Positive correlation
As one variable increases
the other also increases.

Negative correlation
As one variable increases
the other decreases.

No correlation
There is no relationship
between the variables.

Figure 5: Scatter graphs showing positive, negative and no correlation.

Calculating gradients

The gradient of a line is how steep it is. It tells you how quickly the y value
changes if you change the x value.

gradient = change in y ÷ change in x

To measure the gradient of a straight line, start by picking two points on the
line that are easy to read. Draw a vertical line down from one point and a
horizontal line across from the other to make a triangle. The vertical side of
the triangle is the change in y and the horizontal side is the change in x.

Tip: Gradients are used
for working out the rate
of reactions, like on
pages 174-175.

┌ **Example** ── **Maths Skills** ─────────────────

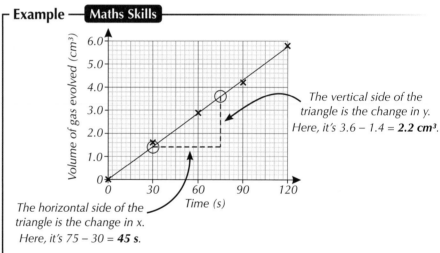

*The vertical side of the
triangle is the change in y.
Here, it's 3.6 – 1.4 = **2.2 cm³**.*

*The horizontal side of the
triangle is the change in x.
Here, it's 75 – 30 = **45 s**.*

Tip: The easiest points
on the line to read are
normally the points at
which the line passes
through the corner of
one of the boxes on the
graph paper.

*Figure 6: Scatter graph showing the volume
of gas evolved from a reaction over time.*

The gradient of the graph in Figure 6 tells you the rate at which gas was
evolved in the experiment.

Gradient = change in y ÷ change in x = 2.2 ÷ 45 = **0.049 cm³ s⁻¹ (2 s.f.)**

     If the line of best fit is a curve, then the gradient will be different at
different places along the curve. This makes it a bit more complicated to
measure the gradient. To find the gradient at a certain point on a curved line
of best fit, you first have to draw a tangent to the line at the point where you
want to find the gradient. To do this, put a ruler on the graph so that it's just
touching the point where you want to find the gradient, and angle the ruler
so that there is equal space between the ruler and the curve on either side of
the point. Then draw a line along the ruler using a sharp pencil. You can then
find the gradient of the tangent in the same way as before.

Example — **Maths Skills**

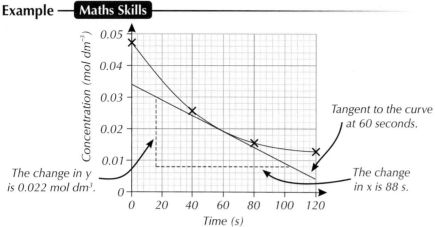

Tip: Always use a ruler and a sharp pencil to draw the tangent to a curve.

The change in y is 0.022 mol dm³.

Tangent to the curve at 60 seconds.

The change in x is 88 s.

Figure 7: A scatter graph showing the change in concentration of sodium hydroxide in its reaction with 2-bromopentane over time.

The gradient at each point along the curve in Figure 9 tells you what the rate of a reaction is at that point in time. The purple line is the tangent to the curve at 60 seconds. So the rate of the reaction at 60 seconds is equal to the gradient of this tangent.

Gradient = change in y ÷ change in x = 0.022 ÷ 88
= 2.5×10^{-4} mol dm⁻³ s⁻¹

Practice Questions — Application

Q1 The graph on the right shows the change in temperature of a reaction mixture in the first ten seconds of the reaction.

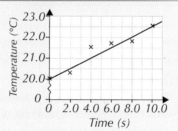

a) Identify any anomalous results.

b) What is the gradient of the graph?

Tip: Remember that anomalous results are ones that don't fit with the other values so are likely to be wrong.

Q2 The graph below shows the change in concentration of $CaCl_2$ in the following reaction: $CaCO_{3(s)} + 2HCl_{(aq)} \rightarrow CaCl_{2(aq)} + H_2O_{(l)} + CO_{2(g)}$.

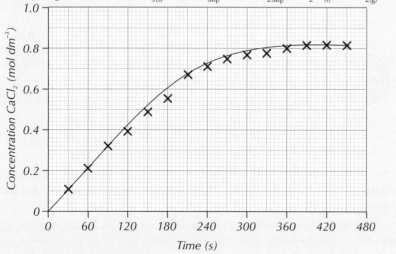

Calculate the gradient after:

a) 60 seconds   b) 180 seconds   c) 360 seconds

Learning Objectives:

- Know how to evaluate results and draw conclusions.
- Know how to analyse and interpret qualitative and quantitative experimental results.
- Understand the precision and accuracy of measurements and data, including margins of error, percentage errors and uncertainties in apparatus.
- Be able to identify the limitations in experimental procedures.
- Be able to refine experimental design by suggestion of improvements to the procedures and apparatus.

Specification Reference 1.1.3, 1.1.4

Tip: Watch out for <u>bias</u> too — for instance, a bottled water company might point these studies out to people without mentioning any of the doubts.

Tip: If an experiment really does confirm that changing one variable causes another to change, we say there's a <u>causal link</u> between them.

Tip: Whoever funded the research may have some influence on what conclusions are drawn from the results, but scientists need to make sure that the conclusions they draw are supported by the data.

5. Conclusions and Evaluations

So you planned your experiment, you've run your tests and you've plotted a nice graph. It's not time to put your feet up yet though, you've got a conclusion to write and an evaluation to do.

Drawing conclusions

When you look at your graph, you may see that there's a **correlation** between two variables. For example, that as one variable increases so does the other. This could lead you to conclude that increasing one variable causes the other to increase. But this isn't necessarily the case — correlation doesn't always mean causation. Ideally, only two quantities would ever change in any experiment — everything else would remain constant. But in experiments or studies outside the lab, you can't usually control all the variables. So even if two variables are correlated, the change in one may not be causing the change in the other. Both changes might be caused by a third variable.

> **Example**
>
> Some studies have found a correlation between drinking chlorinated tap water and the risk of developing certain cancers. So some people argue that this means water shouldn't have chlorine added. But it's hard to control all the variables between people who drink tap water and people who don't. It could be due to many lifestyle factors. Or, the cancer risk could be affected by something else in tap water — or by whatever the non-tap water drinkers drink instead.

You also need to be sure that the conclusion you draw is supported by the data. This may sound obvious but it's easy to jump to conclusions. Conclusions have to be specific — not make sweeping generalisations.

> **Example**
>
> The rate of an enzyme-controlled reaction was measured at 10 °C, 20 °C, 30 °C, 40 °C, 50 °C and 60 °C. All other variables were kept constant, and the results are shown in Figure 1.
>
>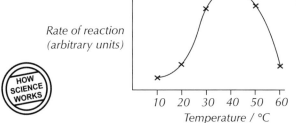
>
> *Rate of reaction (arbitrary units)*
>
> **Figure 1:** *Graph to show the effect of temperature on the rate of an enzyme-controlled reaction.*
>
> *Temperature / °C*

A science magazine concluded from this data that enzyme X works best at 40 °C. The data doesn't prove this. The enzyme could work best at 42 °C or 47 °C but you can't tell from the data because increases of 10 °C at a time were used. The rate of reaction at in-between temperatures wasn't measured. All you know is that it's faster at 40 °C than at any of the other temperatures tested.

Also, the experiment only gives information about this particular enzyme-controlled reaction. You can't conclude that all enzyme-controlled reactions happen faster at a particular temperature — only this one. And you can't say for sure that doing the experiment at, say, a different constant pressure, wouldn't give a different optimum temperature.

Evaluations

There are a few terms that you need to understand. They'll be useful when you're evaluating how convincing your results are.

1. Valid results

Valid results answer the original question, using reliable data. For example, if you haven't controlled all the variables your results won't be valid, because you won't be testing just the thing you wanted to.

2. Accurate results

Accurate results are those that are really close to the true answer.

3. Precise results

Precise results can be consistently reproduced in independent experiments. If results are reproducible they're more likely to be true. If the data isn't precise you can't draw a valid conclusion. For experiments, the more repeats you do, and the closer together the data you get, the more precise it is. If you get the same result twice, it could be the correct answer. But if you get the same result 20 times, it's much more likely to be correct. And it'd be even more precise if everyone in the class gets about the same results using different apparatus.

Tip: <u>Precise</u> results are sometimes called <u>reliable</u> results. So, just like precise results, reliable results are repeatable and reproducible, and you can improve the reliability of an experiment by taking repeat readings and calculating a mean.

Uncertainty

Any measurements you make will have uncertainty in them due to the limits to the sensitivity of the equipment you used. For any piece of equipment you use, the uncertainty will be half the smallest increment the equipment can measure, in either direction.

--- Example — **Maths Skills** ---

If you use a weighing scale that measures to the nearest 0.1 g, then the true weight of any substance you weigh could be up to 0.05 g more than or less than your reading. Your measurement has an uncertainty (or error) of ±0.05 g in either direction.

If you're combining measurements, you'll need to combine their uncertainties. For example, if you're calculating a temperature change by measuring an initial and a final temperature, the total uncertainty for the temperature change will be the uncertainties for both measurements added together.

Tip: The ± sign tells you the range in which the true value could lie. The range can also be called the margin of error.

--- Example — **Maths Skills** ---

In a titration using a burette that measures to the nearest 0.05 cm^3, the initial reading is 10.10 cm^3 and the final reading is 19.75 cm^3.

The uncertainty in each reading will be 0.05 cm^3 ÷ 2 = ±0.025 cm^3.

So the total uncertainty will be 0.025 cm^3 + 0.025 cm^3 = **±0.05 cm^3**.

Percentage error

You can calculate the **percentage error** of a measurement using this equation:

$$\text{percentage error} = \frac{\text{uncertainty}}{\text{reading}} \times 100$$

Tip: Percentage error is sometimes called <u>percentage uncertainty</u>.

Tip: Percentage error means you can directly compare the degree of error in different measurements as a proportion of the total measurement.

Tip: Equipment will also have an error based on how accurately it has been made. The manufacturers should give you these error values — often they'll be written on the equipment somewhere (see Figure 2).

┌─ **Examples** ─ `Maths Skills` ───────────────

Percentage error of a single measurement

A solution is measured to be 16.5 °C by a thermometer that has graduations every 0.5 °C. This reading will have an uncertainty of $0.5 \div 2 = 0.25$ °C so the percentage error is $\frac{0.25}{16.5} \times 100 = \textbf{1.5\,\%}$.

Combining percentage errors

A balance that measures to the nearest 0.2 g is used to measure the change in mass of a substance. The initial mass is measured as 40.4 g. The final mass is measured as 22.0 g.

The change in mass is:

$$40.4 - 22.0 = 18.4 \text{ g}$$

The balance measures to the nearest 0.2 g, so each reading has an uncertainty of ±0.1 g. Two readings have been combined, so the total uncertainty is:

$$0.1 \times 2 = 0.2 \text{ g}$$

So for the change in mass, percentage error $= \frac{0.2}{18.4} \times 100 = \textbf{1.1\%}$

You can reduce errors in your measurements by using the most sensitive equipment available to you. A bit of clever planning can also improve your results. The general principle is that the smaller the measurement, or the larger the increments on your measuring equipment, the larger the percentage error.

┌─ **Example** ───────────────

If you measure out 5 cm³ of liquid in a measuring cylinder that has increments of 0.1 cm³ then the percentage error is (0.05 ÷ 5) × 100 = 1%. But if you measure 10 cm³ of liquid in the same measuring cylinder the percentage error is (0.05 ÷ 10) × 100 = 0.5%. Hey presto — you've just halved the percentage error. So the percentage error can be reduced by planning an experiment so you use a larger volume of liquid.

Figure 2: *A conical flask where the graduations have an error of 5%.*

Types of error

Errors in your results can come from a variety of different sources.

Random errors

Random errors vary — they're what make the results a bit different each time you repeat an experiment. The errors when you make a reading from a burette are random. You have to estimate or round the level when it's between two marks — so sometimes your figure will be above the real one, and sometimes it will be below.

Repeating an experiment and finding the mean of your results helps to deal with random errors. The results that are a bit high will be cancelled out by the ones that are a bit low. So your results will be more precise (reliable).

Systematic errors

Systematic errors are the same every time you repeat the experiment. They may be caused by the set-up or equipment you used. For example, if the 10.00 cm³ pipette you used to measure out a sample for titration actually only measured 9.95 cm³, your sample would have been about 0.05 cm³ too small every time you repeated the experiment.

Repeating your results won't get rid of any systematic errors, so your results won't get more accurate. The best way to get rid of systematic errors is to carefully calibrate any equipment you're using, if possible.

Writing an evaluation

You may well be asked to evaluate a method for an experiment you or somebody else has carried out. In your evaluation you need to think about anything that you could have done differently to improve your results. Here are some things to think about...

1. You need to consider whether the method gives **valid** results. This includes deciding whether the data you collected addressed the aim of the experiment and whether you collected enough data to support your conclusions. You should also think about whether you controlled all the necessary variables to make it a fair test.

2. Next think about how you could have improved the **accuracy** of your results. You should think about whether the apparatus you used was an appropriate scale for your measurements (not too big or too small) and whether you could have used more sensitive equipment to reduce the random errors and uncertainty of your results.

3. Finally, evaluate how **precise** your results are. For most experiments you should have repeated your tests. If so, you should look at whether the results you got were similar, and if you didn't you should consider whether you should repeat your experiment in the future.

Exam Tip
If you think there is a problem with a method, try and explain how you could solve it as well as just stating what it is.

Practice Questions — Application

Q1 a) What is the uncertainty of a measurement made with a measuring cylinder that has graduations every 2.0 cm³?

b) What is the percentage error of a measurement of 8.0 cm³ made with the measuring cylinder in part a)?

c) Suggest how you could reduce the percentage error of the measurement in b).

Q2 A student is investigating the rate at which hydrogen gas is evolved in the reaction between magnesium and hydrochloric acid. She repeats her experiment three times using the following method:

1. Measure out 25.0 cm³ 0.1 mol dm⁻³ hydrochloric acid in a measuring cylinder. Put it in a conical flask fitted with a bung connected to a gas syringe.

2. Put one spatula of magnesium chips into the conical flask, replace the bung and start the timer.

3. Record the volume of gas evolved every five minutes until the reaction is complete.

a) Will the student's results be valid? If not, describe what the student should do instead.

b) The student finds that the volume of gas increases between her readings at five and ten minutes, but there is no change between ten and fifteen minutes, indicating that the reaction is complete. How could the student improve the method to give more accurate results about how the rate changes over the course of the reaction?

Section Summary

Make sure you know...

- The steps involved in planning an experiment.
- The difference between an independent and a dependent variable, and how to identify other variables that will need to be controlled during an experiment.
- The different types of data you might be required to collect in an experiment.
- How to choose what data you should collect in an experiment.
- That the equipment used in an experiment needs to be of the right size, scale and sensitivity.
- How to draw basic laboratory equipment when drawing a diagram of the set-up for an experiment.
- The importance of carrying out a risk assessment for an experiment.
- How to write a detailed method for an experiment.
- How to measure masses of solids, and volumes of liquids and gases, and how to reduce transfer errors associated with moving substances between different containers.
- How to measure the temperature of a substance.
- How to reduce subjectivity when making qualitative measurements.
- What the organic techniques reflux, distillation and separation may be used for.
- How to organise your results into a table of data.
- How to identify anomalous results in your data.
- How to calculate a mean from a data set.
- How to correctly use units and significant figures in your data.
- The different types of graphs you can use, and which one to use for a given set of data.
- That two variables may have a positive, a negative or no correlation.
- How to find gradients from scatter graphs.
- That correlation between variables doesn't always mean that a change in one causes a change in the other, as a third variable may be causing the change.
- How to draw conclusions that are properly backed up by your data.
- What valid, accurate and precise results are.
- How to calculate the uncertainty and percentage error of a measurement.
- How to identify possible errors in a method.
- How to evaluate a method and suggest ways in which it could be improved.

Exam-style Questions

1 What is the error associated with a measurement of 2.45 g on a set of scales that measures to the nearest 0.05 g?

    A   ±0.025 g

    B   ±0.05 g

    C   2.04%

    D   1.02%

(1 mark)

2 The table below shows the results of an experiment to see how long it takes for a reaction to be completed at 30 °C. The experiment was repeated four times.

Temperature (°C)	Time until reaction is complete (s)			
	Repeat 1	Repeat 2	Repeat 3	Repeat 4
30	410	450	398	406

What is the correct value of the mean time taken for the reaction to be completed?

    A   416 s

    B   422 s

    C   405 s

    D   408 s

(1 mark)

3 A student carried out an experiment to find the temperature change of the reaction between 2 g calcium carbonate and 20 ml of 2.0 mol dm^{-3} hydrochloric acid. She measured the temperature of the hydrochloric acid, then added the calcium carbonate and allowed the reaction to run to completion. The reaction was complete when gas was no longer evolved from the reaction vessel. After the reaction had finished, the student took a final temperature measurement and calculated the overall temperature change. The student's result for the total temperature change of the reaction was less than she expected it to be. Which of the following things the student did could have contributed to the temperature change being less than expected?

Action 1: The student used some water to wash the calcium carbonate from the weighing container into the reaction vessel.

Action 2: The student added the calcium carbonate to the reaction vessel two minutes after taking the initial temperature reading.

Action 3: The student left the reaction vessel for ten minutes after the reaction had finished before taking the final reading.

    A   Only action 3

    B   Actions 1, 2 and 3

    C   Actions 1 and 2

    D   Actions 1 and 3

(1 mark)

4   A student makes a standard solution by weighing out a solid and adding it to a volumetric flask. He washes the weighing vessel with some water and pours this water into the volumetric flask. He fills the flask with water until the top of the meniscus is level with the line on the flask. He then puts a cap on the flask and shakes it.

(a) Identify and correct what the student has done wrong in the above method.

(1 mark)

(b) Why does the student wash the weighing vessel into the volumetric flask?

(1 mark)

(c) Why does the student shake the flask?

(1 mark)

5   When calcium carbonate is heated, it decomposes to form a solid and a gas. The table below shows the results of an experiment in which a student investigated the total volume of gas produced by different sized samples of calcium carbonate when heated vigorously.

Mass (g)	Volume gas (cm³)
0.020	4.65
0.040	9.70
0.060	14.45
0.080	16.20
0.100	24.65

(a) Draw a graph of these results, including a line of best fit.

(3 marks)

(b) Describe any correlation in these results.

(1 mark)

(c) The gradient of the graph tells you how many cm³ of gas each gram of calcium carbonate will produce. Calculate the gradient of the graph.

(2 marks)

6   A student carries out an experiment to synthesise the organic compound hexene from hexan-2-ol. Once synthesised, hexene needs to be purified from the reaction mixture. The first step in the purification uses the apparatus in the diagram below.

(a) Name the two pieces of equipment in the diagram above.

(2 marks)

(b) What is the apparatus in the diagram used for?

(1 mark)

1. The Atom

Atoms are the basis of all of chemistry. You learned about them at GCSE and they crop up again here. They're super important.

The structure of the atom

All elements are made of **atoms**. Atoms are made up of 3 types of particle — **protons**, **neutrons** and **electrons**. Figure 1 shows how they are arranged in the atom.

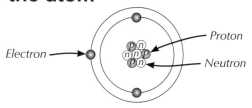

Figure 1: The atom.

Electrons have 1– charge. They whizz around the nucleus in orbitals. The orbitals, and the spaces between them, take up most of the volume of the atom. Most of the mass of the atom is concentrated in the **nucleus**. The diameter of the nucleus is rather titchy compared to the whole atom. The nucleus is where you find the protons and neutrons. The mass and charge of these subatomic particles are really small, so relative mass and relative charge are used instead. The mass of an electron is negligible compared to a proton or a neutron — it's about 2000 times smaller. Figure 2 shows the relative masses and charges of protons, neutrons and electrons.

Subatomic particle	Relative mass	Relative charge
Proton	1	1+
Neutron	1	0
Electron, e^-	$\frac{1}{2000}$	1–

Figure 2: Relative masses and relative charges of subatomic particles.

Nuclear symbols

You can figure out the number of protons, neutrons and electrons from the nuclear symbol.

Figure 3: Nuclear symbol.

Mass (nucleon) number

This is the total number of protons and neutrons in the nucleus of an atom.

Atomic (proton) number

This is the number of protons in the nucleus of an atom — it identifies the element. All atoms of the same element have the same number of protons. Sometimes the atomic number is left out of the nuclear symbol, e.g. ^7Li. You don't really need it because the element's symbol tells you its value.

Learning Objectives:

- Be able to describe atomic structure in terms of the number of protons, neutrons and electrons for atoms and ions given the atomic number, mass number and any ionic charge.
- Know that isotopes are atoms of the same element with different numbers of neutrons and different masses.

Specification Reference 2.1.1

Tip: You can find the symbol and atomic number for each element using the periodic table. The other number in the periodic table isn't the mass number though — it's the relative atomic mass, which is a bit different. (See page 33 for more on relative atomic mass.)

Atoms and ions

For neutral atoms, which have no overall charge, the number of electrons is the same as the number of protons. The number of neutrons is just mass number minus atomic number, i.e. 'top minus bottom' in the nuclear symbol. Figure 4 shows some examples.

Nuclear symbol	Atomic number	Mass number	Protons	Electrons	Neutrons
$^{7}_{3}Li$	3	7	3	3	$7 - 3 = 4$
$^{19}_{9}F$	9	19	9	9	$19 - 9 = 10$
$^{24}_{12}Mg$	12	24	12	12	$24 - 12 = 12$

Figure 4: Calculating the number of neutrons in atoms.

Ions have different numbers of protons and electrons. Negative ions have more electrons than protons and positive ions have fewer electrons than protons. It kind of makes sense if you think about it.

Tip: Ions have the same number of protons and neutrons as atoms do — it's only the number of electrons that changes.

Examples

F^- is a negative ion.

The negative charge means that there's 1 more electron than there are protons. F has 9 protons (see table above), so F^- must have 10 electrons. The overall charge $= + 9 - 10 = -1$.

Mg^{2+} is a positive ion.

The 2+ charge means that there are 2 fewer electrons than there are protons. Mg has 12 protons (see table above), so Mg^{2+} must have 10 electrons. The overall charge $= +12 - 10 = +2$.

Tip: Ions are easy to spot — they've always got a $^+$ or a $^-$ next to them. If they've got a $^+$ it means they've lost electrons. If it's a $^-$ then they've gained electrons. If there's a number next to the sign it means more than one electron has been lost or gained. For example, $^{3+}$ means 3 electrons have been lost, $^{2-}$ means that 2 have been gained.

Isotopes

Isotopes of an element are atoms with the same number of protons but different numbers of neutrons.

Examples

Chlorine-35 and chlorine-37 are examples of isotopes. They have different mass numbers, which means they have different numbers of neutrons. The atomic numbers are the same. Both isotopes have 17 protons and 17 electrons.

Chlorine-35: $^{35}_{17}Cl$

$35 - 17 = 18$ neutrons

Chlorine-37: $^{37}_{17}Cl$

$37 - 17 = 20$ neutrons

Here's another example — naturally occurring magnesium consists of 3 isotopes.

^{24}Mg (79%)	^{25}Mg (10%)	^{26}Mg (11%)
12 protons	12 protons	12 protons
12 neutrons	13 neutrons	14 neutrons
12 electrons	12 electrons	12 electrons

Figure 5: Subatomic particles in Mg isotopes.

Tip: You can show isotopes in different ways. For example, the isotope of magnesium with 12 neutrons can be shown as:

Magnesium-24,

^{24}Mg or $^{24}_{12}Mg$

It's the number and arrangement of electrons that decides the chemical properties of an element. Isotopes have the same configuration of electrons, so they've got the same chemical properties. Isotopes of an element do have slightly different physical properties though, such as different densities, rates of diffusion, etc. This is because physical properties tend to depend more on the mass of the atom.

Practice Questions — Application

Q1 Aluminium has the nuclear symbol: $^{27}_{13}\text{Al}$

a) How many protons does an atom of aluminium have?

b) How many electrons does an atom of aluminium have?

c) How many neutrons does an atom of aluminium have?

Q2 A specific potassium atom has 19 electrons and 20 neutrons.

a) How many protons does this potassium ion have?

b) What is the mass number of this potassium atom?

c) Write the nuclear symbol for potassium.

d) Potassium ions have a charge of 1+. How many electrons does a potassium ion have?

Q3 An isotope of calcium has the nuclear symbol: $^{40}_{20}\text{Ca}$
It forms Ca^{2+} ions.

a) How many electrons does a Ca^{2+} ion have?

b) How many neutrons does a Ca^{2+} ion have?

Q4 Element A has 41 protons and 52 neutrons.

a) Write the nuclear symbol for element A.

b) Another isotope of element A has 53 neutrons.
Write the nuclear symbol for this isotope of element A.

Q5 This question relates to the atoms or ions A to D:

A $^{16}_{8}\text{O}^{2-}$ B $^{17}_{7}\text{N}$ C $^{20}_{10}\text{Ne}$ D $^{18}_{8}\text{O}$

Identify the similarity for each of the following pairs.

a) A and C.

b) A and D.

c) B and C.

d) B and D.

e) Which two of the atoms or ions are isotopes of each other?
Explain your reasoning.

Exam Tip
In your exam you'll have to look at the periodic table to find the nuclear symbol of an element. You usually won't be given it in the question like this.

Tip: Here we mean similarities in the numbers of protons, neutrons or electrons between the two atoms or ions.

Practice Questions — Fact Recall

Q1 Name the three types of particle found in an atom.

Q2 Give the relative masses of these particles.

Q3 State where in the atom each of these particles would be found.

Q4 What is mass number?

Q5 What is atomic number?

Q6 How can you work out the number of neutrons an atom has?

Q7 What are isotopes?

Q8 Why do isotopes have the same chemical properties?

Q9 Explain why isotopes can have different physical properties.

2. Atomic Models

The model of the atom is useful for understanding loads of ideas in chemistry. But it's just a model, and the accepted model of the atom has changed throughout history.

Changes to the atomic model

The Bohr model of the atom (the one on page 31) is the model of the atom you need to know for your exam — it's also one of the currently accepted models. It fits all the observations and evidence we have so far, so we assume it's true until someone shows that it's incomplete or wrong. In the past, completely different models were accepted, because they fitted the evidence available at the time.

Some ancient Greeks thought that all matter was made from indivisible particles. At the start of the 19th century John Dalton described atoms as solid spheres, and said that different types of sphere made up the different elements (see Figure 1).

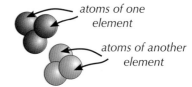

atoms of one element

atoms of another element

Figure 1: *Dalton's model of the atom.*

But as scientists did more experiments, our currently accepted models began to emerge, with modifications or refinements being made to take account of new evidence.

Tip: This topic is all about how science works — scientists come up with a theory which fits the current experimental evidence and that theory changes as more experimental evidence is collected.

Thomson's model

In 1897 J J Thomson did a whole series of experiments and concluded that atoms weren't solid and indivisible. His measurements of charge and mass showed that an atom must contain even smaller, negatively charged particles. He called these particles 'corpuscles' — we call them electrons. The 'solid sphere' idea of atomic structure had to be changed. The new model was known as the '**plum pudding model**' — a positively charged sphere with negative electrons embedded in it.

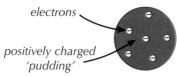

electrons

positively charged 'pudding'

Figure 2: *Thomson's model of the atom.*

Figure 3: *Thomson and Rutherford worked together at Cambridge University.*

Rutherford's model

In 1909 Ernest Rutherford and his students Hans Geiger and Ernest Marsden conducted the famous gold foil experiment. They fired alpha particles (which are positively charged) at an extremely thin sheet of gold. From the plum pudding model, they were expecting most of the alpha particles to be deflected very slightly by the positive 'pudding' that made up most of an atom. In fact, most of the alpha particles passed straight through the gold atoms, and a very small number were deflected backwards through more than 90°. This showed that the plum pudding model couldn't be right. So Rutherford came up with a model that could explain this new evidence — the **nuclear model of the atom**. In this model, there's a tiny, positively charged nucleus at the centre of the atom surrounded by a 'cloud' of negative electrons. Most of the atom's mass is concentrated at the centre and so most of the atom is empty space (see Figure 4).

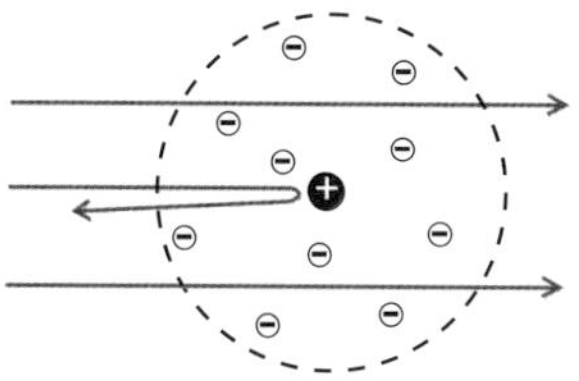

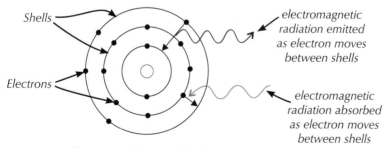

A few alpha particles are deflected very strongly by the nucleus.

Most of the alpha particles pass through empty space.

Figure 4: *Rutherford's model of the atom.*

Tip: This model is closer to the currently accepted model of an atom but still isn't quite right. Read on to find out why...

Modifications to Rutherford's model

Rutherford's model seemed pretty convincing, but Henry Moseley discovered that the charge of the nucleus increased from one element to another in units of one. This led Rutherford to investigate the nucleus further. He finally discovered that it contained positively charged particles that he called protons. The charges of the nuclei of different atoms could then be explained — the atoms of different elements have a different number of protons in their nucleus. There was still one problem with the model — the nuclei of atoms were heavier than they would be if they just contained protons. Rutherford predicted that there were other particles in the nucleus, that had mass but no charge — and the neutron was eventually discovered by James Chadwick.

Tip: See page 27 for more on protons and neutrons.

This is nearly always the way scientific knowledge develops — new evidence prompts people to come up with new, improved ideas. Then other people go through each new, improved idea with a fine-tooth comb as well — modern '**peer review**' is part of this process.

Tip: See page 2 for more on 'peer review'.

Bohr's model

The **Bohr model** (Figure 6) was a further improvement. Scientists realised that electrons in a 'cloud' around the nucleus of an atom, as Rutherford described, would quickly spiral down into the nucleus, causing the atom to collapse. Niels Bohr proposed a new model of the atom with four basic principles:

- Electrons only exist in fixed orbits (shells) and not anywhere in between.
- Each shell has a fixed energy.
- When an electron moves between shells electromagnetic radiation is emitted or absorbed.
- Because the energy of shells is fixed, the radiation will have a fixed frequency.

Figure 5: *Rutherford and Bohr worked together at the University of Manchester.*

Shells

Electrons

electromagnetic radiation emitted as electron moves between shells

electromagnetic radiation absorbed as electron moves between shells

Figure 6: *Bohr's model of the atom.*

The frequencies of radiation emitted and absorbed by atoms were already known from experiments. The Bohr model fitted these observations.

The Bohr model also explained why some elements (the noble gases) are inert. Bohr said that the shells of an atom can only hold fixed numbers of electrons, and that an element's reactivity is due to its electrons. So, when an atom has full shells of electrons it's stable and does not react.

Tip: The term inert just means that it doesn't react with anything.

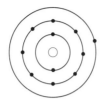

Figure 7: *Atomic structure of sodium (Bohr model).*

Figure 8: *Atomic structure of neon (Bohr model).*

Sodium only has 1 electron in its outer shell. This shell isn't full, so sodium is unstable and will react.

Neon (a noble gas) has full shells of electrons. This means the atom is stable, so neon will not react.

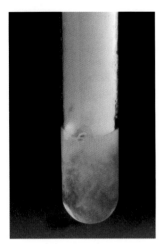

Figure 9: *Sodium reacts vigorously with water as it is very reactive.*

Other atomic models

We now know that the Bohr model is not perfect — but it's still widely used to describe atoms because it is simple and explains many observations from experiments, like bonding and ionisation energy trends. The most accurate model we have today involves complicated quantum mechanics — see Figure 10. Basically, you can never know where an electron is or which direction it's going in at any moment, but you can say how likely it is to be at a certain point in the atom. Oh, and electrons can act as waves as well as particles. But you don't need to worry about that.

Tip: Science is constantly progressing as evidence is found to support or disprove current theories. Some of the atomic models we believe to be accurate today may become outdated in years to come as new evidence is found to disprove them.

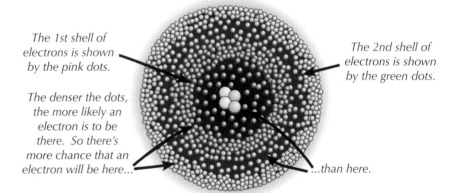

The 1st shell of electrons is shown by the pink dots.

The 2nd shell of electrons is shown by the green dots.

The denser the dots, the more likely an electron is to be there. So there's more chance that an electron will be here...

...than here.

Figure 10: *The quantum model of an atom.*

The **quantum model** might be more accurate, but it's a lot harder to get your head round and visualise. It does explain some observations that can't be accounted for by the Bohr model though. So scientists use whichever model is most relevant to whatever they're investigating.

Practice Questions — Fact Recall

Q1 Describe how J J Thomson's model of the atom was different from Dalton's model.

Q2 What name was given to J J Thomson's model of the atom?

Q3 Name the scientists who conducted the gold foil experiment in 1909.

Q4 Explain how the gold foil experiment provided evidence that Thomson's model was wrong.

Q5 Describe Rutherford's model of the atom.

Q6 Describe the main features of Bohr's model of the atom.

Q7 Is the Bohr model a true representation of the structure of the atom?

3. Relative Mass

The actual mass of an atom is very, very tiny. Don't worry about exactly how tiny for now, but it's far too small to weigh using your average pair of scales. So, the mass of one atom is compared to the mass of carbon–12. This is its relative mass. You need to know about relative atomic mass, relative isotopic mass, relative molecular mass and relative formula mass. Phew... let's get cracking...

Relative atomic mass

The **relative atomic mass**, A_r, is the weighted mean mass of an atom of an element, compared to 1/12 of the mass of an atom of carbon-12. The relative atomic mass of each element is shown in the periodic table (see Figure 1). Relative atomic mass is an average, so it's not usually a whole number.

Relative isotopic mass

Relative isotopic mass is the mass of an atom of an isotope of an element compared to 1/12 of the mass of an atom of carbon-12. At this level, you'll find the relative isotopic mass is usually rounded to a whole number.

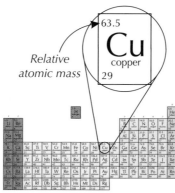

Figure 1: *Location of relative atomic masses on the periodic table.*

Calculating relative atomic mass

You need to know how to calculate the relative atomic mass (A_r) of an element from its isotopic abundances. Different isotopes of an element occur in different quantities, or **isotopic abundances**. The relative atomic mass (A_r) of an element is the average mass of all its isotopes. If you've got the isotopic abundances as percentages, the easiest way to calculate the relative atomic mass is to imagine you have 100 atoms, and then find the average mass. Just follow these steps:

- Multiply each relative isotopic mass by its % relative isotopic abundance and add up the results.
- Divide by 100.

┌─ Example ── **Maths Skills** ─────────────────

Calculating the A_r of boron.
The relative atomic mass of boron is the average mass of all boron atoms. 20.0% of the boron atoms found on Earth have a relative isotopic mass of 10.0, while 80.0% have a relative isotopic mass of 11.0. To calculate the relative atomic mass, just follow the steps above:

- Multiply each relative isotopic mass by its % relative isotopic abundance and add up the results:

  $(10.0 \times 20.0) + (80.0 \times 11.0) = 200 + 880 = 1080$

- Divide this by 100: $1080 \div 100 = 10.8$

So the relative atomic mass of boron is 10.8.

Learning Objectives:

- Be able to define the terms relative isotopic mass and relative atomic mass, based on the mass of an atom of carbon-12.

- Be able to use mass spectra to determine the relative isotopic masses and relative abundances of isotopes.

- Be able to use mass spectra to calculate the relative atomic mass of an element from the relative abundances of its isotopes.

- Be able to use the terms relative molecular mass, M_r, and relative formula mass and calculate their values from relative atomic masses.

Specification Reference 2.1.1

Exam Tip
You could be asked for the definition of relative atomic mass and relative isotopic mass. These are easy marks to get in the exam if you make the effort to learn them now.

Tip: The process of finding an average explains why the relative atomic mass is not usually a whole number.

Figure 2: A scientist using a mass spectrometer to analyse a sample in a research lab.

Relative atomic mass and mass spectra

You might be given your isotopic abundances in the form of a graph, such as a **mass spectrum**. Mass spectra are produced by mass spectrometers — devices which are used to find out what samples are made up of by measuring the masses of their components (see pages 260-263).

- The y-axis gives the abundance of ions, often as a percentage. For an element, the height of each peak gives the relative isotopic abundance.
- The x-axis units are given as a 'mass/charge' ratio.

(see pages 260-263).

On mass spectra like this one you can treat the mass/charge ratio as the isotopic mass because the charge is usually just +1.

Tip: On mass spectra like this one you can treat the mass/charge ratio as the isotopic mass because the charge is usually just +1.

Example — Maths Skills

Calculating the relative atomic mass of chlorine.

The graph on the right shows the mass spectrum of chlorine. As with the example on the last page, the abundances are given as percentages. The peak on the left tells you 75.5% of the chlorine atoms are chlorine-35 atoms, and the peak on the right tells you 24.5% of the atoms are chlorine-37 atoms.

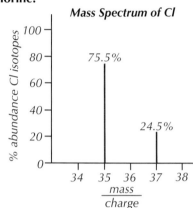

Once you've read the isotopic masses and their relative abundances off the spectrum, you can just follow the same method as before.

- Multiply each relative isotopic mass by its % isotopic abundance and add up the results:

  $(35 \times 75.5) + (37 \times 24.5) = 2642.5 + 906.5 = 3549$

- Divide this by 100: $3549 \div 100 = 35.5$ (1 d.p.)

So the relative atomic mass of chlorine is 35.5.

In some cases, the isotopic abundances on a mass spectrum might not be given as percentages, but as a relative abundance. The method for working out the A_r is very similar:

- Multiply each relative isotopic mass by its relative abundance and add up the results.
- Then divide by the sum of the relative abundances.

Example — Maths Skills

Calculating the relative atomic mass of neon.

The graph on the right shows the mass spectrum for a sample of neon gas. You can use this mass spectrum to calculate the A_r of neon.

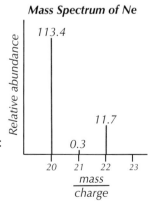

- Multiply each relative isotopic mass by its relative isotopic abundance, and add up the results: $(20 \times 113.4) + (21 \times 0.3) + (22 \times 11.7) = 2531.7$
- Divide by the sum of the relative abundances: Sum of relative abundances = $113.4 + 0.3 + 11.7 = 125.4$
  $2531.7 \div 125.4 = 20.2$ (to 1 d.p.)

So the relative atomic mass of neon is 20.2.

Exam Tip
When calculating the relative atomic mass of an element, it's always worth checking your answer against a periodic table. Under normal conditions, your answer should be the same as, or similar to, the mass (nucleon) number of that element.

Relative molecular mass

The **relative molecular mass**, M_r, is the average mass of a molecule compared to 1/12 of the mass of an atom of carbon-12.
To find the M_r, just add up the relative atomic mass values of all the atoms in the molecule.

Examples — Maths Skills

Calculating the relative molecular mass of C_2H_6O.
In one molecule of C_2H_6O there are 2 atoms of carbon, 6 of hydrogen and 1 of oxygen. The relative atomic masses (A_r) of each atom are shown in Figure 3.

$$M_r \text{ of } C_2H_6O = (2 \times 12) + (6 \times 1) + (1 \times 16) = 46$$

6 H atoms A_r of H
2 C atoms A_r of C   1 O atom A_r of O

Calculating the relative molecular mass of C_4H_{10}.
In one molecule of C_4H_{10} there are 4 atoms of carbon and 10 of hydrogen.

$$M_r \text{ of } C_4H_{10} = (4 \times 12) + (10 \times 1) = 58$$

Atom	A_r
Carbon (C)	12.0
Hydrogen (H)	1.0
Oxygen (O)	16.0
Calcium (Ca)	40.1
Fluorine (F)	19.0

Figure 3: Table of relative atomic masses.

Relative formula mass

Relative formula mass is the average mass of a formula unit, compared to 1/12 of the mass of an atom of carbon-12. It's used for compounds that are ionic (or giant covalent, such as SiO_2). To find the relative formula mass, just add up the relative atomic masses (A_r) of all the ions in the formula unit.

Examples — Maths Skills

Calculating the relative formula mass of CaF_2.
In CaF_2 there is one Ca^{2+} ion for every two F^- ions. The A_r of ions is the same as the A_r of atoms of that element — the electrons are so small that they make no difference to the mass.

A_r of Ca (there's only one calcium ion)

$$M_r \text{ of } CaF_2 = 40.1 + (2 \times 19) = 78.1$$

2 ions of F^- A_r of F

Calculating the relative formula mass of $CaCO_3$.
In $CaCO_3$ there is one Ca^{2+} ion for each CO_3^{2-} ion. The CO_3^{2-} ion contains 1 carbon atom and 3 oxygen atoms, so the A_r values of all these atoms need to be included in the calculation.

$$M_r \text{ of } CaCO_3 = 40.1 + 12 + (3 \times 16) = 100.1$$

Exam Tip
You don't need to know the definitions of relative molecular mass and relative formula mass for your exam, but you do need to be able to calculate them and use the terms correctly.

Tip: Relative molecular mass and relative formula mass are basically the same thing — it's just that ionic compounds aren't made of molecules so they can't have a molecular mass. You work them out the same way though.

Practice Questions — Application

Q1 Find the relative atomic mass of the following elements:
a) Rubidium
b) Mercury
c) Zinc

Q2 A sample of tungsten is 0.100% ^{180}W, 26.5% ^{182}W, 14.3% ^{183}W, 30.7% ^{184}W and 28.4% ^{186}W. Calculate the A_r of tungsten.

Q3 The mass spectrum on the right is for a sample of zirconium. Name all of the isotopes present in the sample of the element.

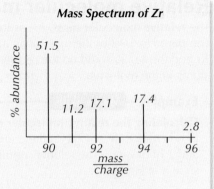

Mass Spectrum of Zr

Tip: You might also see mass/charge as mass ÷ charge, m/z or even m : z.

Q4 The graph on the right shows the mass spectrum of a sample of germanium. Identify the relative abundances of the following isotopes.

a) Germanium-70
b) Germanium 73
c) Germanium-76
d) Germanium-74

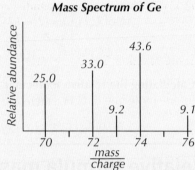

Mass Spectrum of Ge

Tip: There's a periodic table on the inside of the back cover — you might need it to answer these questions.

Q5 The graphs below show the mass spectra for three elements. Use the data in the graphs to calculate the relative atomic mass of each of these elements:

a)

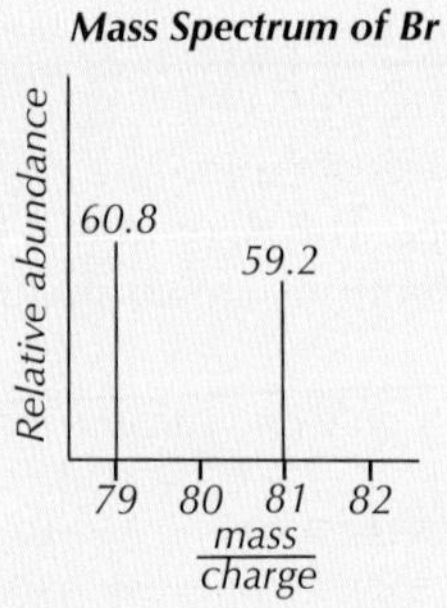

Mass Spectrum of Br

Relative abundance

60.8

59.2

79 80 81 82
mass/charge

b)

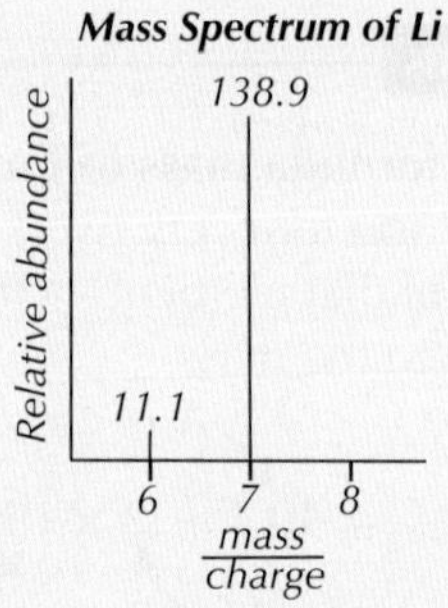

Mass Spectrum of Li

Relative abundance

138.9

11.1

6 7 8
mass/charge

c)

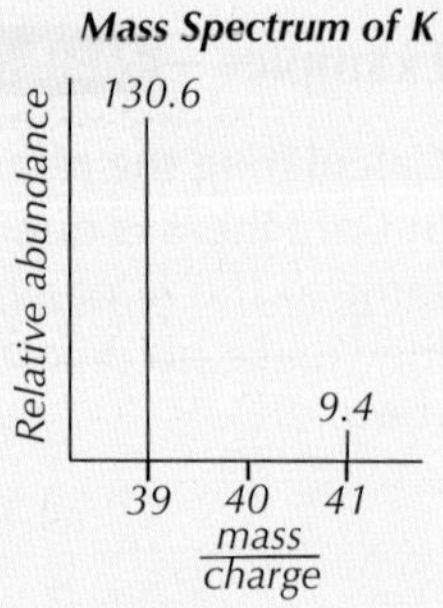

Mass Spectrum of K

Relative abundance

130.6

9.4

39 40 41
mass/charge

Q6 Find the relative molecular mass of the following compounds:
a) NH_3 b) CO_2 c) $C_2H_4O_6N_2$

Q7 Find the relative formula mass of the following compounds:
a) $CaCl_2$ b) $MgSO_4$ c) $NaOH$

Practice Questions — Fact Recall

Exam Tip
You may be asked for the definitions in questions 1 and 2 in the exam, so now's the time to make sure you really know them.

Q1 What is relative atomic mass?
Q2 What is relative isotopic mass?
Q3 What is relative molecular mass?
Q4 What is relative formula mass?

4. The Mole

Amount of substance is a really important idea in chemistry. It's all about working out exactly how much of a chemical you have and what amount of it is reacting with other chemicals. Then you can use that information in all sorts of calculations to do with things like mass, concentration and volume.

What is a mole?

Chemists often talk about 'amount of substance'. Basically, all they mean is 'number of particles'. Amount of substance is measured using a unit called the **mole** (mol for short) and given the symbol n. One mole is 6.02×10^{23} particles (the **Avogadro constant**, N_A). It doesn't matter what the particles are. They can be atoms, molecules, electrons, ions — anything.

Examples ───────────────────

In the reaction $C + O_2 \rightarrow CO_2$:

1 atom of carbon reacts with 1 molecule of oxygen to make
1 molecule of carbon dioxide, so 1 mole of carbon reacts with
1 mole of oxygen molecules to make 1 mole of carbon dioxide.

In the reaction $2Mg + O_2 \rightarrow 2MgO$:

2 atoms of magnesium react with 1 molecule of oxygen to make
2 molecules of magnesium oxide, so 2 moles of magnesium react with
1 mole of oxygen molecules to make 2 moles of magnesium oxide.

Here's a nice simple formula for finding the number of moles from the number of atoms or molecules:

$$\text{Number of moles} = \frac{\text{Number of particles you have}}{\text{Number of particles in a mole}}$$

Example ── **Maths Skills** ───────────────

I have 1.50×10^{24} carbon atoms. How many moles of carbon is this?

$$\text{Number of moles} = \frac{1.50 \times 10^{24}}{6.02 \times 10^{23}} \approx 2.49 \text{ moles}$$

Molar mass

Molar mass, M, is the mass of one mole of something. But the main thing to remember is that molar mass has the same numerical value as the relative molecular mass, M_r (or relative formula mass). The only difference is you stick a 'g mol^{-1}' for grams per mole on the end.

Examples ── **Maths Skills** ───────────────

Find the molar mass of $CaCO_3$.

Relative formula mass, M_r, of $CaCO_3 = 40.1 + 12 + (3 \times 16) = 100.1$
So the molar mass, M, is 100.1 g mol^{-1} (i.e. 1 mole of $CaCO_3$ weighs 100.1 g).

Find the molar mass of $Ni(OH)_2$.

Relative formula mass, M_r, of $Ni(OH)_2 = 58.7 + (2 \times (16 + 1)) = 92.7$
So the molar mass, M, is 92.7 g mol^{-1} (i.e. 1 mole of $Ni(OH)_2$ weighs 92.7 g).

Learning Objectives:

- Be able to explain the term amount of substance.
- Know that a mole (symbol 'mol') is the unit for amount of substance.
- Know that the Avogadro constant, N_A, is the number of particles per mole (6.02×10^{23} mol^{-1}).
- Know that molar mass (units g mol^{-1}) is the mass per mole of a substance.
- Be able to carry out calculations, using amount of substance in mol, involving mass.

Specification Reference 2.1.3

Exam Tip
Make sure you learn this formula — you won't be given it in the exam.

Figure 1: *1 mole of carbon.*

Tip: Remember, to find relative formula mass, all you need to do is add up the relative atomic masses of all the atoms in the formula (see page 35).

Calculations with moles

There's a formula that connects the molar mass of a substance to the number of moles of the substance that you have. It looks like this:

$$\text{Number of moles} = \frac{\text{mass of substance}}{\text{molar mass}}$$

Exam Tip
This formula crops up in all sorts of chemistry calculations — you'll definitely need to know it by heart for your exams.

Examples ─ Maths Skills

How many moles of aluminium oxide are present in 5.1 g of Al_2O_3?

Molar mass of $Al_2O_3 = (2 \times 27.0) + (3 \times 16.0) = 102$ g mol^{-1}

Number of moles of $Al_2O_3 = \dfrac{5.1}{102} = 0.05$ moles

How many moles of calcium bromide are present in 39.98 g of $CaBr_2$?

Molar mass of $CaBr_2 = 40.1 + (2 \times 79.9) = 199.9$ g mol^{-1}

Number of moles of $CaBr_2 = \dfrac{39.98}{199.9} = 0.2$ moles

You can also rearrange the formula and use it to work out either the mass of a substance or its relative molecular mass:

Tip: If it helps you to remember how to rearrange the equation, you could use this formula triangle:

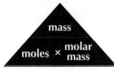

Just cover the thing you want to calculate to find the right formula.

(For example, if you cover mass it will tell you that to calculate mass you multiply moles by molar mass.)

Examples ─ Maths Skills

What is the mass of 2 moles of NaF?

Rearrange the formula to find mass (multiply both sides by molar mass):

mass of substance = number of moles × molar mass

Molar mass of NaF = 23 + 19 = 42 g mol^{-1}
Mass of 2 moles of NaF = 2 × 42 = 84 g

0.050 moles of a compound weighs 2.6 g. Find its relative molecular mass.

Rearrange the formula to find molar mass:

molar mass = mass ÷ number of moles

Molar mass = 2.6 ÷ 0.050 = 52 g mol^{-1}. So, relative molecular mass = 52.

Tip: In this calculation, a '...' is used to show that the number hasn't been rounded — there are extra decimal places that are used in the calculations, but aren't written down.

Multiplying the number of moles in a sample by Avogadro's constant gives you the number of molecules, particles or atoms in the sample.

Example ─ Maths Skills

How many atoms are in 8.5 g of H_2S?

Molar mass of $H_2S = 1 + 1 + 32.1 = 34.1$ g mol^{-1}

Number of moles of $H_2S = \dfrac{8.5}{34.1} = 0.249...$ mol

To work out the number of molecules in 0.249 mol, just multiply it by Avogadro's constant:

Number of molecules of $H_2S = 0.249... \times 6.02 \times 10^{23}$
$$= 1.50... \times 10^{23}$$

The question asks for the number of atoms in 8.5 g of H_2S. There are 3 atoms in each molecule of H_2S (2 hydrogen atoms and 1 sulfur atom), so you need to multiply the number of molecules by 3:

number of atoms = $1.50... \times 10^{23} \times 3$
$$= 4.5 \times 10^{23} \text{ atoms}$$

Exam Tip
The Avogadro constant will be given to you on your data sheet in the exam, so you don't need to worry about learning its numerical value.

Example — Maths Skills

How many chlorine atoms are in 71.0 g of chlorine gas ($Cl_{2\,(g)}$)?

Molar mass of Cl_2 = 35.5 × 2 = 71.0 g mol^{-1}

Number of moles of Cl_2 = $\frac{71.0}{71.0}$ = 1.00 mol

Number of Cl_2 molecules = 1.00 × 6.02 × 10^{23}

$\qquad\qquad\qquad\qquad$ = 6.02 × 10^{23}

There are 2 atoms in one molecule of Cl_2,

so the total number of Cl atoms = 2 × 6.02 × 10^{23}

$\qquad\qquad\qquad\qquad\qquad\qquad$ = 1.20 × 10^{24}

Figure 2: A sample of chlorine, a pale yellow gas.

Practice Questions — Application

Q1 How many atoms are in 1 mole of iron metal ($Fe_{(s)}$)?

Q2 Look at this balanced equation: $4Na + O_2 \rightarrow 2Na_2O$
How many moles of Na_2O are produced when 6 moles of Na react with 1.5 moles of O_2?

Q3 Find the molar mass of:
a) F_2
b) $CaCl_2$
c) $MgSO_4$

Q4 How many moles of sodium nitrate are present in 212.5 g of $NaNO_3$?

Q5 How many moles of zinc chloride are present in 15.5 g of $ZnCl_2$?

Q6 What is the mass of 2 moles of NaCl?

Q7 What is the mass of 0.25 moles of $MgCO_3$?

Q8 1.5 moles of a mystery compound weighs 66 g. Find its molar mass.

Q9 How many O_2 molecules are in 82.1 g of oxygen gas ($O_{2\,(g)}$)?

Q10 A sample of pure magnesium sulfate, $MgSO_4$, contains 3.56 × 10^{24} atoms. What is the mass of the sample?

Tip: Remember — 1 mole of anything always contains the same number of particles.

Tip: You'll need to use the Avogadro constant for some of these questions. It has a value of 6.02 × 10^{23}.

Practice Questions — Fact Recall

Q1 a) How many particles are there in a mole?
b) What's the name for this special number?

Q2 What is the molar mass of a chemical?

Q3 What's the formula that links molar mass and number of moles?

Learning Objectives:
- Know that the molar gas volume (units $dm^3 \, mol^{-1}$) is the gas volume per mole.
- Be able to carry out calculations, using amount of substance in mol, involving mass and gas volume.
- Know and be able to use the ideal gas equation ($pV = nRT$).
- Know the techniques and procedures required during experiments requiring the measurement of gas volumes (PAG 1).

Specification Reference 2.1.3

5. Gas Volumes

Calculations involving gases can be a bit complicated. The volume that a gas occupies varies, depending on conditions such as the temperature and pressure. There are some useful equations to remember, however, that will help you solve tricky, gas-related questions.

Gas Volume

If temperature and pressure stay the same, one mole of any gas always has the same volume — this is known as the molar gas volume. It has units of $dm^3 \, mol^{-1}$. At room temperature and pressure (r.t.p., where temperature is 298 K and pressure is 100 kPa), the molar gas volume is 24 $dm^3 \, mol^{-1}$ (or 24 000 $cm^3 \, mol^{-1}$).

Here are two formulas for working out the number of moles in a volume of gas. Don't forget — only use them for r.t.p.

$$\text{number of moles} = \frac{\text{volume in } dm^3}{24}$$

$$\text{Or: number of moles} = \frac{\text{volume in } cm^3}{24\ 000}$$

You need to be able to use these formulas to find numbers of moles and gas volumes.

Tip: These equations only apply at room temperature and pressure. If you're asked about a gas that isn't under these conditions, you'll have to use a more sophisticated equation (see below).

Examples — Maths Skills

How many moles are there in 6.0 dm^3 of oxygen gas at r.t.p.?
Number of moles = $6.0 \div 24$
$\qquad\qquad\qquad = 0.25$ moles of oxygen molecules

What volume, in cm^3, does 0.020 moles of hydrogen gas occupy at r.t.p.?
Rearrange the formula to find volume (multiply both sides by 24 000):
Volume = number of moles $\times$ 24 000
$\qquad\quad = 0.020 \times 24\ 000 = 480 \ cm^3$

Tip: Remember to be careful when dealing with the units. The equation you'll need to use will depend on whether you're given, or asked for, volume in cm^3 or dm^3.

The ideal gas equation

In the real world, it's not always room temperature and pressure. The **ideal gas equation** lets you find the number of moles in a certain volume at any temperature and pressure:

$p = $ pressure (Pa)
$n = $ number of moles

$$pV = nRT$$

$T = $ temperature (K)
$V = $ volume (m^3)
$R = $ the gas constant ($J \, K^{-1} \, mol^{-1}$)

Exam Tip
The gas constant has a value of 8.314 $J \, K^{-1} \, mol^{-1}$, but this will be on the data sheet in your exam, so you don't need to worry about learning its value.

Working with the ideal gas equation is fairly straightforward — you just have to rearrange the ideal gas equation to put the unknown by itself, and substitute in the rest of the values that you're given in the question. Then it's just a matter of putting it all into your calculator to work out the answer.

Examples — Maths Skills

At what pressure would 0.400 moles of argon gas occupy 0.0100 m³ at 298 K?

Rearrange the equation to find pressure (divide both sides by V):

$$p = \frac{nRT}{V} = \frac{0.400 \times 8.314 \times 298}{0.0100} = 99\,100 \text{ Pa (3 s.f.)}$$

How many moles are there in 0.0600 m³ of hydrogen gas, at 283 K and 50 000 Pa?

Rearrange the equation to find number of moles (divide both sides by RT):

$$n = \frac{pV}{RT} = \frac{50\,000 \times 0.0600}{8.314 \times 283} = 1.28 \text{ moles (3 s.f.)}$$

Tip: Because there's more than one variable on each side of the ideal gas equation, you'll always have to rearrange it before you can use it.

If you're given the values in different units from the ones used in the ideal gas equation you'll need to convert them to the right units first.

- You might be given pressure in kPa (kilopascals). To convert from kPa to Pa you multiply by 1000 (e.g. 2 kPa = 2000 Pa).

- You might be given temperature in °C. To convert from °C to K you add 273 (e.g. 25 °C = 298 K).

- You might be given volume in cm³ or dm³. To convert from cm³ to m³ you multiply by 10^{-6}. To convert from dm³ to m³ you multiply by 10^{-3}. (1 m³ = 1 × 10⁶ cm³ = 1 × 10³ dm³)

Tip: All of these units are S.I. units. That means they're part of an agreed system of measurements used by scientists all over the world.

Example — Maths Skills

What volume would 2.00 moles of argon gas occupy at 27.0 °C and 100 kPa?

First put all the values you have into the right units:
$T = 27.0$ °C = (27.0 + 273) K = 300 K
$p = 100$ kPa = 100 000 Pa

Now rearrange the equation to find volume (divide both sides by pressure):

$$V = \frac{nRT}{p} = \frac{2.00 \times 8.314 \times 300}{100\,000} = 0.0499 \text{ m}^3 \text{ (3 s.f.)}$$

Exam Tip
It's really easy to slip up on units — but using the wrong units will result in an incorrect answer. To prevent yourself losing marks over units in the exam, make sure you learn what units each variable of the gas equation should be in, and how to convert to them.

You might be asked to combine an ideal gas equation calculation with another type of calculation.

Example — Maths Skills

At a temperature of 60.0 °C and a pressure of 250 kPa, a gas occupied a volume of 1100 cm³ and had a mass of 1.59 g.
Find its relative molecular mass.

You've been given temperature, pressure and volume, so you need to find the number of moles:

$$n = \frac{pV}{RT} = \frac{(250 \times 10^3) \times (1.10 \times 10^{-3})}{8.314 \times 333} = 0.0993... \text{ moles}$$

Now you've got the number of moles, you can calculate molar mass using the formula, molar mass = mass ÷ number of moles.

Molar mass = mass ÷ number of moles = 1.59 ÷ 0.0993... = 16.0 g mol⁻¹.

So the relative molecular mass is also 16.0.

Tip: There's a 10³ and a 10⁻³ in this formula because the numbers have been put into standard form. There's more about standard form on pages 277-279.

Tip: This is the formula from page 38 again. Remember that molar mass has the same numerical value as relative molecular mass.

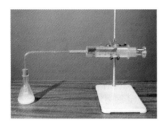

Figure 1: An experimental set-up where gas volume is measured with a gas syringe.

If you ever need to measure gas volumes as part of an experiment, you should use a gas syringe (see Figure 1). The gas syringe can be attached to a reaction container to collect all the gas produced by a reaction. As the gas is produced, the plunger is pushed out of the syringe and the volume of gas collected can be read off the graduations on the side.

PRACTICAL ACTIVITY GROUP **1**

Care should be taken when using a gas syringe to make sure:

- the plunger can move smoothly along the syringe, without getting stuck.
- no gas can escape from the gas syringe.
- the syringe is the correct size for the experiment. If the gas syringe is too big, it may be hard to read off how much gas is produced. If it's too small, the plunger may be blown out of the end of the syringe. Not only does this mean you can't take your readings, but it could also release gas into the atmosphere. If the gas is toxic or flammable, this could be very dangerous.

Tip: It's often good practice to do experiments involving gases in a fume cupboard to prevent gases escaping into the atmosphere.

Practice Questions — Application

Q1   How many moles are there in 2.4 dm³ of carbon dioxide gas at r.t.p.?

Q2   How many moles are in 0.65 dm³ of carbon monoxide gas at r.t.p.?

Q3   How many moles are there in 250 cm³ of sulfur dioxide gas at r.t.p.?

Q4   What volume, in dm³, does 0.21 moles of hydrogen chloride gas occupy at r.t.p.?

Q5   What volume, in dm³, does 1.1 moles of fluorine gas occupy at r.t.p.?

Q6   What volume, in cm³, does 0.028 moles of argon gas occupy at r.t.p.?

Q7   How many moles are there in 0.04 m³ of oxygen gas at a temperature of 350 K and a pressure of 70 000 Pa?

Q8   What volume would 0.65 moles of carbon dioxide gas occupy at a temperature of 280 K and a pressure of 100 000 Pa?

Q9   How many moles are there in 0.55 dm³ of nitrogen gas at a temperature of 35 °C and a pressure of 90 000 Pa?

Q10 At a pressure of 110 000 Pa, 0.05 moles of hydrogen gas occupied a volume of 1200 cm³. What was the temperature in °C?

Q11 What volume would 0.75 moles of helium gas occupy at a temperature of 22 °C and a pressure of 75 kPa?

Q12 At a temperature of 300 K and a pressure of 80 kPa a gas had a volume of 1.5 dm³ and a mass of 2.6 g. Find its relative molecular mass.

Q13 A student had a sample of neon gas, Ne. They heated it to 44 °C. At this temperature the gas had a volume of 0.003 m³. If the pressure was 100 kPa, what was the mass of the neon gas?

Practice Questions — Fact Recall

Q1   What is the formula for calculating the number of moles in a volume of gas in dm³ at r.t.p.?

Q2   What is the formula for calculating the number of moles in a volume of gas in cm³ at r.t.p.?

Q3   Write out the ideal gas equation. Say what the terms mean and give the standard units that each is measured in.

Q4   State why it might be dangerous to use a gas syringe that is too small, when measuring the gas produced by a reaction.

6. Concentration Calculations

The amount of substance is closely linked to the volume of a substance and its concentration. Read on to find out more...

Moles and concentration

The **concentration** of a solution is how many moles (or how many grams) of something are dissolved per 1 dm^3 of solution. The units are mol dm^{-3} (or g dm^{-3}). A solution that has more moles per dm^3 than another is more concentrated. A solution that has fewer moles per dm^3 than another is more dilute. Here's the formula to find the number of moles:

$$\text{Number of moles} = \frac{\text{Concentration} \times \text{Volume (in cm}^3)}{1000}$$

Or: Number of moles = Concentration × Volume (in dm^3)

You need to be able to use these formulas to do calculations in the exam.

┌─ **Examples** ─ **Maths Skills** ─────────────

How many moles of lithium chloride are present in 25 cm^3 of a 1.2 mol dm^{-3} solution of LiCl?

$$\text{Number of moles} = \frac{\text{concentration} \times \text{volume (in cm}^3)}{1000}$$

$$= \frac{1.2 \times 25}{1000} = 0.030 \text{ moles}$$

A solution of $CaCl_2$ contains 0.2 moles of calcium chloride in 0.4 dm^3 water. What is the concentration of the solution?

Rearrange the formula to find concentration (divide both sides by volume):

$$\text{concentration} = \frac{\text{number of moles}}{\text{volume (in dm}^3)}$$

$$= \frac{0.2}{0.4} = 0.5 \text{ mol dm}^{-3}$$

A 0.50 mol dm^{-3} solution of zinc sulfate contains 0.080 moles of $ZnSO_4$. What volume does the solution occupy?

Rearrange the formula to find volume (divide both sides by volume):

$$\text{volume (in dm}^3) = \frac{\text{number of moles}}{\text{concentration}}$$

$$= \frac{0.080}{0.50} = 0.16 \text{ dm}^3$$

You might be asked to combine a concentration calculation with a molar mass calculation. This just means using two formulas, one after the other.

┌─ **Example** ─ **Maths Skills** ─────────────

What mass of sodium hydroxide needs to be dissolved in 50 cm^3 of water to make a 2.0 mol dm^{-3} solution?

First look at the question and see what information it gives you. You've got concentration and volume — so you can work out number of moles.

Learning Objective:

- Be able to carry out calculations, using amount of substance in mol, involving:
  (i) mass,
  (ii) gas volume,
  (iii) solution volume and concentration.

Specification Reference 2.1.3

Tip: This is another formula that you can stick in a formula triangle if it helps you:

Tip: 1 dm^3 is the same as 1000 cm^3 or 1 litre.

Exam Tip
You need to know all of the formulas in this section by heart — so look out for the formula boxes, and learn them.

Exam Tip
Remember to watch out for the units in this type of calculation. Double-check whether the volume you've been given is in cm^3 or dm^3.

Number of moles $= \dfrac{\text{concentration} \times \text{volume (cm}^3)}{1000}$

$= \dfrac{2.0 \times 50}{1000} = 0.10$ moles of NaOH

Then you can use this to work out the mass using the equation
number of moles = mass ÷ molar mass

Molar mass, M, of NaOH $= 23 + 16 + 1 = 40$ g mol^{-1}

Mass = number of moles $\times M = 0.10 \times 40 = 4.0$ g

Practice Questions — Application

Q1 How many moles of potassium phosphate are present in 50 cm^3 of a 2 mol dm^{-3} solution?

Q2 How many moles of sodium chloride are present in 0.5 dm^3 of a 0.08 mol dm^{-3} solution?

Q3 How many moles of silver nitrate are present in 30 cm^3 of a 0.7 mol dm^{-3} solution?

Q4 A solution contains 0.25 moles of copper bromide in 0.5 dm^3. What is the concentration of the solution?

Q5 A solution contains 0.08 moles of lithium chloride in 0.75 dm^3. What is the concentration of the solution?

Q6 A solution contains 0.1 moles of iron oxide in 36 cm^3. What is the concentration of the solution?

Q7 A solution of calcium chloride contains 0.46 moles of $CaCl_2$. The concentration of the solution is 1.8 mol dm^{-3}. What volume does the solution occupy?

Q8 A solution of copper sulfate contains 0.01 moles of $CuSO_4$. The concentration of the solution is 0.55 mol dm^{-3}. What volume does the solution occupy?

Q9 The molecular formula of sodium oxide is Na_2O. What mass of sodium oxide would you have to dissolve in 75 cm^3 of water to make a 0.8 mol dm^{-3} solution?

Q10 The molecular formula of cobalt bromide is $CoBr_2$. What mass of cobalt bromide would you have to dissolve in 30 cm^3 of water to make a 0.5 mol dm^{-3} solution?

Q11 A solution is made by dissolving 4.08 g of a compound in 100 cm^3 of pure water. The solution has a concentration of 1.2 mol dm^{-3}. What is the molar mass of the compound?

Q12 Brine is a solution of sodium chloride, NaCl, in water. What mass of sodium chloride is dissolved in a 50 cm^3 sample of 4.1 mol dm^{-3} brine solution?

Practice Questions — Fact Recall

Q1 What's the formula that links number of moles and concentration? (Write it out twice, once using each volume measurement.)

Q2 How many cm^3 are there in one dm^3?

Section Summary

Make sure you know...

- The structure of an atom in terms of the number of protons, neutrons and electrons.
- That the mass (nucleon) number of an atom is the total number of protons and neutrons it contains.
- That the atomic or proton number of an atom is the number of protons it contains.
- How to work out the number of protons, neutrons and electrons in atoms and ions.
- That isotopes are atoms with the same number of protons but different numbers of neutrons.
- That isotopes of an element have different masses.
- That the relative atomic mass of an element is its mass compared to 1/12 of the mass of an atom of carbon-12.
- That relative isotopic mass is the mass of an isotope of an element compared to 1/12 of the mass of an atom of carbon-12.
- How to calculate relative atomic mass from mass spectra.
- How to determine relative isotopic masses and relative abundances of isotopes from mass spectra.
- What the terms relative molecular mass and relative formula mass mean, and be able to calculate them from relative atomic masses.
- That the term amount of substance means the number of particles.
- That amount of substance is measured using a unit called the mole (mol).
- That the Avogadro constant (6.02×10^{23}) is the number of particles in one mole of a particular substance.
- That the molar mass is the mass of one mole of something and has the units g mol^{-1}.
- How to use the equation: no. of moles = mass of substance ÷ molar mass.
- How to carry out calculations using the amount of substance (in moles).
- How to calculate the volumes and number of moles of gases present at r.t.p.
- How to calculate gas volumes and related quantities, using the ideal gas equation ($pV = nRT$).
- How to carry out calculations using the amount of substance (in moles) and the volumes and concentrations of solutions.

Exam-style Questions

1   Which of these equations shows a form of the ideal gas equation?

    A $pV = RT$

    B $V = \dfrac{nRT}{p}$

    C $p = \dfrac{nV}{RT}$

    D $\dfrac{p}{T} = nRV$

(1 mark)

2   How many protons are in the nucleus of an atom of iodine?

    A   52

    B   73

    C   53

    D   74

(1 mark)

3   How many atoms are in a 6.30 g sample of pure nickel?

    A 6.02×12^{23}

    B 6.46×10^{22}

    C 3.79×10^{24}

    D 5.57×10^{24}

(1 mark)

4   A student is measuring the volume of gas produced by a reaction between a metal and an acid. She uses a gas syringe to collect the gas.

    (a) Before starting her experiment, the student checks that there are no gaps in her apparatus. How might her readings be affected if there are gaps in the apparatus?

(1 mark)

    (b) The gas produced by the experiment is highly flammable.
        Suggest one safety precaution the student should take to reduce the risks associated with the production of a flammable gas.

(1 mark)

    (c) To help her select appropriately sized equipment, the student works out how much gas she expects the reaction to produce before she begins the experiment.
        Why might it be dangerous if the student underestimated the volume of gas produced?

(1 mark)

5   The element silicon (atomic number 14) is commonly used in electronics.
There are three stable isotopes of silicon, ^{28}Si, ^{29}Si and ^{30}Si.

(a) (i)   What are isotopes?

(2 marks)

(ii)   Fill in the table below to show how many protons, neutrons and electrons
each isotope of silicon contains.

	Protons	Neutrons	Electrons
^{28}Si			
^{29}Si			
^{30}Si			

(2 marks)

(b)   The three isotopes of silicon are found naturally with the following isotopic
abundances: ^{28}Si : 92.23%, ^{29}Si : 4.67% and ^{30}Si : 3.10%.

(i)   Define the term relative atomic mass.

(2 marks)

(ii)   Calculate the relative atomic mass of silicon. Give your answer to 2 decimal places.

(2 marks)

(c)   The graph on the right
shows a mass spectrum
for a naturally occurring
sample of an element.
Determine its relative
atomic mass and, therefore,
suggest the identity of the element.

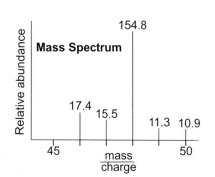

(2 marks)

6   At a temperature of 58.8 °C and a pressure of 178 kPa,
a gas occupied a volume of 7890 cm^3 and had a mass of 22.4 g.

(a)   What is the relative molecular mass of the gas?

(2 marks)

(b)   A molecule of the gas is known to contain 3 atoms, two of which are oxygen.
Give the name of the gas.

(2 marks)

(c)   What volume would the same sample of gas occupy, in dm^3,
at room temperature and pressure?

(1 mark)

Learning Objectives:

- Be able to use the term 'empirical formula' (the simplest whole number ratio of atoms of each element present in a compound).
- Be able to use the term 'molecular formula' (the actual number and type of atoms of each element in a molecule).

Specification Reference 2.1.3

1. Formulas

Now for a few pages about chemical formulas. A formula tells you what atoms are in a compound. Useful, I think you'll agree. There are two types you need to know about — empirical formulas and molecular formulas.

Empirical and molecular formulas

You need to know what's what with empirical and molecular formulas. The **empirical formula** gives just the smallest whole number ratio of atoms of each element in a compound. The **molecular formula** gives the actual numbers of atoms of each type of element in a molecule. The molecular formula is made up of a whole number of empirical units.

Examples

This molecule is butane:

$$H-\overset{\underset{H}{|}}{\underset{}{C}}\overset{\underset{H}{|}}{\underset{}{C}}\overset{\underset{H}{|}}{\underset{}{C}}\overset{\underset{H}{|}}{\underset{}{C}}-H$$

A molecule of butane contains 4 carbon (C) atoms and 10 hydrogen (H) atoms. So its molecular formula is C_4H_{10}.

Butane's empirical formula is C_2H_5. This means that the ratio of carbon atoms to hydrogen atoms in the molecule is 2 : 5. That's as much as you can simplify it.

This molecule is 1,2-dichlorocyclohexane:

A 1,2-dichlorocyclohexane molecule contains:
6 carbon (C) atoms, 10 hydrogen (H) atoms and two chlorine (Cl) atoms.
So its molecular formula is $C_6H_{10}Cl_2$.

1,2-dichlorocyclohexane's empirical formula is C_3H_5Cl.
This means that the ratio of carbon atoms to hydrogen atoms to chlorine atoms in the molecule is 3 : 5 : 1. That's as much as you can simplify it.

Figure 1: *Molecular model of a molecule of butane.*

Tip: There's more information coming up on pages 50-51 about how you can use experimental data to work out empirical and molecular formulas.

If you know the empirical formula and the molecular mass of a compound, you can calculate its molecular formula. Just follow these steps:

1. Find the empirical mass (that's just the mass of the empirical formula).
2. Divide the molecular mass by the empirical mass. This tells you how many multiples of the empirical formula are in the molecular formula.
3. Multiply the empirical formula by that number to find the molecular formula.

Tip: Empirical mass is just like relative formula mass (see page 35).

There are a couple of examples on the next page to show you how it works.

Examples — **Maths Skills**

Tip: There's more on working out molecular formulas on page 52-53.

A molecule has an empirical formula of $C_4H_3O_2$, and a relative molecular mass of 166. Work out its molecular formula.

1. Find the empirical mass — add up the relative atomic mass values of all the atoms in the empirical formula.

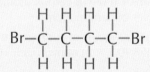

empirical mass = $(4 \times 12) + (3 \times 1) + (2 \times 16) = 83$

4 C atoms A_r of C   2 O atoms A_r of O
3 H atoms A_r of H

2. Divide the molecular mass by the empirical mass. The molecular mass is 166, so there are $(166 \div 83) = 2$ empirical units in the molecule.

3. The molecular formula is the empirical formula × 2, so the molecular formula = $C_8H_6O_4$.

The empirical formula of glucose is CH_2O. Its relative molecular mass is 180. Find its molecular formula.

1. Find the empirical mass of glucose.
   empirical mass = $(1 \times 12) + (2 \times 1) + (1 \times 16) = 30$
2. Divide the molecular mass by the empirical mass. The molecular mass is 180, so there are $(180 \div 30) = 6$ empirical units in the molecule.
3. Molecular formula = $C_6H_{12}O_6$

Figure 2: *Molecular model of a molecule of glucose.*

Practice Questions — Application

Q1 Benzene has the molecular formula C_6H_6. What is the empirical formula of benzene?

Q2 A molecule contains 2 carbon atoms, 6 hydrogen atoms and 4 oxygen atoms. Give the molecular and empirical formulas of this molecule.

Q3 The molecule below is 1,4-dibromobutane.

$$\text{Br}-\overset{\overset{\displaystyle H}{|}}{\underset{\underset{\displaystyle H}{|}}{C}}-\overset{\overset{\displaystyle H}{|}}{\underset{\underset{\displaystyle H}{|}}{C}}-\overset{\overset{\displaystyle H}{|}}{\underset{\underset{\displaystyle H}{|}}{C}}-\overset{\overset{\displaystyle H}{|}}{\underset{\underset{\displaystyle H}{|}}{C}}-\text{Br}$$

a) What is the molecular formula of 1,2-dibromobutane?

b) What is the empirical formula of 1,2-dibromobutane?

Q4 A molecule has the empirical formula C_4H_9, and a relative molecular mass of 114. Find its molecular formula.

Q5 A molecule has the empirical formula $C_3H_5O_2$, and a relative molecular mass of 146. Find its molecular formula.

Q6 A molecule has the empirical formula $C_4H_6Cl_2O$, and a relative molecular mass of 423. Find its molecular formula.

Practice Questions — Fact Recall

Q1 What does the empirical formula of a compound tell you?

Q2 What does the molecular formula of a compound tell you?

- Be able to calculate empirical and molecular formulas, from composition by mass or percentage composition by mass and relative molecular mass.

Specification Reference 2.1.3

2. Calculating Formulas

You can work formulas out using experimental data or percentage compositions. You need to know how to calculate both empirical and molecular formulas, so here's how.

Calculating empirical formulas

There are two different ways of calculating empirical formulas you need to know about — calculating them from experimental data and calculating them from percentage compositions.

Calculating empirical formulas from experimental data

You need to be able to work out empirical formulas from the masses of the roducts created in a reaction. To do this, just follow these steps:

1. Use the equation moles = mass ÷ M_r to work out how many moles of each product has been made.
2. Use the moles of each product made to work out how many moles of each atom you started with.
3. You can then write down the ratio of moles present at the start.
4. Divide by the smallest number of moles to get a whole number ratio.
5. This tells you the empirical formula.

Exam Tip
Make sure you write down all your working for calculation questions. You'll be more likely to spot any mistakes and if you do go wrong you might get some marks for the working.

┌ **Example** ── **Maths Skills** ─────────────

When a hydrocarbon is burnt in excess oxygen, 4.4 g of carbon dioxide and 1.8 g of water are made. What is the empirical formula of the hydrocarbon?

1. The moles of CO_2 and H_2O produced are:
$$\text{moles } CO_2 = \frac{\text{mass}}{M_r} = \frac{4.4}{12 + (16 \times 2)} = \frac{4.4}{44} = 0.10 \text{ moles}$$
$$\text{moles } H_2O = \frac{\text{mass}}{M_r} = \frac{1.8}{(2 \times 1) + 16} = \frac{1.8}{18} = 0.10 \text{ moles}$$

Tip: A hydrocarbon is something that only contains hydrogen and carbon.

2. 1 mole of CO_2 contains 1 mole of carbon atoms, so you must have started with 0.10 moles of carbon atoms.

1 mole of H_2O contains 2 moles of hydrogen atoms, so you must have started with 0.20 moles (0.1 × 2) of hydrogen atoms.

3. If you started with 0.10 moles of C and 0.20 moles of H the C : H ratio is 0.10 : 0.20.

Tip: This method works because the only place the carbon in the carbon dioxide and the hydrogen in the water could have come from is the hydrocarbon.

4. Dividing both sides by 0.10 (the smallest number of moles) gives a whole number C : H ratio of 1 : 2.

5. So the empirical formula of this hydrocarbon is CH_2.

Sometimes there might only be one product and you'll be told the mass of one of the reactants used instead. If this happens you can calculate the mass of the other reactant used with this equation:

Tip: This equation is just the rearranged version of:

mass of products = mass of reactants

mass of reactant A = mass of product − mass of reactant B

Once you know the mass of both reactants you can work out the moles of each reactant used and from there you can use points 4 and 5 above to find the empirical formula.

Example — Maths Skills

2.4 g of magnesium ribbon burns in air to produce a white powder which has a mass of 4.0 g. What is the empirical formula of the white powder?

If 2.4 g of magnesium has burnt to give 4.0 g of magnesium oxide then $4.0 - 2.4 = 1.6$ g of oxygen must be added. So, moles of Mg and O_2 used are:

$$\text{moles Mg} = \frac{\text{mass}}{M_r} = \frac{2.4}{24.3} = 0.10 \text{ moles}$$

$$\text{moles O} = \frac{\text{mass}}{M_r} = \frac{1.6}{16} = 0.10 \text{ moles}$$

So the ratio of Mg to O is $0.10 : 0.10$. Dividing both sides by 0.10 gives a whole number ratio of $1 : 1$, so the empirical formula of magnesium oxide must be MgO.

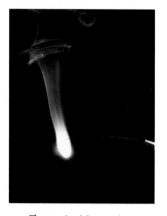

Figure 1: *Magnesium ribbon burning in air.*

Practice Questions — Application

Q1 When a hydrocarbon is burnt in excess oxygen, 17.6 g of carbon dioxide and 10.8 g of water are made. What is the empirical formula of the hydrocarbon?

Q2 When a hydrocarbon is burnt in excess oxygen, 3.52 g of carbon dioxide and 2.88 g of water are made. What is the empirical formula of the hydrocarbon?

Q3 5.52 g of sodium burns in air to produce 7.44 g of sodium oxide. What is the empirical formula of sodium oxide?

Q4 50.2 g of iron reacts with air to produce 69.4 g of an iron oxide. What is the empirical formula of this iron oxide?

Tip: If something is in excess, it means there's much more of it than anything else. This means it doesn't limit the reaction.

Calculating empirical formulas from percentage compositions

You need to know how to work out empirical formulas from the percentages of the different elements. Follow these steps each time:

1. Assume you've got 100 g of the compound — you can turn the percentages straight into masses. Then you can work out how many moles of each element are in 100 g of the compound.

2. Divide each number of moles by the smallest number of moles you found in step 1. This gives you the ratio of the elements in the compound.

3. Apply the numbers from the ratio to the formula.

Tip: Percentage compositions tell you what percentage of the mass of a molecule is made up of each element. So if a molecule contains 26% carbon by mass, 26% of the mass of that molecule is made up of carbon atoms.

Example — Maths Skills

A compound is found to have percentage composition 56.5% potassium, 8.70% carbon and 34.8% oxygen by mass. Calculate its empirical formula.

1. If you had 100 g of the compound you would have 56.5 g of potassium, 8.70 g of carbon and 34.8 g of oxygen. Use the formula, moles = mass ÷ M_r, to work out how many moles of each element that is.

   K: $\frac{56.5}{39.1} = 1.445$ moles   C: $\frac{8.70}{12} = 0.725$ moles   O: $\frac{34.8}{16} = 2.175$ moles

2. Divide each number of moles by the smallest number (0.725 here).

   K: $\frac{1.445}{0.725} = 2.0$ C: $\frac{0.725}{0.725} = 1.0$ O: $\frac{2.175}{0.725} = 3.0$

   This tells you that the ratio of K : C : O in the molecule is $2 : 1 : 3$.

3. So you know the empirical formula's got to be K_2CO_3.

Tip: You should add up the percentages each time there's a question like this to make sure they add up to 100% and you haven't missed out any elements.

Sometimes you might only be given the percentage of some of the elements in the compound. Then you'll have to work out the percentages of the others.

┌─ **Example** ── **Maths Skills** ──────────────────────────────

An oxide of nitrogen contains 26% by mass of nitrogen. Calculate its empirical formula.

1. The compound only contains nitrogen and oxygen, so if it is 26% N it must be $100 - 26 = 74\%$ O. So if you had 100 g of the compound you would have 26 g of nitrogen and 74 g of oxygen.

   N: $\frac{26}{14} = 1.86$ moles   O: $\frac{74}{16} = 4.63$ moles

2. Divide each number of moles by 1.86.

   N: $\frac{1.86}{1.86} = 1.0$ O: $\frac{4.63}{1.86} = 2.5$

   This tells you that the ratio of N : O in the molecule is 1 : 2.5.

3. All the numbers in an empirical formula have to be whole numbers, so you need to multiply the ratio by 2 to put it into its simplest whole number form: $2 \times (1 : 2.5) = 2 : 5$. So the empirical formula is N_2O_5.

Tip: If you don't know one of the percentages, just take the percentages that you do know away from 100 to find it.

Practice Questions — Application

Q1 A compound is found to have percentage composition 5.9% hydrogen and 94.1% oxygen by mass. Find its empirical formula.

Q2 A compound is found to have percentage composition 20.2% aluminium and 79.8% chlorine by mass. Find its empirical formula.

Q3 A compound is found to have percentage composition 8.50% carbon, 1.40% hydrogen and 90.1% iodine by mass. Find its empirical formula.

Q4 A compound containing only vanadium and chlorine is found to be 32.3% vanadium by mass. Find its empirical formula.

Q5 An oxide of chromium contains 31.58% by mass of oxygen. Find its empirical formula.

Tip: Being able to calculate empirical formulas is an important skill in chemistry. It's really useful when analysing the structures of compounds and might crop up in exam questions for later modules, so make sure you understand it.

Calculating molecular formulas

Once you know the empirical formula, you just need the molar mass and you can work out the molecular formula too. Dividing the molar mass by the mass of the empirical formula tells you what factor you need to scale the empirical formula up by to get the molecular formula.

┌─ **Example** ── **Maths Skills** ──────────────────────────────

When 4.6 g of an alcohol, with molar mass 92 g mol⁻¹, is burnt in excess oxygen, it produces 8.8 g of carbon dioxide and 5.4 g of water. Calculate the empirical formula for the alcohol and then its molecular formula.

First, find the empirical formula using the same steps as before:

moles $CO_2 = \dfrac{\text{mass}}{M_r} = \dfrac{8.8}{12 + (16 \times 2)} = \dfrac{8.8}{44} = 0.20$ moles

1 mole of CO_2 contains 1 mole of carbon atoms, so you must have started with 0.20 moles of carbon atoms.

Tip: Alcohols contain carbon, hydrogen and oxygen.

Tip: See page 35 for more on finding relative molecular mass.

$$\text{moles } H_2O = \frac{mass}{M_r} = \frac{5.4}{(2 \times 1) + 16} = \frac{5.4}{18} = 0.30 \text{ moles}$$

1 mole of H_2O contains 2 moles of hydrogen atoms (H), so you must have started with $(0.30 \times 2) = 0.60$ moles of hydrogen atoms.

To find the moles of oxygen coming from the alcohol you first need to find the mass of oxygen you started with. You can find this by using the moles of C and H that you calculated above to find the mass of C and H you started with and then take this away from the total mass of the alcohol:

Mass of C = no. of moles $\times M_r = 0.20 \times 12 = 2.4$ g

Mass of H = no. of moles $\times M_r = 0.60 \times 1 = 0.60$ g

Mass of alcohol = mass of C + mass of H + mass of O, so...

Mass of O = $4.6 - (2.4 + 0.60) = 1.6$ g

moles O in the alcohol = $\dfrac{mass}{M_r} = \dfrac{1.6}{16} = 0.10$ moles

You know the ratio — C : H : O = 0.20 : 0.60 : 0.10 = 2 : 6 : 1
So the empirical formula is C_2H_6O.

The mass of the empirical formula is $(12 \times 2) + (1 \times 6) + 16 = 46$ g

Divide the molar mass of the alcohol by this and you get $92 \div 46 = 2$

So you need to scale the empirical formula up by 2 to get the molecular formula. So the molecular formula of the alcohol is $C_4H_{12}O_2$.

Practice Questions — Application

Q1 3.1 g of phosphorus burns in air to produce 7.1 g of phosphorus oxide which has a molar mass of 284 g mol⁻¹. Calculate the empirical formula of phosphorus oxide and then its molecular formula.

Q2 A hydrocarbon is found to have a percentage composition of 85.7% carbon and 14.3% hydrogen by mass. Find the molecular formula of this hydrocarbon given that it has a molar mass of 56 g mol⁻¹.

Q3 An oxide of chlorine has a molar mass of 167 g mol⁻¹ and contains 42.5% chlorine by mass. Find its molecular formula.

Q4 When 12.8 g of an alcohol, with molar mass 32 g mol⁻¹, is burnt in excess oxygen, it produces 17.6 g of CO_2 and 14.4 g of H_2O. Calculate the empirical and molecular formulas of the alcohol.

Q5 When 2.64 g of an alcohol, with a molar mass 88 g mol⁻¹, is burnt in excess oxygen, it produces 2.16 g of H_2O and 5.28 g of CO_2. Calculate the empirical and molecular formulas of the alcohol.

Practice Questions — Fact Recall

Q1 What equation links the number of moles of a substance to its mass and molecular formula?

Q2 What is meant by the percentage composition of a compound?

Tip: You need to work out the mass of oxygen in this way because you don't know how much oxygen has come from the alcohol itself and how much has come from the air when the alcohol was burnt.

Figure 2: *An alcohol burning in air.*

Tip: If the molar mass of the empirical formula is the same as the molar mass of your substance then the empirical formula is the same as the molecular formula.

3. Chemical Equations

Balancing equations is one of those topics that gets everywhere in chemistry. You'll have done this before, so it should look a bit familiar. Make sure you've got your head round it now though, because you'll definitely need it again.

How to balance equations

Balanced equations have the same number of each atom on both sides. They're.. well... you know... balanced. You can only add more atoms by adding whole reactants or products. You do this by putting a number in front of a substance or changing one that's already there. You can't mess with formulas — ever (e.g. you can change H_2O to $2H_2O$, but never to H_4O).

Examples — ⟨Maths Skills⟩

Balance the equation H_2SO_4 + NaOH → Na_2SO_4 + H_2O.

First you need to count how many of each atom you have on each side.

$$H_2SO_4 + NaOH \rightarrow Na_2SO_4 + H_2O$$

| $H = 3$ | $Na = 1$ | $H = 2$ | $Na = 2$ |
| $O = 5$ | $S = 1$ | $O = 5$ | $S = 1$ |

The left side needs 2 Na's, so try changing NaOH to 2NaOH:

$$H_2SO_4 + 2NaOH \rightarrow Na_2SO_4 + H_2O$$

| $H = 4$ | $Na = 2$ | $H = 2$ | $Na = 2$ |
| $O = 6$ | $S = 1$ | $O = 5$ | $S = 1$ |

Now the right side needs 4 H's, so try changing H_2O to $2H_2O$:

$$H_2SO_4 + 2NaOH \rightarrow Na_2SO_4 + 2H_2O$$

| $H = 4$ | $Na = 2$ | $H = 4$ | $Na = 2$ |
| $O = 6$ | $S = 1$ | $O = 6$ | $S = 1$ |

Both sides have the same number of each atom — the equation is balanced.

Balance the equation C_2H_6 + O_2 → CO_2 + H_2O.

First work out how many of each atom you have on each side.

$$C_2H_6 + O_2 \rightarrow CO_2 + H_2O$$

| $C = 2$ | $H = 6$ | $C = 1$ | $H = 2$ |
| | $O = 2$ | | $O = 3$ |

The right side needs 2 C's, so try $2CO_2$. It also needs 6 H's, so try $3H_2O$.

$$C_2H_6 + O_2 \rightarrow 2CO_2 + 3H_2O$$

| $C = 2$ | $H = 6$ | $C = 2$ | $H = 6$ |
| | $O = 2$ | | $O = 7$ |

The left side needs 7 O's, so try $3\frac{1}{2}O_2$ (you can use ½ to balance equations).

$$C_2H_6 + 3\frac{1}{2}O_2 \rightarrow 2CO_2 + 3H_2O$$

| $C = 2$ | $H = 6$ | $C = 2$ | $H = 6$ |
| | $O = 7$ | | $O = 7$ |

This balances the equation.

Ionic equations

You can write **ionic equations** for any reaction involving ions that happens in solution. In ionic equations, only the reacting particles are included, so you don't have to worry about the rest of the stuff. First, you make sure that both sides of the equation have the same number of atoms — just like a normal equation. Then you just take out anything that appears on both sides.

Work out the ionic equation for the reaction between sodium hydroxide and nitric acid: $HNO_3 + NaOH \rightarrow NaNO_3 + H_2O$

First, you check the full equation is balanced. This one is — there are the same numbers of each type of atom on each side of the equation.

The ionic substances in this equation will dissolve, breaking up into ions in solution. You can now rewrite the equation to show all the ions that are in the reaction mixture:

$$H^+ + NO_3^- + Na^+ + OH^- \rightarrow Na^+ + NO_3^- + H_2O$$

Tip: Leave anything that isn't an ion in solution, like water, as it is.

To get from this to the ionic equation, just cross out any ions that appear on both sides of the equation — in this case, that's the sodium ions and the nitrate ions.

$$H^+ + \cancel{NO_3^-} + \cancel{Na^+} + OH^- \rightarrow \cancel{Na^+} + \cancel{NO_3^-} + H_2O$$

Tip: As long as you use a full, balanced equation to make your ionic equation, the charges in your ionic equation should balance.

So the ionic equation is: $\mathbf{H^+ + OH^- \rightarrow H_2O}$

Once you've written an ionic equation, check that the charges are balanced. In this example, the net charge on the left-hand side is $+1 + (-1) = 0$, and the net charge on the right-hand side is 0 — so the charges balance.

Work out the ionic equation for this reaction:
$$Na_3PO_{4\,(aq)} + CaCl_{2\,(aq)} \rightarrow NaCl_{(aq)} + Ca_3(PO_4)_{2\,(s)}$$

First, balance the equation so there are the same number of atoms on each side. Look back at the last page for more on how to do this.

$$2Na_3PO_4 + 3CaCl_2 \rightarrow 6NaCl + Ca_3(PO_4)_2$$

Tip: The equation shows $Ca_3(PO_4)_2$ is a solid, so you don't need to split it up into its ions.

Now split up everything that dissolves into its constituent ions. Remember to take into account the reaction stoichiometry (see page 56) and the number of atoms of each type in the equation.

$$(2 \times 3)Na^+ + 2PO_4^{3-} + 3Ca^{2+} + (3 \times 2)Cl^- \rightarrow 6Na^+ + 6Cl^- + Ca_3(PO_4)_2$$

And cross out the bits that are on both sides of the equation.

$$\cancel{6Na^+} + 2PO_4^{3-} + 3Ca^{2+} + \cancel{6Cl^-} \rightarrow \cancel{6Na^+} + \cancel{6Cl^-} + Ca_3(PO_4)_2$$

Tip: Make sure you've got the same number of atoms on each side of the equation after each step. It's easy to lose or gain some along the way, especially if your molar ratios aren't 1 : 1 (see next page).

This leaves you with your ionic equation: $\mathbf{2PO_4^{3-} + 3Ca^{2+} \rightarrow Ca_3(PO_4)_2}$

Tip: The net charge on the left-hand side is $(2 \times -3) + (3 \times +2) = 0$. This is the same as the net charge on the right-hand side, so your equation balances.

Practice Questions — Application

Q1 Balance these equations:
a) $Mg + HCl \rightarrow MgCl_2 + H_2$
b) $S_8 + F_2 \rightarrow SF_6$
c) $Ca(OH)_2 + H_2SO_4 \rightarrow CaSO_4 + H_2O$
d) $Na_2CO_3 + HCl \rightarrow NaCl + CO_2 + H_2O$
e) $C_4H_{10} + O_2 \rightarrow CO_2 + H_2O$

Q2 Write out the ionic equations for these reactions:
a) $Fe_{(s)} + CuSO_{4\,(aq)} \rightarrow FeSO_{4(aq)} + Cu_{(s)}$
b) $BaCl_{2\,(aq)} + Na_2SO_{4(aq)} \rightarrow NaCl_{(aq)} + BaSO_{4\,(s)}$
c) $Na_2CO_{3\,(aq)} + HNO_{3\,(aq)} \rightarrow NaNO_{3\,(aq)} + H_2O_{(l)} + CO_{2\,(g)}$

Tip: If you're not sure what the charges on the ions of different elements are, or how to work them out, look at pages 59-60.

- Be able to use stoichiometric relationships in calculations.

- Be able to carry out calculations, using amount of substance in mol, involving mass and gas volume.

- Be able to use state symbols.

Specification Reference 2.1.2, 2.1.3

4. Equations and Calculations

Once you've made sure that an equation is balanced, you can use it to calculate all sorts of things — like how much product a reaction will make...

Calculating masses

Balanced equations (see page 54) show the reaction stoichiometry. The reaction stoichiometry tells you the ratios of reactants to products, i.e. how many moles of product are formed from a certain number of moles of reactants. You can use the balanced equation for a reaction to work out how much product you will get from a certain mass of reactant. Here's how:

1. Write out the balanced equation for the reaction.

2. Work out how many moles of the reactant you have.

3. Use the **molar ratio** from the balanced equation to work out the number of moles of product that will be formed from this much reactant.

4. Calculate the mass of that many moles of product.

Tip: The big numbers in front of substances in the chemical equation show the molar ratio — this is the ratio of the moles of each reactant and product in a balanced chemical equation.

┌─ **Example** ── **Maths Skills** ─────────────────

Calculate the mass of iron(III) oxide produced if 28 g of iron is burnt in air.

1. Write out the balanced equation: $2Fe_{(s)} + 1\frac{1}{2}O_{2\,(g)} \rightarrow Fe_2O_{3\,(s)}$

2. Work out how many moles of iron you have:
   M_r of Fe = 55.8
   Moles = mass $\div M_r$ = 28 $\div$ 55.8 = 0.5 moles of iron

3. The molar ratio of Fe : Fe_2O_3 is 2 : 1. This means that for every 2 moles of Fe that you have, you will produce 1 mole of Fe_2O_3. But you only have 0.5 moles of Fe here.
   So you will produce: 0.5 $\div$ 2 = 0.25 moles of Fe_2O_3.

4. Now find the mass of 0.25 moles of Fe_2O_3:
   M_r of Fe_2O_3 = (2 × 55.8) + (3 × 16) = 159.6
   Mass = moles × M_r = 0.25 × 159.6 = 40 g of iron(III) oxide

Tip: Reactants are the chemicals you start with that get used up during a reaction. Products are the chemicals that are formed during a reaction.

You can use similar steps to work out how much of a reactant you had at the start of a reaction when you're given a certain mass of product:

┌─ **Example** ── **Maths Skills** ─────────────────

Hydrogen gas can react with nitrogen gas to give ammonia (NH_3). Calculate the mass of hydrogen needed to produce 6.8 g of ammonia.

1. $N_{2\,(g)} + 3H_{2\,(g)} \rightarrow 2NH_{3\,(g)}$

2. M_r of NH_3 = 14 + (3 × 1) = 17
   Moles = mass $\div M_r$ = 6.8 $\div$ 17 = 0.40 moles of NH_3

3. From the equation: the molar ratio of NH_3 : H_2 is 2 : 3.
   So to make 0.40 moles of NH_3, you must need to start with (0.40 $\div$ 2) × 3 = 0.60 moles of H_2

4. M_r of H_2 = 2 × 1 = 2
   Mass = moles × M_r = 0.60 × 2 = 1.2 g of hydrogen

Tip: Ammonia is produced from nitrogen and hydrogen by the Haber process. There's more about this on pages 170 and 171.

Q1 3.30 g of zinc is dissolved in hydrochloric acid, producing zinc chloride ($ZnCl_2$) and hydrogen gas.

   a) Write a balanced equation for this reaction.

   b) Calculate the number of moles of zinc in 3.30 g.

   c) How many moles of zinc chloride does the reaction produce?

   d) What mass of zinc chloride does the reaction produce?

Q2 A student burns some ethene gas (C_2H_4) in oxygen, producing carbon dioxide gas and 15.0 g of water.

   a) Write a balanced equation for this reaction.

   b) Calculate the number of moles of water in 15.0 g.

   c) How many moles of ethene did the student begin with?

   d) What mass of ethene did the student begin with?

Q3 Calculate the mass of barium carbonate ($BaCO_3$) produced if 4.58 g of barium chloride ($BaCl_2$) is reacted with sodium carbonate (Na_2CO_3).

Figure 1: *Zinc dissolving in hydrochloric acid.*

Calculating gas volumes

It's pretty handy to be able to work out how much gas a reaction will produce, so that you can use large enough apparatus. Or else there might be a rather large bang. The first three steps of this method are the same as the method on the last page. Once you've found the number of moles of product, the final step is to put that number into one of the gas equations that you saw on page 40.

Examples — Maths Skills

What volume of hydrogen gas is produced when 15 g of sodium is reacted with excess water at r.t.p.?

1. $2Na_{(s)} + 2H_2O_{(l)} \rightarrow 2NaOH_{(aq)} + H_{2(g)}$

2. M_r of Na = 23
   number of moles $= $ mass $\div M_r$
   $\qquad\qquad\qquad = 15 \div 23 = 0.652...$ moles of sodium

3. From the equation: the molar ratio of Na : H_2 is 2 : 1.
   So 0.65 moles of Na must produce $(0.652... \div 2) = 0.326...$ moles of H_2

At room temperature and pressure 1 mole of gas takes up 24 dm³.
Volume in dm³ = number of moles × 24
$\qquad\qquad = 0.326... \times 24 = 7.8$ dm³ of hydrogen gas

What volume of carbon dioxide is produced when 10 g of calcium carbonate reacts with excess hydrochloric acid at r.t.p.?

1. $CaCO_{3(s)} + 2HCl_{(aq)} \rightarrow CaCl_{2(aq)} + CO_{2(g)} + H_2O_{(l)}$

2. M_r of $CaCO_3$ = 40.1 + 12 + (3 × 16) = 100.1
   number of moles $= $ mass $\div M_r$
   $\qquad\qquad\qquad = 10 \div 100.1 = 0.10$ moles of calcium carbonate

3. From the equation: the molar ratio of $CaCO_3$: CO_2 is 1 : 1.
   So 0.10 moles of $CaCO_3$ must produce 0.10 moles of CO_2.

At room temperature and pressure 1 mole of gas takes up 24 dm³.
Volume in dm³ = number of moles × 24
$\qquad\qquad = 0.10 \times 24 = 2.4$ dm³ of carbon dioxide

Tip: 'Excess water' just means that all of the sodium will react.

Tip: In these calculations you need to use the molar ratios which you get from the balanced equation. See the last page for more on molar ratios.

State symbols

State symbols are put after each substance in an equation. They tell you what state of matter things are in:

s = solid,   l = liquid,   g = gas,   aq = aqueous (solution in water).

┌─ **Example** ──

$$CaCO_{3\ (s)} + 2HCl_{(aq)} \rightarrow CaCl_{2\ (aq)} + H_2O_{(l)} + CO_{2\ (g)}$$

solid   aqueous   aqueous   liquid   gas

└──

Practice Questions — Application

Q1 Give the state symbols that you would use in an equation to show the state of the following substances.

   a) a solution of magnesium chloride in water

   b) a piece of magnesium metal

   c) a measured amount of water (at r.t.p.)

   d) a solution of sodium nitrate in water

   e) ethane gas

   f) copper oxide powder

Q2 9.0 g of water is split apart to produce hydrogen gas and oxygen gas.

   a) Write a balanced equation for this reaction.

   b) Calculate the number of moles of water in 9.0 g.

   c) How many moles of oxygen gas does the reaction produce?

   d) What volume of oxygen gas will the reaction produce at r.t.p.?

Q3 7.00 g of zinc sulfide (ZnS) is burnt in oxygen.
This produces solid zinc oxide (ZnO) and sulfur dioxide gas (SO_2).

   a) Write a balanced equation for this reaction.

   b) Calculate the number of moles of zinc sulfide in 7.00 g.

   c) How many moles of sulfur dioxide gas does the reaction produce?

   d) What volume of sulfur dioxide gas will the reaction produce at r.t.p.?

Q4 A sample of hexane gas (C_6H_{14}) is cracked to give butane gas (C_4H_{10}) and ethene gas (C_2H_4). The mass of butane produced is 3.00 g.

   a) Write a balanced equation for this reaction.

   b) Calculate the number of moles of butane in 3.00 g.

   c) How many moles of hexane gas were present in the sample?

   d) What volume would this many moles of hexane gas occupy at r.t.p.?

Q5 Magnesium metal, once ignited, will react with oxygen in the air to produce solid magnesium oxide. Calculate the volume of oxygen, at r.t.p., needed to create 10 g of MgO.

Exam Tip
Make sure any chemical equations you write are balanced. You'll find you use balanced equations in loads of calculations and it's really important you know the right amounts of products compared to reactants.

5. Formulas of Ionic Compounds

The periodic table is a useful tool for predicting how different elements will behave. This includes working out what ions each element is likely to form.

Formation of ions

Ions are formed when electrons are transferred from one atom to another. The simplest ions are single atoms which have either lost or gained electrons so as to have a full outer shell. You don't have to remember what ion each element forms — nope, for many of them you just look at the periodic table. Elements in the same group all have the same number of outer electrons. So they have to lose or gain the same number to get the full outer shell that they're aiming for. And this means that they form ions with the same charges.

Learning Objectives:
- Be able to write the formulas of ionic compounds from ionic charges.
- Be able to predict the ionic charge from the position of an element in the periodic table.
- Know the names and formulas of the following ions: NO_3^-, CO_3^{2-}, SO_4^{2-}, OH^-, NH_4^+, Zn^{2+}, Ag^+.

Specification Reference 2.1.2

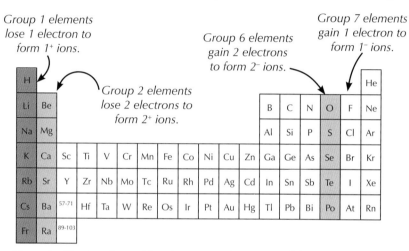

Group 1 elements lose 1 electron to form 1+ ions.

Group 2 elements lose 2 electrons to form 2+ ions.

Group 6 elements gain 2 electrons to form 2– ions.

Group 7 elements gain 1 electron to form 1– ions.

Figure 1: *The ions formed by elements in the groups of the periodic table.*

Tip: You can write half-equations to show the formation of ions. For example:

$$Na \rightarrow Na^+ + e^-$$

$$O + 2e^- \rightarrow O^{2-}$$

Example

What charged ion is sulfur likely to form?

First you need to identify which group sulfur is in by looking at a copy of the periodic table.

Sulfur is in Group 6. Elements in Group 6 gain two electrons to form ions with a –2 charge. So, the sulfur will form a 2– ion (S^{2-}).

Tip: Metals tend to form ions with a charge that's the same as their group number. Non-metals form ions with a charge that's equal to their group number minus eight.

Not all ions are made from single atoms. There are many ions that are made up of a group of atoms with an overall charge. These are called molecular ions. You'll need to learn the names and formulas of the ones in Figure 2.

Name	Formula
Nitrate	NO_3^-
Carbonate	CO_3^{2-}
Sulfate	SO_4^{2-}
Hydroxide	OH^-
Ammonium	NH_4^+

Figure 2: *The names and formulas of common molecular ions.*

Exam Tip
You'll need to remember the charges on some other common ions. You need to know that zinc forms 2+ ions (Zn^{2+}) and that silver forms 1+ ions (Ag^+).

The formulas of ionic compounds

1. **Ionic compounds** are made when positive and negative ions bond together. They do this through **ionic bonding** (see pages 98-100).

2. The charges on an ionic compound must always balance out to zero. For example:
   - In NaCl, the +1 charge on the Na^+ ion balances the -1 charge on the Cl^- ion.
   - In $MgCl_2$, the +2 charge on the Mg^{2+} ion balances the two -1 charges on the two Cl^- ions.

To work out the formula of an ionic compound, you just have to work out the ratio between the positive and negative ions so that the total of all the negative charges is the same as the total of the positive charges.

Figure 3: *Crystals of magnesium chloride, $MgCl_2$.*

Examples

What is the formula of potassium sulfate?

Potassium is in Group 1 of the periodic table, so will form ions with a +1 charge: K^+.

The formula for the sulfate ion is SO_4^{2-}.

For every one sulfate ion, you will need two potassium ions to balance the charge: $(+1 \times 2) + (-2) = 0$.

So the formula is K_2SO_4.

What is the formula of silver nitrate?

The charge on a silver ion is +1 — the formula of the silver ion is Ag^+ (this is unfortunately just a charge you have to learn — you can't work it out from silver's position in the periodic table).

The formula for the nitrate ion is NO_3^-.

Each silver ion exactly balances each nitrate ion, so they exist in a 1 : 1 ratio: $+1 + (-1) = 0$.

So the formula is $AgNO_3$.

Practice Questions — Application

Q1 Use the periodic table to give the charge on the following ions:
   a) hydrogen   b) lithium   c) iodine

Q2 An ionic compound is formed when calcium and chlorine react together. Give the formula of the compound formed.

Q3 Zinc nitrate is an ionic compound.
   a) What is the charge on a zinc ion?
   b) What is the formula of a nitrate ion?
   c) Give the formula of zinc nitrate.

Practice Questions — Fact Recall

Q1 What charge do the ions formed by Group 1 elements have?

Q2 Which elements does the carbonate ion contain?

Q3 What is the charge on a silver ion?

Section Summary

Make sure you know...

- That the empirical formula gives the simplest whole number ratio of atoms of each element present in a compound.
- That the molecular formula gives the actual number of atoms of each element present in a molecule.
- How to calculate empirical and molecular formulas using mass and percentage compositions.
- How to construct balanced equations for chemical reactions, including ionic equations.
- How to use balanced equations to determine stoichiometric relationships in calculations.
- How state symbols are used in chemical equations, and the meaning of the symbols (s), (l), (g) and (aq).
- How to predict the charge on an ion formed by an element, from its position in the periodic table.
- The formulas of the following ions: NO_3^-, CO_3^{2-}, SO_4^{2-}, OH^-, NH_4^+, Zn^{2+} and Ag^+.
- How to work out the formulas of ionic compounds from the charges on the ions.

Exam-style Questions

1 What is the formula of sodium nitrate?

A $NaNO_3$

B $Na(NO)_3$

C Na_2NO_3

D $NaNO_2$

(1 mark)

2 Selenium (Se) is an element in Group 6 of the periodic table.
Which ion is selenium likely to form?

A Se^{-}

B Se^{2-}

C Se^{6+}

D Se^{2+}

(1 mark)

3 A molecule, **X**, has the empirical formula C_3H_4O.
Which of these molecules could be molecule **X**?

A C_6H_8O

B C_2H_2O

C $C_{12}H_{14}O_3$

D $C_{15}H_{20}O_5$

(1 mark)

4 The equation below shows the reaction of magnesium carbonate ions with hydrochloric acid.

$$2HCl_{(aq)} + MgCO_{3\,(s)} \rightarrow CO_{2\,(g)} + H_2O_{(l)} + MgCl_{2\,(aq)}$$

(a) Write an ionic equation for the reaction shown above.

(2 marks)

(b) In a reaction between hydrochloric acid and magnesium carbonate at room temperature and pressure, 496.3 cm^3 of carbon dioxide gas was evolved.
What mass of magnesium carbonate must have reacted?

(4 marks)

5   Alcohols contain the elements carbon, hydrogen and oxygen.
When 9.0 g of an unknown alcohol is burnt in air, 17.6 g of CO_2
and 9.0 g of H_2O are produced.

(a)   Define the term empirical formula.

(1 mark)

(b) (i)   Calculate how many moles of CO_2 and H_2O are produced when this
alcohol is burnt.

(2 marks)

(ii)   Calculate the mass of carbon, hydrogen and oxygen present in the alcohol.

(3 marks)

(iii) Deduce the empirical formula of this alcohol.

(2 marks)

The unknown alcohol has a molar mass of 90 g mol^{-1}.

(c) (i)   Define the term molecular formula.

(1 mark)

(ii)   Deduce the molecular formula of this alcohol.

(2 marks)

6   Sodium hypochlorite (NaClO) is the main chemical in household bleach.
It is made in the Hooker process from chlorine molecules and sodium hydroxide.

(a)   Write a balanced chemical equation for the formation of sodium hypochlorite,
given that the only other products are sodium chloride and water.

(1 mark)

(b)   A student attempts to synthesise a sample of bleach using the same
method as that used in the Hooker process. Calculate the mass of
sodium hydroxide required to make 37.1 g of sodium hypochlorite.

(3 marks)

(c)   Sodium hypochlorite is an ionic compound. Given the chemical formula of
sodium hypochlorite is NaClO, what is the charge on a hypochlorite ion?

(1 mark)

7   A nitrate of iron contains 59.6% by mass of oxygen.

(a)   What is the formula for the nitrate ion?

(1 mark)

(b)   What is the empirical formula of the nitrate of iron?

(5 marks)

Learning Objectives:

- Be able to explain that acids release H+ ions in aqueous solution.
- Be able to explain that alkalis release OH− ions in aqueous solution.
- Know the formulas of the common acids (HCl, H_2SO_4, HNO_3 and CH_3COOH).
- Know the formulas of the common alkalis (NaOH, KOH and NH_3).
- Be able to qualitatively explain strong and weak acids in terms of relative dissociations.
- Be able to describe neutralisation as the reaction of H+ and OH− ions to form H_2O.
- Be able to describe the neutralisation reactions of acids with bases, including carbonates, metal oxides and alkalis (water-soluble bases), to form salts, including full equations.

Specification Reference 2.1.4

1. Acids, Bases and Salts

You met acids and bases at GCSE, but you need to know even more about them now. This section is all about what acids and bases are and how they react with each other to form salts.

What are acids and bases?

Acids are proton donors.
When mixed with water, all acids release hydrogen ions — H+.

--- Examples ---

Sulfuric acid (H_2SO_4) releases hydrogen ions when it is mixed with water:

$$H_2SO_{4(l)} + H_2O_{(l)} \rightarrow 2H^+_{(aq)} + SO_4^{2-}_{(aq)}$$

Hydrochloric acid (HCl) also releases hydrogen ions in water:

$$HCl_{(g)} + H_2O_{(l)} \rightarrow H^+_{(aq)} + Cl^-_{(aq)}$$

Hydrogen atoms only contain one proton and one electron. So H+ ions (which have lost the electron) are just protons. You never get H+ ions by themselves in water — they're always combined with H_2O to form hydroxonium ions (H_3O^+):

$$H^+_{(aq)} + H_2O_{(l)} \rightarrow H_3O^+_{(aq)}$$

Bases do the opposite of acids
— they're proton acceptors and want to grab H+ ions.

--- Examples ---

Ammonia (NH_3) is a base and it can accept hydrogen ions, forming ammonium ions (NH_4^+):

$$NH_{3(aq)} + H^+_{(aq)} \rightarrow NH_4^+_{(aq)}$$

OH− ions act as bases and can accept hydrogen ions to form water:

$$OH^-_{(aq)} + H^+_{(aq)} \rightarrow H_2O_{(l)}$$

So, acids produce $H^+_{(aq)}$ ions in an aqueous solution — i.e. they're proton donors. Bases remove $H^+_{(aq)}$ ions from an aqueous solution — i.e. they're proton acceptors. Bases that are soluble in water are known as **alkalis**. They release OH− ions in solution. You'll need to learn the names and formulas of the acids and bases in Figure 1 for your exam.

Acids	Bases
HCl (hydrochloric acid)	NaOH (sodium hydroxide)
H_2SO_4 (sulfuric acid)	KOH (potassium hydroxide)
HNO_3 (nitric acid)	NH_3 (ammonia)
CH_3COOH (ethanoic acid)	

Figure 1: *The names and formulas of some common acids and bases.*

Ammonia, NH_3, is a base — in fact it dissolves in water, so aqueous ammonia is an alkali. It'll happily accept a proton from an acid to form an ammonium ion — this can then form an ammonium salt.

Writing equations containing ammonium ions is a bit trickier, as ammonia doesn't directly produce hydroxide ions, but aqueous ammonia is still an alkali. This is because the reaction between ammonia and water produces hydroxide ions. As you saw on the last page, ammonia accepts a hydrogen ion from a water molecule, forming an ammonium ion and a hydroxide ion:

$$NH_{3\,(aq)} + H_2O_{(l)} \rightleftharpoons NH_4^{+}{}_{(aq)} + OH^{-}{}_{(aq)}$$

Tip: This equation is really useful as it explains really easily how ammonia acts as an alkali.

The strength of acids and bases

The reaction between an acid and water, or a base and water is reversible, so at any point in time, both the forwards and backwards reactions will be happening. So for the reaction of an acid with water:

$$HA + H_2O \rightleftharpoons H_3O^+ + A^-$$

Both of the following reactions are occurring:
$$HA + H_2O \rightarrow H_3O^+ + A^- \quad \text{and} \quad H_3O^+ + A^- \rightarrow HA + H_2O$$

The same applies for the reaction of a base with water:

$$B + H_2O \rightleftharpoons BH^+ + OH^-$$

In the situation above, both of the following reactions are occurring:
$$B + H_2O \rightarrow BH^+ + OH^- \quad \text{and} \quad BH^+ + OH^- \rightarrow B + H_2O$$

Tip: In these equations, A just represents any acid and B represents any old base.

Strong acids and bases

Acids and bases can be classed as strong or weak, depending on whether the forwards or backwards reaction is more prevalent and to what extent the acid or base is ionised in solution. For strong acids, e.g. HCl, very little of the reverse reaction happens, so nearly all the acid will dissociate (or ionise) in water, and nearly all the H^+ ions are released.

Example

Hydrochloric acid is a strong acid: $HCl_{(aq)} \rightarrow H^+{}_{(aq)} + Cl^-{}_{(aq)}$

The acid is almost 100% ionised in solution (i.e. present as H^+ and Cl^- ions, rather than as HCl), so it's a strong acid.

The same thing applies with strong bases, e.g. NaOH. The forwards reaction is favoured, so nearly all the base dissociates in water and lots of OH^- ions are released.

Example

Sodium hydroxide is a strong base: $NaOH_{(aq)} \rightarrow Na^+{}_{(aq)} + OH^-{}_{(aq)}$

Tip: The reactions of strong acids and bases with water are still reversible. So little of the backwards reaction happens, however, that they're usually written as a non-reversible reaction.

Tip: Don't get strong/weak acids confused with concentrated/dilute acids. The strength is all to do with ionisation, whereas concentration is to do with how much acid or base is dissolved in a solution.

Weak acids and bases

For weak acids, the backwards reaction is favoured, so only a small amount of the acid will dissociate in water and only a few H^+ ions are released. Reactions of weak acids are written as a reversible reaction:

Again, weak bases ionise only slightly in water. The backwards reaction is favoured, so only a small amount of the base dissociates and only a few OH^- ions are released. Again, the reaction is written as a reversible reaction:

Example

Ammonia is a weak base: $NH_{3\,(aq)} + H_2O_{(l)} \rightleftharpoons NH_4^+{}_{(aq)} + OH^-_{(aq)}$

Figure 2: *Some common alkalis.*

Reactions of acids and bases

Acid molecules release their hydrogen ions, so other ions can hop into their places. You get a **salt** if the hydrogen ions are replaced by metal ions or ammonium (NH_4^+) ions.

There are quite a few reactions of acids that produce salts...

Different acids produce different salts:

- Sulfuric acid (H_2SO_4) produces salts called sulfates.
  These contain SO_4^{2-} (sulfate) ions — e.g. $MgSO_4$ is magnesium sulfate.
- Hydrochloric acid (HCl) produces chlorides.
  These contain Cl^- (chloride) ions — e.g. $MgCl_2$ is magnesium chloride.
- Nitric acid (HNO_3) produces nitrates.
  These contain NO_3^- (nitrate) ions — e.g. $Mg(NO_3)_2$ is magnesium nitrate.

Acid-base reactions

When acids react with bases, they neutralise each other.
The general formula for an acid-base (neutralisation) reaction is:

Acid + Base → Salt + Water

The water formed in reactions of acids and bases is formed by the hydrogen ions released by the acid, and the hydroxide ions released by the alkali. These ions combine in solution to form water molecules:

$$H^+_{(aq)} + OH^-_{(aq)} \rightleftharpoons H_2O_{(l)}$$

Example

Sodium hydroxide (NaOH) and nitric acid react to form a salt and water.

This is a reaction between an acid and a base,
so the products will be a salt and water:
Acid + Base → Salt + Water

The salts produced by nitric acid are nitrates, so the salt produced by the reaction of sodium hydroxide and nitric acid will be sodium nitrate:

$$NaOH_{(aq)} + HNO_{3\,(aq)} \rightarrow NaNO_{3\,(aq)} + H_2O_{(l)}$$

The ionic equation for this reaction will be:
$$H^+_{(aq)} + OH^-_{(aq)} \rightarrow H_2O_{(l)}$$

Tip: Acid-base reactions are known as neutralisation reactions because, if the numbers of moles of hydrogen ions and hydroxide ions are equal, the reaction results in a neutral solution.

Tip: Sodium is in Group 1 so forms ions with a 1+ charge. The nitrate ion has a 1– charge, so the ratio of Na to NO_3^- ions in the sodium nitrate salt formed in this reaction is 1:1, and the formula is $NaNO_3$.
Look back at page 60 for more on writing the formulas of ionic compounds.

Tip: See pages 54-55 for more on ionic equations.

Example

The equation of the reaction between aqueous ammonia and sulfuric acid is:

$$2NH_{3\ (aq)} + H_2O_{\ (l)} + H_2SO_{4\ (aq)} \rightarrow (NH_4)_2SO_{4\ (aq)} + H_2O_{\ (l)}$$

But because water is present on both sides of the equation, you can simplify the equation to:

$$2NH_{3\ (aq)} + H_2SO_{4\ (aq)} \rightarrow (NH_4)_2SO_{4\ (aq)}$$

The ionic equation for this reaction is:

$$NH_{3\ (aq)} + H^+_{\ (aq)} \rightarrow NH_4^+_{\ (aq)}$$

> **Tip:** The reaction of ammonia and nitric acid would produce ammonium nitrate. Hydrochloric acid and ammonia would produce ammonium chloride.

Reactions of ammonia and acids produce ammonium salts. The name of the salt in the reaction above is ammonium sulfate.

> **Tip:** The ionic equation is really useful because it applies to all reactions of ammonia with acids.

Reactions of acids with metals

Salts are also produced when acids react with metals. But this time, hydrogen is produced instead of water, so the general equation is:

> Metal + Acid → Salt + Hydrogen

Example

Magnesium reacts with sulfuric acid to produce magnesium sulfate:

$$Mg_{(s)} + H_2SO_{4\ (aq)} \rightarrow MgSO_{4\ (aq)} + H_{2\ (g)}$$

The ionic equation for this reaction is: $Mg_{(s)} + 2H^+_{\ (aq)} \rightarrow Mg^{2+}_{\ (aq)} + H_{2\ (g)}$

> **Tip:** In this reaction magnesium ions are replacing the hydrogen ions in the acid to form a salt.

Acid and metal oxide reactions

Metal oxides react with acids according to the following equation:

> Metal Oxide + Acid → Salt + Water

Example

Magnesium oxide (MgO) reacts with hydrochloric acid to form the salt magnesium chloride ($MgCl_2$) and water. The equation for this reaction is:

$$MgO_{(s)} + 2HCl_{(aq)} \rightarrow MgCl_{2(aq)} + H_2O_{(l)}$$

This is the ionic equation for the reaction:

$$O^{2-}_{\ (s)} + 2H^+_{\ (aq)} \rightarrow H_2O_{\ (l)}$$

In this reaction, the O^{2-} ion accepts two H^+ ions, donated by the acid.

Figure 3: *Magnesium ribbon reacting with acid. The solution fizzes because hydrogen gas is produced.*

Acid and metal hydroxide reactions

Metal hydroxides are usually alkalis. Sodium hydroxide (NaOH) and potassium hydroxide (KOH) are the alkalis you're most likely to meet. Alkalis release OH^- ions in water. These OH^- ions accept H^+ ions (protons) from an acid to form water molecules.
The general equation for this reaction is:

> Metal Hydroxide + Acid → Salt + Water

Example

Potassium hydroxide (KOH) reacts with hydrochloric acid to form the salt potassium chloride (KCl) and water. The equation for this reaction is:

$$KOH_{(aq)} + HCl_{(aq)} \rightarrow KCl_{(aq)} + H_2O_{(l)}$$

Here's the ionic equation for the reaction:

$$OH^-_{(aq)} + H^+_{(aq)} \rightarrow H_2O_{(l)}$$

The ionic equation shows that a proton is transferred from the acid to the hydroxide ion. This ionic equation is the same for all reactions between metal hydroxides and acids.

Reactions of acids with carbonates

When acids react with carbonates, a salt is produced along with water and carbon dioxide. Here's the general equation:

> Metal Carbonate + Acid → Salt + Carbon Dioxide + Water

Example

Sodium carbonate reacts with hydrochloric acid to produce sodium chloride, carbon dioxide and water:

$$Na_2CO_{3\,(s)} + 2HCl_{(aq)} \rightarrow 2NaCl_{(aq)} + CO_{2\,(g)} + H_2O_{(l)}$$

The ionic equation for this reaction is: $CO_3^{2-}{}_{(s)} + 2H^+_{(aq)} \rightarrow CO_{2\,(g)} + H_2O_{(l)}$

Figure 4: *Sodium carbonate reacting with acid. It fizzes because carbon dioxide gas is produced.*

Exam Tip
If you're asked to describe what you'd see when a metal reacts with an acid, you need to say that the metal disappears (dissolves) and bubbles are produced (effervescence).

Tip: If you ever have to include state symbols when writing out equations containing acids and bases, remember — generally, everything will be aqueous, apart from water which is a liquid.

Practice Questions — Application

Q1 Write an equation to show the reaction of hydrochloric acid with:
   a) copper(II) oxide (CuO) to give copper(II) chloride ($CuCl_2$)
   b) sodium hydroxide (NaOH) to give sodium chloride (NaCl)

Q2 Write an equation to show the reaction of sulfuric acid with:
   a) iron (Fe) to give iron(III) sulfate ($Fe_2(SO_4)_3$)
   b) calcium carbonate ($CaCO_3$) to give calcium sulfate ($CaSO_4$)

Q3 Write an equation to show the reaction of nitric acid with:
   a) aluminium oxide (Al_2O_3) to give aluminium nitrate ($Al(NO_3)_3$)
   b) potassium hydroxide (KOH) to give potassium nitrate (KNO_3)
   c) magnesium carbonate ($MgCO_3$) to give magnesium nitrate ($Mg(NO_3)_2$)

Practice Questions — Fact Recall

Q1 a) What is an acid?   b) What is a base?

Q2 Explain the following terms:
   a) a strong acid.   b) a weak base.

Q3 Write down the molecular formula of:
   a) hydrochloric acid.   b) sulfuric acid.   c) nitric acid.
   d) sodium hydroxide.   e) potassium hydroxide. f) ammonia.

Q4 What type of salt do each of the acids in Q3 form when they react?

Q5 What products are formed when an acid reacts with:
   a) a base?   b) a metal carbonate?   c) a metal?

2. Anhydrous and Hydrated Salts

Learning Objectives:

- Be able to explain the terms anhydrous, hydrated and water of crystallisation.
- Be able to calculate the formula of a hydrated salt from percentage composition, mass composition or experimental data (PAG 1).

Specification Reference 2.1.3

Salts are ionic compounds, formed when acids and bases react together. They can come in two different forms — hydrated or anhydrous. Anhydrous salts don't contain water, hydrated salts do.

What are anhydrous and hydrated salts?

All solid salts consist of a **lattice** of positive and negative ions. In some salts, water molecules are incorporated in the lattice too — see Figure 1.

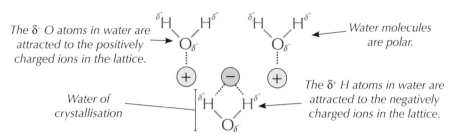

The δ^- O atoms in water are attracted to the positively charged ions in the lattice.

Water molecules are polar.

Water of crystallisation

The δ^+ H atoms in water are attracted to the negatively charged ions in the lattice.

Figure 1: A small part of a lattice in a hydrated salt.

The water in a lattice is called **water of crystallisation**. A solid salt containing water of crystallisation is **hydrated**. A salt is **anhydrous** if it doesn't contain water of crystallisation.

One mole of a particular hydrated salt always has the same number of moles of water of crystallisation — its formula shows how many (it's often a whole number, but not always...).

Tip: See pages 108-115 for more on polar compounds and pages 98-100 for more on lattice structures.

> **Example**
>
> Hydrated copper sulfate has five moles of water for every mole of the salt. So its formula is $CuSO_4.5H_2O$ (see Figures 2 and 3). There's a dot between the $CuSO_4$ and the H_2O to show that they are not joined by a covalent bond.

Figure 2: Anhydrous copper sulfate ($CuSO_4$).

Finding the formulas of hydrated salts

Many hydrated salts lose their water of crystallisation when heated, to become anhydrous. If you know the mass of the salt when hydrated and anhydrous, you can work its formula out. Just follow these steps:

PRACTICAL ACTIVITY GROUP **1**

Figure 3: When water is added, $CuSO_4.5H_2O$ forms, which is blue in colour.

- First you find the mass of water lost by taking the mass of the anhydrous salt away from the mass of the hydrated salt.
- Then you find the number of moles of water lost.
- Next find the number of moles of anhydrous salt that's produced.
- Now you work out the ratio of moles of anhydrous salt to moles of water.
- Scale up or down so that your ratio is in the form 1 : n, round off your answer and you're done.

Tip: To calculate the number of moles you'll need the equation:

$$moles = \frac{mass}{molar\ mass}$$

See page 38 for more on this.

> **Example**
>
> **Heating 3.210 g of hydrated magnesium sulfate, $MgSO_4.XH_2O$, forms 1.567 g of anhydrous magnesium sulfate. Find the value of X and write the formula of the hydrated salt.**
>
> - The mass of water lost is $3.210 - 1.567 = 1.643$ g

- You can now calculate the moles of water present in the hydrated salt:

$$\text{moles } H_2O = \frac{\text{mass}}{M} = \frac{1.643}{16 + (2 \times 1)} = \frac{1.643}{18} = 0.0913 \text{ moles}$$

- And you can calculate the moles of anhydrous magnesium sulfate:

$$\text{moles } MgSO_4 = \frac{1.567}{24.3 + 32.1 + (4 \times 16)} = \frac{1.567}{120.4} = 0.0130 \text{ moles}$$

- So the ratio of $MgSO_4 : H_2O = 0.0130 : 0.0913$.

- Dividing both sides by 0.0130 gives a ratio of 1 : 7.02. This shows that there are 7.02 moles of water for every one mole of $MgSO_4$.

- X must be a whole number, and some errors are to be expected in any experiment, so you can safely round off your result to 1 : 7 — so the formula of the hydrated salt is $MgSO_4.7H_2O$.

Figure 4: Some minerals are made from hydrated salts. This is turquoise, which is hydrated copper-aluminium phosphate $(CuAl_6(PO_4)_4(OH)_8.4H_2O)$.

You could also be given the percentage of the mass that is water. Then, you'd work out the formula by assuming you had 100 g of the hydrated salt and converting the percentages into masses.

Example

Hydrated $CaCl_2$ contains 49.3% H_2O by mass. Find the formula of the hydrated salt.

- If you had 100 g of hydrated $CaCl_2$ then 49.3 g would be water and 50.7 g (100 – 49.3) would be $CaCl_2$.
- Calculating the moles gives

$$\text{moles } CaCl_2 = \frac{\text{mass}}{M} = \frac{50.7}{40.1 + (2 \times 35.5)} = \frac{50.7}{111.1} = 0.456 \text{ moles}$$

$$\text{moles } H_2O = \frac{\text{mass}}{M} = \frac{49.3}{16 + (2 \times 1)} = \frac{49.3}{18} = 2.739 \text{ moles}$$

- So the ratio of $CaCl_2 : H_2O = 0.456 : 2.739$. This is a ratio of 1 : 6, so the formula of the hydrated salt is $CaCl_2.6H_2O$.

Practice Questions — Application

Q1 Heating 57.5 g of hydrated zinc sulfate ($ZnSO_4.XH_2O$) forms 32.3 g of anhydrous zinc sulfate. Find the value of **X** and write down the formula of the hydrated salt.

Q2 35.685 g of hydrated cobalt chloride ($CoCl_2.XH_2O$) contains 16.2 g of water. Find the value of **X** and write down the formula of the hydrated salt.

Q3 Hydrated $BaCl_2$ contains 14.74% H_2O by mass. Find the formula of the hydrated salt.

Q4 Hydrated $Fe(NO_3)_3$ contains 30.87% H_2O by mass. Find the formula of the hydrated salt.

Practice Questions — Fact Recall

Q1 What name is given to the water molecules in a lattice?

Q2 What does anhydrous mean?

Q3 How might a hydrated salt be converted into an anhydrous salt?

3. Titrations

You can do a titration to find the concentration of an acid or an alkali. You'll almost certainly have to do one at some point, so make sure you know how.

Performing titrations

PRACTICAL ACTIVITY GROUP 2

Titrations allow you to find out exactly how much acid is needed to neutralise a quantity of alkali. You measure out some alkali using a pipette and put it in a flask (see Figure 1), along with some indicator, e.g. phenolphthalein.

First of all, do a rough titration to get an idea where the end point is (the point where the alkali is exactly neutralised and the indicator changes colour). To do this, take an initial reading to see how much acid is in the burette to start off with. Then, add the acid to the alkali — giving the flask a regular swirl. Stop when your indicator shows a permanent colour change (the end point) (see Figure 1). Record the final reading from your burette.

Now do an accurate titration. Run the acid in to within 2 cm³ of the end point, then add the acid dropwise. If you don't notice exactly when the solution changed colour you've overshot and your result won't be accurate. Work out the amount of acid used to neutralise the alkali. This is just the final reading minus the initial reading. This volume is known as the titre. It's best to repeat the titration a few times, making sure you get a similar answer each time — your readings should be within 0.1 cm³ of each other. Then calculate a mean, ignoring any anomalous results.

Learning Objectives:

- Know the techniques and procedures used when preparing a standard solution of required concentration and carrying out acid-base titrations (PAG 2).

- Know the techniques and procedures required during experiments requiring the measurement of mass and volumes of solutions (PAG 1, PAG 2).

- Be able to carry out calculations, using amount of substance in mol, involving solution volume and concentration.

Specification Reference 2.1.3, 2.1.4

Tip: Remember to wash out the conical flask between each titration to remove any acid or alkali left in it.

Tip: You can also do titrations the other way round — adding alkali to acid.

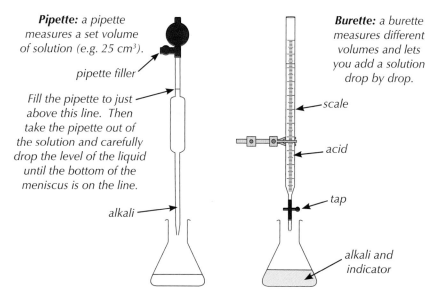

Pipette: *a pipette measures a set volume of solution (e.g. 25 cm³).*

pipette filler

Fill the pipette to just above this line. Then take the pipette out of the solution and carefully drop the level of the liquid until the bottom of the meniscus is on the line.

alkali

Burette: *a burette measures different volumes and lets you add a solution drop by drop.*

scale

acid

tap

alkali and indicator

Figure 1: *The apparatus needed for a titration.*

Indicators

PRACTICAL ACTIVITY GROUP 2

Indicators change colour at certain pHs. In titrations, indicators that change colour quickly over a very small pH range are used so you know exactly when the reaction has ended.

There are two main indicators for acid/alkali reactions:

- methyl orange — turns from yellow to red when adding acid to alkali.

- phenolphthalein — turns from pink to colourless when adding acid to alkali.

Figure 2: *The colour changes observed with phenolphthalein (left) and methyl orange (right).*

Practical techniques

Titrations are all about being precise — you need to be really careful when measuring out solids and liquids. You need to make sure that the volumes and masses you think you have are the volumes and masses you actually have.

Measuring masses

When you're measuring out masses, e.g. when you're making up a standard solution (see below), you should use an accurate balance that reads to a suitable number of decimal places. When weighing out solids you should:

Figure 3: An analytical balance.

PRACTICAL ACTIVITY GROUP **1**

- Reset the balance to zero before you start weighing your solid. This makes sure that the masses you record in your experiment are the actual masses of the things you're weighing.

- Make sure all of the solid you weigh is transferred from your weighing vessel to the apparatus you're using in your experiment. If you're dissolving your solid, you can do this by washing out the weighing vessel with some distilled water to make sure all the solid is transferred to the apparatus. If you're not dissolving the solid, you could compare the mass of the empty weighing vessel before and after weighing out your solid. By doing this, you can work out the mass of any traces of solid left over.

Tip: To work out how much trace solid is left in a weighing vessel, subtract the original mass of the empty weighing vessel from the mass of the vessel after the solid has been transferred from it.

Measuring volumes of solutions

In titrations, burettes are a great way of measuring out liquids. When taking a reading from a burette, you should take the reading from the bottom of the meniscus. You don't have to read to the smallest graduation, e.g. 0.1 cm³. You can make your readings more precise by taking readings to the nearest 0.05 cm³ (see Figure 4).

Tip: For information about precisely measuring gas volumes, look at page 42.

PRACTICAL ACTIVITY GROUP **2**

This is the bottom of the meniscus. This reading would be 0.50 cm³.

The reading is half way between the two graduation marks. This reading would be 0.65 cm³.

Figure 4: *Volume readings using a burette.*

- In titrations, you can also measure volumes using pipettes and volumetric flasks. Unlike burettes, these only measure a fixed volume, e.g. 10 cm³, 50 cm³, etc. For this reason, they're more suited to measuring out volumes for standard solutions or an initial volume of acid or alkali to titrate.

- When measuring volumes with pipettes and volumetric flasks, you'll need to fill the container up exactly to the graduation line. It helps to be at eye-level with the graduation line, so you can see the exact point when the bottom of the meniscus is level with the graduation line.

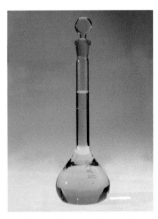

Figure 5: A volumetric flask. A mark on the neck of the flask shows where it should be filled to in order to achieve the desired volume.

Standard Solutions

In a titration, you have one unknown concentration to work out. To work out the concentration of the unknown solution, you have to know the concentration of the solution you're titrating it against.

A solution that has a precisely known concentration is called a **standard solution**. Standard solutions are made by dissolving a known amount of solid in a known amount of water to create a known concentration.

Preparing standard solutions

PRACTICAL ACTIVITY GROUP **2**

To make up a standard solution, follow these steps:

1) Using a precise balance, carefully weigh out the required mass of solid onto a watch glass.

2) Transfer this solid to a beaker. Use some water to wash any bits of solid from the watch glass into the beaker.

3) Add water to the beaker to completely dissolve the solid. Use a glass rod to stir the solution to help the solid dissolve.

4) Once the solid has dissolved, transfer the solution into a volumetric flask. You'll need to use a volumetric flask that's the same size as the volume of solution you want to make up. Rinse the beaker and glass rod with water, transferring this water into the volumetric flask.

5) Use water to fill the volumetric flask up to the graduation line. Use a pipette to add the final few drops to make sure you don't add too much water and overshoot the graduation line.

6) Put the lid on the flask and turn the flask over a few times to thoroughly mix the solution.

Tip: When making standard solutions you should always use distilled water — this is just pure water that contains nothing else.

Calculations involving standard solutions

Titrations are all about concentrations (see pages 43-44). You'll need to be able to work out concentrations, as well as moles and volumes of standard solutions, using this equation:

$$\text{Number of moles} = \frac{\text{Concentration} \times \text{Volume (in cm}^3)}{1000}$$

Tip: This formula pops up all the time. It's one you need to commit to memory and know how to rearrange. If you already have the volume in dm^3, you can use the formula: number of moles = concentration × volume (in dm^3).

Examples — Maths Skills

What mass of solid sodium carbonate, Na_2CO_3, is needed to make 250 cm³ of 0.300 mol dm⁻³ sodium carbonate solution?

Start by working out how many moles of Na_2CO_3 are needed using the equation: moles = concentration × volume

$$n = 0.300 \times \left(\frac{250}{1000}\right) = 0.0750 \text{ moles}$$

Now use the equation mass = moles × M to work out the mass of Na_2CO_3 required to make up the standard solution:

mass = $0.0750 \times [(2 \times 23) + 12.0 + (3 \times 16)] = 0.0750 \times 106 = 7.95$ g

Tip: You need to divide the concentration in cm^3 by 1000 to convert it into dm^3.

What is the concentration of a standard solution formed by dissolving 7.22 g of potassium hydroxide in 250 cm³ water?

Start by working out how many moles of potassium hydroxide are in 7.22 g using the equation:

$$\text{Number of moles} = \frac{\text{mass of substance}}{\text{molar mass}}$$

$$n = \frac{7.22}{(39.1 + 16 + 1)} = 0.128... \text{ moles}$$

Now you just need to work out the concentration of the solution by substituting the number of moles and volume into this equation:

$$\text{concentration} = \frac{\text{moles}}{\text{volume}}$$

$$= \frac{0.128...}{(250 \div 1000)} = 0.515 \text{ mol dm}^{-3} \text{ (3 s.f.)}$$

Tip: This is the formula from page 38. Look back there for more information about molar mass and how to use this formula.

Once you have a standard solution of a known concentration, you can dilute it with distilled water to make further standard solutions of different concentrations using the following method:

- First divide the concentration of the standard solution you want by the concentration of the standard solution you have.

- Then multiply by the volume of new standard solution you want. This gives you the volume of the concentrated solution to use.

- Subtract this volume of concentrated solution from the total volume of dilute standard solution you desire. This gives you the amount of distilled water to use.

Tip: Once you know how much distilled water and solution you need, you can create your dilute standard solution. This is done by first measuring out the volume of concentrated standard solution you need and transferring it to a volumetric flask of the correct size. Then, fill the volumetric flask up to the graduation line with distilled water and mix.

Example — **Maths Skills**

How would you make 250 cm³ of a 3.0 mol dm⁻³ standard solution from a 6.0 mol dm⁻³ standard solution?

First divide the concentration of the standard solution you want by the original concentration of the standard solution:

$$\frac{3.0}{6.0} = 0.50$$

Then multiply by the volume that you want:

$$0.50 \times 250 = 125 \text{ cm}^3$$

This is the volume of old standard solution you would need. In order to make 250 cm³ of this standard solution, you would need to dilute the 125 cm³ of 6.0 mol dm⁻³ with (250 − 125) = 125 cm³ distilled water.

Practice Questions — Application

Q1 How many moles of NaCl are required to make 400 cm³ of a 1.50 mol dm⁻³ solution of NaCl?

Q2 How many moles of NaHSO₄ are required to make 250 cm³ of a 2.0 mol dm⁻³ standard solution?

Q3 What mass of H₂C₂O₄ is needed to make 500.0 cm³ of a 1.250 mol dm⁻³ standard solution?

Q4 A student has 500 cm³ of 1.60 mol dm⁻³ sodium hydroxide solution. They want to make 250 cm³ of a 0.400 mol dm⁻³ solution.

    a) What volume of 1.60 mol dm⁻³ sodium hydroxide solution does the student require to make the 0.400 mol dm⁻³ standard solution?

    b) What volume of distilled water does the student require to make the 0.400 mol dm⁻³ standard solution?

Q5 What quantities of a stock solution of 5.00 mol dm⁻³ HCl solution and distilled water would you need to use to make 100 cm³ of a 1.50 mol dm⁻³ HCl solution?

Figure 6: *A student doing a titration. She is adding acid from the burette to the alkali in the flask. The alkali is coloured because it contains an indicator.*

Practice Questions — Fact Recall

Q1 Which piece of equipment would you use to add an acid of known concentration to a conical flask of alkali, during an acid-base titration?

Q2 Name two indicators used for acid/base titrations.

Q3 What is a standard solution?

4. Titration Calculations

As if knowing how to do a titration wasn't enough, now it's time to learn how to work out concentrations from all the data you collect.

Calculating concentration

You need to be able to use the results of a titration to calculate the concentration of acids and alkalis. There's more on concentration calculations on pages 43-44.

Examples — **Maths Skills**

25 cm³ of 0.50 mol dm⁻³ HCl neutralised 35 cm³ of NaOH solution. Calculate the concentration of the sodium hydroxide solution in mol dm⁻³.

First write a balanced equation and decide what you know and what you need to know:

$$HCl_{(aq)} + NaOH_{(aq)} \rightarrow NaCl_{(aq)} + H_2O_{(l)}$$

Volume:	*25 cm³*	*35 cm³*
Concentration:	*0.50 mol dm⁻³*	*?*

You know the volume and concentration of the HCl, so first work out how many moles of HCl you have:

$$\text{Number of moles HCl} = \frac{\text{concentration} \times \text{volume (cm}^3)}{1000}$$

$$= \frac{0.50 \times 25}{1000} = 0.0125 \text{ moles}$$

From the equation, you know 1 mole of HCl neutralises 1 mole of NaOH.

So 0.0125 moles of HCl must neutralise 0.0125 moles of NaOH.

Now it's a doddle to work out the concentration of NaOH.

$$\text{Concentration of NaOH} = \frac{\text{moles of NaOH} \times 1000}{\text{volume (cm}^3)}$$

$$= \frac{0.0125 \times 1000}{35} = 0.36 \text{ mol dm}^{-3}$$

40 cm³ of 0.25 mol dm⁻³ KOH was used to neutralise 22 cm³ of HNO₃ solution. Calculate the concentration of the nitric acid in mol dm⁻³.

Write out the balanced equation and the information that you have:

$$HNO_{3(aq)} + KOH_{(aq)} \rightarrow KNO_{3(aq)} + H_2O_{(l)}$$

Volume:	*22 cm³*	*40 cm³*
Concentration:	*?*	*0.25 mol dm⁻³*

You know the volume and concentration of the KOH, so now work out how many moles of KOH you have:

$$\text{Number of moles KOH} = \frac{\text{concentration} \times \text{volume (cm}^3)}{1000}$$

$$= \frac{0.25 \times 40}{1000} = 0.010 \text{ moles}$$

From the equation, you know 1 mole of KOH neutralises 1 mole of HNO₃.

So 0.010 moles of KOH must neutralise 0.010 moles of HNO₃.

$$\text{Concentration of HNO}_3 = \frac{\text{moles of HNO}_3 \times 1000}{\text{volume (cm}^3)}$$

$$= \frac{0.010 \times 1000}{22} = 0.45 \text{ mol dm}^{-3}$$

Learning Objective:
- Be able to carry out structured and non-structured titration calculations, based on experimental results of familiar and non-familiar acids and bases.

   Specification Reference 2.1.4

Exam Tip
With long wordy questions like this you might find it helpful to highlight the key bits of information in the question that you're likely to need.

Tip: The volumes in titrations are almost always in cm³ and not dm³, so you need to divide by 1000 when calculating the number of moles.

Tip: In this example, it's an alkali being added to an acid instead.

Exam Tip
You need to be able to work out concentration in g dm⁻³ too. To do this, just convert moles into mass and use:

$$\text{Conc} = \frac{\text{mass (g)} \times 1000}{\text{volume (cm}^3)}$$

Q1 28.0 cm³ of 0.750 mol dm⁻³ hydrochloric acid (HCl) was used to neutralise 40.0 cm³ of potassium hydroxide (KOH) solution.
  a) Write a balanced equation for this reaction.
  b) Calculate the number of moles of HCl used to neutralise the solution.
  c) How many moles of KOH were neutralised by the HCl?
  d) What was the concentration, in mol dm⁻³, of the KOH solution?

Q2 15.3 cm³ of 1.50 mol dm⁻³ sodium hydroxide (NaOH) was used to neutralise 35.0 cm³ of nitric acid (HNO₃). What was the concentration, in mol dm⁻³, of the HNO₃ solution?

Q3 12.0 cm³ of 0.500 mol dm⁻³ HCl solution was used to neutralise 24.0 cm³ of LiOH solution. What was the concentration, in mol dm⁻³, of the LiOH solution?

Tip: You can have polyprotic bases too, such as Ba(OH)₂, which is a diprotic base — it can react with 2 protons.

Polyprotic acids

You may have to do calculations that involve acids that donate more than one proton. These are known as polyprotic acids.

  ▪ Diprotic acids donate two protons, e.g. sulfuric acid (H_2SO_4), carbonic acid (H_2CO_3) and hydrogen sulfide (H_2S).

  ▪ Triprotic acids donate three protons, e.g. phosphoric acid (H_3PO_4).

Compared to a monoprotic acid, you'll need double the number of moles of base to neutralise a diprotic acid. You'll need to triple the number of moles of base to neutralise a triprotic acid compared to a monoprotic acid. So, remember to take this into account when you're working out these sorts of titration calculations.

Tip: All of these calculations are just like the moles, concentration and volume ones back on pages 43-44. You just apply the same method to titrations.

Calculating volumes

You can use a similar method to find the volume of acid or alkali that you need to neutralise a solution. You'll need to use the number of moles = (concentration × volume (cm³)) ÷ 1000 formula again, but this time rearrange it to find the volume:

$$\text{volume (cm}^3) = \frac{\text{number of moles} \times 1000}{\text{concentration}}$$

─ **Example** ── **Maths Skills** ──────────────

20.4 cm³ of a 0.500 mol dm⁻³ solution of sodium carbonate reacts with 1.50 mol dm⁻³ nitric acid. Calculate the volume of nitric acid required to neutralise the sodium carbonate.

Like before, first write a balanced equation for the reaction and decide what you know and what you want to know:

$$Na_2CO_{3(aq)} + 2HNO_{3(aq)} \rightarrow 2NaNO_{3(aq)} + H_2O_{(l)} + CO_{2(g)}$$

Volume: *20.4 cm³*   *?*
Concentration: 0.500 mol dm⁻³   1.50 mol dm⁻³

Now work out how many moles of Na₂CO₃ you've got:

$$\text{Number of moles Na}_2\text{CO}_3 = \frac{\text{concentration} \times \text{volume (cm}^3)}{1000}$$

$$= \frac{0.500 \times 20.4}{1000} = 0.0102 \text{ moles}$$

Tip: See page 68 for more on the reactions of acids with metal carbonates.

1 mole of Na_2CO_3 neutralises 2 moles of HNO_3, so 0.0102 moles of Na_2CO_3 neutralises $(0.0102 \times 2) = 0.0204$ moles of HNO_3.

Now you know the number of moles of HNO_3 and the concentration, you can work out the volume:

$$\text{Volume of } HNO_3 = \frac{\text{number of moles} \times 1000}{\text{concentration}}$$

$$= \frac{0.0204 \times 1000}{1.50} = 13.6 \text{ cm}^3$$

And here's an example where you're finding the volume of alkali used.

Example — **Maths Skills**

18.2 cm³ of a 0.800 mol dm⁻³ H_2SO_4 solution reacts with 0.300 mol dm⁻³ LiOH. Calculate the volume of lithium hydroxide solution required to neutralise the sulfuric acid.

Write out the balanced equation and the information that you have:

$$H_2SO_{4(aq)} + 2LiOH_{(aq)} \rightarrow Li_2SO_{4(aq)} + 2H_2O_{(l)}$$

Volume: 18.2 cm³   ?

Concentration: 0.800 mol dm⁻³   0.300 mol dm⁻³

Now work out how many moles of H_2SO_4 you've got:

$$\text{Number of moles } H_2SO_4 = \frac{\text{concentration} \times \text{volume (cm}^3)}{1000}$$

$$= \frac{0.800 \times 18.2}{1000} = 0.01456 \text{ moles}$$

1 mole of H_2SO_4 neutralises 2 moles of LiOH, so 0.01456 moles of H_2SO_4 neutralises 0.02912 moles of LiOH. Now use this to work out the volume:

$$\text{Volume of LiOH} = \frac{\text{number of moles} \times 1000}{\text{concentration}}$$

$$= \frac{0.02912 \times 1000}{0.300} = 97.1 \text{ cm}^3$$

Figure 1: *A titration where an alkali is being added to an acid. The indicator in the flask is phenolphthalein, so the solution starts colourless and turns pink at the end point.*

Practice Questions — Application

Q1 18.8 cm³ of a 0.200 mol dm⁻³ solution of nitric acid (HNO_3) reacts with 0.450 mol dm⁻³ lithium hydroxide (LiOH) solution.
   a) Write a balanced equation for this reaction.
   b) Calculate the number of moles of HNO_3 present in the acid added.
   c) How many moles of LiOH were in the sample of the alkali?
   d) What volume of LiOH solution was required to neutralise the HNO_3 solution?

Q2 37.3 cm³ of a 0.420 mol dm⁻³ solution of potassium hydroxide (KOH) reacts with 1.10 mol dm⁻³ ethanoic acid (CH_3COOH) solution.
   a) Write a balanced equation for this reaction.
   b) Calculate the number of moles of KOH present in the alkali added.
   c) What volume of CH_3COOH solution was required to neutralise the KOH solution?

Q3 14 cm³ of a 1.0 mol dm⁻³ $Ba(OH)_2$ solution reacts with a 0.50 mol dm⁻³ HCl solution. What volume of HCl solution was required to neutralise the $Ba(OH)_2$ solution?

- Be able to carry out calculations to determine the percentage yield of a reaction, or related quantities.

Specification Reference 2.1.3

Tip: The limiting reactant is the one that you have a limited amount of (i.e. the reactant that's not in excess).

Tip: The theoretical yield is the amount of product you would expect to form. The actual yield is the amount of product that is actually obtained.

Figure 1: A student pouring and filtering a solution. Some chemicals will be left on the glassware and some will be left on the filter paper.

5. Chemical Yield

If you're making a chemical (in a lab or a factory), it helps to know how much of it you can expect to get. In real life you'll never manage to make exactly that much — but percentage yield can give you an idea of how close you got.

Calculating theoretical yield

The **theoretical yield** is the mass of product that should be formed in a chemical reaction. It assumes no chemicals are 'lost' in the process. You can use the masses of reactants and a balanced equation to calculate the theoretical yield for a reaction. It's a bit like calculating reacting masses (see page 56) — here are the steps you have to go through:

1. Work out how many moles of the limiting reactant you have.

2. Use the equation to work out how many moles of product you would expect that much reactant to make.

3. Calculate the mass of that many moles of product — and that's the theoretical yield.

┌─ **Example** ── **Maths Skills** ──────────────

Ethanol can be oxidised to form ethanal:

$$C_2H_5OH + [O] \rightarrow CH_3CHO + H_2O$$

9.2 g of ethanol was reacted with an oxidising agent in excess. Calculate the theoretical yield of this reaction.

1. Ethanol is the limiting reactant so work out how many moles of ethanol you have:
   Molar mass of $C_2H_5OH = (2 \times 12) + (5 \times 1) + 16 + 1 = 46$ g mol^{-1}
   Number of moles C_2H_5OH = mass ÷ molar mass
   $= 9.2 \div 46 = 0.20$ moles.

2. Work out how many moles of product you would expect to make:
   From the equation, you know that 1 mole of C_2H_5OH produces 1 mole of CH_3CHO, so 0.20 moles of C_2H_5OH should produce 0.20 moles of CH_3CHO.

3. Now calculate the mass of that many moles of product:
   Molar mass of $CH_3CHO = (2 \times 12) + (4 \times 1) + 16 = 44$ g mol^{-1}
   Theoretical yield = number of moles × molar mass
   $= 0.20 \times 44 = 8.8$ g

Calculating percentage yield

For any reaction, the actual mass of product obtained (the actual yield) will always be less than the theoretical yield. There are many reasons for this. For example, sometimes not all the 'starting' chemicals react fully. And some chemicals are always 'lost', e.g. some solution gets left on filter paper, or is lost during transfers between containers. Once you've found the theoretical yield and the actual yield, you can work out the **percentage yield** — the actual amount of product you collect, written as a percentage of the theoretical yield. You can work out the percentage yield with this formula:

$$\text{Percentage Yield} = \frac{\text{Actual Yield}}{\text{Theoretical Yield}} \times 100$$

Examples — Maths Skills

In the ethanal example on the previous page, the theoretical yield was 8.80 g. Say you weighed the ethanal produced and found the actual yield was 2.10 g.

Then to work out the percentage yield you just have to plug the numbers into the formula:

$$\text{Percentage yield} = \frac{\text{Actual yield}}{\text{Theoretical yield}} \times 100$$

$$= (2.10 \div 8.80) \times 100 = 23.9\ \%$$

Here's another example:

5.00 g of ethanoyl chloride reacted with water to produce ethanoic acid. The theoretical yield of this reaction was 3.82 g. When the ethanoic acid was weighed it was found to have a mass of 2.46 g.

Calculate the percentage yield of this reaction.

All you need to do here is put the right numbers into the formula:

$$\text{Percentage yield} = \frac{\text{Actual yield}}{\text{Theoretical yield}} \times 100$$

$$= (2.46 \div 3.82) \times 100 = 64.4\%$$

Exam Tip
If you get a question in the exam on percentage yield and you've never heard of the compounds involved, don't be put off. You can just ignore the names — all you need are the theoretical and actual yields.

Exam Tip
This is a percentage yield, so it can never be more than 100%. If your answer is bigger than 100%, check the working for mistakes.

Practice Questions — Application

Q1 The theoretical yield of a reaction used in an experiment was 3.24 g. The actual yield was 1.76 g. Calculate the percentage yield of the reaction.

Q2 In an experiment nitrobenzene was reduced to produce phenylamine. The theoretical yield of this reaction was 6.10 g. The phenylamine produced had a mass of 3.70 g. Calculate the percentage yield of this reaction.

Q3 3.00 g of ethanoic anhydride reacts with water to give ethanoic acid:

$$(CH_3CO)_2O + H_2O \rightarrow 2CH_3COOH$$

   a) How many moles of ethanoic anhydride are there in 3.00 g?

   b) Calculate the theoretical yield of ethanoic acid for this reaction.

   c) Calculate the percentage yield if 2.80 g of ethanoic acid is made.

Q4 Propene reacts with HCl to produce 1-chloropropane:

$$CH_3CHCH_2 + HCl \rightarrow CH_3CH_2CH_2Cl$$

   a) How much 1-chloropropane would you expect to get from 50.0 g of propene?

   b) Calculate the percentage yield if only 54.0 g is made.

Q5 4.70 g of methanoic acid reacts to form 3.60 g of methanoic anhydride. The equation for this reaction is:

$$2HCOOH \rightarrow (CHO)_2O + H_2O$$

Calculate the percentage yield of this reaction.

Exam Tip
Percentage yields can be calculated for organic or inorganic reactions. The method is exactly the same, so don't be put off if you're asked to calculate the percentage yield of an inorganic reaction in your exam.

Practice Questions — Fact Recall

Q1 What is meant by the 'theoretical yield' of a reaction?

Q2 Write down the formula for percentage yield.

- Be able to calculate the atom economy of a reaction.
- Be able to discuss the benefits for sustainability of developing chemical processes with a high atom economy.

Specification Reference 2.1.3

6. Atom Economy

Atom economy is one way to work out how efficient a reaction is. Efficient reactions are better for the environment and save the chemical industry money.

What is atom economy?

The efficiency of a reaction is often measured by the percentage yield. This tells you how wasteful the process is — it's based on how much of the product is lost because of things like reactions not completing or losses during collection and purification. But percentage yield doesn't measure how wasteful the reaction itself is. A reaction that has a 100% yield could still be very wasteful if a lot of the atoms from the reactants wind up in by-products rather than the desired product. **Atom economy** is a measure of the proportion of reactant atoms that become part of the desired product (rather than by-products) in the balanced chemical equation.

Calculating atom economy

Atom economy is calculated using this formula:

$$\% \text{ atom economy} = \frac{\text{Molecular mass of desired product}}{\text{Sum of molecular masses of all products}} \times 100$$

To calculate the atom economy for a reaction, you just need to find the molecular mass of the product you're interested in, add up the molecular masses of the products, and put them both into the formula.

Exam Tip
This is another equation you'll have to learn for your exam. Atom economy can never be more than 100%, so if you get answers over 100% (or less than 0%), then you've either got the equation wrong or you've slipped up in the calculation somewhere.

┌ **Example** ─────────────────────

Bromomethane is reacted with sodium hydroxide to make methanol:

$$CH_3Br + NaOH \rightarrow CH_3OH + NaBr$$

Calculate the percentage atom economy for this reaction.

First, find the mass of the desired product — that's the methanol:

Mass of desired product = $12 + (3 \times 1) + 16 + 1 = 32$

Then, calculate the total mass of the products — add up the relative molecular masses of everything on the right side of the balanced equation:

Total mass of products = $32 + (23 + 79.9) = 134.9$

Now you can find the % atom economy:

$$\% \text{ atom economy} = \frac{\text{Molecular mass of desired product}}{\text{Sum of molecular masses of all products}} \times 100$$

$$= \frac{32}{134.9} \times 100 = 23.7\%$$
└──────────────────────────────

When you calculate the masses, you should use the number of moles of each compound that is in the balanced equation (e.g. the mass of '$2H_2$' should be $2 \times (2 \times 1) = 4$). Here's a quick example:

┌ **Example** ─────────────────────

Ethanol can be produced by fermenting glucose:

$$C_6H_{12}O_6 \rightarrow 2C_2H_5OH + 2CO_2$$

Calculate the percentage atom economy for this reaction.

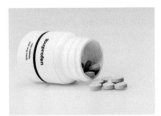

Figure 1: *Tablets of the painkiller ibuprofen. Ibuprofen was originally made using a reaction with a 40% atom economy. Now a new way of making it with a 77% atom economy is used. This produces much less waste.*

First, find the mass of the desired product (2 moles of ethanol):

Mass of desired product = 2 × ((12 × 2) + (5 × 1) + 16 + 1) = 92

Then calculate the total mass of the products:

Total mass of products = 92 + 2(12 + (16 × 2)) = 180

So, % atom economy = $\dfrac{\text{Molecular mass of desired product}}{\text{Sum of molecular masses of all products}}$ × 100

$$= \frac{92}{180} \times 100 = 51.1\%$$

Exam Tip
If you're asked to calculate atom economy in an exam, make sure that you start from the balanced equation.

Addition and substitution reactions

In an **addition reaction**, the reactants combine to form a single product. The atom economy for addition reactions is always 100% since no atoms are wasted.

Example

Ethene (C_2H_4) and hydrogen react to form ethane (C_2H_6) in an addition reaction: $C_2H_4 + H_2 \rightarrow C_2H_6$

The only product is ethane — the desired product. So no reactant atoms are wasted — the atom economy is 100%.

Tip: Any reaction where there's only one product will have a 100% atom economy because the mass of reactants has to equal the mass of product — atoms can't go anywhere else.

A **substitution reaction** is one where some atoms from one reactant are swapped with atoms from another reactant. This type of reaction always results in at least two products — the desired product and at least one by-product. So the atom economy of substitution reactions is always less than 100%.

Example

The reaction of bromoethane with sodium hydroxide to make methanol (on the previous page), is a substitution reaction and has a low atom economy.

Atom economy and percentage yield

Atom economy and percentage yield measure different things — so a reaction that has a high percentage yield might have a really low atom economy.

Example

0.475 g of CH_3Br reacts with an excess of NaOH in this reaction:

$$CH_3Br + NaOH \rightarrow CH_3OH + NaBr$$

0.153 g of CH_3OH is produced. What is the percentage yield?

Number of moles = mass of substance ÷ molar mass

Moles of CH_3Br = 0.475 ÷ (12 + 3 × 1 + 80) = 0.475 ÷ 95 = 0.005 moles

The reactant : product ratio is 1 : 1, so the maximum number of moles of CH_3OH is 0.005.

Theoretical yield = 0.005 × M_r(CH_3OH) = 0.005 × (12 + (3 × 1) + 16 + 1)
    = 0.005 × 32 = 0.160 g

percentage yield = $\dfrac{\text{actual yield}}{\text{theoretical yield}}$ × 100% = $\dfrac{0.153}{0.160}$ × 100% = 95.6%

Tip: See pages 78-79 for more about calculating percentage yield.

So this reaction has a very high percentage yield, but, as you saw on the previous page, the atom economy is low.

Atom economy in industry

Companies in the chemical industry will often choose to use reactions with high atom economies. High atom economy has environmental and economic benefits.

- Reactions with low atom economies are less sustainable. Many raw materials are in limited supply, so it makes sense to use them efficiently so they last as long as possible. Also, waste has to go somewhere — it's better for the environment if less is produced.

- A low atom economy means there's lots of waste produced. It costs money to separate the desired product from the waste products and more money to dispose of the waste products safely so they don't harm the environment. Companies will usually have paid good money to buy the reactant chemicals. It's a waste of money if a high proportion of them end up as useless products.

But reactions with a low atom economy may still be used if the waste products can be sold and used for something else (waste products like gases, salts and acids can often be useful reactants for other reactions).

Figure 2: *Chemical waste disposal site. Disposing of chemicals is expensive, so reactions with high atom economies and less waste are better in industry.*

Practice Questions — Application

Q1 Chlorine gas can react with excess methane to make chloromethane:
$$CH_4 + Cl_2 \rightarrow CH_3Cl + HCl$$
a) Find the molecular mass of the chloromethane produced.
b) Find the total molecular mass of the products in this reaction.
c) Calculate the percentage atom economy of this reaction.
d) A company wants to use this reaction to make chloromethane, despite its low atom economy. Suggest one way that they could increase their profit and reduce the waste they produce.

Q2 Ethanol can be produced using this reaction:
$$C_2H_4 + H_2O \rightarrow C_2H_5OH$$
What is the percentage atom economy of this reaction?

Q3 Ethene can be produced from ethanol in a dehydration reaction:
$$C_2H_5OH \rightarrow C_2H_4 + H_2O$$
Calculate the percentage atom economy of this reaction.

Q4 In industry, ammonia (NH_3) is usually produced using this reaction:
Reaction 1: $N_2 + 3H_2 \rightarrow 2NH_3$
It can also be made using this reaction:
Reaction 2: $2NH_4Cl + Ca(OH)_2 \rightarrow CaCl_2 + 2NH_3 + 2H_2O$
a) Calculate the percentage atom economy of both reactions.
b) Give one reason why reaction 1 is used to produce ammonia industrially rather than reaction 2.

Practice Questions — Fact Recall

Q1 What is meant by the 'atom economy' of a reaction?
Q2 Write down the formula for calculating % atom economy.
Q3 Give two reasons why reactions with a low atom economy are not used in industry.

7. Oxidation Numbers

Oxidation numbers are really useful in chemistry. They help you work out what's going on in chemical reactions. You need to know how to assign oxidation numbers to atoms in elements, compounds and ions. This is done using a simple set of rules. Read on to find out more...

Assigning oxidation numbers

Atoms use electrons to form bonds with other atoms. The **oxidation number** of an element tells you the total number of electrons it has donated or accepted to form an ion or to form part of a compound. Oxidation numbers are also called oxidation states. There are lots of rules for working out oxidation numbers. Take a deep breath...

Uncombined elements have an oxidation number of 0 — they haven't accepted or donated any electrons. Elements just bonded to identical atoms also have an oxidation number of 0.

Learning Objectives:

- Be able to apply rules for assigning and calculating oxidation number for atoms in elements, compounds and ions.
- Be able to write formulas using oxidation numbers.
- Be able to use Roman numerals to indicate the magnitude of the oxidation number when an element may have compounds or ions with different oxidation numbers.

Specification Reference 2.1.5

--- Examples ---

Uncombined elements — oxidation number = 0

Elements bonded to identical elements — oxidation number = 0

The oxidation number of a simple monatomic ion is the same as its charge.

--- Examples ---

oxidation number = +1   *oxidation number = +2*

Monatomic ions

For molecular ions (see page 59), each of the constituent atoms has an oxidation number of its own and the sum of their oxidation numbers equals the overall oxidation number. This overall oxidation number is equal to the overall charge on the ion.

Figure 1: *Nuggets of gold, silver and copper. These are all uncombined elements with oxidation numbers of 0.*

--- Example ---

Combined oxygen has an oxidation number of –2 (apart from in O_2 where it's 0). There are 4 oxygen atoms in SO_4^{2-}, so the total oxidation number from oxygens is $4 \times -2 = -8$.

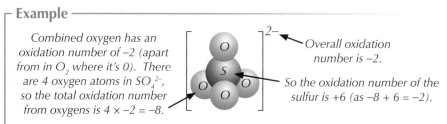

Overall oxidation number is –2.

So the oxidation number of the sulfur is +6 (as $-8 + 6 = -2$).

Figure 2: *Oxidation numbers of elements in the SO_4^{2-} ion.*

The sum of the oxidation numbers for a neutral compound is 0 (see Figure 3). If the compound is made up of more than one element, each element will have its own oxidation number.

Tip: All atoms are treated as ions when you're finding oxidation numbers, even if they're covalently bonded.

--- Example ---

The oxidation number of the chloride ion is –1.

The oxidation number of the magnesium ion is +2.

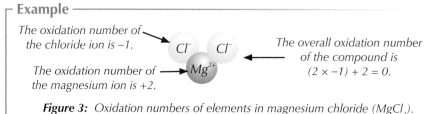

The overall oxidation number of the compound is $(2 \times -1) + 2 = 0$.

Figure 3: *Oxidation numbers of elements in magnesium chloride ($MgCl_2$).*

Oxygen nearly always has an oxidation number of –2, except in peroxides (O_2^{2-}) where it's –1, and molecular oxygen (O_2) where it's 0.

Hydrogen always has an oxidation number of +1, except in metal hydrides (MH_x, M = metal) where it's –1 and in molecular hydrogen (H_2) where it's 0.

Examples

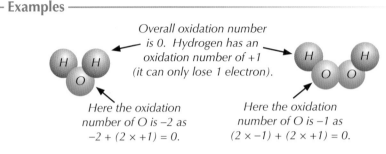

Overall oxidation number is 0. Hydrogen has an oxidation number of +1 (it can only lose 1 electron).

Here the oxidation number of O is –2 as $-2 + (2 \times +1) = 0$.

Here the oxidation number of O is –1 as $(2 \times -1) + (2 \times +1) = 0$.

Figure 4: Oxidation numbers of hydrogen and oxygen in water (H_2O) and hydrogen peroxide (H_2O_2).

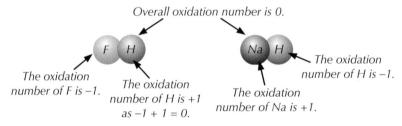

Overall oxidation number is 0.

The oxidation number of F is –1.

The oxidation number of H is +1 as $-1 + 1 = 0$.

The oxidation number of Na is +1.

The oxidation number of H is –1.

Figure 5: Oxidation numbers of hydrogen in hydrogen fluoride (HF) and sodium hydride (NaH).

Finding oxidation numbers

You can work out oxidation numbers from formulas or systematic names.

Finding oxidation numbers from formulas

In your exam, you may get a question asking you to work out the oxidation number of one element in a compound. To do this you just have to follow all the rules on the previous page and above and you'll be fine.

Examples

Find the oxidation number of Zn in $Zn(OH)_2$.

- $Zn(OH)_2$ is neutral (it has no charge), so its overall oxidation number is 0.
- Oxygen's oxidation number is usually –2, and hydrogen's is usually +1.
- So the oxidation number of the $(OH)_2$ bit of the molecule is $2 \times (-2 + 1) = -2$.
- So the oxidation number of Zn in $Zn(OH)_2$ is $0 - (-2) = +2$.

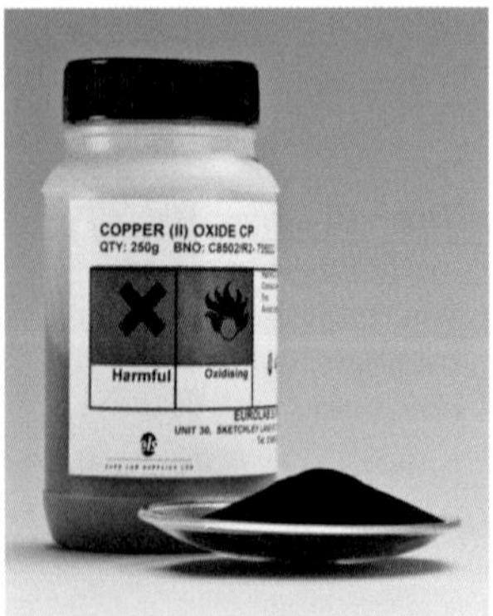

Finding oxidation numbers from systematic names

If an element can have multiple oxidation numbers, or isn't in its 'normal' oxidation state, its oxidation number can be shown by using Roman numerals, e.g. (I) = +1, (II) = +2, (III) = +3 and so on. The Roman numerals are written after the name of the element they correspond to.

Examples

In iron(II) sulfate, iron has an oxidation number of +2. Formula = $FeSO_4$

In iron(III) sulfate, iron has an oxidation number of +3. Formula = $Fe_2(SO_4)_3$

COPPER (II) OXIDE CP
QTY: 250g   BNO: C8602RO-7002

Harmful   Oxidising

Figure 6: A bottle of copper(II) oxide. The Roman numerals show that the copper has an oxidation number of +2.

This is particularly useful when looking at -ate ions. Ions with names ending in -ate (e.g. sulfate, nitrate, carbonate) contain oxygen, as well as another element. For example, sulfates contain sulfur and oxygen, nitrates contain nitrogen and oxygen... and so on. But sometimes the 'other' element in the ion can exist with different oxidation numbers, and so form different '-ate ions'. You can use the systematic name to work out the formula of the ion.

Tip: The oxidation number in sulfate ions applies to the sulfur, not the oxygen, because oxygen always has an oxidation number of -2 in -ate ions.

--- Examples ---

In sulfate(VI) ions the sulfur has oxidation number $+6$. This is the SO_4^{2-} ion.
In sulfate(IV) ions, the sulfur has oxidation number $+4$. This is the SO_3^{2-} ion.
In nitrate(III), nitrogen has an oxidation number of $+3$. This is the NO_2^- ion.

Tip: Several ions have widely used common names that are different from their correct systematic names. E.g. the sulfate(IV) ion (SO_3^{2-}) is often called the sulfite ion.

Using oxidation numbers

If you know the oxidation numbers of the elements in a compound, you can use them to work out the systematic name for that compound or its formula.

Working out systematic names

You might have to work out the systematic name for a compound, given its formula. To do this you have to find the oxidation numbers of the elements in the compound and then add in Roman numerals where needed.

--- Examples ---

What is the systematic name of KNO_3?
This is potassium nitrate, but for the systematic name to be complete you need to give the oxidation number of the nitrogen. You know that potassium always forms K^+ ions, so the charge on the nitrate ion must be $1-$.
Each oxygen atom in the NO_3^- ion has oxidation number -2.
This gives $3 \times -2 = -6$. Then, since the ion has an overall oxidation number of -1, the nitrogen must be in the $+5$ state.
So the compound is potassium nitrate(V).

What is the systematic name for ClO_2^-?
This formula contains chlorine and oxygen, so it's a chlorate.
Oxygen usually exists with an oxidation number of -2. There are 2 oxygens, so this will make the total charge from oxygens $-2 \times 2 = -4$.
The overall charge on the ion is -1, so chlorine must have an oxidation number of $+3$, since $-4 + 3 = -1$.
So, the systematic name is chlorate(III).

Tip: It'll help if you learn the charges of the three main -ate ions you'll come across in the exam. Sulfate ions (SO_4^{2-}) are always $2-$, nitrate ions (NO_3^-) are always $1-$ and carbonate ions (CO_3^{2-}) are always $2-$.

Working out formulas

You can also use oxidation numbers to work out the formula of a compound given its systematic name.

--- Example ---

What is the formula of iron(III) sulfate?
From the systematic name, you can tell iron has an oxidation number of $+3$.
The formula of the sulfate ion is SO_4^{2-} and it has an overall charge of -2.
The overall charge of the compound is 0, so you need to find a ratio of $Fe^{3+} : SO_4^{2-}$ that will make the overall charge 0.
$$(+3 \times 2) + (-2 \times 3) = 6 + -6 = 0$$
The ratio of $Fe : SO_4$ is $2 : 3$.
So the formula is $Fe_2(SO_4)_3$.

Figure 7: *Chlorates are powerful oxidising agents (see page 87). Potassium chlorate(V) is frequently used in pyrotechnics, such as fireworks.*

Tip: Iron(III) sulfate is uncharged so has an overall oxidation number of 0.

Working out the formula of compound ions is just the same except the oxidation numbers won't add up to 0 — they'll add up to the charge of the ion instead. You'll be told the charge of the ion in the question.

Exam Tip
Don't forget to include the charge of the ion after you've worked out its formula. If you just put PO_3 here you wouldn't get any marks.

---- Example ----

Find the formula of a phosphate(III) ion given that it has a charge of 3–.
As it's a phosphate ion it must contain phosphorus and oxygen. Oxygen has an oxidation number of –2 and you know from the systematic name that the phosphorus has an oxidation number of +3. The overall oxidation number of the ion is –3. So for the oxidation number to add up to –3 you need 3 oxygen atoms (giving a total of –6) and one phosphorus atom (+3). So the formula of a phosphate(III) ion is PO_3^{3-}.

Practice Questions — Application

Q1 Give the oxidation numbers of the following ions.

    a) Na^+ b) F^- c) Ca^{2+}

Q2 Give the overall oxidation numbers of the following ions.

    a) OH^- b) CO_3^{2-} c) NO_3^-

Exam Tip
Finding oxidation numbers is easy when you know how. Just make sure you learn the rules for the exam and you'll be fine.

Q3 Work out the oxidation numbers of all the elements in the following compounds and compound ions.

    a) HCl b) CO_3^{2-} c) ClO_4^- d) HSO_4^-

Q4 Work out the oxidation numbers of carbon in the following.

    a) CO b) CCl_4 c) $CaCO_3$ d) C_3H_6

Q5 Work out the oxidation numbers of phosphorus in the following.

    a) P_4 b) PH_3 c) PO_4^{2-} d) P_2F_4

Q6 a) What is the oxidation number of iron in iron(III) chloride?

    b) What is the oxidation number of chlorine in chlorate(VII) ions?

Q7 Give the systematic names of the following compounds.

    a) $FeSO_4$ b) $MnCO_3$ c) CuO

Q8 Give the formulas of the following compounds and compound ions.

    a) Copper(II) sulfate.

    b) Iron(II) oxide.

    c) Nitrate(III) ions with an overall charge of –1.

    d) Chromate(VI) ions with an overall charge of –2.

Practice Questions — Fact Recall

Q1 Give the oxidation number of an element bonded to an identical atom.

Q2 What is the sum of the oxidation numbers for a neutral compound?

Q3 What is the oxidation number of oxygen in a peroxide?

Q4 Give the oxidation number of hydrogen in a metal hydride.

8. Redox Reactions

This'll probably ring a bell from GCSE, but don't go thinking you know it all already — there's plenty to learn about redox reactions.

What are redox reactions?

A loss of electrons is called **oxidation**. A gain in electrons is called **reduction**. Reduction and oxidation happen simultaneously — hence the term "**redox**" reaction. An **oxidising agent** accepts electrons and gets reduced. A **reducing agent** donates electrons and gets oxidised.

┌─ **Example** ────────────────────────────────

Here's a redox reaction between sodium and chlorine to form sodium chloride:

Sodium is the reducing agent — it donates electrons and gets oxidised.

Chlorine is the oxidising agent — it accepts electrons and gets reduced.

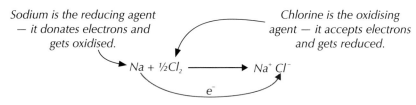

$$Na + \tfrac{1}{2}Cl_2 \longrightarrow Na^+ Cl^-$$

e^-

└──

Changing oxidation numbers

Oxidation numbers go up or down as electrons are lost or gained.

* The oxidation number for an atom will increase by 1 for each electron lost.

* The oxidation number will decrease by 1 for each electron gained.

When metals form compounds, they generally donate electrons to form positive ions — this is accompanied by an increase in oxidation number. When non-metals form compounds, they generally gain electrons and form negative ions — this is accompanied by a decrease in oxidation number.

┌─ **Examples** ───────────────────────────────

Zinc (a metal) can lose electrons to form Zn^{2+} ions. When this happens, its oxidation number increases from 0 to +2.

Bromine (a non-metal) can gain an electron to form Br^- ions. When this happens, its oxidation number decreases from 0 to –1.

└──

In a redox reaction, some oxidation numbers will change — something will lose electrons and end up with an increased oxidation number and something will gain electrons and end up with a decreased oxidation number.

┌─ **Example** ────────────────────────────────

In this reaction between iron(III) oxide and carbon(II) oxide (a.k.a. carbon monoxide), the products are the element iron and carbon(IV) oxide (more commonly known as carbon dioxide).

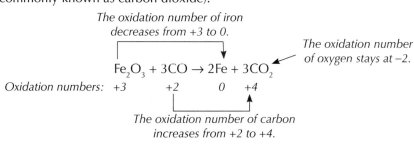

The oxidation number of iron decreases from +3 to 0.

The oxidation number of oxygen stays at –2.

$$Fe_2O_3 + 3CO \rightarrow 2Fe + 3CO_2$$

Oxidation numbers: +3   +2   0   +4

The oxidation number of carbon increases from +2 to +4.

└──

Learning Objectives:

* Be able to describe the terms oxidation and reduction in terms of electron transfer and changes in oxidation number.

* Know the redox reactions of metals with acids to form salts, including full equations.

* Be able to interpret redox equations and unfamiliar redox reactions to make predictions in terms of oxidation numbers and electron loss and gain.

Specification Reference 2.1.5

Tip: Now's your chance to learn the most famous memory aid thingy in the world...

OIL RIG
Oxidation Is Loss
Reduction Is Gain
(of electrons)

Tip: When an element is reduced, it's oxidation number is also reduced.

Tip: Look back at the rules for assigning oxidation numbers on pages 83-84 if you're unsure about this.

Tip: Remember — oxidising agents get reduced while reducing agents get oxidised.

Once you have identified how the oxidation numbers of elements and ions change in a reaction, you can work out which substance in a reaction acts as a reducing or oxidising agent.

Examples

Identify the oxidising and reducing agents in this reaction:
$4Fe + 3O_2 \rightarrow 2Fe_2O_3$

Iron has gone from having an oxidation number of 0 to an oxidation number of +3. It's lost electrons and has been oxidised. This makes it the reducing agent in this reaction.

Oxygen has gone from having an oxidation number of 0 to an oxidation number of –2. It's gained electrons and has been reduced. This means it's the oxidising agent in this reaction.

Identify the oxidising and reducing agents in this reaction:
$2Na + Cl_2 \rightarrow 2NaCl$

Sodium has gone from having an oxidation number of 0 to an oxidation number of +1. It's lost an electron and has been oxidised, so it's a reducing agent.

Chlorine has gone from having an oxidation number of 0 to an oxidation number of –1. It's gained an electron and has been reduced, so it's an oxidising agent.

When asked about oxidation and reduction, it's always worth working out the oxidation numbers of each atom or ion to see exactly how the electrons are moving around. But as a rule:

- When metals form compounds, they generally donate electrons to form positive ions — meaning they usually have positive oxidation numbers.
- When non-metals form compounds, they generally gain electrons — meaning they usually have negative oxidation numbers.

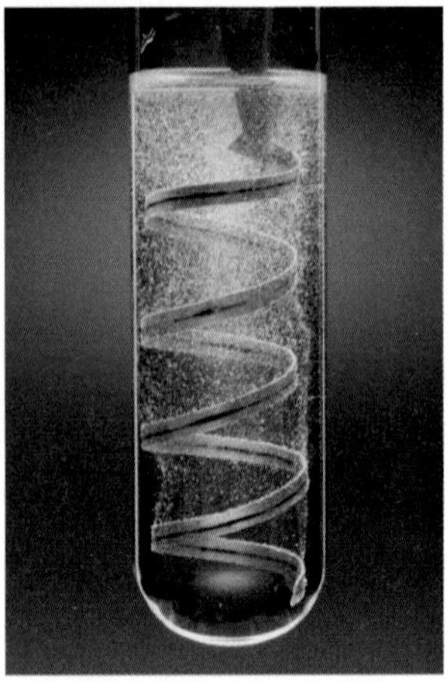

Figure 1: Magnesium ribbon reacting with hydrochloric acid. The bubbles are the hydrogen gas molecules that are being formed.

Reactions of dilute acids with metals

On page 67 you saw how metals react with acids to produce a salt and hydrogen gas. Well this is a redox reaction. The metal atoms are oxidised, losing electrons to form positive metal ions (in salts). The hydrogen ions in solution are reduced, gaining electrons and forming hydrogen molecules.

Example

Magnesium reacts with dilute hydrochloric acid like this:

The oxidation number of magnesium increases from 0 to +2.

The oxidation number of chlorine stays at –1.

$$Mg_{(s)} + 2HCl_{(aq)} \rightarrow MgCl_{2(aq)} + H_{2(g)}$$

Oxidation numbers: 0   +1   +2   0

The oxidation number of hydrogen decreases from +1 to 0.

---- Example --

If you use sulfuric acid instead of hydrochloric acid, exactly the same processes of oxidation and reduction take place.

Potassium is oxidised to K^+ ions in the reaction with dilute sulfuric acid like this:

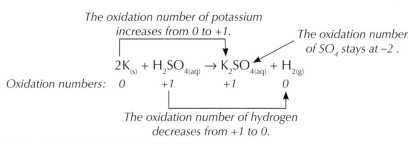

The oxidation number of potassium increases from 0 to +1.

The oxidation number of SO_4 stays at −2 .

$$2K_{(s)} + H_2SO_{4(aq)} \rightarrow K_2SO_{4(aq)} + H_{2(g)}$$

Oxidation numbers: 0   +1   +1   0

The oxidation number of hydrogen decreases from +1 to 0.

Practice Questions — Application

Q1 Describe the changes in oxidation number that occur in each of the following reactions between metals and acids.

   a) $Mg + H_2SO_4 \rightarrow MgSO_4 + H_2$

   b) $2V + 6HCl \rightarrow 2VCl_3 + 3H_2$

   c) $2Fe + 3H_2SO_4 \rightarrow Fe_2(SO_4)_3 + 3H_2$

Q2 This is a redox reaction: $MnO_2 + 4HCl \rightarrow MnCl_2 + Cl_2 + 2H_2O$

   a) Describe the changes in oxidation number that occur in this reaction.

   b) Identify the oxidising and reducing agents in this reaction.

Tip: If you're asked to describe the changes in oxidation number in a reaction you have to say which elements change oxidation numbers and what the change is.

Practice Questions — Fact Recall

Q1 What is oxidation?

Q2 What is reduction?

Q3 Describe the role of an oxidising agent in a redox reaction.

Q4 Describe the role of a reducing agent in a redox reaction.

Q5 What happens to the oxidation number when an atom loses an electron?

Q6 What happens to the oxidation number when an atom gains an electron?

Tip: The oxidation number of an atom doesn't always change when it reacts, so don't be alarmed if your answer is the same for the beginning and end of the reaction.

Section Summary

Make sure you know...

- That acids release protons in aqueous solution and bases absorb H^+ ions in aqueous solution.
- That alkalis are soluble bases that release OH^- ions in aqueous solution.
- The formulas of the common acids HCl, H_2SO_4, HNO_3 and CH_3COOH.
- The formulas of the common alkalis $NaOH$, KOH and NH_3.
- The definition and nature of strong and weak acids and bases.
- That a salt is produced when the H^+ ion in an acid is replaced by a metal ion or NH_4^+.
- That in neutralisation reactions between acids and bases, H^+ ions from the acid and OH^- ions from the base react together to form water.
- That metal oxides, metal hydroxides and ammonia can all act as bases.
- That acids react with bases, alkalis, metals and metal carbonates to form salts.
- What the terms anhydrous, hydrated and water of crystallisation mean in terms of salts.
- How to calculate the formula of a hydrated salt from mass compositions or percentage compositions.
- How to perform acid-base titrations and carry out structured titrations.
- Some of the appropriate indicators used for acid-base titrations.
- The techniques for precisely measuring the masses of solids, and the volumes of liquids and gases.
- The procedure for making a standard solution from a solid and from a more concentrated solution.
- How to calculate unknown concentrations and volumes using data collected from a titration.
- How to calculate the percentage yield of a reaction, from the chemical equation.
- How to calculate atom economy from a chemical equation.
- The industrial advantages of using reactions with high atom economies, in terms of cost and sustainability.
- How to assign oxidation numbers to atoms in elements, compounds and ions.
- How to use Roman numerals to determine the oxidation number of an element in a compound.
- How to write formulas using oxidation numbers.
- That oxidation is a loss of electrons and reduction is a gain in electrons.
- That oxidation and reduction result in changes in oxidation number.
- How to interpret redox equations and redox reactions to make predictions about oxidation numbers and about electron loss and gain.

Exam-style Questions

1   What is the formula of iron(III) sulfate?

A $FeSO_4$

B $Fe(SO_4)_2$

C Fe_2SO_4

D $Fe_2(SO_4)_3$

(1 mark)

2   Which of these equations **does not** show a redox reaction?

A $Mg + 2HCl \rightarrow MgCl_2 + H_2$

B $Fe_2O_3 + 3CO \rightarrow 2Fe + 3CO_2$

C $Ca(OH)_2 + 2HCl \rightarrow CaCl_2 + 2H_2O$

D $Ag + H_2S \rightarrow Ag_2S + H_2$

(1 mark)

3   What is the oxidation number of chromium in the compound $Cr_2(SO_4)_3$?

A   +3

B   +2

C   −3

D   +1

(1 mark)

4 (a)   Silicon is most commonly found as silicon dioxide (SiO_2).

(i)   State the oxidation state of silicon in SiO_2.

(1 mark)

(ii)   Give the systematic name of silicon dioxide.

(1 mark)

(b)   Silicon dioxide reacts with sodium hydroxide (NaOH), as shown by the equation below.

$$SiO_2 + 2NaOH \rightarrow Na_2SiO_3 + H_2O$$

Use your knowledge of oxidation states to determine whether the reaction above is a redox reaction. Explain you answer.

(2 marks)

5   Hydrogen can be made by reacting a metal with an acid.

(a)   Zinc metal and hydrochloric acid are reacted together.

(i)   Write a balanced equation to show the reaction between zinc and hydrochloric acid.
You should include state symbols in your answer.

(2 marks)

(ii) Use your answer to **(i)** to calculate the atom economy for this reaction.

(2 marks)

(b)   Hydrogen is produced on an industrial scale through steam reformation.
This involves reacting methane with steam.

$$CH_{4(g)} + H_2O_{(g)} \rightarrow CO_{(g)} + 3H_{2(g)}$$

(i)   What is the atom economy of the reaction above?

(2 marks)

(ii) With reference to your answers to **a (ii)** and **b (i)**, suggest two reasons
why steam reformation is preferred as a method for producing
hydrogen, compared to reacting a metal with an acid.

(2 marks)

6   A student is doing an experiment into *water of crystallisation*.
She heats an 8.93 g sample of *hydrated* iron(II) sulfate to form 4.88 g
of *anhydrous* iron(II) sulfate.

(a)   Define the following terms:

(i)   *water of crystallisation*.

(ii) *hydrated*.

(iii) *anhydrous*.

(3 marks)

(b)   What is the oxidation number of iron in the hydrated iron(II) sulfate compound?

(1 mark)

(c)   The formula of the hydrated iron complex can be expressed
as $FeSO_4 \bullet xH_2O$, where **x** represents a whole number.
Find the value of **x** and write the formula of the hydrated salt.

(3 marks)

7   This question is about the reactions of acids.

(a)   When an acid is added to a base, a neutralisation reaction occurs.
In a titration, 26.0 cm³ of 0.600 mol dm⁻³ hydrochloric acid was needed
to exactly neutralise 20.0 cm³ of a sodium hydroxide solution.

   (i)   Write an equation for the reaction between hydrochloric acid and
sodium hydroxide. Include state symbols in your answer.

(2 marks)

   (ii)   Calculate how many moles of hydrochloric acid were added to the
sodium hydroxide solution.

(2 marks)

   (iii)   Calculate the concentration of the sodium hydroxide solution used
in this titration.

(2 marks)

(b)   Acids react with metals to produce salts. When aluminium (Al) reacts
with hydrochloric acid, aluminium(III) chloride is produced.

   (i)   What is the oxidation number of aluminium in aluminium(III) chloride?

(1 mark)

   (ii)   Use your knowledge of oxidation numbers to work out the chemical formula
of aluminium(III) chloride.

(1 mark)

(c)   The reactions of acids with metals are redox reactions.
Below is the reaction of sodium with sulfuric acid:

$$2Na + H_2SO_4 \rightarrow Na_2SO_4 + H_2$$

   (i)   How does the oxidation number of sodium change during this reaction?

(1 mark)

   (ii)   What is the role of sodium in this reaction?

(1 mark)

(d)   The reaction of dilute nitric acid with calcium produces a salt called
calcium nitrate $(Ca(NO_3)_2)$.
Hydrated calcium(II) nitrate contains 30.5% water by mass.
The hydrated salt has the formula $Ca(NO_3)_2.xH_2O$. Find the value of **x**.

(4 marks)

(e)   A student wants to make 250 cm³ of a standard solution of calcium(II) nitrate.
He uses a volumetric flask to accurately measure 250 cm³ of water and adds it to
a beaker containing the correct mass of calcium(II) nitrate, dissolved in water.
What has the student done wrong and how will this error affect the
concentration of the standard solution made?

(2 marks)

Learning Objectives:

- Know how many orbitals make up the s, p and d sub-shells and how many electrons can fill s, p and d sub-shells.

- Recall how many electrons can fill the first four shells.

- Understand that atomic orbitals are a region around the nucleus that can hold up to two electrons, with opposite spins.

- Know the shapes of s- and p-orbitals.

- Understand that electrons fill the first three shells and the 4s and 4p orbitals in order of increasing energy.

- Know that electrons occupy orbitals of the same energy singly before pairing.

- Deduce the electron configurations of atoms, given their atomic number, up to Z = 36 and ions, given their atomic number and ionic charge, limited to s- and p-block ions, up to Z = 36.

Specification Reference 2.2.1

1. Electronic Structure

Electronic structure is all about how electrons are arranged in atoms.

Electron shells

In the currently accepted model of the atom, electrons have fixed energies. They move around the nucleus in certain regions of the atom called **shells** or **energy levels**. Each shell is given a number called the principal quantum number. The further a shell is from the nucleus, the higher its energy and the larger its principal quantum number — see Figure 1.

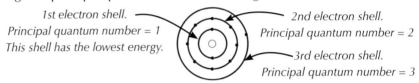

1st electron shell.
Principal quantum number = 1
This shell has the lowest energy.

2nd electron shell.
Principal quantum number = 2

3rd electron shell.
Principal quantum number = 3

Figure 1: A sodium atom.

These shells are divided up into **sub-shells**. Different electron shells have different numbers of sub-shells, which each have a different energy. Sub-shells can be s sub-shells, p sub-shells, d sub-shells or f sub-shells.

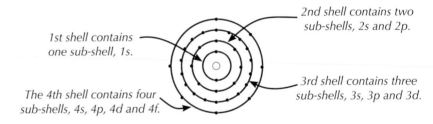

1st shell contains one sub-shell, 1s.

2nd shell contains two sub-shells, 2s and 2p.

The 4th shell contains four sub-shells, 4s, 4p, 4d and 4f.

3rd shell contains three sub-shells, 3s, 3p and 3d.

Figure 2: A bromine atom.

These sub-shells have different numbers of **orbitals** which can each hold up to 2 electrons. The table below shows the number of orbitals and electrons in each sub-shell. You can use it to work out how many electrons each shell can hold.

Sub-shell	Number of orbitals	Maximum electrons
s	1	2
p	3	6
d	5	10
f	7	14

Figure 3: The number of electrons that can fill each sub-shell.

Tip: Don't get confused by notation like 2s or 4f. The letter shows what type of sub-shell it is, the number shows what shell it's in. So 3p means a p sub-shell in the 3rd electron shell.

Example

The third shell contains 3 sub-shells: 3s, 3p and 3d.

- An s sub-shell contains 1 orbital, so can hold 2 electrons (1 × 2).
- A p sub-shell contains 3 orbitals, so can hold 6 electrons (3 × 2).
- A d sub-shell contains 5 orbitals, so can hold 10 electrons (5 × 2).

So the total number of electrons the third shell can hold is 2 + 6 + 10 = **18**.

The table on the right shows the number of electrons that the first four electron shells can hold.

Shell	Sub-shells	Total number of electrons	
1st	1s	2	= 2
2nd	2s 2p	$2 + (3 \times 2)$	= 8
3rd	3s 3p 3d	$2 + (3 \times 2) + (5 \times 2)$	= 18
4th	4s 4p 4d 4f	$2 + (3 \times 2) + (5 \times 2) + (7 \times 2)$	= 32

Exam Tip
Make sure you learn how many electrons each electron shell can hold — you won't get far with electronic structures if you don't know these numbers.

Orbital shapes

An orbital is the bit of space that an electron moves in (see Figure 4). Orbitals within the same sub-shell have the same energy. If there are two electrons in an orbital, they must 'spin' in opposite directions — this is called spin-pairing.

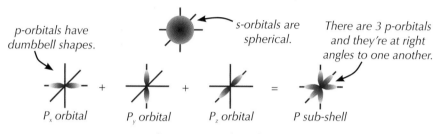

p-orbitals have dumbbell shapes.

s-orbitals are spherical.

There are 3 p-orbitals and they're at right angles to one another.

P_x orbital + P_y orbital + P_z orbital = P sub-shell

Figure 4: s- and p-orbitals.

Tip: Electrons have a property called 'spin'. Spin just has to do with the momentum that an electron has (and that's all you need to know about it for now). Two electrons in the same orbital will have opposite spins — one is called 'down' and the other 'up'.

Showing electron configurations

The number of electrons that an atom or ion has, and how they are arranged, is called its **electron configuration**. Electron configurations can be shown in different ways. For example, an atom of neon has 10 electrons — two electrons are in the 1s sub-shell, two are in the 2s sub-shell and six are in the 2p sub-shell. You can show this electron configuration in three different ways...

1. Sub-shell notation

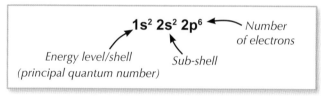

1s² 2s² 2p⁶ ← Number of electrons

Energy level/shell (principal quantum number)

Sub-shell

Tip: Dumbbell-shaped just means it looks like this:

So if you're asked to draw the shape of a p-orbital, draw this.

2. Electrons in boxes

Each of the boxes represents one orbital. Each of the arrows represents one electron. The up and down arrows represent the electrons spinning in opposite directions. Two electrons can only occupy the same orbital if they have opposite spin.

1s 2s 2p
[↑↓] [↑↓] [↑↓|↑↓|↑↓]

Exam Tip
In the exam you'll only have to do electron configurations up to the d sub-shell (so don't worry about the f sub-shell).

3. Energy level diagrams

These show the energy of the electrons in different orbitals, as well as the number of electrons and their arrangement.

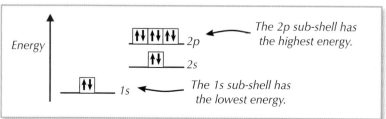

Energy

[↑↓|↑↓|↑↓] 2p ← The 2p sub-shell has the highest energy.

[↑↓] 2s

[↑↓] 1s ← The 1s sub-shell has the lowest energy.

Exam Tip
Electron configurations are normally shown using sub-shell notation or electrons in boxes, so make sure you're confident using both these methods.

Working out electron configurations

You can figure out most electronic configurations pretty easily, so long as you know a few simple rules:

Rule 1

Electrons fill up the lowest energy sub-shells first.

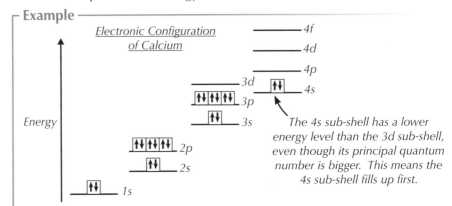

Tip: Even though the 4s sub-shell fills up before the 3d sub-shell, the 3d electrons are usually shown first when you write the configurations down. So the electron configuration of Ca is usually shown as:

$1s^2\ 2s^2\ 2p^6\ 3s^2\ 3p^6\ 4s^2$

and the electron configuration of Sc is:

$1s^2\ 2s^2\ 2p^6\ 3s^2\ 3p^6\ 3d^1\ 4s^2$

Example

Electronic Configuration of Calcium

The 4s sub-shell has a lower energy level than the 3d sub-shell, even though its principal quantum number is bigger. This means the 4s sub-shell fills up first.

Rule 2

Electrons fill orbitals with the same energy singly before they start sharing.

Examples

Nitrogen   Oxygen

Rule 3

For the configuration of ions from the s and p blocks of the periodic table, just add or remove the electrons to or from the highest energy occupied sub-shell.

Tip: Elements with their outer electrons in an s sub-shell are called s block elements. Elements with their outer electrons in a p sub-shell are called p-block elements.

Examples

Mg atom: $1s^2\ 2s^2\ 2p^6\ 3s^2$ Cl atom: $1s^2\ 2s^2\ 2p^6\ 3s^2\ 3p^5$

Mg^{2+} ion: $1s^2\ 2s^2\ 2p^6$ Cl$^-$ ion: $1s^2\ 2s^2\ 2p^6\ 3s^2\ 3p^6$

Shortened electron configurations

Noble gas symbols in square brackets, such as [Ar], are sometimes used in electron configurations. For example, calcium ($1s^2\ 2s^2\ 2p^6\ 3s^2\ 3p^6\ 4s^2$) can be written as [Ar]4s^2, where [Ar] = $1s^2\ 2s^2\ 2p^6\ 3s^2\ 3p^6$.

Theories of electronic structure

You saw on pages 30-32 that it took a long time for our current theory of the structure of the atom to be developed. It took scientists even longer to work out how the electrons were arranged.

HOW SCIENCE WORKS

The Bohr model (see pages 31-32) was a good starting point. It proposed that electrons orbit the nucleus in spherical shells with fixed energy levels. The model helped to explain why atoms only absorb or emit energy at certain frequencies (see Figure 5) — these are the frequencies that correspond to the energy difference between two of the energy levels.

Whilst the Bohr model is a good approximation, it doesn't explain some of the finer details of absorption and emission spectra. The model was later refined so that the shells didn't have to be spherical. This caused the idea of sub-shells and orbitals to be developed.

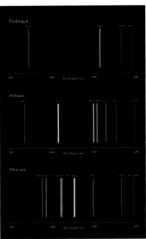

Figure 5: *The emission spectra of hydrogen, helium and mercury show distinct lines corresponding to the differences in energy between electron shells.*

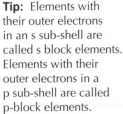

In 1927, Werner Heisenberg came up with the theory that you cannot know the speed of an electron and its exact position at the same time — this is known as Heisenberg's uncertainty principle. As a result, scientists now think of orbitals as an area where electrons are most likely to be found, rather than where they will definitely be.

Investigations into electronic structure has led to the development of an area of science called quantum mechanics. This uses maths to explain how very small particles, such as electrons, behave. It's also allowed scientists to develop theories that explain and predict the properties of atoms, such as their spectra and the way they bond to other atoms to form molecules.

Figure 6: Werner Heisenberg was a German scientist who helped to develop the model of electronic structure scientists use today.

Practice Questions — Application

Q1 Use sub-shell notation to show the full electron configurations of the elements listed below.
   a) Lithium
   b) Titanium
   c) Gallium
   d) Nitrogen

Q2 Draw arrows in boxes to show the electron configurations of the elements listed below.
   a) Calcium
   b) Nickel
   c) Sodium
   d) Oxygen

Q3 Draw energy level diagrams to show the electron configurations of the elements listed below.
   a) Magnesium
   b) Argon
   c) Carbon
   d) Arsenic

Q4 Use sub-shell notation to show the electron configurations of the ions listed below.
   a) Na^+
   b) O^{2-}
   c) Al^{3+}
   d) Cl^-

Q5 Which elements have the electron configurations given below?
   a) $[Ar]3d^{10}\ 4s^2\ 4p^5$
   b) $[Ne]3s^2\ 3p^3$
   c) $[Ar]3d^3\ 4s^2$

Exam Tip
Writing electron configurations using noble gas symbols can save you loads of time. Just make sure you've got your head round sub-shell notation before you start to use it — otherwise you're likely to get confused. And if a question asks you to give the full configuration then make sure that's what you do.

Practice Questions — Fact Recall

Q1 How many orbitals does a p sub-shell contain?

Q2 How many electrons can a p sub-shell hold?

Q3 How many electrons can the 3rd electron shell hold in total?

Q4 Describe the shape of:
   a) an s-orbital.
   b) a p-orbital.

Q5 What does "electron configuration" mean?

Q6 Which electron shells are filled up first?

Q7 The electron configuration shown below is wrong. Explain why.

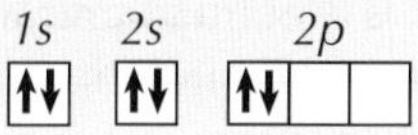

1s   2s   2p
[↑↓] [↑↓] [↑↓][ ][ ]

- Describe the term ionic bonding as the electrostatic attraction between positive and negative ions.

- Be able to construct 'dot-and-cross' diagrams for ionic compounds.

- Explain that the solid structures of giant ionic lattices result from oppositely charged ions strongly attracted in all directions, e.g. NaCl.

- Explain the effect of structure and bonding on the physical properties of ionic compounds, including melting and boiling points, solubility and electrical conductivity in solid, liquid and aqueous states.

Specification Reference 2.2.2

2. Ionic Bonding

When atoms join together, they form a bond. There are two main types of bonding — ionic and covalent. First up is ionic bonding.

Ionic compounds

Ions form when atoms lose or gain electrons to become positively or negatively charged. **Electrostatic attraction** holds positive and negative ions together — it's very strong. When atoms are held together like this, it's called ionic bonding. So, an **ionic bond** is an electrostatic attraction between two oppositely charged ions.

When oppositely charged ions form an ionic bond you get an **ionic compound**. The formula of a compound tells you what ions that compound has in it. The positive charges in the compound balance the negative charges exactly — so the total overall charge is zero. This is a dead handy way of checking the formula.

Example

In the compound Fe_2O_3, there are three oxygen ions, each with a charge of -2. So the total negative charge is $3 \times (-2) = -6$.

To balance this out and make the compound neutral, the two iron ions must have a combined charge of $+6$.

So each iron ion has a charge of $(+6) \div 2 = +3$.

Dot-and-cross diagrams

You can use 'dot-and-cross' diagrams to show how ionic bonding works in ionic compounds. Dot-and-cross diagrams show the arrangement of electrons in an atom or ion. Each electron is represented by a dot or a cross. They can also show which atom the electrons in a bond originally came from.

Examples

Sodium chloride
The formula of sodium chloride is NaCl. It just tells you that sodium chloride is made up of Na^+ ions and Cl^- ions (in a 1:1 ratio). In NaCl, the single positive charge on the Na^+ ion balances the single negative charge on the Cl^- ion (see Figure 2).

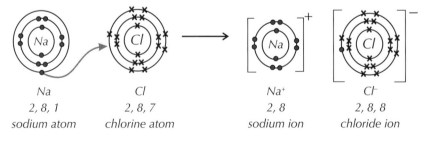

Na	Cl	Na⁺	Cl⁻
2, 8, 1	2, 8, 7	2, 8	2, 8, 8
sodium atom	chlorine atom	sodium ion	chloride ion

Figure 2: *Formation of sodium chloride from a sodium atom and a chlorine atom.*

Here the dots represent the Na electrons and the crosses represent the Cl electrons. All electrons are really identical, but this is a good way of following their movement. It's clear to see how the sodium atom loses an electron to form a sodium ion (Na^+), whilst the chlorine atom gains an electron to form a chloride ion (Cl^-). Both the ions have full outer shells.

Figure 1: *The reaction between sodium and chlorine to form sodium chloride.*

Magnesium oxide

Magnesium oxide, MgO, is another example of an ionic compound. The formation of magnesium oxide involves the transfer of two electrons — see Figure 3. The formula tells you that magnesium oxide is made up of Mg^{2+} ions and O^{2-} ions in a 1:1 ratio. Figure 3 shows outer electrons only.

Tip: You can often use an atom's position in the periodic table to predict what charge ion it will form — atoms in the s-block will lose electrons, and atoms in the p-block will normally gain or lose electrons until they have a full outer shell (see page 59).

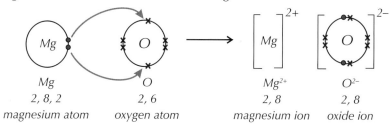

Mg	O		Mg^{2+}	O^{2-}
2, 8, 2	2, 6		2, 8	2, 8
magnesium atom	oxygen atom		magnesium ion	oxide ion

Figure 3: *Formation of magnesium oxide from a magnesium atom and an oxygen atom.*

Magnesium chloride

Magnesium chloride ($MgCl_2$) is different again. In this compound, the 2+ charge on the Mg^{2+} ion balances the two individual charges on the two Cl^- ions — see Figure 4.

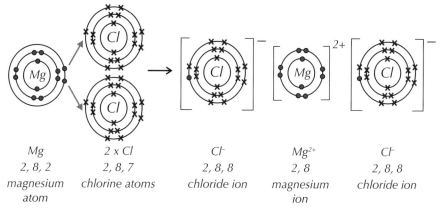

Mg	2 x Cl	Cl^-	Mg^{2+}	Cl^-
2, 8, 2	2, 8, 7	2, 8, 8	2, 8	2, 8, 8
magnesium atom	chlorine atoms	chloride ion	magnesium ion	chloride ion

Figure 4: *Formation of magnesium chloride from a magnesium atom and two chlorine atoms.*

Exam Tip
You can simplify dot-and-cross diagrams by only showing the outer shell of electrons on each atom (see Figure 3). Most of the time it doesn't matter if dot-and-cross diagrams show all the shells or just the outer ones, but if you're asked to draw them a certain way in the exam then make sure you do.

Giant ionic lattices

Ionic crystals are **giant lattices** of ions. A lattice is just a regular structure. The structure's called 'giant' because it's made up of the same basic unit repeated over and over again. It forms because each ion is electrostatically attracted in all directions to ions of the opposite charge. The sodium chloride lattice is cube shaped (see Figures 5 and 6).

The Na⁺ and Cl⁻ ions alternate.

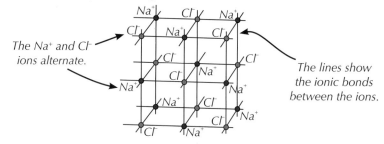

The lines show the ionic bonds between the ions.

Figure 5: *The structure of sodium chloride.*

Figure 6: *Crystals of sodium chloride (table salt).*

Different ionic compounds have different shaped structures, but they're all still giant lattices.

Tip: These physical
properties are sometimes
called 'macroscopic'
properties — that's just
a fancy way of saying
properties that result
from lots of particles
interacting with each
other. For example,
you couldn't say an
individual atom has
a melting point, but a
compound made up of
lots of atoms does.
You should be able to
explain how ionic bonds
cause the macroscopic
properties of ionic
compounds.

*Figure 7: Water doesn't
conduct electricity (see top).
When the ionic compound
sodium chloride is added
to the water (above), it
dissolves and the free
Na^+ and Cl^- ions allow
a current to flow.*

Behaviour of ionic compounds

The structure and bonding of ionic compounds decides their
physical properties — things like their electrical conductivity,
melting point and solubility.

Electrical conductivity

Ionic compounds conduct electricity when they're molten or dissolved —
but not when they're solid. The ions in a liquid are free to move (and they
carry a charge). In a solid they're fixed in position by the strong ionic bonds.

Melting and boiling points

Ionic compounds have high melting and boiling points. The giant ionic
lattices are held together by strong electrostatic forces. It takes loads of energy
to overcome these forces, so melting and boiling points are very high
(801 °C and 1413 °C respectively for sodium chloride).

Solubility

Ionic compounds tend to dissolve in water. Water molecules are polar — part
of the molecule has a small negative charge, and the other bits have small
positive charges (see page 109). The water molecules pull the ions away from
the lattice and cause it to dissolve.

Practice Questions — Application

Q1 Fluorine and lithium react together to form lithium fluoride, an ionic
compound that contains F^- and Li^+ ions.

a) Give the formula of the compound formed.

b) Describe how an ionic bond forms between a fluorine atom and a
lithium atom.

c) Draw a 'dot and cross' diagram to show the formation of an ionic
bond between fluorine and lithium.

Q2 Potassium reacts with oxygen to form the ionic compound potassium
oxide, which has the formula K_2O.

a) Given that the oxide ion has a charge of –2, what is the charge on
a potassium ion?

b) Draw a dot-and-cross diagram to show the formation of potassium
oxide from potassium and oxygen atoms.

Q3 Draw a dot-and-cross diagram to show the formation of the ionic
compound sodium bromide, NaBr, from sodium and bromine atoms.
Your diagram should show the outer electrons only.

Practice Questions — Fact Recall

Q1 What effect does electrostatic attraction have on oppositely
charged ions?

Q2 Explain what an ionic lattice is.

Q3 Draw the structure of the sodium chloride lattice.

Q4 Explain why ionic compounds conduct electricity when molten.

Q5 Magnesium chloride is an ionic compound. Apart from the changes
to its electrical conductivity when in different states, describe three
physical properties you would expect magnesium chloride to have.

3. Covalent Bonding

Ionic bonding done — now it's on to covalent bonding.

Molecules

Molecules are formed when two or more atoms bond together — it doesn't matter if the atoms are the same or different. Chlorine gas (Cl_2), carbon monoxide (CO), water (H_2O) and ethanol (C_2H_5OH) are all molecules. Molecules are held together by strong **covalent bonds**. A covalent bond is the strong electrostatic attraction between a shared pair of electrons and the nuclei of the bonded atoms. Usually each of the atoms in a molecule ends up with eight electrons in its outer shell. This is good for the atoms — it's a very stable arrangement.

Dot-and-cross diagrams

Dot-and-cross diagrams can be used to show how electrons behave in covalent bonds. The bonded atoms are drawn with their outer atomic orbitals overlapping. The shared electrons that make up the covalent bond are drawn within the overlapping area. Dot-and-cross diagrams can show single or multiple covalent bonds.

Single bonds

In a single covalent bond, the atoms share one pair of electrons. In general, each atom donates one electron to the bonding pair.

> **Examples**
>
> Two chlorine atoms (Cl) bond covalently to form a molecule of chlorine (Cl_2) — see Figure 1. (These diagrams don't show all the electrons — just the ones in the outer shells.)
>
>
>
> *Figure 1: Formation of a molecule of chlorine.*
>
> A chlorine molecule can also be drawn as:
>
> $$Cl-Cl$$
>
> *Figure 2: Use of lines to represent covalent bonds.*
>
> The diagrams below show other examples of covalent molecules.
>
>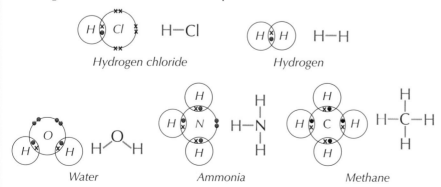
>
> *Figure 3: Examples of covalent molecules.*

Learning Objectives:

- Be able to define a covalent bond as the strong electrostatic attraction between a shared pair of electrons and the nuclei of the bonded atoms.

- Be able to construct 'dot-and-cross' diagrams of molecules and ions to show single covalent bonds, multiple covalent bonds and dative covalent (coordinate) bonds.

- Be able to construct 'dot-and-cross' diagrams for molecules with up to six electron pairs (including lone pairs) surrounding the central atom.

- Understand that average bond enthalpy can be used as a measurement of covalent bond strength.

Specification Reference 2.2.2

Tip: The outer electrons in hydrogen are in the first electron shell, which only needs two electrons to be filled.

Tip: Just like with dot-and-cross diagrams for ionic compounds, you can use the dots and crosses to show which atom the electrons in the bonds originally came from.

Double and triple bonds

Atoms in covalent molecules don't just form single bonds — double or even triple covalent bonds can form too. In double bonds, the atoms share two pairs of electrons, and in triple bonds the atoms share three pairs of electrons.

┌─ **Examples** ─────────────────

Double bonds

The oxygen atoms in O_2 are connected via a double bond. It forms because each oxygen atom has six electrons in its outer shell, so needs another two to get a full outer shell of electrons. This happens if each oxygen atom shares two electrons, forming a double bond.

$$O=O$$

Carbon dioxide contains two $C=O$ double bonds. Carbon has 4 electrons in its outer shell, so it needs another 4 to have a full outer shell. This means each oxygen atom must share two electrons.

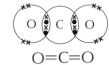

$$O=C=O$$

Triple bonds

Nitrogen has 5 electrons in its outer shell, so it needs another 3 to have a full outer shell. The only way of doing this in N_2 is if each nitrogen atom shares three electrons, resulting in a triple bond.

$$N\equiv N$$

Dative covalent bonding

In a normal single covalent bond, atoms share a pair of electrons — with one electron coming from each atom. In **dative covalent**, also known as **coordinate**, bonding, one of the atoms provides both of the shared electrons.

┌─ **Example** ─────────────────

The ammonium ion

The ammonium ion (NH_4^+) is formed by dative covalent bonding. It forms when the nitrogen atom in an ammonia molecule donates a pair of electrons to a proton (H^+) — see Figure 4.

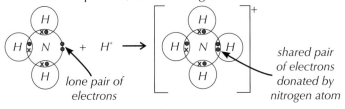

Figure 4: Dative bonding in NH_4^+.

Dative covalent bonding can also be shown in diagrams by an arrow, pointing away from the 'donor' atom (see Figure 5).

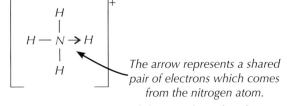

Figure 5: An alternative way of showing dative bonding in NH_4^+.

Special cases

There are always a few pesky exceptions to make life that bit trickier. For example, a few compounds contain atoms with fewer than 8 electrons in their outer shell.

Tip: Make sure you know these exceptions, and are able to draw dot-and-cross diagrams to represent their bonding.

─ Example ─────────────────────────────

In boron trifluoride, boron only has 6 electrons in its outer shell.

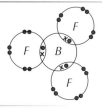

And a few compounds can use d-orbitals to 'expand the octet'. This means they contain atoms with more than 8 electrons in their outer shell.

─ Example ─────────────────────────────

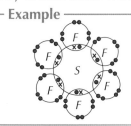

In sulfur hexafluoride, sulfur has 12 electrons in its outer shell.

Figure 6: *A molecular model of sulfur hexafluoride.*

Covalent bond strength

Not all covalent bonds are the same strength — they differ depending on how much the outer atomic orbitals of the bonded atoms overlap, and how strongly the atomic nuclei are attracted to the shared electrons.

You can find out the strength of a covalent bond by looking at its **average bond enthalpy**. Average bond enthalpy measures the energy required to break a covalent bond. The stronger a bond is, the more energy is required to break it, and so the greater the value of the average bond enthalpy.

Tip: 'Enthalpy' is just a posh word for energy.

- Know the relative repulsive strengths of bonded pairs and lone pairs of electrons.
- Be able to draw the shapes of, and state the bond angles in, molecules and ions with up to six electron pairs (including lone pairs) surrounding the central atom as predicted by electron pair repulsion.
- Be able to use electron pair repulsion to explain the following shapes of molecules and ions: linear, non-linear, trigonal planar, pyramidal, tetrahedral and octahedral.

Specification Reference 2.2.2

4. Shapes of Molecules

There's a lot of variation in molecular shape and you need to understand how to work out the shape of any molecule or molecular ion. Don't worry though, the next few pages have lots of advice to help you along.

Electron pair repulsion

Molecules and molecular ions come in loads of different shapes. The shape depends on the number of pairs of electrons in the outer shell of the central atom. Pairs of electrons can be shared in a covalent bond or can be unshared. Shared electrons are called bonding pairs, unshared electrons are called **lone pairs** or non-bonding pairs.

Electrons are all negatively charged, so electron pairs will repel each other as much as they can. This sounds straightforward, but the type of electron pair affects how much it repels other electron pairs. Lone pairs repel more than bonding pairs. So, the greatest angles are between lone pairs of electrons, and bond angles between bonding pairs are often reduced because they are pushed together by lone pair repulsion. This is known as '**electron pair repulsion theory**'. Figure 1 shows the electron pairs in water.

Lone pair/lone pair bond angles are the biggest.

Lone pair/bonding pair bond angles are the second biggest.

Bonding pair/bonding pair bond angles are the smallest.

Figure 1: *Angles between electron pairs in water.*

Tip: The area where an electron pair is most likely to be found is called a 'charge cloud'. Charge clouds repel each other so that they're as far away as possible.

Drawing shapes of molecules

It can be tricky to draw molecules showing their shapes — but one way to do it is to show which way the bonds are pointing. In a molecular diagram, use wedges to show a bond pointing towards you, and a broken (or dotted) line to show a bond pointing away from you (see Figure 2).

A broken line shows a bond pointing away from you.

Lines show bonds that aren't pointing towards you or away from you.

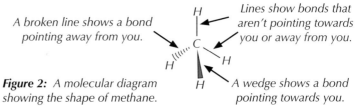

Figure 2: *A molecular diagram showing the shape of methane.*

A wedge shows a bond pointing towards you.

Calculating the number of electron pairs

To work out the shape of a molecule or an ion you need to know how many lone pairs and how many bonding pairs of electrons are on the central atom. Follow these steps:

1. Find the central atom — it's the one all the other atoms are bonded to.

2. Work out how many electrons are in the outer shell of the central atom. Use the periodic table to do this.

3. The formula of the molecule or ion will tell you how many atoms are bonded to the central atom so you can work out the number of electrons donated to the central atom by other atoms.

Tip: Unless one of the bonds is a dative covalent bond, each single bond to the central atom donates one electron, each double bond donates two electrons and each triple bond donates three electrons.

4. Add up the electrons and divide by 2 to find the number of electron pairs surrounding the central atom. If you're dealing with an ion, you need to take into account its charge, as it will affect the number of electrons involved in the bonding.

5. Compare the number of electron pairs to the number of bonds to find the number of lone pairs and the number of bonding pairs.

Tip: Double bonds count as two bonds, and triple bonds count as three bonds.

┌─ Examples ─────────────────────────────

Carbon tetrafluoride, CF_4

1. The central atom in this molecule is carbon.

2. Carbon's in Group 4 — so it has four electrons in its outer shell.

3. There are four covalent bonds bonding the central atom to fluorine atoms, so there are four electrons coming from the fluorine atoms.

4. There are 8 electrons in total, so there are 4 electron pairs.

5. 4 pairs of electrons are involved in bonding the fluorine atoms to the carbon so there must be four bonding pairs of electrons. That accounts for all the electrons — there are no lone pairs (see Figure 3).

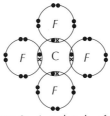

Tip: Elements that are in Group 7 (e.g. fluorine) can form one covalent bond with another atom to complete their outer shell. See pages 101-103 for more on covalent bonding.

Figure 3: *A molecule of CF_4.*

Phosphorus trihydride, PH_3

1. The central atom in this molecule is phosphorus.

2. It's in Group 5 — so it has five electrons in its outer shell.

3. Phosphorus forms three covalent bonds with hydrogen, so there are three electrons coming from the hydrogen atoms.

4. There are 8 electrons in total which means 4 electron pairs.

5. Three electron pairs are involved in bonding with the hydrogen atoms (bonding pairs) and so there's one lone pair of electrons (see Figure 4).

Tip: The number of bonds the central atom forms is also called its coordination number.

One lone pair ⟶
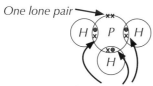
Three bonding pairs

Figure 4: *Electron pairs in a molecule of PH_3.*

Tip: A hydrogen atom will form one covalent bond with another atom to complete its outer shell.

Working out the shapes of molecules

(HOW SCIENCE WORKS)

Once you know how many electron pairs are on the central atom, you can work out the shape of the molecule.

Central atoms with two electron pairs

Molecules with two electron pairs have a bond angle of 180° and have a **linear** shape. This is because the pairs of bonding electrons repel each other, so they are positioned as far away from each other as possible.

Tip: You need to know how to calculate the number of electron pairs before you try and learn this bit. Make sure you've got that sorted before you go any further.

┌─ Examples ─ **Maths Skills** ─────────────

Beryllium chloride, $BeCl_2$

Beryllium has two bonding pairs of electrons and no lone pairs so the bond angle in $BeCl_2$ is 180° and it has a linear shape.

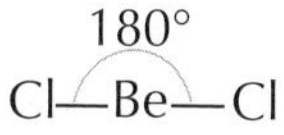

$180°$
Cl—Be—Cl

Carbon dioxide, CO_2

Carbon has four bonding pairs of electrons (found in two carbon-oxygen double bonds). You treat the double bonds like single bonds so CO_2 will have a linear shape.

$$180°$$
$$O{=}C{=}O$$

Central atoms with three electron pairs

Molecules that have three electron pairs around the central atom don't always have the same shape — the shape depends on the combination of bonding pairs and lone pairs of electrons. If there are three bonding pairs of electrons the repulsion of the charge clouds is the same between each pair and so the bond angles are all 120°. The shape of the molecule is **trigonal planar**.

┌ **Example** ── **Maths Skills** ──────────────

Boron trifluoride, BF_3

The central boron atom has three bonding pairs of electrons, so the bond angle in BF_3 is 120° and it has a trigonal planar shape.

If there are two bonding pairs of electrons and one lone pair in a molecule you'll get a squished trigonal planar shape which is called **non-linear**. The bond angle will be a bit less than 120°.

Central atoms with four electron pairs

If there are four pairs of bonding electrons and no lone pairs on a central atom, all the bond angles are 109.5° — the charge clouds all repel each other equally. The shape of the molecule is **tetrahedral**.

┌ **Example** ── **Maths Skills** ──────────────

Methane, CH_4

The carbon atom has four bonding pairs of electrons so the shape of CH_4 is tetrahedral.

Ammonium ion, NH_4^+

The nitrogen atom has four bonding pairs of electrons so the shape of NH_4^+ is tetrahedral.

If there are three bonding pairs of electrons and one lone pair, the lone-pair/bonding-pair repulsion will be greater than the bonding-pair/bonding-pair repulsion and so the angles between the atoms will change. There'll be smaller bond angles between the bonding pairs of electrons and larger angles between the lone pair and the bonding pairs. The bond angle is 107° and the shape of the molecule is **trigonal pyramidal**.

┌ **Example** ── **Maths Skills** ──────────────

Ammonia, NH_3

The nitrogen has three bonding pairs of electrons and a lone pair, so the shape of NH_3 is trigonal pyramidal.

Figure 5: A molecular model of ammonia, showing it to be a trigonal pyramidal shape.

If there are two bonding pairs of electrons and two lone pairs of electrons the lone-pair/lone-pair repulsion will squish the bond angle even further. The bond angle is 104.5° and the shape of the molecules is **non-linear**.

Tip: Take a look back at the electron pair repulsion theory (page 104) for why more lone pairs means smaller bond angles.

Example — Maths Skills

Water, H_2O

The oxygen atom has two bonding pairs shared with hydrogen atoms and two lone pairs, so the shape of H_2O is non-linear (bent).

$$\overset{\times\times}{O}\overset{\times\times}{}$$
$$H\ \underset{104.5°}{\diagup\diagdown}\ H$$

Central atoms with five or six electron pairs

Some central atoms can use d orbitals and can 'expand the octet' — which means they can have more than eight bonding electrons. A molecule with five bonding pairs will be **trigonal bipyramidal**. Repulsion between the bonding pairs means that three of the atoms will form a trigonal planar shape with bond angles of 120° and the other two atoms will be at 90° to them.

Example — Maths Skills

Phosphorus pentachloride, PCl_5

The phosphorus atom has five bonding pairs so it has a trigonal bipyramidal shape.

Exam Tip
You could be asked to name the shape of a molecule so learn the different names — some of the names are quite similar so make sure you spell them correctly.

A molecule with six bonding pairs will be **octahedral**. All of the bond angles in the molecule are 90°.

Example — Maths Skills

Sulfur hexafluoride, SF_6

Sulfur has six bonding pairs making its shape **octahedral**.

Practice Questions — Application

Q1 a) How many electron pairs are on the central atom of an H_2S molecule?

  b) How many lone pairs does a molecule of H_2S have?

  c) Draw and name the shape of an H_2S molecule.

  d) Suggest the bond angle between bonding pairs in H_2S.

Q2 Draw and name the shape of a molecule of CCl_2F_2. Explain your answer.

Q3 Predict the shape and relevant bond angles of the bonds surrounding each of the labelled atoms in the molecule on the right:

atom B

$$H-C=C-C-OH$$

atom A   atom C

Exam Tip
In the exam you could be asked to draw the shape of a molecule you've never met before. Don't panic, just take it step by step. Work out how many electron pairs the molecule has, then work out how many of those are lone pairs. Decide what the bond angles are in the molecule, then draw the molecule and make sure you label it neatly.

Practice Questions — Fact Recall

Q1 What is the bond angle between electron pairs in a trigonal planar molecule?

Q2 Name the structure that a molecule will have if it has six bonding pairs on the central atoms.

5. Polarisation

Polarisation of bonds occurs because of the nature of different atomic nuclei — some are just more attractive than others.

Electronegativity

Very few compounds come even close to being purely ionic. Similarly, only bonds between atoms of a single element, like diatomic gases such as hydrogen (H_2) or oxygen (O_2), can be purely covalent. In reality, most compounds come somewhere in between the two extremes — meaning they've often got ionic and covalent properties, e.g. covalent hydrogen chloride gas molecules dissolve to form hydrochloric acid, which is an ionic solution.

Whether a bond has more covalent or ionic character depends on the difference in **electronegativity** between the bonded atoms. Electronegativity is just the ability of an atom to attract the bonding electrons in a covalent bond. Electronegativity is measured on the Pauling Scale. A higher number means an element is better able to attract the bonding electrons. Ignoring the noble gases and hydrogen, electronegativity tends to increase across periods and decrease down groups. This means that fluorine is the most electronegative element (see Figure 1). Oxygen, nitrogen and chlorine are also very strongly electronegative — see Figure 2.

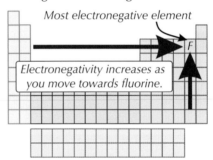

Most electronegative element

Electronegativity increases as you move towards fluorine.

Figure 1: Trends of increasing electronegativity in the periodic table

Element	Electronegativity (Pauling Scale)
H	2.20
C	2.55
N	3.04
Cl	3.16
O	3.44
F	3.98

Figure 2: The electronegativity of different elements.

Polar and non-polar bonds

The covalent bonds in diatomic gases (e.g. H_2, Cl_2) are **non-polar** because the atoms have equal electronegativities and so the electrons are equally attracted to both nuclei (see Figure 3). Some elements, like carbon and hydrogen, have pretty similar electronegativities, so bonds between them are essentially non-polar.

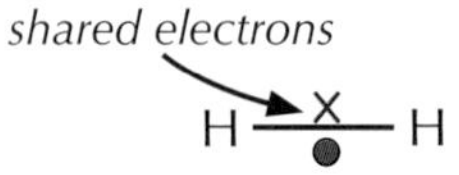

shared electrons

H — X — H

Figure 3: A non-polar covalent bond in a hydrogen molecule.

In a covalent bond between two atoms of different electronegativities, the bonding electrons are pulled towards the more electronegative atom. This makes the bond **polar** (see Figure 4).

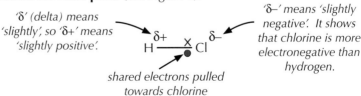

'δ' (delta) means 'slightly', so 'δ+' means 'slightly positive'.

'δ–' means 'slightly negative'. It shows that chlorine is more electronegative than hydrogen.

shared electrons pulled towards chlorine

Figure 4: A polar covalent bond in a hydrogen chloride molecule.

In a polar bond, the difference in electronegativity between the two atoms causes a **permanent dipole**. A dipole is a difference in charge between the two atoms caused by a shift in electron density in the bond. So what you need to remember is that the greater the difference in electronegativity, the more polar the bond.

Polar molecules

Polar molecules have an **overall dipole**. The arrangement of polar bonds in a molecule determines whether or not the molecule will have an overall dipole.

In simple molecules, such as hydrogen chloride, the one polar bond causes a single permanent dipole, which gives the whole molecule an overall dipole (see Figure 5).

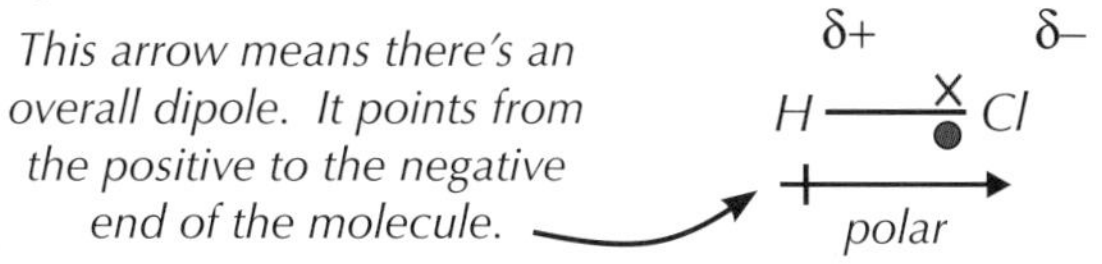

This arrow means there's an overall dipole. It points from the positive to the negative end of the molecule.

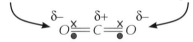

Figure 5: Overall dipole in a molecule of hydrogen chloride.

More complicated molecules might have several polar bonds. The shape of the molecule will decide whether or not it has an overall dipole and so whether or not it will be polar. If the polar bonds are arranged symmetrically so that the dipoles cancel each other out, such as in carbon dioxide, then the molecule has no overall dipole and is non-polar — see Figure 6.

The two polar C=O bonds exactly cancel each other out, so the molecule has no overall dipole.

Figure 6: A molecule of carbon dioxide has no overall dipole.

If the polar bonds are arranged so that they all point in roughly the same direction, they won't cancel each other out and the charge will be arranged unevenly across the whole molecule. The molecule will have an overall dipole and so it will be polar.

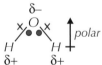

Figure 7: The overall dipole in a molecule of water.

Predicting bond types

Bonds between atoms of different elements are rarely purely ionic or purely covalent. Instead, there's a gradual transition from ionic to covalent bonding, and you can use the differences in electronegativities between two elements to predict the type of bonds that will form between them — the greater the difference, the less covalent and more ionic the bond will be. In general, bonds where the electronegativity difference between the two atoms is less than about 0.4 will be non-polar covalent bonds. If the electronegativity difference is between about 0.4 and 2.0, then the bonds will be polar but still mainly covalent in character. If the difference in electronegativity values for the two elements in the bond is more than 2.0 then the bonding will be mainly ionic in character.

Figure 8: Linus Pauling was the chemist who came up with the concept of electronegativity. In 1954 he was awarded the Nobel Prize for Chemistry for this work, as well as his other research into the properties of chemical bonds.

Tip: Looking at electronegativity differences isn't a foolproof way of working out the type of bonding in a compound but it's useful for getting a rough idea of what's likely to be happening.

Examples

Oxygen has a Pauling electronegativity value of 3.44. It can form non-polar covalent, polar covalent or ionic bonds depending upon the element it is bonded to. For example:

With nitrogen:
Nitrogen has a Pauling electronegativity value of 3.04. The difference in electronegativity values is 0.4, so the nitrogen-oxygen bond in nitrogen monoxide (NO) is likely to be covalent, and either non-polar or only very slightly polar.

With hydrogen:
Hydrogen has a Pauling electronegativity value of 2.20. The difference in electronegativity values is 1.24, so the hydrogen-oxygen bonds in water (H_2O) are likely to be covalent, but quite polar in character.

With magnesium:
Magnesium has a Pauling electronegativity value of 1.31. The difference in electronegativity is 2.13, so the magnesium-oxygen bonds in magnesium oxide (MgO) are mainly ionic in character.

Element	*Electronegativity (Pauling Scale)*
B	*2.04*
P	*2.19*
H	*2.20*
C	*2.55*
N	*3.04*
Cl	*3.16*
O	*3.44*
F	*3.98*

Figure 9: *The electronegativity of different elements.*

Practice Questions — Application

You may need to use Figure 9 when answering the following questions.

Q1 Predict whether or not the following bonds have a permanent dipole:
a) C–O
b) N–Cl
c) B–F

Q2 Copy out the diagrams of the following molecules and mark any permanent dipoles on the atoms. Use this to predict whether or not the molecules are polar:
a) Nitrogen trifluoride: 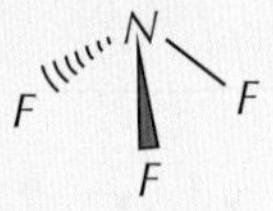

b) E-dichloroethene: 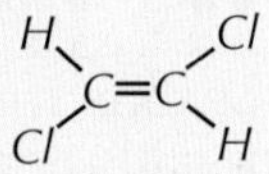

Tip: Have a look back at pages 104-107 to find the rules for drawing the shapes of molecules.

Q3 Draw the shapes of the following molecules, and predict whether or not they are polar:
a) BCl_3
b) CH_2Cl_2
c) PF_3

Practice Questions — Fact Recall

Q1 Chlorine is more electronegative than hydrogen. Explain what this means.
Q2 Explain why the H–F bond is polarised.
Q3 What is a dipole?

6. Intermolecular Forces

Molecules don't just exist independently — they can interact with each other. And you need to know how they interact.

What are intermolecular forces?

Intermolecular forces are forces between molecules. They're much weaker than covalent, ionic or metallic bonds. There are three types you need to know about: induced dipole-dipole interactions, permanent dipole-dipole interactions and hydrogen bonding (this is the strongest type).

Induced dipole-dipole interactions

Induced dipole-dipole interactions cause all atoms and molecules to be attracted to each other. Electrons in charge clouds are always moving really quickly. At any particular moment, the electrons in an atom are likely to be more to one side than the other. At this moment, the atom would have a temporary dipole. This dipole can cause another temporary (induced) dipole in the opposite direction on a neighbouring atom (see Figure 1). The two dipoles are then attracted to each other. The second dipole can cause yet another dipole in a third atom. It's a domino effect. Because the electrons are constantly moving, the dipoles are being created and destroyed all the time. Even though the dipoles keep changing, the overall effect is for the atoms to be attracted to each other.

nucleus   *charge cloud*

At this moment, the electrons in the charge cloud are to one side of the positively-charged nucleus. This is a temporary dipole...

...which induces a temporary dipole in another atom.

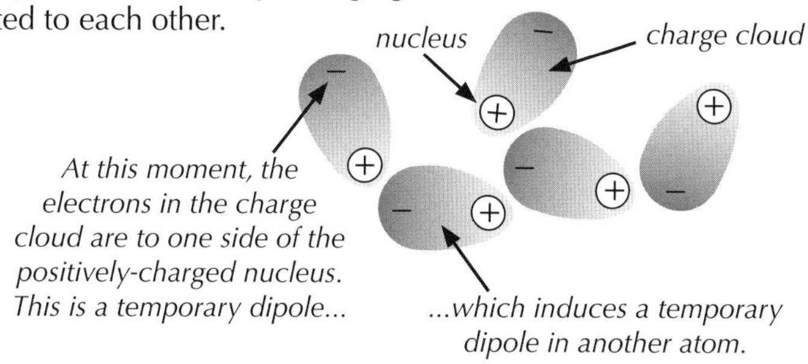

Figure 1: *Temporary dipoles in a liquid resulting in induced dipole-dipole interactions.*

Example

Induced dipole-dipole interactions are responsible for holding iodine molecules together in a lattice. Iodine atoms are held together in pairs by strong covalent bonds to form molecules of I_2 (see Figure 2). But the molecules are then held together in a simple molecular lattice arrangement by induced dipole-dipole interactions (see Figure 3).

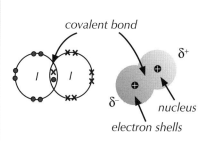

Figure 2: *A dot-and-cross diagram and a diagram showing electron density in a molecule of iodine.*

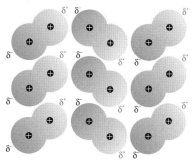

Figure 3: *Lattice of iodine molecules held together by induced dipole-dipole interactions.*

Learning Objectives:

- Understand how intermolecular forces are based on induced dipole-dipole interactions and permanent dipole-dipole interactions.

- Explain the solid structures of simple molecular lattices as covalently bonded molecules attracted by intermolecular forces, e.g. I_2 or ice.

- Understand that hydrogen bonding is intermolecular bonding between molecules containing N, O or F and the H atom of -NH, -OH or HF.

- Explain the anomalous properties of H_2O, such as its relatively high melting and boiling points and the low density of ice compared to water, as resulting from hydrogen bonding.

- Explain the effect of structure and bonding on the physical properties of covalent compounds with simple molecular lattice structures including melting and boiling points, solubility and electrical conductivity.

Specification Reference 2.2.2

Tip: Induced dipole-dipole interactions can also be called induced dipole-dipole forces.

Figure 4: The adhesive ability of a gecko's foot is thought to be due to induced dipole-dipole interactions.

Not all induced dipole-dipole interactions are the same strength — larger molecules have larger electron clouds, meaning stronger induced dipole-dipole interactions. Molecules with greater surface areas also have stronger induced dipole-dipole interactions because they have a more exposed electron cloud.

When you boil a liquid, you need to overcome the intermolecular forces, so that the particles can escape from the liquid surface. It stands to reason that you need more energy to overcome stronger intermolecular forces, so liquids with stronger induced dipole-dipole interactions will have higher boiling points. Induced dipole-dipole interactions affect other physical properties, such as melting point and viscosity too.

> ┌ **Example**
>
> Induced dipole-dipole interactions are the only forces between noble gas atoms, so the boiling points of the gases depend on them. As you go down the group of noble gases, the number of electrons increases and the atomic size also increases. This means larger temporary dipoles are able to form, so the induced dipole-dipole interactions between particles increase in strength and therefore the boiling points increase (see Figure 5).
>
>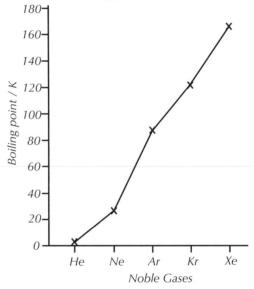
>
> *Figure 5: Graph showing the boiling points of noble gases.*

Tip: Induced dipole-dipole interactions can also be called London (dispersion) forces.

Tip: Remember — there are induced dipole-dipole interactions between all atoms and molecules.

Tip: Sometimes the term 'van der Waals' forces' is used to refer to both induced dipole-dipole interactions and permanent dipole-dipole interactions.

Exam Tip
When you're drawing dipoles in the exam, make sure you include the δ+ and δ– symbols to show the charges.

Tip: Using the electrostatic attraction between pairs of dipoles to explain the intermolecular forces in an entire substance is a great example of how science works.

Permanent dipole-dipole interactions

The δ+ and δ– charges on polar molecules cause weak electrostatic forces of attraction between molecules. These are called permanent dipole-dipole interactions. Permanent dipole-dipole interactions happen in addition to (not instead of) induced dipole-dipole interactions.

> ┌ **Example**
>
> Hydrogen chloride gas has polar molecules due to the difference in electronegativity of hydrogen and chlorine.
>
>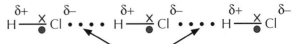
>
> *The molecules have weak electrostatic forces between them because of the shift in electron density.*
>
> *Figure 6: Permanent dipole-dipole interactions in hydrogen chloride gas.*

Hydrogen bonding

Hydrogen bonding only happens when hydrogen is covalently bonded to fluorine, nitrogen or oxygen. Hydrogen has a high charge density because it's so small and fluorine, nitrogen and oxygen are very electronegative. The bond is so polarised that a weak bond forms between the hydrogen of one molecule and a lone pair of electrons on the fluorine, nitrogen or oxygen in another molecule. Molecules which have hydrogen bonding usually contain -OH or -NH groups.

Tip: Charge density is just a measure of how much positive or negative charge there is in a certain volume.

Examples

Water and ammonia both have hydrogen bonding (see Figures 7 and 8).

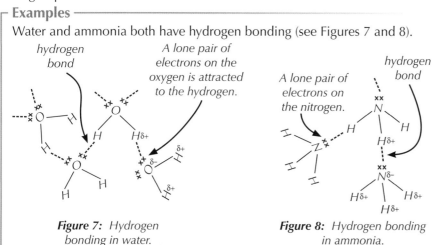

Figure 7: Hydrogen bonding in water.

Figure 8: Hydrogen bonding in ammonia.

Exam Tip
Hydrogen bonding is a special case scenario — it only happens in specific molecules. In the exam, you could be asked to compare intermolecular forces in different substances, so you'll need to know the different intermolecular forces and their relative strengths. Don't forget that not every molecule with hydrogen in it makes hydrogen bonds.

Hydrogen bonding has a huge effect on the properties of substances. They are soluble in water and have higher boiling and melting points than molecules of a similar size that are unable to form hydrogen bonds. Water and ammonia have very high boiling points if you compare them with other hydrides in their groups, because of the extra energy needed to break the H bonds — see Figure 9.

Exam Tip
If you're asked to draw a diagram to show hydrogen bonding you'll need to include the lone pairs of electrons on the electronegative atom (O, N or F). You may also have to show the partial charges — the δ+ goes on the H atom and the δ− goes on the electronegative atom.

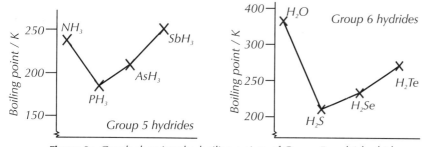

Figure 9: Graph showing the boiling points of Group 5 and 6 hydrides.

In ice, molecules of H_2O are held together in a lattice by hydrogen bonds — see Figure 10. When ice melts, hydrogen bonds are broken, so ice has more hydrogen bonds than liquid water. Since hydrogen bonds are relatively long, the molecules in ice will, on average, be further apart than in liquid water. This makes ice less dense than liquid water. This is unusual — most substances get denser when they freeze.

Exam Tip
You don't need to learn the actual boiling points of the substances in Figure 9, but you should be able to explain the shapes of the graphs.

Figure 10: Lattice of water molecules in ice held together by hydrogen bonds.

Figure 11: Icebergs float because ice is less dense than water.

Figure 12: Iodine is made up of non-polar molecules, so is only slightly soluble in water. Most of the iodine crystals are undissolved at the bottom of the test tube.

Behaviour of simple covalent compounds

Simple covalent compounds have strong bonds within molecules but weak forces between the molecules. Their physical properties, such as electrical conductivity, melting point and solubility, are determined by the bonding in the compound.

Electrical conductivity

Even though some covalent molecules have permanent dipoles, overall covalent molecules are uncharged. This means they can't conduct electricity.

Melting and boiling points

The intermolecular forces that hold together the molecules in simple covalent compounds are weak so don't need much energy to break. This means their melting and boiling points are normally low — they are often liquids or gases at room temperature. As intermolecular forces get stronger, melting and boiling points increase.

Solubility

Water is a polar molecule, so only tends to dissolve other polar substances well. Compounds with hydrogen bonds, such as ammonia, can form hydrogen bonds with water molecules, so will be soluble. Molecules that aren't polar, such as methane, will be insoluble or, at best, only slightly soluble in water.

Trends in melting and boiling points

In general, the main factor that determines the boiling point of a substance will be the strength of the induced dipole-dipole forces (unless the molecule can form hydrogen bonds).

Example

As you go down the Group 7 hydrides from HCl to HI, there are two competing factors that could affect the overall strength of the intermolecular forces, and so the boiling points:

- The polarity of the molecules decreases, so the strength of the permanent dipole-dipole interactions decreases.
- The number of electrons in the molecules increases, so the strength of the induced dipole-dipole interactions increases.

As you can see from Figure 13, the boiling points of the Group 7 hydrides increase from HCl to HI. So the increasing strength of the induced dipole-dipole interactions has a greater effect on the boiling point than the decreasing strength of the permanent dipole-dipole interactions.

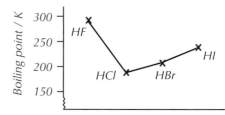

Figure 13: Boiling points of the Group 7 hydrides.

If you have two molecules with a similar number of electrons, then the strength of their induced dipole-dipole interactions will be similar. So if one of the substances has molecules that are more polar than the other, it will have stronger permanent dipole-dipole interactions and so a higher boiling point.

Practice Questions — Application

Q1 What intermolecular force(s) exist(s) in H_2?

Q2 Draw a diagram to show the intermolecular forces between three molecules of hydrogen bromide, HBr. Include bonding electrons and any partial charges in your diagram. Hydrogen has an electronegativity value of 2.20 and bromine has a value of 2.96.

Q3 The table in Figure 14 shows the electronegativity values of some elements.

a) Use the table to explain why there are hydrogen bonds between H_2O molecules but not between HCl molecules.

b) Why does water have a higher boiling point than hydrogen chloride?

c) Identify one other element from the table that would form hydrogen bonds when covalently bonded to hydrogen.

d) Name one other element from the table that would not form hydrogen bonds when covalently bonded to hydrogen.

Q4 Hydrogen has an electronegativity value of 2.20 on the Pauling scale, nitrogen has a value of 3.04 and phosphorus has a value of 2.19.

a) The boiling point of NH_3 is –33 °C and the boiling point of PH_3 is –88 °C. Explain why the boiling point of PH_3 is lower.

b) Arsenic (As) has an electronegativity value of 2.18. Would you expect the boiling point of AsH_3 to be higher or lower than that of NH_3?

Q5 Put the following compounds in order of increasing boiling point. Explain your prediction in terms of intermolecular forces: CH_3OH, CH_4, CH_3I, CH_3Cl.

Element	Electronegativity (Pauling Scale)
H	2.20
C	2.55
Cl	3.16
O	3.44
F	3.98

Figure 14:
The electronegativity of different elements.

Exam Tip
It's quite likely you'll be asked to identify and compare the intermolecular forces in different substances in the exam. You'll also need to know the effects that the intermolecular forces have on the properties of the substances, so make sure you know all this stuff inside out.

Practice Questions — Fact Recall

Q1 Name three types of intermolecular forces.

Q2 Describe the bonding within and between iodine molecules.

Q3 What are permanent dipole-dipole forces?

Q4 a) What is the strongest intermolecular force in ammonia?

b) Draw a diagram to show this intermolecular force between two ammonia molecules.

Q5 Explain why ice is less dense than liquid water.

Q6 Chlorine (Cl_2) is a simple covalent molecule.

a) Explain why chlorine is only slightly soluble in water.

b) Would you expect chlorine to conduct electricity? Explain your answer.

Section Summary

Make sure you know...

- How many electrons each of the first four shells in atoms can contain.
- How many orbitals make up the s, p and d sub-shells and how many electrons go in each of them.
- That an orbital is the bit of space that an electron moves in and that each orbital can hold up to two electrons with opposite spins.
- What shapes the s- and p-orbitals are.
- The relative energy levels of the s-, p- and d-orbitals of the first 4 electron shells.
- That electrons fill orbitals of lower energies first and that they fill orbitals with the same energy singly before they start sharing.
- How to write electron configurations using both sub-shell notation and 'electrons in boxes'.
- How to work out electron configurations of the first 36 elements from the periodic table.
- How different theories of electronic structure developed over time.
- That electrostatic attraction holds ions together and that this is called ionic bonding.
- How to draw dot-and-cross diagrams to show ionic bonding.
- That giant ionic lattices, such as sodium chloride, are regular repeating structures resulting from oppositely charged ions strongly attracted to each other in all directions.
- How the structure and bonding of ionic compounds decides their physical properties — their electrical conductivity, melting and boiling points and solubility.
- That a covalent bond is the strong electrostatic attraction between a shared pair of electrons and the nuclei of the bonded atoms.
- That dative covalent bonds form when one atom donates both the shared electrons in a bond.
- How to draw dot-and-cross diagrams to show single, multiple and dative covalent bonds between atoms, for molecules with up to six electron pairs around the central atom.
- That the larger the value of the average bond enthalpy, the stronger a covalent bond will be.
- How the repulsion between electron pairs on a central atom affects the shape of simple molecules.
- How to use electron pair repulsion theory to predict the shapes of molecules that have central atoms with 2, 3, 4, 5 and 6 electron pairs, including their bond angles and shape names.
- How to draw 3-D diagrams to illustrate the shapes of molecules and ions.
- That electronegativity is the ability to attract the bonding electrons in a covalent bond.
- That electronegativity increases towards fluorine in the periodic table.
- How differences in electronegativities between bonding atoms causes polarisation and permanent dipoles in covalent bonds.
- The difference between polar and non-polar bonds.
- How the shape of a molecule and the polarity of its bonds affects whether or not it has an overall dipole and is a polar molecule.
- How to use Pauling electronegativity values to predict the type of bond that will form between atoms.
- What permanent dipole-dipole interactions and induced dipole-dipole interactions are, and what causes them.
- That solid structures of simple molecular substances contain covalently bonded molecules attracted to each other by intermolecular forces.
- How hydrogen bonds form and their effect on the properties of compounds.
- How the structure and bonding of covalent compounds with simple molecular structures decides their physical properties — their electrical conductivity, melting and boiling points and solubility.

Exam-style Questions

1   Which of the options below gives the correct electron configuration
for the specified atom?

                1s   2s   2p

   A   Oxygen: ↑↓ ↑↓ ↑↓ ↑↓ ☐

                1s   2s   2p

   B   Nitrogen: ↑↓ ↑↓ ↑ ↑ ↑

                1s   2s   2p

   C   Carbon: ↑↓ ↑ ↑ ↑ ↑

                1s   2s   2p

   D   Boron: ↑↓ ↑↓ ↑ ↑ ☐

(1 mark)

2   Which of the following statements about hydrogen selenide, H_2Se, is correct?

   A   Hydrogen selenide is a linear molecule.

   B   Hydrogen selenide has a higher boiling point that hydrogen sulfide (H_2S).

   C   There is one lone pair and two bonding pairs around the central Se atom in H_2Se.

   D   Hydrogen selenide is able to form hydrogen bonds.

(1 mark)

3   Potassium oxide, K_2O, has a melting point of 740 °C. It is an electrical insulator
when it is a solid, but once molten or dissolved it can carry an electrical current.

Silicon dioxide, SiO_2, has a melting point of 1600 °C.
It is an electrical insulator and is insoluble in water.

From the table below, select the option that gives the correct
structure for both compounds.

	K_2O	SiO_2
A	ionic	metallic
B	giant covalent	ionic
C	metallic	giant covalent
D	ionic	giant covalent

(1 mark)

4   Which of the following molecules does **not** have a trigonal pyramidal shape?

   A H_3O^+

   B NCl_3

   C BCl_3

   D PF_3

(1 mark)

5   The table below shows the electronegativities of some elements.

Element	C	H	Cl	O	F
Electronegativity (Pauling Scale)	2.55	2.20	3.16	3.44	3.98

(a) (i)   Define the term electronegativity.

(1 mark)

(ii)   Explain how electronegativity can give rise to permanent dipole-dipole interactions.

(2 marks)

(b) (i)   Use the information in the table to name all the intermolecular forces in each of the following compounds:
HCl
CH_4
HF

(3 marks)

(ii)   Draw a diagram to show the strongest intermolecular forces between two HF molecules. Include partial charges and all lone pairs.

(3 marks)

(iii)   Explain why the only forces between Cl_2 molecules are induced dipole-dipole interactions.

(1 mark)

6   Calcium is an element that can react to form ionic bonds with negatively charged ions.

(a)   Calcium can react with oxygen to form the ionic compound calcium oxide, CaO.

(i)   State what is meant by the term ionic bond.

(1 mark)

(ii)   Give the electronic configuration of the calcium ion, Ca^{2+}, using sub-shell notation.

(1 mark)

(iii)   Draw a dot-and-cross diagram to show the bonding in CaO.
Show the outer electrons only.

(2 marks)

(b)   Calcium can also form the ionic compound calcium carbonate. Calcium carbonate decomposes when heated to form calcium oxide and carbon dioxide.
State the shape and bond angle of a molecule of carbon dioxide.
Explain why carbon dioxide has this shape.

(3 marks)

(c)   Predict, with reasoning, whether calcium oxide or carbon dioxide will have a higher boiling point.

(2 marks)

7 The Group 5 elements include nitrogen, phosphorus, arsenic and antimony.
They can form covalent bonds with hydrogen.

(a) The graph below shows the boiling points of some Group 5 hydrides.

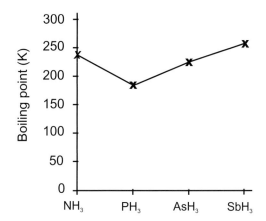

Explain the trend in boiling points shown by the graph for NH_3, PH_3, AsH_3 and SbH_3.

(4 marks)

(b) Draw the shape of a molecule of PH_3, labelling the size of the bond angles.

(2 marks)

(c) Explain why ammonia, NH_3, is the most soluble of the Group 5 hydrides.

(2 marks)

8 Fluorine can form covalent bonds with sulfur, S_8, to produce the molecule SF_6 and boron to form the molecule BF_3.

(a) Draw a dot-and-cross diagram to show the bonding in SF_6.
Use your diagram to explain the shape of the molecule.

(4 marks)

(b) A fluorine ion, F^-, can react with BF_3 to form the BF_4^- ion.
A dative covalent bond forms between F^- and BF_3.

(i) State the bond angle in BF_3.

(1 mark)

(ii) Explain what is meant by the term dative covalent bond.

(1 mark)

(iii) Draw a dot-and-cross diagram to show the bonding in a BF_4^- ion.
Your diagram should show the outer electrons only.

(1 mark)

(iv) Predict the shape of the BF_4^- ion. Explain your answer.

(2 marks)

1. The Periodic Table

You'll remember from GCSE that the periodic table isn't just arranged how it is by chance. There are well-thought-out reasons behind it, and you can use it to predict what the properties of an element might be. Read on...

Grouping the elements

In the early 1800s, there were only two ways to categorise elements — by their physical and chemical properties and by their **relative atomic mass**. (The modern periodic table is arranged by proton number, but back then, they knew nothing about protons or electrons. The only thing they could measure was relative atomic mass.)

In 1817, Johann Döbereiner attempted to group similar elements — these groups were called Döbereiner's triads. He saw that chlorine, bromine and iodine had similar characteristics. He also realised that other properties of bromine (e.g. atomic weight) fell halfway between those of chlorine and iodine. He found other such groups of three elements (e.g. lithium, sodium and potassium), and called them triads. It was a start.

An English chemist called John Newlands had the first good stab at making a table of the elements in 1863. He noticed that if he arranged the elements in order of mass, elements with similar chemical and physical properties appeared at regular intervals — every eighth element was similar. He called this the law of octaves, and he listed some known elements in rows of seven so that the similar elements lined up in columns — see Figure 1. The law of octaves later developed into the Periodic Law which states that if you arrange elements in order of increasing atomic number then their chemical and physical properties will repeat in a systematic way that can be predicted.

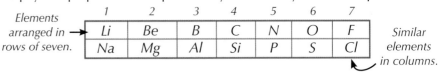

	1	2	3	4	5	6	7
Elements arranged in rows of seven.	Li	Be	B	C	N	O	F
	Na	Mg	Al	Si	P	S	Cl

Similar elements in columns.

Figure 1: *The arrangement of elements by John Newlands.*

The problem was, the pattern broke down on the third row, with many transition metals like Fe, Cu and Zn messing it up completely.

Mendeleev's table

In 1869, Russian chemist Dmitri Mendeleev produced a much better table, which wasn't far off the one we have today. He arranged all the known elements by atomic mass (like Newlands did), but the clever thing he did was to leave gaps in the table where the next element didn't seem to fit. By putting in gaps, he could keep elements with similar chemical properties in the same group — see Figure 2.

He also predicted the properties of undiscovered elements that would go in the gaps. When elements were later discovered (e.g. germanium, scandium and gallium) with properties that matched Mendeleev's predictions, it showed that clever old Mendeleev had got it right.

	Group 1	Group 2	Group 3	Group 4	Group 5	Group 6	Group 7
1	H						
2	Li	Be	B	C	N	O	F
3	Na	Mg	Al	Si	P	S	Cl
4	K	Ca	?	Ti	V	Cr	Mn
	Cu	Zn	?	?	As	Se	Br
5	Rb	Sr	Y	Zr	Nb	Mo	?
	Ag	Cd	In	Sn	Sb	Te	I
6	Cs	Ba	La	?	Ta	W	?
	Au	Hg	Tl	Pb	Bi	?	?

Figure 2: *Dmitri Mendeleev's table of elements. The question marks show gaps in the table which were later filled when new elements were discovered.*

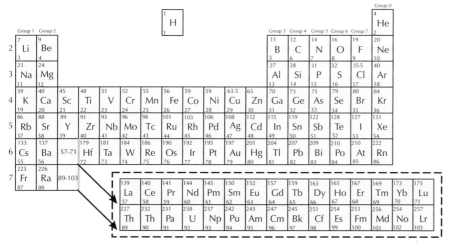

Figure 3: *Dmitri Mendeleev (1834-1907) was a Russian chemist who developed the periodic table.*

The modern periodic table

The modern periodic table is pretty much the one produced by Henry Moseley around 1914. He arranged the elements according to increasing atomic number rather than by mass. This fixed a few elements that Mendeleev had put out of place using atomic mass. He also added the noble gases (Group 0) which had been discovered in the 1890s. The final big change was a result of the work of Glenn Seaborg. He suggested how the f-block elements fit into the periodic table (though they're usually shown separated from the main part of the table). The modern periodic table is shown in Figure 4.

Tip: The atomic number is the number of protons in the nucleus — so it's also known as the proton number.

Figure 4: *The modern periodic table.*

Exam Tip
You'll be given a periodic table in your exam, so you'll have a copy to refer to. It's a good idea to be familiar with how it works <u>before</u> you go into the exam though.

Periods and rows

The periodic table is arranged into **periods** (rows) and **groups** (columns). All the elements within a period have the same number of electron shells (if you don't worry about the sub-shells).

Tip: When you arrange elements by atomic number, there are a few that no longer go in order of atomic mass. For example, Ar would go after K if you put the elements in order of atomic mass. But Ar comes before K in the modern periodic table.

─ Example ───────────

The elements in Period 2 all have 2 electron shells:

The first three elements in Period 2.

All have two electron shells.

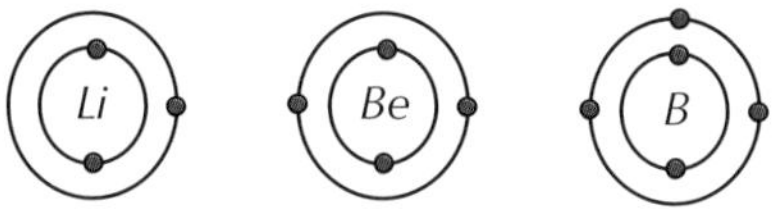

This results in repeating patterns of physical and chemical properties across a period (this is known as **periodicity**).

Tip: The elements of Period 1 (hydrogen and helium) both have 1 electron shell.

All the elements within a group have the same number of electrons in their outer shell. This means they have similar physical and chemical properties. The group number tells you the number of electrons in the outer shell.

┌─ Examples ─────────────────────────────────────

Group 1 elements have 1 electron in their outer shell:

As a result the elements in Group 1 all have similar properties. For example, they all react strongly with water (see Figure 5).

Group 4 elements have 4 electrons in their outer shell and so on.

The only elements where the group number doesn't tell you how many electrons are in their outer shells are the Group 0 elements — they have full outer shells.

Figure 5: The Group 1 elements potassium (top left), sodium (top right) and lithium (bottom) all react strongly with water.

Electron configurations

You can use the periodic table to work out electron configurations. The period number tells you how many electron shells the element has and the group number tells you how many electrons an element has in its outer electron shell. But to make things even easier the periodic table can be split into an s-block, d-block and p-block (see Figure 6). Doing this shows you which sub-shells all the electrons go into.

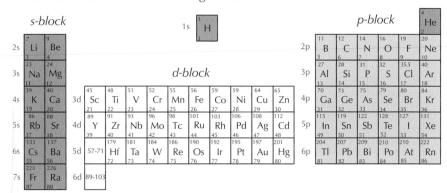

Figure 6: The periodic table showing the s-block, p-block and d-block.

s-block elements

The s-block elements have an outer shell electron configuration of of s^1 or s^2.

┌─ Examples ─────────────────────────────────────

Lithium is in Group 1 and Period 2:

Its electron configuration is: 1s^2 **2s^1**

group number

period number

Magnesium is in Group 2 and Period 3:

Its electron configuration is: 1s^2 2s^2 2p^6 **3s^2**

period number   *group number*

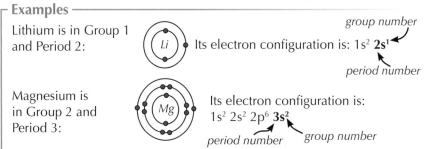

p-block elements

The p-block elements have an outer shell configuration of s^2 p^1 to s^2 p^6.

Example

Chlorine is in Group 7 and Period 3:

Its electron configuration is:

2 + 5 = 7 = group number

$1s^2\ 2s^2\ 2p^6\ \mathbf{3s^2\ 3p^5}$

period number

d-block elements

The d-block elements have electron configurations in which d sub-shells are being filled. They're a bit trickier — you don't always write the sub-shells in the order they're filled. Instead, you write them in order of increasing period number.

Example

The electron configuration of cobalt is: $1s^2\ 2s^2\ 2p^6\ 3s^2\ 3p^6\ \mathbf{3d^7\ 4s^2}$

Even though the 3rd sub-shell fills last in cobalt, it's not written at the end of the line.

Tip: Watch out for the fact that 3d is on the same row as 4s and 4p in the periodic table. Remember that the 4s sub-shell is of lower energy than the 3d sub-shell so it fills first. Sneaky.

Working out the electron configuration of an element

When you've got the periodic table labelled with the shells and sub-shells, it's pretty easy to read off the electron structure of any element by starting at the top and working your way across and down until you get to your element.

Example

To work out the electron structure of phosphorus (P), you can use the periodic table to see that it's in Group 5 and Period 3. Starting with Period 1, the electron configuration of a full shell is $1s^2$. For Period 2 it's $2s^2\ 2p^6$. However, phosphorus' outer shell is only partially filled — it's got 5 outer electrons in the configuration $3s^2\ 3p^3$.

So: Period 1 — $1s^2$
      Period 2 — $2s^2\ 2p^6$
      Period 3 — $3s^2\ 3p^3$

The full electron structure of phosphorus is: $1s^2\ 2s^2\ 2p^6\ 3s^2\ 3p^3$.

Tip: It doesn't really matter how you work out the electron configurations of elements, whether you use the rules on page 96 or whether you read them off the periodic table like on this page. The important thing is that you get them right — so find a method you're happy with and stick with it.

Practice Questions — Application

Q1 How many electron shells do atoms of the following elements have?

   a) Sulfur, S   b) Bromine, Br   c) Rubidium, Rb

Q2 How many electrons are in the outer shell of atoms of these elements?

   a) Selenium, Se   b) Aluminium, Al   c) Potassium, K

Q3 Work out the electron configurations of the following elements:

   a) Sodium, Na   b) Calcium, Ca   c) Chlorine, Cl

   d) Arsenic, As   e) Vanadium, V   f) Scandium, Sc

Tip: Don't forget that you always write the sub-shells in electron configurations in order of increasing period number, even if this isn't the order that they're filled in.

Practice Questions — Fact Recall

Q1 a) How did Mendeleev arrange the elements in his version of the periodic table?

   b) How are elements arranged in the modern periodic table?

Q2 a) What is a period?

   b) What is a group?

   c) Define the term periodicity.

Q3 Explain why elements in a group have similar chemical properties.

- Define the term first ionisation energy.
- Explain the trend in first ionisation energies across Periods 2 and 3, and down a group, in terms of attraction, nuclear charge and atomic radius.
- Understand how trends in ionisation energies support the Bohr model of the atom.

Specification Reference 3.1.1

Tip: An endothermic process is one that takes in heat — see page 155 for more on this.

Exam Tip
Make sure you know the definition of first ionisation energy — it could come up in your exam.

2. First Ionisation Energy

More stuff on electron configurations coming up. The title may be first ionisation energy, but it's still all about electrons and how they're arranged.

Ionisation energy

When electrons have been removed from an atom or molecule, it's been ionised. The energy you need to remove the first electron is called the **first ionisation energy**.

> The first ionisation energy is the energy needed to remove 1 mole of electrons from 1 mole of gaseous atoms.

You have to put energy in to ionise an atom or molecule, so it's an endothermic process. You can write equations for this process — here's the equation for the first ionisation of oxygen:

$$O_{(g)} \rightarrow O^+_{(g)} + e^- \qquad \text{1st ionisation energy} = +1314 \text{ kJ mol}^{-1}$$

Here are a few rather important points about ionisation energies:

- You must use the gas state symbol, (g), because ionisation energies are measured for gaseous atoms.
- Always refer to 1 mole of atoms, as stated in the definition, rather than to a single atom.
- The lower the ionisation energy, the easier it is to form an ion.

Factors affecting ionisation energy

A high ionisation energy means there's a strong attraction between the electron and the nucleus, so more energy is needed to overcome the attraction and remove the electron. Three things can affect ionisation energy:

1. Nuclear charge

The more protons there are in the nucleus, the more positively charged the nucleus is and the stronger the attraction for the electrons.

2. Atomic radius

Attraction falls off very rapidly with distance. An electron close to the nucleus will be much more strongly attracted than one further away.

3. Shielding

As the number of electrons between the outer electrons and the nucleus increases, the outer electrons feel less attraction towards the nuclear charge. This lessening of the pull of the nucleus by inner shells of electrons is called shielding.

Example 1

The distance between the nucleus and the electron being removed is greater in the sodium atom.

There are only two electrons between the nucleus and the outer electron in a lithium atom.

There are ten electrons between the nucleus and the outer electron in a sodium atom — the shielding effect is greater.

Figure 1: *A lithium atom and a sodium atom.*

This means that lithium has a higher first ionisation energy (519 kJ mol⁻¹) than sodium (496 kJ mol⁻¹). (The shielding and the atomic radius have a bigger effect than the nuclear charge in this example.)

Example 2

As the number of protons increases, the positive charge of the nucleus increases. This means electrons are pulled closer to the nucleus, making the atomic radius smaller.

Tip: You can only really see the effect of nuclear charge on ionisation energy if you're looking at atoms with equal shielding effects. This only really happens when you're looking at elements in the same period of the Periodic Table.

Na and Cl have the same number of electrons in the first and second shells, so the shielding is the same.

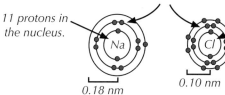

11 protons in the nucleus.

17 protons in the nucleus — the positive charge of the nucleus in Cl is greater than in Na, so the attraction of the electrons to the nucleus is greater and the atomic radius is smaller.

0.18 nm   0.10 nm

Figure 2: *A sodium atom and a chlorine atom.*

This means that chlorine has a higher first ionisation energy (1256 kJ mol^{-1}) than sodium (496 kJ mol^{-1}). (The nuclear charge and the atomic radius determine this, as the shielding is the same.)

Figure 3: *Cut sodium metal.*

Trend in ionisation energy down a group

As you go down a group in the periodic table, ionisation energies generally fall, i.e. it gets easier to remove outer electrons (see Figure 4).

This is because elements further down a group have extra electron shells compared to ones above. The extra shells mean that the atomic radius is larger, which greatly reduces the attraction to the nucleus. The extra inner shells also shield the outer electrons from the attraction of the nucleus. Both of these factors make it easier to remove outer electrons, resulting in a lower ionisation energy. The positive charge of the nucleus does increase as you go down a group (due to the extra protons), but this effect is overridden by the effect of the extra shells.

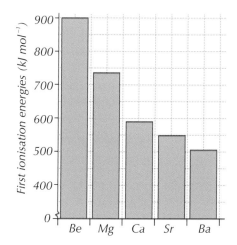

Figure 4: *First ionisation energies of the first five elements of Group 2.*

Exam Tip
If you're asked about trends in ionisation energy in a group or across a period, you can work them out by thinking about how the three factors that affect ionisation energy (atomic radius, nuclear charge and shielding) change.

Periodicity of ionisation energy

As you move across a period, the general trend is for the ionisation energies to increase — i.e. it gets harder to remove the outer electrons. This is because the number of protons is increasing, which means a higher nuclear charge, so a smaller atomic radius and a stronger attraction. All the extra electrons are at roughly the same energy level, even if the outer electrons are in different orbital types. This means there's generally little extra shielding effect to lessen the attraction from the nucleus.

Examples

In Period 2 the first ionisation energies generally increase from lithium to neon and in Period 3 the first ionisation energies generally increase from sodium to argon (see Figure 5).

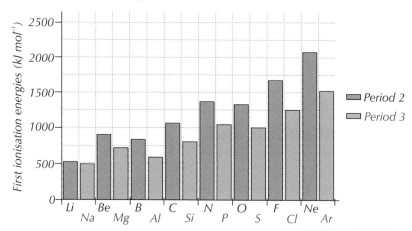

Figure 5: *The trend in first ionisation energies across Periods 2 and 3.*

As you go across Period 2 or Period 3, the number of protons in the nucleus increases. This means the overall attraction between the electrons and the nucleus increases, the atomic radius decreases and the outer electrons get more difficult to remove.

You might have spotted that in Figure 5, the ionisation energies across a period don't always increase — there are small drops between Groups 2 and 3, and 5 and 6.

The drop between Groups 2 and 3 is due to the outer electrons in Group 3 elements being in a p-orbital rather than an s-orbital.

Example

Mg $1s^2 2s^2 2p^6 3s^2$ 1st ionisation energy = 738 kJ mol^{-1}
Al $1s^2 2s^2 2p^6 3s^2 3p^1$ 1st ionisation energy = 578 kJ mol^{-1}

- Aluminium's outer electron is in a 3p orbital rather than a 3s. The 3p orbital has a slightly higher energy than the 3s orbital, so the electron is, on average, to be found further from the nucleus.
- The 3p orbital also has additional shielding provided by the $3s^2$ electrons.

Both these factors together are strong enough to override the effect of the increased nuclear charge, resulting in the ionisation energy dropping slightly. This pattern in ionisation energies provides evidence for the theory of electron sub-shells.

Tip: This is an example of how real-life data (the first ionisation energies of atoms) can provide evidence for a theory (Bohr's model of the atom). See page 31 for more.

HOW SCIENCE WORKS

The drop between Groups 5 and 6 is due to electron repulsion.

Example

Phosphorus: $1s^2\ 2s^2\ 2p^6\ 3s^2\ 3p^3$ 1st ionisation energy = 1012 kJ mol^{-1}

Sulfur: $1s^2\ 2s^2\ 2p^6\ 3s^2\ 3p^4$ 1st ionisation energy = 1000 kJ mol^{-1}

The shielding is identical in the phosphorus and sulfur atoms, and in both cases the electron is being removed from an orbital in the 3p sub-shell.

In phosphorus's case, the electron is being removed from a singly-occupied orbital. But in sulfur, the electron is being removed from an orbital containing two electrons.

Phosphorus: [Ne] 3s 3p

Sulfur: [Ne] 3s 3p

The repulsion between two electrons in an orbital means that electrons are easier to remove from shared orbitals. Yup, yet more evidence for the electronic structure model.

Tip: Writing out or drawing the electronic configurations of elements can help you work out why their ionisation energies are what they are.
For example, drawing

will show you that the electron being removed is paired, so there will be repulsion. Drawing

will show you how much shielding there is.

Practice Questions — Application

Q1 a) Write an equation for the first ionisation energy of chlorine.

  b) Write an equation for the first ionisation energy of silicon.

Q2 a) Explain why the atomic radius of aluminium is larger than the atomic radius of sulfur.

  b) Name a Period 3 element with a larger atomic radius than aluminium.

Q3 The first ionisation energy of aluminium is 578 kJ mol^{-1}. The first ionisation energy of silicon is 787 kJ mol^{-1}. Explain why there is a difference between these ionisation energies.

Q4 a) Would you expect strontium to have a larger or smaller atomic radius than rubidium? Explain your answer.

  b) Would you expect bromine to have a higher or lower first ionisation energy than selenium? Explain your answer.

Q5 The first ionisation energy of nitrogen is 1402 kJ mol^{-1}. The first ionisation energy of oxygen is 1314 kJ mol^{-1}. Explain why there is a difference between these ionisation energies.

Q6 The first ionisation energy of beryllium is 900 kJ mol^{-1}. The first ionisation energy of boron is 801 kJ mol^{-1}. Explain why there is a difference between these ionisation energies.

Exam Tip
If you get a question in the exam asking you to compare ionisation energies, make sure you remember the 3 factors that affect ionisation energy. Work out how the factors differ between each element, and you should have a very good idea of your answer.

Practice Questions — Fact Recall

Q1 Define first ionisation energy.

Q2 How does the number of protons affect the first ionisation energy?

Q3 Give two other factors that affect the first ionisation energy.

Q4 Explain why first ionisation energies decrease down a group.

Q5 a) Describe the general trend in ionisation energy across a period of the periodic table.

  b) Explain this trend.

Exam Tip
If you're asked about a specific trend, it might help you to roughly sketch out the shape of the relevant graph. That way you'll easily be able to see how the values for the elements compare to each other.

Learning Objectives:

- Understand the term successive ionisation energy.
- Predict from successive ionisation energies the number of electrons in each shell of an atom, and the group of the element.

Specification Reference 3.1.1

3. Successive Ionisation Energies

First ionisation energy is the energy needed to remove 1 mole of electrons from 1 mole of gaseous atoms. You'll now see second, third and all other ionisation energies, collectively known as successive ionisation energies.

What are successive ionisation energies?

You can remove all the electrons from an atom, leaving only the nucleus. Each time you remove an electron, there's a **successive ionisation energy**. These are called second ionisation energy, third ionisation energy... and so on. For example, the **second ionisation energy** is the energy needed to remove 1 electron from each ion in 1 mole of gaseous 1+ ions to form 1 mole of gaseous 2+ ions.

Here's the equation for the second ionisation of oxygen :

$$O^+_{(g)} \rightarrow O^{2+}_{(g)} + e^-$$ 2nd ionisation energy = +3388 kJ mol^{-1}

Ionisation energies and shell structure

If you have the successive ionisation energies of an element you can work out the number of electrons in each shell of the atom and which element the group is in. A graph of successive ionisation energies provides evidence for the shell structure of atoms (see Figure 1).

Tip: The y-axis of this graph has a log (logarithmic) scale. Log scales go up in powers of a number (e.g. 1, 10, 100, etc.) rather than in units (1, 2, 3, etc.). Log scales are often used for graphs like this because ionisation energy values have such a huge range.

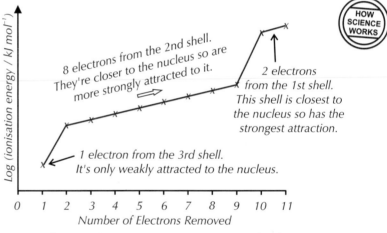

Figure 1: *Successive ionisation energies of sodium.*

Within each shell, successive ionisation energies increase. This is because electrons are being removed from an increasingly positive ion — there's less repulsion amongst the remaining electrons, so more energy is needed to remove the next electron. The big jumps in ionisation energy happen when a new shell is broken into — an electron is being removed from a shell closer to the nucleus.

Graphs like the one in Figure 1 can tell you which group of the periodic table an element belongs to. Just count how many electrons are removed before the first big jump to find the group number.

Example

In Figure 1, one electron is removed before the first big jump — sodium is in Group 1.

These graphs can be used to predict the electronic structure of an element. Working from right to left, count how many points there are before each big jump to find how many electrons are in each shell, starting with the first.

Example

Working from right to left in Figure 1, the graph has 2 points on the right-hand side, then a jump, then 8 points, a jump, and 1 final point. Sodium has 2 electrons in the first shell, 8 in the second and 1 in the third.

Practice Questions — Application

Q1 a) Write an equation for the second ionisation energy of boron.

b) Write an equation for the second ionisation energy of chlorine.

c) Write an equation for the third ionisation energy of chlorine.

Q2 Here is an ionisation energy equation for sulfur.

$$S^{4+}_{(g)} \rightarrow S^{5+}_{(g)} + e^-$$

Which ionisation energy does the equation show?

Q3 The graph below shows the successive ionisation energies of an element.

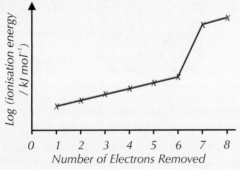

a) Which group is this element in?

b) State the number of electrons it has in each shell.

c) Name the element.

Q4 a) Sketch a graph showing the successive ionisation energies of magnesium.

b) Explain the shape of the graph.

Exam Tip
Make sure you use your periodic table to help you on questions like this. It can also help to write out electron configurations so that you can see what shell and orbital an electron is being removed from for each successive ionisation energy.

Learning Objectives:

- Explain the solid giant covalent lattices of carbon (diamond, graphite and graphene) and silicon as networks of atoms bonded by strong covalent bonds.

- Be able to use ideas about bonding to explain the strength and conductive properties of graphene, and its potential applications and benefits.

- Explain the physical properties of giant covalent lattices, including melting and boiling points, solubility and electrical conductivity in terms of structure and bonding.

Specification Reference 3.1.1

Tip: 'Delocalised' means an electron isn't attached to a particular atom — it can move around between atoms.

Tip: 'Sublimes' means it changes straight from a solid to a gas, skipping out the liquid stage.

Tip: Tetrahedral is a molecular shape — see pages 104-107 for more on shapes of molecules.

Tip: You can 'cut' diamond to form gemstones (see Figure 3). Its structure makes it refract light a lot, which is why it sparkles.

4. Giant Covalent Lattices

Atoms can form giant structures as well as tiny ones. Silicon and carbon both form giant structures — giant compared to other atomic structures, anyway...

Bonding in giant covalent lattices

Giant covalent lattices are huge networks of covalently bonded atoms. (They're sometimes called **macromolecular** structures.) Carbon and silicon atoms can form this type of structure because they can each form four strong, covalent bonds. Different forms of the same element in the same state are called **allotropes**. There are three carbon allotropes you need to know about — graphite, diamond and graphene.

Graphite

The carbon atoms in graphite are arranged in sheets of flat hexagons covalently bonded with three bonds each (see Figure 1). The fourth outer electron of each carbon atom is delocalised. The sheets of hexagons are bonded together by weak induced dipole-dipole forces (see pages 111-112).

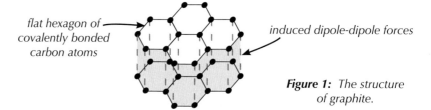

flat hexagon of covalently bonded carbon atoms

induced dipole-dipole forces

Figure 1: The structure of graphite.

Graphite's structure means it has certain properties:

- The weak forces between the layers in graphite are easily broken, so the sheets can slide over each other — graphite feels slippery and is used as a dry lubricant and in pencils.
- The 'delocalised' electrons in graphite are free to move along the sheets, so an electric current can flow.
- The layers are quite far apart compared to the length of the covalent bonds, so graphite has a low density and is used to make strong, lightweight sports equipment.
- Because of the strong covalent bonds in the hexagon sheets, graphite has a very high melting point (it sublimes at over 3900 K).
- Graphite is insoluble in any solvent. The covalent bonds in the sheets are too difficult to break.

Diamond

Diamond is also made up of carbon atoms. Each carbon atom is covalently bonded to four other carbon atoms (see Figure 2). The atoms arrange themselves in a tetrahedral shape — its crystal lattice structure.

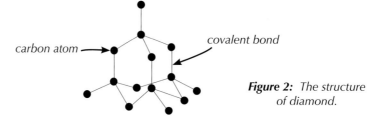

carbon atom

covalent bond

Figure 2: The structure of diamond.

Because it has lots of strong covalent bonds:

- Diamond has a very high melting point — it actually sublimes at over 3800 K.
- Diamond is extremely hard — it's used in diamond-tipped drills and saws.
- Vibrations travel easily through the stiff lattice, so it's a good thermal conductor.
- It can't conduct electricity — all the outer electrons are held in localised bonds.
- Like graphite, diamond won't dissolve in any solvent.

Figure 3: A cut and polished diamond. Oooh, sparkly.

Silicon

Silicon is in the same periodic group as carbon. Each silicon atom can also form four strong, covalent bonds. It makes a crystal lattice structure like diamond, and has similar properties.

Graphene

Graphene is just one layer of graphite — it's a sheet of carbon atoms joined together in hexagons. The sheet is one atom thick, making it a two-dimensional compound.

Each carbon atom has three covalent bonds...

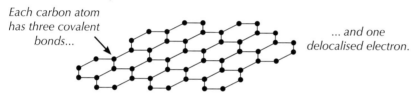

... and one delocalised electron.

Figure 4: The structure of graphene.

Graphene's structure gives it some pretty useful properties:

- Like in graphite, the delocalised electrons in graphene are free to move along the sheet. Without layers, they can move quickly above and below the sheet, making graphene the best known electrical conductor.
- The delocalised electrons also strengthen the covalent bonds between the carbon atoms. This makes graphene extremely strong.
- A single layer of graphene is transparent and incredibly light.

Due to its high strength, low mass, and good electrical conductivity, graphene has potential applications in high-speed electronics and aircraft technology. Its flexibility and transparency also make it a potentially useful material for touchscreens on smartphones and other electronic devices.

Tip: Properties that can be directly perceived, like the fact that graphite is slippery or diamond is hard are called <u>macroscopic</u> properties. Finding explanations for macroscopic properties is important in science.

Tip: Like diamond and graphite, graphene has high melting and boiling points and it's insoluble due to its strong covalent bonds.

Tip: When new substances, like graphene, are discovered, scientists can start to consider how the properties of the material could be applied and what its benefits could be.

Practice Questions — Fact Recall

Q1 a) Describe the structure of diamond.

  b) Explain why the structure of diamond means it can't conduct electricity.

Q2 Describe the structure of graphite.

Q3 a) Describe the structure of graphene.

  b) Explain why the structure of graphene makes it a good electrical conductor.

  c) Give an example of a potential application of graphene.

5. Metallic Bonding

You'll be familiar with metallic bonding from GCSE, but there's more to know...

Metallic bonding

Metal elements exist as giant metallic lattice structures. The outermost electrons of a metal atom are delocalised — the electrons are free to move about the metal. This leaves a positive metal cation, e.g. Na^+, Mg^{2+}, Al^{3+}. The metal cations are electrostatically attracted to the delocalised electrons — they form a lattice of closely packed cations in a sea of delocalised electrons — this is metallic bonding (see Figure 1).

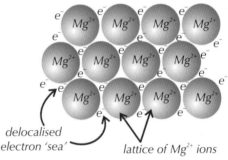

delocalised electron 'sea'   *lattice of Mg^{2+} ions*

Figure 1: *Metallic bonding in magnesium.*

Metallic bonding explains the properties of metals — for example, their melting and boiling points, their ability to be shaped, their conductivity and their solubility.

Melting and boiling points

The number of delocalised electrons per atom affects the melting and boiling points. The more there are, the stronger the bonding will be and the higher the melting and boiling points. Mg^{2+} has two delocalised electrons per atom, so it's got higher melting and boiling points than Na^+, which only has one. The size of the metal ion and the lattice structure also affect the melting and boiling points. A smaller ionic radius will hold the delocalised electrons closer to the nuclei.

Ability to be shaped

As there are no bonds holding specific ions together, the metal ions can slide over each other when the structure is pulled, so metals are malleable (can be shaped) and ductile (can be drawn into a wire, see Figure 2).

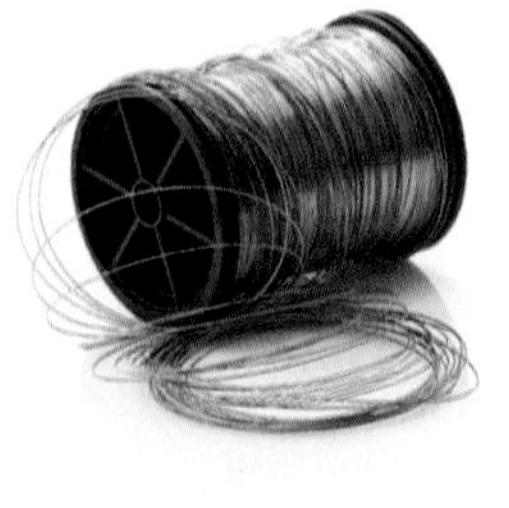

Conductivity

The delocalised electrons can pass kinetic energy to each other, making metals good thermal conductors. Metals are good electrical conductors because the delocalised electrons can carry a current.

Solubility

Metals are insoluble, except in liquid metals, because of the strength of the metallic bonds.

Figure 2: *Copper pulled into a wire.*

Practice Questions — Fact Recall

Q1 Describe the structure of magnesium.

Q2 What type of bonding can be found in magnesium?

Q3 Explain the following:

  a) Copper can be drawn into wires.

  b) Copper is a good thermal conductor.

6. Periodic Trends in Melting and Boiling Points

Melting and boiling points have periodicity, due to structure and bonding.

Melting and boiling points

If you look at how the melting and boiling points change across the periods, the trend isn't immediately obvious. The melting and boiling points of the Period 2 and 3 elements generally increase from the first to the fourth elements in the period, but then decrease from the fourth to the eighth elements (see Figures 1 and 2).

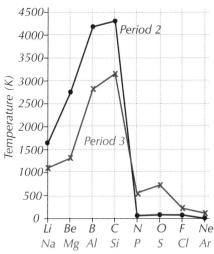

Figure 1: The trend in boiling points across Periods 2 and 3.

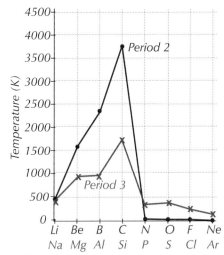

Figure 2: The trend in melting points across Periods 2 and 3.

Once you start looking at the bond strengths and structures of the elements in Periods 2 and 3, the reasons for the trends become clear. As you go across a period, the type of bonding between the atoms of an element and the type of structure changes. It changes from giant metallic to giant covalent and then to a simple molecular lattice.

Metals

For the metals (Li and Be, Na, Mg and Al), melting and boiling points increase across the period because the metal-metal bonds get stronger. The bonds get stronger because the metal ions have a greater charge, an increasing number of **delocalised electrons** and a decreasing ionic radius. This leads to a higher **charge density**, which attracts the ions together more strongly (see Figure 3).

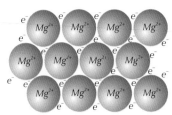

The magnesium ions have a larger radius and a charge of 2+ so there are two delocalised electrons for each ion...

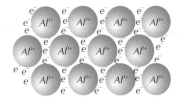

...whereas the aluminium ions have a smaller radius and a charge of 3+ so there are three delocalised electrons for each ion.

Figure 3: The structures of magnesium and aluminium.

Learning Objectives:

- Explain the variation in melting and boiling points across Periods 2 and 3 in terms of structure and bonding.
- Understand the trend in structure from giant metallic to giant covalent to simple molecular lattice.

Specification Reference 3.1.1

Tip: The charge density is the amount of charge in relation to the size of an ion. Smaller ions have greater charge densities than larger ions with the same charge.

Giant covalent structures

The elements with giant covalent lattice structures (B, C and Si) have strong covalent bonds linking all their atoms together. A lot of energy is needed to break these bonds. So, for example, carbon and silicon have the highest melting and boiling points in their periods.

Simple molecular structures

Next come the simple molecular substances (N_2, O_2 and F_2 in Period 2 and P_4, S_8 and Cl_2 in Period 3). The covalent bonds between the atoms in a molecule are very strong but the melting and boiling points depend upon the strength of the induced dipole-dipole forces between their molecules. These forces are weak and easily overcome so these elements have low melting and boiling points.

Tip: See pages 111-115 for lots more about intermolecular forces.

More atoms in a molecule mean stronger induced dipole-dipole forces. For example, in Period 3 sulfur is the biggest molecule (S_8), so it's got higher melting and boiling points than phosphorus or chlorine — see Figure 4.

Figure 5: Sulfur is a solid at room temperature.

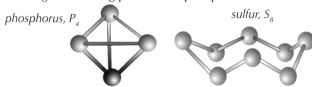

phosphorus, P_4   *sulfur, S_8*

Figure 4: The structures of phosphorus and sulfur.

The noble gases (neon and argon) have the lowest melting and boiling points because they exist as individual atoms (they're monatomic) resulting in very weak induced dipole-dipole forces.

Practice Questions — Application

Q1 a) Explain why the boiling point of lithium is higher than the boiling point of nitrogen.

   b) Explain why the boiling point of beryllium is higher than that of lithium.

Q2 a) Explain why magnesium has a higher melting point than sodium.

   b) Explain why sulfur has a higher melting point than phosphorus.

Q3 The melting point of silicon is 1414 °C and the melting point of phosphorus is 44 °C.

   a) Explain why the melting point of phosphorus is lower than the melting point of silicon.

   b) Name a Period 3 element with a lower melting point than phosphorus.

Q4 Would you expect calcium to have a higher or lower boiling point than potassium? Explain your answer.

Practice Questions — Fact Recall

Q1 Describe the trend in melting and boiling points that occurs across Period 2 of the periodic table.

Q2 Name two Period 2 elements that have giant covalent lattice structures.

Q3 Name the Period 3 element that has the lowest melting point.

7. Group 2 — The Alkaline Earth Metals

Learning Objectives:
- Know that the outer shell electron configuration of elements in Group 2 is s².
- Understand that the Group 2 elements lose their outer s² electrons in redox reactions to form 2+ ions.
- Know the relative reactivities of the Group 2 elements (from Mg to Ba) shown by their redox reactions with oxygen, water and dilute acids.
- Explain the trend in reactivity in terms of the first and second ionisation energies of Group 2 elements down the group.
- Know the effect of water on Group 2 oxides and the approximate pH of any resulting solutions, including the trend of increasing alkalinity.
- Know uses of some Group 2 compounds as bases, including equations. For example, the use of $Ca(OH)_2$ in agriculture to neutralise acid soils and the use of $Mg(OH)_2$ and $CaCO_3$ as 'antacids' for treating indigestion.

Specification Reference 3.1.2

The alkaline earth metals are in the s-block of the periodic table. You have to know some trends in their properties as you go down Group 2 and some of the reactions of Group 2 elements and their compounds.

Trend in reactivity down Group 2

When Group 2 elements react they lose electrons, forming positive ions (cations). The easier it is to lose electrons (i.e. the lower the first and second ionisation energies), the more reactive the element. So because ionisation energy decreases down the group, reactivity increases down the group.

Reactions of Group 2 elements

Group 2 elements all have two electrons in their outer shell (s²). They can lose their two outer electrons to form 2+ ions. Their ions then have every atom's dream electronic structure — that of a **noble gas** (see Figure 1).

Element	Electronic structure	Ion	Electronic structure
Be	$1s^2\,2s^2$	Be^{2+}	$1s^2$
Mg	$1s^2\,2s^2\,2p^6\,3s^2$	Mg^{2+}	$1s^2\,2s^2\,2p^6$
Ca	$1s^2\,2s^2\,2p^6\,3s^2\,3p^6\,4s^2$	Ca^{2+}	$1s^2\,2s^2\,2p^6\,3s^2\,3p^6$

Figure 1: *Electronic structures of Group 2 atoms and ions.*

So, when Group 2 elements react, they are oxidised from a state of 0 to +2.

$$M \rightarrow M^{2+} + 2e^-$$

Oxidation state: $\quad 0 \rightarrow +2$

In this equation, M is used to represent any Group 2 metal.

Examples

$$Mg \rightarrow Mg^{2+} + 2e^- \quad Ca \rightarrow Ca^{2+} + 2e^- \quad Be \rightarrow Be^{2+} + 2e^-$$

Oxidation number: $\quad 0 \quad\;\; +2 \qquad\quad 0 \quad\;\; +2 \qquad\quad 0 \quad\;\; +2$

Reactions with water

The Group 2 metals react with water to give a metal hydroxide and hydrogen.

$$M_{(s)} + 2H_2O_{(l)} \rightarrow M(OH)_{2\,(aq)} + H_{2\,(g)}$$

Oxidation state: $\quad 0 \qquad\qquad\qquad \rightarrow +2$

The metal hydroxide that forms dissolves in water to produce hydroxide ions (OH^-). These make the solutions strongly alkaline, with a pH of about 12-13.

Example

Calcium reacts with water to form calcium hydroxide and hydrogen.

$$Ca_{(s)} + 2H_2O_{(l)} \rightarrow Ca^{2+}_{(aq)} + 2OH^-_{(aq)} + H_{2(g)}$$

Oxidation state: $\quad 0 \qquad\qquad\qquad \rightarrow +2$

The hydrogen gas forms bubbles in the solution.

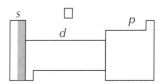

Figure 2: *The s-, p- and d-blocks of the periodic table (see page 122 for more). Group 2 is highlighted in grey.*

The elements react more readily down the group because the ionisation energies decrease (see Figure 4). This is due to the increasing size of the atomic radii and the increasing shielding effect (see page 124).

Figure 3: *Magnesium (left) and calcium (right) reacting with water. Calcium is more reactive so reacts quicker.*

Figure 5: *Calcium burns in air, producing an orange flame.*

Tip: It's because their oxides form alkaline solutions that the Group 2 elements are also known as the alkaline earth metals.

Tip: An <u>alkali</u> is a base that's <u>soluble</u> in water. The oxides and hydroxides of Group 2 metals are bases. Most of them are also alkalis.

Group 2 element	1st ionisation energy / kJ mol⁻¹	Rate of reactivity with water
Be	900	doesn't react
Mg	738	VERY slow
Ca	590	quite quick
Sr	550	quick
Ba	503	rapid

Figure 4: *Comparison of first ionisation energies and reactivity with water for Group 2 elements.*

Reactions with oxygen

When Group 2 metals burn in oxygen, you get solid white oxides. Here's the general equation for the reaction of a Group 2 metal (M) with oxygen.

$$2M_{(s)} + O_{2(g)} \rightarrow 2MO_{(s)}$$

Examples

Calcium burns in air to produce calcium oxide (CaO). The equation for this reaction is:

$$2Ca_{(s)} + O_{2\,(g)} \rightarrow 2CaO_{(s)}$$

Beryllium burns in air to produce beryllium oxide (BeO).
Here's the equation:

$$2Be_{(s)} + O_{2\,(g)} \rightarrow 2BeO_{(s)}$$

As with the other reactions of Group 2 elements, during this reaction the oxidation state of the Group 2 element increases from 0 to +2.

The oxides of the Group 2 metals react readily with water to form metal hydroxides, which dissolve. The hydroxide ions, OH⁻, make these solutions strongly alkaline (e.g. pH 12 - 13).

Example

Calcium oxide reacts with water to form calcium hydroxide. The calcium hydroxide then dissolves in the water, releasing OH⁻ ions and Ca²⁺ ions. So,

$$CaO_{(s)} + H_2O_{(l)} \rightarrow Ca^{2+}_{(aq)} + 2OH^-_{(aq)}$$

The OH⁻ ions make the solution strongly alkaline.

Magnesium oxide is an exception — it only reacts slowly and the hydroxide isn't very soluble. The oxides form more strongly alkaline solutions as you go down the group, because the hydroxides get more soluble.

Reactions with dilute acids

When Group 2 metals react with dilute hydrochloric acid, you get a metal chloride and hydrogen. Here's the general equation for the reaction of a Group 2 metal (M) with dilute hydrochloric acid.

$$M_{(s)} + 2HCl_{(aq)} \rightarrow MCl_{2\,(aq)} + H_{2\,(g)}$$

Oxidation state: 0   → +2

Examples

Calcium reacts with dilute hydrochloric acid to produce calcium chloride ($CaCl_2$). The equation for this reaction is:

$$Ca_{(s)} + 2HCl_{(aq)} \rightarrow CaCl_{2(aq)} + H_{2(g)}$$

Strontium reacts with dilute hydrochloric acid to produce strontium chloride ($SrCl_2$). The equation for this reaction is:

$$Sr_{(s)} + 2HCl_{(aq)} \rightarrow SrCl_{2(aq)} + H_{2(g)}$$

Tip: The reactions of Group 2 metals with dilute acid get more vigorous as you go down the group — this is the same trend as with water.

Different acids will produce different salts. For example, if you use dilute sulfuric acid, you'll get a metal sulfate.

$$M_{(s)} + H_2SO_{4(aq)} \rightarrow MSO_{4(aq)} + H_{2(g)}$$

Example

Magnesium reacts with dilute sulfuric acid to produce magnesium sulfate ($MgSO_4$). The equation for this reaction is:

$$Mg_{(s)} + H_2SO_{4(aq)} \rightarrow MgSO_{4(aq)} + H_{2(g)}$$

Uses of Group 2 compounds

Group 2 elements are known as the **alkaline earth metals**, and many of their common compounds are used for neutralising acids. Here are a couple of common examples:

- Calcium hydroxide (slaked lime, $Ca(OH)_2$) is used in agriculture to neutralise acid soils. It has to be used in moderation though, otherwise the soils will become too alkaline to support crop growth.
- Magnesium hydroxide ($Mg(OH)_2$) and calcium carbonate ($CaCO_3$) are used in some indigestion tablets as **antacids** — these neutralise excess stomach acid.

In both cases, the ionic equation for the neutralisation is:

$$H^+_{(aq)} + OH^-_{(aq)} \rightarrow H_2O_{(l)}$$

Figure 6: *Tractors are used to spread slaked lime to neutralise acid soil.*

Practice Questions — Application

Q1 When calcium reacts with water, calcium hydroxide is produced.

a) Write an equation for this reaction.

b) How does the oxidation state of calcium change during this reaction?

c) State what you would see when this reaction takes place.

d) How would the rate of the reaction be different if strontium was used instead of calcium?

Q2 Strontium burns in air to form strontium oxide.

a) Write an equation for this reaction.

b) Describe the appearance of strontium oxide.

c) Write an equation to show what would happen if water was added to strontium oxide.

d) Give an approximate pH of the solution formed when water and strontium oxide are mixed.

Tip: When writing equations for reactions don't forget to make sure they're balanced.

Q3 Calcium reacts with hydrochloric acid to form calcium chloride.

a) Write an equation for this reaction.

b) How does the oxidation state of calcium change during this reaction?

c) State what you would see when this reaction takes place.

d) Predict how the rate of reaction would be different if barium was used instead of calcium.

Practice Questions — Fact Recall

Q1 Explain why reactivity increases down Group 2.

Q2 a) What charge do Group 2 ions usually have?

b) Explain why Group 2 ions normally have this charge.

Q3 What change in oxidation state do Group 2 metals usually undergo when they react?

Q4 What pH would you expect a Group 2 metal hydroxide solution to have?

Q5 Which, out of barium oxide and strontium oxide, would you expect to be more alkaline?

Q6 Describe the trend in the reactivity of the Group 2 elements with dilute acids as you go down the group.

Q7 Give two uses of Group 2 hydroxides.

8. Group 7 — The Halogens

The halogens are highly-reactive non-metals found in Group 7 of the periodic table. You need to know about their properties, trends and reactions.

Properties of halogens

The table below gives some of the main properties of the first four halogens, at room temperature. They exist as diatomic molecules (molecules made up of two atoms).

halogen	formula	colour	physical state	electronic structure
fluorine	F_2	pale yellow	gas	$1s^2\ 2s^2\ 2p^5$
chlorine	Cl_2	green	gas	$1s^2\ 2s^2\ 2p^6\ 3s^2\ 3p^5$
bromine	Br_2	red-brown	liquid	$1s^2\ 2s^2\ 2p^6\ 3s^2\ 3p^6\ 3d^{10}\ 4s^2\ 4p^5$
iodine	I_2	grey	solid	$1s^2\ 2s^2\ 2p^6\ 3s^2\ 3p^6\ 3d^{10}\ 4s^2\ 4p^6\ 4d^{10}\ 5s^2\ 5p^5$

Figure 1: *Some properties of the first four halogens.*

Trend in boiling points

The boiling and melting points of the halogens increase down the group. This is due to the increasing strength of the **induced dipole-dipole** (London) **forces** as the number of electrons increases when the size and relative mass of the atoms increases. This trend is shown in the changes of physical state from fluorine to iodine (see Figure 2). A substance is said to be **volatile** if it has a low boiling point. So you could also say that volatility decreases down the group.

Figure 2: *At room temperature and pressure, chlorine (left) is a gas, bromine (centre) is a liquid and iodine (right) is a solid.*

Trend in reactivity

Halogen atoms react by gaining an electron in their outer shell. This means they're reduced. When halogens are reduced, **halide** ions are formed. The general equation for the reduction of a halogen (X) to a halide ion (X⁻) is shown below:

$$X + e^- \rightarrow X^-$$

$$\text{oxidation number:} \qquad 0 \qquad\qquad -1$$

As the halogens are reduced, they oxidise another substance (it's a redox reaction — see pages 87-89) — so they're **oxidising agents**.

As you go down the group, the atomic radius increases so the outer electrons are further from the nucleus. The outer electrons are also shielded more from the attraction of the positive nucleus, because there are more inner electrons. This makes it harder for larger atoms to attract the electron needed to form an ion (despite the increased charge on the nucleus), so larger atoms are less reactive. Another way of saying that the halogens get less reactive down the group is to say that they become less oxidising.

Learning Objectives:

- Know that halogens exist as diatomic molecules.

- Explain the trend in the boiling points of Cl_2, Br_2 and I_2 in terms of induced dipole-dipole interactions.

- Know the outer shell configuration of Group 7 elements and that they'll gain one electron in many redox reactions to form 1– ions.

- Understand the trend in reactivity of the halogens Cl_2, Br_2 and I_2, illustrated by reactions with other halide ions.

- Explain the trend in reactivity in terms of attraction, atomic radius and electron shielding.

- Know the precipitation reactions of the aqueous anions Cl^-, Br^- and I^- with aqueous silver ions, followed by aqueous ammonia, and their use as a test for different halide ions.

- Be able to use apparatus to carry out qualitative tests for ions, and make and record your observations (PAG 4).

Specification Reference 3.1.3

Tip: <u>Halogen</u> should be used when describing the atom (X) or molecule (X_2), but <u>halide</u> is used to describe the negative ion (X⁻).

Displacement reactions

The halogens' relative oxidising strengths can be seen in their **displacement reactions** with halide ions. More reactive halogens will oxidise and displace the halide ions of less reactive halogens. Reactivity decreases down the group so a halogen will displace a halide from solution if the halide is below it in the periodic table. You need to know which halogens displace what and the **ionic equations** for these displacement reactions.

Tip: The displacement reactions of the halogens can be used to identify them in solution. See the next page for more.

Tip: These are ionic equation — they only show the reacting particles.

Halogen	Displacement reactions	Ionic equations
Cl	chlorine (Cl_2) will displace bromide (Br^-) and iodide (I^-)	$Cl_{2(aq)} + 2Br^-_{(aq)} \rightarrow 2Cl^-_{(aq)} + Br_{2(aq)}$ $Cl_{2(aq)} + 2I^-_{(aq)} \rightarrow 2Cl^-_{(aq)} + I_{2(aq)}$
Br	bromine (Br_2) will displace iodide (I^-)	$Br_{2(aq)} + 2I^-_{(aq)} \rightarrow 2Br^-_{(aq)} + I_{2(aq)}$
I	no reaction with F^-, Cl^-, Br^-	

Figure 3: Some displacement reactions of the halogens.

When these displacement reactions happen, there are colour changes — you can see what happens by following them.

Examples

Bromine water and potassium iodide

If you mix bromine water, $Br_{2\,(aq)}$, with potassium iodide solution, the bromine displaces the iodide ions (it oxidises them), giving iodine (I_2) and potassium bromide solution, $KBr_{(aq)}$. The equation for this reaction is:

$$Br_{2(aq)} + 2I^-_{(aq)} \rightarrow 2Br^-_{(aq)} + I_{2(aq)}$$

Oxidation number of Br: 0 $\rightarrow$ -1

Oxidation number of I: -1 $\rightarrow$ 0

Iodine water ($I_{2\,(aq)}$) is brown and bromine water ($Br_{2\,(aq)}$) is orange. So when bromine displaces the iodide ions in potassium iodide, the solution changes colour from orange to brown.

Chlorine water and potassium bromide

If you mix chlorine water, $Cl_{2\,(aq)}$, with potassium bromide, $KBr_{(aq)}$, the solution changes from colourless to orange. The chlorine displaces the bromide ions, forming bromine water ($Br_{2(aq)}$), which is orange.

$$Cl_{2(aq)} + 2Br^-_{(aq)} \rightarrow 2Cl^-_{(aq)} + Br_{2(aq)}$$

Oxidation number of Cl: 0 $\rightarrow$ -1

Oxidation number of Br: -1 $\rightarrow$ 0

Figure 4: Iodine mixed with hexane (an organic solvent). The top layer shows the violet colour of the solution formed when iodine dissolves in hexane. The bottom layer is an aqueous solution of I_2.

Brown and orange can sometimes look a bit similar. You can make the changes easier to see by shaking the reaction mixture with an organic solvent like hexane. The halogen that's present will dissolve readily in the organic solvent, which settles out as a distinct layer (called the solvent layer) above the aqueous solution. The different halogens are very different colours when they are dissolved in organic solvent so you can easily see which halogen has been produced.

- A violet/pink colour shows the presence of iodine (see Figure 4).
- An orange/red colour shows bromine.
- A very pale yellow/green shows chlorine.

Tip: Make sure you learn all of these colour changes. You'll need them for the exam.

The table on the next page summarises the colour changes you'll see when different displacement reactions take place.

	Potassium chloride solution ($KCl_{(aq)}$)	Potassium bromide solution ($KBr_{(aq)}$)	Potassium iodide solution ($KI_{(aq)}$)
Chlorine water ($Cl_{2(aq)}$) – colourless		orange/red solution (Br_2) formed with organic solvent	violet/pink solution (I_2) formed with organic solvent
Bromine water ($Br_{2(aq)}$) – orange	No reaction		violet/pink solution (I_2) formed with organic solvent
Iodine solution ($I_{2(aq)}$) – brown	No reaction	No reaction	

Figure 5: *The results of some reactions between halogens and halide compounds.*

Figure 6: *The initial (left) and final (right) appearance of a test tube when an organic solvent is added to bromine water. Notice the red/orange colour of the solvent layer which settles at the top of the test tube.*

Identifying halogens in solution

The halogen displacement reactions can be used to help identify which halogen or halide is present in a solution. All you have to do is mix your unknown solution with some known halogen solutions and watch to see what colour changes take place.

┌─ Examples ─────────────────────────────

Chlorine water is added to a solution of an unknown potassium halide. When hexane is added, an organic solvent layer forms which is violet in colour. Identify the halide ions present in the unknown solution.

Because the organic solvent layer turns violet, you know that I_2 must have been formed. So, I⁻ ions must have been present in the unknown solution. When the chlorine water is added the following reaction occurs:

$$Cl_{2(aq)} + 2I^-_{(aq)} \rightarrow 2Cl^-_{(aq)} + I_{2(aq)}$$

An unknown halogen solution is added to solutions of KBr and KCl. A colour change occurs with KBr but not with KCl. Identify the halogen present in the unknown solution.

Because there is a colour change when the halogen solution is added to KBr, you know that a displacement reaction has occurred and Br_2 has been formed. So the halogen can't be I_2 or Br_2 because neither of these can displace Br⁻ ions. Because no colour change happens when the unknown halogen solution is added to KCl you know the halogen can't be F_2 (because this would displace the Cl⁻ ions). So the unknown halogen must be Cl_2.

Testing for halides

The halogens are pretty distinctive to look at. Unfortunately, halide ions aren't so easily identifiable. Luckily, you can test for halides using the silver nitrate test — it's dead easy.

PRACTICAL ACTIVITY GROUP **4**

- If you're testing solid substances for halide ions, you'll first need to dissolve each of them separately in distilled water to make solutions.
- Once you've got solutions of the substances that you're testing, use a pipette to add about 3 cm³ of each solution to separate test tubes.
- Label each test tube so that you don't get confused about which solution is which.

Exam Tip
You could be asked to identify any halogen or halide solution in your exam so make sure you learn which reactions happen and what the colour changes are.

Tip: When identifying halogen or halide solutions, looking at which reactions don't happen is as important as looking at the reactions that do happen.

Tip: You won't ever be asked to identify fluorine in school or college — it's too hazardous. But it's still worth knowing how to identify it.

Tip: Remember, you should carry out a risk assessment before doing any practicals, and take any necessary precautions.

Tip: You can't use hydrochloric acid instead of nitric acid because the silver nitrate would just react with the chloride ions from the HCl — and that would mess up your results completely.

Tip: Be careful when handling $AgNO_3$ — it can stain skin and clothing. Also take great care with concentrated NH_3 as it's corrosive.

Figure 8: *Results of silver nitrate tests for solutions containing (L-R) fluoride, chloride, bromide and iodide ions.*

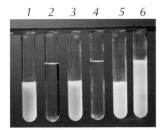

Figure 9: *The chloride, bromide and iodide test tubes from Figure 8 (1, 3 and 5), and the same tubes with concentrated $NH_{3(aq)}$ added (2, 4 and 6).*

- Prepare a table to record your results. You'll need to include each sample that you're testing, and leave space to record whether a precipitate is formed with silver nitrate.

- Using a pipette, add a few drops of dilute nitric acid (HNO_3) to each test tube. This gets rid of any unwanted ions that might otherwise mess up the test results.

- Again using a pipette, add a few drops of aqueous silver nitrate ($AgNO_{3(aq)}$) to each test tube. If there are chloride, iodide or bromide ions present a precipitate of the silver halide will be formed.

$$Ag^+_{(aq)} + X^-_{(aq)} \rightarrow AgX_{(s)} \quad \text{...where X is Cl, Br or I}$$

The colour of the precipitate identifies the halide (see Figures 7 and 8). You should record your observations in your results table.

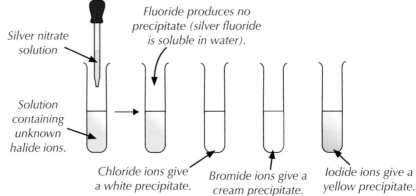

Silver nitrate solution

Fluoride produces no precipitate (silver fluoride is soluble in water).

Solution containing unknown halide ions.

Chloride ions give a white precipitate.

Bromide ions give a cream precipitate.

Iodide ions give a yellow precipitate.

Figure 7: *The silver nitrate test for identifying an unknown halide ion in solution.*

It isn't always easy to tell the difference between silver halide precipitates — some of them look very similar (see Figure 8). So there's a further test that you can carry out using dilute or concentrated ammonia that makes it much easier to tell the halides apart. Before you start, you'll have to add a column to your results table to record your observations for what happens to each of the halide precipitates when dilute or concentrated ammonia solution is added.

- Using a pipette, add dilute ammonia (NH_3) to each of the silver halide precipitate suspensions. You should add about the same amount of ammonia as the amount of silver halide precipitate suspension you have.

- Stir the mixtures using a glass rod and record whether any precipitates dissolve in the ammonia.

- If any precipitates haven't dissolved, add concentrated ammonia to the solution. Add roughly the same volume of concentrated ammonia as you did dilute ammonia.

- Again, stir the mixtures using a glass rod, and record whether the precipitates dissolve.

- You should now be able to identify which halides were in your samples. Each silver halide has a different solubility in ammonia — the larger the ion is, the more difficult it is to dissolve (see Figures 9 and 10).

Halide	Result
Chloride Cl⁻	precipitate dissolves in dilute $NH_{3(aq)}$
Bromide Br⁻	precipitate doesn't dissolve in dilute $NH_{3(aq)}$ but will dissolve in conc. $NH_{3(aq)}$
Iodide I⁻	precipitate is insoluble in dilute and conc. $NH_{3(aq)}$

Figure 10: *Solubility of silver halide precipitates in ammonia.*

Practice Questions — Application

Q1 Explain why the boiling point of bromine is lower than that of iodine.

Q2 Chlorine water is mixed with potassium iodide.

    a) Write out the ionic equation for the reaction, along with the change in oxidation numbers of both halogens.

    b) Hexane is added to the solution. What do you expect to see?

Q3 Fluorine is the most reactive of the halogens. Explain why the other halogens are less reactive than fluorine.

Q4 When bromine is added to an unknown solution of halide ions and an organic solvent is added, the solvent layer turns violet.

    a) Identify the halide ions present in the solution.

    b) Write an equation for the displacement reaction that occurs.

Q5 An experiment is carried out to identify the halide ions in three different solutions. The results are shown in the table below.

Sample	Colour of precipitate following addition of silver nitrate	Effect of adding concentrated NH_3 solution to the precipitate
A	yellow	no change
B	no precipitate	no change
C	cream	precipitate dissolves

Identify the halide ion in each sample.

Practice Questions — Fact Recall

Q1 What is a diatomic molecule?

Q2 Describe and explain the trend in the boiling points of the halogens.

Q3 Explain why the halogens get less reactive as you go down the group.

Q4 Which halide ions are displaced by reaction with chlorine water?

Q5 What colour is the organic layer when an organic solvent is added to:

    a) chlorine water   b) bromine water   c) iodine water

Q6 Briefly describe a test for distinguishing between different halide solutions.

9. Disproportionation and Water Treatment

Disproportionation doesn't have a snappy name and it's got far more letters than you expect, but it is quite handy — and you have to know all about it for your exam.

Disproportionation reactions

Disproportionation is when a single element is simultaneously oxidised and reduced. The halogens undergo disproportionation when they react with cold dilute alkali solutions (e.g. NaOH or KOH). The general equation for the reaction of a halogen (X) with sodium hydroxide (NaOH) is shown below:

Full equation:	X_2 + 2NaOH	$\rightarrow$ NaXO + NaX + H_2O
Ionic equation:	X_2 + 2OH$^-$	$\rightarrow$ XO$^-$ + X$^-$ + H_2O
Oxidation number of X:	0	+1 −1

All of the halogens, except fluorine, can exist in oxidation states other than the 0 and −1 oxidation states.

−1	0	+1
Cl$^-$	Cl$_2$	ClO$^-$
chloride	chlorine	chlorate(I)

Figure 1: *Some of the oxidation states of chlorine.*

--- Example ---

Bromine reacts with NaOH to give sodium bromate(I), sodium bromide and water:

$$Br_{2(aq)} + 2NaOH_{(aq)} \rightarrow NaBrO_{(aq)} + NaBr_{(aq)} + H_2O_{(l)}$$

As Br_2, bromine has an oxidation state of 0. In NaBrO the oxidation state of bromine is +1, so when bromine forms NaBrO it is oxidised. In NaBr the oxidation state of bromine is −1, so when bromine forms NaBr it is reduced. So in the reaction above, the bromine is simultaneously oxidised and reduced and it is a disproportionation reaction.

Making bleach

If you mix chlorine gas with cold, dilute aqueous sodium hydroxide, you get sodium chlorate(I) solution, NaClO$_{(aq)}$, which just happens to be common household bleach. In this reaction some of the chlorine is oxidised and some of it is reduced so it's a disproportionation reaction.

$$2NaOH_{(aq)} + Cl_{2(g)} \rightarrow NaClO_{(aq)} + NaCl_{(aq)} + H_2O_{(l)}$$

Chlorine is bonded to chlorine so its oxidation state is 0.

ClO$^-$ is the chlorate(I) ion. Chlorine's oxidation state is +1 in this ion.

Here, chlorine's oxidation state is −1.

The sodium chlorate(I) solution (bleach) has loads of uses — it's used in water treatment, to bleach paper and textiles... and it's good for cleaning toilets, too. Handy...

Chlorine and water

When you mix chlorine with water, it undergoes disproportionation. You end up with a mixture of hydrochloric acid and chloric(I) acid (also called hypochlorous acid).

$$Cl_{2(g)} + H_2O_{(l)} \rightleftharpoons HCl_{(aq)} + HClO_{(aq)}$$

Chlorine's oxidation state is 0.   *In hydrochloric acid, chlorine's oxidation state is –1.*   *In chloric(I) acid, chlorine's oxidation state is +1.*

Aqueous chloric(I) acid ionises to make chlorate(I) ions (also called hypochlorite ions):

$$HClO_{(aq)} + H_2O_{(l)} \rightleftharpoons ClO^-_{(aq)} + H_3O^+_{(aq)}$$

Tip: Bromine and iodine can both react with water in similar equilibrium reactions to produce HX and HXO (where X is a halogen).

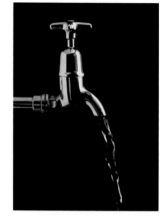

Figure 2: Chlorine is used to treat tap water in the UK.

Water treatment

Chlorate(I) ions kill bacteria. So, adding chlorine (or a compound containing chlorate(I) ions) to water can make it safe to drink or swim in. In the UK our drinking water is treated to make it safe.

Chlorine is an important part of water treatment. It kills disease-causing microorganisms (and some chlorine persists in the water and prevents reinfection further down the supply). It also prevents the growth of algae, eliminating bad tastes and smells, and removes discolouration caused by organic compounds.

(HOW SCIENCE WORKS)

However, there are risks from using chlorine to treat water. Chlorine gas is toxic. It's very harmful if it's breathed in — it irritates the respiratory system. Liquid chlorine on the skin or eyes causes severe chemical burns. Accidents involving chlorine could be really serious, or fatal. Water contains a variety of organic compounds, e.g. from the decomposition of plants. Chlorine reacts with these compounds to form chlorinated hydrocarbons, e.g. chloromethane (CH_3Cl), and many of these chlorinated hydrocarbons are carcinogenic (cancer-causing). However, this increased cancer risk is small compared to the risks from untreated water — a cholera epidemic, say, could kill thousands of people. There are ethical considerations too. We don't get a choice about having our water chlorinated — some people object to this as forced 'mass medication'.

Tip: See page 4 for more about weighing up the benefits and risks of scientific techniques (like using chlorine to treat drinking water).

Figure 3: The distinctive 'swimming pool smell' is due to the chlorine in the water.

Alternatives to chlorine

There are other methods of purifying drinking water. And just like chlorine, they have their advantages and disadvantages.

- Ozone (O_3) is a strong oxidising agent, which makes it great at killing microorganisms. However, it's expensive to produce and its short half-life in water means that treatment isn't permanent.

- Ultraviolet light kills microorganisms by damaging their DNA, but it is ineffective in cloudy water and, like O_3, it won't stop the water being contaminated further down the line.

Practice Questions — Application

Q1 When iodine is mixed with dilute potassium hydroxide solution (KOH) a disproportionation reaction occurs.

    a) Write an equation to show the reaction of iodine with KOH.

    b) Using oxidation states, explain why this reaction is a disproportionation reaction.

Q2 The equation below shows the decomposition of hydrogen peroxide (H_2O_2) to water and oxygen:

$$2H_2O_2 \rightarrow 2H_2O + O_2$$

    Is this a disproportionation reaction? Explain your answer.

Q3 The equation below shows the reaction of chlorine gas with water:

$$Cl_{2(g)} + H_2O_{(l)} \rightleftharpoons HCl_{(aq)} + HClO_{(aq)}$$

    a) Write an equation to show how chlorate(I) ions can be produced from one of the products of this reaction.

    b) Explain why chlorate(I) ions are added to water.

Tip: The oxidation state of oxygen in H_2O_2 is –1, the oxidation state of oxygen in H_2O is –2 and the oxidation state of oxygen in O_2 is 0.

Practice Questions — Fact Recall

Q1 What is disproportionation?

Q2 a) Name the three products of the reaction between sodium hydroxide and chlorine.

    b) Give the balanced equation for this reaction.

Q3 Describe the reactions that occur when chlorine is mixed with water.

Q4 a) Explain why chlorine is used to treat water.

    b) Describe the disadvantages of using chlorine to treat water.

Q5 Ozone is sometimes used in water treatment.

    a) Why is ozone good for water treatment?

    b) What are the drawbacks of using ozone?

    c) Name another alternative to chlorine in water treatment.

10. Tests for Ions

If you're given something and asked to find out what's in it, there are loads of different tests that you can do — here are just a few...

False positives

When you're carrying out tests to identify an unknown substance you need to be wary of creating false positive results. A false positive is a result that suggests that a particular ion is present when it actually isn't. This can happen if there are ions present that will interfere with the test you are carrying out. To prevent false positive you can sometimes add a substance to your sample to remove problematic ions. You also need to be careful about what substances you add during the test — it's important not to add any ions that will lead to false positives. To help prevent false positives, you should do the three tests below in the following order:

> Test for carbonates ⟶ Test for sulfates ⟶ Test for halides

Test for carbonates

If you have an unknown solution and you want to test it for carbonates (CO_3^{2-}), add a dilute strong acid (e.g. dilute nitric acid or dilute hydrochloric acid). If carbonates are present then carbon dioxide will be released. The ionic equation for the reaction of a carbonate and an acid is:

$$CO_3^{2-}{}_{(s)} + 2H^+{}_{(aq)} \rightarrow CO_2{}_{(g)} + H_2O_{(l)}$$
carbonate + acid → carbon dioxide + water

--- Example ---

Calcium carbonate reacts with hydrochloric acid to produce carbon dioxide, water and calcium chloride. The equation for this reaction is:

$$CaCO_3{}_{(s)} + 2HCl_{(aq)} \rightarrow CO_2{}_{(g)} + H_2O_{(l)} + CaCl_2{}_{(aq)}$$

You can test to see if the gas produced is carbon dioxide using limewater. Figure 1 shows the apparatus needed for this test.

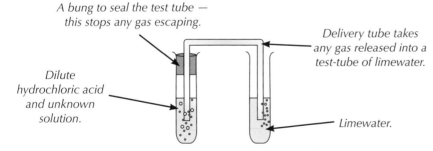

A bung to seal the test tube — this stops any gas escaping.

Delivery tube takes any gas released into a test-tube of limewater.

Dilute hydrochloric acid and unknown solution.

Limewater.

Figure 1: *Apparatus for carrying out a test for carbonate ions.*

Any gas created by the reaction is delivered into limewater — if it's CO_2, then it'll react and turn the limewater cloudy (see Figure 2).

Learning Objectives:

- Understand how to use qualitative analysis to identify the ions in an unknown compound on a test-tube scale.

- Be able to use apparatus to carry out qualitative tests for ions, and make and record your observations (PAG 4).

- Be able to identify CO_3^{2-} ions by reaction with $H^+{}_{(aq)}$, forming $CO_2{}_{(g)}$.

- Be able to identify SO_4^{2-} ions by precipitation with $Ba^{2+}{}_{(aq)}$.

- Be able to identify Cl^-, Br^- and I^- ions.

- Be able to identify NH_4^+ ions by reaction with warm $NaOH_{(aq)}$ forming NH_3.

Specification Reference 2.1.4, 3.1.3, 3.1.4

Tip: Think about any safety precautions you might need to consider before doing these tests.

Tip: Carrying out experiments and investigations correctly is an important part of scientific enquiry.

HOW SCIENCE WORKS

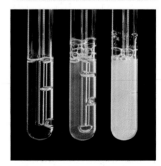

Figure 2: *Limewater turns cloudy when carbon dioxide is added to it.*

Tip: You can carry out the test for carbonates on solids as well as solutions — just add a small amount of your solid to a test-tube containing the acid.

Tip: You could also test for sulfates by using barium chloride solution, $BaCl_{2(aq)}$, instead of barium nitrate solution.

Tip: You don't need to remember this equation, but you need to understand why you have to avoid this reaction when testing for sulfates.

Figure 3: Barium sulfate is a white precipitate.

Tip: You test for halides after you test for sulfates because silver sulfate (Ag_2SO_4) is insoluble. If you tested for halides before testing to see if the anions were sulfate, then any precipitate you see might be a false positive — it could be silver sulfate rather than a silver halide.

Tip: Silver fluoride is soluble, so it won't give any precipitate.

You can carry out this test on a test-tube scale, so you'll only need to use small volumes of the substances. Transfer the liquids into the test tubes using teat pipettes. Make sure you place the bung connected to the transfer tube on to the test tube quickly after adding the acid to the solution, so that you don't lose too much of any gas produced.

Test for sulfates

If you carried out the test for carbonates and didn't get a positive result, i.e. no CO_2 was produced, then you can move on to test for sulfates ions. Most sulfates are soluble in water, but barium sulfate is insoluble. So, to test for a sulfate ion (SO_4^{2-}), add a few drops of barium nitrate solution, $Ba(NO_3)_{2(aq)}$, to a solution of the unknown substance. If you get a white precipitate it'll be barium sulfate, which tells you your mystery substance is a sulfate (see Figure 3). However, you need to be careful you don't end up with a false positive due to carbonate or sulfite ions.

Example

Sodium sulfite reacts with $Ba(NO_3)_2$ solution to give barium sulfite and sodium nitrate:

$$Na_2SO_{3(s)} + Ba(NO_3)_{2(aq)} \rightarrow BaSO_{3(s)} + 2NaNO_{3(aq)}$$

Barium sulfite is a white precipitate, which will confuse the results of a test for sulfates.

In the test for carbonates, you add a dilute strong acid to your substance. The acid will react with any carbonates or sulfites present, which makes sure that they won't interfere with the test for sulfates and cause a false positive. So if you haven't done the test for carbonates on your sample already, you'll need to add dilute acid before you add any barium nitrate, in order to remove any carbonate or sulfite ions that may be in the solution.

Now that you've got rid of any carbonates or sulfites, if a white precipitate is formed from the reaction with barium nitrate solution, it can only mean that sulfate ions are present. The ionic equation for this reaction is:

$$SO_4^{2-}{}_{(aq)} + Ba^{2+}{}_{(aq)} \rightarrow BaSO_{4(s)}$$
$$\text{sulfate} + \text{barium} \rightarrow \text{barium sulfate}$$
$$\text{anion} \qquad \text{cation}$$

Example

Sodium sulfate reacts with $Ba(NO_3)_2$ solution to give barium sulfate and sodium nitrate:

$$Na_2SO_{4(s)} + Ba(NO_3)_{2(aq)} \rightarrow BaSO_{4(s)} + 2NaNO_{3(aq)}$$

If no precipitate is formed, you don't have any sulfate ions present and you can then move on to the last test.

Test for halides

To test for halide ions just add nitric acid, then silver nitrate solution. If chloride, bromide or iodide is present, a precipitate will form. The colour of the precipitate depends on the halide present — silver chloride (AgCl) is a white precipitate, silver bromide (AgBr) is a cream precipitate and silver iodide (AgI) is a yellow precipitate.

It might not be easy to distinguish between the different colours of precipitate, so you can test the solubility of them in ammonia to help you tell them apart — look back at pages 141-142 for more details about this test.

Test for ammonium ions

Ammonia gas (NH_3) is alkaline, so you can check for it using a damp piece of red litmus paper. If there's ammonia present, the paper will turn blue (see Figure 4). You'll also be able to smell ammonia — it has a distinctive, pungent smell.

You can use this to test whether a substance contains ammonium ions (NH_4^+). Add a few drops of aqueous sodium hydroxide to your mystery substance in a test tube and warm the mixture. Hold a piece of damp litmus paper near the top of the test-tube. If the paper turns blue it means ammonia is being given off and there are ammonium ions in your substance. The ionic equation for this reaction is:

$$NH_4{}^+{}_{(aq)} + OH^-{}_{(aq)} \rightarrow NH_{3(g)} + H_2O_{(l)}$$

$$\text{ammonium} + \text{hydroxide} \rightarrow \text{ammonia} + \text{water}$$
$$\text{ion} \qquad \text{ion}$$

─ **Example** ─────────────────

Ammonium chloride reacts with sodium hydroxide to give ammonia, water and sodium chloride.

$$NH_4Cl_{(aq)} + NaOH_{(aq)} \rightarrow NH_{3(g)} + H_2O_{(l)} + NaCl_{(aq)}$$

HEAT

Figure 4: *Ammonia will come out of solution when heated and turn damp litmus paper blue.*

Tip: If you used barium chloride solution in the test for sulfates, or have added hydrochloric acid at any point, then you'll need to carry out the test for halides using a fresh sample of the unknown substance. This is because the chloride ions you've introduced to the sample could give a false positive.

Tip: The litmus paper needs to be damp so the ammonia gas can dissolve and make the colour change.

Exam Tip
If you're asked how to test for a particular ion in the exam, or you're asked to draw conclusions from a set of results, you need to think about what ions could be present that could give false positives. Have they been dealt with or could they interfere with the test? Also, remember to always consider the effect that adding substances during a test could have. Have ions been added that will affect the results?

Practice Questions — Application

Q1 An unknown solution is run through a series of tests to determine what ions are present.
Firstly, dilute hydrochloric acid is added. The gas produced is delivered into limewater. The limewater does not change.
Next, barium chloride is added to the solution.
A white precipitate is formed.

What ions are present in the unknown solution?

Q2 A student adds barium nitrate solution to an unknown solution to try and determine what ions are present. A white precipitate is formed and he concludes that there are sulfate ions in the unknown solution.

a) Explain why he might be wrong.

b) Suggest how he should carry out the test to correctly determine the presence of sulfate ions.

Practice Questions — Fact Recall

Q1 What is the correct order in which you should carry out the tests for:
    sulfates,   carbonates,   halides?

Q2 Name a dilute acid used in the test for:
    a) carbonates   b) sulfates   c) halides

Q3 What colour will red litmus paper go in the presence of ammonia?

Section Summary

Make sure you know...

- How the periodic table was developed, and its acceptance by the scientific community.
- That in the modern periodic table the elements are arranged in order of increasing atomic number.
- That the modern periodic table is organised into periods (rows), groups (columns) and blocks (e.g. the s-block, p-block and d-block).
- That the elements within a period all have the same number of electron shells (ignoring sub-shells).
- That periods show repeating trends in physical and chemical properties and that this is known as periodicity.
- That the elements within a group all have the same number of electrons in their outer shell and as a result have similar physical and chemical properties.
- How the periodic table can be used to work out the electron configuration of an element.
- What first ionisation energy and successive ionisation energies are.
- Why first ionisation energy generally increases across a period and decreases down a group.
- Why first ionisation energy decreases between Groups 2 and 3, and between Groups 5 and 6.
- That trends in ionisation energy support the Bohr model of the atom.
- How to use successive ionisation energies of an element to work out how many electrons are in each of its shells and what group it's in.
- That carbon (as diamond, graphite and graphene) and silicon have giant covalent lattice structures.
- How the properties of the allotropes of carbon can be explained by their structure and bonding.
- That metals have a giant metallic structure that's held together by electrostatic attraction between cations and delocalised electrons and how this determines its properties.
- The variation in melting and boiling points as you move across Periods 2 and 3.
- How to explain the variation in melting and boiling points across Periods 2 and 3 in terms of structure and bonding.
- That the Group 2 elements generally form M^{2+} ions when they react because this gives them a stable electron configuration (that of a noble gas).
- Why the Group 2 elements get more reactive as you move down the group.
- That the Group 2 elements undergo redox reactions with water to form metal hydroxides and hydrogen gas, that they burn in air to form metal oxides, and that they react with dilute acids to form metal salts and hydrogen gas.
- That the Group 2 oxides are solid white powders which react with water to form alkaline solutions with a pH of 12–13.
- That some Group 2 compounds are bases that can be used to neutralise soil and as antacids.
- Why the boiling and melting points of the halogens increase as you move down Group 7.
- Why the halogens get less reactive as you move down Group 7.
- How halogen and halide ion solutions can be identified using displacement reactions.
- How to use silver nitrate and ammonia solution to test for halide ions.
- That a disproportionation reaction is a reaction where a single element is simultaneously oxidised and reduced.
- How bleach is formed, using chlorine and sodium hydroxide, and its uses.
- The equations for the reactions of chlorine with water.
- The benefits and risks of using chlorine in water treatment.
- How to test for carbonates, sulfates and halides, and in which order the tests should be carried out.
- How to test for ammonium ions.

Exam-style Questions

1   The table below shows the first six ionisation energies of a Period 3 element.

ionisation number	1st	2nd	3rd	4th	5th	6th
ionisation energy (kJ mol^{-1})	577.5	1816.7	2744.8	11577	14842	18379

What is the element?

A   Sodium

B   Aluminium

C   Phosphorus

D   Chlorine

(1 mark)

2   When chlorine undergoes disproportionation with potassium hydroxide, the reaction produces potassium chloride, potassium chlorate and water.

Which of the options below gives the correct oxidation states of chlorine in each molecule?

	Cl_2	KCl	KClO
A	0	−1	+1
B	−1	−1	0
C	0	+1	−1
D	−1	0	+1

(1 mark)

3   Below are four statements about ionisation energies.

1.   The increase in ionisation energy between Groups 5 and 6 is due to electron repulsion.

2.   The 3rd ionisation energy of an element is always higher than the 2nd ionisation energy.

3.   The drop in ionisation energy between Groups 2 and 3 is due to the electrons that are removed being in different orbitals.

4.   The number of neutrons in the nucleus of an atom affects its ionisation energies.

Which of these statements are true?

A   Only 1, 2 and 3.

B   Only 2 and 3.

C   Only 1 and 3.

D   Only 2 and 4.

(1 mark)

4   The periodic table is a table of elements arranged into periods and groups.

(a) (i)   Identify the fifteenth element in Period 4 of the periodic table.
State which block of the periodic table this element is in.

(1 mark)

(ii) Use your knowledge of the periodic table to write the electronic
configuration for this element.

(1 mark)

(b)   Strontium and barium are both in Group 2 of the periodic table.
Both react with oxygen forming solid white oxides.

(i)   Write equations, including state symbols, for the reactions of strontium and
barium with oxygen.

(2 marks)

(ii) Use your knowledge of the periodic table to explain why strontium and
barium react with oxygen in similar ways.

(2 marks)

(iii) Explain how the rate of the reaction of strontium with oxygen is
likely to be different from the reaction of barium with oxygen.

(2 marks)

5   The elements in Group 2 of the periodic table are commonly known as
the alkaline earth metals.
The alkaline earth metals react with water to form metal hydroxides.

(a) (i)   Write a balanced equation for the reaction of calcium with water.

(1 mark)

(ii) Give the electron configuration of the calcium species
before and after it reacts with water.

(1 mark)

(iii) Describe what you would see when this reaction takes place.

(2 marks)

(iv) State the approximate pH of the resulting calcium hydroxide solution.

(1 mark)

(b) (i)   Give one use of calcium hydroxide.

(1 mark)

(ii) Write an ionic equation for the reaction that takes place when calcium
hydroxide is used in this way.

(1 mark)

6 A student was demonstrating that an unknown potassium halide solution was potassium bromide.

   (a) He mixed some of the solution with chlorine water ($Cl_{2(aq)}$) and added hexane. Then he observed the results.

      (i) Write an ionic equation for the displacement reaction that would occur if the solution was potassium bromide.

(1 mark)

      (ii) State how the colour of the organic solvent layer could be used to distinguish between a solution of potassium bromide and potassium iodide.

(2 marks)

   (b) The student's results confirmed that the solution was potassium bromide. The student further confirmed his results using the silver nitrate test.

      (i) Describe how the student could perform a silver nitrate test to confirm that bromide ions were present in the unknown solution.

(2 marks)

      (ii) Write an ionic equation, including state symbols, for the reaction that occurs when a silver nitrate test is used to detect bromide ions.

(1 mark)

      (iii) Explain how the student could double-check his results.

(2 marks)

7 Carbon is the first element of Group 4.

   (a) Different forms of the same element in the same state are called allotropes. Carbon has three common allotropes.

      (i) Name three common allotropes of carbon.

(1 mark)

      (ii) Silicon is also a Group 4 element.
      Which allotrope of carbon has the same structure as silicon?

(1 mark)

      (iii) Describe the lattice structure of silicon.

(2 marks)

   (b) Carbon and nitrogen are both in Period 2.

      (i) Explain why the first ionisation energy of carbon is lower than that of nitrogen.

(3 marks)

      (ii)* Carbon has the highest melting point of all the elements in Period 2.

      Explain why the melting points of Period 2 elements change as you move across the period.

      Your answer should include details of the structure and bonding of the Period 2 elements.

(6 marks)

*The quality of your response will be assessed in this question.

Learning Objectives:

- Explain and use the terms standard conditions and standard states.

- Define and use the terms enthalpy change of reaction, enthalpy change of formation, enthalpy change of combustion and enthalpy change of neutralisation.

- Explain that some chemical reactions are accompanied by enthalpy changes that can be exothermic (ΔH negative) or endothermic (ΔH positive).

- Construct an enthalpy profile diagram for a reaction to show the difference in the enthalpy of the reactants compared with that of the products.

- Explain qualitatively, using enthalpy profile diagrams, the term activation energy.

Specification Reference 3.2.1

1. Enthalpy Changes

When chemical reactions happen, some bonds are broken and some bonds are made. More often than not, this'll cause a change in energy. The souped-up chemistry term for this is enthalpy change.

Enthalpy notation

Enthalpy change, ΔH (delta H), is the heat energy transferred in a reaction at constant pressure. The units of ΔH are kJ mol^{-1}. You write $\Delta H^\ominus$ to show that the measurements were made under **standard conditions** and that the elements were in their **standard states** (i.e. their physical states under standard conditions). Standard conditions are 100 kPa (about 1 atm) pressure and a temperature of 298 K (25 °C). Sometimes the notation will also include a subscript to signify the type of reaction. See below for more on this notation.

Conditions for enthalpy changes

You can't directly measure the actual enthalpy of a system. In practice, that doesn't matter, because it's only ever enthalpy change that matters. You can find enthalpy changes either by experiment or in data books. Enthalpy changes you find in data books are usually standard enthalpy changes — enthalpy changes under standard conditions (298 K and 100 kPa). This is important because changes in enthalpy are affected by temperature and pressure — using standard conditions means that everyone can know exactly what the enthalpy change is describing.

The different types of ΔH

Standard enthalpy change of reaction

Standard enthalpy change of reaction, $\Delta_r H^\ominus$, is the enthalpy change when a reaction occurs in the molar quantities shown in the chemical equation, under standard conditions with all reactants and products in their standard states.

Standard enthalpy change of formation

Standard enthalpy change of formation, $\Delta_f H^\ominus$, is the enthalpy change when 1 mole of a compound is formed from its elements in their standard states under standard conditions, e.g. $2C_{(s)} + 3H_{2(g)} + \frac{1}{2}O_{2(g)} \rightarrow C_2H_5OH_{(l)}$.

Standard enthalpy change of combustion

Standard enthalpy change of combustion, $\Delta_c H^\ominus$, is the enthalpy change when 1 mole of a substance is completely burned in oxygen under standard conditions with all reactants and products in their standard states.

Standard enthalpy change of neutralisation

Standard enthalpy change of neutralisation, $\Delta_{neut} H^\ominus$, is the enthalpy change when solutions of an acid and an alkali react together to form 1 mole of water, under standard conditions.

Exothermic reactions

Exothermic reactions give out energy to their surroundings. The products of the reaction end up with less energy than the reactants. This means that the enthalpy change for the reaction, ΔH, will be negative.

Oxidation is usually exothermic. Here are two examples:

The combustion of a fuel like methane:

$$CH_{4(g)} + 2O_{2(g)} \rightarrow CO_{2(g)} + 2H_2O_{(l)} \qquad \Delta_c H^\ominus = -890 \text{ kJ mol}^{-1}$$

ΔH is negative so the reaction is **exothermic**.

The oxidation of carbohydrates, like glucose, in respiration is exothermic.

Endothermic reactions

Endothermic reactions take in energy from their surroundings. This means that the products of the reaction have more energy than the reactants, so the enthalpy change for the reaction, ΔH, is positive.

Examples

The thermal decomposition of calcium carbonate is endothermic.

$$CaCO_{3(s)} \rightarrow CaO_{(s)} + CO_{2(g)} \qquad \Delta_r H^\ominus = +179 \text{ kJ mol}^{-1}$$

ΔH is positive so the reaction is **endothermic**.

The main reactions of photosynthesis are also endothermic — sunlight supplies the energy.

Figure 1: Photosynthesis in plants is endothermic — the products have more energy than the reactants.

Enthalpy profile diagrams

Enthalpy profile diagrams show you how the enthalpy (energy) changes during a reaction (see Figure 2). A substance is most stable when it has lost all of its internal energy. So, lower positions on an enthalpy profile diagram will be more stable than higher positions.

The **activation energy**, E_a, is the minimum amount of energy needed to begin breaking reactant bonds and start a chemical reaction. On an enthalpy diagram, E_a is the difference between the highest point and the energy of the reactants (see Figure 2).

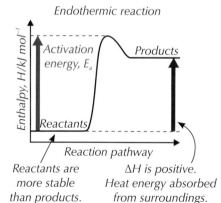

Figure 2: Enthalpy profile diagrams.

Practice Questions — Fact Recall

Q1 Give the notation for an enthalpy change under standard conditions.

Q2 Define the 'standard enthalpy change of reaction'.

Q3 Describe the difference between exothermic and endothermic reactions.

Q4 a) Sketch an enthalpy profile diagram for an endothermic reaction.

b) Draw an arrow on the diagram to show E_a and explain the term.

2. Bond Enthalpies

Reactions involve breaking and making bonds. The enthalpy change for a reaction depends on which bonds are broken and which are made.

What are bond enthalpies?

In ionic bonding, positive and negative ions are attracted to each other. In covalent molecules, the positive nuclei are attracted to the negative charge of the shared electrons in a covalent bond. You need energy to break this attraction. The amount of energy you need per mole is called the **bond dissociation enthalpy**. (Of course it's got a fancy name — this is chemistry.) Bond dissociation enthalpies always involve bond breaking in gaseous compounds. This makes comparisons between different bond dissociation enthalpies fair.

Breaking and making bonds

When reactions happen, reactant bonds are broken and product bonds are formed. You need energy to break bonds, so bond breaking is **endothermic** (ΔH is positive). Stronger bonds take more energy to break. Energy is released when bonds are formed, so this is **exothermic** (ΔH is negative). Stronger bonds release more energy when they form. The enthalpy change for a reaction is the overall effect of these two changes. If you need more energy to break bonds than is released when bonds are made, ΔH is positive. If it's less, ΔH is negative.

> **Example**
> Nitrogen reacts with hydrogen to form ammonia in this reaction:
> $$N_2 + 3H_2 \rightarrow 2NH_3$$
> The energy needed to break all the bonds in N_2 and H_2 = 2253 kJ mol⁻¹.
> The energy released when forming the bonds in NH_3 = 2346 kJ mol⁻¹.
> The amount of energy released is bigger than the amount needed, so the reaction is exothermic and ΔH is negative. (See page 157 for full calculation.)

Average bond enthalpies

We tend to use **average bond enthalpies** in calculations because the energy required to break an individual bond can change depending on where it is.

> **Example**
> Water (H_2O) has two O–H bonds (see Figure 1). You'd think it'd take the same amount of energy to break them both, but it doesn't.
>
> The first bond, H–OH$_{(g)}$: $E(\text{H–OH}) = +492$ kJ mol⁻¹
> The second bond, H–O$_{(g)}$: $E(\text{H–O}) = +428$ kJ mol⁻¹
> (OH⁻ is a bit easier to break apart because of the extra electron repulsion.)
>
> So, the average bond enthalpy for O–H bonds in water is:
> $$\frac{492 + 428}{2} = +460 \text{ kJ mol}^{-1}.$$
>
> The data book says the bond enthalpy for O–H is +463 kJ mol⁻¹. It's a bit different than the one calculated above because it's the average for a much bigger range of molecules, not just water. For example, it includes the O–H bonds in alcohols and carboxylic acids too.

Learning Objectives:

- Explain exothermic and endothermic reactions in terms of enthalpy changes associated with the breaking and making of chemical bonds.
- Explain the term average bond enthalpy.
- Be able to calculate an enthalpy change of reaction and related qualities from average bond enthalpies.

Specification Reference 3.2.1

Tip: You can look up the average bond enthalpies for different bonds in a data book, or calculate them from given data. In an exam you'll be given any bond enthalpies you need.

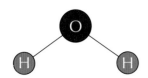

Figure 1: The bonds in a water molecule.

So when you look up an average bond enthalpy, what you get is the energy needed to break one mole of bonds in the gas phase, averaged over many different compounds.

Tip: This explanation of average bond energy is really important so make sure you learn it.

Calculating enthalpy changes

In any chemical reaction, energy is absorbed to break bonds and given out during bond formation. The difference between the energy absorbed and released is the enthalpy change of reaction:

Enthalpy change of reaction = Total energy absorbed – Total energy released

- To calculate the enthalpy change for a reaction, first calculate the total energy needed to break the bonds in the reactants. You'll usually be given the average bond enthalpies for each type of bond, so just multiply each value by the number of each bond present. This total will be the total energy absorbed in the reaction.

- To find the total energy released by the reaction, calculate the total energy needed to form all the new bonds in the products. Use the average bond enthalpies to do this.

- The overall enthalpy change for the reaction can then be found by subtracting the total energy released from the total energy absorbed.

Bond	Bond Enthalpy (Average value except where stated)
N≡N	+945 kJ mol^{-1}
H–H	+436 kJ mol^{-1}
N–H	+391 kJ mol^{-1}
O=O	+498 kJ mol^{-1}
O–H (water)	+460 kJ mol^{-1}

Figure 2: *Table of bond enthalpies.*

Examples — Maths Skills

Calculate the enthalpy change for the following reaction:

$$N_2 + 3H_2 \rightarrow 2NH_3$$

Use the bond enthalpy values shown in Figure 2.

You might find it helpful to draw a sketch of the molecules in the reaction:

Tip: Draw sketches to show the bonds present in the reactants and products to make sure you include them all in your calculations.

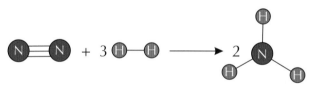

Bonds broken: 1 × N≡N bond broken = 1 × 945 = 945 kJ mol^{-1}
3 × H–H bonds broken = 3 × 436 = 1308 kJ mol^{-1}

Total Energy Absorbed = 945 + 1308 = 2253 kJ mol^{-1}

Bonds formed: 6 × N–H bonds formed = 6 × 391 = 2346 kJ mol^{-1}
Total Energy Released = 2346 kJ mol^{-1}

Now you just subtract 'total energy released' from 'total energy absorbed':

Enthalpy change of reaction = 2253 – 2346 = –93 kJ mol^{-1}.

The negative sign tells you that the reaction is exothermic. More energy is released when the N–H bonds are made than is needed to break the N≡N and H–H bonds.

Tip: If you can't remember which value to subtract from which, just take the smaller number from the bigger one then add the sign at the end — positive if 'bonds broken' was the bigger number (endothermic), negative if 'bonds formed' was bigger (exothermic).

Exam tip
Always double check you've multiplied the enthalpy values by the right number of bonds. It's really easy to make a mistake and end up losing marks.

Tip: You can ignore any bonds that don't actually change during the reaction. Just work out which bonds actually break and which new bonds form. You'll still get the same value if you break and form all of the bonds, but it'll save you time if you don't have to.

Bond	Bond Enthalpy (Average value except where stated)
C–H	+413 kJ mol^{-1}
C=C	+612 kJ mol^{-1}
C–C	+347 kJ mol^{-1}
C–O	+358 kJ mol^{-1}
C–Cl	+346 kJ mol^{-1}
C=O (in CO$_2$)	+805 kJ mol^{-1}
C–N	+286 kJ mol^{-1}
H–Cl	+432 kJ mol^{-1}
Cl–Cl	+243 kJ mol^{-1}

Figure 3: *Table of bond enthalpies.*

Calculate the overall enthalpy change for the following reaction:
$$H_{2(g)} + \tfrac{1}{2}O_{2(g)} \rightarrow H_2O_{(g)}$$
The molecules present are shown below:

Bonds broken: 1 × H–H bond broken = 1 × 436 = 436 kJ mol^{-1}
  ½ × O=O bond broken = ½ × 498 = 249 kJ mol^{-1}

Total Energy Absorbed = 436 + 249 = 685 kJ mol^{-1}

Bonds formed: 2 × O–H bonds formed = 2 × 460 = 920 kJ mol^{-1}
Total Energy Released = 920 kJ mol^{-1}

Enthalpy change of reaction = 685 – 920 = –235 kJ mol^{-1}.

Practice Questions — Application

Q1 Use the average bond enthalpies shown in Figures 2 and 3 to calculate the enthalpy changes for the following reactions:

Q2 Calculate the enthalpy change for the complete combustion of ethene (C$_2$H$_4$) using the bond enthalpies given in Figures 2 and 3. (The products of complete combustion are CO$_2$ and H$_2$O.)

Q3 Calculate the standard enthalpy change of reaction for 1 mole of hydrogen (H$_{2(g)}$) reacting with 1 mole of chlorine (Cl$_{2(g)}$) to form hydrogen chloride (HCl$_{(g)}$) using the bond enthalpies given in Figures 2 and 3.

Q4 The enthalpy change for the following reaction is –181 kJ mol^{-1}:
$$2NO_{(g)} \rightarrow N_{2(g)} + O_{2(g)}$$
Use this value for $\Delta_r H^{\ominus}$, along with the data in Figure 2, to estimate a value for the average bond enthalpy for the bond between nitrogen and oxygen in NO.

Practice Questions — Fact Recall

Q1 Is bond breaking exothermic or endothermic?

Q2 In an exothermic reaction, which is larger — the energy required to make bonds or the energy required to break bonds?

Q3 What is average bond enthalpy?

Q4 Give the formula for calculating the enthalpy change of a reaction.

3. Measuring Enthalpy Changes

A lot of the data we have on enthalpy changes has come from someone, somewhere, measuring the enthalpy change of a reaction in a lab.

Measuring enthalpy changes in the lab

To measure the enthalpy change for a reaction, there are only two things you need to find out — the number of moles of the stuff that's reacting, and the change in temperature. How you go about doing the experiment depends on what type of reaction it is. Some reactions will quite happily take place in solution, such as neutralisation or displacement, and you can just stick a thermometer in to find out the temperature change. Use an insulated container like a polystyrene beaker, so that you don't lose or gain much heat through the sides (see Figure 1).

> PRACTICAL ACTIVITY GROUP **3**

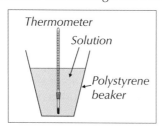

Figure 1: Simple equipment used to measure the enthalpy change of reaction.

Combustion reactions are trickier because the reactant is burned in air. A copper calorimeter containing a known mass of water is often used (see Figure 2). You burn a known mass of the reactant and record the temperature change of the water.

Ideally all the heat given out by the fuel as it burns would be absorbed by the water — allowing you to work out the enthalpy change of combustion (see page 154). In practice though, you always lose some heat (as you heat the apparatus and the surroundings).

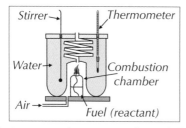

Figure 2: A copper calorimeter used to measure the enthalpy change of combustion.

A 'bomb' calorimeter, like the one shown in Figure 3, is a much more accurate piece of equipment, but works on the same principle.

Using the equation $q = mc\Delta T$

The equation for enthalpy change is:

$$q = mc\Delta T$$

q = heat lost or gained (in J). This is the same as the enthalpy change if the pressure is constant.

m = mass (in g) of solution in the insulated container (or mass of water in the calorimeter).

ΔT = the change in temperature (in K or °C) of the solution / water.

c = specific heat capacity of the solution / water ($4.18\ J\,g^{-1}K^{-1}$).

Learning Objective:

- Describe the techniques and procedures used to determine enthalpy changes directly.

- Be able to calculate enthalpy changes directly from appropriate experimental results, including use of the relationship: $q = mc\Delta T$.

- Be able to determine enthalpy changes from temperature measurements (PAG 3).

Specification Reference 3.2.1

Tip: Learning how to carry out experiments is an important part of science. We wouldn't get very far without experiments.

> HOW SCIENCE WORKS

Tip: Before carrying out experiments in the lab, remember to carry out a risk assessment.

Figure 3: A bomb calorimeter.

Tip: The specific heat capacity of a substance is the amount of heat energy it takes to raise the temperature of 1 g of that substance by 1 K.

Tip: $\Delta H^{\ominus}$ is the standard enthalpy change of a reaction carried out at 100 kPa with all reactants and products in their standard states (see page 154). If the experiment was carried out under different conditions, this method wouldn't give you the value for $\Delta H^{\ominus}$.

Figure 4: *A combustion reaction — glucose burning.*

Tip: M_r is the relative molecular mass — and it's exactly the same as the molar mass (M), except M_r doesn't have any units.

Exam Tip
You might be asked to suggest why a measured enthalpy change value is different to one in a data book. It's usually to do with heat losses to the surroundings, but it can also be due to things like incomplete combustion.

Calculating the standard enthalpy change of combustion

To calculate the standard enthalpy change of combustion, $\Delta_c H^{\ominus}$, using data from a laboratory experiment, follow these steps:

Step 1: Calculate the amount of heat lost or gained during the combustion using $q = mc\Delta T$ and your measured or given values of m and ΔT. You'll then need to change the units of q from joules to kilojoules.

Step 2: Calculate the number of moles of fuel that caused this enthalpy change, from the mass that reacted. Use the equation:

$$n = \frac{mass}{M}$$ n is the number of moles of fuel burned.
M is the fuel's molar mass (see page 37).

Step 3: Calculate the standard enthalpy change of combustion, $\Delta_c H^{\ominus}$ (in kJ mol^{-1}), using the actual heat change for the reaction, q (in kJ), and the number of moles of fuel that burned, n. Use the equation:

$$\Delta_c H^{\ominus} = \frac{q}{n}$$

Example ── Maths Skills

Calculating the standard enthalpy change of combustion:

In a laboratory experiment, 1.16 g of an organic liquid fuel was completely burned in oxygen. The heat formed during this combustion raised the temperature of 100 g of water from 295.3 K to 357.8 K. Calculate the standard enthalpy of combustion, $\Delta_c H^{\ominus}$, of the fuel. Its M_r is 58.0.

Step 1: Calculate the amount of heat given out by the fuel using $q = mc\Delta T$. Remember that m is the mass of water, not the mass of fuel.

$q = mc\Delta T$
$q = 100 \times 4.18 \times (357.8 - 295.3) = 26\ 125$ J
Change the amount of heat from J to kJ: $q = 26.125$ kJ.

Step 2: Find out how many moles of fuel produced this heat:

$$n = \frac{mass}{M} = \frac{1.16\ \text{g}}{58.0\ \text{g mol}^{-1}} = 0.0200 \text{ moles of fuel.}$$

Step 3: The standard enthalpy of combustion involves 1 mole of fuel.

$$\text{So } \Delta_c H^{\ominus} = \frac{q}{n} = \frac{-26.125\ \text{kJ}}{0.0200\ \text{mol}} \approx -1310 \text{ kJ mol}^{-1} \text{ (3 s.f.).}$$

(Note: q is negative because combustion is an exothermic reaction.)

The actual $\Delta_c H^{\ominus}$ of this compound is -1615 kJ mol^{-1} — loads of heat has been lost and not measured. E.g. it's likely a fair bit would escape through the copper calorimeter and also the fuel might not combust completely.

Calculating the standard enthalpy change of reaction

The standard enthalpy change of a reaction, $\Delta_r H^{\ominus}$, is calculated in a slightly different way. Instead of calculating the enthalpy change per mole of substance reacted, you need to find the enthalpy change for the number of moles shown in the balanced chemical equation. Step 1 is exactly the same as step 1 for calculating the standard enthalpy change of combustion. It's steps 2 and 3 that are a bit different...

Step 2: Calculate the number of moles of one of the reactants that caused this enthalpy change, from the mass of it that reacted. Use the equation $n = $ mass $\div M$ again.

Step 3: Calculate the standard enthalpy change of reaction, $\Delta_r H^\ominus$ (in kJ mol^{-1}) using the actual heat change for the reaction, q (in kJ), and the number of moles that reacted, n, using the equation:

$\Delta_r H^\ominus = \dfrac{q}{n}$ (× number of moles reacting in balanced chemical equation)

Tip: When finding the standard enthalpy change of a reaction, always write out a balanced equation for the reaction so you can see the correct molar quantities.

Example ─ Maths Skills

Calculating the standard enthalpy change of reaction:

30.0 g of ammonium chloride ($NH_4Cl_{(s)}$) is dissolved in water in a polystyrene beaker. The temperature of the contents of the beaker decreases from 298.0 K to 296.0 K. The total mass of the solution is 980 g. Calculate the standard molar enthalpy change for the reaction.

The balanced reaction is: $NH_4Cl_{(s)} \rightarrow NH_4^+{}_{(aq)} + Cl^-{}_{(aq)}$

The molar mass, M, of NH_4Cl = 14.0 + (4 × 1.0) + 35.5 = 53.5 g mol^{-1}.

Step 1: $q = mc\Delta T = 980 \times 4.18 \times (298.0 - 296.0) = 8192.8$ J = 8.1928 kJ

Step 2: $n = \dfrac{30.0 \text{ g}}{53.5 \text{ g mol}^{-1}} = 0.5607$ moles of NH_4Cl.

Step 3: The balanced reaction involves one mole of NH_4Cl so:

$$\Delta_r H^\ominus = \dfrac{q}{n} = \dfrac{8.1928 \text{ kJ}}{0.5607 \text{ mol}} \approx +14.6 \text{ kJ mol}^{-1} \text{ (3 s.f.)}.$$

Tip: It doesn't matter whether you're measuring the temperature of pure water or a solution of something, always make the assumption that $c = 4.18$ J g^{-1} K^{-1}.

Practice Questions — Application

Q1 0.0500 mol of a compound dissolves in water, causing the temperature of the solution to increase from 298 K to 301 K. The total mass of the solution is 220 g. Calculate the enthalpy change for the reaction in kJ mol^{-1}. Assume $c = 4.18$ J g^{-1} K^{-1}.

Q2 A calorimeter, containing 200 g of water ($c = 4.18$ J g^{-1} K^{-1}), was used to measure the enthalpy change of combustion of pentane ($C_5H_{12(l)}$, $M_r = 72.0$). 0.500 g of pentane was burnt, which increased the temperature of the water by 29.0 K.

   a) Calculate the enthalpy change of combustion of pentane. Give your answer in kJ mol^{-1}.

   b) Suggest reasons why this value may be different to the standard enthalpy change of combustion of pentane given in a data book.

Q3 The standard enthalpy of combustion of octane ($C_8H_{18(l)}$, $M_r = 114$) is −5512 kJ mol^{-1}. Some octane was burnt in a calorimeter containing 300 g of water ($c = 4.18$ J g^{-1} K^{-1}). The temperature of the water went up by 55.0 K. Calculate an estimate of the mass of octane burnt.

Tip: If the temperature has increased during the reaction (i.e. it's exothermic), you need to use a negative value for q in your calculations.

Practice Questions — Fact Recall

Q1 What measurements need to be made in order to calculate the enthalpy change for a reaction in a laboratory?

Q2 Sketch and label a calorimeter that could be used in the lab to measure the enthalpy change of a combustion.

Q3 In the equation $q = mc\Delta T$, state what 'q' stands for and give its units.

Q4 What conditions are needed to measure the standard enthalpy change of a reaction, $\Delta_r H^\ominus$?

Q5 Explain how you would calculate $\Delta_r H^\ominus$ for a reaction, given a value for q and the number of moles, n, of a reactant used in the reaction.

- Describe the techniques and procedures used to determine enthalpy changes indirectly.

- Use Hess' law to construct enthalpy cycles and carry out calculations to determine an enthalpy change of reaction, using either enthalpy changes of combustion, enthalpy changes of formation or an unfamiliar enthalpy cycle.

Specification Reference 3.2.1

4. Hess's Law

For some reactions, there is no easy way to measure enthalpy changes in the lab. For these, we can use Hess's Law.

What is Hess's Law?

Hess's Law says that:

> The total enthalpy change of a reaction is always the same, no matter which route is taken.

This law is handy for working out enthalpy changes that you can't find directly by doing an experiment — for example, the enthalpy change of the reaction that breaks down NO_2 into N_2 and O_2. We can call this reaction 'route 1'. But we can also think of the reaction as NO_2 breaking down into NO and O_2, and then reacting further to form N_2 and O_2. This longer route, with an intermediate step, can be called 'route 2' (see Figure 1).

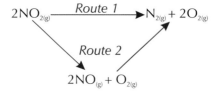

Figure 1: *Two possible routes for the formation of nitrogen and oxygen from nitrogen dioxide.*

Hess's Law says that the total enthalpy change for route 1 is the same as for route 2. So if you know the enthalpy changes for the stages of route 2, you can calculate the enthalpy change for route 1, as shown in the example below.

┌─ **Example** ── **Maths Skills** ────────────────────

Use Hess's Law to calculate the enthalpy change, $\Delta_r H^\ominus$, for route 1 of the reaction shown below.

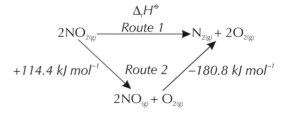

The total enthalpy change for route 1 is the same as the total enthalpy change for route 2. So the enthalpy change for route 1 is the sum of the steps in route 2:

$\Delta_r H^\ominus = 114.4$ kJ $+ (-180.8$ kJ$) = -66.4$ kJ mol^{-1}.

Using enthalpies of formation

You can find enthalpy changes of formation for hundreds of various compounds listed in data books. They're handy because you can use them (along with Hess's Law) to find enthalpy changes for all kinds of reactions.

Tip: It doesn't matter what you label as route 1 and route 2, or which routes you choose, the two routes will always be equal. It's just like magic — but less cool.

Tip: As it says at the top of the page, you can't measure the enthalpy change for every reaction. So how did Hess prove that his Law worked? By building on already established theories — in this case, the principle of conservation of energy. Scientists knew that energy couldn't be created or destroyed, so if you start with the same reactants and end with the same products, it follows that the energy (or enthalpy) change has to be the same.

You need to know $\Delta_f H^\circ$ for all the reactants and products that are compounds. The value of $\Delta_f H^\circ$ for elements is zero — the element's being formed from the element, so there's no change in enthalpy. The standard enthalpy changes are all measured at 298 K.

Examples — Maths Skills

Calculate $\Delta_r H^\circ$ for this reaction using the enthalpies of formation in Figure 2:

$$SO_{2(g)} + 2H_2S_{(g)} \rightarrow 3S_{(s)} + 2H_2O_{(l)}$$

- Write under the reaction a list of all the elements present in the reaction, balanced in their correct molar quantities, as shown below:

Compound	$\Delta_f H^\circ$
$SO_{2(g)}$	−297 kJ mol⁻¹
$H_2S_{(g)}$	−20.2 kJ mol⁻¹
$H_2O_{(l)}$	−286 kJ mol⁻¹

Figure 2: Table of enthalpies of formation for three compounds.

Reactants   *Products*

$SO_{2(g)} + 2H_2S_{(g)} \longrightarrow 3S_{(s)} + 2H_2O_{(l)}$

$3S_{(s)} + 2H_{2(g)} + O_{2(g)}$
Elements

- Enthalpies of formation ($\Delta_f H^\circ$) tell you the enthalpy change going from the elements to the compounds. The enthalpy change of reaction ($\Delta_r H^\circ$) is the enthalpy change going from the reactants to the products. Draw and label arrows to show this on your diagram:

Reactants $\Delta_r H^\circ$ *Products*

$SO_{2(g)} + 2H_2S_{(g)} \longrightarrow 3S_{(s)} + 2H_2O_{(l)}$

$\Delta_f H^\circ_{(reactants)}$ $\Delta_f H^\circ_{(products)}$

$3S_{(s)} + 2H_{2(g)} + O_{2(g)}$
Elements

- The calculation is often simpler if you keep the arrows end to end, so make both routes go from the elements to the products. Route 1 gets there via the reactants (and includes $\Delta_r H^\circ$), whilst route 2 gets there directly. Label the enthalpy changes along each arrow, as shown below. There are 2 moles of H_2O and 2 moles of H_2S, so their enthalpies of formation will need to be multiplied by 2. $\Delta_f H^\circ$ of sulfur is zero because it's an element, but you can still label it on the diagram.

Tip: You don't have to pick a route that follows the direction of the arrows. If your route goes against an arrow you can just change the signs (so negative enthalpies become positive and positive enthalpies become negative). There's an example of this on pages 165-166.

Reactants $\Delta_r H^\circ$ *Products*

$SO_{2(g)} + 2H_2S_{(g)} \longrightarrow 3S_{(s)} + 2H_2O_{(l)}$
Route 1

$\Delta_f H^\circ_{[reactants]} = \Delta_f H^\circ_{[SO_2]} + 2 \times \Delta_f H^\circ_{[H_2S]}$ *Route 2* $\Delta_f H^\circ_{[products]} = 3 \times \Delta_f H^\circ_{[S]} + 2 \times \Delta_f H^\circ_{[H_2O]}$

$3S_{(s)} + 2H_{2(g)} + O_{2(g)}$
Elements

- Use Hess's Law, Route 1 = Route 2, and plug the numbers from Figure 2 into the equation:

$\Delta_f H^\circ_{[SO_2]} + 2\Delta_f H^\circ_{[H_2S]} + \Delta_r H^\circ = 3\Delta_f H^\circ_{[S]} + 2\Delta_f H^\circ_{[H_2O]}$

$-297 + (2 \times -20.2) + \Delta_r H^\circ = (3 \times 0) + (2 \times -286)$

$\Delta_r H^\circ = [(3 \times 0) + (2 \times -286)] - [-297 + (2 \times -20.2)]$
$= -235$ kJ mol⁻¹ (3 s.f.)

Compound	$\Delta_f H^\circ$
$NH_4NO_{3(s)}$	-365 kJ mol^{-1}
$CO_{2(g)}$	-394 kJ mol^{-1}
$H_2O_{(l)}$	-286 kJ mol^{-1}

Figure 3: *Table of enthalpies of formation for three compounds.*

Calculate $\Delta_r H^\circ$ for this reaction using the enthalpies of formation in Figure 3:

$$2NH_4NO_{3(s)} + C_{(s)} \rightarrow 2N_{2(g)} + CO_{2(g)} + 4H_2O_{(l)}$$

- Draw and label your diagram:

- Label the enthalpy changes along each arrow.

- Use Hess's Law, Route 1 = Route 2, and plug the numbers from Figure 3 into the equation:

$$2\Delta_f H^\circ_{[NH_4NO_3]} + \Delta_f H^\circ_{[C]} + \Delta_r H^\circ = 2\Delta_f H^\circ_{[N_2]} + \Delta_f H^\circ_{[CO_2]} + 4\Delta_f H^\circ_{[H_2O]}$$
$$(2 \times -365) + 0 + \Delta_r H^\circ = 0 + -394 + (4 \times -286)$$
$$\Delta_r H^\circ = -394 + (-1144) - (-730) = -808 \text{ kJ mol}^{-1}.$$

Compound	$\Delta_f H^\circ$
$Mg(OH)_{2(s)}$	-925 kJ mol^{-1}
$H_2O_{(l)}$	-286 kJ mol^{-1}
$CO_{2(g)}$	-394 kJ mol^{-1}
$CaO_{(s)}$	-635 kJ mol^{-1}
$CaCO_{3(s)}$	-1207 kJ mol^{-1}
$N_2O_{5(s)}$	-41 kJ mol^{-1}
$NO_{2(g)}$	33 kJ mol^{-1}

Figure 4: *Table of enthalpies of formation for five compounds.*

Practice Questions — Application

Q1 Use Hess's Law and the diagram below to calculate $\Delta_r H^\circ$ for the reaction between magnesium and water. The enthalpies of formation needed are given in Figure 4.

Q2 Calculate $\Delta_r H^\circ$ for the following reactions using Hess's Law, and the enthalpies of formation given in Figure 4:

a) $CaCO_{3(s)} \rightarrow CaO_{(s)} + CO_{2(g)}$

b) $2N_2O_{5(g)} \rightarrow 4NO_{2(g)} + O_{2(g)}$

Using enthalpies of combustion

You can use a similar method to find an enthalpy change from enthalpy changes of combustion, instead of using enthalpy changes of formation. There's a lovely example of this coming up on the next page...

Example — **Maths Skills**

Calculate $\Delta_f H^\circ$ of ethanol using the enthalpies of combustion in Figure 5.

- The desired reaction in this case is the formation of ethanol from its elements, so write out the balanced equation:

  Reactants   Product
  $$2C_{(s)} + 3H_{2(g)} + \tfrac{1}{2}O_{2(g)} \longrightarrow C_2H_5OH_{(l)}$$

Substance	$\Delta_c H^\circ$
$C_{(s)}$	-394 kJ mol^{-1}
$H_{2(g)}$	-286 kJ mol^{-1}
$C_2H_5OH_{(l)}$	-1367 kJ mol^{-1}

Figure 5: *Table of enthalpies of combustion for three substances.*

- Figure 5 tells you the enthalpy change when each of the 'reactants' and 'products' is burned in oxygen. Add these combustion reactions to your diagram, making sure they are balanced, as shown below:

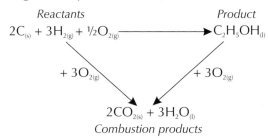

Tip: The products of a complete combustion of a CHO compound in oxygen are carbon dioxide (CO_2) and water (H_2O).

- Choose which reactions will form which route. Label the diagram with the enthalpy changes along each arrow as before (taking into account molar quantities):

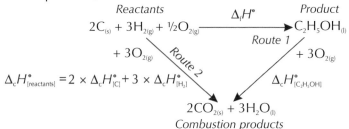

Tip: You can ignore the enthalpy change of combustion of oxygen in these calculations. Oxygen <u>doesn't have</u> an enthalpy change of combustion — you <u>can't</u> burn 1 mole of oxygen in oxygen.

- Use Hess's Law as follows: Route 1 = Route 2

  $$\Delta_f H^\circ_{[ethanol]} + \Delta_c H^\circ_{[C_2H_5OH]} = 2\Delta_c H^\circ_{[C]} + 3\Delta H^\circ_{c\,[H_2]}$$
  $$\Delta_f H^\circ_{[ethanol]} + (-1367) = (2 \times -394) + (3 \times -286)$$
  $$\Delta_f H^\circ_{[ethanol]} = -788 + -858 - (-1367) = -279 \text{ kJ mol}^{-1}.$$

Using enthalpies of reaction

You can also use Hess's Law to calculate enthalpy changes using a group of linked reactions, where all but one of the enthalpy changes for the reactions are known. The following example shows how to do this, this time choosing routes where the arrows don't run end to end.

Example — **Maths Skills**

Calculate $\Delta_r H^\circ$ for the reaction below using the data given in Figure 6.

$$H^+_{(g)} + Br^-_{(g)} \xrightarrow{\Delta_r H^\circ} H^+_{(aq)} + Br^-_{(aq)}$$

$$\uparrow \Delta H_1 \qquad\qquad \downarrow \Delta H_3$$

$$H_{(g)} + Br_{(g)} \xrightarrow{\Delta H_2} HBr_{(g)}$$

Reaction	$\Delta_r H^\circ$
ΔH_1	$+987$ kJ mol^{-1}
ΔH_2	-366 kJ mol^{-1}
ΔH_3	-85 kJ mol^{-1}

Figure 6: *Table of enthalpies of reaction for three reactions.*

You are given three of the four enthalpies for these reactions, so use Hess's Law to find the unknown $\Delta_r H^\ominus$. First though, choose and label the two routes. For this example we will choose routes that go against the direction of the arrows, to show how this method works:

$$H^+_{(g)} + Br^-_{(g)} \xrightarrow[\text{Route 1}]{\Delta_r H^\circ} H^+_{(aq)} + Br^-_{(aq)}$$

$$-\Delta H_1 \Big\uparrow \Big\downarrow \Delta H_1 \qquad\qquad \Delta H_3 \Big\uparrow$$

$$H_{(g)} + Br_{(g)} \xrightarrow[\text{Route 2}]{\Delta H_2} HBr_{(g)}$$

The first step in the chosen route 2 goes against the direction of the arrow for ΔH_1. The enthalpy change for a backwards reaction is exactly the same size as for the forwards reaction — but with the opposite sign. So the enthalpy change for the first step in route 2 will be $-\Delta H_1$, as shown.

Now just use Hess's Law as before:

Route 1 = Route 2

$\Delta_r H^\ominus = -\Delta H_1 + \Delta H_2 + \Delta H_3$

$\Delta_r H^\ominus = -987 + (-366) + (-85) = -1438$ kJ mol^{-1}.

Practice Questions — Application

Q1   Calculate $\Delta_f H^\ominus$ for the following organic compounds using Hess's Law, and the enthalpies of combustion given in Figure 7 and below:

a) propan-1-ol (C_3H_7OH): $\Delta_c H^\ominus = -2021$ kJ mol^{-1}.

b) ethane-1,2-diol ($C_2H_4(OH)_2$): $\Delta_c H^\ominus = -1180$ kJ mol^{-1}.

c) butan-2-one (C_4H_8O): $\Delta_c H^\ominus = -2442$ kJ mol^{-1}.

Q2   The reaction scheme below involves 7 unknown substances, A-G:

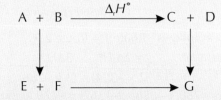

Element	$\Delta_c H^\ominus$
$C_{(s)}$	-394 kJ mol^{-1}
$H_{2(g)}$	-286 kJ mol^{-1}

Figure 7: Enthalpies of combustion for carbon and hydrogen.

Reaction	ΔH (kJ mol^{-1})
A + B → E + F	-837
E + F → G	$+89$
C + D → G	$+424$

Use Hess's Law, along with the data in the table, to calculate the enthalpy change, $\Delta_r H^\ominus$, for the reaction A + B → C + D.

5. Reaction Rates

The rate of a reaction is how quickly the reaction happens.

Collision theory and activation energy

Particles in liquids and gases are always moving and colliding with each other. They don't react every time though — only when the conditions are right. **Collision theory** says that a reaction won't take place between two particles unless they collide in the right direction (they need to be facing each other the right way) and they collide with at least a certain minimum amount of kinetic (movement) energy.

The minimum amount of kinetic energy particles need to react is called the **activation energy**. The particles need this much energy to break the bonds to start the reaction. Reactions with low activation energies often happen pretty easily. But reactions with high activation energies don't. You need to give the particles extra energy by heating them.

Enthalpy profile diagrams

To make things a bit clearer, we can draw an enthalpy profile diagram like the one shown below in Figure 1 (see page 155 for more on enthalpy profile diagrams).

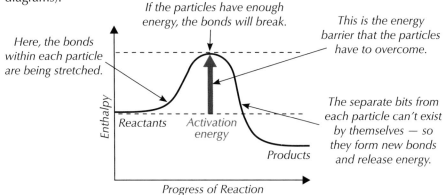

Figure 1: *An enthalpy profile diagram.*

Enthalpy profile diagrams can be used to work out the enthalpy change (ΔH) of a reaction, and whether it is exothermic or endothermic (see pages 154-155). ΔH is the difference between the enthalpy of the reactants and the enthalpy of the products on the diagram. If the products have a lower enthalpy than the reactants, the reaction is exothermic. If the products have a higher enthalpy than the reactants, the reaction is endothermic.

Tip: Remember, for exothermic reactions ΔH is negative. For endothermic reactions, ΔH is positive.

Example

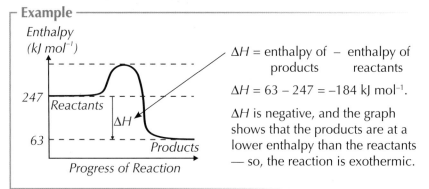

ΔH = enthalpy of − enthalpy of products reactants

$\Delta H = 63 - 247 = -184$ kJ mol^{-1}.

ΔH is negative, and the graph shows that the products are at a lower enthalpy than the reactants — so, the reaction is exothermic.

Boltzmann distributions

Imagine looking down on Oxford Street when it's teeming with people. You'll see some people ambling along slowly, some hurrying quickly, but most of them will be walking with a moderate speed. It's the same with the molecules in a liquid or gas. Some don't have much kinetic energy and move slowly. Others have loads of kinetic energy and whizz along. But most molecules are somewhere in between. If you plot a graph of the numbers of molecules in a substance with different kinetic energies you get a **Boltzmann distribution**. The Boltzmann distribution is a theoretical model that has been developed to explain scientific observations (see page 1). It looks like this:

Figure 2: *Ludwig Boltzmann, the Austrian physicist who developed the ideas on the energy distribution of gas molecules.*

Tip: In science, it's important to be able to look at theoretical models and use the ideas behind them to explain the results of experiments.

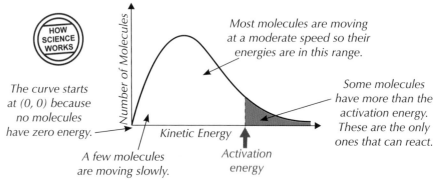

Figure 3: *A Boltzmann distribution curve showing the different kinetic energies of molecules in a gas.*

The effect of temperature on reaction rate

If you increase the temperature of a substance, the molecules will, on average, have more kinetic energy and will move faster. So, a greater proportion of molecules will have at least the activation energy and be able to react. This changes the shape of the Boltzmann distribution curve — it pushes it over to the right (see Figure 4). The total number of molecules is still the same, which means the area under each curve must be the same.

Exam Tip
You need to be able to draw distribution curves for different temperatures so remember — if the temperature increases the curve moves to the right, if it decreases the curve moves to the left.

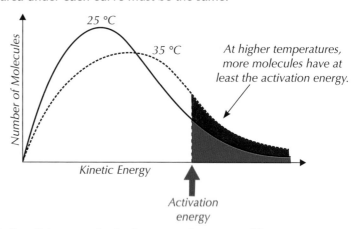

Figure 4: *Two Boltzmann distribution curves for a gas at different temperatures. Increasing the temperature of the gas shifts the distribution of the kinetic energies of the molecules.*

Exam Tip
When drawing Boltzmann distribution curves, make sure your line starts at the origin, but doesn't end touching the x-axis.

Because the molecules are flying about faster, they'll collide more often. This is another reason why increasing the temperature makes a reaction faster. So, small temperature increases can lead to large increases in reaction rate.

The effect of concentration on reaction rate

If you increase the concentration of reactants in a solution, the particles will on average be closer together. If they're closer, they'll collide more often. If there are more collisions, they'll have more chances to react.

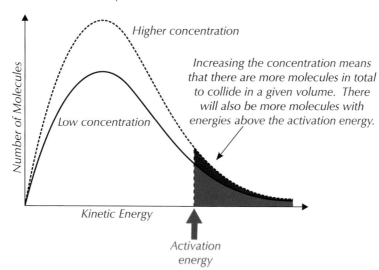

Figure 5: Two Boltzmann distribution curves for a solution at different concentrations.

Tip: Figure 5 refers to the number of molecules in a given volume. Changing the volume as well as the concentration means that two variables in the experiment have changed — you wouldn't be able to tell what was causing the change in the Boltzmann distribution. See page 5 for more on variables.

If any of your reactants are gases, increasing the pressure will increase the rate of reaction. It's pretty much the same as increasing the concentration of a solution — at higher pressures, the particles will be closer together, increasing the chance of collisions. As a result there'll be more successful collisions.

Tip: If one of the reactants is a solid, increasing its surface area makes the reaction faster too.

Practice Questions — Application

Q1 Look at the enthalpy profile diagram below.

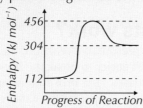

Is the reaction exothermic or endothermic? Explain your answer.

Q2 The two Boltzmann distribution curves shown in Figure 6 are for the same volume of the same gas. Which curve, A or B, is for the gas at a higher temperature? Explain your answer.

Number of Molecules

A

B

Kinetic Energy

Figure 6: Two Boltzmann distribution curves for a volume of gas at different temperatures.

Practice Questions — Fact Recall

Q1 What conditions are required for a collision between two particles to result in a reaction?

Q2 What does the term 'activation energy' mean?

Q3 Explain why a small increase in temperature can lead to a large increase in reaction rate.

Q4 Describe and explain the effect that increasing the concentration of a solution has on the rate of a reaction involving that solution.

Learning Objectives:

- Explain the role of a catalyst in increasing reaction rate without being used up by the overall reaction.

- Explain the role of a catalyst in allowing a reaction to proceed via a different route with lower activation energy, as shown by enthalpy profile diagrams.

- Interpret catalytic behaviour in terms of the Boltzmann distribution.

- Know that a heterogeneous catalyst is in a different phase to the reactants and that a homogeneous catalyst is in the same phase as the reactants.

- Explain that catalysts have great economic importance.

- Explain the benefits of using catalysts for increased sustainability by lowering temperatures and reducing energy demand from combustion of fossil fuels with resulting reduction in CO_2 emissions.

Specification Reference 3.2.2

6. Catalysts

Sometimes you need to speed up a reaction, but you can't (or don't want to) increase the temperature, concentration or pressure any further. That's where catalysts come in.

What is a catalyst?

You can use **catalysts** to make chemical reactions happen faster. A catalyst increases the rate of a reaction by providing an alternative reaction pathway with a lower activation energy. The catalyst is chemically unchanged at the end of the reaction.

Catalysts are great. They don't get used up in reactions, so you only eed a tiny bit of catalyst to catalyse a huge amount of stuff. They do take part in reactions, but they're remade at the end. Catalysts are very fussy about which reactions they catalyse. Many will usually only work on a single reaction. Catalysts save heaps of money in industrial processes.

Example

The Haber-Bosch process uses an iron catalyst to increase the rate of forming ammonia from nitrogen and hydrogen in the following reaction:

$$N_{2(g)} + 3H_{2(g)} \rightleftharpoons 2NH_{3(g)}$$

This reaction has a very high activation energy, due to a very strong N≡N bond in N_2. For the reaction rate to be high enough to make ammonia in any great quantity, the temperature and pressure would have to be extremely high — too high to be practical or profitable.

In reality, the reaction is performed with the use of an iron catalyst, which increases the reaction rate at a workable temperature and pressure (around 400-500 °C and 20 MPa).

How do catalysts work?

When a suitable catalyst is present in a reaction, the reactant molecules bind to the catalyst. This makes it easier to break the bonds, and so the activation energy of the reaction decreases. The broken reactant molecules then form product molecules, and break away from the catalyst.

Enthalpy profiles (see Figure 1) and Boltzmann distribution curves (Figure 2 — next page) can help illustrate how catalysts work.

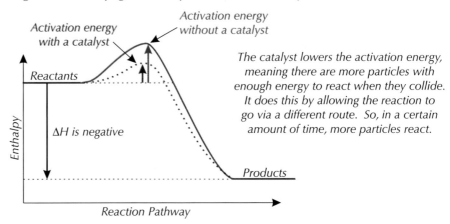

The catalyst lowers the activation energy, meaning there are more particles with enough energy to react when they collide. It does this by allowing the reaction to go via a different route. So, in a certain amount of time, more particles react.

Figure 1: *Enthalpy profile diagram for a reaction with and without a catalyst.*

With a catalyst present, the molecules still have the same amount of energy, so the Boltzmann distribution curve is unchanged. But because the catalyst lowers the activation energy, more of the molecules have energies above this threshold and are able to react, as shown in Figure 2.

Tip: Catalysts speed up the reaction in a different way to increasing temperature, concentration or pressure. These things all change the energy distribution but the addition of a catalyst does not.

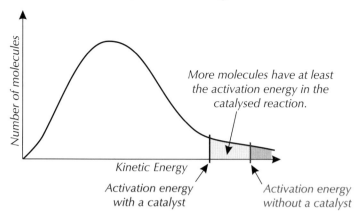

More molecules have at least the activation energy in the catalysed reaction.

Activation energy with a catalyst

Activation energy without a catalyst

Figure 2: *A Boltzmann distribution curve for a reaction with and without a catalyst.*

Homogeneous and heterogeneous catalysts

A **heterogeneous** catalyst is one that is in a different phase from the reactants — i.e. in a different physical state. For example, in the Haber Process (see the previous page), gases are passed over a solid iron catalyst. The reaction happens on the surface of the heterogeneous catalyst. So, increasing the surface area of the catalyst increases the number of molecules that can react at the same time, increasing the rate of the reaction.

Homogeneous catalysts are in the same physical state as the reactants. Usually a homogeneous catalyst is an aqueous catalyst for a reaction between two aqueous solutions. A homogeneous catalyst works by forming an intermediate species. One or more reactants combine with the catalyst to make the intermediate species, which then reacts to form the products and reform the catalyst.

Catalysts in industry

Loads of industries rely on catalysts. They can dramatically lower production costs, and help make better products.

Examples

Using a catalyst changes the properties of poly(ethene).

	Made without a catalyst	Made with a catalyst (a Ziegler-Natta catalyst to be precise)
Properties of poly(ethene)	▪ less dense ▪ less rigid	▪ more dense ▪ more rigid ▪ higher melting point

Figure 3: *A table showing the properties of poly(ethene) made with and without a Ziegler-Natta catalyst.*

Iron is used as a catalyst in ammonia production (see page 170).

Tip: Interesting fact — the chemists Karl Ziegler and Giulio Natta shared the Nobel Prize for chemistry in 1963 for their work developing the Ziegler-Natta catalyst. Fascinating.

Catalysts and the environment

Using catalysts means that lower temperatures and pressures can be used. So energy is saved, meaning less CO_2 is released, and fossil fuel reserves are preserved. They can also reduce waste by allowing a different reaction to be used with a better atom economy. (See page 80 for more on atom economy.)

┌─ Example ──
Making the painkiller ibuprofen by the traditional method involves 6 steps and has an atom economy of 32%. Using catalysts, it can be made in 3 steps with an atom economy of 77%.

Figure 4: *Tablets of the painkiller ibuprofen.*

Catalytic converters on cars are made from alloys of platinum, palladium and rhodium. They reduce the pollution released into the atmosphere by speeding up the following reaction:

$$2CO + 2NO \rightarrow 2CO_2 + N_2$$

But catalysts don't last forever. All catalysts eventually need to be disposed of. The trouble is, many contain nasty toxic compounds, which may leach into the soil if they're sent directly to landfill. So it's important to try to recycle them, or convert them to non-leaching forms. If catalysts contain valuable metals, such as platinum, it's worth recovering and recycling it — and there are special companies eager to do this. The decision whether to recycle the catalyst or to send it to landfill is made by balancing the economic and environmental factors.

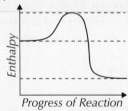

Tip: 'Uncatalysed' just means that no catalyst has been used.

Practice Question — Application

Q1 The enthalpy profile diagram shown below is for an uncatalysed chemical reaction to produce 'Product X'.

Enthalpy vs *Progress of Reaction*

A company wants to produce 'Product X' on a large scale. They are considering using a catalyst.

a) Draw a sketch to show how the addition of a catalyst would affect the enthalpy profile diagram for the reaction.

b) The uncatalysed reaction will only take place at temperatures above 1000 °C. Suggest how adding a catalyst would improve the industrial process.

Exam Tip
You need to be able to give a full description of what a catalyst is.

Practice Questions — Fact Recall

Q1 What is a catalyst?

Q2 Explain why catalysts are used in many industrial processes.

Q3 Explain how a catalyst can speed up the rate of a reaction.

Q4 What's the difference between homogeneous and heterogeneous catalysts?

7. Calculating Reaction Rates

Understanding all about the rates of chemical reactions is a really important part of chemistry. You've already learnt a bit about reaction rates, but now it's time to cover things in a bit more detail.

What are reaction rates?

The **reaction rate** is how fast a reaction takes place. It is defined as the change in the amount of reactants or products per unit time (normally per second). The units for the rate of a reaction will be 'what you're measuring per unit of time'. E.g. $g \, s^{-1}$ or $cm^3 \, s^{-1}$:

$$\text{rate of reaction} = \frac{\text{amount of reactant used or product formed}}{\text{time}}$$

Measuring the progress of a reaction

If you want to find the rate of a reaction, you need to be able to follow the reaction as it's occurring. Although there are quite a few ways to follow reactions, not every method works for every reaction. You've got to pick a property that changes as the reaction goes on. Here are a few examples:

Change in mass

When the product is a gas, its formation can be measured using a mass balance.

PRACTICAL ACTIVITY GROUP **9**

Time (s)	Mass (g)
0	280.0
30	279.3
60	278.7
90	278.2
120	278.0
150	277.9
180	277.8
210	277.7
240	277.7
270	277.7

Figure 2: *Results of the experiment carried out in Figure 1.*

— Example —

This would work for the reaction between an acid and a carbonate in which carbon dioxide gas is given off.

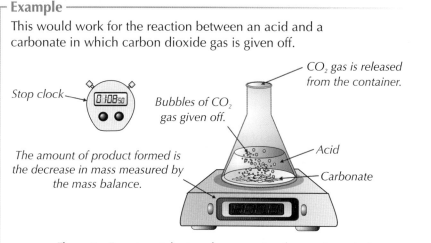

Stop clock

Bubbles of CO_2 gas given off.

CO_2 gas is released from the container.

Acid

Carbonate

The amount of product formed is the decrease in mass measured by the mass balance.

Figure 1: *Experimental set-up for measuring the reaction rate by monitoring the change in mass of a reaction mixture.*

When the reaction starts, you should start a stop clock or timer. Then take mass measurements at regular time intervals. Make a table with a column for 'time' and a column for 'mass' and fill it in as the reaction goes on (see Figure 2). You'll know the reaction is finished when the reading on the mass balance stops decreasing. This method is very accurate and easy to use but does release gas into the room, which could be dangerous if the gas is toxic or flammable. So it's best to carry out the experiment in a fume cupboard.

Tip: Acids can be dangerous and releasing gases into the lab (even in a fume cupboard) is potentially hazardous, so make sure you carry out a risk assessment before carrying out these experiments.

Time (s)	Volume (cm³)
0	0.0
30	6.1
60	10.9
90	15.2
120	17.7
150	20.0
180	21.1
210	21.9
240	22.0
270	22.0

Figure 4: *Results of the experiment carried out in Figure 3.*

Gas volume

If a gas is given off, you could collect it in a gas syringe and record how much you've got at regular time intervals.

PRACTICAL ACTIVITY GROUP 9

┌ **Example** ─────

This would work for the reaction between magnesium and an acid in which hydrogen gas is given off.

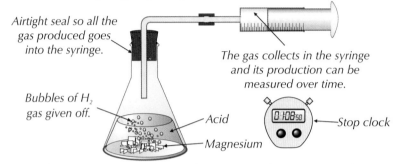

Airtight seal so all the gas produced goes into the syringe.

The gas collects in the syringe and its production can be measured over time.

Bubbles of H₂ gas given off.

Acid

Magnesium

Stop clock

Figure 3: *Experimental set-up for measuring the reaction rate by monitoring the volume of gas given off by a reaction mixture.*

The experiment is carried out in a similar way as when measuring the change in mass but this time you're measuring the volume of the gas in the syringe rather than the mass from the balance (see Figure 4). This method is accurate but vigorous reactions can blow the plunger out of the syringe. Because no gas escapes, this method can be used for toxic or flammable gases.

Other methods

There are a few other ways to measure the amount of reactant used or product formed. For example, you can monitor changes in pressure (for gases), changes in colour (for solutions) or changes in conductivity. The best method depends on the reaction you're looking at.

Working out reaction rates

If you draw a graph where the x-axis is time and the y-axis is a measure of either the amount of reactant or product, then the reaction rate is just the gradient of the graph. If the graph's a curve, you have to draw a **tangent** to the curve and find the gradient of that. A tangent is a line that just touches a curve and has the same gradient as the curve does at that point. Figure 5 shows how a graph of the mass of a reaction vessel against time might look.

Tip: The rate of reaction slows down as time progresses. This is because the reactants get used up, and so collisions between reactant molecules become less likely.

Tip: When you're drawing a tangent, try to do it so that the gaps between the graph line and the tangent on either side of the point are as even as possible. i.e.

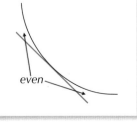

even

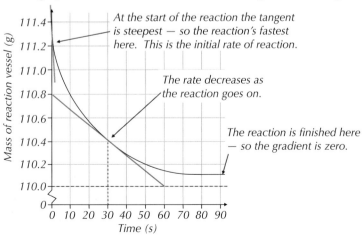

At the start of the reaction the tangent is steepest — so the reaction's fastest here. This is the initial rate of reaction.

The rate decreases as the reaction goes on.

The reaction is finished here — so the gradient is zero.

Figure 5: *Graph showing the mass of a reaction vessel against time.*

The gradient of a tangent is the change in vertical height (Δy) divided by the change in horizontal width (Δx).

Tip: Don't forget, the x-axis is the horizontal axis and the y-axis is the vertical axis.

— Example — **Maths Skills**

On the mass-time graph in Figure 5, the gradient of the blue tangent is the rate of reaction at 30 seconds. This tangent makes a triangle. The change in y is –0.8 and the change in x is 60, so:

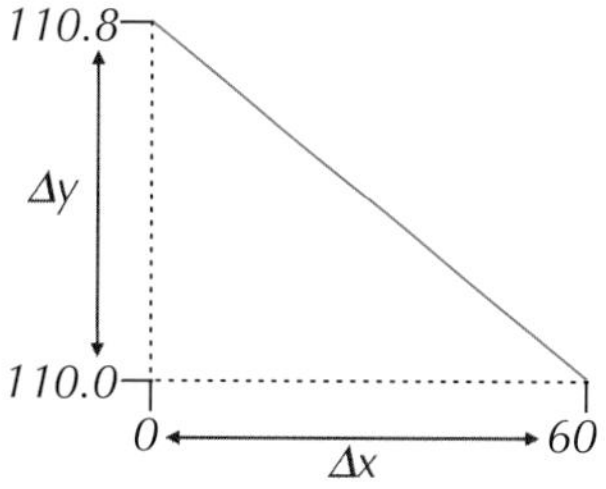

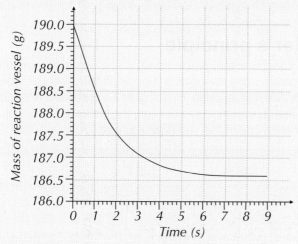

$$\text{Gradient} = \frac{\Delta y}{\Delta x} = \frac{-0.8}{60} = -0.013 \text{ g s}^{-1}$$

This means that the rate of reaction at 30 seconds is 0.013 g s^{-1}.

In this context, the sign of the gradient doesn't really matter — it's a negative gradient when you're measuring the mass of a reaction vessel because the reactant decreases. If you measured the volume of gas produced, it'd be a positive gradient.

Practice Question — Application

Q1 The mass-time graph for a reaction is shown below:

Exam Tip
Don't be afraid to draw on the graphs you're given in the exam — you'll need to draw tangents to find the gradients of curves.

Determine the rate of this reaction after:
a) 1 second,
b) 2 seconds,
c) 4 seconds.

Practice Questions — Fact Recall

Q1 What is a reaction rate?

Q2 Give an example of a unit of reaction rate.

Q3 Suggest two ways in which the progress of a reaction could be measured.

Q4 a) Describe the experimental procedure used to produce a mass-time graph for a reaction.

b) Explain how you could determine the rate of a reaction at a particular time using a mass-time graph.

8. Reversible Reactions

Learning Objectives:

- Explain that a dynamic equilibrium exists in a closed system when the rate of the forward reaction is equal to the rate of the reverse reaction and the concentrations of reactants and products do not change.

- Be able to apply Le Chatelier's principle to deduce qualitatively (from appropriate information) the effect of a change in temperature, concentration or pressure, on the position of equilibrium in a homogeneous system in equilibrium.

- Explain that a catalyst increases the rate of both forward and reverse reactions in an equilibrium by the same amount, resulting in an unchanged equilibrium position.

- Be able to explain the importance in the chemical industry of a compromise between chemical equilibrium and reaction rate in deciding the operational conditions.

- Describe the techniques and procedures used to investigate changes to the position of equilibrium for changes in concentration and temperature.

**Specification
Reference 3.2.3**

We usually think of a reaction as a one-way process to make products from reactants. In reality though, many reactions are reversible.

Dynamic equilibrium

Lots of chemical reactions are reversible — they go both ways. To show a reaction's reversible, you stick in a $\rightleftharpoons$.

> **Example**
>
> Hydrogen will react with iodine to produce hydrogen iodide:
>
> $$H_{2(g)} + I_{2(g)} \rightleftharpoons 2HI_{(g)}$$
>
> This reaction can go in either direction —
>
> forwards: $H_{2(g)} + I_{2(g)} \rightarrow 2HI_{(g)}$ ...or backwards: $2HI_{(g)} \rightarrow H_{2(g)} + I_{2(g)}$

As the reactants get used up, the forward reaction slows down — and as more product is formed, the reverse reaction speeds up. After a while, the forward reaction will be going at exactly the same rate as the backward reaction so the concentration of reactants and products won't be changing any more — it'll seem like nothing's happening. It's a bit like you're digging a hole while someone else is filling it in at exactly the same speed. This is called a **dynamic equilibrium**. At equilibrium, the concentrations of reactants and products stay constant. A dynamic equilibrium can only happen in a **closed system**. This just means nothing can get in or out.

Le Chatelier's principle

If you change the concentration, pressure or temperature of a reversible reaction, you're going to alter the position of equilibrium. This just means you'll end up with different amounts of reactants and products at equilibrium. If the position of equilibrium moves to the left, the backwards reaction is faster than the forwards reaction, and so you'll get more reactants.

> **Example**
>
> If the position of equilibrium in the reaction $H_{2(g)} + I_{2(g)} \rightleftharpoons 2HI_{(g)}$ shifts to the left, the backwards reaction is fastest, so more H_2 and I_2 are produced:
>
> $$H_{2(g)} + I_{2(g)} \leftharpoondown 2HI_{(g)}$$

If the position of equilibrium moves to the right, the forwards reaction is faster than the backwards reaction, and so you'll get more products.

> **Example**
>
> If the position of equilibrium in the reaction $H_{2(g)} + I_{2(g)} \rightleftharpoons 2HI_{(g)}$ shifts to the right, the forwards reaction is fastest, so more HI is produced:
>
> $$H_{2(g)} + I_{2(g)} \rightharpoonup 2HI_{(g)}$$

Le Chatelier's principle tells you how the position of equilibrium will change if a condition changes:

> If there's a change in concentration, pressure or temperature, the equilibrium will move to help counteract the change.

So, basically, if you raise the temperature, the position of equilibrium will shift to try to cool things down. And, if you raise the pressure or concentration, the position of equilibrium will shift to try to reduce it again. Catalysts have no effect on the position of equilibrium.

Using Le Chatelier's principle

Changing concentration

If you increase the concentration of a reactant, the equilibrium tries to get rid of the extra reactant. It does this by making more product. So the equilibrium's shifted to the right. If you increase the concentration of the product, the equilibrium tries to remove the extra product. This makes the reverse reaction go faster. So the equilibrium shifts to the left. Decreasing the concentrations has the opposite effect.

─ Examples ─────────────────────────────

Sulfur dioxide reacts with oxygen to produce sulfur trioxide:

$$2SO_{2(g)} + O_{2(g)} \rightleftharpoons 2SO_{3(g)}$$

If you increase the concentration of SO_2 or O_2, the equilibrium tries to get rid of it by making more SO_3, so the equilibrium shifts to the right. If you increase the concentration of SO_3, the equilibrium shifts to the left to make the backwards reaction faster to get rid of the extra SO_3.

In the Haber process, nitrogen reacts with hydrogen to produce ammonia:

$$N_{2(g)} + 3H_{2(g)} \rightleftharpoons 2NH_{3(g)}$$

If you increase the concentration of N_2 or H_2, the equilibrium shifts to the right and you'll make more NH_3. If you increase the concentration of NH_3, the equilibrium shifts to the left and you'll make more N_2 and H_2.

Figure 1: *Henri Le Chatelier, the French physical chemist who developed Le Chatelier's principle in the 1880s.*

Changing pressure

Changing the pressure only affects equilibria involving gases. Increasing the pressure shifts the equilibrium to the side with fewer gas molecules. This reduces the pressure. Decreasing the pressure shifts the equilibrium to the side with more gas molecules. This raises the pressure again.

─ Examples ─────────────────────────────

When sulfur dioxide reacts with oxygen you get sulfur trioxide:

$$2SO_{2(g)} + O_{2(g)} \rightleftharpoons 2SO_{3(g)}$$

There are 3 moles on the left, but only 2 on the right. So, an increase in pressure shifts the equilibrium to the right, making more SO_3 and reducing the pressure. Decreasing the pressure favours the backwards reaction, so the equilibrium shifts to the left and more SO_2 and O_2 will be made to increase the pressure.

Methane reacts with steam to produce carbon monoxide and hydrogen:

$$CH_{4(g)} + H_2O_{(g)} \rightleftharpoons CO_{(g)} + 3H_{2(g)}$$

There are 2 moles on the left and 4 on the right. So for this reaction an increase in pressure shifts the equilibrium to the left, making more CH_4 and H_2O. Decreasing the pressure shifts the equilibrium to the right to make more CO and H_2. This reaction is used in industry to produce hydrogen. It is best performed at a low pressure to favour the forwards reaction so that more H_2 is produced.

Tip: If there are the same number of moles of gas on each side of the equation, changing the pressure won't change the position of equilibrium.

Changing temperature

Increasing the temperature means adding heat energy. The equilibrium shifts in the endothermic (positive ΔH) direction to absorb this energy. Decreasing the temperature removes heat energy. The equilibrium shifts in the exothermic (negative ΔH) direction to try to replace the heat energy. If the forward reaction is endothermic, the reverse reaction will be exothermic, and vice versa.

This reaction's exothermic in the forward direction, which means it is endothermic in the backward direction.

Exothermic→

$$2SO_{2(g)} + O_{2(g)} \rightleftharpoons 2SO_{3(g)} \qquad \Delta H = -197 \text{ kJ mol}^{-1}.$$

←Endothermic

If you increase the temperature, the equilibrium shifts to the left (the endothermic direction) to absorb the extra heat. This means more SO_2 and O_2 are produced. If you decrease the temperature, the equilibrium shifts to the right (the exothermic direction) to produce more heat. This means more SO_3 is produced.

This reaction's endothermic in the forward direction (and so exothermic in the backward direction).

Endothermic→

$$C_{(s)} + H_2O_{(g)} \rightleftharpoons CO_{(g)} + H_{2(g)} \qquad \Delta H = +131 \text{ kJ mol}^{-1}.$$

←Exothermic

Increasing the temperature will shift the equilibrium to the right, producing more CO and H_2. Decreasing the temperature shifts the equilibrium to the left, producing more C and H_2O.

Adding a catalyst

Catalysts have no effect on the position of equilibrium. They speed up the forward and reverse reactions by the same amount. They can't increase yield — but they do mean equilibrium is reached faster.

Ethanol production

HOW SCIENCE WORKS

The industrial production of ethanol is a good example of why Le Chatelier's principle is important in real life. Ethanol is produced via a reversible exothermic reaction between ethene and steam:

$$C_2H_{4(g)} + H_2O_{(g)} \rightleftharpoons C_2H_5OH_{(g)} \qquad \Delta H = -46 \text{ kJ mol}^{-1}$$

The industrial conditions for the reaction are:

- a pressure of 60-70 atmospheres
- a temperature of 300 °C
- a phosphoric acid catalyst.

Because it's an exothermic reaction, lower temperatures favour the forward reaction. This means that at lower temperatures more ethene and steam is converted to ethanol — you get a better **yield**. But lower temperatures mean a slower rate of reaction. You'd be daft to try to get a really high yield of ethanol if it's going to take you 10 years. So the 300 °C is a compromise between maximum yield and a faster reaction.

Higher pressures favour the forward reaction, so a pressure of 60-70 atmospheres is used — high pressure moves the reaction to the side with fewer molecules of gas. Increasing the pressure also increases the rate of reaction. Cranking up the pressure as high as you can sounds like a great idea so far. But high pressures are expensive to produce. You need stronger pipes and containers to withstand high pressure. And, in this process, increasing the pressure can also cause side reactions to occur. So the 60-70 atmospheres is a compromise between maximum yield and expense. In the end, it all comes down to minimising costs.

Tip: An enthalpy change given with a reversible reaction always refers to the forwards reaction, unless you're told otherwise.

Exam Tip
In an exam question, make it clear exactly how the equilibrium shift opposes a temperature change — i.e. by removing or producing heat.

Tip: A lot of exam questions on this section ask about the effect of increasing temperature, pressure and concentration. But their effect on reaction rate is different to their effect on the position of equilibrium. Make sure you're clear which one you're being asked about.

Tip: The yield is the amount of product you get from a reaction. Increasing the reaction rate will give you a higher yield in a given time, but you need to shift the equilibrium to increase the maximum yield.

Only a small proportion of the ethene reacts each time the gases pass through the catalyst. To save money and raw materials, the unreacted ethene is separated from the liquid ethanol and recycled back into the reactor. Thanks to this, around 95% of the ethene is eventually converted to ethanol.

Investigating equilibrium position

Some experiments can be used to investigate how equilibrium position changes with changing conditions. The best experiments to highlight these changes are ones where a change in equilibrium position brings about a colour change.

Changing temperature

In a closed system, an increase in temperature will push a reaction at equilibrium in the endothermic direction and a decrease in temperature will push the equilibrium in the exothermic direction.

Figure 2: *Equilibrium between $NO_{2(g)}$ (brown) and $N_2O_{4(g)}$ (colourless). The tube in the middle is at room temperature. The tube on the left is in a warm water bath. The tube on the right is cooled in ice.*

Example

The brown gas NO_2 exists in equilibrium with the colourless gas N_2O_4. This reversible reaction can be used to investigate the effect of changing temperature on equilibrium position. The forward reaction is exothermic, which means the reverse reaction is endothermic.

Exothermic→

$$2NO_{2(g)} \rightleftharpoons N_2O_{4(g)} \qquad \Delta H = -57.2 \text{ kJ mol}^{-1}$$
brown   colourless

←Endothermic

HOW SCIENCE WORKS

To carry out the experiment, place two sealed tubes containing the equilibrium mixture in water baths — one in a warm water bath and one in an ice bath, and observe the colours of the mixtures. The tube in the warm water bath will change to a darker brown colour (Figure 2) as the equilibrium shifts to the left to absorb the extra heat by favouring the endothermic reaction. The tube in the ice bath will go a paler colour (Figure 2) as the equilibrium shifts to the right to replace the lost heat by favouring the exothermic reaction.

Tip: NO_2 is extremely toxic and can be lethal. If a tube breaks during this experiment, the lab should be evacuated. Remember to carry out a full risk assessment before the experiment.

Changing concentration

In a closed system, changing the concentrations of either the reactants or products will change the equilibrium position. Adding more reactants will move the equilibrium to the right. Adding more products will move the equilibrium to the left.

Tip: It might seem weird that if you add more product you end up with more reactant and vice versa. Make sure you're comfortable with Le Chatelier's principle and it will make more sense.

Example

Mixing iron(III) nitrate (yellow) and potassium thiocyanate (colourless) solutions results in a reversible reaction where the product is iron(III) thiocyanate (blood red). You end up with the following equilibrium...

$$Fe^{3+}_{(aq)} + SCN^-_{(aq)} \rightleftharpoons Fe(SCN)^{2+}_{(aq)}$$
yellow   colourless   blood red

HOW SCIENCE WORKS

The equilibrium mixture is a reddish colour. You can investigate what happens to the equilibrium position when the concentrations of reactants or products are changed by monitoring the colour of the solution.

Figure 3: *Test tubes 2, 3 and 4 from the iron(III) thiocyanate equilibrium experiment.*

Add equal amounts of the equilibrium mixture to four test tubes.

- Test tube 1 is the 'control' and nothing is added to it. It keeps its initial reddish colour.
- Add a few drops of iron(III) nitrate solution to test tube 2. The mixture turns a deep red colour (Figure 3).
- Add a few drops of potassium thiocyanate solution to test tube 3. The mixture turns a deep red colour (Figure 3).
- Add a few drops of iron(III) thiocyanate solution to test tube 4. The mixture turns a yellow colour (Figure 3).

When more reactants are added, the equilibrium moves to the right to remove them. The forward reaction is favoured and more product is made (as seen by the deep red colour in test tubes 2 and 3).
When more product is added, the equilibrium moves to the left to remove them. The reverse reaction is favoured and more reactants are made (as seen by the yellowish colour in test tube 4).

Practice Questions — Application

Q1 An industrial process uses the following reversible reaction:

$$A_{(g)} + 2B_{(g)} \rightleftharpoons C_{(g)} + D_{(g)} \qquad \Delta H = -189 \text{ kJ mol}^{-1}.$$

a) Explain the effect of increasing the concentration of A on the position of the equilibrium.

b) Explain the effect of increasing the pressure on the position of the equilibrium.

c) Explain the effect of increasing the temperature on the position of the equilibrium.

d) Briefly outline the best reaction conditions (in terms of high or low concentration, pressure and temperature) to maximise the production of product D.

Q2 What will be the effect of increasing the pressure on the position of equilibrium of the following reaction?

$$H_{2(g)} + I_{2(g)} \rightleftharpoons 2HI_{(g)}$$

Explain your answer.

Exam Tip
You may get asked why the ideal conditions for a reaction aren't used in reality. Often the answer is to do with the cost of generating the conditions or their safety.

Practice Questions — Fact Recall

Q1 What does it mean if a reaction is in dynamic equilibrium?

Q2 What is Le Chatelier's principle?

Q3 How does the addition of a catalyst affect the position of equilibrium in a reversible reaction?

Q4 Ethanol is produced using a reaction that gives you a higher yield at a low temperature. Explain why a low temperature is not used to produce ethanol industrially.

9. The Equilibrium Constant

Equilibrium constants are important when you're looking at reversible reactions. The next few pages are all about them.

Learning Objectives:

- Deduce expressions for the equilibrium constant, K_c, for homogeneous reactions.
- Calculate the values of the equilibrium constant, K_c, from provided equilibrium concentrations.
- Estimate the position of equilibrium from the magnitude of K_c.

Specification Reference 3.2.3

The equilibrium constant, K_c

When you have a homogeneous reaction (where all the reactants and products are in the same physical state) that's reached dynamic equilibrium, you can work out the **equilibrium constant**, K_c, using the concentrations of the products and reactants at equilibrium. K_c gives you an idea of how far to the left or right the equilibrium is. Before you can calculate K_c, you have to write an expression for it. Here's how:

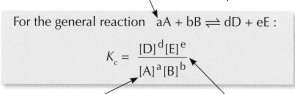

The lower-case letters a, b, d and e are the number of moles of each substance in the equation.

For the general reaction $aA + bB \rightleftharpoons dD + eE$:

$$K_c = \frac{[D]^d [E]^e}{[A]^a [B]^b}$$

The square brackets, [ ], mean concentration in mol dm⁻³.

The products go on the top line and the reactants go on the bottom line.

--- **Example** ---

For the reaction $H_{2(g)} + I_{2(g)} \rightleftharpoons 2HI_{(g)}$ there are two reactants (H_2 and I_2) and one product (HI). There's one mole of each of the reactants and two moles of the product so the expression for K_c is:

$$K_c = \frac{[HI]^2}{[H_2]^1 [I_2]^1} = \frac{[HI]^2}{[H_2][I_2]}$$

Calculating K_c

If you know the equilibrium concentrations, just bung them in your expression. Then with a bit of help from the old calculator, you can work out the value for K_c. The units are a bit trickier though — they vary, so they're not the same for every reaction.

--- **Example** — **Maths Skills** ---

For the hydrogen iodide example above, the equilibrium concentrations are: [HI] = 0.80 mol dm⁻³, [H_2] = 0.10 mol dm⁻³ and [I_2] = 0.10 mol dm⁻³ at 640 K. What is the equilibrium constant for this reaction at 640 K?

Just stick the concentrations into the expression for K_c:

$$K_c = \frac{[HI]^2}{[H_2][I_2]} = \frac{0.8^2}{0.1 \times 0.1} = 64$$

To work out the units of K_c put the units in the expression instead of the numbers:

$$K_c = \frac{(\text{mol dm}^{-3})^2}{(\text{mol dm}^{-3})(\text{mol dm}^{-3})} = \frac{\cancel{(\text{mol dm}^{-3})}\cancel{(\text{mol dm}^{-3})}}{\cancel{(\text{mol dm}^{-3})}\cancel{(\text{mol dm}^{-3})}}$$

The concentration units cancel, so there are no units and K_c is just **64**.

Exam Tip
In exam questions on K_c you'll often be told the temperature. You don't need this value for your calculation — it's just so you know the temperature is constant.

Tip: Don't forget — when you're calculating K_c the products go on the top line and the reactants go on the bottom line.

Exam Tip
K_c has no units in this example but this won't always be the case. You <u>won't</u> be expected to work out the units if you're taking the AS level exam but you <u>will</u> need to know how to do it if you're doing A level.

Tip: If the units end up as (1 / mol dm⁻³), you write that as mol⁻¹ dm³.

A change in temperature can change the position of equilibrium so K_c varies with temperature. That's why you'll often be asked what K_c is at a specific temperature.

Estimating the position of equilibrium

K_c will increase when the quantities of the products increase and the quantities of the reactants decrease. So an increase in K_c means the equilibrium has shifted to the right. If K_c decreases, that means the quantities of reactants have increased and the quantities of products have decreased, so the equilibrium has moved to the left. The greater the increase or decrease in K_c is, the more the equilibrium has moved.

Practice Questions — Application

Q1 The following equilibrium exists under certain conditions:

$$C_2H_4 + H_2O \rightleftharpoons C_2H_5OH$$

Write out the expression for the equilibrium constant, K_c, for this reaction.

Q2 Under certain conditions the following equilibrium is established:

$$2SO_2 + O_2 \rightleftharpoons 2SO_3$$

a) Write out an expression for K_c for this reaction.

At a certain temperature the equilibrium concentrations for the three reagents were found to be:

$SO_2 = 0.250$ mol dm^{-3} , $O_2 = 0.180$ mol dm^{-3} , $SO_3 = 0.360$ mol dm^{-3}

b) Calculate K_c for this equilibrium.

Practice Questions — Fact Recall

Q1 Write out an expression for K_c for the general reaction:
$$aA + bB \rightleftharpoons dD + eE$$

Q2 Why is K_c often given at a certain, stated temperature?

Q3 K_c for a certain reaction at equilibrium is 0.012 at 298 K. For the same reaction at 350 K, the value of K_c was found to be 2.048. What is the effect of increasing the temperature on the position of equilibrium for this reaction?

Section Summary

Make sure you know...

- That 'standard conditions' mean 100 kPa and 298 K and 'standard state' means the physical state of a substance under standard conditions.

- That enthalpy change, ΔH (in kJ mol^{-1}), is the heat energy transferred in a reaction at constant pressure.

- That $\Delta H^\ominus$ is the enthalpy change for a reaction where the reactants and products are in their standard states and the measurements are made at 100 kPa pressure and a stated temperature (usually 298 K).

- That $\Delta_r H^\ominus$ is the enthalpy change when a reaction occurs in the molar quantities shown in the chemical equation, under standard conditions with all reactants and products in their standard states.

- That $\Delta_f H^\ominus$ is the enthalpy change when 1 mole of a compound is formed from its elements in their standard states under standard conditions.

- That $\Delta_c H^\ominus$ is the enthalpy change when 1 mole of a substance is completely burned in oxygen under standard conditions.

- That $\Delta_{neut} H^\ominus$ is the enthalpy change when solutions of an acid and an alkali react together to form 1 mole of water, under standard conditions.

- That exothermic reactions give out energy, so ΔH is negative.

- That endothermic reactions absorb energy, so ΔH is positive.

- How to draw and interpret an enthalpy profile diagram for a reaction, identifying the activation energy, the enthalpy change of the reaction, and whether the reaction is exothermic or endothermic.

- That the minimum amount of kinetic energy required for a reaction is called the activation energy.

- That average bond enthalpies tell us the energy needed to break one mole of bonds in the gas phase, averaged over many different compounds.

- How to use average bond enthalpies to calculate enthalpy changes for reactions, using the equation:
Enthalpy change of reaction = Total energy absorbed – Total energy released.

- How to measure enthalpy changes directly in the lab.

- How to calculate the heat lost or gained (q) by a reaction in the laboratory using the equation $q = mc\Delta T$, where m is the mass of the reaction mixture, c is its specific heat capacity, and ΔT is the temperature change due to the reaction.

- That Hess's Law says that:
The total enthalpy change of a reaction is always the same, no matter which route is taken.

- How to use Hess's Law to calculate enthalpy changes for reactions from other enthalpies of reaction.

- How to use Hess's Law to calculate enthalpy changes for reactions from enthalpies of formation.

- How to use Hess's Law to calculate enthalpy changes for reactions from enthalpies of combustion.

- That the Boltzmann distribution describes the spread of energies of the molecules in a liquid or gas.

- How to draw and interpret Boltzmann distribution curves for substances at different temperatures.

- That increasing the concentration of reactants (or the pressure if they're gases) will increase the reaction rate, because the molecules will be closer together and so more likely to collide and react.

- That a catalyst is a substance that increases the rate of a reaction by providing an alternative pathway with a lower activation energy, and is chemically unchanged at the end of the reaction.

- That catalysts do not change the shape of Boltzmann distribution curves.

- That heterogeneous catalysts are in a different physical state to the reactants and homogeneous catalysts are in the same physical state as the reactants.

- That catalysts have a great economic importance.

- That using catalysts has benefits in terms of environmental sustainability.

- How to measure the rates of chemical reactions, including the measurement of mass and gas volume.

- How to calculate the rate of a reaction using the gradient of a graph showing how a physical quantity changes over time.
- That reversible reactions can reach an equilibrium, where the concentrations of reactants and products stay constant and the forwards and backwards reactions have the same reaction rate.
- That Le Chatelier's principle states that "if there's a change in concentration, pressure or temperature, the equilibrium will move to help counteract the change."
- That increasing the concentration of a reactant shifts the equilibrium to remove the extra reactant.
- That increasing the pressure shifts the equilibrium in favour of the reaction that produces the fewest moles of gas, in order to reduce the pressure.
- That increasing the temperature shifts the equilibrium in favour of the endothermic reaction, to remove the excess heat. (Low temperatures favour exothermic reactions.)
- That a catalyst does not affect the position of equilibrium in a reversible reaction.
- Why there sometimes has to be a compromise between chemical equilibrium and reaction rate in industry.
- How to describe the experimental techniques used to investigate how changes in concentration and temperature affect the position of equilibrium.
- That K_c is the equilibrium constant.
- How to deduce expressions for the equilibrium constant, K_c.
- How to calculate K_c and its units from the equilibrium concentrations for a reaction.
- How to estimate the position of equilibrium from the magnitude of K_c.

Exam-style Questions

1 Two Boltzmann energy distributions for molecules of a gas are shown below.

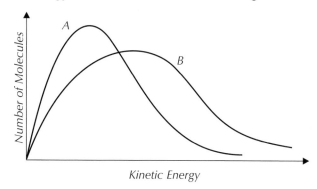

(a) What does the kinetic energy value at the maximum height on curve A represent?

    A The total number of molecules in the distribution.

    B The most likely energy of molecules in the distribution.

    C The activation energy of the reaction.

    D The enthalpy change of formation for the molecule.

(1 mark)

(b) What does distribution B represent?

    A Distribution A at lower concentration.

    B Distribution A at lower temperature.

    C Distribution A at higher temperature.

    D Distribution A at higher concentration.

(1 mark)

2 1.5 g of magnesium is added to a conical flask containing 40 cm^3 1.0 mol dm^{-3} hydrochloric acid and the volume of hydrogen gas given off is measured, over time, using a gas syringe. A series of identical experiments is then carried out with increasing concentrations of hydrochloric acid to see what effect this has on the rate of reaction. Which of the following variables is the independent variable in the experiment?

    A Concentration of hydrochloric acid.

    B Volume of hydrochloric acid.

    C Mass of magnesium added.

    D Volume of hydrogen gas produced.

(1 mark)

3   A chemical factory produces ethanol (C_2H_5OH) from ethene (C_2H_4) and steam, using the following reversible reaction:

$$C_2H_{4(g)} + H_2O_{(g)} \rightleftharpoons C_2H_5OH_{(g)} \qquad \Delta H = -46 \text{ kJ mol}^{-1}$$

The reaction is carried out under the following conditions:

Pressure = 60 atm
Temperature = 300 °C
Catalyst = phosphoric acid

(a)   Without the phosphoric acid catalyst the rate of reaction is so slow that dynamic equilibrium takes a very long time to be reached.

Describe what it means for a reaction to be at dynamic equilibrium.

(2 marks)

(b)   The conditions for the reaction were chosen with consideration to Le Chatelier's principle. Explain why the pressure chosen for the process is a compromise.

(3 marks)

(c)   A leak in one of the pipes reduces the amount of steam in the reaction mixture.

Explain the effect this has on the maximum yield of ethanol.

(3 marks)

(d)   The equilibrium concentrations are: $[C_2H_5OH]$ = 2.70 mol dm^{-3}, $[C_2H_4]$ = 0.400 mol dm^{-3} and $[H_2O]$ = 0.400 mol dm^{-3}.

Calculate the equilibrium constant for this reaction at 60 atm and 300 °C.

(2 marks)

4   Two gases react together in an exothermic reaction.
The reaction has an activation energy of 90 kJ mol^{-1}.
The enthalpy change for the reaction is −150 kJ mol^{-1}.

(a) (i)   In terms of collision theory, what is meant by the term 'activation energy'?

(2 marks)

(ii)   Sketch the enthalpy profile diagram for the reaction.
Label your diagram to show the axis labels, the activation energy and the enthalpy change of the reaction.

(4 marks)

(b)   The reactants are heated.
Explain the effect this will have on the rate of the reaction.

(3 marks)

(c)   Explain the effect that lowering the pressure has on the rate of the reaction.

(3 marks)

(d) A catalyst is added to the reaction.

(i) Define the term catalyst.

(1 mark)

(ii) Explain how a catalyst increases the rate of reaction using an enthalpy profile diagram and a Boltzmann distribution curve.

You should organise your answer and use the correct technical terms.

(6 marks)

5 The table below shows the standard enthalpy change of combustion, $\Delta_c H^\ominus$, for carbon, hydrogen and octane ($C_8H_{18(l)}$).

The standard enthalpy of formation of octane can be calculated from this data using Hess's Law.

	$\Delta_c H^\ominus$
$C_{(s)}$	-394 kJ mol^{-1}
$H_{2(g)}$	-286 kJ mol^{-1}
$C_8H_{18(l)}$	-5470 kJ mol^{-1}

(a) Write a balanced chemical equation for the complete combustion of octane.

(1 mark)

(b) (i) Use your answer to part **(a)** and the data in the table above to calculate the standard enthalpy change of formation of octane, $\Delta_f H^\ominus$.

(3 marks)

(ii) State whether the formation of octane is exothermic or endothermic.

Explain your answer.

(2 marks)

(c) A calorimeter, containing 325 g of water ($c = 4.18$ J g^{-1} K^{-1}), was used to measure the enthalpy change of combustion of octane ($M_r = 114$). 0.4503 g of octane was burnt, which increased the temperature of the water by 13.0 K.

(i) Calculate the measured enthalpy change of combustion of octane.

(2 marks)

(ii) Give two possible reasons why the measured enthalpy change of combustion is different to the value given in the table above.

(2 marks)

6 Alkenes are very important in the chemical industry.

(a) The structure of the alkene but-1-ene is shown below.

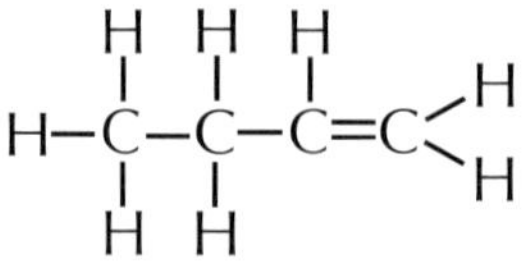

$$H-\overset{\overset{\displaystyle H}{|}}{\underset{\underset{\displaystyle H}{|}}{C}}-\overset{\overset{\displaystyle H}{|}}{\underset{\underset{\displaystyle H}{|}}{C}}-\overset{\overset{\displaystyle H}{|}}{C}=C\overset{\nearrow H}{\searrow H}$$

But-1-ene will burn completely in oxygen to produce CO_2 and H_2O.

The table below shows bond enthalpies for the bonds present in the reactants and products of this combustion reaction.

Bond	Bond Enthalpy (Average value except where stated)
C–H	+413 kJ mol^{-1}
C=C	+612 kJ mol^{-1}
C–C	+347 kJ mol^{-1}
O=O	+498 kJ mol^{-1}
C=O (in CO_2)	+805 kJ mol^{-1}
O–H (in H_2O)	+460 kJ mol^{-1}

These bond enthalpies can be used to calculate the standard enthalpy change of combustion for but-1-ene.

(i) State the meaning of the term 'standard enthalpy change of combustion', $\Delta_c H^\circ$.

(3 marks)

(ii) Use the data in the table to calculate a value for the standard enthalpy change of combustion for but-1-ene.

(3 marks)

(iii) The standard enthalpy change of combustion for but-1-ene calculated from the average bond enthalpies is different to the value given in the data book. Suggest why.

(1 mark)

(b) 0.0215 mol of another alkene are burned. The energy released heats 200 cm³ water from 21.0 °C to 53.8 °C.

(density of water = 1.00 g cm^{-3}, specific heat capacity of water = 4.18 J g^{-1} K^{-1})

(i) Calculate the amount of energy released in kJ when the alkene is burned.

(2 marks)

(ii) Calculate the enthalpy change of combustion, $\Delta_c H^\circ$, of the alkene.

(2 marks)

(iii) Explain, in terms of making and breaking bonds, why the combustion of the alkene is exothermic.

(2 marks)

7   When calcium is reacted with water, calcium hydroxide and hydrogen gas are produced, according to the equation below.

$$Ca_{(s)} + H_2O_{(l)} \rightarrow CaO_{(s)} + H_{2(g)}$$

(a)   Describe a method which could be used to measure the volume of hydrogen gas released over time.

(2 marks)

(b)   The reaction was carried out and the volume of hydrogen produced was measured at 30 second intervals. A graph showing the results is given below.

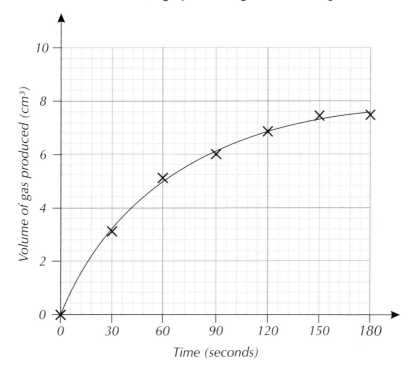

Calculate the rate of reaction at 1 minute.

(3 marks)

1. Organic Chemistry

Organic chemistry is the study of carbon-containing compounds. Here's a brief introduction to some of the basic concepts you'll need to get your head around before you can study organic chemistry in more detail.

The basics

There are a few basic concepts in organic chemistry which you need to nderstand to really get on with this module.

Nomenclature

There are thousands, if not millions, of known organic compounds and it would be pretty silly if we didn't have an easy way to describe them. That's where **nomenclature** comes in. Don't be put off by the long name, all it means is naming molecules using specific rules. These rules (known as the IUPAC system for naming organic compounds) allow scientists to discuss organic chemistry safe in the knowledge that they're all talking about the same molecules. It means that some molecules end up with really long and complicated looking names (e.g. 1,2-dichloro-3-methylbutane) but once you know the rules, it's easy to work out what they all mean. There's more about nomenclature on pages 199-201.

Formulas

Picturing molecules can be pretty difficult when you can't see them all around you. We can use the elemental symbols from the periodic table to help visualise molecules. For example, a molecule of methane is one carbon atom attached to four hydrogen atoms. You could show this by giving its molecular formula, CH_4, or you could draw its displayed formula like this: ⟶

There's more on formulas on pages 191-193. This isn't exactly what methane looks like, but visualising it like this lets us compare it to other molecules and means we can predict its properties and how it might react with other molecules. Molecular models can also be used to represent molecules (see Figure 1).

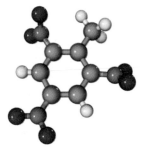

Figure 1: *A molecular model of a TNT molecule. Each grey sphere represents a carbon atom, each white sphere represents a hydrogen atom, the purple ones represent nitrogen atoms and the red ones oxygen atoms.*

Tip: That stuff about carbon atoms making four bonds, hydrogen making one bond and oxygen making two is right <u>most</u> of the time, but isn't always the case. The good news is that you don't need to worry about that right now.

Functional groups

The functional group of a molecule is the group of atoms that's responsible for its characteristic reactions — it's where all the interesting stuff happens. They're usually pretty easy to spot because they're the bits which aren't just hydrogen and carbon atoms (e.g. bromine atoms, oxygen atoms, etc.). You'll come across a few different functional groups in this Module — here are a few examples...

−OH	$-\overset{\overset{\displaystyle O}{\|}}{C}-OH$	C=C
Functional groups of... *alcohols*	*carboxylic acids*	*alkenes*

For now, remember that carbon atoms have four bonds, hydrogen atoms have one bond and oxygen atoms have two bonds joining them to other atoms.

So there you go. That's pretty much all you need to know to get started.

2. Formulas

Organic compounds can be represented in lots of different ways, using different types of formulas. You need to be familiar with what these formulas show and how to switch between them.

Types of formulas

General formulas and homologous series

A **general formula** is an algebraic formula that can describe any member of a family of compounds. For example, alcohols have the general formula $C_nH_{2n+1}OH$. Organic chemistry is more about groups of similar chemicals than individual compounds. These groups are called **homologous series**. A homologous series is a family of compounds that have the same functional group and general formula. Consecutive members of a homologous series differ by $-CH_2-$.

> **Example**
>
> The simplest homologous series is the alkanes. They're straight chain molecules that contain only carbon and hydrogen atoms. There are always twice as many hydrogen atoms as carbon atoms, plus two more. So the general formula for alkanes is C_nH_{2n+2}. You can use this formula to work out how many hydrogen atoms there are in any alkane if you know the number of carbon atoms. For example...
>
> - If an alkane has 1 carbon atom, n = 1.
>   This means the alkane will have $(2 \times 1) + 2 = 4$ hydrogen atoms.
>   So the molecular formula of this alkane would be CH_4 (you don't need to write the 1 in C_1).
> - If an alkane has 5 carbon atoms, n = 5.
>   This means the alkane will have $(2 \times 5) + 2 = 12$ hydrogen atoms.
>   So its molecular formula would be C_5H_{12}.
> - If an alkane has 15 carbon atoms, n = 15.
>   This means the alkane will have $(2 \times 15) + 2 = 32$ hydrogen atoms.
>   So its molecular formula is $C_{15}H_{32}$.

Molecular formulas

A molecular formula gives the actual number of atoms of each element in a molecule.

> **Examples**
>
> Ethane has the molecular formula C_2H_6 — each molecule is made up of 2 carbon atoms and 6 hydrogen atoms.
> - Pentene has the molecular formula C_5H_{10} — each molecule is made up of 5 carbon atoms and 10 hydrogen atoms.
> - 1,4-dibromobutane has the molecular formula $C_4H_8Br_2$ — each molecule is made up of 4 carbon atoms, 8 hydrogen atoms and 2 bromine atoms.
> - 1,3-dichloropropane has the molecular formula $C_3H_6Cl_2$ — each molecule is made up of 3 carbon atoms, 6 hydrogen atoms and 2 chlorine atoms.

Learning Objectives:

- Know that a general formula is the simplest algebraic formula of a member of a homologous series.
- Be able to define a homologous series as a series of organic compounds with the same functional group but where each successive member differs by CH_2.
- Be able to use the general formula of a homologous series to predict the formula of any member of the series.
- Know that a structural formula gives the minimal detail that shows the arrangement of atoms in a molecule.
- Know that a displayed formula shows the relative positioning of atoms and the bonds between them.
- Know that a skeletal formula is a simplified organic formula, shown by removing hydrogen atoms from alkyl chains, leaving just a carbon skeleton and associated functional groups.

Specification Reference 4.1.1

Tip: Molecular formulas tell you what atoms are in a molecule, but they don't tell you which atoms are bonded to which.

Empirical formulas

An empirical formula gives the simplest whole number ratio of atoms of each element in a compound. To find the empirical formula you have to divide the molecular formula by the smallest number of atoms for a given element in the molecule. For example, if the molecular formula is $C_2H_4Cl_2$, the smallest number of atoms is 2 (for both C and Cl). So you divide the molecular formula by 2 and get the empirical formula CH_2Cl. The number of each type of atom in the empirical formula needs to be a whole number. So if you divide the molecular formula by the smallest number of atoms and end up without whole numbers, the molecular formula will be the same as the empirical formula.

┌ Examples ─────────────

Name	Molecular Formula	Divide by...	Empirical Formula
Ethane	C_2H_6	2	CH_3
Pentene	C_5H_{10}	5	CH_2
1,4-dichlorobutane	$C_4H_8Cl_2$	2	C_2H_4Cl
1,3-dichloropropane	$C_3H_6Cl_2$	-	$C_3H_6Cl_2$
1,2,3-trichloroheptane	$C_7H_{13}Cl_3$	-	$C_7H_{13}Cl_3$

In the last two examples in the table, the molecular formula is the same as the empirical formula — you can't divide by the smallest number of atoms for a given element and still get whole numbers.

Structural formulas

A structural formula shows the atoms carbon by carbon, with the attached hydrogens and functional groups.

┌ Examples ─────────────
Ethane has the structural formula CH_3CH_3.

Pentene has the structural formula $CH_3CH_2CH_2CHCH_2$.

1,4-dibromobutane has the structural formula $BrCH_2CH_2CH_2CH_2Br$.

1,3-dichloropropane has the structural formula $ClCH_2CH_2CH_2Cl$.

Displayed formulas

A displayed formula shows how all the atoms are arranged, and all the bonds between them.

┌ Examples ── **Maths Skills** ──

Displayed formula of ethane:

H H
| |
H─C─C─H
| |
H H

Displayed formula of pentene:

H H H H
| | | | H
H─C─C─C─C=C
| | | H
H H H

Displayed formula of 1,4-dibromobutane:

H H H H
| | | |
Br─C─C─C─C─Br
| | | |
H H H H

Displayed formula of 1,3-dichloropropane:

H H Cl
| | |
Cl─C─C─C─H
| | |
H H H

Skeletal formulas

A skeletal formula shows the bonds of the carbon skeleton only, with any functional groups. The hydrogen and carbon atoms that are part of the main carbon chain aren't shown. This is handy for drawing large complicated structures, like cyclic hydrocarbons. The carbon atoms are found at each junction between bonds and at the end of bonds (unless there's already a functional group there). Each carbon atom has enough hydrogen atoms attached to make the total number of bonds from the carbon up to four.

Examples — Maths Skills

Displayed and skeletal formulas of 1,5-difluoropentane:

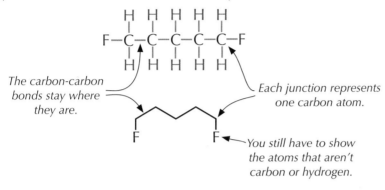

The carbon-carbon bonds stay where they are.

Each junction represents one carbon atom.

You still have to show the atoms that aren't carbon or hydrogen.

Skeletal formula of hex-1-ene:

A double line represents a carbon-carbon double bond.

This carbon atom only has one carbon-carbon bond drawn on the molecule. This means that it has three hydrogen atoms attached to make the number of bonds up to four.

This carbon atom has a carbon-carbon double bond, so it must have two hydrogen atoms attached to make the number of bonds up to four.

Exam Tip
Skeletal formulas are notoriously difficult to draw in an exam without making any mistakes... If you're not 100% happy with them stick to displayed formulas — you don't want to introduce silly errors into your answers. Of course, if the exam question asks for a skeletal formula you've got no choice — just give it your best shot.

Tip: You have to draw skeletal formulas as zig-zag lines, otherwise you can't tell where one bond ends and the next begins.

Tip: The various types of formula have different levels of detail, so which one you use depends on what you're trying to show. The trick is to know which formula will give all the information you're trying to show, without being over-complicated.

Practice Questions — Application

Q1 2-bromopropane has the structural formula $CH_3CHBrCH_3$. Draw the displayed formula of 2-bromopropane.

Q2 Here is the structure of 3-ethyl-2-methylpentane.

$$H-\underset{\underset{H}{|}}{\overset{\overset{H}{|}}{C}}-\underset{\underset{H}{|}}{\overset{\overset{H}{|}}{C}}-\underset{\underset{CH_2}{|}}{\overset{\overset{H}{|}}{C}}-\underset{\underset{H}{|}}{\overset{\overset{CH_3}{|}}{C}}-\underset{\underset{H}{|}}{\overset{\overset{H}{|}}{C}}-H$$

$$CH_3$$

Write down the molecular formula for 3-ethyl-2-methylpentane.

Q3 Write down the empirical formula of the following compounds:

a) C_2H_4

b) $C_8H_{14}Br_2$

c) $C_9H_{17}Cl_3$

Tip: Drawing a displayed formula from a structural formula is dead easy — just draw it out exactly as it's written:

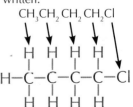

Q4 Alkenes have the general formula C_nH_{2n}.
  a) Butene is an alkene with 4 carbon atoms.
    Write the molecular formula of butene.
  b) Heptene is an alkene with 7 carbon atoms.
    How many hydrogen atoms does it contain?

Q5 1,2-dibromopropane has the structural formula $CH_3CHBrCH_2Br$.
  a) Write down the molecular formula of 1,2-dibromopropane.
  b) Draw the displayed formula of 1,2-dibromopropane.
  c) Write the empirical formula of 1,2-dibromopropane.

Q6 Here is the displayed formula of pent-1-ene.

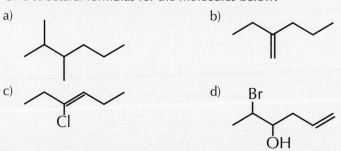

  a) Write down the molecular formula of pent-1-ene.
  b) Write down the structural formula of pent-1-ene.
  c) What is the empirical formula of pent-1-ene?

Q7 Draw skeletal formulas of the molecules below:
  a)
  b)
  c)
  d)

Q8 Give structural formulas for the molecules below:
  a)
  b)
  c)
  d)

Practice Questions — Fact Recall

Q1 What is the formula used to represent a homologous series called?

Q2 What is a homologous series?

Q3 What does a displayed formula show?

Q4 The symbols of which atoms aren't shown in a skeletal formula?

3. Carbon Skeletons

All organic compounds have a carbon skeleton. This is just the arrangement of all the carbon atoms in the molecule, ignoring any functional groups. Carbon skeletons can be split into two groups — aromatic and aliphatic.

Aromatic compounds

Aromatic compounds contain a benzene ring. All you need to know about benzene for now is how you recognise or draw it (see Figure 1).

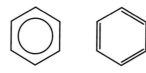

Figure 1: *Two representations of a benzene ring.*

Aliphatic compounds

Aliphatic compounds contain carbon and hydrogen joined together in straight chains, branched chains or non-aromatic rings (see Figure 2). If an aliphatic compound contains a (non-aromatic) ring, then it can be called **alicyclic**.

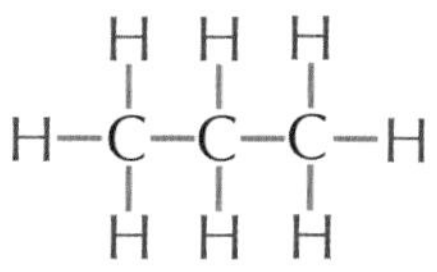

Propane has a straight chain carbon skeleton.

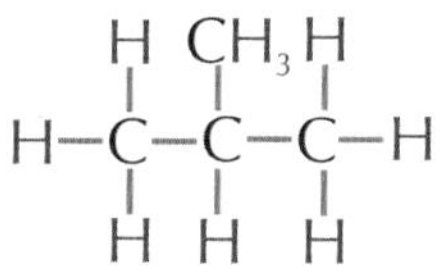

2-methylpropane has a branched chain carbon skeleton.

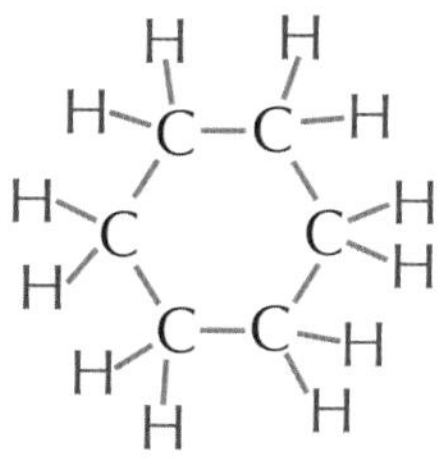

Cyclohexane is alicyclic.

Figure 2: *Different types of aliphatic compound.*

In compounds with a branched carbon skeleton, any hydrocarbon branched chains are called **alkyl groups**. Alkyl groups have the general formula C_nH_{2n+1}.

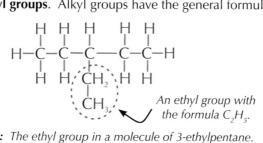

An ethyl group with the formula C_2H_5.

Figure 3: *The ethyl group in a molecule of 3-ethylpentane.*

Organic compounds can have **saturated** or **unsaturated** carbon skeletons. Saturated compounds only contain carbon-carbon single bonds — like alkanes. Unsaturated compounds can have carbon-carbon double bonds, triple bonds or aromatic groups.

Practice Questions — Application

Q1 A propyl group is an alkyl group containing three carbon atoms. What is the molecular formula of a propyl group?

Q2 The organic compound butene contains a C=C double bond. Is it saturated or unsaturated?

Tip: The representations of benzene in Figure 1 show its skeletal formula (see page 193). Each point represents a carbon atom, and the lines are the bonds between them. There is also a hydrogen bonded to each carbon, but these aren't shown in skeletal formulas.

Learning Objectives:

- Know that structural isomers are compounds with the same molecular formula but different structural formulas.
- Be able to determine the possible structural formulas of an organic molecule, given its molecular formula.

Specification Reference 4.1.1

Figure 1: Molecular models showing two chain isomers of C_4H_{10} — butane (left) and methylpropane (right).

Exam Tip
You don't always have to draw all of the bonds when you're drawing a molecule — writing CH_3 next to a bond is just as good as drawing out the carbon atom, three bonds and three hydrogen atoms. But if you're asked for a displayed formula you <u>must</u> draw out all of the bonds to get the marks.

Tip: If the chlorine atom was attached to the carbon atom on the left, it would still be the <u>same molecule</u> — just drawn the other way round. It would still be 1-chlorobutane.

4. Structural Isomers

You can put the same atoms together in different ways to make completely different molecules. Two molecules are isomers if they have the same molecular formula but the atoms are arranged differently.

What are structural isomers?

In structural isomers, the molecular formula is the same, but the structural formula is different. There are three different types of structural isomer.

1. Chain isomers

The carbon skeleton can be arranged differently — for example, as a straight chain, or branched in different ways. Molecules that have different arrangements of the carbon skeleton are called **chain isomers**.

┌─ **Examples** ─ **Maths Skills** ─────────────────────────

There are different chain isomers of C_4H_{10}. The diagrams below show the straight chain isomer butane and a branched chain isomer methylpropane.

Here the longest carbon chain is 3 carbon atoms.

Here the longest carbon chain is 4 carbon atoms.

butane   methylpropane

There are different chain isomers of $C_4H_8O_2$. The diagrams below show the straight chain isomer butanoic acid and a branched chain isomer methylpropanoic acid.

Here the longest carbon chain is 4 carbon atoms.

Here the longest carbon chain is 3 carbon atoms.

butanoic acid   methylpropanoic acid

Chain isomers have similar chemical properties — but their physical properties, like boiling point, will be different because of the change in shape of the molecule.

2. Positional isomers

The skeleton and the functional group could be the same, only with the functional group attached to a different carbon atom. These are called **positional isomers**.

┌─ **Example** ─ **Maths Skills** ─────────────────────────

There are two positional isomers of C_4H_9Cl. The chlorine atom is attached to different carbon atoms in each isomer.

The Cl is attached to the first carbon atom.

1-chlorobutane

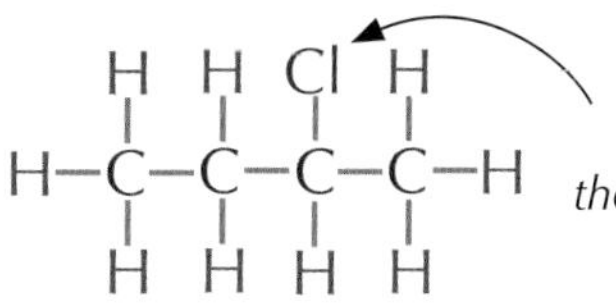

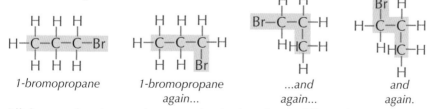

2-chlorobutane

Positional isomers also have different physical properties, and the chemical properties might be different too.

3. Functional group isomers

Functional group isomers have the same atoms arranged into different functional groups.

— **Example** — **Maths Skills** —

The formulas below show two functional group isomers of C_6H_{12}.

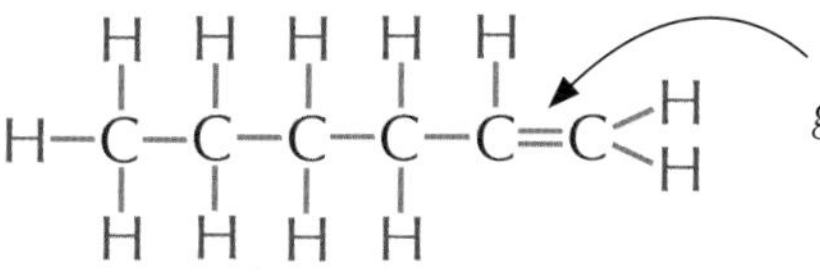

The functional group is the C=C — it's an alkene.

hex-1-ene

This molecule is an alkane.

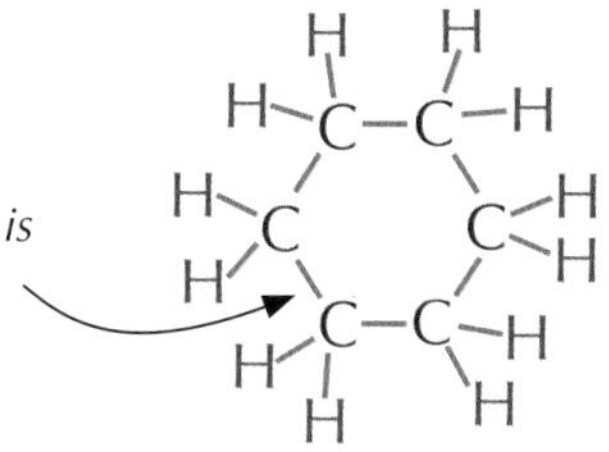

cyclohexane

Functional group isomers have very different physical and chemical properties.

Identifying isomers

Atoms can rotate as much as they like around single C–C bonds. Remember this when you work out structural isomers — sometimes what looks like an isomer, isn't.

— **Examples** — **Maths Skills** —

There are only two positional isomers of C_3H_7Br:

1-bromopropane

The Br is always on the first carbon atom.

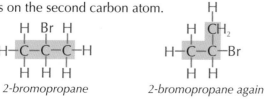

1-bromopropane   *1-bromopropane again...*   *...and again...*   *and again.*

All these molecules are the same, they're just drawn differently.

2-bromopropane

The Br is always on the second carbon atom.

2-bromopropane   *2-bromopropane again*

Tip: Number the carbon atoms — it makes it easier to see what the longest carbon chain is and where side chains and atoms are attached:

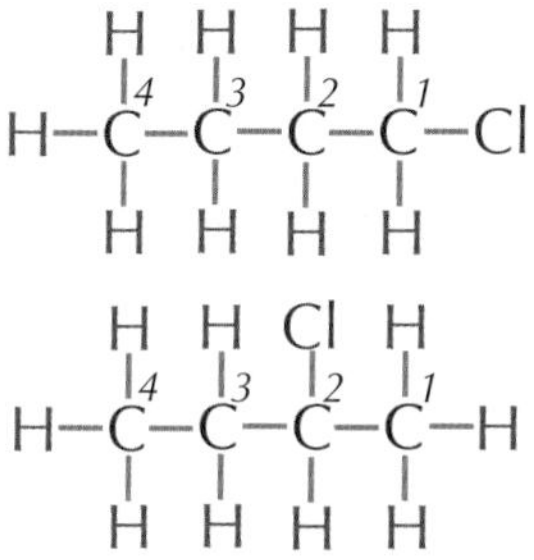

Exam Tip
To avoid mistakes when you're identifying isomers in an exam, draw the molecule so the longest carbon chain goes left to right across the page. This will make it easier to see the isomers.

Tip: In propane, the Br can only really go on the first or second carbon atom. If it was on the "third" it would be the same as being on the first again because you start counting from whichever end the Br is on.

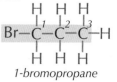

1-bromopropane

Practice Questions — Application

Q1 Here is an isomer of chloro-2-methylpropane.

$$CH_3$$
$$H_3C-\overset{|}{\underset{|}{C}}-CH_3$$
$$Cl$$

Draw the other positional isomer of chloro-2-methylpropane.

Q2 Draw all the chain isomers of C_5H_{12}.

Q3 Here is the displayed formula of propanal.

$$H \quad H \quad O$$
$$H-\overset{|}{\underset{|}{C}}-\overset{|}{\underset{|}{C}}-\overset{\parallel}{C}-H$$
$$H \quad H$$

Propanal has the functional group $\overset{O}{\overset{\parallel}{C}}-H$.

Draw an isomer of propanal with the functional group $\overset{O}{\overset{\parallel}{C}}$.

Q4 Here is the displayed formula of 1-chlorohexane.

$$H \quad H \quad H \quad H \quad H \quad H$$
$$H-\overset{|}{\underset{|}{C}}-\overset{|}{\underset{|}{C}}-\overset{|}{\underset{|}{C}}-\overset{|}{\underset{|}{C}}-\overset{|}{\underset{|}{C}}-\overset{|}{\underset{|}{C}}-Cl$$
$$H \quad H \quad H \quad H \quad H \quad H$$

a) Which of the molecules (**A–D**) are isomers of 1-chlorohexane?

A
$$H \quad Cl \quad H \quad H$$
$$H-\overset{|}{\underset{|}{C}}-\overset{|}{\underset{|}{C}}-\overset{|}{\underset{|}{C}}-\overset{|}{\underset{|}{C}}-H$$
$$H \quad H \quad CH_2H$$
$$CH_3$$

B
$$H \quad Cl \quad CH_3H$$
$$H-\overset{|}{\underset{|}{C}}-\overset{|}{\underset{|}{C}}-\overset{|}{\underset{|}{C}}-\overset{|}{\underset{|}{C}}-H$$
$$H \quad H \quad CH_3H$$

C
$$H \quad H \quad H \quad H$$
$$H-\overset{|}{\underset{|}{C}}-\overset{|}{\underset{|}{C}}-\overset{|}{\underset{|}{C}}-\overset{|}{\underset{|}{C}}-H$$
$$H \quad H \quad CH_2H$$
$$CH_3$$

D
$$H \quad H \quad Cl \quad H \quad H$$
$$H-\overset{|}{\underset{|}{C}}-\overset{|}{\underset{|}{C}}-\overset{|}{\underset{|}{C}}-\overset{|}{\underset{|}{C}}-\overset{|}{\underset{|}{C}}-H$$
$$H \quad H \quad H \quad H \quad H$$

b) State the type of isomerism shown in part a).

Exam Tip
Be really careful when you're drawing out functional group isomers that you do draw a different isomer and not just the same isomer again in a slightly different way — numbering the carbons and making sure the functional group's on a different one might help.

Exam Tip
If you get confused between different isomers of a molecule, try drawing the structure of the molecule out again in a slightly different way — everything might become clear.

Practice Questions — Fact Recall

Q1 What are isomers?

Q2 What are structural isomers?

5. Alkanes and Nomenclature

Alkanes are molecules with hydrogen atoms, carbon atoms and single bonds. Nomenclature is just a fancy word for naming organic compounds.

Learning Objectives:

- Know that alkanes are saturated hydrocarbons that only contain single C–C and C–H bonds.
- Be able to use the IUPAC rules of nomenclature to systematically name organic compounds.

Specification Reference 4.1.1, 4.1.2

Structure of alkanes

Alkanes have the general formula C_nH_{2n+2}. They've only got carbon and hydrogen atoms, so they're **hydrocarbons**. Every carbon atom in an alkane has four single bonds with other atoms. It's impossible for carbon to make more than four bonds, so alkanes are **saturated**.
Here are a few examples of alkanes —

methane   ethane   propane

You get **cycloalkanes** too. They have a ring of carbon atoms with two hydrogens attached to each carbon. Cycloalkanes have two fewer hydrogens than other alkanes (assuming they have only one ring) so cycloalkanes have a different general formula from that of normal alkanes (C_nH_{2n}), but they are still saturated.

cyclohexane, C_6H_{12}

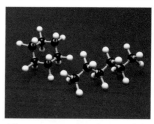

Figure 1: *Molecular models of cyclohexane (left) and hexane (right).*

Rules of nomenclature

The IUPAC system for naming organic compounds is the agreed international language of chemistry. Years ago, organic compounds were given whatever names people fancied, such as acetic acid and ethylene. But these names caused confusion between different countries.

HOW SCIENCE WORKS

IUPAC (The International Union of Pure and Applied Chemistry) is a group founded in 1919 with the aim of creating international standards in Chemistry so that research could be shared more easily across the world. Amongst other things, this included making rules for naming organic molecules.

There are a few rules to learn before you meet any specific compounds.

1. Count the carbon atoms in the longest continuous chain to give you the stem.

Number of Carbon Atoms	Stem
1	meth-
2	eth-
3	prop-
4	but-
5	pent-
6	hex-
7	hept-
8	oct-
9	non-
10	dec-

Figure 2: *The stems for carbon chains up to ten carbon atoms long.*

Tip: The skeletal formula of cyclohexane looks like this:

Tip: The IUPAC naming system may seem like a foreign language at the moment, but you'll get loads of practice at naming organic compounds during this Module.

Tip: Be careful, the longest carbon chain may not be in a straight line:

$$H-\overset{\overset{\displaystyle H}{|}}{\underset{\underset{\displaystyle H}{|}}{C}}_{1}-\overset{\overset{\displaystyle Cl}{|}}{\underset{\underset{\displaystyle H}{|}}{C}}_{2}-\overset{\overset{\displaystyle H}{|}}{\underset{\underset{\displaystyle CH_2H}{|}}{C}}_{3}-\overset{\overset{\displaystyle H}{|}}{\underset{\underset{\displaystyle H}{|}}{C}}-H$$

$$\overset{|}{\underset{5}{CH_3}}$$

Tip: Always number the longest continuous carbon chain so that the name contains the lowest numbers possible. For example, you could number this chain:

$$H-\overset{\overset{\displaystyle H}{|}}{\underset{\underset{\displaystyle H}{|}}{C}}_{1}-\overset{\overset{\displaystyle H}{|}}{\underset{\underset{\displaystyle H}{|}}{C}}_{2}-\overset{\overset{\displaystyle H}{|}}{\underset{\underset{\displaystyle CH_3}{|}}{C}}_{3}-\overset{\overset{\displaystyle H}{|}}{\underset{\underset{\displaystyle H}{|}}{C}}_{4}-H$$

which would make it 3-methylbutane. But you should actually number it in the opposite direction to get 2-methylbutane.

$$H-\overset{\overset{\displaystyle H}{|}}{\underset{\underset{\displaystyle H}{|}}{C}}_{4}-\overset{\overset{\displaystyle H}{|}}{\underset{\underset{\displaystyle H}{|}}{C}}_{3}-\overset{\overset{\displaystyle H}{|}}{\underset{\underset{\displaystyle CH_3}{|}}{C}}_{2}-\overset{\overset{\displaystyle H}{|}}{\underset{\underset{\displaystyle H}{|}}{C}}_{1}-H$$

2. The main functional group of the molecule usually tells you what homologous series the molecule is in, and so gives you the prefix or suffix. For example, alcohols all have the suffix '-ol', and chloroalkanes have the prefix 'chloro-'. You'll learn the prefix or suffix for each homologous series as you meet them in this Module.

3. Number the longest carbon chain so that the main functional group has the lowest possible number. If there's more than one longest chain, pick the one with the most side-chains.

4. Any side-chains or less important functional groups are added as prefixes at the start of the name. Put them in alphabetical order, after the number of the carbon atom each is attached to.

5. If there's more than one identical side-chain or functional group, use di- (2), tri- (3) or tetra- (4) before that part of the name — but ignore this when working out the alphabetical order.

Naming alkanes

Alkanes are the simplest type of molecules to name. There are two types you need to learn to name — straight chain alkanes and branched chain alkanes.

Straight-chain alkanes

There are two parts to the name of a straight-chain alkane. The first part (the stem) states how many carbon atoms there are in the molecule. The second part is always "-ane". It's the "-ane" bit that lets people know it's an alkane.

┌─ **Example** ─────────────────────────────────
This molecule is pentane:

$$H-\overset{\overset{\displaystyle H}{|}}{\underset{\underset{\displaystyle H}{|}}{C}}-\overset{\overset{\displaystyle H}{|}}{\underset{\underset{\displaystyle H}{|}}{C}}-\overset{\overset{\displaystyle H}{|}}{\underset{\underset{\displaystyle H}{|}}{C}}-\overset{\overset{\displaystyle H}{|}}{\underset{\underset{\displaystyle H}{|}}{C}}-\overset{\overset{\displaystyle H}{|}}{\underset{\underset{\displaystyle H}{|}}{C}}-H$$

The stem is pent-, which tells you that the molecule has 5 carbons in it, and the -ane bit at the end tells you it's an alkane.

Branched alkanes

Branched alkanes have side chains. These are the carbon atoms that aren't part of the longest continuous chain. To name branched alkanes you first need to count how many carbon atoms are in the longest chain and work out the stem (just like you would for a straight-chain alkane). Once you've done that you can name the side chains. The side chains are named according to how many carbon atoms they have (see Figure 3) and which carbon atom they are attached to. If there's more than one side chain in a molecule, you place them in alphabetical order. So but-groups come before eth- groups which come before meth- groups.

Number of Carbon Atoms	Side Chain Prefix
1	methyl-
2	ethyl-
3	propyl-
4	butyl-
5	pentyl-
6	hexyl-

Figure 3: Names of carbon side chains.

Examples

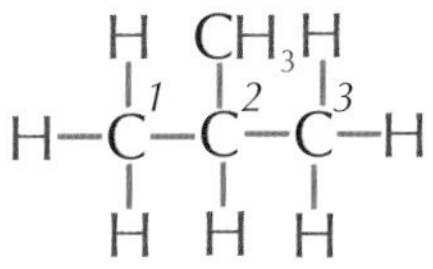

2-methylpropane

The longest continuous carbon chain is 3 carbon atoms, so the stem is propane.

There's one side chain, which has one carbon atom so it's a methyl group.

It's joined to the main carbon chain at the 2nd carbon atom, so it's a 2-methyl group.

The alkane is called 2-methylpropane.

Exam Tip
Always number each carbon on a drawing of your molecule — it makes it much easier to name molecules where there are lots of branches or functional groups.

The longest continuous carbon chain is 5 carbon atoms, so the stem is pentane.

There are two side chains.

One side chain is a methyl group joined to the 2nd carbon atom: 2-methyl-.

The other is an ethyl group (2 carbons) joined to the 3rd carbon atom: 3-ethyl-.

Side chains go in alphabetical order, so the alkane is 3-ethyl-2-methylpentane.

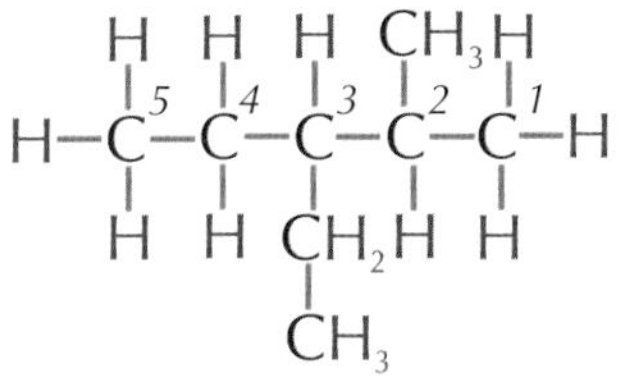

3-ethyl-2-methylpentane

Some alkanes have two or more of the same side chain. Remember that you just need to put a prefix before that part of the name to tell you how many of that side chain there are. You ignore these prefixes when putting the groups in alphabetical order (so 'dimethyl' would still come after 'ethyl').

Tip: When you're naming molecules commas are put between numbers (for example 2,2) and dashes are put between numbers and letters (for example 2-methyl).

Examples

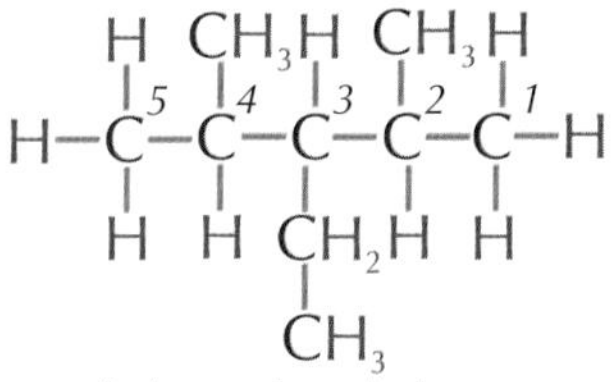

3-ethyl-2,4-dimethylpentane

The longest carbon chain is five carbons, so the stem is pent-. You could choose two different routes to number the main chain — one way has three branches off the main chain, and the other way has two (see Figure 4).

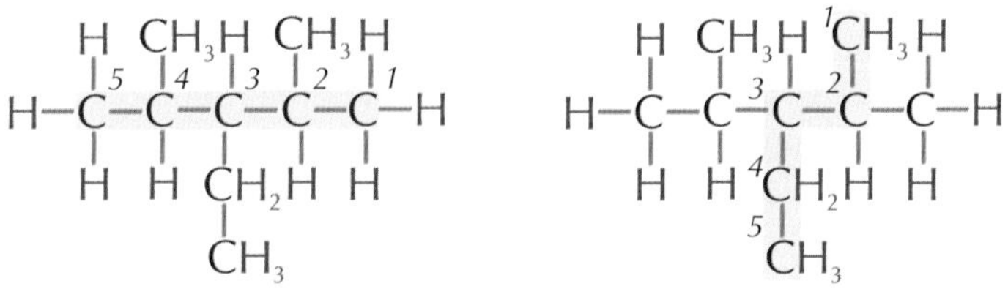

Figure 4: *Two possible ways of numbering the longest carbon chain in a molecule*

The numbering in the left hand diagram is correct — this way the main carbon chain has the most branches.

There are two methyl side chains, one attached to the second carbon and one attached to the fourth carbon, so there will be a 'dimethyl' prefix. There is also one ethyl group attached to the third carbon, so there'll also be an 'ethyl' prefix.

Side chains go in alphabetical order, ignoring any 'di' or 'tri' prefixes, so the molecule is 3-ethyl-2,4-dimethylpentane.

Tip: When you write down the numbers of the carbons that groups of the same type are attached to, you should write them in ascending order. So the molecule on the left is 3-ethyl-2,4-dimethylpentane, rather than 3-ethyl-4,2-dimethylpentane.

Practice Questions — Application

Q1 Name the alkanes shown below.

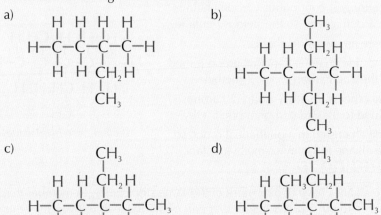

a)

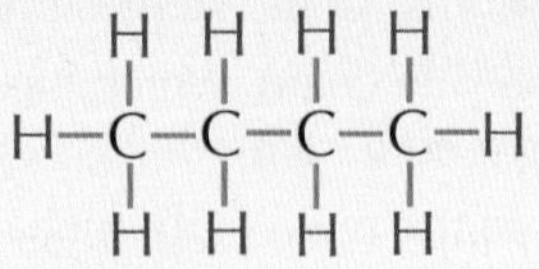

H H H H
| | | |
H–C–C–C–C–H
| | | |
H H H H

b)

H H
| |
H–C–C–H
| |
H H

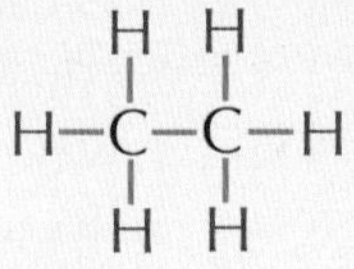

c)

H
|
H–C–H
|
H

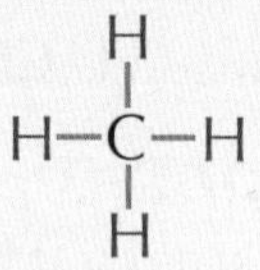

d) C_9H_{20} e) C_7H_{16} f) $C_{10}H_{22}$

Q2 Name the following branched alkanes:

a)

H H H H
| | | |
H–C–C–C–C–H
| | | |
H H CH$_2$H
|
CH$_3$

b)

CH$_3$
|
H H CH$_2$H
| | | |
H–C–C–C–C–H
| | | |
H H CH$_2$H
|
CH$_3$

c)

CH$_3$
|
H H CH$_2$H
| | | |
H–C–C–C–C–CH$_3$
| | | |
H H CH$_2$H
|
H$_3$C–CH$_2$

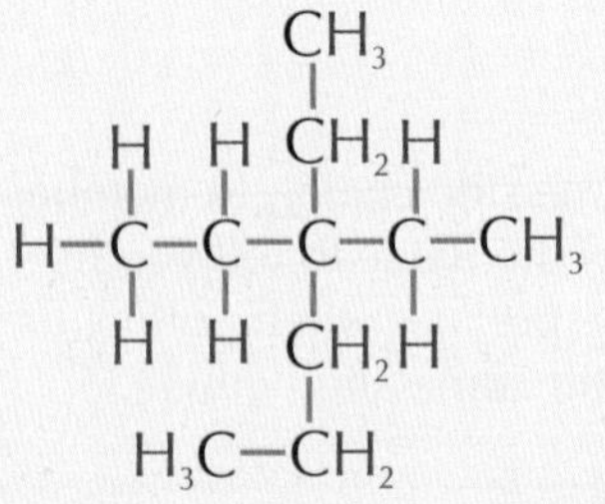

d)

CH$_3$
|
H CH$_3$CH$_2$H
| | | |
H–C–C–C–C–CH$_3$
| | | |
H H CH$_2$H
|
H$_3$C–CH$_2$

Exam Tip
If you're asked to name a molecule from its molecular formula, it can help to draw it out first.

Practice Questions — Fact Recall

Q1 What is an alkane?

Q2 Give the general formula for an alkane.

Q3 What is the stem for a carbon chain containing six carbon atoms?

Q4 What is the name for a carbon side chain containing two carbon atoms?

Q5 If there are two methyl- side chains what prefix should you add to methyl- when naming the molecule?

6. Properties of Alkanes

You need to know a little bit about the physical and chemical properties of the alkanes. Luckily for you, the next few pages happen to be about just that.

Shapes of alkane molecules

In an alkane molecule, each carbon atom has four pairs of bonding electrons around it. They all repel each other equally. So the molecule forms a **tetrahedral shape** around each carbon. The bond angles around each carbon will be 109.5°

Examples — **Maths Skills**

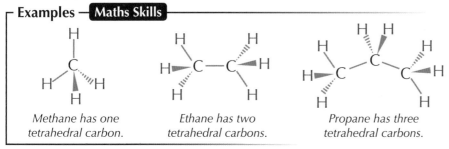

Methane has one tetrahedral carbon.

Ethane has two tetrahedral carbons.

Propane has three tetrahedral carbons.

Bonding in alkanes

The C–C and C–H bonds in alkanes are all single covalent bonds. You can use the 'orbital overlap' model to explain how the bonds are formed. The model states that covalent bonds can form between two atoms if they're arranged so that the outer atomic orbitals overlap. The orbitals then combine to form a shared orbital that forms a bond between the atoms. How well the orbitals overlap determines how strong the bond is. In alkanes, atomic orbitals on carbon and hydrogen atoms are positioned so that they overlap to form a new, shared orbital lying directly between the bonded atoms. This type of covalent bond is called a sigma (σ-) bond.

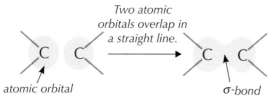

Two atomic orbitals overlap in a straight line.

atomic orbital

σ-bond

Figure 1: *The formation of a sigma (σ-) bond.*

The high electron density between the nuclei means there is a strong electrostatic attraction between the nuclei and the shared pair of electrons. This means that σ-bonds have a high bond enthalpy — they are the strongest type of covalent bonds. The bonded atoms are free to rotate around the σ-bond as whichever way the atoms point, the atomic orbitals between them will always overlap.

Reactivity of alkanes

Alkanes are pretty unreactive. They will combust with oxygen (see page 205), and undergo substitution reactions with highly reactive free radical species (see page 209), but that's about it.

The low reactivity of alkanes can be explained by the bonding in alkane molecules. The C–C and C–H σ-bonds all have a large bond enthalpy, making them very strong and therefore difficult to break. The bonds are also non-polar. This means that they won't attract any positively or negatively charged particles to react with them.

Learning Objectives:

- Be able to explain the tetrahedral shape and bond angle around each carbon atom in alkanes in terms of electron pair repulsion.

- Know that the single bonds in alkanes are σ- (sigma) bonds which form from the overlap of orbitals directly between the bonding atoms.

- Know that atoms are able to rotate freely around σ-bonds.

- Be able to explain the low reactivity of alkanes with many reagents in terms of the high bond enthalpy and very low polarity of the σ-bonds present.

- Be able to explain the variations in boiling points of alkanes with different carbon-chain length and branching, in terms of induced dipole–dipole interactions.

- Describe the complete combustion of alkanes, as used in fuels, and the incomplete combustion of alkane fuels in a limited supply of oxygen with the resulting potential dangers from CO.

Specification Reference 4.1.2

Tip: If you draw lines joining up the Hs in tetrahedral molecules, you get a tetrahedron:

Boiling points of alkanes

The boiling point of an alkane depends on its size and shape. The smallest alkanes, like methane, are gases at room temperature and pressure — they've got very low boiling points. Larger alkanes are liquids — they have higher boiling points. This is due to differences in their intermolecular forces.

Alkanes have covalent bonds inside the molecules. Between the molecules, there are **induced dipole-dipole interactions** (also called London forces) which hold them all together (see pages 111-112). The longer the carbon chain, the more induced dipole-dipole interactions there are. This is because they have a larger molecular surface area so there is more surface contact between the molecules and there are more electrons to interact. So as the molecules get longer, it takes more energy to overcome the induced dipole-dipole interactions and separate them, and the boiling point rises.

— **Example** —————————————————————————————

Methane is a very small molecule so there is little surface contact between the molecules. This means that the induced dipole-dipole interactions between the molecules are weak and the boiling point of methane is very low. Propane has a much higher boiling point because the molecules are much larger so have more surface contact with each other. Therefore, the induced dipole-dipole interactions between the molecules are stronger.

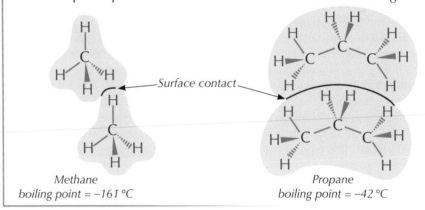

Methane
boiling point = −161 °C

Propane
boiling point = −42 °C

***Figure 2:** The alkane propane is a gas at room temperature and pressure.*

You can use your knowledge about the strength of induced dipole-dipole interactions to explain trends in boiling points of different sized alkanes.

— **Example** — **Maths Skills** —————————————

The boiling points of the first six alkanes are shown in Figure 3.

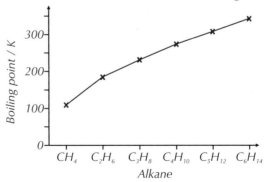

***Figure 3:** The boiling points of the first six alkanes.*

As the alkane chains get longer, the number of electrons in the molecules and the surface contact between molecules increase. So the induced dipole-dipole interactions are stronger, and so the boiling points increase.

A branched-chain alkane has a lower boiling point than its straight-chain isomer. Branched-chain alkanes can't pack closely together and they have smaller molecular surface areas — so the induced dipole-dipole interactions are reduced.

Tip: Butane and methylpropane are chain isomers — they've got the same molecular formula but their structural formulas are different.

Example

Butane and methylpropane are both isomers of C_4H_{10}. Butane has a higher boiling point than methylpropane because the molecules can pack closely together, therefore have more surface contact and so have more induced dipole-dipole interactions holding the molecules together.

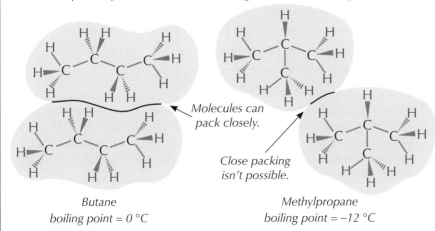

Molecules can pack closely.

Close packing isn't possible.

Butane
boiling point = 0 °C

Methylpropane
boiling point = −12 °C

Complete combustion of alkanes

If you burn (oxidise) alkanes with enough oxygen, you get carbon dioxide and water — this is a **complete combustion** reaction.

Examples

Here's the equation for the complete combustion of propane:

$$C_3H_{8(g)} + 5O_{2(g)} \rightarrow 3CO_{2(g)} + 4H_2O_{(g)}$$

This is the equation for the complete combustion of heptane:

$$C_7H_{16(g)} + 11O_{2(g)} \rightarrow 7CO_{2(g)} + 8H_2O_{(g)}$$

Tip: You only get complete combustion when there's loads of oxygen around. If oxygen is in short supply, you'll get incomplete combustion instead. There's more on incomplete combustion on the next page.

Complete combustion reactions happen between gases, so liquid alkanes have to be vaporised first. Smaller alkanes turn into gases more easily (they're more **volatile**), so they'll burn more easily too.

Alkanes and fuels

When alkanes burn, some energy is used to break the covalent bonds but more energy is released by forming the new product bonds in CO_2 and H_2O. This means that larger alkanes release more energy per mole than smaller alkanes, because more CO_2 and H_2O are formed. Because they release so much energy when they burn, alkanes make excellent fuels.

Examples

- Propane is used as a central heating and cooking fuel.
- Butane is bottled and sold as camping gas.
- Petrol and diesel are both made up of a mixture of alkanes too (and additives) — these are used as fuels for transport.

Figure 4: *A butane gas camping stove. The blue flame indicates that the combustion is complete.*

Identifying an unknown hydrocarbon

Complete combustion reactions happen between gases. All gases at standard temperature and pressure have the same molar volume — 24 dm^3. This means you can use the ratio of the volumes of gases reacting together to calculate the molar ratios, and then work out what hydrocarbon is combusting.

Example — Maths Skills

30 cm^3 of an unknown hydrocarbon, X, combusts completely with 240 cm^3 oxygen to form 150 cm^3 carbon dioxide. You can use this information to identify the molecular formula of X by following these steps:

- Using the volumes provided, a reaction equation can be written.

$$30X + 240O_2 \rightarrow 150CO_2 + ?H_2O$$

- This can be simplified by dividing everything by 30.

$$X + 8O_2 \rightarrow 5CO_2 + nH_2O$$

Tip: Have look back at page 54 for more about balancing equations.

- All the oxygen atoms in molecules on the right-hand side of the equation come from the oxygen molecules on the left-hand side (none come from the hydrocarbon). You can use this fact to balance the oxygen atoms on the right-hand side of the equation, and so work out how much water is produced.

    8 moles of oxygen react to form 5 moles of carbon dioxide and n moles of water. So any oxygen atoms that don't end up in CO_2 must be in H_2O.

    This means that $n = (8 \times 2) - (5 \times 2) = $ **6**.

- Write down the reaction equation again, including your value for n.

$$X + 8O_2 \rightarrow 5CO_2 + 6H_2O$$

Tip: This method will give you the molecular formula of the hydrocarbon, but if that hydrocarbon forms isomers you won't know which isomer was used.

- Now all you need to do to find the formula of X is to balance the left-hand side of the equation with the right-hand side.

    All the carbon atoms from X end up in carbon dioxide, and all the hydrogen atoms from X end up in water, so the number of carbon atoms in X is 5 and the number of hydrogen atoms in X is 12.

    The molecular formula of X is C_5H_{12}.

Incomplete combustion of alkanes

Tip: Not all incomplete combustion reactions will only produce water and carbon monoxide. Some will produce particulate carbon or small amounts of carbon dioxide as well. Just make sure your equation <u>balances</u> and you should be fine.

If there isn't much oxygen around, an alkane will still burn, but it will produce carbon monoxide and water. This is an **incomplete combustion** reaction.

Examples

Here's the reaction that occurs when methane is burnt in a limited supply of oxygen:

$$2CH_{4(g)} + 3O_{2(g)} \rightarrow 2CO_{(g)} + 4H_2O_{(g)}$$

And here's the equation for the incomplete combustion of ethane:

$$2C_2H_{6(g)} + 5O_{2(g)} \rightarrow 4CO_{(g)} + 6H_2O_{(g)}$$

Carbon monoxide poisoning

Incomplete combustion is a problem because carbon monoxide is poisonous. The oxygen in your bloodstream is carried around by haemoglobin. Carbon monoxide is better at binding to haemoglobin than oxygen is. So if you breathe in air with a high concentration of carbon monoxide it will bind to the haemoglobin in your bloodstream before the oxygen can. This means that less oxygen will reach your cells. You will start to suffer from symptoms associated with oxygen deprivation — things like fatigue, headaches, and nausea. At very high concentrations, carbon monoxide can even be fatal.

Any appliance that burns alkanes can produce carbon monoxide. This includes things like gas- or oil-fired boilers and heaters, gas stoves, and coal or wood fires. Cars also produce carbon monoxide. All appliances that use an alkane-based fuel need to be properly ventilated. They should be checked and maintained regularly, and their sources of ventilation should never be blocked. If you have any alkane burning appliances it's a good idea to have a carbon monoxide detector around.

Tip: Carbon monoxide is a colourless, odourless gas. This makes it very dangerous because you don't know it's there until it's too late.

Figure 5: *A carbon monoxide detector.*

Practice Questions — Application

Q1 Propane (C_3H_8) and octane (C_8H_{18}) are both alkanes.
   a) Explain why octane has a higher boiling point than propane.
   b) Write equations for the complete and incomplete combustion of octane.

Q2 Pentane and 2,2-dimethylpropane both have the molecular formula C_5H_{12}. Which has the higher boiling point? Explain your answer.

Q3 20 cm³ of an unknown hydrocarbon burns completely in 130 cm³ oxygen to produce 80 cm³ CO_2. What is the molecular fomula of the unknown hydrocarbon?

Practice Questions — Fact Recall

Q1 Describe the molecular shape around each carbon atom in an alkane.

Q2 Describe how a σ-bond is formed.

Q3 Name two factors that affect the boiling point of an alkane.

Q4 What are the products of the complete and incomplete combustion of alkanes?

Q5 Explain why carbon monoxide is poisonous.

- Be able to describe heterolytic fission in terms of one bonding atom receiving both electrons from the bonded pair.
- Be able to describe homolytic fission in terms of each bonding atom receiving one electron from the bonded pair, forming two radicals.
- Be able to describe a radical as a species with an unpaired electron and use 'dots' to represent species that are radicals in mechanisms.
- Know that a 'curly arrow' describes the movement of an electron pair and can show either heterolytic fission or formation of a covalent bond.
- Know how to write reaction mechanisms, using diagrams, to show clearly the movement of an electron pair with 'curly arrows' and relevant dipoles.

Specification Reference 4.1.1

7. Bond Fission

Before you go on to meet more organic reactions, you need to know a bit about the different types of bond fission and how the breaking and forming of bonds can be shown using reaction mechanisms. Here's a quick summary...

Homolytic and heterolytic bond fission

Breaking a covalent bond is called **bond fission**. A single covalent bond is a shared pair of electrons between two atoms. It can break in two ways.

Heterolytic fission

In heterolytic fission the bond breaks unevenly with one of the bonded atoms receiving both electrons from the bonded pair. Two different substances are formed — a positively charged cation (X^+), and a negatively charged anion (Y^-). The general equation for heterolytic fission is:

$$XY \rightarrow X^+ + Y^-$$

Homolytic fission

In homolytic fission, the bond breaks evenly and each bonding atom receives one electron from the bonded pair. Two electrically uncharged **radicals** are formed. Radicals are particles that have an unpaired electron. The unpaired electron is shown by a dot after the radical. The general equation for homolytic fission is:

$$XY \rightarrow X\bullet + Y\bullet$$

Because of the unpaired electron, these radicals are very reactive.

Reaction mechanisms

Reactions occur via a series of different processes. These processes can be shown step by step using a reaction mechanism. Reaction mechanisms use curly arrows to show the movement of electrons during a reaction. A curly arrow ($\curvearrowright$) shows the movement of a pair of electrons. You can use curly arrows to show how covalent bonds are broken.

> ### Example
> During heterolytic fission a pair of electrons shared in a covalent bond moves onto one of the species, giving it a negative charge. This leaves the other species with a positive charge.
>
> $$X \overset{\curvearrowright}{\underset{\cdot\cdot}{}} Y \rightarrow X^+ + Y^-$$
>
> *Curly arrows show the movement of a pair of electrons.*

Reaction mechanisms come up a lot in chemistry — it's much easier to explain what's happening in a reaction by drawing diagrams than by using words.

Practice Questions — Fact Recall

Q1 What is bond fission?

Q2 a) Name the two different types of bond fission.

    b) Describe how the two different types of bond fission are different.

Q3 What is a radical?

Q4 In a reaction mechanism, how do you show that a particle is a radical?

Q5 What do curly arrows show?

Tip: You can use filled in arrows (like this: →) or line arrows (like this: →) to show the movement of an electron pair. They mean the same thing.

Tip: There are lots of reaction mechanisms using curly arrows on pages 218-222.

8. Substitution Reactions

A substitution reaction is a reaction where an atom in a compound gets swapped with another atom. This section is all about how haloalkanes can be formed by substituting a hydrogen in an alkane with a halogen.

Formation of haloalkanes

Haloalkanes are formed when halogens react with alkanes in photochemical reactions. **Photochemical reactions** are reactions that are started by light. During the formation of haloalkanes a hydrogen atom is substituted (replaced) by a halogen such as chlorine or bromine in a **radical substitution reaction**.

There are lots of reactions between halogens and alkanes to form different haloalkanes, but one of the most industrially important free radical substitution reactions is the synthesis of chloromethane.

Synthesis of chloromethane

A mixture of methane and chlorine will not react on its own but when exposed to UV light it reacts with a bit of a bang to form chloromethane. The overall equation for this reaction is shown below.

$$CH_4 + Cl_2 \xrightarrow{UV} CH_3Cl + HCl$$

The reaction mechanism for the synthesis of chloromethane by a photochemical reaction has three stages — initiation, propagation and termination.

Initiation

In the initiation step, radicals are produced. Sunlight provides enough energy to break some of the Cl–Cl bonds — this is **photodissociation**.

$$Cl_2 \xrightarrow{UV} 2Cl\bullet$$

The bond splits equally and each atom gets to keep one electron (homolytic fission). These atoms are highly reactive radicals, $Cl\bullet$, because each one has an unpaired electron.

Propagation

During propagation, radicals are used up and created in a chain reaction. First, $Cl\bullet$ attacks a methane molecule:

$$Cl\bullet + CH_4 \rightarrow CH_3\bullet + HCl$$

The new methyl radical, $CH_3\bullet$, can then attack another Cl_2 molecule:

$$CH_3\bullet + Cl_2 \rightarrow CH_3Cl + Cl\bullet$$

The new $Cl\bullet$ can attack another CH_4 molecule, and so on, until all the Cl_2 or CH_4 molecules are used up.

Termination

In the termination step, radicals are mopped up. If two radicals join together, they make a stable molecule — this terminates the chain reaction. Many radical chain reactions have heaps of possible termination reactions. Here are some from the synthesis of chloromethane, there are three:

$$CH_3\bullet + Cl\bullet \rightarrow CH_3Cl \qquad CH_3\bullet + CH_3\bullet \rightarrow C_2H_6 \qquad Cl\bullet + Cl\bullet \rightarrow Cl_2$$

Learning Objectives:

- Be able to describe the reaction of alkanes with Cl_2 and Br_2 by radical substitution using ultraviolet radiation, including a mechanism involving homolytic fission and radical reactions in terms of initiation, propagation and termination.

- Understand the limitations of radical substitution in synthesis due to the formation of a mixture of organic products, in terms of further substitution and reactions at different positions in a carbon chain.

Specification Reference 4.1.2

Tip: The reaction between bromine and methane works in the same way as the reaction between chlorine and methane — you just swap Cl for Br. The overall equation is then:

$$CH_4 + Br_2 \xrightarrow{UV} CH_3Br + HBr$$

The mechanism is exactly the same too.

Exam Tip
When you write radical equations, make sure that there are the <u>same number</u> of radicals on each side (or that two radicals are combining to create a non-radical).

Problems with radical substitution

The big problem with radical substitution if you're trying to make a particular product is that you don't only get the product you're after, but a mixture of products. For example, if you're trying to make chloromethane, and there's too much chlorine in the reaction mixture, some of the remaining hydrogen atoms on the chloromethane molecule will be swapped for chlorine atoms. The propagation reactions happen again, this time to make dichloromethane (CH_2Cl_2):

$$Cl\bullet + CH_3Cl \rightarrow CH_2Cl\bullet + HCl$$
$$CH_2Cl\bullet + Cl_2 \rightarrow CH_2Cl_2 + Cl\bullet$$

It doesn't stop there. Another substitution reaction can take place to form trichloromethane ($CHCl_3$):

$$Cl\bullet + CH_2Cl_2 \rightarrow CHCl_2\bullet + HCl$$
$$CHCl_2\bullet + Cl_2 \rightarrow CHCl_3 + Cl\bullet$$

Tetrachloromethane (CCl_4) is formed in the last possible substitution. There are no more hydrogens attached to the carbon atom, so the substitution process has to stop. So the end product is a mixture of CH_3Cl, CH_2Cl_2, $CHCl_3$ and CCl_4. This is a nuisance, because you have to separate the chloromethane from the other three unwanted by-products.

The best way of reducing the chance of these by-products forming is to have an excess of methane. This means there's a greater chance of a chlorine radical colliding only with a methane molecule and not a chloromethane molecule.

Another problem with radical substitution is that it can take place at any point along the carbon chain. So a mixture of isomers can be formed. For example, reacting propane with chlorine will produce a mixture of 1-chloropropane and 2-chloropropane.

Practice Questions — Application

Q1 Bromine reacts with methane to form bromomethane in a three-stage reaction mechanism.

   a) Give the names of the three stages of this reaction mechanism.

   b) Write equations to show what happens at each of these stages.

   c) What other products besides bromomethane are likely to be in the reaction mixture?

Q2 Ethane (C_2H_6) reacts with chlorine to form chloroethane (C_2H_5Cl).

   a) What name is given to the mechanism for this reaction?

   b) Describe this reaction mechanism.

   c) This reaction gives a mixture of products. How could the concentration of chloroethane in the final mixture be increased?

Practice Questions — Fact Recall

Q1 Write an equation for the production of chloromethane from chlorine and methane.

Q2 What type of fission occurs in the initiation step of a free radical substitution reaction?

Q3 Give two reasons why a mixture of products is formed during free radical substitution reactions.

9. Alkenes and their Properties

The alkenes are another group of hydrocarbons. They're really similar to alkanes but they contain a carbon-carbon double bond. This topic is all about alkenes and how to name them.

What are alkenes?

Alkenes have the general formula C_nH_{2n}. They're just made of carbon and hydrogen atoms, so they're hydrocarbons. Alkene molecules all have at least one C=C double covalent bond. Molecules with C=C double bonds are **unsaturated** because they can make more bonds with extra atoms in addition reactions.

┌─ **Examples** ─────────────────────────────

Here are a few pretty diagrams of alkenes:

propene

penta-1,3-diene

cyclopentene

A cyclic alkene has two fewer hydrogen atoms than an open-chain alkene. Carbons can only have four bonds — a double bond means that the carbons can make one less bond with a hydrogen.

Naming alkenes

Alkenes are named in the same way as alkanes (see pages 199-201), but the -ane ending is changed to an -ene ending — see Figure 2.

No. of Carbon Atoms	Stem	Alkene
2	eth-	ethene (C_2H_4)
3	prop-	propene (C_3H_6)
4	but-	butene (C_4H_8)
5	pent-	pentene (C_5H_{10})
6	hex-	hexene (C_6H_{12})

Figure 2: *Naming some alkenes.*

For alkenes with more than three carbons, you need to say which carbon the double bond starts from.

┌─ **Example** ──────────────────────────────

The longest chain is 5 carbons, so the stem of the name is pent-.

The functional group is C=C, so it's pentene. Number the carbons from right to left (so the double bond starts on the lowest possible number). The first carbon in the double bond is carbon 2. So this molecule is pent-2-ene.

pent-2-ene

Learning Objectives:

- Be able to use the IUPAC rules of nomenclature to systematically name alkenes.

- Know that alkenes are unsaturated hydrocarbons containing a C=C bond.

- Know that a C=C bond comprises a π-bond and a σ-bond and that there is restricted rotation of the π-bond.

- Be able to explain the reactivity of alkenes in terms of the relatively low bond enthalpy of the π-bond.

- Be able to explain the trigonal planar shape and bond angle around each carbon in the C=C of alkenes in terms of electron pair repulsion.

Specification Reference 4.1.1, 4.1.3

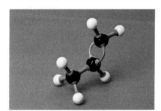

Figure 1: *A molecular model of propene.*

Tip: When you're naming alkenes the stem is based on the longest continuous carbon chain <u>containing a double bond</u> — even if there is a carbon chain that is longer.

If the alkene has two double bonds the suffix becomes diene. The stem of the name usually gets an extra 'a' too (e.g. buta-, penta-, not but-, pent-) when there's more than one double bond. And you might see the numbers written first.

┌─ **Example** ──────────────────

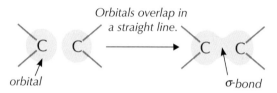

This molecule can be named as buta-1,3-diene or 1,3-butadiene.

Structure of a double bond

A double bond is made up of a **sigma (σ-) bond** and a **pi (π-) bond**. The σ-bond is formed in the same way as it is in alkanes (see page 203) — two orbitals overlap in a straight line which gives the highest possible electron density between the two nuclei (see Figure 3). This is a single covalent bond.

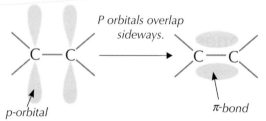

Figure 3: The formation of a sigma (σ-) bond.

A π-bond is formed when two p orbitals overlap sideways. It's got two parts to it — one 'above' and one 'below' the molecular axis. This is because the p orbitals which overlap are dumb-bell shaped — see Figure 4.

Figure 4: The formation of a pi (π-) bond.

π-bonds are weaker than σ-bonds because the electron density is spread out above and below the nuclei. This means that the electrostatic attraction between the nuclei and the shared pair of electrons is weaker, so π-bonds have a relatively low bond enthalpy. This means that a double bond (π-bond + σ-bond) is not twice as strong as a single bond (just a σ-bond).

Reactivity of the alkenes

Each double bond in an alkene is a bit like a hot dog. The π-bond is the bun and the σ-bond is sandwiched in the middle like the sausage — see Figure 5.

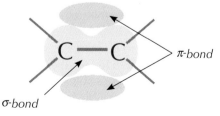

Figure 5: Structure of a double bond.

Because there are two pairs of electrons in the bond, the C=C double bond has a really high electron density. This makes alkenes pretty reactive. Another reason for the high reactivity is that the π-bond sticks out above and below the rest of the molecule. So, the π-bond is likely to be attacked by particles that have a low electron density and can accept a pair of electrons — these particles are called **electrophiles**. The low bond enthalpy of the π-bond also contributes to the reactivity of alkenes. Because the double bond's so reactive, alkenes are handy starting points for making other organic compounds and for making petrochemicals (organic compounds made from petroleum).

Tip: See page 218 for more on electrophiles.

Double bond rotation

Carbon atoms in a C=C double bond and the atoms bonded to these carbons all lie in the same plane (they're planar). The three bonds repel each other as much as possible and arrange themselves into a trigonal planar shape — the atoms attached to each double-bond carbon are at the corners of an imaginary equilateral triangle — see Figure 6.

Tip: Because of the double bond, alkenes are much more reactive than alkanes, which don't contain a double bond.

The bond angles in the planar unit are all 120°.

Figure 6: The trigonal planar shape around each carbon of C=C bonds in alkenes.

Ethene, C_2H_4 (as in Figure 6) is completely planar, but in larger alkenes, only the >C=C< unit is planar.

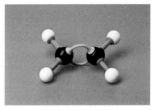

Figure 7: A molecular model of ethene. All of the atoms are in the same plane.

Example

This molecule is but-1-ene. The carbon-carbon double bond section of the molecule is planar and the carbon-carbon single bond section is non-planar.

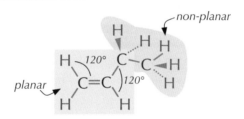

Tip: The C–C single bond section isn't planar because the bonding electron pairs repel each other giving a tetrahedral shape. The bond angles in a tetrahedral molecule are 109.5°.

Another important thing about C=C double bonds is that atoms can't rotate around them like they can around single bonds. This is because the p orbitals have to stay in the same position to overlap and form a π-bond. Double bonds are also fairly rigid — they don't bend much. Even though atoms can't rotate about the double bond, things can still rotate about any single bonds in the molecule.

Tip: See pages 104-107 for loads more about the shapes of molecules.

Example

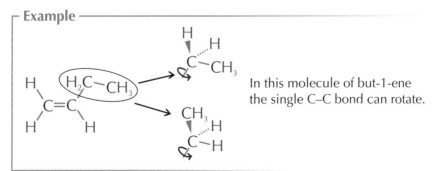

In this molecule of but-1-ene the single C–C bond can rotate.

The restricted rotation around the C=C double bond is what causes alkenes to form stereoisomers (see page 215).

Practice Questions — Application

Q1 Name the alkenes below:

a)

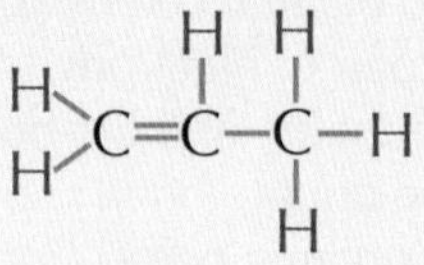

$$H_2C=C(H)-C(H_2)-H$$

(structure showing: H₂C=CH–CH₂–H with H's drawn explicitly)

b)

$$H-C(H_2)-C(H)=C(H)-C(H_2)-H$$

c)

$$H-C(H_2)-C(H_2)-C(H)=C(H)-C(H)=C(H_2)$$

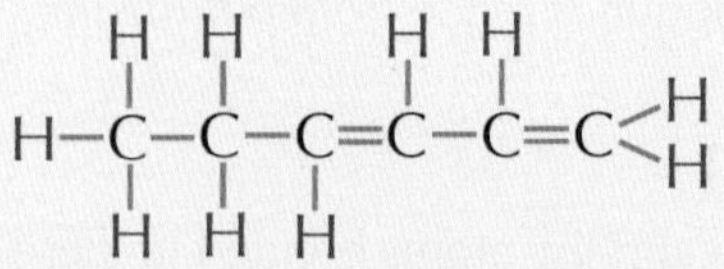

d)

$$H-C(H_2)-C(CH_3)=C(H_2)$$

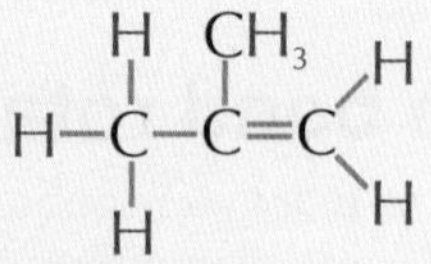

Q2 Propene is more reactive than propane. Explain why.

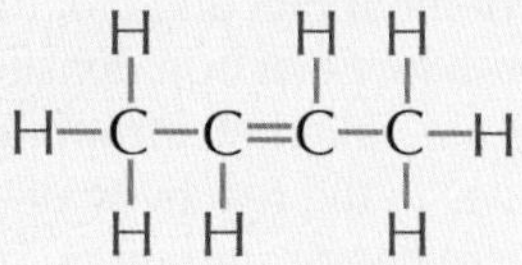

Q3 The table below shows the average bond enthalpies of single and double carbon-carbon bonds:

Type of bond	Average bond enthalpy (kJ mol⁻¹)
C–C	+347
C=C	+612

Using your knowledge of the structure of C=C double bonds, explain why the average bond enthalpy of a C=C double bond is not twice as large as that of a C–C single bond.

Practice Questions — Fact Recall

Q1 What is the general formula of an alkene?

Q2 a) Draw a diagram to show how a sigma bond is formed.

   b) Draw a diagram to show how a pi bond is formed.

Q3 Are C=C double bonds susceptible to attack by nucleophiles or electrophiles?

Q4 a) What does the term trigonal planar mean?

   b) Which part of an alkene molecule is trigonal planar?

10. Stereoisomers

Learning Objectives:

- Be able to define stereoisomers as compounds with the same structural formula but with a different arrangement in space.

- Be able to describe *E/Z* isomerism as an example of stereoisomerism, in terms of restricted rotation about a double bond and the requirement for two different groups to be attached to each carbon atom of the C=C group.

- Be able to use the Cahn–Ingold–Prelog (CIP) priority rules to identify the *E* and *Z* stereoisomers.

- Be able to describe cis-trans isomerism as a special case of *E/Z* isomerism in which two of the substituent groups attached to each carbon atom of the C=C group are the same.

- Be able to determine the possible E/Z or cis–trans stereoisomers of an organic molecule, given its structural formula.

Specification Reference 4.1.3

Structural isomers aren't the only isomers you need to know about. You also need to know all about stereoisomers... which is what this topic is about.

E/Z isomerism

Stereoisomers have the same structural formula but a different arrangement in space. Some alkenes have stereoisomers — this is because there's a lack of rotation around the C=C double bond. When the double-bonded carbon atoms each have two different atoms or groups attached to them, you get an 'E-isomer' and a 'Z-isomer'.

Each of the groups linked to the double-bonded carbons is given a priority. If the two carbon atoms have their 'higher priority groups' on opposite sides, then it's an *E*-isomer. If the two carbon atoms have their 'higher priority groups' on the same side, then it's a Z-isomer — see Figure 1.

Figure 1: *E-isomers and Z-isomers.*
In these diagrams X and Y are the higher priority groups.

Examples — Maths Skills

The double-bonded carbon atoms in but-2-ene (C_4H_8) each have an H and a CH_3 group attached. H groups are always the lowest priority, so the CH_3 groups on each of the carbons will be the highest priority.

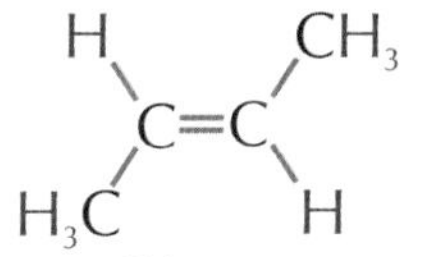

When the CH_3 groups are across the double bond then it's the *E*-isomer.

This molecule is *E*-but-2-ene.

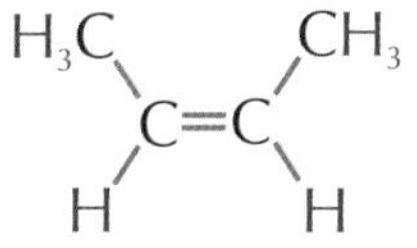

When the CH_3 groups are both above or both below the double bond then it's the *Z*-isomer.

This molecule is Z-but-2-ene.

In pent-2-ene (C_5H_{10}) one of the double-bonded carbon atoms has an H and a CH_3 group attached to it. The other has an H and a CH_2CH_3 group attached.

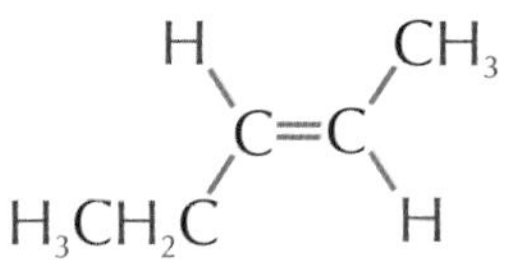

The high priority groups (CH_3 and CH_2CH_3) are across the double bond so it's the *E*-isomer.

This molecule is *E*-pent-2-ene.

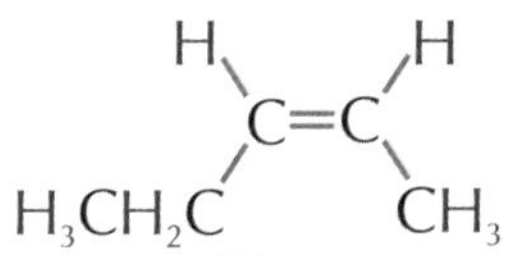

The high priority groups are both below the double bond so it's the *Z*-isomer.

This molecule is Z-pent-2-ene.

Tip: See page 213 for more about why double bonds can't rotate.

Tip: In alkanes, the groups are free to rotate around the single C-C bonds, so they don't form *E/Z* isomers.

Cahn-Ingold-Prelog priority rules

Figure 2: *Sir Christopher Ingold was one of the Chemists who developed the Cahn-Ingold-Prelog priority rules.*

When the carbons on either end of a double bond both have the same groups attached, then it's easy to work out which is the *E*-isomer and which is the *Z*-isomer (like in the example on the last page). It only starts to get problematic if the carbon atoms both have totally different groups attached. Fortunately, three clever people (Mr Cahn, Mr Ingold and Mr Prelog) came up with a solution to this problem. Using the **Cahn-Ingold-Prelog (CIP) rules** you can work out which is the *E*-isomer and which is the *Z*-isomer for any alkene. They're really simple, and they work every time.

The highest priority group on each of the C=C carbons is the one which has the atom with the highest atomic number directly bonded to the carbon atom. If the higher priority groups on each of the C=C atoms are positioned on the same side of the double bond, then the molecule is the *Z*-isomer, and if they're on opposite sides then it's the *E*-isomer.

Tip: If the two groups connected to one of the double-bonded carbons in an alkene are the same, then it won't have *E/Z* isomers. So neither propene nor but-1-ene have *E/Z* isomers. Try drawing them out if you're not sure.

Example — Maths Skills

The molecule on the right shows one of the stereoisomers of 1-bromo-1-chloro-2-fluoroethene. The atoms directly attached to carbon-1 are bromine and chlorine. Bromine has an atomic number of 35 and chlorine has an atomic number of 17. So bromine is the higher priority group. The atoms directly attached to carbon-2 are fluorine and hydrogen. Fluorine has an atomic number of 9 and hydrogen has an atomic number of 1. So fluorine is the higher priority group.

In this stereoisomer of 1-bromo-1-chloro-2-fluoroethene, the higher priority groups (bromine and fluorine) are positioned across the double bond from one another. So it's the **E-isomer**.

In the *Z*-isomer, the higher priority groups are positioned on the same side of the double bond:

Exam Tip
An easy way to remember which isomer is which is to remember that in the *Z*-isomer, the groups are on 'ze zame zide', but in the *E*-isomer, they are 'enemies'.

Sometimes, the atoms directly bonded to the carbon are the same. For example, a methyl group and an ethyl group both have a carbon atom directly bonded to the C=C carbon. If this is the case then you have to look at the next atom along in each group to work out which has the higher priority.

Example — Maths Skills

In the isomer of 1-bromo-1-chloro-2-methylbut-1-ene shown below, the atoms directly attached to carbon-1 are bromine and chlorine. Bromine has an atomic number of 35 and chlorine has an atomic number of 17. So bromine is the higher priority group.

Meanwhile, carbon-2 is directly bonded to two carbon atoms, so you need to go further along the chain to work out the ordering. The methyl carbon is only attached to hydrogen atoms, but the ethyl carbon is attached to another carbon atom. So the ethyl group is higher priority. The higher priority groups (ethyl and bromine) are positioned across the double bond from one another. So it's the **E-isomer**.

Cis-trans isomerism

Cis-trans isomerism is a special type of *E/Z* isomerism where the two carbon atoms either side of the double bond have at least one group in common. The cis-isomer is the one that has the two identical groups on the same side of the C=C double bond. The *trans*-isomer is the one that has the two identical groups on opposite sides of the C=C double bond — see Figure 4.

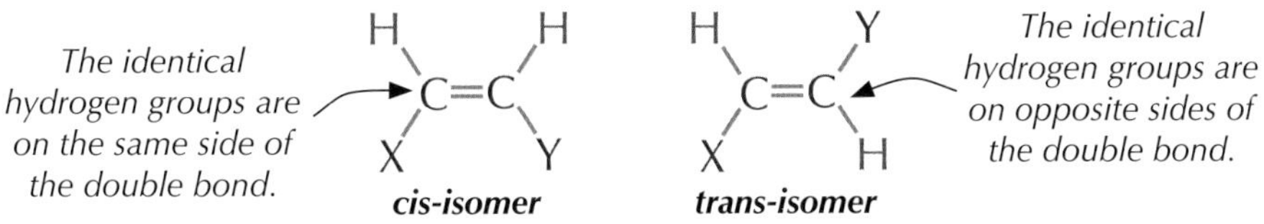

Tip: Because *cis-trans* isomerism is a type of *E/Z* isomerism, any molecule that shows *cis-trans* isomerism will also show *E/Z* isomerism.

The identical hydrogen groups are on the same side of the double bond.

The identical hydrogen groups are on opposite sides of the double bond.

cis-isomer   *trans-isomer*

Figure 4: Cis-isomers and trans-isomers.

Tip: To remember which is the *trans*-isomer and which is the *cis*-, it can be helpful to remember that the trans-Siberian railway goes <u>across</u> Siberia — so in the *trans*-isomer the same groups are <u>across</u> the double bond. And in the <u>c</u>is isomer, the same groups are on the <u>s</u>ame <u>s</u>ide.

--- Example ---

This is *cis*-1-fluoropropene:

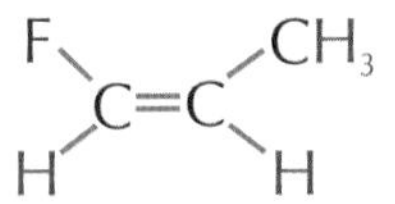

1-fluoropropene shows *cis-trans* isomerism because both of the carbons around the double bond have a hydrogen atom and another group (F or CH_3) attached to them.

You can't use the *cis-trans* system if there are more than two different groups (other than hydrogen atoms) attached around the double bond because you can't tell which isomer is which.

--- Example ---

Here is the structure of 1-bromo-1-fluoropropene:

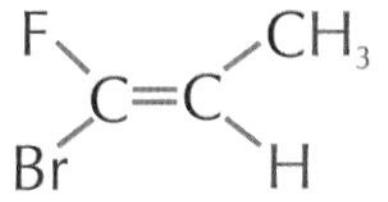

1-bromo-1-fluoropropene has more than two different groups (other than hydrogen atoms) attached around the double bond. As a result the *cis–trans* system doesn't work. The *E/Z* system keeps on working though. In the *E/Z* system, Br has a higher priority than F, so the names depend on where the Br atom is in relation to the CH_3 group (which has a higher priority than the H atom).

Tip: If all this isomer stuff is a bit confusing, try to get your hands on a molecular modelling kit and have a go making the isomers yourself — it should make it all a bit clearer.

Practice Questions — Application

Q1 For each of the molecules below, state if it is:

a) an *E*-isomer or a *Z*-isomer.

b) a *cis*-isomer or a *trans*-isomer.

i)

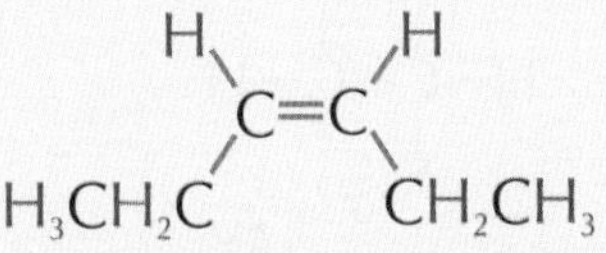

ii)

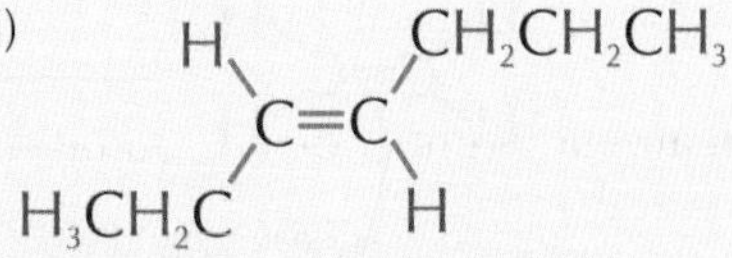

Q2 Draw the two stereoisomers of 3-methylhex-2-ene and label which is the *E*-isomer and which is the *Z*-isomer.

11. Reactions of Alkenes

Remember those alkenes from page 211 — well they're back and this time they're reacting.

Electrophilic addition reactions

Electrophilic addition reactions aren't too complicated. The double bond in an alkene opens up and atoms are added to the carbon atoms. Electrophilic addition reactions happen because the double bond has got plenty of electrons and is easily attacked by **electrophiles**. Electrophiles are electron pair acceptors — they're usually a bit short of electrons, so they're attracted to areas where there's lots of them about.

┌─ **Examples** ─────────────────────────────
Here are a few examples of electrophiles.

Positively charged ions are electrophiles. ⟶ NO_2^+

H^+

$$\underset{\underset{H}{|}}{\overset{\overset{H}{|}}{H-C}}-\underset{\underset{H}{|}}{\overset{\overset{H}{|}}{\overset{\delta+}{C}}}-\overset{\delta-}{Br}$$

Polar molecules can also be electrophiles — the δ+ atom is attracted to places with lots of electrons.

The double bond is also nucleophilic — it's attracted to places that don't have enough electrons.

You need to learn the mechanism for electrophilic addition. Here is the general electrophilic addition reaction equation, using ethene as an example:

$$H_2C=CH_2 + X-Y \rightarrow CH_2XCH_2Y$$

$$\underset{H}{\overset{H}{\diagdown}}\underset{1}{C}=\underset{2}{C}\underset{H}{\overset{H}{\diagup}}$$

$$\overset{\delta+}{X}-\overset{\delta-}{Y}$$

The carbon-carbon double bond repels the electrons in the X–Y bond, which polarises the X–Y bond (or the bond could already be polar, like in HBr).

Two electrons from the carbon-carbon double bond attack the δ+ X atom, creating a new bond between carbon 1 and the X atom. The X–Y bond breaks (heterolytic fission) and the electrons from the bond are taken by the Y atom to form a negative ion with a lone pair of electrons. Carbon 2 is left electron deficient — when the double bond was broken carbon 1 took the electrons to form a bond with the X atom, which left carbon 2 as a positively charged **carbocation** intermediate.

$$\underset{H}{\overset{H}{\diagdown}}\underset{1}{C}=\underset{2}{C}\underset{H}{\overset{H}{\diagup}} \longrightarrow H-\underset{\underset{X}{|}}{\overset{\overset{H}{|}}{C}}-\underset{+}{\overset{\overset{H}{|}}{C}}-H$$

$$\overset{\delta+}{X}-\overset{\delta-}{Y} \qquad \qquad \bar{:}Y$$

The Y⁻ ion then acts as a **nucleophile**, attacking the positively charged carbocation intermediate, donating its lone pair of electrons and forming a new bond with carbon 2.

Learning Objectives:

- Be able to define and use the term electrophile as an electron pair acceptor.

- Know the mechanism of electrophilic addition in alkenes by heterolytic fission.

- Be able to describe the addition reactions of alkenes with:

  (i) hydrogen in the presence of a suitable catalyst, e.g. Ni, to form alkanes.

  (ii) halogens to form dihaloalkanes, including the use of bromine to detect the presence of a double C=C bond as a test for unsaturation in a carbon chain (PAG 7).

  (iii) steam in the presence of an acid catalyst, e.g. H_3PO_4, to form alcohols.

  (iv) hydrogen halides to form haloalkanes.

- Be able to use Markownikoff's rule to predict formation of a major organic product in addition reactions of H–X to unsymmetrical alkenes, in terms of the relative stabilities of carbocation intermediates in the mechanism.

  Specification Reference 4.1.3

Tip: A nucleophile is an electron pair donor.

Tip: A carbocation is an organic ion containing a positively charged carbon atom.

So overall, the X–Y molecule has been added to the alkene across the double bond to form a saturated compound.

Exam Tip
You <u>must</u> draw the curly arrows coming from the <u>lone pair</u> of electrons or from the <u>bond</u>. If you don't — you won't get all the marks for the mechanism in the exam.

Producing alkanes

Alkenes react with hydrogen gas to produce alkanes. The reaction needs a catalyst and a high temperature though. For example, ethene will react with hydrogen gas and a nickel catalyst at 150 °C to produce ethane. Here's the equation for the reaction:

$$H_2C=CH_2 + H_2 \xrightarrow[150\ °C]{Ni} CH_3CH_3$$

Reactions with halogens

Alkenes react with halogens to form dihaloalkanes. The halogens add across the double bond, and each of the carbon atoms ends up bonded to one halogen atom. It's an electrophilic addition reaction. The general reaction, using ethene as an example, is:

$$H_2C=CH_2 + X_2 \rightarrow CH_2XCH_2X$$

The mechanism for the reaction is shown below. Bromine is used as an example, but chlorine and iodine react in the same way.

Figure 1: *Unsaturated vegetable oils are reacted with hydrogen to form margarine.*

─ Example ───────────────

When you shake ethene with orange bromine water, the solution turns from orange to colourless. Here's the equation for this reaction:

$$H_2C=CH_2 + Br_2 \rightarrow CH_2BrCH_2Br$$

Here's the mechanism...

The double bond repels the electrons in Br$_2$, polarising Br–Br. This is called an induced dipole.

Heterolytic (unequal) fission of Br$_2$. The closer Br gives up its bonding electrons to the other Br and bonds to the C atom.

...and bonds to the other C atom, forming 1,2-dibromoethane.

You get a positively charged carbocation intermediate. The Br⁻ now zooms over...

Tip: The reaction mechanism is the same for any reaction between an alkene and a halogen. You can use it to predict what the product will be when an alkene you've never seen before reacts with a halogen.

Exam Tip
You could get asked to draw the mechanism for the reaction between any halogen and any alkene — not just bromine and ethene. It's not too hard though — the mechanism is the same for all alkenes, and you'll always end up with a halogen atom added to each of the carbon atoms that were double bonded. Simple as that.

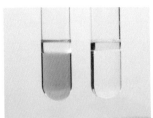

Figure 2: Bromine water has been added to two test tubes. The one on the right contains a compound with a C=C that has decolourised the bromine water. The one on the left contains a substance that doesn't react with bromine.

Tip: If you don't notice anything happen when you add your hydrocarbon to the bromine water, you should record 'no change' in your table of results as this is still an observation.

Tip: The reaction between steam and alkenes is also an electrophilic addition reaction. You don't need to worry about the mechanism though — it's a bit different because there's a catalyst involved.

Exam Tip
Other alkenes react in a similar way with HBr. Don't be put off if they give you a different alkene in the exam — the mechanism works in exactly the same way.

Test for unsaturation

The reaction between alkenes and bromine forms the basis of a test that can be used to distinguish between compounds that contain a double bond (like alkenes) and compounds that don't (like alkanes).

> PRACTICAL ACTIVITY GROUP **7**

- Use a pipette to add about 2 cm³ of orange bromine water to a test tube.
- Use a second, clean pipette to add about 2 cm³ of your unknown hydrocarbon sample to the same test tube.
- Stopper the test tube and give it a quick shake.
- Record any observations in a table of results.

Figure 3: Adding bromine water to a solution containing a carbon-carbon double bond turns the bromine water colourless.

If your unknown hydrocarbon is an alkene, then when you shake it with bromine water you should see the solution quickly turn from orange to colourless (see Figures 2 and 3). This is because the bromine is added across the double bond to form a colourless dibromoalkane — this happens by electrophilic addition.

Synthesising alcohols

Alkenes can be hydrated by steam at 300 °C and at a pressure of 60-70 atm. The reaction needs a solid phosphoric(V) acid catalyst. The reaction is used industrially to produce ethanol from ethene. Here's the equation for the reaction:

$$H_2C=CH_{2(g)} + H_2O_{(g)} \underset{\substack{300\,°C \\ 60\,atm}}{\overset{H_3PO_4}{\rightleftharpoons}} CH_3CH_2OH_{(g)}$$

The reaction's reversible and the reaction yield is low — with ethene it's only about 5%. This sounds rubbish, but you can recycle the unreacted ethene gas, making the overall yield of ethene a much more profitable 95%.

Synthesising haloalkanes

Alkenes undergo electrophilic addition reactions with hydrogen halides to form haloalkanes.

Example

This is the reaction between ethene and hydrogen bromide.

$$H_2C=CH_2 + HBr \rightarrow C_2H_5Br$$

It's an electrophilic addition reaction and the mechanism is very similar to the one for the addition of halogens on page 219.

Markownikoff's rule

If the hydrogen halide adds to a symmetrical alkene like ethene, only one product can be formed. But if the hydrogen halide adds to an unsymmetrical alkene, there are two possible products.

Tip: This electrophilic addition mechanism crops up in loads of different reactions, so make sure you've got it nailed.

― Example ―――――――――――――――――――

If you add hydrogen bromide to propene, the bromine atom could add to either the first carbon or the second carbon. This means you could produce 1-bromopropane or 2-bromopropane.

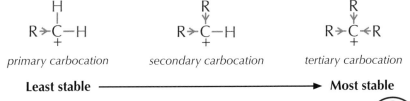

propene

1-bromopropane

2-bromopropane

The amount of each product formed depends on how stable the carbocation formed in the middle of the reaction is. The three possible carbocations are:

primary carbocation
(one R group)

secondary carbocation
(two R groups)

tertiary carbocation
(three R groups)

Tip: The alkyl groups don't give up their electrons to the carbon atom — they just move some of their negatively charged electrons nearer to it, which helps to stabilise the positive charge.

R is an alkyl group — an alkane with a hydrogen removed, e.g. CH_3.

Carbocations with more alkyl groups are more stable because the alkyl groups feed electrons towards the positive charge. You can show that an alkyl group is donating electrons by drawing an arrow on the bond that points to where the electrons are donated.

primary carbocation

secondary carbocation

tertiary carbocation

Least stable ――――――――――――――――→ **Most stable**

As a rule, more stable carbocations are much more likely to form than less stable ones. This is because the first step of the mechanism is more likely to lead to the formation of the most stable carbocation. So there will be more of the product formed via the more stable carbocation than there is via the less stable carbocation. This rule can be applied in order to explain what the major product will be when a hydrogen halide reacts with an unsymmetrical alkene.

This can be summed up by Markownikoff's rule, which says that the major product from addition of a hydrogen halide (HX) to an unsymmetrical alkene is the one where hydrogen adds to the carbon with the most hydrogens already attached. The reaction to form this product will have occurred via the most stable carbocation intermediate.

HOW SCIENCE WORKS

Figure 4: *Vladimir Markownikoff.*

Here's how hydrogen bromide reacts with propene:

$$H_2C=CHCH_3 + HBr \rightarrow CH_3CHBrCH_3 \qquad H_2C=CHCH_3 + HBr \rightarrow CH_2BrCH_2CH_3$$

2-bromopropane
major product

1-bromopropane
minor product

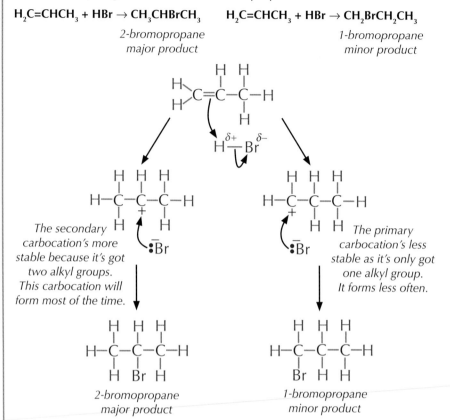

Tip: The product that there's most of is called the <u>major</u> product, or the <u>Markownikov</u> product — after the Russian scientist Vladimir Markownikov who came up with the theory that the product formed most often is the one where the hydrogen adds to the carbon atom with the most hydrogen atoms already attached.

The secondary carbocation's more stable because it's got two alkyl groups. This carbocation will form most of the time.

The primary carbocation's less stable as it's only got one alkyl group. It forms less often.

Tip: When you're drawing mechanisms make sure the charges balance. That way you'll know if you've managed to lose electrons along the way.

2-bromopropane
major product

1-bromopropane
minor product

Here's how hydrogen bromide reacts with 2-methylbut-2-ene:

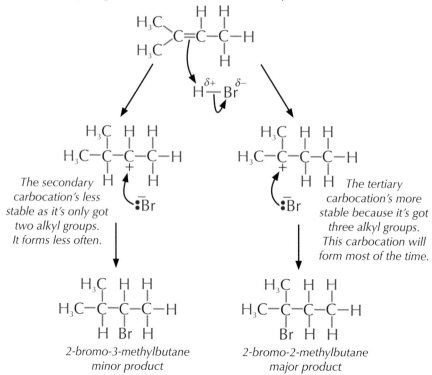

Exam Tip
It makes it easier to see what the main product is if you draw out all the possible cations each time — then there's less chance of making a mistake.

The secondary carbocation's less stable as it's only got two alkyl groups. It forms less often.

The tertiary carbocation's more stable because it's got three alkyl groups. This carbocation will form most of the time.

2-bromo-3-methylbutane
minor product

2-bromo-2-methylbutane
major product

Practice Questions — Application

Q1 Predict the product of the reaction between pent-2-ene and hydrogen gas at 150 °C with a nickel catalyst.

Q2 When propene is added to bromine water, the solution decolourises.

a) Write an equation for the reaction that is occurring.

b) Name and outline the mechanism for this reaction.

c) Bromine water does not decolourise when added to an unknown chemical. What does this tell you about the unknown compound?

Q3 Outline the mechanism for the reaction between but-2-ene and hydrogen bromide.

Q4 a) Draw and name the two different products that could be produced when hydrogen bromide reacts with but-1-ene.

b) Predict, with reasoning, the major product of the reaction.

Q5 The structure of penta-1,3-diene is shown below:

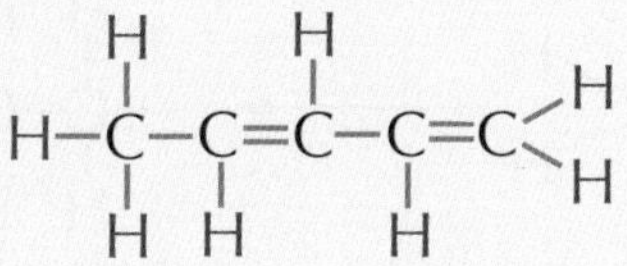

Draw the products formed when this alkene reacts with HBr.

Tip: Q5 is a bit tricky so here's a hint. If there are two double bonds in an alkene, the addition could occur at either or both of the double bonds, so you'll get more than two products.

Practice Questions — Fact Recall

Q1 What is an electrophile?

Q2 Give two examples of electrophiles.

Q3 What could you react with ethene to produce bromoethane?

Q4 What can you use bromine water to test for?

Q5 Write the equation for the hydration of ethene by steam. Include the conditions for this reaction and the state symbols of all the substances in your answer.

Q6 What does Markownikoff's rule state?

- Be able to describe the addition polymerisation of alkenes and substituted alkenes.
- Be able to deduce the repeat unit of an addition polymer from a given monomer.
- Be able to identify the monomer that would produce a given section of an addition polymer.
- Understand the benefits for sustainability of processing waste polymers by combustion for energy production and use as an organic feedstock for the production of plastics and other organic chemicals.
- Understand the need for the removal of toxic waste products, e.g. removal of HCl formed during disposal by combustion of halogenated plastics (e.g. PVC).
- Understand the benefits to the environment of development of biodegradable and photodegradable polymers.

Specification Reference 4.1.3

12. Addition Polymers

Lots of small molecules (called monomers) can join together to form really long molecules (called polymers). You need to know how alkenes come together to form addition polymers. Read on...

Addition polymers

The double bonds in alkenes can open up and join together to make long chains called **polymers**. It's kind of like they're holding hands in a big line. The individual, small alkenes are called **monomers**. This is called addition polymerisation.

─ Example ─────────────────────

Poly(ethene) is made by the addition polymerisation of ethene.

ethene monomers   *a section of poly(ethene)*

────────────────────────────────

Addition polymerisation reactions can be written like this...

monomer   *polymer*

...where the *n* stands for a very large number of repeat units (monomers) in the polymer — there can be as many as 10 000.

To find the monomer used to form an addition polymer, take the repeat unit and add a double bond.

─ Example ─────────────────────

To find the monomer used to make the polymer below you first need to look for the repeat unit.

polymer   *repeating unit*

Then replace the horizontal carbon-carbon bond with a double bond and remove the unnecessary side bonds to find the monomer.

repeat unit   *monomer — propene*

────────────────────────────────

Tip: The bit inside the brackets is the repeat unit of the polymer. The formula of the polymer is the bit with the brackets and the *n*.

Q1 Draw the repeating units of the polymers that would be formed from each of these alkenes:

Q2 Draw the alkenes that would form each of these polymers:

The widespread use of polymers

Synthetic polymers have loads of advantages, so they're incredibly widespread these days — we take them pretty much for granted. Just imagine what you'd have to live without if there were no polymers (see Figure 1).

Figure 1: *Some of the many items that are made out of synthetic polymers.*

Biodegradability of polymers

One of the really useful things about many everyday polymers is that they're very unreactive. This means food doesn't react with the PTFE coating on pans, plastic windows don't rot, plastic crates can be left out in the rain and they'll be okay, and so on. But this lack of reactivity also leads to a problem. Most polymers aren't biodegradable, and so they're really difficult to dispose of.

Disposing of waste plastics

In the UK over 2 million tonnes of plastic waste are produced each year. It's important to find ways to get rid of this waste while minimising environmental damage. There are various possible approaches (Figure 2).

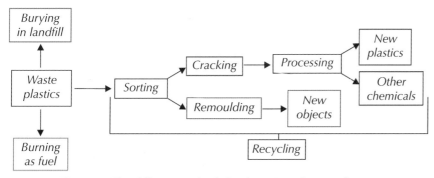

Figure 2: *The different methods for disposing of waste plastic.*

Burying waste plastic

Landfill is one option for dealing with waste plastics. This means taking waste to a landfill site, compacting it, and then covering it with soil. It is generally used when the plastic is:

- Difficult to separate from other waste.
- Not in sufficient quantities to make separation financially worthwhile.
- Too difficult technically to recycle.

But because the amount of waste we generate is becoming more and more of a problem, there's a need to reduce landfill as much as possible.

Recycling plastics

Because many plastics are made from non-renewable oil fractions, it makes sense to recycle plastics as much as possible. There's more than one way to recycle plastics. After sorting into different types, some plastics (poly(propene), for example) can be melted and remoulded, while others can be cracked into monomers which can be used as an organic feedstock to make more plastics or other chemicals.

Burning waste plastic

If recycling isn't possible for whatever reason, waste plastics can be burned — and the heat can be used to generate electricity. This process needs to be carefully controlled to reduce toxic gases. For example, polymers that contain chlorine (such as PVC) produce HCl when they're burned — this has to be removed. Waste gases from the combustion are passed through scrubbers which can neutralise gases such as HCl by allowing them to react with a base.

Making biodegradable polymers

Scientists can now make biodegradable polymers — ones that naturally decompose. Biodegradable polymers decompose pretty quickly in certain conditions — because organisms can digest them.

Biodegradable polymers can be made from materials such as starch (from maize and other plants) and from the hydrocarbon isoprene (2-methyl-1,3-butadiene). So, biodegradable polymers can be produced from renewable raw materials or from oil fractions.

Advantages of using renewable raw materials

Using renewable raw material has several advantages:

- Renewable raw materials aren't going to run out like oil will.
- When polymers biodegrade, carbon dioxide (a greenhouse gas) is produced. If your polymer is plant-based, then the CO_2 released as it decomposes is the same CO_2 absorbed by the plant when it grew. But with an oil-based biodegradable polymer, you're effectively transferring carbon from the oil to the atmosphere.
- Over their 'lifetime' some plant-based polymers save energy compared to oil-based plastics.

But whatever raw material you use, at the moment the energy for making polymers usually comes from fossil fuels.

Figure 3: A landfill site — burying waste plastic is one way of disposing of it.

Tip: See page 4 for more on how society makes decisions about things like recycling and waste plastic.

Exam Tip
Weighing up the advantages and disadvantages of things is an important skill in chemistry. You may be asked to do it in your exam, so make sure it's a skill you've mastered.

Tip: Releasing extra CO_2 into the atmosphere adds to the greenhouse effect and warms the Earth. See page 249 for loads more on the greenhouse effect.

Disadvantages of using biodegradable polymers

Although biodegradable polymers sound like a fab idea, there are a few disadvantages of using biodegradable plastics over the standard non-biodegradable ones.

Even though they're biodegradable, these polymers still need the right conditions before they'll decompose. You couldn't necessarily just put them in a landfill and expect them to perish away — because there's a lack of moisture and oxygen under all that compressed soil. You need to chuck them on a big compost heap. This means that you still need to collect and separate the biodegradable polymers from non-biodegradable plastics. At the moment, they're also more expensive than oil-based equivalents.

Figure 4: *A compostable plastic bag.*

Uses of biodegradable polymers

There are various potential uses — e.g. plastic sheeting used to protect plants from the frost can be made from poly(ethene) with starch grains embedded in it. In time the starch is broken down by microorganisms and the remaining poly(ethene) crumbles into dust. There's no need to collect and dispose of the old sheeting.

Other things scientists can do

Developing biodegradable plastics isn't the only thing that chemists can do to decrease the environmental damage caused by waste plastics. Other potential developments to solve the problem include:

- Continuing to develop photodegradable polymers (polymers which can be chemically broken down by light), and introducing them into everyday use.

- Developing better techniques for cracking polymers so that recycling polymers becomes more efficient.

- Finding new ways of making polymers from plant-based substances to reduce the use of finite raw materials like crude oil.

- Using processes with higher atom economy to reduce the amount of waste produced during manufacturing processes.

- Developing new, more efficient ways of sorting and recycling polymers.

Tip: See pages 80-82 for more on atom economy and why high atom economy processes are important.

Practice Questions — Fact Recall

Q1 What types of polymers are formed from alkenes?

Q2 Describe the process that leads to the formation of polymers from alkenes.

Q3 a) Explain why it is good for everyday polymers to be unreactive.

   b) What problem does the fact that plastics are unreactive cause?

Q4 Give two ways in which plastics can be recycled.

Q5 Burning plastic produces toxic gases.

   a) What toxic gas is produced when poly(chloroethene), also known as PVC, is burnt?

   b) How can this toxic gas be removed?

Q6 Give three advantages of making plastic from renewable raw materials rather than non-renewable materials such as oil.

Q7 Suggest two disadvantages of using biodegradable polymers.

Section Summary

Make sure you know...

- That a functional group is a group of atoms responsible for the characteristic reactions of a compound.
- What general formulas, homologous series, structural formulas, displayed formulas, and skeletal formulas are and how to use them.
- How you can use the general formula of a homologous series to predict the formula of any member of the series.
- What aromatic compounds, aliphatic compounds, alicyclic compounds, alkyl groups, saturated compounds and unsaturated compounds are.
- That structural isomers have the same molecular formula but different structural formulas.
- That alkanes are saturated hydrocarbons that only contain single C–C and C–H bonds.
- How to name alkanes using the IUPAC rules of nomenclature.
- Why atoms form a tetrahedral shape around each carbon atom in alkanes.
- That the single bonds in alkanes are called sigma (σ-) bonds, and they form from the overlap of orbitals directly between the bonding atoms.
- That atoms are free to rotate around sigma bonds.
- That the low reactivity of alkanes is due to the high bond enthalpy and low polarity of the C–C and C–H bonds.
- Why long or linear alkanes have higher boiling points than short or branched alkanes.
- How alkanes may undergo complete or incomplete combustion.
- Why carbon monoxide (CO) is toxic to humans.
- What heterolytic and homolytic fission are.
- That a radical is a species with an unpaired electron, and is represented in mechanisms by a dot next to the species' formula.
- What curly arrows show in reaction mechanisms and how to use them in diagrams.
- How haloalkanes are formed from alkanes in radical substitution reactions.
- The mechanism of radical substitution including initiation, propagation and termination.
- Why you can get a mixture of products in free radical substitution reactions.
- What alkenes are and how to name them.
- The structure of a C=C double bond in terms of pi (π-) and sigma (σ-) bonds.
- How to explain the relatively high reactivity of alkenes due to the low bond enthalpy of the pi bond.
- Why atoms form a trigonal planar shape around each carbon of the C=C double bond of alkenes.
- That stereoisomers have the same structural formula but different arrangements of the atoms in space.
- That *E/Z* isomerism and *cis-trans* isomerism are types of stereoisomerism, and why they occur.
- How to use the Cahn-Ingold-Prelog priority rules to identify *E* and *Z* stereoisomers.
- That an electrophile is an electron-pair acceptor.
- The mechanism of electrophilic addition in alkenes and how alkenes react with halogens, halides, steam and hydrogen.
- How to use Markownikoff's rule to predict the formation of a major organic product in addition reactions of H–X to unsymmetrical alkenes.
- How alkenes can join together to form addition polymers.
- How to work out the repeat unit of a polymer given its monomer and how to work out the monomer of a polymer given its repeat unit.
- The benefits for sustainability of processing waste polymers and the potential problems.
- The benefits to the environment of biodegradable and photodegradable polymers.

Exam-style Questions

1 2-methylpropene is an alkene that can react with chlorine or hydrogen chloride in an electrophilic addition reaction. From the table below, choose the correct option which shows the major products for each of these two reactions.

	Reaction with hydrogen chloride	Reaction with chlorine
A	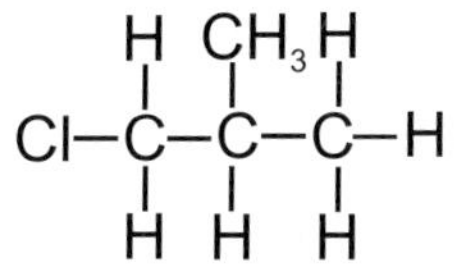	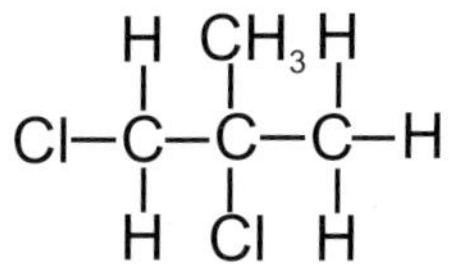
B	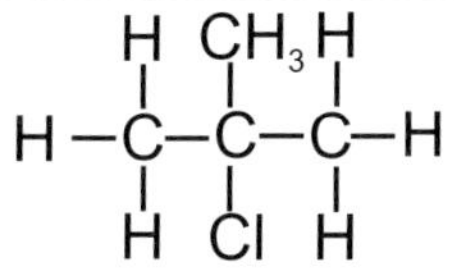	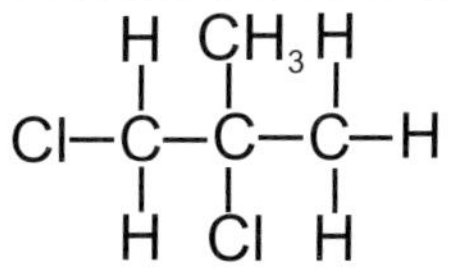
C	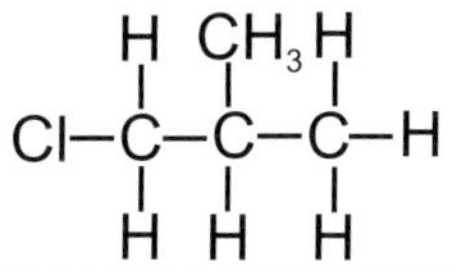	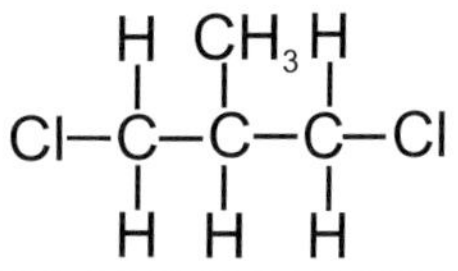
D	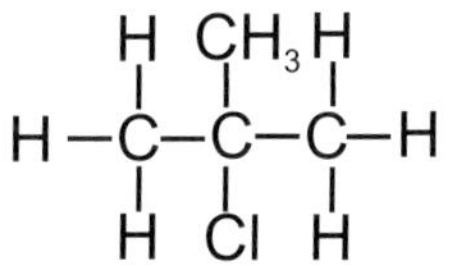	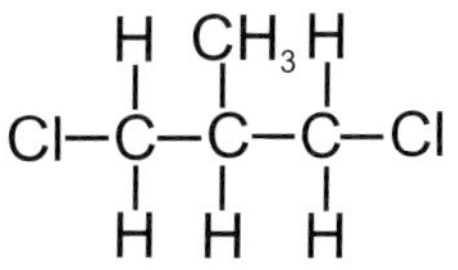

(1 mark)

2 Which of the following options shows the structural formula of methylbutane?

A $CH_3CH(CH_3)CH_2CH_3$

B C_5H_{12}

C

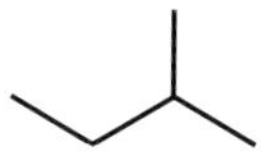

D

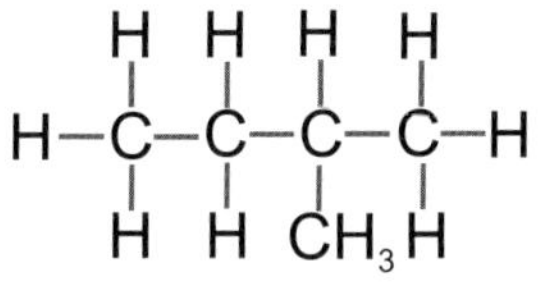

(1 mark)

3 When bromine is exposed to UV light, the Br–Br bond breaks and two radicals are formed.

(a) (i) What are radicals?

(1 mark)

(ii) What name is given to the type of bond fission that produces radicals?

(1 mark)

(b) Bromine reacts with ethane under UV light to form bromoethane.

(i) Write an equation for the formation of bromoethane.

(1 mark)

(ii) Outline the   chanism for this reaction, naming each step.

(3 marks)

(c) Suggest two haloalkanes other than bromoethane that could be produced during this reaction.

(2 marks)

4 The scheme below shows some reactions involving propene (C_3H_6):

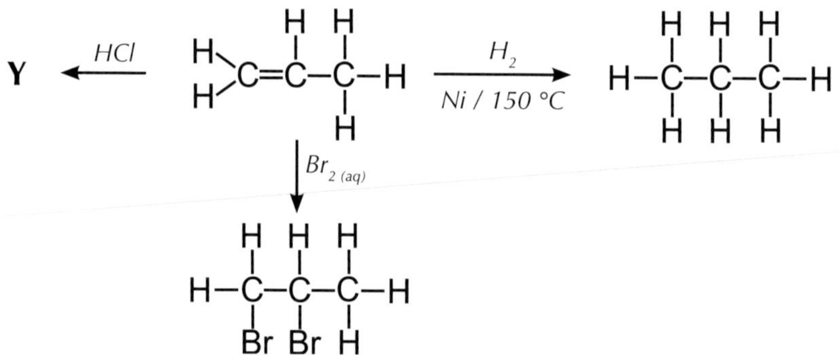

(a) Alkenes like propene are susceptible to attack by electrophiles.

(i) Draw a diagram to illustrate the structure of a carbon-carbon double bond.

(2 marks)

(ii) Explain why alkenes are susceptible to attack by electrophiles.

(2 marks)

(b) When propene is added to bromine water, 1,2-dibromopropane is produced.

(i) Outline the mechanism for this reaction, including dipoles where relevant.

(4 marks)

(ii) State what you would observe when this reaction takes place.

(1 mark)

(c) When propene reacts with HCl, molecule **Y** is formed.

Suggest two possible structures for molecule **Y**.

(2 marks)

5   2,2,4-trimethylpentane is a branched alkane widely used in petrol.
It is an isomer of the straight-chain alkane octane.

(a) (i) Draw the displayed formula of 2,2,4-trimethylpentane.

(1 mark)

(ii) The boiling point of 2,2,4-trimethylpentane is 372 K. Predict, with reasoning, whether you expect the boiling point of octane to be higher or lower than this.

(4 marks)

(b) Write an equation for the complete combustion of 2,2,4-trimethylpentane.

(1 mark)

(c) Alkanes are used as fuel in household appliances. Use your knowledge of combustion to explain the importance of an adequate supply of oxygen to the appliances.

(3 marks)

6   This question is about alkenes and their polymers.

(a) One of the stereoisomers of 1-bromo-1,3-butadiene is shown below:

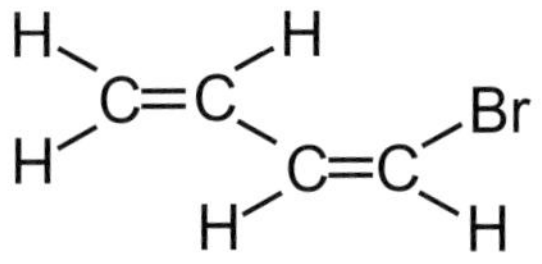

(i) What is stereoisomerism?

(1 mark)

(ii) Draw one other E/Z isomer of 1-bromo-1,3-butadiene and state whether the isomer you have drawn is the E-isomer or the Z-isomer.

(2 marks)

(b) Polyvinylacetate (PVA) is a synthetic polymer. It is one of the main components of PVA glue. The repeating unit of PVA is shown below:

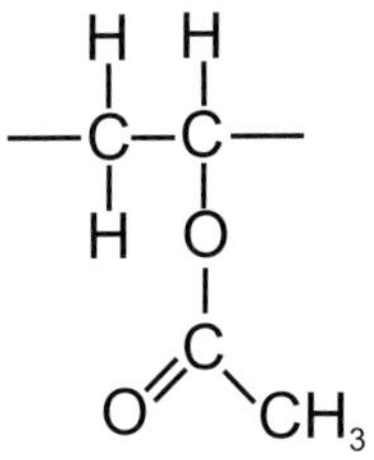

(i) What type of polymer is PVA?

(1 mark)

(ii) Draw the structure of the monomer that gives rise to PVA.

(1 mark)

(c) Alkene-based polymers are extremely useful, but disposing of waste polymers is a big problem. Discuss the advantages and disadvantages of using biodegradable polymers.

(4 marks)

Learning Objectives:

- Be able to use the IUPAC rules of nomenclature to systematically name alcohols.

- Be able to classify alcohols as primary, secondary and tertiary alcohols.

- Be able to explain the polarity of alcohols.

- Be able to explain, in terms of hydrogen bonding, the water solubility and the relatively low volatility of alcohols compared with alkanes.

Specification Reference 4.1.1, 4.2.1

Tip: It's pretty easy naming alcohols with saturated carbon chains. But if an alcohol is unsaturated (i.e. contains an alkene group), you need to remember to include it in the name too. E.g.:

H–C=C–C–C–H (with H H H on top, H H OH on bottom)

This molecule has a name based on 'butene' — it's 3-buten-1-ol.

Tip: If the alcohol functional group (-OH) is the most important one then the name ends in -ol, like in these examples. Otherwise, the molecule gets a hydroxy- prefix instead. For example, 1-hydroxypropanone.

1. Properties of Alcohols

Alcohols are organic compounds that contain an -OH functional group. This dramatically affects their physical properties compared to alkanes. Before you get on to that though, you need to know how to name them.

Nomenclature of alcohols

The **alcohol** homologous series has the general formula $C_nH_{2n+1}OH$. Alcohols are named using the same IUPAC naming rules as alkanes (see pages 199-201), but the suffix -ol is added in place of the -e on the end of the name.
You also need to indicate which carbon atom the alcohol functional group is attached to — the carbon number(s) comes before the -ol suffix.
If there are two -OH (hydroxyl) groups the molecule is a -diol, and if there are three it's a -triol.

┌ Examples

ethanol

The molecule is a saturated hydrocarbon where the longest continuous carbon chain is 2 carbon atoms, so the stem is eth- and the name will be based on 'ethane'.

There's one -OH attached to the carbon chain, so the suffix is -ol.

No matter which carbon atom the -OH group is attached to, the molecule will be exactly the same (-OH will always be attached to carbon atom 1), so there's no need to put a number.

So, the alcohol is called ethanol.

The molecule is a saturated hydrocarbon where the longest continuous carbon chain is 3 carbon atoms, so the stem is prop- and the name will be based on 'propane'.

There's one -OH attached to the carbon chain, so the suffix is -ol.

It's attached to the second carbon, so there's a 2 before the -ol.

There's also a methyl group attached to the second carbon, so there's a 2-methyl- prefix.

The alcohol is called 2-methylpropan-2-ol.

2-methylpropan-2-ol

ethane-1,2-diol

The molecule is a saturated hydrocarbon where the longest continuous carbon chain is 2 carbon atoms, so the stem is eth- and the name will be based on 'ethane'.

There are two -OH groups attached to the carbon chain, so the suffix is -diol.

There's one -OH attached to each carbon atom, so there's a 1,2- before the -diol.

So, the alcohol is called ethane-1,2-diol.

Primary, secondary and tertiary alcohols

An alcohol can be primary, secondary or tertiary, depending on which carbon atom the hydroxyl group -OH is bonded to. Primary alcohols are given the notation 1° and the -OH group is attached to a carbon with one alkyl group attached. Secondary alcohols are given the notation 2° and the -OH group is attached to a carbon with two alkyl groups attached. Tertiary alcohols are given the notation 3° (you can see where I'm going with this) and the -OH group is attached to a carbon with three alkyl groups attached (see Figure 1).

Tip: Remember that an alkyl group is an alkane with a hydrogen removed, for example CH_3 or CH_3CH_2.

Tip: 'R' just means any alkyl group.

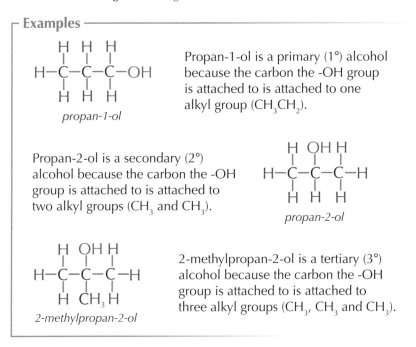

| primary alcohol | secondary alcohol | tertiary alcohol |

Figure 1: Diagrams of 1°, 2° and 3° alcohols.

Examples

Propan-1-ol is a primary (1°) alcohol because the carbon the -OH group is attached to is attached to one alkyl group (CH_3CH_2).

propan-1-ol

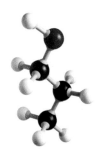

Figure 2: A molecular model of propan-1-ol.

Propan-2-ol is a secondary (2°) alcohol because the carbon the -OH group is attached to is attached to two alkyl groups (CH_3 and CH_3).

propan-2-ol

Tip: Alcohols can react in different ways depending on whether they are primary, secondary or tertiary — so it's important that you know the difference between them.

2-methylpropan-2-ol is a tertiary (3°) alcohol because the carbon the -OH group is attached to is attached to three alkyl groups (CH_3, CH_3 and CH_3).

2-methylpropan-2-ol

Physical properties of alcohols

Alcohols are generally polar molecules due to the electronegative hydroxyl group which pulls the electrons in the C–OH bond away from the carbon atom. The hydroxyl group (-OH) is also polar, with a δ– charge on the oxygen atom and a δ+ charge on the hydrogen atom (see Figure 3).

Tip: Electronegativity is the ability of an atom to attract the bonding electrons in a covalent bond. There's more about it on page 108.

$$\overset{\delta+}{R_1}-\overset{\delta-}{O}-\overset{\delta+}{H}$$

Figure 3: Charge distribution in an alcohol.

The partial positive charge on the hydrogen atom in the hydroxyl group can attract the lone pairs on an oxygen from a neighbouring molecule, forming **hydrogen bonds**. This gives alcohols certain properties...

When you mix an alcohol with water, hydrogen bonds form between the -OH group and H_2O — see Figure 4.

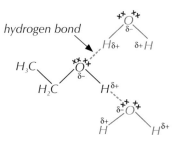

Figure 4: Hydrogen bonding of ethanol in water.

If it's a small alcohol (e.g. methanol, ethanol or propan-1-ol), hydrogen bonding lets it mix freely with water — it's soluble in water. In larger alcohols, most of the molecule is a non-polar carbon chain, so there's less attraction for the polar H_2O molecules. This means that as alcohols increase in size, their solubility in water decreases.

    Alcohols also form hydrogen bonds with each other. Hydrogen bonding is the strongest kind of intermolecular force, so it gives alcohols a relatively low volatility (they don't evaporate easily into a gas) and relatively high boiling points compared to non-polar compounds of similar sizes, e.g. alkanes.

Tip: The volatility of a substance is its tendency to evaporate (turn into a gas).

Tip: Their relatively high boiling points mean that alcohols are liquids at room temperature.

Practice Questions — Application

Q1 Name the following alcohols.

a) H H H OHH
H–C–C–C–C–C–H
H H H H H

b) H H OHH
H–C–C–C–C–H
H H CH₃H

c) H CH₃H OH
H–C–C–C–C–H
H H CH₃H

d) H H H CH₃H
H–C–C–C–C–C–H
H H CH₂H OH
CH₂OH

Tip: Remember — name molecules so that the names include the lowest numbers possible.

Tip: When you're naming diols, the stem of the name must come from the longest carbon chain that includes both hydroxy groups.

Q2 State whether each of the alcohols in Question 1, parts a), b) and c), are primary (1°), secondary (2°) or tertiary (3°) alcohols.

Q3 Which alcohol is more soluble in water: propan-1-ol or octan-1-ol? Explain your answer.

Q4 Which of these molecules will have a higher boiling point: butane or butan-1-ol? Explain your answer.

Tip: When you're naming diols, you keep the 'e' at the end of the alkane name. You lose it when naming alcohols with only one -OH group. For example:
• butanol (not butaneol),
• hexanediol (not hexandiol).

Practice Questions — Fact Recall

Q1 What suffix is added to a molecule's name if an -OH functional group is the highest priority group in the molecule?

Q2 What is a secondary alcohol?

Q3 Draw a diagram to show the hydrogen bonding present between a molecule of ethanol and water.

2. Reactions of Alcohols

Learning Objectives:
- Know that alcohols undergo substitution reactions with halide ions in the presence of acid (e.g. NaBr/H_2SO_4) to form haloalkanes.
- Know that H_2O can be eliminated from alcohols in the presence of an acid catalyst (e.g. H_3PO_4 or H_2SO_4) and heat to form alkenes.

Specification Reference 4.2.1

Alcohols can react in a number of different ways. In substitution reactions, the hydroxyl group is replaced by a different functional group, and in elimination reactions the alcohol loses a molecule of water to form an alkene.

Substitution reactions of alcohols

Alcohols will react with compounds containing halide ions (such as NaBr) in a **substitution reaction**. The hydroxyl (-OH) group is replaced by the halide, so the alcohol is transformed into a **haloalkane**. The reaction also requires an acid catalyst, such as H_2SO_4. A general reaction is shown in Figure 1.

$$R-OH + NaX \xrightarrow{H^+ \text{ (catalyst)}} R-X + Na^+ + H_2O$$

alcohol   haloalkane

Figure 1: *The general equation for the reaction of a sodium halide with an alcohol.*

Tip: 'X' just represents any halogen, for example Cl or Br.

Example

To make 2-bromo-2-methylpropane you just need to shake 2-methylpropan-2-ol (a tertiary alcohol) with sodium bromide and concentrated sulfuric acid at room temperature.

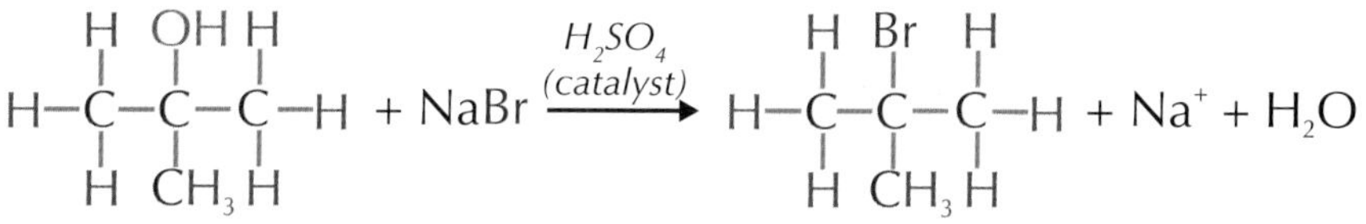

2-methylpropan-2-ol   2-bromo-2-methylpropane

Tip: Catalysts speed up a reaction without being used up themselves (see page 170). In the acid-catalysed substitution of alcohols by halide compounds, the water that forms can dissociate to form H^+ and OH^- ions, so the H^+ ions that catalyse the reaction are regenerated.

Elimination reactions of alcohols

Alkenes are really useful organic chemicals that can be used as starting products for lots of organic chemicals such as polymers (see pages 224-227). You can make alkenes by eliminating water from alcohols in an **elimination reaction**. The alcohol is mixed with an acid catalyst — either concentrated sulfuric acid (H_2SO_4) or concentrated phosphoric acid (H_3PO_4). The mixture is then heated. Water is eliminated from the alcohol, so this reaction is sometimes called a dehydration reaction. The general reaction for the dehydration of alcohols is shown in Figure 2.

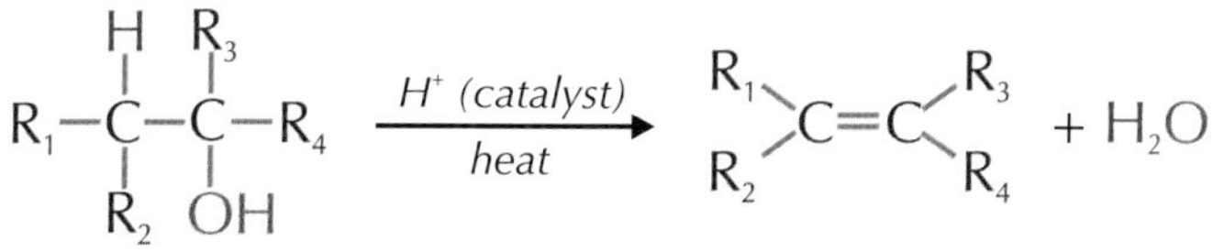

alcohol   alkene

Figure 2: *The general equation for the dehydration of an alcohol to form an alkene.*

Tip: In a dehydration reaction water is lost from one of the reactants. It's the opposite of the hydration reaction on page 220.

Example

You can make ethene by eliminating water from ethanol in a dehydration reaction. The ethanol is mixed with an acid catalyst and heated to 170 °C.

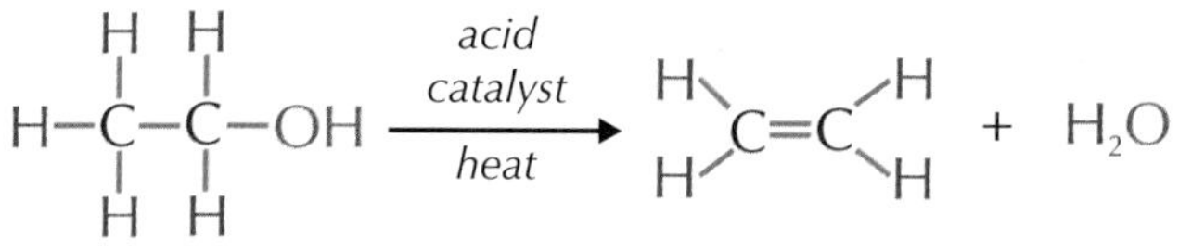

ethanol   ethene

The water molecule that is eliminated from an alcohol when it forms an alkene is made up from the hydroxyl group and a hydrogen atom that was bonded to a carbon atom adjacent to the hydroxyl carbon. This means that often there are two possible alkene products from one elimination reaction depending on which side of the hydroxyl group the hydrogen is eliminated from. Sometimes an alkene product can form E/Z isomers (see page 215) — if this is the case then a mixture of both isomers will form.

Example

When butan-2-ol is heated with concentrated phosphoric acid, elimination can occur between the hydroxyl group and the hydrogen either on carbon-1 or carbon-3. This results in the formation of a mixture of alkene products — but-1-ene, E-but-2-ene and Z-but-2-ene.

Tip: But-1-ene doesn't form E/Z isomers because there are two identical (hydrogen) groups attached to one of the C=C carbons:

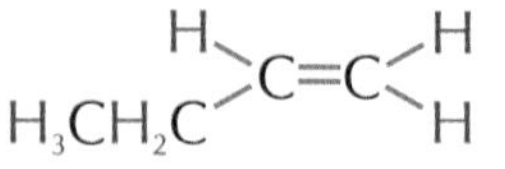

- Elimination between the hydroxyl group and a hydrogen on carbon-1 results in the formation of but-1-ene.

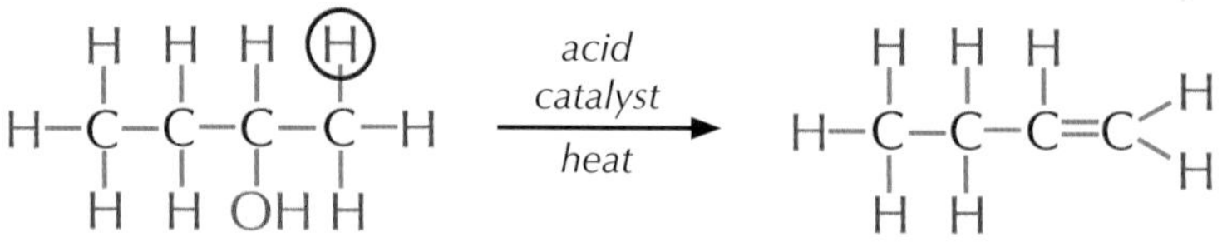

butan-2-ol → but-1-ene

Tip: The mixture of E and Z isomers doesn't have to be an equal ratio — often you'll end up with more of one isomer than the other.

- Elimination between the hydroxyl group and a hydrogen on carbon-3 results in the formation of but-2-ene. Since but-2-ene is able to form E/Z isomers, a mixture of E-but-2-ene and Z-but-2-ene will form.

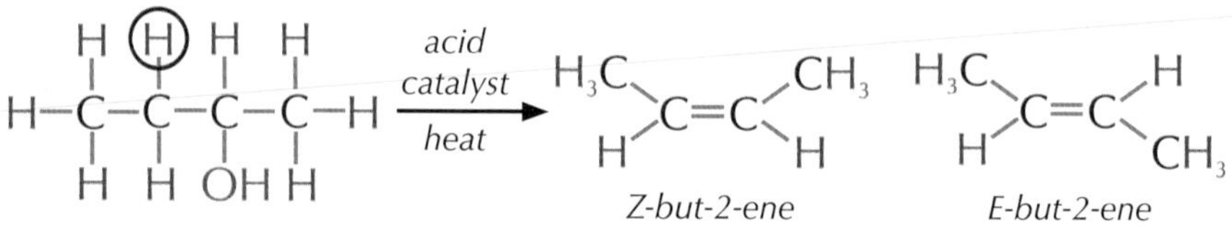

Z-but-2-ene   E-but-2-ene

Practice Questions — Application

Q1 2-chloro-2-methyl-propane can be synthesised from an alcohol in a one-step reaction.
Give the reagents and conditions needed for this reaction.

Q2 Draw and name all the organic products formed when 4-methyl-hexan-3-ol is heated with concentrated phosphoric acid.

Tip: You may need to have a look back at pages 211-212 for the IUPAC rules on naming alkenes.

Practice Questions — Fact Recall

Q1 a) Write the equation for the general reaction between an alcohol and a sodium halide.

b) What type of reaction is this?

Q2 a) Write down the equation for the dehydration of ethanol.

b) Name the products of this reaction.

c) Name a catalyst that could be used to catalyse this reaction.

Q3 Explain why the elimination reaction of an alcohol can result in the formation of a mixture of organic products.

3. Oxidising Alcohols

You can oxidise alcohols by burning them. But that's not all. You can also oxidise primary and secondary alcohols with certain oxidising agents to create molecules containing a carbon-oxygen double bond. Substances that contain these carbon-oxygen double bonds are known as carbonyl compounds.

Combustion of alcohols

The simple way to oxidise alcohols is to burn them. It doesn't take much to set ethanol alight and it burns with a pale blue flame. The C–C and C–H bonds are broken as the ethanol is completely oxidised to make carbon dioxide and water. This is a **combustion** reaction (see page 205).

$$C_2H_5OH_{(l)} + 3O_{2(g)} \rightarrow 2CO_{2(g)} + 3H_2O_{(g)}$$

But if you want to end up with something more interesting, you need a more sophisticated way of oxidising. You can use the oxidising agent acidified potassium dichromate(VI) ($K_2Cr_2O_7/H_2SO_4$) to mildly oxidise alcohols.

Primary alcohols are oxidised to **aldehydes** and then to **carboxylic acids**. Secondary alcohols are oxidised to **ketones** only. In these reactions, the orange dichromate(VI) ion, $Cr_2O_7^{2-}$, is reduced to the green chromium(III) ion, Cr^{3+}. Tertiary alcohols won't be oxidised, so a solution containing dichromate(VI) ions and a tertiary alcohol will stay orange. These colour changes can be used as a test to distinguish tertiary alcohols from primary and secondary alcohols (see page 240).

Aldehydes, ketones and carboxylic acids

Aldehydes and ketones are carbonyl compounds — they have the functional group C=O. Their general formula is $C_nH_{2n}O$. Aldehydes have a hydrogen and one alkyl group attached to the **carbonyl** carbon atom...

This is the aldehyde functional group.

Aldehydes have the suffix -al. You don't have to say which carbon the functional group is on — it's always on carbon-1. Naming aldehydes follows very similar rules to the naming of alcohols (see page 232).

Examples

propanal

The molecule has a saturated carbon skeleton, and the longest continuous carbon chain is 3 carbon atoms, so the stem is prop- and the name is based on 'propane'.

So, the aldehyde is called propanal.

The molecule has a saturated carbon skeleton, and the longest continuous carbon chain is 4 carbon atoms, so the stem is butane.

There's a methyl group attached to the second carbon atom, so there's a 2-methyl- prefix.

So, the aldehyde is called 2-methylbutanal.

2-methylbutanal

Learning Objectives:

- Be able to describe the combustion of alcohols.
- Be able to use the IUPAC rules of nomenclature to systematically name aldehydes, ketones and carboxylic acids.
- Know that you can oxidise alcohols using an oxidising agent, such as $Cr_2O_7^{2-}/H^+$ (i.e. $K_2Cr_2O_7/H_2SO_4$).
- Be able to describe the oxidation of primary alcohols to form aldehydes and carboxylic acids.
- Be able to describe how you can control the oxidation product of a primary alcohol using different reaction conditions.
- Be able to describe the oxidation of secondary alcohols to form ketones.
- Know that tertiary alcohols are resistant to oxidation.
- Be able to carry out qualitative tests to distinguish tertiary alcohols from primary and secondary alcohols (PAG 7).

Specification Reference 4.1.1, 4.2.1

Tip: Remember that a suffix comes at the end of a name and a prefix comes at the beginning.

Ketones have two alkyl groups attached to the carbonyl carbon atom.

H—C—C—C—H *This is the ketone functional group.*

The suffix for ketones is -one. For ketones with five or more carbons, you always have to say which carbon the functional group is on. (If there are other groups attached, such as methyl groups, you have to say what carbon the ketone group is on for ketones with a stem of four or more carbons too.)

Examples

propanone

The molecule has a saturated carbon skeleton and the longest continuous carbon chain is 3 carbon atoms, so the stem is prop- and the name is based on 'propane'.

So, the ketone is called propanone.

Figure 1: *The ketone propanone (also known as acetone) is commonly used as a nail varnish remover.*

The molecule has a saturated carbon skeleton and the longest continuous carbon chain is 5 carbon atoms, so the stem is pent- and the name is based on 'pentane'.

The carbonyl is found on the second carbon atom.

So, the ketone is called pentan-2-one.

pentan-2-one

Tip: The carboxylic acid functional group is written as COOH and not CO_2H to show that the two oxygens are different — one is part of a carbonyl group (CO) and the other is part of an OH group.

The same idea applies to aldehydes — you always write the functional group out as CHO (not COH) so it doesn't look like an alcohol.

Carboxylic acids have a COOH group at the end of their carbon chain.

H—C—C—C—OH *This is the carboxylic acid functional group.*

The suffix for carboxylic acids is -oic, and you also add the word 'acid' to the end of the name.

Examples

propanoic acid

The carbon skeleton is saturated and the longest continuous carbon chain is 3 carbon atoms, so the stem is prop- and the name is based on 'propane'.

So, the carboxylic acid is called propanoic acid.

Tip: As with diols, dicarboxylic acids keep the 'e' at the end of the alkane stem.
So the example on the right is propane**dioic** acid, and not propandioic acid.

The carbon skeleton is saturated and the longest continuous carbon chain is 3 carbon atoms, so the stem is prop- and the name is based on 'propane'.

There's a COOH group at each end of the carbon chain so it has a -dioic acid suffix.

So, the carboxylic acid is called propanedioic acid.

HO—C—C—C—OH

propanedioic acid

Oxidation of primary alcohols

A primary alcohol is first oxidised to an aldehyde. This aldehyde can then be oxidised to a carboxylic acid. You can use the notation [O] to represent an oxidising agent — this saves you having to write down acidified potassium dichromate(VI) every time you write out a reaction, which is handy. This means you can write equations like this:

$$R-CH_2-OH \xrightarrow{[O]} \underset{\text{aldehyde}}{R-\overset{\displaystyle O}{\overset{\|}{C}}-H} + H_2O \xrightarrow{[O]} \underset{\text{carboxylic acid}}{R-\overset{\displaystyle O}{\overset{\|}{C}}-OH}$$

primary alcohol   aldehyde   + H_2O carboxylic acid

You can control how far the alcohol is oxidised by controlling the reaction conditions.

Oxidising primary alcohols to aldehydes

Gently heating ethanol with potassium dichromate(VI) solution and sulfuric acid in a test tube should produce "apple" smelling ethanal (an aldehyde).

$$\underset{\text{ethanol}}{H-\overset{\displaystyle H}{\underset{\displaystyle H}{C}}-\overset{\displaystyle H}{\underset{\displaystyle H}{C}}-OH} + [O] \xrightarrow[\text{distillation}]{H_2SO_4} \underset{\text{ethanal}}{H-\overset{\displaystyle H}{\underset{\displaystyle H}{C}}-\overset{\displaystyle O}{\overset{\|}{C}}-H} + H_2O$$

However, it's really tricky to control the amount of heat and the aldehyde is usually oxidised to form "vinegar" smelling ethanoic acid. To get just the aldehyde, you need to get it out of the oxidising solution as soon as it's formed. You can do this by gently heating excess alcohol with a controlled amount of oxidising agent in a distillation apparatus (see Figure 2), so the aldehyde (which boils at a lower temperature than the alcohol) is distilled off immediately.

Oxidising primary alcohols to carboxylic acids

To produce the carboxylic acid, the alcohol has to be vigorously oxidised.

$$\underset{\text{ethanol}}{H-\overset{\displaystyle H}{\underset{\displaystyle H}{C}}-\overset{\displaystyle H}{\underset{\displaystyle H}{C}}-OH} + 2[O] \xrightarrow{\text{reflux}} \underset{\text{ethanoic acid}}{H-\overset{\displaystyle H}{\underset{\displaystyle H}{C}}-\overset{\displaystyle O}{\overset{\|}{C}}-OH} + H_2O$$

The alcohol is mixed with excess oxidising agent and heated under **reflux** (see Figure 3). Heating under reflux means you can increase the temperature of an organic reaction to boiling without losing volatile solvents, reactants or products. Any vaporised compounds are cooled, condense and drip back into the reaction mixture.

Oxidation of secondary alcohols

Refluxing a secondary alcohol with acidified dichromate(VI) will produce a ketone.

$$\underset{\text{secondary alcohol}}{R_1-\overset{\displaystyle R_2}{\underset{\displaystyle H}{C}}-OH} + [O] \xrightarrow[\substack{\text{acidic}\\\text{conditions}}]{\text{reflux}} \underset{\text{ketone}}{R_1-\overset{\displaystyle O}{\overset{\|}{C}}-R_2} + H_2O$$

Exam Tip
Make sure you learn the conditions required to produce aldehydes and carboxylic acids — it can be pretty easy to mix them up.

Tip: Make sure you balance the oxidising agents when you're writing these equations.

Tip: There's loads more about distillation, reflux and other organic techniques on pages 267-269.

Figure 2: *Distillation apparatus.*

Tip: Heating the alcohol under reflux means that, although you still make an aldehyde first, it stays in the reaction vessel with the oxidising agent — so it oxidises further to give a carboxylic acid.

Figure 3: *Reflux apparatus.*

┌─ **Example** ─────────────────────────

H—C—C—C—H + [O] —reflux→ H—C—C—C—H + H_2O
              acidic
              conditions

propan-2-ol   *propanone*

───────────────────────────────────────

Ketones can't be oxidised easily, so even prolonged refluxing won't produce anything more.

Oxidation of tertiary alcohols

Tertiary alcohols don't react with acidified potassium dichromate(VI) at all — the solution stays orange. The only way to oxidise tertiary alcohols is by burning them.

You can use the resistance of tertiary alcohols to oxidation to distinguish them from primary and secondary alcohols. If you heat a sample of an unknown alcohol in a test tube with a few drops of orange potassium dichromate(VI) and a few drops of concentrated sulfuric acid then the solution will stay orange if the alcohol is a tertiary alcohol because they can't be oxidised. If it's a secondary or a primary alcohol the solution will turn green as the alcohol is oxidised and the orange dichromate(VI) ions are reduced to green chromium(III) ions (see Figures 4a and 4b).

> PRACTICAL ACTIVITY GROUP **7**

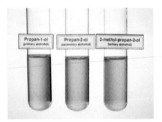

Figure 4a: A primary alcohol (left), a secondary alcohol (middle) and a tertiary alcohol (right) at the start of a reaction with acidified potassium dichromate(VI).

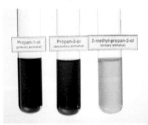

Figure 4b: Primary (left) and secondary (middle) alcohols are oxidised, causing a colour change from orange to green as Cr(VI) is reduced to Cr(III). Tertiary alcohols are resistant to oxidation, so no colour change is seen (right).

Practice Questions — Application

Q1 Name the following molecules:

a) H—C—C—C—C—H

b) H—C—OH (with O double bond)

c) H—C—C—C—C—C—H

d) H—C—C—C—C—C—C—H

Q2 Draw the structures of the organic products of the following reactions.

a) A reaction between butan-2-ol and acidified potassium dichromate(VI) under reflux.

b) A reaction between butan-1-ol and acidified potassium dichromate(VI) using distillation apparatus.

c) A reaction between butan-1-ol and acidified potassium dichromate(VI) under reflux.

Practice Questions — Fact Recall

Q1 Write an equation for the complete combustion of ethanol.

Q2 Give the functional groups of the following compounds:

a) aldehydes   b) ketones   c) carboxylic acids

Q3 Write a general equation for the reaction of a primary alcohol with an oxidising agent under reflux.

4. Haloalkanes

Haloalkanes pop up a lot in chemistry, so it's important that you know exactly what they are and how they behave. You'll meet a fair few reactions and mechanisms over the next few pages, but they're all pretty similar so you don't need to fret too much about it.

What are haloalkanes?

A **haloalkane** is an alkane with at least one halogen atom in place of a hydrogen atom.

Examples

dichloromethane   *2-iodopropane*   *1,2-dibromo-1-fluoroethane*

Naming haloalkanes

You name haloalkanes in exactly the same way that alkanes are named (see pages 199-201), but you have to add a prefix before the name of the alkane (see Figure 1). The prefixes are always placed in alphabetical order. If you have multiple halogens of the same type within a molecule, you use the prefixes di- (for two) or tri- (for three), as you have done when naming other organic compounds. These prefixes don't affect the order that you write the halogens in. For example, trichloro- would still be written before iodo-.

Halogen	Prefix
Fluorine	*fluoro-*
Chlorine	*chloro-*
Bromine	*bromo-*
Iodine	*iodo-*

***Figure 1:** Prefixes for naming haloalkanes.*

Examples

The molecule is saturated and the longest carbon chain is 1 carbon atom, so the stem is meth- and the name is based on methane.

There's one chlorine atom attached to the carbon atom, so it has a chloro- prefix: chloromethane.

chloromethane

2-bromo-1,1-dichloroethane

The molecule is saturated and the longest carbon chain is 2 carbon atoms, so the stem is eth- and the name is based on ethane.

There's one bromine atom attached to the second carbon atom, so it has a bromo- prefix.

There are two chlorine atoms attached to the first carbon, so it also has the prefix dichloro-.

So the molecule is 2-bromo-1,1-dichloroethane.

Learning Objectives:

- Be able to apply IUPAC rules of nomenclature to systematically name haloalkanes.

- Be able to define and use the definition of the term nucleophile (an electron pair donor).

- Know that haloalkanes can be hydrolysed in substitution reactions by aqueous alkali and by water.

- Understand the mechanism of nucleophilic substitution in the hydrolysis of primary haloalkanes with aqueous alkali.

- Be able to explain the trend in the rates of hydrolysis of primary haloalkanes in terms of the bond enthalpies of carbon–halogen bonds.

- Know that the hydrolysis of haloalkanes by water in the presence of $AgNO_3$ and ethanol can be used to compare experimentally the rates of hydrolysis of different carbon-halogen bonds.

- Be able to carry out qualitative tests to identify the halogen present in a haloalkane (PAG 7).

Specification Reference 4.1.1, 4.2.2

Polarity of haloalkanes

Halogens are generally much more electronegative than carbon, so the carbon-halogen bond is **polar**.

Example

$$-\overset{|}{\underset{|}{C}}\overset{\delta+}{-}\overset{\delta-}{Br}$$

The bromine atom is more electronegative than the carbon atom and so withdraws electron density from the carbon-bromine bond. This leaves the carbon atom with a partial positive charge and the bromine atom with a partial negative charge.

The δ+ carbon is electron deficient (it doesn't have enough electrons). This means it can be attacked by a **nucleophile**. A nucleophile's an electron-pair donor. It donates an electron pair to somewhere without enough electrons.

Examples

Here are some nucleophiles that will react with haloalkanes.

$:\overline{C}N$ $:NH_3$ $:\overline{O}H$

cyanide ion   ammonia   hydroxide ion

The pairs of dots represent lone pairs of electrons.
Water's a nucleophile too, but it reacts slowly.

There are examples of reactions where nucleophiles react with haloalkanes on the next few pages.

Nucleophilic substitution reactions

Mechanisms are step-by-step sequences of how reactions work. They're often shown as diagrams. They show how the bonds in molecules are made and broken, how the electrons are transferred and how you get from the reactants to the products. Haloalkanes react in **nucleophilic substitution reactions**. In a nucleophilic substitution reaction, a nucleophile attacks a polar molecule, kicks out a functional group and settles itself down in its place. The general equation for a nucleophilic substitution reaction of a haloalkane is:

$$RX + Nu^- \rightarrow RNu + X^-$$

The reaction mechanism explains how and why haloalkanes will react this way:

The carbon-halogen bond is polar. The tiny charges on the atoms are shown by δ+ and δ– signs.

The X stands for one of the halogens (F, Cl, Br or I).

:Nu⁻ stands for a nucleophile (e.g. :OH⁻).
The ':' represents the lone pair of electrons and the '–' shows that it has a negative charge.

The lone pair of electrons on the nucleophile attacks the slightly positive charge on the carbon to create a new bond. This is shown by a curly arrow.

Sidebar tips

Tip: Nucleophiles are often negative ions which, because they form by gaining electrons, have extra electrons that they can donate. Nucleophiles don't <u>have</u> to be ions though. For example, NH_3 is a nucleophile — it's got a non-bonding pair of electrons that it can donate.

Exam Tip
If you're asked to outline a mechanism using a nucleophile that you're not familiar with — don't panic. Just follow this general mechanism and you'll be fine.

Tip: If the nucleophile isn't charged, don't just go ahead and write a negative charge. It will just be :Nu (e.g. :NH_3).

Tip: In mechanism diagrams, curly arrows always show the movement of an electron pair (see page 208).

Tip: The bond breaking between the carbon atom and the halogen atom is <u>heterolytic</u> bond breaking — both of the bonding electrons are taken by the halogen.

The carbon can only be bonded to four other atoms so the addition of the nucleophile breaks the bond between the carbon and the halogen — this is shown by another curly arrow. The pair of electrons from the carbon-halogen bond are taken by the halogen and become a lone pair.

Exam Tip
You <u>must</u> draw the curly arrows coming from the <u>lone pair</u> of electrons or from the <u>bond</u>.
If you don't, you won't get the marks for the mechanism in the exam.

Hydrolysis of haloalkanes

In **hydrolysis** reactions, molecules are split up by water molecules (which also split apart). Haloalkanes can be hydrolysed to make alcohols. There's a couple of ways of doing this.

1. Hydrolysis with aqueous alkali

Haloalkanes are hydrolysed by warm aqueous alkali, such as sodium hydroxide (NaOH) solution or potassium hydroxide (KOH) solution, in a nucleophilic substitution reaction. The general equation for this reaction is:

$$RX + {}^-OH \rightarrow ROH + X^-$$

R represents an alkyl group. X stands for one of the halogens (Cl, Br or I). As it's a nucleophilic substitution reaction, the nucleophile ($^-$OH) kicks out the halogen (X) from the RX molecule and takes its place.

Tip: This reaction is usually called hydrolysis, even though it's $^-$OH ions from the alkali that are reacting, not water molecules. That's because the product is the same as when you use water as a nucleophile (see below).

--- Example ---

Bromoethane can be hydrolysed to ethanol in a nucleophilic substitution reaction with warm aqueous sodium hydroxide or potassium hydroxide. Here's the equation for this reaction:

$$CH_3CH_2Br \ + \ {}^-OH \ \xrightarrow{\ reflux\ } \ CH_3CH_2OH \ + \ Br^-$$

Here's how it happens:

1. The $C^{\delta+}$ from a polar C–Br bond attracts a lone pair of electrons from an OH$^-$ ion.

3. The C–Br bond breaks heterolytically — both the electrons are taken by the Br.

4. A new bond forms between the C and the OH$^-$ ion.

2. The OH$^-$ ion acts as a nucleophile — it provides a pair of electrons for the $C^{\delta+}$.

5. The Br$^-$ falls off as the OH$^-$ bonds to the carbon.

Tip: The C–F bond in fluoroalkanes is very strong (see page 244), so they can't be hydrolysed.

Tip: <u>Refluxing</u> is a method for heating a reaction to boiling point without losing volatile solvents, reactants or products (see page 267).

Tip: When you're drawing mechanisms make sure the charges balance. That way you'll know if you've lost track of any electrons along the way. In this example, the left-hand side has one negative charge on the hydroxide ion and the right-hand side has one negative charge from a bromide ion — so it's balanced.

2. Hydrolysis with water

The water molecule is a weak nucleophile, but it will eventually substitute for the halogen — it's just a much slower reaction than the one using a warm aqueous alkali. You get an alcohol produced again. The general equation is:

$$RX + H_2O \ \rightarrow \ ROH + H^+ + X^-$$

Example

Bromoethane reacts slowly with water in a hydrolysis reaction to form ethanol. The equation for this reaction is:

$$CH_3CH_2Br + H_2O \rightarrow CH_3CH_2OH + H^+ + Br^-$$

Bond enthalpy and hydrolysis

How quickly different haloalkanes are hydrolysed depends on bond enthalpy — see page 156 for more on this. Weaker carbon-halogen bonds break more easily — so they react faster. Iodoalkanes have the weakest bonds, so they hydrolyse the fastest. Fluoroalkanes have the strongest bonds, so they're the slowest at hydrolysing (see Figure 2).

Bond	Bond Enthalpy (kJ mol^{-1})
C–F	467
C–Cl	346
C–Br	290
C–I	228

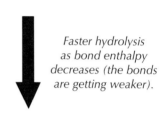

Faster hydrolysis as bond enthalpy decreases (the bonds are getting weaker).

Figure 2: *Carbon-halogen bond enthalpies.*

Tip: If you've got a molecule with more than one halogen in it, the halogen with the lowest bond enthalpy will get replaced first.

Tip: To hydrolyse haloalkanes with high bond enthalpies you need to use harsher reaction conditions — for example, a higher temperature.

Comparing hydrolysis rates of haloalkanes

You saw on the last page that when haloalkanes are mixed with water they will be slowly hydrolysed to form alcohols. This is the overall reaction:

PRACTICAL ACTIVITY GROUP 7

$$RX + H_2O \rightarrow ROH + H^+ + X^-$$

If you put silver nitrate solution in the mixture too, the silver ions will react with the halide ions as soon as they form, giving a silver halide precipitate (see pages 141-142). This is the equation for that reaction:

$$Ag^+{}_{(aq)} + X^-{}_{(aq)} \rightarrow AgX_{(s)}$$

You can use this reaction to compare the reactivities of different haloalkanes. To do this, set up four flasks each containing the same amount of a different haloalkane, ethanol (as a solvent) and dilute silver nitrate solution. You can 'measure' the rates of the reactions by timing how quickly each silver halide is precipitated, using the good old 'timing how long it takes the cross to disappear' method (not its official name...). Just stick a piece of paper with a cross on it under each flask and measure how long it takes until you can't see the cross any more (see Figure 3).

Tip: You use water as the nucleophile in this reaction — if you used an alkali the hydroxide ions would react with the silver nitrate to form a precipitate and mess up your results.

Tip: Remember to always do a risk assessment before you carry out any experiments in class.

Tip: The hydrolysis of haloalkanes by water can be very slow. So, you can warm all the reaction flasks to the same temperature to make the reactions in this experiment occur more quickly.

bromoalkane *chloroalkane*

iodoalkane

fluoroalkane

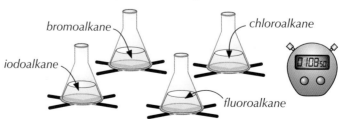

Figure 3: *Experimental set-up for measuring the rate of reaction of hydrolysis.*

If all the conditions are the same (e.g. temperature, concentration of reactants, the carbon skeleton of the haloalkane, etc.), then you'll find that iodoalkanes react the fastest to form a precipitate, bromoalkanes are a bit slower to react, and chloroalkanes take ages to form a precipitate. Fluoroalkanes aren't hydrolysed at all. These observations match what you know about the bond enthalpies of the different carbon-halogen bonds (see last page).

Identifying unknown haloalkanes

PRACTICAL ACTIVITY GROUP **7**

Sometimes, you can't use the relative reaction rates to identify the halogen present in a haloalkane. This may be the case if you only have one sample, or if you have samples where the carbon chains are different. Instead, you react a sample of the haloalkane in a test tube with water in the presence of silver nitrate solution and ethanol. The colour of the precipitate that forms will tell you what halogen is present in the haloalkane — yellow means it's an iodoalkane, cream means it's a bromoalkane and white means it's a chloroalkane (see Figures 4 and 6). The method for the experiment is similar to the one on the previous page.

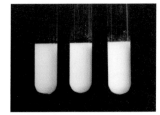

Figure 4: The result of adding silver nitrate solution to a chloroalkane (left), a bromoalkane (middle) and an iodoalkane (right).

Tip: You can only be sure that the identity of the halogen is what influences the relative rate of reaction between each sample if you keep <u>everything</u> else the same.

─ Example ─────────────────────────────

Three haloalkanes are labelled A, B and C. One is an iodoalkane, one is a bromoalkane and one is a chloroalkane. You can distinguish between them by comparing the colours of the precipitates formed when a sample of each haloalkane is warmed with water in the presence of silver nitrate and ethanol. The set-up for the reaction is shown in Figure 5.

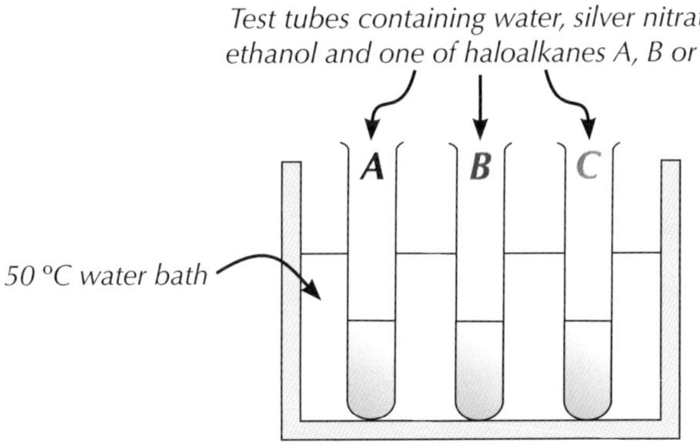

Test tubes containing water, silver nitrate, ethanol and one of haloalkanes A, B or C.

50 °C water bath

Figure 5: The set-up of an experiment to determine the identity of the halogen in three unknown haloalkanes.

The identity of each haloalkane can be determined once a precipitate has formed in each of the test tubes.

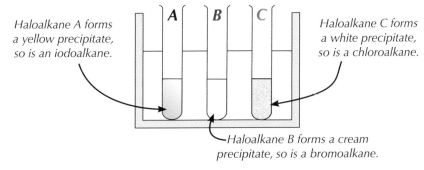

Haloalkane A forms a yellow precipitate, so is an iodoalkane.

Haloalkane C forms a white precipitate, so is a chloroalkane.

Haloalkane B forms a cream precipitate, so is a bromoalkane.

Figure 6: The colours of the precipitates formed when different haloalkanes are reacted with water in the presence of silver nitrate and ethanol.

Tip: You can't just use the difference in reaction rates to identify the haloalkanes. If their carbon skeletons are different, or each molecule contains different numbers of halogen atoms, then this will affect the reaction rate as well.

Tip: You may need to look at the rates as well as the colours of the precipitates to successfully identify an unknown haloalkane.

Tip: Always do a risk assessment before you do any experiments in the lab to make sure you're working safely. For example, silver nitrate solution can irritate your skin and eyes, so you should wear a lab coat, gloves and goggles if you do an experiment like this in class.

Tip: Remember that skeletal formulas only show the bonds of the carbon skeleton and any functional groups on the molecule. The hydrogen atoms aren't shown at all.

Q1 Draw skeletal formulas for the following haloalkanes:
a) 1-bromobutane
b) 2,3-difluoropentane
c) 1-bromo-2-chloropropane
d) 1-iodohexane

Q2 Draw the mechanism for the hydrolysis of chloroethane by warm aqueous sodium hydroxide. The structure of chloroethane is shown below.

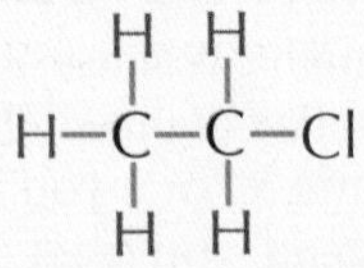

$$H-\underset{\underset{H}{|}}{\overset{\overset{H}{|}}{C}}-\underset{\underset{H}{|}}{\overset{\overset{H}{|}}{C}}-Cl$$

Exam Tip
When drawing any mechanism, double-check that you've drawn all the necessary curly arrows, lone pairs and partial charges. You'll lose marks in the exam if you've missed one out.

Q3 Which of the following reactions, **A**, **B** or **C**, would be quickest? Explain your answer.
A $CH_3CH_2Cl + H_2O \rightarrow CH_3CH_2OH + HCl$
B $CH_3CH_2Br + H_2O \rightarrow CH_3CH_2OH + HBr$
C $CH_3CH_2I + H_2O \rightarrow CH_3CH_2OH + HI$

Q4 Three unknown haloalkanes, A, B and C, are reacted separately with water in the presence of silver nitrate solution and ethanol. The time taken for an 'X' on a piece of card behind each test tube to disappear is recorded. The haloalkanes all have the same carbon skeleton, but one is a chloroalkane, one is a bromoalkane and one is an iodoalkane. Apart from the identity of the haloalkane, all the other variables in each reaction are kept the same. The results of each reaction are shown in the table below.

Haloalkane	Time for X to disappear (s)
A	240
B	7
C	567

a) Use the table to identify the halogen present in each of the haloalkanes, A, B and C.

b) Explain why variables such as the concentration of reactants need to be kept the same between the different samples.

Practice Questions — Fact Recall

Q1 What property of haloalkanes causes them to be attacked by nucleophiles?

Q2 Briefly describe what a nucleophilic substitution reaction is.

Q3 Name a substance that you could react with bromoethane to produce ethanol.

Q4 Explain why fluoroalkanes are hydrolysed more slowly than other haloalkanes.

Q5 Write an equation for the reaction of bromoethane with hydroxide ions.

Q6 Describe a test you could carry out to identify whether a haloalkane is a chloroalkane, a bromoalkane or an iodoalkane.

Tip: There's loads of stuff about how to plan experiments and analyse data in the Practical Skills section on pages 5-23.

5. Chlorofluorocarbons

Chlorofluorocarbons are a family of haloalkanes. They were once used for loads of things, before it was discovered that they were destroying the ozone layer...

Chlorofluorocarbons

Chlorofluorocarbons (CFCs) are well-known haloalkanes. They contain only chlorine, fluorine and carbon — all the hydrogens have been replaced. They're very stable, volatile, non-flammable and non-toxic. They were used a lot — e.g. in fridges, aerosol cans, dry cleaning and air-conditioning — until scientists realised they were destroying the ozone layer.

Chlorofluorocarbons and the ozone layer

The **ozone layer** is in a layer of the atmosphere called the stratosphere. It contains most of the atmosphere's ozone molecules, O_3, and acts as a chemical sunscreen. It absorbs a lot of the ultraviolet radiation which can cause sunburn or even skin cancer. Ozone's formed naturally when an oxygen molecule is broken down into two free radicals by ultraviolet radiation:

$$O_2 + h\nu \rightarrow O + O$$

The free radicals attack other oxygen molecules, forming ozone:

$$O_2 + O \rightarrow O_3$$

In the 1970s and 1980s, scientists discovered that the ozone layer above Antarctica was getting thinner — in fact, it was thinning very rapidly. The ozone layer over the Arctic has been found to be thinning too. These 'holes' in the ozone layer are bad because they allow more harmful UV radiation to reach the Earth. The 'holes' are formed because when CFCs travel up into the upper atmosphere they absorb high-energy UV radiation and split to form chlorine free radicals. For example:

$$CF_2Cl_{2(g)} + h\nu \rightarrow CF_2Cl\bullet_{(g)} + Cl\bullet_{(g)}$$

These free radicals catalyse the destruction of ozone — they destroy ozone molecules and are then regenerated to destroy more ozone. One chlorine atom can destroy 10 000 ozone molecules before it forms a stable compound. Here's what happens:

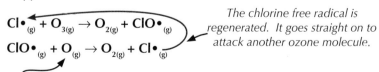

The chlorine free radical is regenerated. It goes straight on to attack another ozone molecule.

The O radical comes from the breakdown of oxygen by ultraviolet radiation.

Because the Cl• free radical is regenerated, it only takes one little chlorine free radical to destroy loads of ozone molecules. So, the overall reaction is...

$$O_{3(g)} + O_{(g)} \rightarrow 2O_{2(g)} \qquad \text{... and Cl• is the catalyst.}$$

Learning Objectives:

- Be able to explain how halogen radicals are produced by the action of ultraviolet (UV) radiation on CFCs in the upper atmosphere.

- Understand how halogen radicals can catalyse the breakdown of the Earth's protective ozone layer.

- Be able to write equations to represent the production of halogen radicals and the catalysed breakdown of ozone by Cl• and other radicals, e.g. •NO.

Specification Reference 4.2.2

Tip: The hv in the first equation is the notation for a quantum of UV radiation — a photon. It just means that the reaction needs to be initiated by electromagnetic radiation.

Tip: CFCs are really stable, so they don't get broken down in the lower atmosphere. Instead they can travel all the way up to the ozone layer, where they wreak havoc.

Tip: The chlorine radicals are homogeneous catalysts because they're in the same phase as the ozone molecules.

Nitrogen oxides and the ozone layer

Chlorine radicals often get blamed for destroying the ozone layer, but there are other radicals that are also catalysing the breakdown of ozone. For example, NO• free radicals from **nitrogen oxides** destroy ozone too. Nitrogen oxides are produced by car and aircraft engines, and thunderstorms. NO• free radicals affect ozone in the same way as chlorine radicals.

Tip: NO• and Cl• aren't the only culprits — free radicals are produced from haloalkanes containing other halogens too.

The reactions showing how ozone is broken down can be represented by equations where **R** represents any radical, for example Cl• or NO•.

$$R + O_3 \rightarrow RO + O_2$$
$$RO + O \rightarrow R + O_2$$

In both cases, the free radicals act as **catalysts** for the destruction of the ozone. The overall reaction is:

$$O_3 + O \rightarrow 2O_2$$

Alternatives to CFCs

Tip: Scientific evidence was used as a basis by governments to draw up an international agreement that banned the use of CFCs.

HOW SCIENCE WORKS

Scientific evidence showed that the advantages of CFCs couldn't outweigh the environmental problems they were causing, so they were banned. The Montreal Protocol of 1987 was an international treaty to phase out the use of CFCs and other ozone-destroying haloalkanes by the year 2000. There were a few permitted uses, such as in medical inhalers and in fire extinguishers used in submarines. Scientists supported the treaty, and worked on finding alternatives to CFCs.

HCFCs and HFCs

HCFCs (hydrochlorofluorocarbons) and HFCs (hydrofluorocarbons) are being used as temporary alternatives to CFCs until safer products are developed. Hydrocarbons are also used.

The problem with CFCs is that they hang around in the atmosphere causing disruption for ages — it takes an average of 90 years for them to leave the atmosphere. HCFCs are broken down in the atmosphere in 10-20 years. They still damage the ozone layer, but their effect is much smaller than that of CFCs. HFCs are broken down in the atmosphere too and they don't contain chlorine, so they don't affect the ozone layer.

Unfortunately, HFCs and HCFCs are greenhouse gases (see page 249) — they contribute towards the warming of the Earth. Some hydrocarbons are being used in fridges, but these are greenhouse gases too. Nowadays, most aerosols have been replaced by pump spray systems or use nitrogen as the propellant. Many industrial fridges and freezers now use ammonia as the coolant gas, and carbon dioxide is used to make expanded polymers.

These substances do have drawbacks, but they're currently the least environmentally damaging of all the alternatives. The ozone holes still form in the spring but are slowly shrinking — so things are looking up.

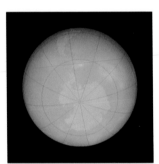

Figure 1: *Satellite image of the ozone layer over Antarctica in 1979.*

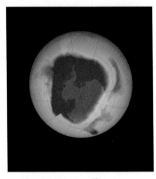

Figure 2: *Satellite image of the ozone layer over Antarctica in 2013. The 'hole' is shown by the blue area.*

Practice Questions — Fact Recall

Q1 What is a chlorofluorocarbon (CFC)?

Q2 Write equations to show how chlorofluorocarbons can catalyse the breakdown of ozone in the stratosphere.

Q3 Name one type of chemical that is used as an alternative to CFCs.

6. Global Warming

Global warming, the greenhouse effect and climate change seem to crop up in every subject, at every level. Here's the chemistry spin on them, including how chemists are involved in measuring, monitoring and fighting back.

Learning Objectives:

- Know that atmospheric gases containing C=O, O–H and C–H bonds (e.g. H_2O, CO_2 and CH_4) are able to absorb infrared radiation.

- Understand why H_2O, CO_2 and CH_4 are suspected to be linked to global warming.

- Understand how energy usage has changed as a result of the suspected link between H_2O, CO_2 and methane with global warming.

Specification Reference 4.2.4

Greenhouse gases

Some of the electromagnetic radiation from the Sun reaches the Earth and is absorbed. The Earth then re-emits it as infrared radiation (heat). Various gases in the **troposphere** (the lowest layer of the atmosphere) absorb some of this infrared radiation... and re-emit it in all directions — including back towards Earth, keeping us warm (see Figure 1). This is called the '**greenhouse effect**' (even though a real greenhouse doesn't actually work like this, annoyingly).

Visible and UV radiation from the Sun

Some infrared radiation emitted by the Earth is absorbed by greenhouse gases

Some infrared radiation emitted by the Earth escapes

Figure 1: *The greenhouse effect.*

The main **greenhouse gases** are water vapour, carbon dioxide and methane. The C=O, O–H and C–H bonds in these molecules absorb infrared (IR) radiation (see page 255) and this makes the bonds in the molecule vibrate more. This extra energy is passed on to other molecules in the air by collisions, giving the other molecules more kinetic energy and raising the overall temperature.

Not all greenhouse gases contribute the same amount to the greenhouse effect. The contribution of any particular gas depends on a number of factors, including:

- How much IR radiation one molecule of the gas absorbs.

- How much of that gas there is in the atmosphere.

- How long the gas stays in the atmosphere for.

> **Example**
>
> One methane molecule traps far more heat than one carbon dioxide molecule, but there's much less methane in the atmosphere, so its overall contribution to the greenhouse effect is smaller. A molecule of methane also spends much less time in the atmosphere, before it's broken down, than a molecule of carbon dioxide.

Figure 2: *Methane is released from cows...*

What is global warming?

Over the last 150 years or so, the world's human population has shot up and we've become more industrialised. We've been burning fossil fuels, releasing tonnes of CO_2, and we've been chopping down forests which used to absorb CO_2 by photosynthesis.

Methane levels have also risen as we've grown more food. Cows produce large amounts of methane (from both ends). Paddy fields, in which rice is grown, kick out a fair bit of it too.

Figure 3: *...and from paddy fields (fields where rice is grown).*

These human activities have caused a rise in greenhouse gas concentrations, which enhances the greenhouse effect. More heat is being trapped and the Earth is getting warmer — this is **global warming**.

Evidence for global warming

Scientists have collected data to provide evidence for if and why global warming and climate change are happening, e.g. from analysing air samples and seawater samples.

The evidence shows that the Earth's average temperature has increased dramatically in the last 50 years, and that CO_2 levels have increased at the same time — see Figure 4.

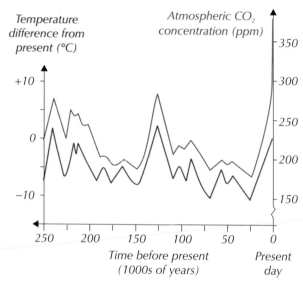

Figure 4: *Graph showing the correlation between atmospheric CO_2 concentration and temperature.*

The correlation between CO_2 and temperature is pretty clear, but there's been debate about whether rising carbon dioxide levels have caused the recent temperature rise. Just showing a correlation doesn't prove that one thing causes another — there has to be a plausible mechanism for how one change causes the other (in this case, the explanation is the enhanced greenhouse effect). There's now a consensus among climate scientists that the link is causal, and that recent warming is largely anthropogenic — this means that human activities are to blame.

Consequences of global warming

Global warming won't just make everywhere a bit warmer and affect the skiing — warmer oceans will expand and massive ice sheets in the polar regions could melt, causing sea levels to rise and leading to more flooding. The climate in any region of the world depends on a really complicated system of ocean currents, winds, etc. Global warming means there's more heat energy in the system. This could lead to stormier, less predictable weather. In some places there could be much less rainfall, with droughts and crop failures causing famines and forcing entire populations to become refugees. In other regions, increased rainfall and flooding could bring diseases like cholera.

Efforts to prevent global warming

Scientific evidence has persuaded governments to form a global agreement that climate change could be damaging for people, the environment and economies, and that we should try to **limit** it.

Tip: See pages 1-4 for more on how scientists collect evidence and use it to support their claims.

In 1997 the **Kyoto protocol** was signed — industrialised countries (including the UK) promised to reduce their greenhouse gas emissions to agreed levels. This agreement came to an end in 2012, and currently has no replacement, though many governments agree that they need to reduce CO_2 emissions by around 50% by 2050.

In the UK, the government has created policies to use more **renewable energy resources**, such as through wind and solar farms, in order to reduce the country's emissions. This has reduced the need for coal-burning power stations, which are a major source of carbon dioxide pollution and used to be one of the main sources of electricity in the UK. The government have also encouraged the use of more energy-efficient alternatives to everyday objects, such as energy-saving light bulbs and electric cars.

Figure 5: Wind turbines use wind energy, a renewable energy resource, to generate electricity.

Practice Questions — Fact Recall

Q1 What type of radiation do greenhouse gases absorb?

Q2 Name three greenhouse gases.

Q3 How is the greenhouse effect linked to global warming?

Q4 Explain why global warming is a problem.

Q5 How are governments working to limit global warming?

Section Summary

Make sure you know...

- How to use the IUPAC rules of nomenclature to name alcohols.
- What primary, secondary and tertiary alcohols are and how to spot them.
- That alcohols are polar molecules and are able to form hydrogen bonds.
- How hydrogen bonding affects the water solubility, volatility and boiling points of alcohols.
- That alcohols can undergo nucleophilic substitution reactions with halide ions to form haloalkanes.
- That water can be eliminated from alcohols to form a mixture of alkene products, and if these alkenes have E/Z isomers then both isomers will form.
- How to describe the combustion of alcohols.
- What aldehydes, ketones and carboxylic acids are.
- How to use the IUPAC rules of nomenclature to name aldehydes, ketones and carboxylic acids.
- That you can oxidise primary and secondary alcohols using acidified potassium dichromate(VI).
- How to oxidise primary alcohols to form aldehydes and carboxylic acids.
- How to oxidise secondary alcohols to form ketones.
- That tertiary alcohols can only be oxidised by burning.
- That you can use acidified potassium dichromate(VI) as a test to distinguish tertiary alcohols from primary and secondary alcohols.
- How to use the IUPAC rules of nomenclature to name haloalkanes.
- That carbon-halogen bonds are polar so they can be attacked by nucleophiles.
- That a nucleophile is an electron-pair donor.
- The basic mechanism for a nucleophilic substitution reaction.
- That haloalkanes can be hydrolysed by warm aqueous alkali or, much more slowly, by water.
- That hydrolysis of a haloalkane is a nucleophilic substitution reaction.
- The mechanism for the reaction of a haloalkane with a warm aqueous alkali.
- That the hydrolysis rate of haloalkanes depends on the bond enthalpy of the carbon-halogen bond.
- How you can compare the rate of hydrolysis of haloalkanes experimentally using water in the presence of silver nitrate and ethanol.
- How to identify different haloalkanes by observing the colour of the precipitate formed when the haloalkane is warmed with silver nitrate and ethanol.
- That CFCs are volatile, non-toxic, non-flammable and not very reactive.
- That CFCs produce halogen radicals in the upper atmosphere which catalyse the breakdown of the ozone layer.
- That other radicals, such as NO•, also catalyse the breakdown of ozone.
- How to write equations to show how radicals can catalyse the breakdown of ozone.
- That scientists are working to find less harmful alternatives to CFCs (e.g. hydrocarbons, HFCs and HCFCs).
- The mechanism behind the greenhouse effect.
- That atmospheric gases containing C=O, C–H and O–H bonds (such as CO_2, CH_4 and H_2O) can all absorb infrared (IR) radiation.
- That the rise in atmospheric levels of CO_2, CH_4 and H_2O is suspected to be linked to global warming, and energy use has changed as a result.

Exam-style Questions

1 When 2,2,4-trimethylpentan-3-ol is reacted with hot, concentrated phosphoric acid, how many different alkene products are formed?

    A 1

    B 2

    C 3

    D 4

(1 mark)

2 Which of the following organic compounds can be refluxed with acidified potassium dichromate(VI) to form 3-methylbutanone?

    A

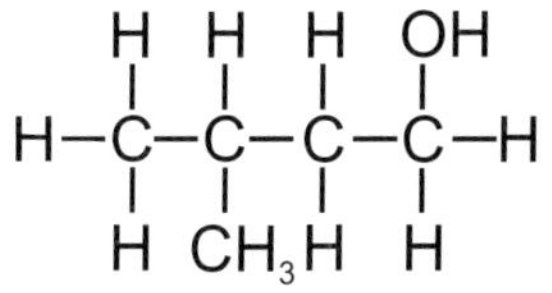

    B

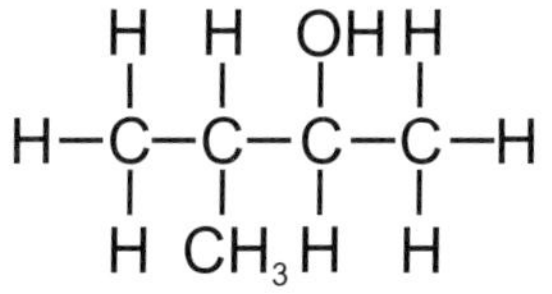

    C

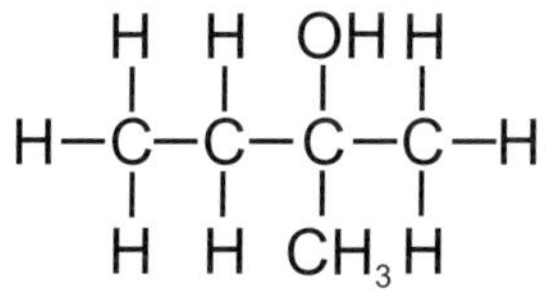

    D

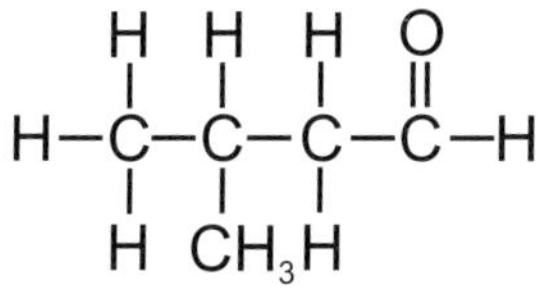

(1 mark)

3 Which of the following statements about global warming is correct?

    A The correlation between rising carbon dioxide levels and rising global temperatures proves that carbon dioxide is causing global warming.

    B The greenhouse effect is caused by increased levels of gases that absorb infrared radiation in the atmosphere.

    C Global warming is largely man-made.

    D The amount a greenhouse gas contributes to the greenhouse effect only depends on its concentration in the atmosphere.

(1 mark)

4 Ethanol is a simple alcohol that can be used as a solvent and as a starting point for many organic synthesis reactions. Its structure is shown below.

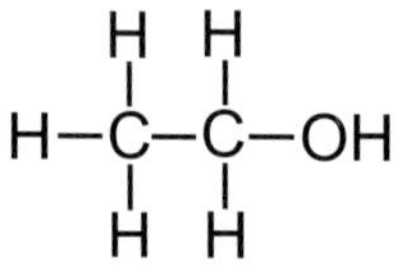

$$H-\underset{\underset{H}{|}}{\overset{\overset{H}{|}}{C}}-\underset{\underset{H}{|}}{\overset{\overset{H}{|}}{C}}-OH$$

(a) Ethanol can be made by reacting bromoethane with warm aqueous sodium hydroxide.

(i) Write the equation for this reaction.

(1 mark)

(ii) Draw the mechanism for the reaction between bromoethane and hydroxide ions.

(3 marks)

(iii) Ethanol can also be made by reacting iodoethane with warm aqueous sodium hydroxide. Which of the reactions would proceed more quickly? Explain your answer.

(2 marks)

(b) Ethanol is soluble in water.

(i) Explain why ethanol is soluble in water.

(1 mark)

(ii) Explain why butan-1-ol is less soluble in water than ethanol.

(1 mark)

5 A scientist has synthesised a molecule — molecule **A**.
The molecule was synthesised by reacting $^-$OH ions with 1-bromopropane.
The structure of 1-bromopropane is shown below.

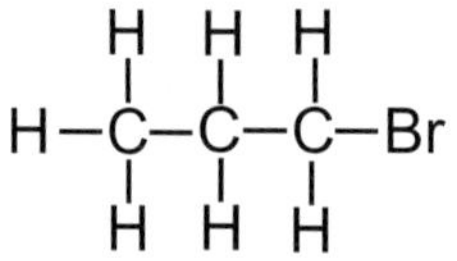

$$H-\underset{\underset{H}{|}}{\overset{\overset{H}{|}}{C}}-\underset{\underset{H}{|}}{\overset{\overset{H}{|}}{C}}-\underset{\underset{H}{|}}{\overset{\overset{H}{|}}{C}}-Br$$

(a) Draw the displayed structure of molecule **A** and give its systematic name.

(2 marks)

(b) Suggest what reagents and conditions would be needed to produce a carboxylic acid from molecule **A**.

(2 marks)

6 CFCs are molecules that have been linked to the destruction of ozone in the upper atmosphere.

(a) Explain why the ozone layer is an important part of the atmosphere.

(1 mark)

(b) What role do CFCs play in the destruction of ozone?

(2 marks)

(c) NO• is another species that has been linked to the breakdown of ozone molecules. Write equations to show how ozone can be broken down in the presence of NO•. You don't need to show how NO• is formed, but you should include an overall equation for the reaction.

(3 marks)

1. Infrared Spectroscopy

Infrared spectroscopy is an analytical technique which can help you to identify a compound. The bonds of different functional groups absorb different frequencies of infrared light. This means we can use an infrared spectrum of a molecule to identify its functional groups.

The basics

In **infrared (IR) spectroscopy**, a beam of IR radiation is passed through a sample of a chemical. The IR radiation is absorbed by the covalent bonds in the molecules, increasing their vibrational energy (they vibrate more). Bonds between different atoms absorb different frequencies of IR radiation. Bonds in different places in a molecule absorb different frequencies too — so the O–H bond in an alcohol and the O–H in a carboxylic acid absorb different frequencies. Figure 1 shows what frequencies different bonds absorb — you don't need to learn this data, but you do need to understand how to use it. Wavenumber is the measure used for the frequency (it's just 1/wavelength).

Bond	Where it's found	Frequency / Wavenumber (cm⁻¹)
C–C	alkanes, alkyl chains	750 – 1100
C–X	haloalkanes	500 – 800
C–F	fluoroalkanes	1000 – 1350
C–O	alcohols, carboxylic acids	1000 – 1300
C=C	alkenes	1620 – 1680
C=O	aldehydes, ketones, carboxylic acids	1630 – 1820
C–H	most organic molecules	2850 – 3100
O–H	carboxylic acids	2500 – 3300 (broad)
O–H	alcohols	3200 – 3600

Figure 1: *Infrared absorption for different bonds in organic molecules.*

An infrared spectrometer produces a graph, known as a spectrum, that shows you what frequencies of radiation the bonds in a molecule are absorbing. So you can use it to identify the functional groups in the molecule. The peaks show you where radiation is being absorbed — the 'peaks' on IR spectra are upside down.

Learning Objectives:

- Know that infrared (IR) radiation causes covalent bonds to vibrate more and absorb energy.

- Be able to use the infrared spectrum of an organic compound to identify an alcohol from an absorption peak of the O–H bond, an aldehyde or ketone from an absorption peak of the C=O bond, and a carboxylic acid from an absorption peak of the C=O bond and a broad absorption peak of the O–H bond.

- Be able to interpret and predict the infrared spectrum of a familiar or unfamiliar substance using supplied data.

- Know how infrared spectroscopy is used to monitor gases causing air pollution (e.g. CO and NO from car emissions) and in modern breathalysers.

Specification Reference 4.2.4

Exam Tip
You'll get a table like the one in Figure 1 on the data sheet in your exam. So there's no need to memorise all those numbers — yay.

Example — **Maths Skills**

Here is the structure and the infrared spectrum of ethanal:

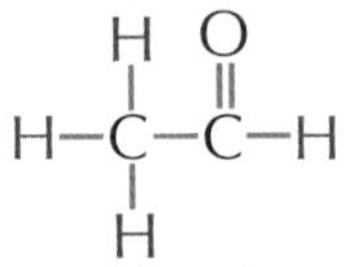

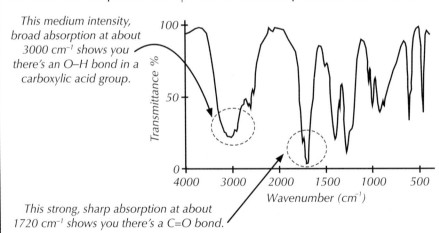

ethanal

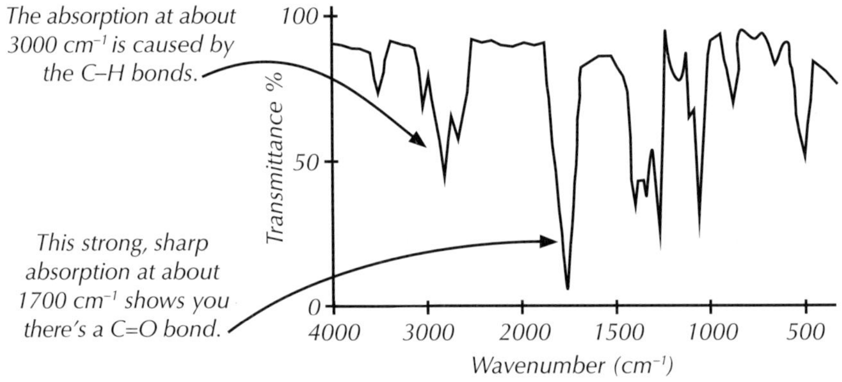

Tip: Most organic molecules will have loads of C–H bonds in them. This means the region at ~3000 cm^{-1} on an IR spectrum isn't always very useful when it comes to identifying what an organic molecule could be.

The absorption at about 3000 cm^{-1} is caused by the C–H bonds.

This strong, sharp absorption at about 1700 cm^{-1} shows you there's a C=O bond.

Interpreting IR spectra

Infrared spectroscopy is a powerful tool for identifying molecules. By looking at the peaks in the IR spectrum of an unknown molecule, you can identify what functional groups it's likely to contain.

Example — **Maths Skills**

An unknown compound has $M_r = 60$. Its infrared spectrum is shown below:

Tip: When you're reading an infrared spectrum, always double-check the scale. The wavenumbers increase from <u>right to left</u> — don't get caught out.

This medium intensity, broad absorption at about 3000 cm^{-1} shows you there's an O–H bond in a carboxylic acid group.

This strong, sharp absorption at about 1720 cm^{-1} shows you there's a C=O bond.

Tip: You can use infrared spectroscopy to tell if a functional group has changed during a reaction. For example, if you oxidise an alcohol to an aldehyde you'll see the O–H absorption disappear from the spectrum, and a C=O absorption appear.

The peaks on the IR spectrum tell you that the molecule must contain a carboxylic acid group (this accounts for the C=O group and the carboxylic acid O–H group). There's only one carboxylic acid with $M_r = 60$ — ethanoic acid.

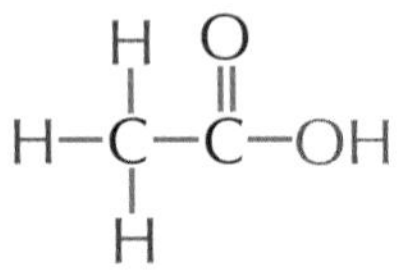

ethanoic acid

Predicting infrared spectra

As well as using an infrared spectrum to identify an unknown molecule, you can use the structure of a molecule to predict what peaks will be present in its infrared spectrum. All you have to do is work out what functional groups are in the molecule, and then use the values on the data sheet to predict roughly where the absorption peaks will be.

Tip: You won't be able to predict exactly where each peak will be, but a rough range is fine.

Example — Maths Skills

Here is the structure of 3-hydroxybutanoic acid:

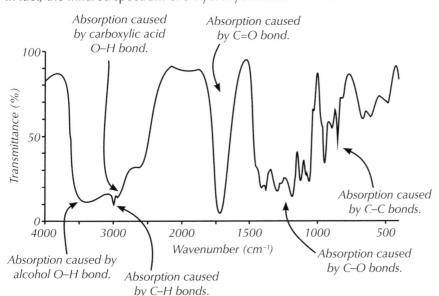

The molecule contains C–C, C–H, C–O, O–H (alcohol), C=O and O–H (carboxylic acid) bonds that are all able to absorb infrared radiation.

Once you've identified all the different bonds in the molecule, all that's left to do is use your data sheet to look up where the peaks for each of these bonds appear on an infrared spectrum.

So, the infrared spectrum of 3-hydroxybutanoic acid is likely to have peaks at the following wavenumbers:

Bond	Frequency / Wavenumber (cm⁻¹)
C–C	750 – 1100
C–O	1000 – 1300
C=O	1630 – 1820
C–H	2850 – 3100
O–H (carboxylic acid)	2500 – 3300 (broad)
O–H (alcohol)	3200 – 3600

In fact, the infrared spectrum of 3-hydroxybutanoic acid looks like this:

Exam Tip
If you're asked to predict what the infrared spectrum for a molecule will look like, it helps to draw out the displayed structure of the molecule. This will help to make sure you don't miss out any bonds when working out what peaks will be in the spectrum.

Tip: Again, you don't have to remember all these numbers. The data sheet, which you'll be given in your exam, will tell you the wavenumbers of all the peaks you need to know.

Tip: It's hard to identify each of the peaks on this spectrum, as some of them appear at very similar wavenumbers. The alcohol O–H peak, the C–H peak and the carboxylic acid O–H peak all overlap and so are merged together in the spectrum:

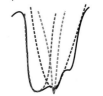

Applications of IR spectroscopy

As well as being used by scientists to identify unknown compounds, IR spectroscopy also has uses outside the lab.

Breathalysers

If a person's suspected of drink-driving, they're breathalysed. First, a very quick test is done by the roadside — if it says that the driver's over the limit, they're taken into a police station for a more accurate test using infrared spectroscopy. The amount of ethanol vapour in the driver's breath is found by measuring the intensity of the peak corresponding to the C–H bond in the IR spectrum. It's chosen because it's not affected by any water vapour in the breath. The IR spectrum from the breathalyser test is kept and can be used as evidence in court during the offender's trial.

Figure 2: *A man undergoing a drink-driving breath test at a police station.*

Tip: You can't use the intensity of the O–H bond peak to measure the amount of alcohol in a breath sample. This is because water also contains O–H bonds, so the size of this peak will be affected by how much water is in the breath sample as well as how much alcohol there is.

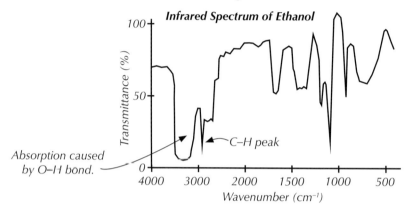

Figure 3: *The infrared absorption spectrum of ethanol.*

Monitoring pollutants

Infrared spectroscopy is used to monitor the concentrations of **polluting gases** in the atmosphere. These include carbon monoxide (CO) and nitrogen monoxide (NO), which are both present in car emissions. The intensity of the peaks corresponding to the C≡O or N=O bonds can be studied to monitor their levels.

Practice Questions — Application

Q1 The spectrum below is the infrared spectrum of a carboxylic acid with $M_r = 74$.

Tip: You can use the data table on page 255 to help you with all of these questions.

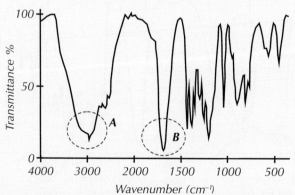

Tip: Remember that displayed formulas have to show all of the bonds present in a molecule.

a) Identify the bonds that create the peaks marked **A** and **B** in the diagram.

b) Draw the displayed formula of the molecule.

Q2 The infrared spectrum of an unknown molecule is shown below. Use the spectrum to identify one important bond that can be found in the molecule.

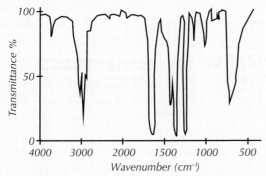

Q3 One of the infrared spectra below is the infrared spectrum of propan-2-ol. Identify which spectrum (**A** or **B**) it is.

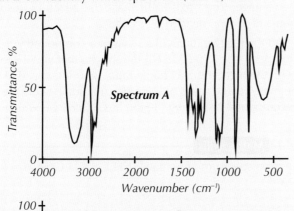

Exam Tip
Remember — if you're asked to predict the spectrum of a molecule in the exam, it may help to draw the molecule out so it's easy to spot the functional groups and other bonds.

Q4 Predict the wavenumbers of the peaks you would expect to see in the infrared spectrum of the molecule prop-2-enal:

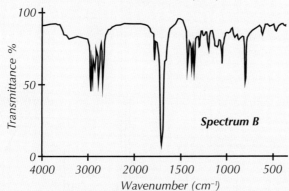

Practice Questions — Fact Recall

Q1 Give a brief explanation of how an infrared spectrum is created.

Q2 Describe one application of infrared spectroscopy.

- Be able to use a mass spectrum of an organic compound to identify the molecular ion peak and hence to determine molecular mass.
- Be able to analyse fragmentation peaks in a mass spectrum to identify parts of structures.

Specification Reference 4.2.4

Figure 1: *Mass spectrometer.*

Tip: The M+1 peak arises mainly because, in a given sample, a small percentage of the organic molecules will contain atoms of the carbon isotope carbon-13. If you're given a question containing a spectrum with an M+1 peak, you can just ignore it when working out the M_r of the molecule from its mass spectrum.

2. Mass Spectrometry

This topic deals with another analytical technique — mass spectrometry. Mass spectrometry uses the mass of a compound to identify it. It's not quite as simple as it sounds though... you'll have to learn about something called 'fragmentation'. Read on to find out more...

Finding relative molecular mass

You saw on page 34 how you can use a **mass spectrum** showing the relative isotopic abundances of an element to work out its relative atomic mass. You need to make sure you can remember how to do this. You can also get mass spectra for molecular samples.

A mass spectrum is produced by a mass spectrometer. The molecules in the sample are bombarded with electrons and a molecular ion, $M^+_{(g)}$, is formed when the bombarding electrons remove an electron from the molecule. On a mass spectrum the *y*-axis gives the abundance of the ions, often as a percentage. The *x*-axis is the mass/charge ratio. This is just the molecular mass of the ion divided by its charge.

To find the relative molecular mass of a compound you look at the molecular ion peak (the M peak). For the spectra that you'll see, the M peak is the one with the highest mass/charge ratio, ignoring any M+1 peak (see below). The mass/charge value of the molecular ion peak is the molecular mass of the compound (assuming the ion has +1 charge, which it normally will have).

Example — **Maths Skills**

Here's the mass spectrum of pentane ($CH_3CH_2CH_2CH_2CH_3$).

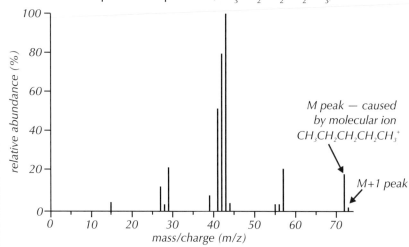

Its M peak is at 72 — so the compound's M_r is 72.

Fragmentation

The bombarding electrons make some of the molecular ions break up into fragments. The fragments that are ions show up on the mass spectrum, making a fragmentation pattern. **Fragmentation patterns** are actually pretty cool because you can use them to identify molecules and even their structure.

For propane ($CH_3CH_2CH_3$), the molecular ion is $CH_3CH_2CH_3^+$, and the fragments it breaks into include CH_3^+ ($M_r = 15$) and $CH_3CH_2^+$ ($M_r = 29$).

$$CH_3CH_2CH_3^+ \nearrow \quad \begin{array}{cc} CH_3CH_2\bullet & + & CH_3^+ \\ \textit{free radical} & & \textit{ion} \end{array}$$

$$\searrow \quad \begin{array}{cc} CH_3CH_2^+ & + & CH_3\bullet \\ \textit{ion} & & \textit{free radical} \end{array}$$

Tip: Only the ions show up on the mass spectrum — the free radicals are 'lost' because they are uncharged.

To work out the structural formula, you've got to work out what ion could have made each peak from its *m/z* value. (You can assume that the *m/z* value of a peak matches the mass of the ion that made it.)

Tip: Being able to analyse and interpret the mass spectrum of a molecule is a vital part of organic chemistry. It's an important technique used by research scientists for identifying unknown compounds or confirming the identity of a product in organic synthesis.

Example — Maths Skills

The mass spectrum below is for a molecule with the molecular formula C_2H_6O. Use the mass spectrum to work out the structure of the molecule.

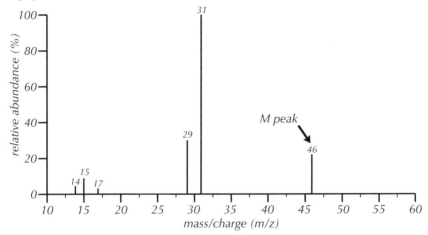

Tip: The little numbers above the peaks here are their exact *m/z* values.

First you need to identify the fragments — you can use Figure 2 to help you identify some common ions.

- This molecule's got a peak at *m/z* = 15, so it's likely to have a CH_3 group. It has a peak at *m/z* = 29, so it's likely to have a CH_3CH_2 group. It's also got a peak at *m/z* = 17, so it's likely to have an OH group.

- To find the other fragments you just have to add combinations of 12 (the mass of carbon), 1 (the mass of hydrogen) and 16 (the mass of oxygen) until you come up with sensible fragment ions.

Other ions are matched to the peaks here:

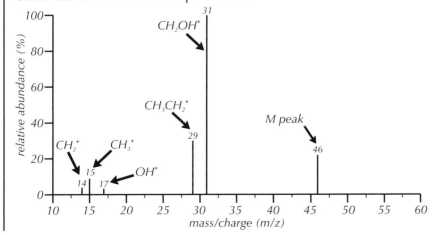

Fragment	m/z
CH_3^+	15
$CH_3CH_2^+$	29
$CH_3CH_2CH_2^+$ or $CH_3CHCH_3^+$	43
OH^+	17
$C{=}O^+$	28
$COCH_3^+$	43

Figure 2: *Common fragment ions.*

Exam Tip
You won't be given a common fragments table in the exam. But don't worry — if you can't remember an *m/z* value, you can work it out by finding the M_r of the ion For example:
$OH^+ = 16 + 1 = 17$.

The next step is piecing them together to form a molecule with the correct M_r. Ethanol has all the fragments on this spectrum.

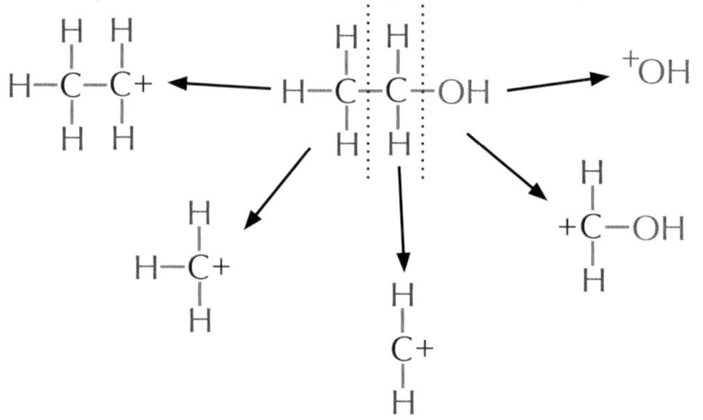

$$H-\overset{\overset{\displaystyle H}{|}}{\underset{\underset{\displaystyle H}{|}}{C}}-\overset{\overset{\displaystyle H}{|}}{\underset{\underset{\displaystyle H}{|}}{C}}+ \quad \longleftarrow \quad H-\overset{\overset{\displaystyle H}{|}}{\underset{\underset{\displaystyle H}{|}}{C}}-\overset{\overset{\displaystyle H}{|}}{\underset{\underset{\displaystyle H}{|}}{C}}-OH \quad \longrightarrow \quad {}^+OH$$

$$H-\overset{\overset{\displaystyle H}{|}}{\underset{\underset{\displaystyle H}{|}}{C}}+ \qquad \overset{\overset{\displaystyle H}{|}}{\underset{\underset{\displaystyle H}{|}}{C}}+ \qquad {}^+\overset{\overset{\displaystyle H}{|}}{\underset{\underset{\displaystyle H}{|}}{C}}-OH$$

Ethanol's formula is C_2H_6O, and its molecular mass is 46 — the same as the m/z value of the M peak. So, this is the mass spectrum of ethanol.

Differentiating between similar molecules

Even if two different compounds contain the same atoms, you can still tell them apart with mass spectrometry because they won't produce exactly the same set of fragments.

─ Example ─

The formulas of propanone and propanal are shown below.

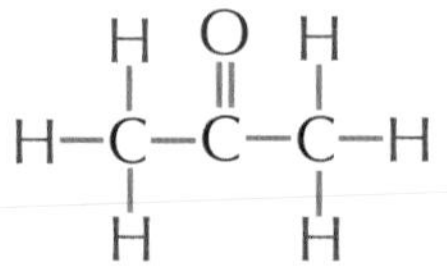

propanone   *propanal*

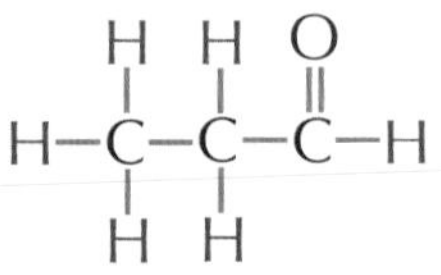

They've got the same M_r, but different structures, so they produce some different fragments.

Propanone

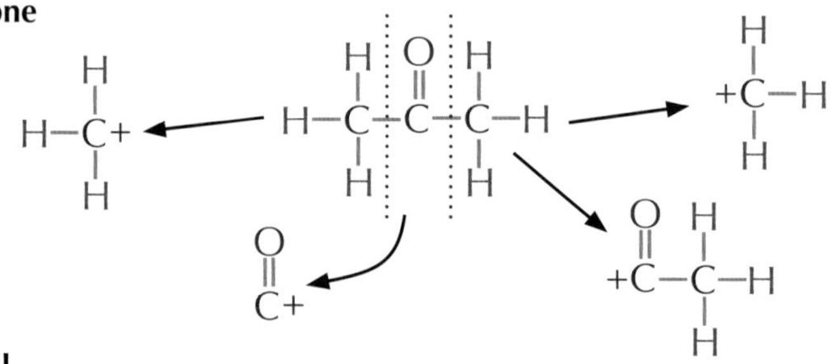

Propanal

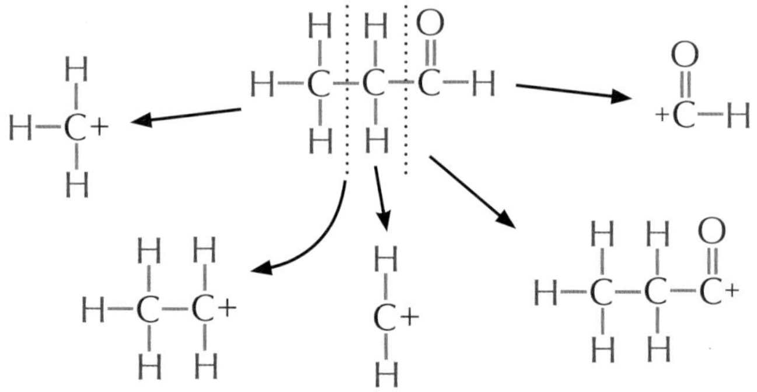

Every compound produces a different mass spectrum — so the spectrum's like a fingerprint for the compound. Large computer databases of mass spectra can be used to identify a compound from its spectrum.

Practice Questions — Application

Q1 Write down three possible fragment ions of propan-1-ol. The structure of propan-1-ol is shown on the right.

$$H-\overset{\overset{\displaystyle H}{|}}{\underset{\underset{\displaystyle H}{|}}{C}}-\overset{\overset{\displaystyle H}{|}}{\underset{\underset{\displaystyle H}{|}}{C}}-\overset{\overset{\displaystyle H}{|}}{\underset{\underset{\displaystyle H}{|}}{C}}-OH$$

Q2 Use the mass spectrum below to work out the structure of the molecule. HINT: The molecule is an alkene.

Tip: You can use Figure 2 on page 261 to help with this question if you like.

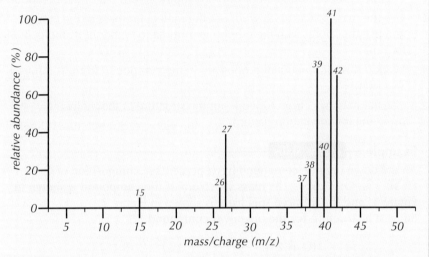

Tip: If you're struggling to work out what fragments a molecule might produce, draw it out. You'll find it's so much easier to divide the molecule up into fragments when you can see all the atoms and bonds.

Q3 Identify a fragment ion that will appear in the mass spectrum of butan-2-ol but won't appear in the mass spectrum of butan-1-ol.

Practice Questions — Fact Recall

Q1 What do the x-axis and the y-axis on a mass spectrum tell you?

Q2 What information does the m/z value of the M peak give you?

Q3 If you have a peak at an m/z of 15, what is the most likely fragment ion of an organic compound that it will correspond to?

<table>
<tr><td>

Learning Objective:

- Be able to deduce the structures of organic compounds from different analytical data including elemental analysis, mass spectra and IR spectra.

  Specification Reference 4.2.4

</td><td>

3. Combined Techniques

Often, it can help to use more than one analytical technique to work out what an organic compound is. Before you start this topic, make sure you're confident working out the formula of a compound from its percentage composition, and you understand how to interpret IR and mass spectra.

</td></tr>
</table>

Identifying compounds

In the exam, you may be asked to identify a compound from a combination of its mass or percentage composition, IR spectrum and mass spectrum.
You may have to do some of the following steps:

1. Use the composition to work out the empirical formula of the compound.

2. Use the mass spectrum to work out the molecular mass of the compound, and use this along with the empirical formula to work out its molecular formula.

3. Work out what functional groups are in the compound from its infrared spectrum.

4. Use the mass spectrum to work out the structure of the molecule using the fragmentation pattern.

Exam Tip
If you're asked to use a variety of methods to identify a compound, make sure you refer to all the sources of data in your answer. So if you're asked to identify a compound using a mass spectrum and an IR spectrum, make sure you write about what both the spectra show you, even if you can figure it out from just one of them.

┌─ **Example** ── Maths Skills ─────────

An unknown organic compound has a percentage composition of C: 62.1%, H: 10.3%, O: 27.6%. The mass spectrum of the compound is shown in Figure 1, and the infrared spectrum is shown in Figure 2. Suggest a structure for the unknown compound.

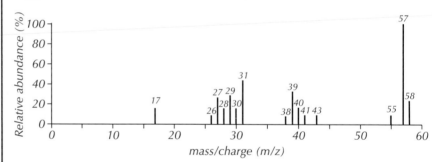

Figure 1: The mass spectrum of an organic compound.

Tip: Being able to predict what a compound is from one type of analytical technique is fine, but if you get the same answer using more than one technique as evidence then you can be more confident of your answer.

HOW SCIENCE WORKS

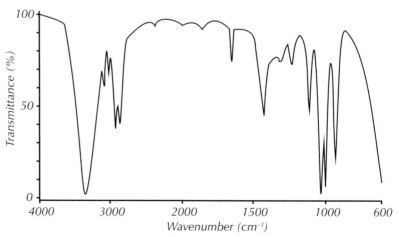

Figure 2: The infrared spectrum of an organic compound.

First, work out the empirical formula using the percentage composition of the compound:

- If you had 100 g of the compound, there would be 62.1 g of carbon, 10.3 g of hydrogen and 27.6 g of oxygen.
  Using the formula moles = mass ÷ M_r, you can work out how many moles of each element that is:

  C: $\frac{62.1}{12}$ = 5.18 mol   H: $\frac{10.3}{1}$ = 10.3 mol   O: $\frac{27.6}{16}$ = 1.73 mol

- Divide each number of moles by the smallest number (here it's 1.73):

  C: $\frac{5.18}{1.73} \approx 3$ H: $\frac{10.3}{1.73} \approx 6$ O: $\frac{1.73}{1.73} = 1$

- This tells you that the ratio of the elements C : H : O in the compound is 3 : 6 : 1. So the empirical formula is **C_3H_6O**.

Tip: There's more about calculating the formula of a compound from its percentage composition on pages 51-52.

Next, use the mass spectrum to find the molecular mass of the compound:

- The peak with the highest mass (the M peak) in Figure 1 has an m/z of 58, so the molecular mass of the compound is 58.
- The empirical formula has $M_r = (3 \times 12) + (6 \times 1) + (1 \times 16) = 58$. Since the empirical mass is the same as the molecular mass of the compound, the molecular formula will be **C_3H_6O**.

The easiest way to identify the functional groups in the molecule is by looking at the IR spectrum.

- The spectrum shows a peak at about 3200 cm^{-1}, which is likely to be due to an -OH group.
- There is also a peak at about 3000 cm^{-1} due to the vibrations of the C–H bonds and a peak at about 1650 cm^{-1}, which is likely to be due to vibrations of C=C bonds. These peaks imply that the molecule is an **alcohol** and also has an **alkene** group.

Tip: The molecule must be an alcohol or a carbonyl — it can't be a carboxylic acid as there's only one oxygen atom in the molecular formula.

You can now start piecing together the information to draw some potential structures for your compound. The following structural isomers all have a hydroxyl group, an alkene group and a molecular formula of C_3H_6O:

1-propen-1-ol   *1-propen-2-ol*   *2-propen-1-ol*

Tip: Look back at pages 199-200 for the rules on how to name organic molecules.

Now it's time to go back to the mass spectrum to identify what fragments are in the molecule:

- The peak at $m/z = 31$ is likely to be a CH_2OH^+ fragment.
- The peak at $m/z = 27$ is likely to be a CH_2CH^+ fragment.
- The spectrum doesn't have a peak at $m/z = 15$, so it's unlikely that there's a CH_3 fragment in the molecule.

The spectrum shows that the compound must be **2-propen-1-ol**, as this is the only isomer that has a CH_2OH fragment, a CH_2CH fragment and no CH_3 fragment.

Q1 Explain which of the compounds A, B or C is represented by the data below:

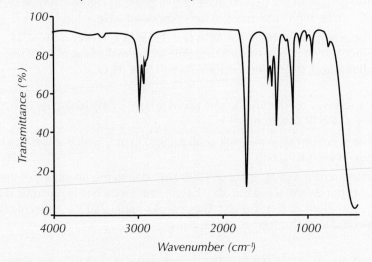

A

H CH₃ H
H—C—C—C—H
H CH₃ H

B

H H O H
H—C—C—C—C—H
H H H

C

H O H
H—C—C—C—H
H H

The mass spectrum of the compound has a molecular ion peak at an *m/z* of 72.

The infrared spectrum of the compound is:

Q2 An organic compound that can be made by oxidising a primary alcohol has percentage composition: C: 54.5%, H: 9.01%, O: 36.4%. Its mass spectrum is shown below.
Predict, with reasoning, the identity of the organic compound.

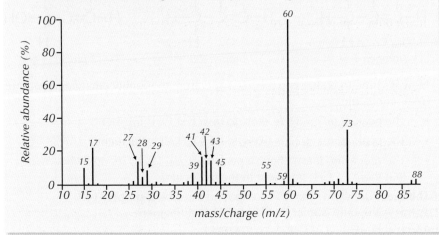

Tip: Don't get confused between IR spectroscopy and mass spectrometry. Remember — if you're given an IR spectrum, you want to be looking at the functional groups in a molecule. But if you're given a mass spectrum, you need to look at the structure and what fragments you're likely to get.

Tip: Use the table on page 255 to help identify the IR peaks.

Tip: Remember that you don't have to assign every peak to a fragment in a mass spectrum.

4. Practical Techniques in Organic Synthesis

PRACTICAL ACTIVITY GROUP 5

There are some practical techniques that get used a lot in organic chemistry. They may be used during the synthesis of a product, or to purify it from unwanted by-products or unreacted reagents once it's been made.

Reflux

Organic reactions are slow and the substances are usually flammable and volatile (they've got low boiling points). If you stick the reactants in a beaker and heat them with a Bunsen burner they'll evaporate or catch fire before they have time to react. You can **reflux** a reaction to get round this problem.

When you carry out a reaction under reflux, the mixture's heated in a flask fitted with a vertical **Liebig condenser**. This means the mixture can be continuously boiled, and as the vapours evaporate into the condenser they condense and are recycled back into the flask, giving them time to react.

The heating is usually electrical — hotplates, heating mantles or electrically controlled water baths are normally used. This avoids naked flames that might ignite the compounds.

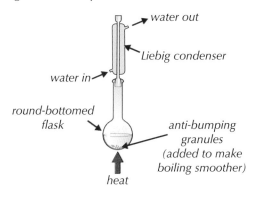

Figure 1: Reflux apparatus.

water out

Liebig condenser

water in

round-bottomed flask

anti-bumping granules (added to make boiling smoother)

heat

--- Example ---

The reaction between butan-2-ol and acidified potassium dichromate(VI) to make butanone is slow at room temperature, so it needs to be heated.

Butanone has a boiling point of 80 °C and butan-2-ol has a boiling point of about 100 °C, so if you were to heat the reaction in a beaker then lots of the reactant and product compounds would evaporate out of the mixture and be lost.

By heating the reaction under reflux, the rate of the reaction is increased but neither the starting materials nor the product can evaporate out of the apparatus, so the yield isn't reduced.

Distillation

Distillation separates liquids with different boiling points. It works by gently heating a mixture in a distillation apparatus. The substances will evaporate out of the mixture in order of increasing boiling point.

Learning Objectives:

- Be able to describe and use the techniques and procedures for the use of Quickfit apparatus, including for distillation and heating under reflux (PAG 5).

- Be able to describe and use the techniques and procedures for the preparation and purification of an organic liquid, including how to use a separating funnel to remove an organic layer from an aqueous layer, how to dry an organic layer with an anhydrous salt (e.g. $MgSO_4$, $CaCl_2$), and redistillation (PAG 5).

Specification Reference 4.2.3

Tip: The chemicals you use in organic reactions are often hazardous. You should always carry out a full risk assessment before you do any reactions in the lab.

Figure 2: Two students carrying out a reflux reaction.

A thermometer is placed at the neck of the condenser and shows the boiling point of the substance that is evaporating at any given time. If you know the boiling point of your pure product, you can use the thermometer to tell you when it's evaporating and therefore when it's condensing.

If the product of a reaction has a lower boiling point than the starting materials, then the reaction mixture can be heated in a distillation apparatus so that the product evaporates from the reaction mixture as it forms. As long as the temperature is controlled, the starting materials won't evaporate from the reaction mixture.

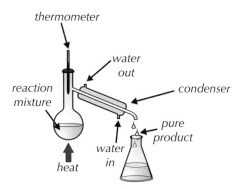

Figure 3: *Distillation apparatus.*

Tip: Secondary alcohols are oxidised to ketones by acidified potassium dichromate(VI) solution. Primary alcohols are oxidised first to aldehydes and then to carboxylic acids. There's more on this on pages 239-240.

Example

Hexan-1-ol reacts with acidified dichromate(VI) solution to form hexanal. However, hexanal can be further oxidised by acidified dichromate(VI) to form hexanoic acid.

By heating the reaction in a distillation apparatus at a temperature of around 131 °C (the boiling point of hexanal), any hexanal that is produced will immediately evaporate out of the reaction mixture. Hexan-1-ol, which has a boiling point of about 155 °C, won't evaporate, so stays in the reaction mixture and can react fully to form hexanal. The hexanal that is distilled out of the reaction mixture can be collected in a separate vessel. This prevents it from being oxidised further to hexanoic acid.

Redistillation

Mixtures that contain volatile liquids can be purified using a technique called **redistillation**. If a product and its impurities have different boiling points, then redistillation can be used to separate them. You just use the same distillation apparatus as shown above, but this time you're heating an impure product, instead of the reaction mixture.

When the liquid you want boils (this is when the thermometer is at the boiling point of the liquid), you place a flask at the open end of the condenser ready to collect your product. When the thermometer shows the temperature is changing, put another flask at the end of the condenser because a different liquid is about to be delivered.

Separation

Tip: Water-soluble impurities might include salts (such as NaCl) or short-chain organic compounds that are capable of forming hydrogen bonds (such as alcohols, carbonyls and carboxylic acids).

If the product is insoluble in water then you can use a separating funnel to remove any impurities that do dissolve in water, such as salts or water-soluble organic compounds (e.g. alcohols).

Once the reaction is completed, the mixture is poured into the separating funnel, and water is added. The funnel is shaken and then allowed to settle (see Figure 4). The organic layer is normally less dense than the aqueous layer, so should float on top. Most of the water-soluble impurities should have dissolved in the lower aqueous layer. You can then open the stopper on the separating funnel, run off the aqueous layer and collect your product.

Tip: Your product won't necessarily be pure after separation — any organic impurities that don't dissolve in water will still be in the organic layer alongside your product. You'll probably need to remove them by redistillation. There may also be a few water soluble impurities left in the organic layer. To get rid of these, you'll need to repeat the separation.

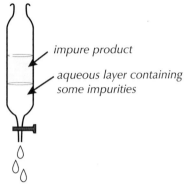

impure product

aqueous layer containing some impurities

Figure 4: *Separating apparatus.*

Figure 5: *A student using a separating funnel to separate an organic and an aqueous layer.*

Drying agents

If you use separation to purify a product, the organic layer will end up containing trace amounts of water, so it has to be dried. To do this you can add an anhydrous salt such as magnesium sulfate ($MgSO_4$) or calcium chloride ($CaCl_2$). The salt is used as a **drying agent** — it binds to any water present to become hydrated. The drying agent will become lumpy when you first add it to the organic layer — this means you need to add more. You know that all the water has been removed when you can swirl the mixture and it looks like a snow globe. The mixture, which may have looked cloudy due to the presence of tiny water droplets at the beginning, should also go clear when it's dry and the drying agent has settled to the bottom. You can filter the mixture to remove the solid drying agent.

Practice Questions — Application

Q1 Suggest how you could separate a mixture of hexane and ethanol into its component parts.

Q2 A student wants to make the compound 4-hydroxypentan-2-one by heating pentane-2,4-diol with acidified potassium dichromate(VI). If the reaction is left for too long, the starting material ends up being oxidised twice to form a compound with two carbonyl groups. Suggest a method the student could use to prevent the starting material from being over-oxidised.

Tip: If you're asked about how you could go about separating a mixture, you need to think about the properties of the different compounds. For example, hexane is insoluble in water and has a boiling point of 68 °C. Ethanol is soluble in water and has a boiling point of 78 °C.

Practice Questions — Fact Recall

Q1 Draw a labelled diagram of the apparatus used to reflux a reaction.

Q2 What physical property is used to separate compounds in redistillation?

Q3 Name two compounds that can be used as drying agents.

Exam Tip
Always remember to label diagrams if you have to draw them in the exam.

Learning Objectives:

5. Organic Synthesis

In the exam, you might have to explain how you could synthesise one compound from another, so here's a summary of all the homologous series and reactions you've met so far. It might look like a lot of information, but don't panic — you've seen most of it before.

Typical reactions of functional groups

The different properties of functional groups influence their reactivity — for example, nucleophiles don't react with the electron-rich double bond in alkenes, but they do attack the $\delta+$ carbon in haloalkanes. Figure 1 is a summary of all the functional groups you've studied so far, along with how to name them and how they'll typically react:

Homologous series	Functional group	Prefix/ suffix	Properties	Typical reactions
Alkane	only C–C and C–H	-ane	Non-polar, unreactive	Radical substitution
Alkene	C=C	-ene	Non-polar, electron-rich double bond	Electrophilic addition
Alcohol	C–OH	-ol (or hydroxy-)	Polar C–OH bond	Nucleophilic substitution/ Dehydration/ Elimination/Oxidation
Haloalkane	C–X	halo- (e.g. chloro-)	Polar C–X bond	Nucleophilic substitution
Ketone	C=O	-one	Polar C=O bond	—
Aldehyde	HC=O	-al	Polar C=O bond	Oxidation
Carboxylic acid	-COOH	-oic acid	Electron-deficient carbon centre	—

Figure 1: *The homologous series and organic reactions in Module 4.*

Tip: Now you've learnt about lots of organic reactions, you can use them to work out how you could make one compound from another. That's what organic chemistry's all about.

Synthetic Routes

Chemists need to be able to make one compound from another. It's vital for things such as designing medicines. It's not always possible to synthesise a desired product from a starting material in just one reaction. A synthetic route shows how you get from one compound to another. It shows all the reactions with the intermediate products, and the reagents needed for each reaction.

┌ **Example** ─────

You can't produce propanone from 2-bromopropane via one reaction. Instead you first have to make propan-2-ol. The synthetic route is:

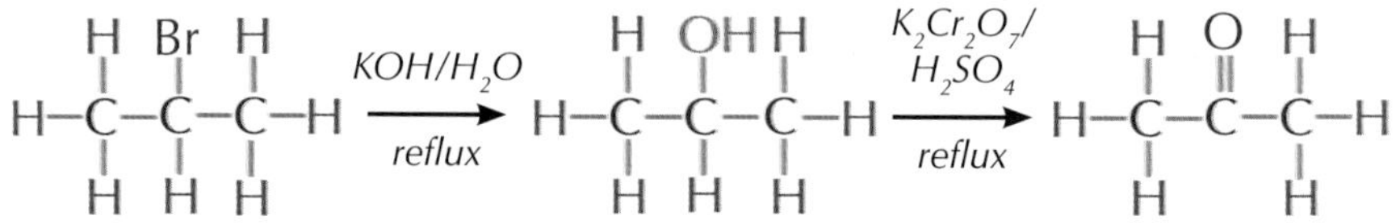

$$
\begin{array}{ccc}
\underset{\substack{H\ Br\ H \\ | \ | \ | \\ H-C-C-C-H \\ | \ | \ | \\ H\ H\ H}}{} & \xrightarrow[\text{reflux}]{KOH/H_2O} & \underset{\substack{H\ OH\ H \\ | \ | \ | \\ H-C-C-C-H \\ | \ | \ | \\ H\ H\ H}}{} & \xrightarrow[\text{reflux}]{K_2Cr_2O_7/ H_2SO_4} & \underset{\substack{H\ O\ H \\ | \ || \ | \\ H-C-C-C-H \\ | \quad | \\ H\quad\ H}}{}
\end{array}
$$

Here are all the organic reactions you've met so far:

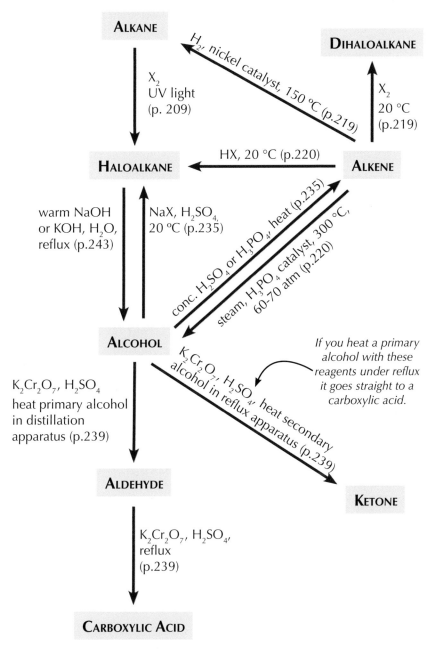

Figure 2: *A summary of organic reactions that could be used in synthetic routes.*

If you're asked how to make one compound from another in the exam, make sure you include:

- Any special procedures, such as refluxing.
- The conditions needed, e.g. high temperature or pressure, or the presence of a catalyst.

Tip: The reaction between an alkene and a halogen to form a dihaloalkane using bromine water ($Br_{2\,(aq)}$) can be used as a test for unsaturation (see page 220).

Tip: To form an alcohol from a haloalkane, you could also use H_2O in the presence of $AgNO_3$. This reaction is used to test the strength of different carbon-halogen bonds (see page 244).

Tip: If it says a reaction is carried out at 20 °C, it just means it's done at room temperature.

Tip: Remember — aldehydes form from primary alcohols and ketones from secondary alcohols.

Tip: Hydrocarbons (organic molecules that contain only hydrogen and carbon) also combust in oxygen to form carbon dioxide and water (page 205).

Tip: When you're planning a synthetic route, you should aim to get from the first compound to the last in as few steps as possible.

Tip: The summary diagram on page 271 will be really useful for these questions.

Q1 Name all the functional groups in the following molecule:

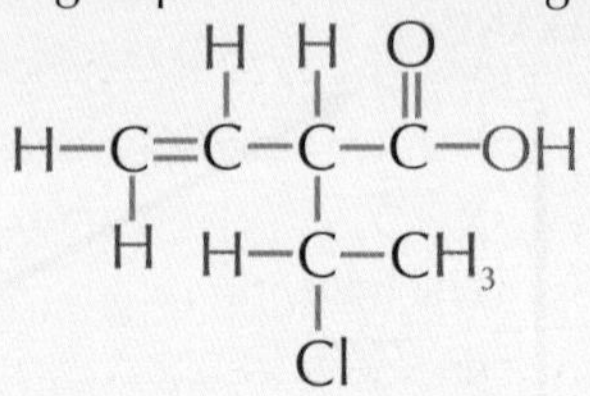

Q2 The diagram below shows how some haloalkanes can be produced from an alcohol:

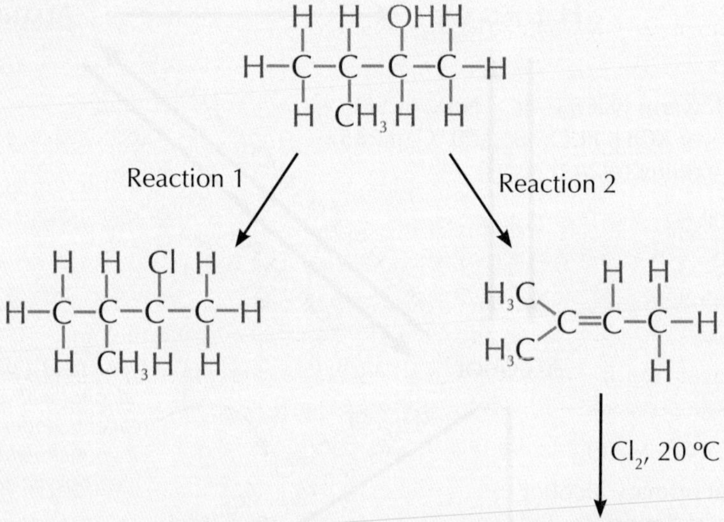

Reaction 1

Reaction 2

Cl_2, 20 °C

Compound X

Exam Tip
If a question asks for a synthetic route, remember to give <u>all</u> the special procedures, conditions and reagents you need. Missing out any could cost you valuable marks...

a) What reagents and conditions are needed in Reaction 1?

b) What reagents and conditions are needed in Reaction 2?

c) Draw the structure of Compound X.

Q3 Devise a two-stage synthetic route that could be used to produce pentanoic acid from 1-bromopentane.

Q1 Name the homologous series that contain the following functional groups:

a)

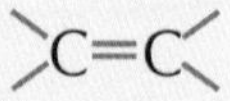

b)

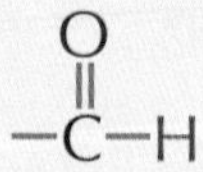

c)

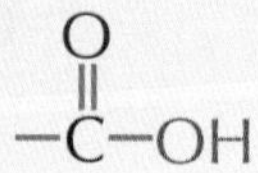

Q2 Give one of the typical reactions of the following compounds:

a) a haloalkane

b) an alkane

c) an alcohol

Q3 What conditions and reagents are required to synthesise an alkane from an alkene?

Q4 What would happen if you heated a primary alcohol under reflux with potassium dichromate(VI) in acidic conditions?

Section Summary

Make sure you know...

- That absorption of infrared radiation causes covalent bonds to vibrate.
- How to identify an alcohol, an aldehyde, a ketone and a carboxylic acid from the absorption peaks in an infrared spectrum.
- How to interpret and predict the infrared spectra of unfamiliar molecules.
- That modern breathalysers measure ethanol in the breath using infrared spectroscopy.
- That gases causing air pollution, such as CO and NO, can be monitored using infrared spectroscopy.
- How to use the molecular ion peak on a mass spectrum to determine the molecular mass of a molecule.
- How to use the fragmentation pattern of a mass spectrum to identify the structure of a molecule.
- How to use a combination of analysis techniques, such as elemental analysis, infrared spectra and mass spectra, in order to deduce the structures of organic compounds.
- How to prepare an organic liquid by heating under reflux and by distillation.
- How to purify an organic liquid by redistillation.
- That you can purify an organic liquid by using a separating funnel to remove aqueous impurities.
- How to use anhydrous salts, such as anhydrous $MgSO_4$ or anhydrous $CaCl_2$, to dry organic liquids.
- The different functional groups in an organic molecule and how to identify them.
- How to predict the properties and reactions of an organic molecule based on its functional groups.
- How to devise a two-stage synthetic route to prepare an organic compound.

Exam-style Questions

1 Identify which of the steps in the following method for purifying an organic compound that is immiscible with water from water-soluble impurities is incorrect:

A Pour the organic mixture into a separating funnel and add water.

B Put a stopper in the separating funnel and shake it. Remove the stopper and allow the layers to settle.

C Run out the lower, aqueous, layer and discard it.

D Run out the upper, organic, layer and dry it with hydrated magnesium sulfate.

(1 mark)

2 Predict which compound is represented by the infrared spectrum shown below.

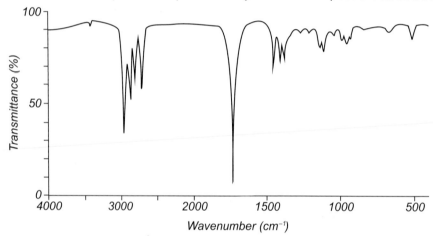

A butanol

B butanal

C butanoic acid

D butene

(1 mark)

3 Which of the following is not a valid one-stage synthetic route?

A alcohol → carboxylic acid

B dihaloalkane → haloalkane

C alcohol → alkene

D alkene → alkane

(1 mark)

4   A student synthesises the alcohol hexan-3-ol from an alkene in a one-stage synthesis.

   (a)   Name an alkene that could be used as the starting material for synthesising hexan-3-ol.

   (1 mark)

   (b)   Give the reagents and conditions needed to synthesise hexan-3-ol from an alkene.

   (2 marks)

   (c)   Give one difference that you would expect to see between the infrared spectra of the starting alkene and hexan-3-ol.

   (1 mark)

   (d)   The student purifies her product by redistillation.
   Draw a labelled diagram of the apparatus used in redistillation.

   (3 marks)

   (e)   Once the student has carried out her reaction, she records a mass spectrum of the purified product, shown below. Use the spectrum to confirm whether hexan-3-ol was successfully synthesised. Explain your answer.

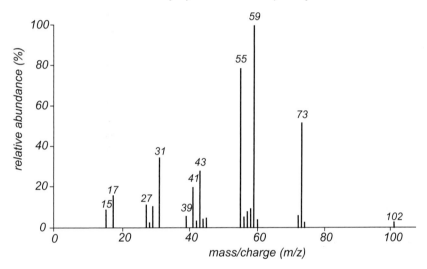

   (3 marks)

5   1,2-dichloroethane is an organic molecule, used in part of the manufacturing process of the polymer PVC.

   (a)   Describe a synthetic route which could be used to successfully produce 1,2-dichloroethane from ethanol. You should include details of any reaction conditions, reagents and intermediates formed in your synthetic route.

   (4 marks)

   (b)   A student successfully synthesises 1,2-dichloroethane from ethanol, but finds her product contains trace amounts of unreacted ethanol.
   Suggest a technique the student could use to purify her product.

   (1 mark)

6   Mass spectrometry and infrared spectrometry are two analytical techniques that are used to identify unknown compounds.

(a)   Describe how infrared spectroscopy can help to catch drunk drivers.

(2 marks)

(b)   Briefly outline why mass spectrometry can be used to differentiate between similar molecules.

(1 mark)

(c)   Molecule **J** is a hydrocarbon. The mass spectrum of molecule **J** is shown below. Identify the structure of molecule **J**. Explain your reasoning.

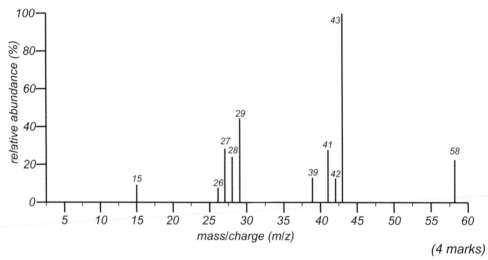

(4 marks)

(d)   Molecule **K** contains only carbon, oxygen and hydrogen atoms. It has the infrared spectrum shown below.

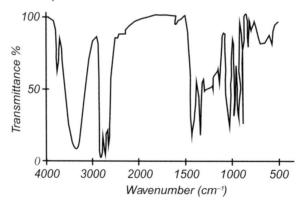

The mass spectrum of molecule **K** shows that the M_r of the molecule is 74.

If you react molecule **K** with acidified potassium dichromate(VI), you produce a ketone.

Use your knowledge of organic chemistry and analytical techniques along with the table on page 255 to identify the structure of molecule **K**. Explain your reasoning.

(4 marks)

Maths skills for AS and A Level Chemistry

Maths crops up quite a lot in AS and A Level Chemistry so it's really important that you've mastered all the maths skills you'll need before sitting your exams. Maths skills are covered throughout this book but here's an extra little section, just on maths, to help you out.

Exam Tip
Around 20% of the marks in the exams will depend on your maths skills. That's a lot of marks so it's definitely worth making sure you're up to speed.

1. Calculations

There's no getting away from those pesky calculations...

Showing your working

When you're doing calculations the most important thing to remember is to show your working. You've probably heard it a million times before but it makes perfect sense. It only takes a few seconds more to write down what's in your head and it'll stop you from making silly errors and losing out on easy marks. You won't get a mark for a wrong answer but you could get marks for the method you used to work out the answer.

Tip: All the examples in this book that include the kind of maths you could get in your exam are clearly marked. You can spot them by the big label that says...

Maths Skills

Units

Make sure you always give the correct units for your answer (see pages 282-283 for more on units).

┌─ **Example** ── **Maths Skills** ──────────

Here's an example of a question where you need to change the units so they match the answer the examiner wants.

1   A student measures the enthalpy change of reaction **A**. The temperature of the water increased by 2 °C during the reaction.

     a)   Calculate the heat given out in the reaction in kJ.

(2 marks)

When you use $q = mc\Delta T$ to calculate the heat given out you'll get an answer in joules. Make sure you convert the units to kilojoules by dividing by 1000.

Exam Tip
You'll need to know what units your figures need to be in for different formulas — see page 280 for the units used in different formulas and pages 282-283 for how to convert between units.

Standard form

You might need to use numbers written in standard form in calculations. Standard form is used for writing very big or very small numbers in a more convenient way. Standard form must always look like this:

This number must always be between 1 and 10. ➤ $A \times 10^n$ ◀ *This number is the number of places the decimal point moves.*

Tip: '*A*' can be 1 or any number <u>up to</u> 10 but it can't <u>be</u> 10 — it has to be a single digit.

You need to be able to convert numbers written in ordinary form into standard form.

Examples — Maths Skills

Here's how to write 3 500 000 in standard form.

- First write the non-zero digits with a decimal point after the first number and a '× 10' after it:
$$3.5 \times 10$$

- Then count how many places the decimal point has moved to the left. This number sits to the top right of the 10, as a superscript.

$$3\,5\,0\,0\,0\,0\,0 = 3.5 \times 10^6$$

- Et voilà... that's 3 500 000 written in standard form.

Here are some more examples.

- You can write 450 000 as 4.5×10^5.

- The number 0.000056 is 5.6×10^{-5} in standard form — the n is negative because the decimal point has moved to the right instead of the left.

- You can write 0.003456 as 3.456×10^{-3}.

Exam Tip

If you're asked specifically to give a number in ordinary or standard form then you'll need to make sure you've written it in the correct way. If you're not told how to write a number then give it in the form that the numbers in the question are in.

You also need to be able to convert numbers written in standard form into ordinary form.

Examples — Maths Skills

Here's how to write 7.2×10^3 in ordinary form.

- Take the number in standard form, move the decimal point 3 places to the right and fill in the gaps with zeros.

$$7\,2\,0\,0 = 7200$$

- There you go... that's 7.2×10^3 written in standard form.

Here are some more examples.

- You can write 9.1×10^5 as 910 000.

- The number 3.3×10^{-4} is 0.00033 in ordinary form — the n is negative so the decimal point has moved to the left instead of the right.

- You can write 1.765×10^{-3} as 0.001765.

Tip: It can be tricky to remember which way to move the decimal point. If n is positive then it means the number you're converting is a high number, and you'll need to move the decimal point to the right — you need more digits in front of the decimal point. If n is negative then you're dealing with a very low number and the decimal point needs to move to the left.

You can do calculations with numbers that are in ordinary form and numbers that are in standard form.

┌─ Example ─ **Maths Skills** ─────────────────────────────────

How many atoms are there in 5.00 moles of carbon?

To work this out you need to use the Avogadro constant (which is written in standard form) and the equation for calculating the number of particles in an amount of substance.

The Avogadro constant $= 6.02 \times 10^{23}$

no. of particles = no. moles × the Avogadro constant

So...   number of atoms in 5.00 moles of carbon $= 5.00 \times (6.02 \times 10^{23})$
$= 3.01 \times 10^{24}$

Significant figures

Use the number of significant figures given in the question as a guide for how many to give in the answer. You should always give your answer to the lowest number of significant figures (s.f.) given in the question — if you're really unsure, write down the full answer and then round it to 3 s.f. It always helps to write down the number of significant figures you've rounded to after your answer — it shows the examiner you haven't just made a mistake in your calculation. There's more information on how to use significant figures on page 16.

When you're converting between ordinary and standard form, you need to make sure the number you've converted to has the same number of significant figures as the number you've converted from. So if you've got 2 significant figures when the value is in ordinary form it also needs to be written to 2 significant figures in standard form.

┌─ Example ─ **Maths Skills** ─────────────────────────────────

Convert 0.00310 mol dm⁻³ from ordinary form to standard form.

- First write the non-zero digits with a decimal point after the first digit and a '× 10' after it: 3.1×10

- Then count how many places the decimal point has moved. This number needs to go as a superscript on the 10.

$$0.00310 = 3.1 \times 10^{-3}$$

- In ordinary form, the value is given to 3 significant figures. So it needs to have 3 significant figures when it's written in standard form. So 0.00310 mol dm⁻³ is the same as:

$$3.10 \times 10^{-3} \text{ mol dm}^{-3}$$

Exam Tip
Make sure you know how to use standard form on your calculator — it'll make these kinds of calculations much easier.

Exam Tip
It's so easy to mistype numbers into a calculator when you're under pressure in an exam. Always double check your calculations and make sure the answer looks sensible.

Exam Tip
You might get told in the question how many significant figures or decimal places to give your answer to. If you are, make sure that you follow the instructions — you'll lose marks if you don't.

Tip: Make sure you get the sign of the superscript correct when you're converting from ordinary form to standard form — it'll be negative for small numbers and positive for large numbers.

2. Formulas and Equations

A big part of the maths you need to do in chemistry involves using formulas and equations. So here's a nice page with them all neatly summarised for you.

Formulas

First up is perhaps a couple of the most useful equations of all...

Tip: M_r is relative molecular mass (or relative formula mass). You work it out by adding up all the A_rs (atomic masses) of all the atoms in the compound.

$$\text{Number of moles} = \frac{\text{Number of particles you have}}{\text{Number of particles in a mole}}$$

$$\text{Number of moles} = \frac{\text{Mass of substance}}{\text{Molar mass}} \qquad \text{also written as...} \quad n = \frac{m}{M_r}$$

You'll need these ones when you're dealing with solutions...

$$\text{Number of moles} = \frac{\text{Concentration (in mol dm}^{-3}\text{)} \times \text{Volume (in cm}^3\text{)}}{1000}$$

$$\text{Number of moles} = \text{Concentration (in mol dm}^{-3}\text{)} \times \text{Volume (in dm}^3\text{)}$$

...and these when you've got gases at room temperature and pressure.

$$\frac{\text{Number}}{\text{of moles}} = \frac{\text{Volume (in dm}^3\text{)}}{24} \qquad \frac{\text{Number}}{\text{of moles}} = \frac{\text{Volume (in cm}^3\text{)}}{24\ 000}$$

Tip: In the formula for working out the number of moles of a gas, the "24" comes from the fact that at room temperature and pressure one mole of any gas occupies 24 dm^3. See page 40 for more on this.

These two are handy when you're working out how much stuff you have...

$$\%\text{ atom economy} = \frac{\text{Molecular mass of desired product}}{\text{Sum of molecular masses of reactants}} \times 100$$

$$\%\text{ yield} = \frac{\text{Actual yield}}{\text{Theoretical yield}} \times 100$$

Here's the ideal gas equation.

$$\underset{\text{(Pa)}}{\overset{\text{(m}^3\text{)}}{pV}} = \underset{\text{(moles)}}{\overset{\text{(8.314 J K}^{-1}\text{mol}^{-1}\text{)}}{nRT}} \text{(K)}$$

Exam Tip
All these formulas are really important — you have to learn them because they won't be given to you in the exam.

There are two formulas you need to calculate enthalpy changes of a reaction. Here's one:

$$\underset{\text{(J)}}{q} = \underset{\text{(J g}^{-1}\text{K}^{-1}\text{)}}{\overset{\text{(g)}}{mc\Delta T}} \text{(K or °C)}$$

It doesn't matter whether the temperature is in K or °C — it's the <u>change</u> in temperature that goes into the formula, and that will be the same no matter what the units are.

And the slightly easier:

Enthalpy change of reaction = Total energy absorbed − Total energy released

And finally, here's the equation for the equilibrium constant (K_c).

For the general reaction $aA + bB \rightleftharpoons dD + eE$:

$$K_c = \frac{[D]^d[E]^e}{[A]^a[B]^b}$$

Tip: The lower-case letters a, b, d and e are the number of moles of each substance in the equation. The square brackets, [ ], mean concentration in mol dm^{-3}.

Rearranging formulas

You'll often need to change the subject of a formula. To do this you'll need to rearrange it. The crucial thing to remember here is that whatever you do to one side of the formula you need to do exactly the same to the other side.

Example — Maths Skills

Use the ideal gas equation to calculate the number of moles of gas present in 1.23 m^3 at a pressure of 100 000 Pa and a temperature of 298 K.

The ideal gas equation is $pV = nRT$

You need to rearrange it to make n (number of moles) the subject. To get n on its own you divide it by RT. Because you're dividing the right hand side of the equation by RT you also need to divide the left hand side by RT:

$\dfrac{pV}{RT} = \dfrac{nRT}{RT}$ You can cancel out RT on the right hand side... $\dfrac{pV}{RT} = \dfrac{n\cancel{RT}}{\cancel{RT}}$

...which leaves you with: $\dfrac{pV}{RT} = n$ You can then plug in the values given in the question to work out the answer.

Tip: The <u>subject</u> of an equation is the component on its own on one side of the equation. So for $q = mc\Delta T$, q is the subject. For $n = \text{mass} \div M_r$, n is the subject. You'll usually want to rearrange formulas so that the thing you've been asked to <u>calculate</u> is the subject.

Formula triangles are really useful tools for changing the subject of an equation. If three things are related by a formula like this:

$$a = b \times c \quad \text{or like this: } b = \frac{a}{c}$$

...then you can put them into a formula triangle. The components that are multiplied together go on the bottom of the triangle. Any components that are divided go on the top. To use the formula triangle to write out a formula just cover up the component that you want to make the subject of the equation, and write down what's left.

Example — Maths Skills

The equation 'number of moles (n) = concentration (c) × volume (V)' can be put into this formula triangle:

c = concentration (in mol/dm^3) — n = number of moles — V = volume (in dm^3)

If you want to make V the subject of the equation, just cover it up in the triangle and you're left with n over c, which is n divided by c. So $V = n \div c$

Tip: You don't have to use formula triangles to rearrange equations — if you're happy rearranging equations without them, then that's fine. You <u>do</u> need to know how to rearrange equations <u>without</u> a formula triangle though, as you may need to rearrange equations that don't fit nicely into a triangle. E.g. $q = mc\Delta T$

Symbols

You'll need to know the symbols which might be used in equations in the exam. You'll have seen many of these before but here's a quick refresher:

Symbol	Meaning
<	less than
<<	much less than
>	greater than
>>	much greater than

Symbol	Meaning
=	equal to
$\propto$	proportional to
~	approximately
$\rightleftharpoons$	reversible

3. Units

Units can trip you up if you're not sure which ones to use or how to convert between them. Here are the ones you're likely to have to deal with.

Exam Tip
You need to practise these conversions until you're sick of them. It'll save you loads of time in the exam if you're confident changing between units.

Volume

Volume can be measured in m^3, dm^3 and cm^3.

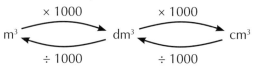

Examples — Maths Skills

Write 6 dm³ in m³ and cm³.

First, to convert 6 dm^3 into m^3 you need to divide by 1000.
$$6 \text{ dm}^3 \div 1000 = 0.006 \text{ m}^3 = 6 \times 10^{-3} \text{ m}^3$$
Then, to convert 6 dm^3 into cm^3 you need to multiply by 1000.
$$6 \text{ dm}^3 \times 1000 = 6000 \text{ cm}^3 = 6 \times 10^3 \text{ cm}^3$$

Write 0.4 cm³ in dm³ and m³.

First, to convert 0.4 cm^3 into dm^3 you need to divide by 1000.
$$0.4 \text{ cm}^3 \div 1000 = 0.0004 \text{ dm}^3 = 4 \times 10^{-4} \text{ dm}^3$$
Then, to convert 0.0004 dm^3 into m^3 you need to divide by 1000.
$$0.0004 \text{ dm}^3 \div 1000 = 0.0000004 \text{ m}^3 = 4 \times 10^{-7} \text{ m}^3$$

Tip: Standard form (that's showing numbers as, for example, 6×10^{-3}) is covered on pages 277 and 278.

Temperature

Temperature can be measured in K and °C.

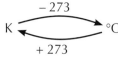

Examples — Maths Skills

Write 21 °C in Kelvin.

To convert 21 °C into K you need to add 273:   21 °C + 273 = 294 K

Write 298 K in °C.

To convert 298 K into °C you need to subtract 273:   298 K – 273 = 25 °C

Figure 1: A calculator. In an exam your brain can turn to mush and you can forget how to do the most simple maths. Don't be afraid to put every calculation into the calculator (even if it's just 2 × 10). If it stops you making mistakes then it's worth it.

Pressure

Pressure can be measured in Pa and kPa.

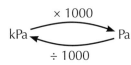

Examples — Maths Skills

Write 2100 Pa in kPa.

To convert 2100 Pa into kPa you need to divide by 1000:
$$2100 \text{ Pa} \div 1000 = 2.1 \text{ kPa}$$

Mass

Mass can be measured in kg and g.

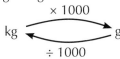

Examples — Maths Skills

Write 4.6 kg in g.

To convert 4.6 kg into g you need to multiply by 1000.

$$4.6 \text{ kg} \times 1000 = 4600 \text{ g}$$

Write 320 g in kg.

To convert 320 g into kg you need to divide by 1000.

$$320 \text{ g} \div 1000 = 0.32 \text{ kg}$$

Tip: If you're unsure about converting between units like these just think about a conversion you know and use that to help you. For example, if you know that 1 kg is 1000 g you know that to get from kg to g you must have to multiply by 1000 — simple.

Energy

Energy can be measured in kJ and J.

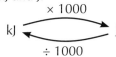

Examples — Maths Skills

Write 56 kJ in J.

To convert 56 kJ into J you need to multiply by 1000.

$$56 \text{ kJ} \times 1000 = 56\,000 \text{ J} = 5.6 \times 10^4 \text{ J}$$

Write 48 000 J in kJ.

To convert 48 000 J into kJ you need to divide by 1000.

$$48\,000 \text{ J} \div 1000 = 48 \text{ kJ}$$

Tip: A kJ is bigger than a J, so you'd expect the number to get smaller when you convert from J to kJ — each unit is worth more so you'll have fewer of them.

Concentration

Concentration can be measured in mol dm^{-3} and mol cm^{-3}.

$$\text{mol cm}^{-3} \quad \underset{\div 1000}{\overset{\times 1000}{\rightleftarrows}} \quad \text{mol dm}^{-3}$$

Examples — Maths Skills

Write 0.2 mol cm^{-3} in mol dm^{-3}.

To convert 0.2 mol cm^{-3} into mol dm^{-3} you need to multiply by 1000.

$$0.2 \text{ mol cm}^{-3} \times 1000 = 200 \text{ mol dm}^{-3}$$

Write 34 mol dm^{-3} in mol cm^{-3}.

To convert 34 mol dm^{-3} into mol cm^{-3} you need to divide by 1000.

$$34 \text{ mol dm}^{-3} \div 1000 = 0.034 \text{ mol cm}^{-3}$$

Exam Tip
Always, always, always give units with your answer. It's really important that the examiner knows what units you're working in — 10 g is very different from 10 kg.

4. Graphs

How to construct and interpret graphs is covered on pages 17-19. But you might be asked to go a little further and estimate a value from a graph. Here's how you go about it:

Extrapolation

Extrapolation sounds complicated but all it is is estimating a value on a graph which is outside the range of measured values.

Tip: If you're having trouble remembering what extrapolation is, then remember that the original meaning of the word 'extra' is 'outside' or 'beyond'. So you're looking for an estimate 'outside' the measurements.

Examples — **Maths Skills** ────────────────

The concentration of product A was measured over the first 8 minutes of a chemical reaction. The results are plotted on the graph below.

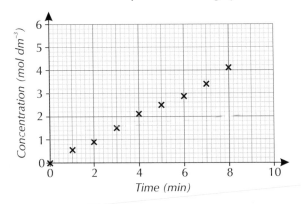

Estimate the concentration of product A at 10 minutes into the reaction.

- Draw a line of best fit through the data points on the graph.

Tip: Remember, a line of best fit doesn't have to go through every data point. It's the line which, on average, is closest to all of the data points.

- Continue drawing the line of best fit beyond the data points — it needs to go at least as far as the value on the x-axis where you've been asked to estimate a value. In this example, that's 10 minutes.

- Read off the concentration value from the line of best fit at 10 minutes.

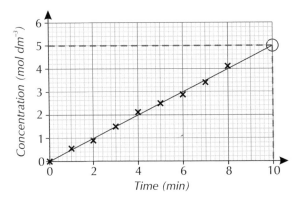

Exam Tip
If you're ever having trouble drawing a line of best fit then it's a good idea to double check that you've plotted all your points correctly. If you've got any of them wrong it'll make it tricky to draw a line of best fit, and even if you do manage it it's likely to be inaccurate.

From the line of best fit, the concentration of product A at 10 minutes would be 5 mol dm^{-3}.

Extrapolation isn't always accurate because the graph can change between the last measurement and the point you're estimating at. In the example here, the concentration could level off somewhere between 8 and 10 minutes.

Interpolation

Interpolation is a bit like extrapolation except you're being asked to estimate a value between two points on a graph, rather than outside a range of values.

Tip: The word '<u>inter</u>' means '<u>between</u>'. So interpolation means making an estimation '<u>between</u>' data points.

Examples — Maths Skills

The concentration of reactant B was measured over the first 10 minutes of a chemical reaction. The results are plotted on the graph below.

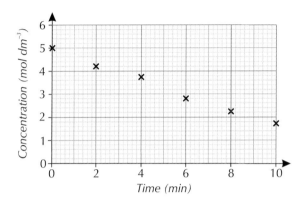

Tip: Remember — not all graphs produced by experiments are nice straight lines. It could be a line which tails off, or a curve, or something completely different.

Estimate the concentration of reactant B at 7 minutes into the reaction.

- Draw a line of best fit through the data points on the graph.
- Read off the concentration value from the line of best fit at 7 minutes.

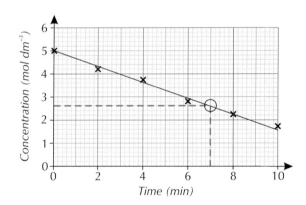

Exam Tip
Always use a <u>sharp</u> pencil for plotting points and drawing lines of best fit. If it's not sharp you'll end up with a thick line and any readings you take using it will be inaccurate.

From the line of best fit, the concentration of reactant B at 7 minutes would be 2.6 mol dm^{-3}.

Interpolation is usually more accurate than extrapolation — this is because the line of best fit is likely to be more accurate as it just goes through measured data points. The closer together the data points are on the graph, the more accurate the results of interpolation will be.

Exam Help

1. Exam Structure and Technique

Figure 1: *Chemistry lesson — witness the joy.*

Passing exams isn't all about revision — it really helps if you know how the exam is structured and have got your exam technique nailed so that you pick up every mark you can. These pages are about the AS Level exams.

Course structure

OCR A AS level Chemistry is split into four modules:

Module 1 — Development of practical skills in chemistry

Module 2 — Foundations in chemistry

Module 3 — Periodic table and energy

Module 4 — Core organic chemistry

Exam structure

For OCR A AS Level Chemistry you're gonna have to sit through two exams:

- Paper 1 — Breadth in chemistry
- Paper 2 — Depth in chemistry

Both exams are 1 hour and 30 minutes long and they cover content from all four modules, so you need to learn everything for both exams. Each exam is worth 70 marks and they have equal weighting — they're each worth 50% of your total mark.

- Paper 1 is split up into two sections. Section A has 20 marks' worth of multiple choice questions. Section B has 50 marks' worth of short and extended answer questions.
- Paper 2 has 70 marks' worth of short and extended answer questions, including Level of Response questions (see below).

Level of Response questions

Both exam papers include some extended response questions, where you'll usually be asked to explain or describe something at a bit more length. Two of these questions in Paper 2 will be marked using a Level of Response marking scheme. All this means is that you'll receive marks based on the quality of your response — not just its scientific content. So the more fully explained, better structured and more coherent your answer is, the more marks you'll get.

These questions will be clearly marked on your paper, so make sure you know which ones they are and write full and well thought out answers.

Synoptic assessment

Both exam papers will contain some synoptic assessment. This sounds complicated but don't worry, all it means is that you could be asked to draw together and apply different bits of chemistry knowledge in the same question.

Bringing together knowledge from different parts of the course.

You might be given a certain molecule and asked to calculate its enthalpy of formation, and then be asked about the electronic structure and shape of the molecule. This draws together knowledge from Modules 2 and 3.

Applying knowledge from different areas to a new context.

You might be asked to draw on your knowledge of structural isomerism to identify the isomers of an organic drug molecule you've not seen before.

Time management

This is one of the most important exam skills to have. How long you spend on each question is really important in an exam — it could make all the difference to your grade. Some questions will require lots of work for only a few marks but other questions will be much quicker. Don't spend ages struggling with questions that are only worth a couple of marks — move on. You can come back to them later when you've bagged loads of other marks elsewhere.

─ Example ──────────────────────────────────────

The questions below are both worth the same number of marks but require different amounts of work.

1 (a) Define the term 'standard enthalpy change of combustion'.

(2 marks)

2 (a) Draw a structural isomer of molecule **B** and state the type of structural isomerism it shows.

(2 marks)

Question 1 (a) only requires you to write down a definition — if you can remember it this shouldn't take you too long.

Question 2 (a) requires you to draw an isomer and then work out what type of isomer it is — this may take you a lot longer than writing down a definition, especially if you have to draw out a few structures before getting it right.

So, if you're running out of time it makes sense to do questions like 1(a) first and come back to 2 (a) if you've got time at the end.

It's worth keeping in mind that the multiple choice questions in Section A of Paper 1 are all only worth 1 mark, even though some of them could be quite tricky and time-consuming. Don't make the mistake of spending too much time on these. If you're struggling with some of them, move on to the written answer questions where there are more marks available and then go back to the harder multiple choice questions later.

Command words

Command words are just the bit of the question that tell you what to do. You'll find answering exam questions much easier if you understand exactly what they mean, so here's a brief summary table of the most common command words:

Command word:	What to do:
Give / Name / State	Give a brief one or two word answer, or a short sentence.
Identify	Say what something is.
Describe (an observation)	Write about what you would expect to happen in a reaction, e.g. colour change or the formation of a precipitate.
Explain	Give reasons for something.
Suggest / Predict	Use your scientific knowledge to work out what the answer might be.
Outline / Describe (an experiment)	Write about each step in an experiment — including any equipment you would use, the reagents required and any reaction conditions (e.g. temperature, presence of a catalyst). If you are identifying a substance, you should also include any physical changes you would expect to see, such as a precipitate being formed.
Calculate	Work out the solution to a mathematical problem.
Deduce / Determine	Use the information given in the question to work something out.
Compare	Give the similarities and differences between two things.
Contrast	Give the differences between two things.

Exam Tip
Some questions might contain more than one command word. For example, a question could start 'state and explain'. In this case, you should treat the question a little bit like two questions rolled into one. Make sure you clearly state what the question asks for and then go on to the explanation.

Some questions will also ask you to answer 'using the information / data provided' (e.g. a graph, table, equation, etc.). When that's the case, you must use the information given and you may need to refer to it in your answer to get all the marks. Some questions may also ask you to answer 'using your calculation' — it's the same here, you need to use your answer to a particular calculation, otherwise you won't get the marks. Not all of the questions will have command words — instead they may just ask a which / what / how type of question.

Exam data sheet

When you sit your exams, you'll be given a data sheet as an insert within the exam paper. On it you'll find some useful information to help you with your exam, including...

- the molar gas volume at room temperature and pressure
- Avogadro's constant
- the specific heat capacity of water
- the relationship between tonnes and grams
- the gas constant
- the characteristic infrared absorptions of some common functional groups.

Exam Tip
The same data sheet is used in the AS and A Level exams, so if you're sitting AS there'll be some information on the data sheet that you may not be familiar with. Don't be put off by it — it's there for people sitting the A Level exams and you won't need to use it. Phew!

The data sheet will also contain a copy of the periodic table. You might have seen a few slightly different versions of the periodic table — for example, some tables include the lanthanides and actinides, and others don't. In the exam, make sure you use the information from the periodic table on the data sheet, even if you think it's slightly different to something you've seen elsewhere. The information on the data sheet will be what the examiners use to mark the exam papers.

Exam Tip
It's a good idea to have a look at an exam data sheet before going in to the exam — you should be able to find it on the OCR website.

2. Diagrams

When you're asked to draw diagrams or mechanisms in an exam it's important that you draw everything correctly and include all the details that are needed.

Organic reaction mechanisms

Organic reaction mechanisms are used to show what happens during a chemical reaction. One of the most common mistakes with these is to get the curly arrows wrong.

Example

When you're drawing organic reaction mechanisms the curly arrows must come from either a lone pair of electrons or from a bond, like this:

The mechanisms below are incorrect — you wouldn't get marks for them:

You won't get marks if the curly arrows come from atoms, like this...

or this...

Tip: It's important that the curly arrows come from a lone pair or a bond because that's where the electrons are found. Remember, curly arrows are supposed to show the movement of electrons.

Exam Tip
Make sure that you draw carbocations with a full positive charge (+) and dipoles clearly as dipoles (δ+) — you will lose marks in the exam if it's not clear which you mean.

Displayed and skeletal formulas

Displayed formulas show how all the atoms are connected in a molecule. It's surprisingly easy to make mistakes when drawing them.

Examples

If a question asks you for a displayed formula you have to show all of the bonds and all of the atoms in the molecule. That means you have to draw displayed formulas like this:

And not like this:

Some of the bonds between the carbon atoms and the hydrogen atoms haven't been shown, so it's not a displayed formula and you wouldn't get the marks.

If you're not asked specifically for a displayed formula then either of the diagrams above will do. Just make sure that the bonds are always drawn between the right atoms. For example, ethanol should be drawn like this:

And not like this:

It's the oxygen that's bonded to the carbon, not the hydrogen, so drawing it like this is just wrong.

Tip: A displayed formula shows how all the atoms are arranged and all the bonds between them. See page 192 for more on displayed formulas.

Skeletal formulas are handy when you're drawing larger organic molecules. There's a pretty good chance that you'll have to draw skeletal formulas in your exam, so you need to be able to draw them properly. Remember — bonds between carbon atoms are shown by a line and carbon atoms are found at each end. Atoms that aren't carbon or hydrogen have to be drawn on:

Exam Tip
If you're not totally comfortable drawing skeletal formulas draw out the displayed formula first and that'll help you to see what atoms need to be drawn in the skeletal formula.

Example

1,5-difluoropentane (FCH$_2$CH$_2$CH$_2$CH$_2$CH$_2$F)

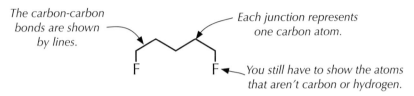

The carbon-carbon bonds are shown by lines.

Each junction represents one carbon atom.

You still have to show the atoms that aren't carbon or hydrogen.

You don't draw any carbon or hydrogen atoms from the main carbon chain when you're drawing skeletal formulas, so the diagrams below are both wrong.

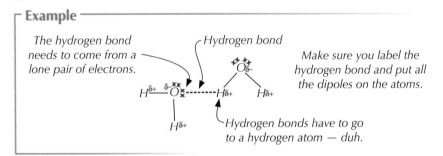

You don't show the carbon atoms or the hydrogen atoms.

Exam Tip
Make sure you've got everything the question asks for in your answer. For example, if the question asks you to include lone pairs and dipoles in a diagram, don't forget to include them

Hydrogen bonds

Drawing hydrogen bonds is a common exam question. You need to know how to draw them properly to pick up all the marks you can.

Example

The hydrogen bond needs to come from a lone pair of electrons.

Hydrogen bond

Make sure you label the hydrogen bond and put all the dipoles on the atoms.

$H^{\delta+}$ —$\overset{xx}{\underset{xx}{O}}^{\delta-}$ - - - - - - $H^{\delta+}$ $H^{\delta+}$

$H^{\delta+}$

$O^{\delta-}$

Hydrogen bonds have to go to a hydrogen atom — duh.

General advice

These pages cover some of the types of diagram that are likely to come up in your exams. But you could be asked to draw other diagrams. Whatever diagram you're drawing, make sure it's really clear. A small scribble in the bottom corner of a page isn't going to show enough detail to get you the marks. Draw the diagrams nice and big, but make sure that you stay within the space given for that answer. If you've drawn a diagram incorrectly don't scribble part of it out and try to fix it — it'll look messy and be really hard for the examiner to figure out what you're trying to show. Cross the whole thing out and start again. And always double check that you've included all the things that you should have done.

3. The Periodic Table — Facts and Trends

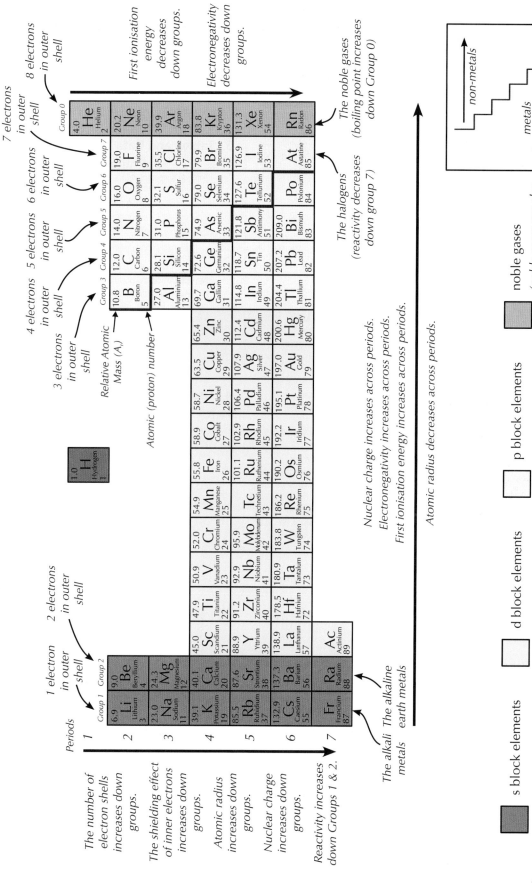

Nuclear charge increases across periods.
Electronegativity increases across periods.
First ionisation energy increases across periods.

Atomic radius decreases across periods.

The number of electron shells increases down groups.

The shielding effect of inner electrons increases down groups.

Atomic radius increases down groups.

Nuclear charge increases down groups.

Reactivity increases down Groups 1 & 2.

The alkali metals

The alkaline earth metals

1 electron in outer shell
2 electrons in outer shell
3 electrons in outer shell
4 electrons in outer shell
5 electrons in outer shell
6 electrons in outer shell
7 electrons in outer shell
8 electrons in outer shell

First ionisation energy decreases down groups.

Electronegativity decreases down groups.

The noble gases (boiling point increases down Group 0)

The halogens (reactivity decreases down group 7)

Relative Atomic Mass (Aᵣ)

Atomic (proton) number

s block elements

d block elements

p block elements

noble gases
(noble gases are also p block elements)

non-metals

metals

Answers

Module 1

Development of Practical Skills

1. Planning Experiments

Page 10 — Application Questions

Q1 a)

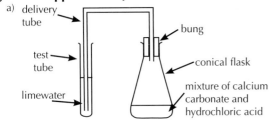

delivery tube

bung

test tube

conical flask

limewater

mixture of calcium carbonate and hydrochloric acid

  b) E.g. the chemicals used in this reaction might be harmful, so a lab coat, goggles and gloves should be used when carrying out the experiment. The hydrochloric acid should be dilute, as the more concentrated it is, the more hazardous it will be.

Q2 E.g. using test tubes means that the student won't be able to measure precisely how much gas has been given off in the experiment. He should use an appropriately sized gas syringe instead.

Q3 a) The independent variable is whether the haloalkane is a bromoalkane or a chloroalkane.

  b) E.g. you could place a piece of card with an 'X' on it beneath each reaction vessel, and time how long it takes for the 'X' to disappear as the solution goes cloudy as the precipitate forms.

  c) Any two from, e.g.: the temperature of the reaction / the concentration of the reactants / the volume of the reactants / the carbon skeleton of the two haloalkanes / the volume of the reaction vessel.

Page 10 — Fact Recall Questions

Q1 An independent variable is the thing you change during an experiment.

Q2 categoric

Q3 E.g. all the dangers in the experiment, who is at risk from these hazards and what you can do to reduce this risk.

2. Practical Techniques

Page 14 — Application Questions

Q1 E.g. they could put a piece of paper marked with an X under or behind the reaction vessel, and time how long it takes until they can no longer see the X.

Q2 a) A volumetric flask.

  b) E.g. he could wash out the weighing vessel into the volumetric flask using the solvent used in the standard solution.

Page 14 — Fact Recall Questions

Q1 E.g. you could reweigh the weighing vessel after you transfer the solid, so you can work out the exact mass you transferred.

Q2 E.g. a pipette / a burette / a volumetric flask.

Q3 A mixture is gently heated so that the compounds evaporate off in order of increasing boiling point and can be collected separately.

3. Tables and Data

Page 16 — Application Questions

Q1 After 0 s, mean = (18.7 cm³ + 18.4 cm³ + 19.0 cm³) ÷ 3
= 56.1 cm³ ÷ 3 = **18.7 cm³**

After 20 s, mean = (22.0 cm³ + 21.7 cm³ + 21.8 cm³) ÷ 3
= 65.5 cm³ ÷ 3 = **21.8 cm³ (3 s.f.)**

After 40 s, mean = (24.6 cm³ + 25.0 cm³ + 24.8 cm³) ÷ 3
= 74.4 cm³ ÷ 3 = **24.8 cm³**

Q2 First, calculate the average mass of water lost from the sample: (0.35 + 0.36 + 0.33) ÷ 3 = 0.34666...

Remember not to round your answer until right at the end.
Now use the formula moles = mass ÷ molar mass to calculate how many moles of water were lost from the sample: 0.34666... ÷ 18.0 = **0.019 mol (2 s.f.)**

The mass changes are shown to 2 significant figures, and the molar masses are shown to 3 significant figures, so your final answer should be shown to 2 significant figures.

4. Graphs and Charts

Page 19 — Application Questions

Q1 a) The result at 4 s (21.5 cm³) is anomalously high.

  b)

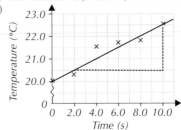

E.g. The change in x is 8.0 s and the change in y is 2.0 °C. So the gradient is change in y ÷ change in x
= 2 ÷ 8 = **0.25 °C s⁻¹**.

Q2

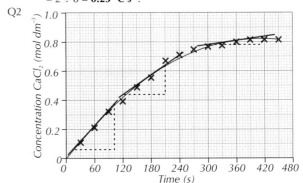

  a) E.g. change in x = 84 s and change in y = 0.32 mol dm⁻³.

Gradient = $\dfrac{\text{change in } y}{\text{change in } x} = \dfrac{0.32}{84}$

= **0.0038 mol dm⁻³ s⁻¹ (2 s.f.)**

b) Change in x = 90 s and change in y = 0.22 mol dm^{-3}
Gradient = $\dfrac{\text{change in } y}{\text{change in } x} = \dfrac{0.22}{90}$
= **0.0024 mol dm^{-3} s^{-1} (2 s.f.)**
c) Change in x = 112 s and change in y = 0.06 mol dm^{-3}.
Gradient = $\dfrac{\text{change in } y}{\text{change in } x} = \dfrac{0.06}{112}$
= **0.0005 mol dm^{-3} s^{-1} (1 s.f.)**

5. Conclusions and Evaluations
Page 23 — Application Questions
Q1 a) 2.0 cm^3 ÷ 2 = 1.0 cm^3, so the uncertainty is **±1.0 cm^3**.
b) Percentage error = $\dfrac{\text{uncertainty}}{\text{reading}} \times 100 = \dfrac{1.0}{8.0} \times 100$
= **12.5%**
c) E.g. use a measuring cylinder that has smaller increments.
Q2 a) E.g. the results will not be valid because she hasn't controlled the mass of magnesium chips. She just uses 'one spatula' which is not an accurate measurement so the mass of magnesium chips could vary between repeats. Instead, she should weigh out the same mass of magnesium to be used in each repeat.
b) She could take readings more regularly (e.g. every minute).

Exam-style Questions — pages 25-26
1 A *(1 mark)*
2 C *(1 mark)*
  The result of 450 s is anomalously high so should be ignored when calculating the mean.
3 D *(1 mark)*
4 a) The student filled the flask until the top of the meniscus was level with the line, when he should have filled it until the bottom of the meniscus was level with the line *(1 mark)*.
b) To make sure that all the solid has been transferred from the weighing vessel into the volumetric flask / To reduce transfer errors *(1 mark)*.
c) To make sure the solution is mixed evenly *(1 mark)*.
5 a)

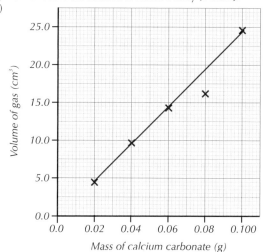

(3 marks — 1 mark for correct, labelled axes on an appropriate scale, 1 mark for correctly plotted points, 1 mark for line of best fit ignoring anomalous point at 0.08 g.)

b) There is a positive correlation *(1 mark)*.
c) E.g. change in x = 0.01 g, change in y = 2.5 *(1 mark)* gradient = 2.5 ÷ 0.01 = **250 cm^3 g^{-1}** *(1 mark)* (allow between 210 and 290 cm^3)
6 a) A separating funnel *(1 mark)* and a conical flask *(1 mark)*.
b) Separating organic compounds from water soluble impurities / separating liquids of different densities *(1 mark)*.

Module 2

Section 1 — Atoms and Moles

1. The Atom
Page 29 — Application Questions
Q1 a) 13
b) 13
c) 27 − 13 = **14**
Q2 a) 19
b) 19 + 20 = **39**
c) $^{39}_{19}\text{K}$
d) 19 − 1 = **18**
Q3 a) 20 − 2 = **18**
b) 40 − 20 = **20**
Q4 a) $^{93}_{41}\text{A}$ or $^{93}_{41}\text{Nb}$
(mass number = 41 + 52 = 93)
b) $^{94}_{41}\text{A}$ or $^{94}_{41}\text{Nb}$
The atomic number must be the same, but the mass number must be different as an isotope will have a different number of neutrons.
Q5 a) A and C both have 10 electrons.
b) A and D both have 8 protons.
c) B and C both have 10 neutrons.
(17 − 7 = 10 and 20 − 10 = 10)
d) B and D both have 10 neutrons.
(17 − 7 = 10 and 18 − 8 = 10)
e) A and D are isotopes of each other because they have the same number of protons (8) but different numbers of neutrons.
(A has 16 − 8 = 8 and D has 18 − 8 = 10)

Page 29 — Fact Recall Questions
Q1 proton, neutron, electron
Q2 proton: 1, neutron: 1, electron: 1/2000
Q3 Protons and neutrons are found in the nucleus. Electrons are found in orbitals around the nucleus.
Q4 The total number of protons and neutrons in the nucleus of an atom.
Q5 The number of protons in the nucleus of an atom.
Q6 By subtracting the atomic number from the mass number.
Q7 Atoms with the same number of protons but different numbers of neutrons.
Q8 Chemical properties of an element are decided by the number and arrangement of electrons. Isotopes have the same configuration of electrons so have the same chemical properties.
Q9 Physical properties depend on the mass of an atom. Isotopes have different masses so can have different physical properties.

2. Atomic Models
Page 32 — Fact Recall Questions
Q1 Dalton described atoms as solid spheres.
J J Thomson suggested that atoms were not solid spheres — he thought they contained small negatively charged particles (electrons) in a positively charged "pudding".

Q2 the plum pudding model

Q3 Ernest Rutherford, Hans Geiger and Ernest Marsden.

Q4 If Thomson's model was correct the alpha particles fired at the sheet of gold should have been deflected very slightly by the positive "pudding" that made up most of the atom. Instead, most of the alpha particles passed straight through the gold atoms, and a very small number were deflected backwards. So the plum pudding model couldn't be right.

Q5 Rutherford's model has a tiny positively charged nucleus at the centre surrounded by a "cloud" of negative electrons. Most of the atom is empty space.

Q6 In Bohr's model the electrons only exist in fixed shells and not anywhere in between. Each shell has a fixed energy. When an electron moves between shells electromagnetic radiation is emitted or absorbed. Because the energy of the shells is fixed, the radiation will have a fixed frequency.

Q7 No

3. Relative Mass
Pages 35-36 — Application Questions
Q1 a) 85.5
b) 200.6
c) 65.4
You can just read these A_rs off the periodic table. There's one on the inside of the back cover of this book.

Q2 $A_r = ((0.100 \times 180) + (26.5 \times 182) + (14.3 \times 183) + (30.7 \times 184) + (28.4 \times 186)) \div 100 = 183.891 \approx \mathbf{183.9}$

Q3 Zirconium-90 (^{90}Zr), zirconium-91 (^{91}Zr), zirconium-92 (^{92}Zr), zirconium-94 (^{94}Zr) and zirconium-96 (^{96}Zr).

Q4 a) 25.0
b) 9.2
c) 9.1
d) 43.6

Q5 a) $A_r = ((79 \times 60.8) + (81 \times 59.2)) \div 120 = 79.986 \approx \mathbf{80.0}$
b) $A_r = ((6 \times 11.1) + (7 \times 138.9)) \div 150 = 6.926 \approx \mathbf{6.9}$
c) $A_r = ((39 \times 130.6) + (41 \times 9.4)) \div 140 = 39.134 \approx \mathbf{39.1}$

Q6 a) $14 + (3 \times 1) = \mathbf{17}$
b) $12 + (16 \times 2) = \mathbf{44}$
c) $(12 \times 2) + (1 \times 4) + (16 \times 6) + (14 \times 2) = \mathbf{152}$

Q7 a) $40.1 + (35.5 \times 2) = \mathbf{111.1}$
b) $24.3 + 32.1 + (16 \times 4) = \mathbf{120.4}$
c) $23 + 16 + 1 = \mathbf{40}$

Page 36 — Fact Recall Questions
Q1 The weighted mean mass of an atom of an element compared to 1/12 of the mass of an atom of carbon-12.

Q2 The mass of an atom of an isotope of an element compared to 1/12 of the mass of an atom of carbon-12.

Q3 The average mass of a molecule compared to 1/12 of the mass of an atom of carbon-12.

Q4 The average mass of a formula unit compared to 1/12 of the mass of an atom of carbon-12.

4. The Mole
Page 39 — Application Questions
Q1 6.02×10^{23} atoms

Q2 4 moles of Na react with 1 mole of O_2 to give 2 moles of Na_2O. So 6 moles of Na must react with 1.5 moles of oxygen to give **3 moles** of Na_2O.

Q3 a) $M_r = 19 + 19 = 38$
$M = \mathbf{38 \ g \ mol^{-1}}$
b) $M_r = 40.1 + (35.5 \times 2) = 111.1$
$M = \mathbf{111.1 \ g \ mol^{-1}}$
c) $M_r = 24.3 + 32.1 + (4 \times 16) = 120.4$
$M = \mathbf{120.4 \ g \ mol^{-1}}$

Q4 $M = 23 + 14 + (16 \times 3) = 85 \ g \ mol^{-1}$
number of moles $= 212.5 \div 85 = \mathbf{2.5 \ moles}$

Q5 $M = 65.4 + (35.5 \times 2) = 136.4 \ g \ mol^{-1}$
number of moles $= 15.5 \div 136.4 = \mathbf{0.114 \ moles}$

Q6 $M = 23 + 35.5 = 58.5 \ g \ mol^{-1}$
Mass $= 58.5 \times 2 = \mathbf{117 \ g}$

Q7 $M = 24.3 + 12 + (3 \times 16) = 84.3 \ g \ mol^{-1}$
Mass $= 84.3 \times 0.25 = \mathbf{21.1 \ g}$

Q8 $M = 66 \div 1.5 = \mathbf{44 \ g \ mol^{-1}}$

Q9 $M = 16 + 16 = 32 \ g \ mol^{-1}$
number of moles $= 82.1 \div 32 = 2.565... \ mol$
number of molecules $= 2.565... \times 6.02 \times 10^{23} = \mathbf{1.54 \times 10^{24}}$

Q10 number of moles of atoms $= 3.56 \times 10^{24} \div 6.02 \times 10^{23}$
$= 5.913... \ mol$
There are 6 atoms in 1 molecule of $MgSO_4$, so moles of $MgSO_4 = 5.931... \div 6 = 0.985...$
$M = 24.3 + 32.1 + (16 \times 4) = 120.4 \ g \ mol^{-1}$
mass $= 0.985... \times 120.4 = \mathbf{119 \ g}$ (3 s.f.)

Page 39 — Fact Recall Questions
Q1 a) 6.02×10^{23}
b) The Avogadro constant.

Q2 The mass of one mole of the chemical.

Q3 Number of moles = mass of substance ÷ molar mass

5. Gas Volumes
Page 42 — Application Questions
Q1 Number of moles $= 2.4 \div 24 = \mathbf{0.10 \ moles}$

Q2 Number of moles $= 0.65 \div 24 = \mathbf{0.027 \ moles}$

Q3 Number of moles $= 250 \div 24 \ 000 = \mathbf{0.010 \ moles}$

Q4 Volume $= 0.21 \times 24 = \mathbf{5.04 \ dm^3}$

Q5 Volume $= 1.1 \times 24 = \mathbf{26.4 \ dm^3}$

Q6 Volume $= 0.028 \times 24 \ 000 = \mathbf{672 \ cm^3}$

Q7 $n = pV \div RT$
$= (70 \ 000 \times 0.04) \div (8.314 \times 350) = \mathbf{0.96 \ moles}$

Q8 $V = nRT \div p$
$= (0.65 \times 8.314 \times 280) \div 100 \ 000 = \mathbf{0.015 \ m^3}$

Q9 $0.55 \ dm^3 = 0.55 \times 10^{-3} \ m^3$ $35 \ °C = 308 \ K$
$n = pV \div RT$
$= (90 \ 000 \times (0.55 \times 10^{-3})) \div (8.314 \times 308)$
$= \mathbf{0.019 \ moles}$

Q10 $1200 \ cm^3 = 1200 \times 10^{-6} \ m^3 = 1.2 \times 10^{-3} \ m^3$
$T = pV \div nR$
$= (110 \ 000 \times (1.2 \times 10^{-3})) \div (0.05 \times 8.314) = 317.5 \ K$
$317.5 \ K = (317.7 - 273) \ °C = \mathbf{44.5 \ °C}$

Q11 $75 \ kPa = 75 \ 000 \ Pa$ $22 \ °C = 295 \ K$
$V = nRT \div p$
$= (0.75 \times 8.314 \times 295) \div 75 \ 000 = \mathbf{0.025 \ m^3}$

Q12 $80 \ kPa = 80 \ 000 \ Pa$ $1.5 \ dm^3 = 1.5 \times 10^{-3} \ m^3$
$n = pV \div RT$
$= (80 \ 000 \times (1.5 \times 10^{-3})) \div (8.314 \times 300)$
$= 0.048 \ moles$
Molar mass = mass ÷ moles $= 2.6 \div 0.048 = 54 \ g \ mol^{-1}$
So the relative molecular mass is **54**.

Q13 $44 \ °C = 317 \ K$ $100 \ kPa = 100 \ 000 \ Pa$
$n = pV \div RT$
$= (100 \ 000 \times 0.003) \div (8.314 \times 317)$
$= 0.114 \ moles$
Molar mass of neon = 20.2
mass = number of moles × molar mass
$= 0.114 \times 20.2 = \mathbf{2.30 \ g}$

Page 42 — Fact Recall Questions

Q1 number of moles = volume in dm^3 ÷ 24
Q2 number of moles = volume in cm^3 ÷ 24 000
Q3 $pV = nRT$
    p = pressure measured in pascals (Pa)
    V = volume measured in m^3
    n = number of moles
    $R = 8.314$ J K^{-1} mol^{-1}. R is the gas constant.
    T = temperature measured in kelvin (K)
Q4 If the gas syringe is too small, the plunger may be blown out of the end of the gas syringe during the experiment/ reaction. This could release toxic or flammable gases into the atmosphere, which is highly dangerous.

6. Concentration Calculations

Pages 44 — Application Questions

Q1 Number of moles = (2 × 50) ÷ 1000 = **0.1 moles**
Q2 Number of moles = 0.08 × 0.5 = **0.04 moles**
Q3 Number of moles = (0.7 × 30) ÷ 1000 = **0.021 moles**
Q4 Concentration = 0.25 ÷ 0.5 = **0.5 mol dm^{-3}**
Q5 Concentration = 0.08 ÷ 0.75 = **0.11 mol dm^{-3}**
Q6 Concentration = 0.1 ÷ (36 ÷ 1000) = **2.8 mol dm^{-3}**
    Dividing a volume in cm^3 by 1000 converts it to dm^3. Then you can stick it into the equation concentration = number of moles ÷ volume (dm^3).
Q7 Volume = 0.46 ÷ 1.8 = **0.26 dm^3**
Q8 Volume = 0.01 ÷ 0.55 = **0.02 dm^3**
Q9 Number of moles = concentration × volume (dm^3)
        = 0.8 × (75 ÷ 1000) = 0.06
    M of Na_2O = (23 × 2) + 16 = 62 g mol^{-1}
    Mass = moles × molar mass = 0.06 × 62 = **3.72 g**
Q10 Number of moles = concentration × volume (dm^3)
        = 0.5 × (30 ÷ 1000) = 0.015
    M of $CoBr_2$ = 58.9 + (79.9 × 2) = 218.7 g mol^{-1}
    Mass = number of moles × molar mass
        = 0.015 × 218.7 = **3.3 g**
Q11 Number of moles = concentration × volume (dm^3)
        = 1.2 × (100 ÷ 1000) = 0.12
    molar mass = mass ÷ number of moles
        = 4.08 ÷ 0.12 = **34 g mol^{-1}**
Q12 Number of moles = concentration × volume (dm^3)
        = 4.1 × (50 ÷ 1000) = 0.205
    M of sodium chloride (NaCl) = 23 + 35.5 = 58.5
    mass = molar mass × number of moles
        = 58.5 × 0.205 = **12.0 g**

Page 44 — Fact Recall Questions

Q1 Number of moles = $\dfrac{\text{concentration} \times \text{volume (in } cm^3)}{1000}$
    Number of moles = concentration × volume (dm^3)
Q2 1000

Exam-style Questions — pages 46–47

1 B *(1 mark)*
2 C *(1 mark)*
3 B *(1 mark)*
4 a) Her readings would be lower than expected *(1 mark)*.
   b) E.g. Do the reaction in a fume cupboard *(1 mark)*.
   c) If the student underestimates the volume of gas in the experiment, she may select a gas syringe that is too small. The plunger may be blown out of the end of the syringe, allowing the gas to escape into the atmosphere *(1 mark)*.

5 a) (i) Isotopes are atoms of the same element which have the same number of protons / same atomic number *(1 mark)* but different numbers of neutrons / different mass numbers *(1 mark)*.
     (ii)

	Protons	Neutrons	Electrons
^{28}Si	14	14	14
^{29}Si	14	15	14
^{30}Si	14	16	14

     (1 mark for protons and electrons correct, 1 mark for all neutrons correct).
   b) (i) The weighted mean mass of an atom of an element *(1 mark)* compared to 1/12 of the mass of an atom of carbon-12 *(1 mark)*.
    Make sure you talk about atoms here and not just elements or isotopes. If you say 'the mean mass of an element' or 'the mean mass of an isotope' you won't get the marks.
     (ii) A_r = [(28 × 92.23) + (29 × 4.67) + (30 × 3.10)] ÷ 100 *(1 mark)* = 28.11 *(1 mark)*
   c) A_r = [(46 × 17.4) + (47 × 15.5) + (48 × 154.8) + (49 × 11.3) + (50 × 10.9)] ÷ (17.4 + 15.5 + 154.8 + 11.3 + 10.9) = **47.9** *(1 mark)*
    The element is titanium *(1 mark)*.
6 a) $n = pV ÷ RT$
    T = 58.8 + 273 = 331.8 K
    n = [(178 × 10^3) × (7.89 × 10^{-3})] ÷ (8.314 × 331.8)
    = 0.509... moles *(1 mark)*
    M_r = mass ÷ moles
    = 22.4 ÷ 0.509... = **44.0** (3 s.f.) *(1 mark)*
   b) 44 – (16 × 2) = 12 *(1 mark)*
    12 corresponds to a single atom of carbon. Therefore the gas is carbon dioxide *(1 mark)*.
   c) At r.t.p., volume in dm^3 = moles × 24.
    From part (a), moles of CO_2 = 0.509... mol.
    volume in dm^3 = 0.509... × 24 = **12.2 dm^3** (3 s.f.)
    (1 mark)

Section 2 — Formulas and Equations

1. Formulas

Page 49 — Application Questions

Q1 CH
Q2 Molecular formula: $C_2H_6O_4$, empirical formula: CH_3O_2.
Q3 a) $C_4H_8Br_2$
   b) C_2H_4Br
Q4 empirical mass = (4 × 12) + (9 × 1) = 57
    molecular mass = 114, so there are (114 ÷ 57) = 2 empirical units in the molecule.
    molecular formula = **C_8H_{18}**
Q5 empirical mass = (3 × 12) + (5 × 1) + (2 × 16) = 73
    M_r = 146, so there are (146 ÷ 73) = 2 empirical units in the molecule.
    molecular formula = **$C_6H_{10}O_4$**
Q6 empirical mass = (4 × 12) + (6 × 1) + (2 × 35.5) + (1 × 16) = 141
    M_r = 423, so there are (423 ÷ 141) = 3 empirical units in the molecule.
    molecular formula = **$C_{12}H_{18}Cl_6O_3$**

Page 49 — Fact Recall Questions

Q1 The empirical formula gives the smallest whole number ratio of atoms of each element in a compound.
Q2 The molecular formula gives the actual numbers of atoms of each type of element in a molecule.

2. Calculating Formulas

Page 51 — Application Questions

Q1 moles CO_2 = mass ÷ M_r = 17.6 ÷ 44 = 0.40 mol
moles H_2O = mass ÷ M_r = 10.8 ÷ 18 = 0.60 mol
There is 1 mole of C in 1 mole of CO_2 so you must have
started with 0.40 moles of C.
There are 2 moles of H in 1 mole of H_2O so you must have
started with 2 × 0.60 = 1.2 moles of H.
So, the ratio of C : H = 0.40 : 1.2 = 1 : 3 and the empirical
formula is **CH_3**.

Q2 moles CO_2 = mass ÷ M_r = 3.52 ÷ 44 = 0.080 mol
moles H_2O = mass ÷ M_r = 2.88 ÷ 18 = 0.16 mol
There is 1 mole of C in 1 mole of CO_2 so you must have
started with 0.080 moles of C.
There are 2 moles of H in 1 mole of H_2O so you must have
started with 2 × 0.16 = 0.32 moles of H.
So, the ratio of C : H = 0.080 : 0.32 = 1 : 4 and the
empirical formula is **CH_4**.

Q3 If 5.52 g of sodium burns to give 7.44 g of sodium oxide
then 7.44 − 5.52 = 1.92 g of oxygen must be added.
moles Na = mass ÷ M_r = 5.52 ÷ 23 = 0.24 mol
moles O = mass ÷ M_r = 1.92 ÷ 16 = 0.12 mol
So, the ratio of Na : O = 0.24 : 0.12 = 2 : 1 and the
empirical formula is **Na_2O**.

Q4 If 50.2 g of iron burns to give 69.4 g or iron oxide then
69.4 − 50.2 = 19.2 g of oxygen must be added.
moles Fe = mass ÷ M_r = 50.2 ÷ 55.8 = 0.90 mol
moles O = mass ÷ M_r = 19.2 ÷ 16 = 1.2 mol
So, the ratio of Fe : O = 0.90 : 1.2 = 3 : 4 and the empirical
formula is **Fe_3O_4**.

*In this question the highest number of moles isn't divisible by
the lowest number of moles. So to get the whole number ratio
you have to divide by a common factor — in this case 0.3.*

Page 52 — Application Questions

Q1 Mass of each element:
H = 5.9 g   O = 94.1 g
Moles of each element:
H = (5.9 ÷ 1) = 5.9 moles
O = (94.1 ÷ 16) = 5.9 moles
Divide each by 5.9:
H = (5.9 ÷ 5.9) = 1   O = (5.9 ÷ 5.9) = 1
The ratio of H : O is 1 : 1.
So the empirical formula is **HO**.

Q2 Mass of each element:
Al = 20.2 g   Cl = 79.8 g
Moles of each element:
Al = (20.2 ÷ 27) = 0.748 moles
Cl = (79.8 ÷ 35.5) = 2.248 moles
Divide each by 0.748:
Al = (0.748 ÷ 0.748) = 1   Cl = (2.248 ÷ 0.748) = 3
The ratio of Al : Cl is 1 : 3.
So the empirical formula is **$AlCl_3$**.

Q3 Mass of each element:
C = 8.50 g   H = 1.40 g   I = 90.1 g
Moles of each element:
C = (8.50 ÷ 12) = 0.708 moles
H = (1.40 ÷ 1) = 1.40 moles
I = (90.1 ÷ 126.9) = 0.710 moles
Divide each by 0.708:
C = (0.708 ÷ 0.708) = 1
H = (1.40 ÷ 0.708) = 2
I = (0.710 ÷ 0.708) = 1
The ratio of C : H : I is 1 : 2 : 1.
So the empirical formula is **CH_2I**.

Q4 % V = 32.3   % Cl = 100 − 32.3 = 67.7
Mass of each element:
V = 32.3 g   Cl = 67.7 g
Moles of each element:
V = (32.3 ÷ 50.9) = 0.635 moles
Cl = (67.7 ÷ 35.5) = 1.91 moles
Divide each by 0.635:
V = (0.635 ÷ 0.635) = 1   Cl = (1.91 ÷ 0.635) = 3
The ratio of V : Cl is 1 : 3.
So the empirical formula is **VCl_3**.

Q5 % O = 31.58   % Cr = 100 − 31.58 = 68.42
Mass of each element:
O = 31.58 g   Cr = 68.42 g
Moles of each element:
O = (31.58 ÷ 16) = 1.974 moles
Cr = (68.42 ÷ 52) = 1.316 moles
Divide each by 1.316:
O = (1.974 ÷ 1.316) = 1.5   Cr = (1.316 ÷ 1.316) = 1
The ratio of Cr : O is 1 : 1.5.
Multiply by 2... 2 × (1 : 1.5) = 2 : 3.
So the empirical formula is **Cr_2O_3**.

Page 53 — Application Questions

Q1 mass O in oxide = 7.1 − 3.1 = 4.0 g
moles O = mass ÷ M_r = 4.0 ÷ 16 = 0.25 mol
moles P = mass ÷ M_r = 3.1 ÷ 31 = 0.10 mol
So, the ratio of P : O = 0.10 : 0.25 = 2 : 5 and the empirical
formula is P_2O_5.
mass of empirical formula is (31 × 2) + (5 × 16) = 142 g mol^{-1}
284 ÷ 142 = 2 so the empirical formula is scaled up by a
factor of 2 and the molecular formula is **P_4O_{10}**.

Q2 Mass of each element:
C = 85.7 g   H = 14.3 g
Moles of each element:
C = (85.7 ÷ 12) = 7.14 moles
H = (14.3 ÷ 1) = 14.3 moles
Divide each by 7.14:
C = (7.14 ÷ 7.14) = 1   O = (14.3 ÷ 7.14) = 2
The ratio of C : H is 1 : 2. So the empirical formula is CH_2.
mass of empirical formula is 12 + (2 × 1) = 14 g mol^{-1}.
56 ÷ 14 = 4 so the empirical formula is scaled up by a factor
of 4 and the molecular formula is **C_4H_8**.

Q3 Mass of each element:
Cl = 42.5 g   O = 100 − 42.5 = 57.5 g
Moles of each element:
Cl = (42.5 ÷ 35.5) = 1.20 moles
O = (57.5 ÷ 16) = 3.59 moles
Divide each by 1.20:
Cl = (1.20 ÷ 1.20) = 1   O = (3.59 ÷ 1.20) = 3
The ratio of Cl : O is 1 : 3. So the empirical formula is ClO_3.
mass of empirical formula is 35.5 + (3 × 16) = 83.5 g mol^{-1}.
167 ÷ 83.5 = 2 so the empirical formula is scaled up by a
factor of 2 and the molecular formula is **Cl_2O_6**.

Q4 moles CO_2 = mass ÷ M_r = 17.6 ÷ 44 = 0.40 mol
moles H_2O = mass ÷ M_r = 14.4 ÷ 18 = 0.80 mol
There is 1 mole of C in 1 mol of CO_2 so you must have
started with 0.40 moles of C.
There are 2 moles of H in 1 mol of H_2O so you must have
started with 2 × 0.80 = 1.6 moles of H.
mass of C in alcohol = moles × M_r = 0.40 × 12 = 4.8 g
mass of H in alcohol = moles × M_r = 1.6 × 1 = 1.6 g
mass of O in alcohol = 12.8 − (4.8 + 1.6) = 6.4 g
moles O = mass ÷ M_r = 6.4 ÷ 16 = 0.40 mol
So, the ratio of C : H : O = 0.4 : 1.6 : 0.4 = 1 : 4 : 1 and the
empirical formula is CH_4O.
mass of empirical formula is 12 + (4 × 1) + 16 = 32 g mol^{-1}
32 ÷ 32 = 1 so the empirical formula is not scaled up and
the molecular formula is **CH_4O**.

Q5 moles CO_2 = mass $\div M_r$ = 5.28 $\div$ 44 = 0.12 mol
moles H_2O = mass $\div M_r$ = 2.16 $\div$ 18 = 0.12 mol
There is 1 mole of C in 1 mole of CO_2 so you must have started with 0.12 moles of C.
There are 2 moles of H in 1 mole of H_2O so you must have started with 2 $\times$ 0.12 = 0.24 moles of H.
mass of C in alcohol = moles $\times M_r$ = 0.12 $\times$ 12 = 1.44 g
mass of H in alcohol = moles $\times M_r$ = 0.24 $\times$ 1 = 0.24 g
mass of O in alcohol = 2.64 – (1.44 + 0.24) = 0.96 g
moles O = mass $\div M_r$ = 0.96 $\div$ 16 = 0.060 mol
So, the ratio of C : H : O = 0.12 : 0.24 : 0.060 = 2 : 4 : 1 and the empirical formula is C_2H_4O.
mass of empirical formula is (12 $\times$ 2) + (4 $\times$ 1) + 16 = 44 g mol^{-1}. 88 $\div$ 44 = 2 so the empirical formula is scaled up by a factor of 2 and the molecular formula is **$C_4H_8O_2$**.

Page 53 — Fact Recall Questions
Q1 moles = mass $\div M_r$
Q2 The percentage composition tells you what percentage of the mass of the compound is made up of each element.

3. Chemical Equations
Page 55 — Application Questions
Q1 a) $Mg + 2HCl \rightarrow MgCl_2 + H_2$
b) $S_8 + \mathbf{24}F_2 \rightarrow \mathbf{8}SF_6$
c) $Ca(OH)_2 + H_2SO_4 \rightarrow CaSO_4 + \mathbf{2}H_2O$
d) $Na_2CO_3 + 2HCl \rightarrow 2NaCl + CO_2 + H_2O$
e) $C_4H_{10} + \mathbf{6\frac{1}{2}}O_2 \rightarrow \mathbf{4}CO_2 + \mathbf{5}H_2O$
  If you wanted to double the numbers to get rid of the half in this equation that would be fine too (making it $2C_4H_{10} + 13O_2 \rightarrow 8CO_2 + 10H_2O$).
Q2 a) $Fe + Cu^{2+} \rightarrow Fe^{2+} + Cu$
b) $Ba^{2+} + SO_4^{2-} \rightarrow BaSO_4$
  This reaction looks like it has the same ions on each side of the equation, so wouldn't have an ionic equation. But the state symbols show you that $BaSO_4$ is a solid, so you shouldn't split it up into ions when writing your ionic equation.
c) $CO_3^{2-} + 2H^+ \rightarrow H_2O + CO_2$

4. Equations and Calculations
Page 57 — Application Questions
Q1 a) $Zn + 2HCl \rightarrow ZnCl_2 + H_2$
b) M_r of Zn = 65.4
  number of moles = mass $\div M_r$ = 3.30 $\div$ 65.4
  = **0.0505 moles**
c) The molar ratio of Zn : $ZnCl_2$ is 1 : 1. So 0.0505 moles of Zn will give **0.0505 moles** of $ZnCl_2$.
d) M_r of $ZnCl_2$ = 65.4 + (2 $\times$ 35.5) = 136.4
  mass = number of moles $\times M_r$ = 0.0505 $\times$ 136.4 = **6.89 g**
Q2 a) $C_2H_4 + 3O_2 \rightarrow 2CO_2 + 2H_2O$
b) M_r of H_2O = (2 $\times$ 1) + 16 = 18
  number of moles = mass $\div M_r$ = 15.0 $\div$ 18 = **0.833 moles**
c) The molar ratio of H_2O : C_2H_4 is 2 : 1.
  So 0.833 moles of H_2O must be made from (0.833 $\div$ 2) = **0.417 moles** of C_2H_4.
d) M_r of C_2H_4 = (2 $\times$ 12) + (4 $\times$ 1) = 28
  mass = number of moles $\times M_r$ = 0.417 $\times$ 28 = **11.7 g**
Q3 $Na_2CO_3 + BaCl_2 \rightarrow 2NaCl + BaCO_3$
M_r of $BaCl_2$ = 137.3 + (2 $\times$ 35.5) = 208.3
number of moles = mass $\div M_r$ = 4.58 $\div$ 208.3 = 0.0220 mol
The molar ratio of $BaCl_2$: $BaCO_3$ is 1 : 1.
So 0.0220 moles of $BaCO_3$ must be made from 0.0220 moles of $BaCl_2$.
M_r of $BaCO_3$ = 137.3 + 12 + (16 $\times$ 3) = 197.3
mass = number of moles $\times M_r$ = 0.0220 $\times$ 197.3 = **4.34 g**

Page 58 — Application Questions
Q1 a) aq
b) s
c) l
d) aq
e) g
f) s
Q2 a) $2H_2O_{(l)} \rightarrow 2H_{2\,(g)} + O_{2\,(g)}$
b) M_r of H_2O = (2 $\times$ 1) + 16 = 18
  number of moles = mass $\div M_r$ = 9.0 $\div$ 18 = **0.50 moles**
c) The molar ratio of H_2O to O_2 is 2 : 1.
  So 0.50 moles of H_2O will produce (0.50 $\div$ 2) = **0.25 moles** of O_2.
d) At room temperature and pressure 1 mole of gas takes up 24 dm^3.
  Volume in dm^3 = number of moles $\times$ 24
  Volume of O_2 = 0.25 $\times$ 24 = **6.0 dm^3**
Q3 a) $ZnS_{(s)} + 1\frac{1}{2}O_{2\,(g)} \rightarrow ZnO_{(s)} + SO_{2\,(g)}$
b) M_r of ZnS = 65.4 + 32.1 = 97.5
  number of moles = mass $\div M_r$ = 7.00 $\div$ 97.5
  = **0.0718 moles**
c) The molar ratio of ZnS to SO_2 is 1 : 1.
  So 0.0718 moles of ZnS will give **0.0718 moles** of SO_2.
d) At room temperature and pressure 1 mole of gas takes up 24 dm^3.
  Volume in dm^3 = number of moles $\times$ 24
  Volume of SO_2 = 0.0718 $\times$ 24 = **1.72 dm^3**
Q4 a) $C_6H_{14\,(g)} \rightarrow C_4H_{10\,(g)} + C_2H_{4\,(g)}$
b) M_r of C_4H_{10} = (4 $\times$ 12) + (10 $\times$ 1) = 58
  number of moles = mass $\div M_r$ = 3.00 $\div$ 58
  = **0.0517 moles**
c) The molar ratio of C_4H_{10} to C_6H_{14} is 1 : 1.
  So 0.0517 moles of C_4H_{10} must be made from **0.0517 moles** of C_6H_{14}.
d) At room temperature and pressure 1 mole of gas takes up 24 dm^3.
  Volume in dm^3 = number of moles $\times$ 24
  Volume of C_6H_{14} = 0.0517 $\times$ 24 = **1.24 dm^3**
Q5 $2Mg_{(s)} + O_{2\,(g)} \rightarrow 2MgO_{(s)}$
M_r of MgO = 24.3 + 16.0 = 40.3
number of moles = mass $\div M_r$ = 10 $\div$ 40.3 = 0.25 moles
The molar ratio of MgO : O_2 is 2 : 1.
So 0.25 moles of MgO is made from 0.125 moles of O_2.
At room temperature and pressure 1 mole of gas takes up 24 dm^3.
Volume in dm^3 = number of moles $\times$ 24
Volume of O_2 = 0.125 $\times$ 24 = **3.0 dm^3**

5. Formulas of Ionic Compounds
Page 60 — Application Questions
Q1 a) +1
b) +1
c) –1
Q2 Calcium is in group 2 so loses 2 electrons to form Ca^{2+} ions. Chlorine is in group 7 so gains 1 electron to form Cl^- ions. For every calcium ion, you need two chloride ions to balance the charge: (+2) + (–1 $\times$ 2) = 0. So the ratio of calcium to chloride ions is 1 : 2. The formula is **$CaCl_2$**.
Q3 a) +2
b) NO_3^-
c) $Zn(NO_3)_2$

Page 60 — Fact Recall Questions
Q1 +1
Q2 Carbon and oxygen.
Q3 +1

Exam-style Questions — pages 62–63

1   A *(1 mark)*
2   B *(1 mark)*
3   D *(1 mark)*
4   a) $2HCl + MgCO_3 \rightarrow CO_2 + H_2O + MgCl_2$ *(1 mark)*
        $2H^+ + 2Cl^- + Mg^{2+} + CO_3^{2-} \rightarrow CO_2 + H_2O + Mg^{2+} + 2Cl^-$
        $2H^+ + CO_3^{2-} \rightarrow CO_2 + H_2O$ *(1 mark)*
     b) At r.t.p., moles = volume ÷ 24 000 (cm³) *(1 mark)*
        = 496.3 ÷ 24 000 = 0.0206... mol *(1 mark)*
        From the balanced equation, 1 mole of $MgCO_3$ produced
        1 mole of CO_2. So 0.0206... moles of CO_2 is produced
        by 0.0206... moles of $MgCO_3$ *(1 mark)*.
        M_r $MgCO_3$ = 24.3 + 12.0 + (16.0 × 3) = 84.3 g mol⁻¹
        mass = moles × molar mass
           = 0.0206... × 84.3 = **1.74 g** (3 s.f.) *(1 mark)*
5   a) The empirical formula is a formula giving the simplest
        whole number ratio of atoms of each element present in
        a compound *(1 mark)*.
     b) (i) moles CO_2 = mass ÷ M_r = 17.6 ÷ 44 = **0.40 moles**
            moles H_2O = mass ÷ M_r = 9.0 ÷ 18 = **0.50 moles**
            (1 mark for each correct number of moles).
        (ii) There is 1 mole of C in 1 mole of CO_2 so must have
            started with 0.40 moles of C.
            mass C = moles × M_r = 0.40 × 12 = **4.8 g**
            There are 2 moles of H in 1 mole of H_2O so must
            have started with 0.50 × 2 = 1.0 moles of H.
            mass H = 1.0 × 1 = **1 g**
            mass O = total mass – (mass of C + mass of H)
            = 9 – (4.8 + 1.0) = **3.2 g**
            (1 mark for each correct mass).
        (iii) moles O = mass ÷ M_r = 3.2 ÷ 16 = 0.2 moles
            (1 mark). So the ratio of C : H : O = 0.4 : 1.0 : 0.2
            = 2 : 5 : 1 so the empirical formula is **C_2H_5O**
            (1 mark).
     c) (i) The molecular formula is a formula giving the actual
            number of atoms of each element present in a
            molecule *(1 mark)*.
        (ii) The formula mass of the empirical formula is
            (12 × 2) + (5 × 1) + 16 = 45 *(1 mark)*.
            90 ÷ 45 = 2 so the empirical formula is scaled up by
            a factor of 2 and the molecular formula is **$C_4H_{10}O_2$**
            (1 mark).
6   a) $Cl_2 + 2NaOH \rightarrow NaClO + NaCl + H_2O$ *(1 mark)*
     b) M_r of NaClO = 23 + 35.5 + 16 = 74.5 g mol⁻¹
        moles NaClO = 37.1 ÷ 74.5 = 0.497... moles *(1 mark)*
        From the balanced equation, 2 moles of NaOH react to
        produce 1 mole of NaClO, so 0.995... moles of NaOH
        must react to produce 0.497... moles of NaClO *(1 mark)*.
        M_r NaOH = 23 + 16 + 1 = 40 g mol⁻¹
        mass NaOH = 40 × 0.995... = **39.8 g** *(1 mark)*
     c) –1 *(1 mark)*
7   a) NO_3^- *(1 mark)*
     b) In 100 g, 59.6 g will be O.
        So moles O = 59.6 ÷ 16 = 3.725 moles *(1 mark)*
        For each mole of O, you must have:
        3.725 ÷ 3 = 1.241... moles N *(1 mark)*.
        So % composition N = 1.241... × 14 = 17.38...%
        So % composition of nitrate = 17.38... + 59.6
                     = 76.98...% *(1 mark)*
        So, % composition of iron = 100 – 76.98... = 23.01...%
        So ratio of Fe : NO_3 =
        (23.01... ÷ M_r(Fe)) : (76.98... ÷ M_r(NO_3)) = 1 : 3 *(1 mark)*
        Therefore the formula of the
        iron nitrate is **$Fe(NO_3)_3$** *(1 mark)*.

Section 3 — Reactions and Calculations

1. Acids, Bases and Salts
Page 68 — Application Questions
Q1 a) $CuO_{(s)} + 2HCl_{(aq)} \rightarrow CuCl_{2(aq)} + H_2O_{(l)}$
     b) $NaOH_{(aq)} + HCl_{(aq)} \rightarrow NaCl_{(aq)} + H_2O_{(l)}$
     *Don't forget to balance your equations. You'll lose marks in the
     exam if you don't.*
Q2 a) $2Fe_{(s)} + 3H_2SO_{4(aq)} \rightarrow Fe_2(SO_4)_{3(aq)} + 3H_{2(g)}$
     b) $CaCO_{3(s)} + H_2SO_{4(aq)} \rightarrow CaSO_{4(aq)} + CO_{2(g)} + H_2O_{(l)}$
Q3 a) $Al_2O_{3(s)} + 6HNO_{3(aq)} \rightarrow 2Al(NO_3)_{3(aq)} + 3H_2O_{(l)}$
     b) $KOH_{(aq)} + HNO_{3(aq)} \rightarrow KNO_{3(aq)} + H_2O_{(l)}$
     c) $MgCO_{3(s)} + 2HNO_{3(aq)} \rightarrow Mg(NO_3)_{2(aq)} + H_2O_{(l)} + CO_{2(g)}$

Page 68 — Fact Recall Questions
Q1 a) A substance that releases H^+ ions in aqueous solution (a
        proton donor).
     b) A substance that removes H^+ ions from an aqueous
        solution (a proton acceptor).
Q2 a) An acid that almost completely ionises/dissociates in an
        aqueous solution.
     b) A base that only slightly ionises/dissociates in an
        aqueous solution.
Q3 a) HCl
     b) H_2SO_4
     c) HNO_3
     d) NaOH
     e) KOH
     f) NH_3
Q4 a) chloride
     b) sulfate
     c) nitrate
Q5 a) A salt and water.
     b) A salt, carbon dioxide and water.
     c) A salt and hydrogen.

2. Anhydrous and Hydrated Salts
Page 70 — Application Questions
Q1 mass H_2O in hydrated salt = 57.5 – 32.3 = 25.2 g
    *This is the mass of the hydrated salt minus the mass of the
    anhydrous salt.*
    moles $ZnSO_4$ = mass ÷ M = 32.3 ÷ 161.5 = 0.20 mol
    moles H_2O = mass ÷ M = 25.2 ÷ 18 = 1.4 mol
    So, the ratio of $ZnSO_4$: H_2O in the hydrated salt =
    0.20 : 1.4 = 1 : 7 so **X = 7** and the formula of the hydrated
    salt is **$ZnSO_4.7H_2O$**.
Q2 mass $CoCl_2$ in hydrated salt = 35.685 – 16.200 = 19.485 g
    *This is the mass of the hydrated salt minus the mass of the
    water in the hydrated salt.*
    moles $CoCl_2$ = mass ÷ M = 19.485 ÷ 129.9 = 0.1500 mol
    moles H_2O = mass ÷ M = 16.2 ÷ 18 = 0.90 mol
    So, the ratio of $CoCl_2$: H_2O in the hydrated salt =
    0.1500 : 0.90 = 1 : 6 so **X = 6** and the formula of the
    hydrated salt is **$CoCl_2.6H_2O$**.
Q3 % mass $BaCl_2$ = 100 – 14.74 = 85.26%.
    Assuming you have 100 g of hydrated salt it would contain
    85.26 g of $BaCl_2$ and 14.74 g of water.
    moles $BaCl_2$ = mass ÷ M = 85.26 ÷ 208.3 = 0.41 mol
    moles H_2O = mass ÷ M = 14.74 ÷ 18 = 0.82 mol
    So, the ratio of $BaCl_2$: H_2O in the hydrated salt =
    0.41 : 0.82 = 1 : 2 so the formula of the hydrated salt is
    $BaCl_2.2H_2O$.

Q4 % mass $Fe(NO_3)_3$ = 100 − 30.87 = 69.13%.
Assuming you have 100 g of hydrated salt it would contain 69.13 g of $Fe(NO_3)_3$ and 30.87 g of water.
moles $Fe(NO_3)_3$ = mass ÷ M = 69.13 ÷ 241.8 = 0.290 mol
moles H_2O = mass ÷ M = 30.87 ÷ 18 = 1.72 mol
So, the ratio of $Fe(NO_3)_3$: H_2O in the hydrated salt = 0.290 : 1.72 = 1 : 6 and so the formula of the hydrated salt is **$Fe(NO_3)_3.6H_2O$**.

Page 70 — Fact Recall Questions
Q1 Water of crystallisation.
Q2 Anhydrous means that a substance doesn't contain water of crystallisation.
Q3 By heating — hydrated salts lose their water of crystallisation and become anhydrous when they are heated.

3. Titrations
Page 74 — Application Questions
Q1 moles NaCl = 1.50 × (400 ÷ 1000) = **0.600 moles**
Q2 moles $NaHSO_4$ = 2.0 × (250 ÷ 1000) = **0.50 moles**
Q3 moles $H_2C_2O_4$ = 1.250 × (500.0 ÷ 1000) = 0.6250 moles
M_r $H_2C_2O_4$ = (2 × 1) + (2 × 12) + (4 × 16) = 90 g mol^{-1}
mass $H_2C_2O_4$ = 0.6250 × 90 = **56.25 g**
Q4 a) 0.400 ÷ 1.60 = 0.250
0.250 × 250 = **62.5 cm³**
b) 250 − 62.5 = **187.5 cm³**
Q5 Volume of stock HCl solution required: 1.50 ÷ 5.00 = 0.300
0.300 × 100 = 30 cm³ of 5.00 mol dm^{-3} solution
Volume of distilled water required: 100 − 30 = 70 cm³.
So, to make the 1.50 mol dm^{-3} solution, you would mix **30 cm³ of 5.00 mol dm^{-3} HCl solution** with **70 cm³ distilled water**.

Page 74 — Fact Recall Questions
Q1 A burette.
Q2 E.g. methyl orange and phenolphthalein.
Q3 A solution that has a precisely known concentration.

4. Titration Calculations
Page 76 — Application Questions
Q1 a) $HCl_{(aq)} + KOH_{(aq)} \rightarrow KCl_{(aq)} + H_2O_{(l)}$
b) moles HCl = (conc. × volume (cm³)) ÷ 1000
= (0.750 × 28) ÷ 1000 = **0.0210 moles**
c) 1 mole of HCl reacts with 1 mole of KOH.
So 0.0210 moles of HCl must react with **0.0210 moles** of KOH.
d) concentration = (moles KOH × 1000) ÷ vol. (cm³)
= (0.0210 × 1000) ÷ 40.0 = **0.525 mol dm^{-3}**
Q2 $NaOH_{(aq)} + HNO_{3 (aq)} \rightarrow NaNO_{3 (aq)} + H_2O_{(l)}$
moles NaOH = (conc. × volume (cm³)) ÷ 1000
= (1.50 × 15.3) ÷ 1000 = 0.02295 moles
1 mole of NaOH reacts with 1 mole of HNO_3.
So 0.02295 moles of NaOH must react with 0.02295 moles of HNO_3.
concentration = (moles HNO_3 × 1000) ÷ vol. (cm³)
= (0.02295 × 1000) ÷ 35.0 = **0.656 mol dm^{-3}**
Q3 $LiOH_{(aq)} + HCl_{(aq)} \rightarrow LiCl_{(aq)} + H_2O_{(l)}$
moles HCl = (conc. × volume (cm³)) ÷ 1000
= (0.500 × 12.0) ÷ 1000 = 0.00600 moles
1 mole of HCl reacts with 1 mole of LiOH, so 0.00600 moles of HCl must react with 0.00600 moles of LiOH.
concentration = (moles LiOH × 1000) ÷ vol. (cm³)
= (0.00600 × 1000) ÷ 24.0 = **0.250 mol dm^{-3}**

Page 77 — Application Questions
Q1 a) $HNO_3 + LiOH \rightarrow LiNO_3 + H_2O$
b) moles HNO_3 = (conc. × volume (cm³)) ÷ 1000
= (0.200 × 18.8) ÷ 1000 = **0.00376 moles**
c) 1 mole of HNO_3 reacts with 1 mole of LiOH.
So 0.00376 moles of HNO_3 must react with **0.00376 moles** of LiOH.
d) volume = (moles LiOH × 1000) ÷ concentration
= (0.00376 × 1000) ÷ 0.450 = **8.36 cm³**
Q2 a) $KOH + CH_3COOH \rightarrow CH_3COOK + H_2O$
b) moles KOH = (conc. × volume (cm³)) ÷ 1000
= (0.420 × 37.3) ÷ 1000 = **0.0157 moles**
c) 1 mole of KOH reacts with 1 mole of CH_3COOH.
So 0.0157 moles of KOH must react with 0.0157 moles of CH_3COOH.
volume = (moles CH_3COOH × 1000) ÷ conc.
= (0.0157 × 1000) ÷ 1.10 = **14.3 cm³**
Q3 $Ba(OH)_2 + 2HCl \rightarrow BaCl_2 + 2H_2O$
moles of $Ba(OH)_2$ = (conc. × volume (cm³)) ÷ 1000
= (14 × 1) ÷ 1000 = 0.014 moles
1 mole of $Ba(OH)_2$ reacts with 2 moles of HCl. So, 0.014 moles of $Ba(OH)_2$ must react with 0.028 moles of HCl.
volume of HCl = (moles HCl × 1000) ÷ conc.
= (0.028 × 1000) ÷ 0.50 = **56 cm³**

5. Chemical Yield
Page 79 — Application Questions
Q1 % yield = (actual yield ÷ theoretical yield) × 100
= (1.76 ÷ 3.24) × 100 = **54.3%**
Q2 % yield = (actual yield ÷ theoretical yield) × 100
= (3.70 ÷ 6.10) × 100 = **60.7%**
Q3 a) Molar mass of $(CH_3CO)_2O$ = 2 × ((12 + (3 × 1) + 12 + 16)) + 16 = 102 g mol^{-1}
Number of moles $(CH_3CO)_2O$ = mass ÷ molar mass
= 3.00 ÷ 102 = **0.0294 moles**
b) From the equation: 1 mole of $(CH_3CO)_2O$ produces 2 moles of CH_3COOH, so 0.0294 moles of $(CH_3CO)_2O$ will produce (0.0294 × 2) = 0.0588 moles of CH_3COOH.
Molar mass of CH_3COOH = 12 + (3 × 1) + 12 + 16 + 16 + 1 = 60 g mol^{-1}
Theoretical yield = moles CH_3COOH × molar mass
= 0.0588 × 60 = **3.53 g**
c) % yield = (actual yield ÷ theoretical yield) × 100
= (2.80 ÷ 3.53) × 100 = **79.3%**
Q4 a) Molar mass of CH_3CHCH_2 =
12 + (3 × 1) + 12 + 1 + 12 + (2 × 1) = 42 g mol^{-1}
Number of moles CH_3CHCH_2 = mass ÷ molar mass
= 50 ÷ 42 = 1.19... moles
From the equation: 1 mole of CH_3CHCH_2 produces 1 mole of $CH_3CH_2CH_2Cl$, so 1.19 ... moles of CH_3CHCH_2 will produce 1.19 ... moles of $CH_3CH_2CH_2Cl$.
Molar mass of $CH_3CH_2CH_2Cl$ = 12 + (3 × 1) + 12 + (2 × 1) + 12 + (2 × 1) + 35.5 = 78.5 g mol^{-1}
Theoretical yield = moles $CH_3CH_2CH_2Cl$ × molar mass
= 1.19 ... × 78.5 = **93.5 g**
b) % yield = (actual yield ÷ theoretical yield) × 100
= (54 ÷ 93.5) × 100 = **57.8%**
Q5 Molar mass of HCOOH = 1 + 12 + 16 + 16 + 1 = 46 g mol^{-1}
Number of moles HCOOH = mass ÷ molar mass
= 4.70 ÷ 46 = 0.102... moles
From the equation: 2 moles of HCOOH produce 1 mole of $(CHO)_2O$, so 0.102... moles of NaOH will produce (0.102... ÷ 2) = 0.0510... moles of $(CHO)_2O$.
Molar mass of $(CHO)_2O$ = (2 × (12 + 1 + 16)) + 16 = 74 g mol^{-1}

Theoretical yield = moles $(CHO)_2O$ × molar mass
= 0.0510... × 74 = 3.78 g
% yield = (actual yield ÷ theoretical yield) × 100
= (3.60 ÷ 3.78...) × 100 = **95.2%**

Page 79 — Fact Recall Questions

Q1 The theoretical yield is the mass of product that should be formed in a chemical reaction, assuming no chemicals are 'lost' in the process.

Q2 percentage yield = $\dfrac{\text{actual yield}}{\text{theoretical yield}}$ × 100

6. Atom Economy

Page 82 — Application Questions

Q1 a) mass of CH_3Cl = 12 + (3 × 1) + 35.5 = **50.5**
    b) mass of products = (12 + (3 × 1) + 35.5) + (1 + 35.5) = **87**
    c) % atom economy = $\dfrac{M_r \text{ of desired product}}{\text{Total mass of all products}}$ × 100
       = (50.5 ÷ 87) × 100 = **58.0%**
    d) E.g. sell the HCl so it can be used in other chemical reactions / use the HCl as a reactant in another reaction.

Q2 mass of product = (2 × 12) + (5 × 1) + 16 + 1 = 46
   % atom economy = $\dfrac{M_r \text{ of desired product}}{\text{Total mass of all products}}$ × 100
   = (46 ÷ 46) × 100 = **100%**
   Award yourself an extra chocolate biscuit if you spotted that this reaction has 100% atom economy before you did the calculations — any reaction where there's only one product will have 100% atom economy.

Q3 mass of C_2H_4 = (2 × 12) + (4 × 1) = 28
   mass of H_2O = (2 × 1) + 16 = 18
   total mass of products = 28 + 18 = 46
   % atom economy = $\dfrac{M_r \text{ of desired product}}{\text{Total mass of all products}}$ × 100
   = (28 ÷ 46) × 100 = **60.9%**

Q4 a) Reaction 1:
       total mass of products = 2 × (14 + (3 × 1)) = 34
       % atom economy = $\dfrac{M_r \text{ of desired product}}{\text{Total mass of all products}}$ × 100
       = (34 ÷ 34) × 100 = **100%**
       Reaction 2:
       mass of $CaCl_2$ = 40.1 + (35.5 × 2) = 111.1
       mass of $2NH_3$ = 2 × (14 + (3 × 1)) = 34
       mass of $2H_2O$ = 2 × ((2 × 1) + 16) = 36
       total mass of products = 181.1
       % atom economy = $\dfrac{M_r \text{ of desired product}}{\text{Total } M_r \text{ of all products}}$ × 100
       = (34 ÷ 181.1) × 100 = **18.8%**
    b) E.g. reaction 1 has a much higher atom economy / produces no waste.

Page 82 — Fact Recall Questions

Q1 Atom economy is a measure of the proportion of reactant atoms that become part of the desired product (rather than by-products) in the balanced chemical equation.

Q2 % atom economy = $\dfrac{M_r \text{ of desired product}}{\text{Total } M_r \text{ of all products}}$ × 100

Q3 Any two from: e.g. for low atom economy reactions there's lots of waste produced / it costs money to separate the desired product from waste / it costs money to dispose of waste products safely / reactant chemicals are expensive so it wastes money if a high proportion of them end up as useless products / high atom economy reactions are more sustainable.

7. Oxidation Numbers

Page 86 — Application Questions

Q1 a) +1
    b) −1
    c) +2
Q2 a) −1
    b) −2
    c) −1
Q3 a) H: +1, Cl: −1
    b) C: +4, O: −2
    c) Cl: +7, O: −2
    d) H: +1, S: +6, O: −2
    Oxygen has an oxidation number of −2. There are 4 oxygen atoms here so the total is −8. The overall oxidation number of the ion is −1. Hydrogen has an oxidation number of +1. So, sulfur must have an oxidation number of +6 (as −8 + 1 + 6 = −1).
Q4 a) +2
    b) +4
    c) +4
    Calcium forms Ca^{2+} ions so has an oxidation number of +2. Oxygen has an oxidation number of −2. There are 3 oxygen atoms here so the total is −6. The overall oxidation number of the compound is 0. So, carbon must have an oxidation number of +4 (as −6 + 4 = −2).
    d) −2
    Hydrogen has an oxidation number of +1. So, in C_3H_6, carbon must have an oxidation number of −2 (as (6 × +1) + (3 × −2) = 0).
Q5 a) 0
    b) −3
    c) +6
    d) +2
    Fluorine is the most electronegative element so its oxidation number is equal to its ionic charge, −1. There are 4 fluorine atoms here so the total is −4. So, phosphorus must have an oxidation number of +2 (as (4 × −1) + (2 × +2) = 0).
Q6 a) +3
    b) +7
Q7 a) iron(II) sulfate
    b) manganese(II) carbonate
    c) copper(II) oxide
Q8 a) $CuSO_4$
    b) FeO
    c) NO_2^-
    d) CrO_4^{2-}

Page 86 — Fact Recall Questions

Q1 0
Q2 0
Q3 −1
Q4 −1

8. Redox Reactions

Page 89 — Application Questions

Q1 a) The oxidation number of magnesium increases from 0 to +2. The oxidation number of hydrogen decreases from +1 to 0.
    b) The oxidation number of vanadium increases from 0 to +3. The oxidation number of hydrogen decreases from +1 to 0.
    c) The oxidation number of iron increases from 0 to +3. The oxidation number of hydrogen decreases from +1 to 0.

Q2 a) The oxidation number of manganese decreases from +4 to +2. The oxidation number of two of the chlorine atoms increases from –1 to 0.
Only two of the chlorine atoms show an increase in oxidation number. The other two stay with an oxidation number of –1.
b) MnO_2 is the oxidising agent. It accepts electrons and gets reduced. HCl is the reducing agent. It donates electrons and gets oxidised.

Page 89 — Fact Recall Questions
Q1 Oxidation is a loss of electrons.
Q2 Reduction is a gain of electrons.
Q3 An oxidising agent accepts electrons from another reactant and is reduced.
Q4 A reducing agent donates electrons to another reactant and is oxidised.
Q5 It increases by 1.
Q6 It decreases by 1.

Exam-style Questions — pages 91–93
1   D *(1 mark)*
2   C *(1 mark)*
3   A *(1 mark)*
4   a) (i) +4 *(1 mark)*
        (ii) silicon(IV) oxide *(1 mark)*
    b) This is not a redox reaction *(1 mark)*. There are no changes in oxidation state during this reaction *(1 mark)*.
5   a) (i) $Zn_{(s)} + 2HCl_{(aq)} \rightarrow ZnCl_{2\,(aq)} + H_{2\,(g)}$ *(1 mark for correct balanced equation, 1 mark for correct state symbols)*
        (ii) atom economy = M_r desired product ÷ M_r all products × 100%
              = $(2 \times 1) \div ((2 \times 1) + (65.4 + (35.5 \times 2)) \times 100\%$
              (1 mark)
              = **1.45%** *(1 mark)*
    b) (i) $(3 \times (2 \times 1)) \div ((3 \times (2 \times 1)) + (12 + 16)) \times 100\%$
              (1 mark) = **17.6%** *(1 mark)*
        (ii) Any two from: e.g. Steam reformation has a higher atom economy. This means it's more sustainable/ less waste is produced. / It costs money to dispose of waste products. / Reagents are often expensive, so it's wasteful if a high proportion of them are converted to waste products. *(2 marks — 1 mark for each appropriate reason.)*
6   a) (i) Water of crystallisation is the water contained in an ionic lattice *(1 mark)*.
        (ii) A salt is hydrated if it contains water of crystallisation *(1 mark)*.
        (iii) A salt is anhydrous if it doesn't contain any water of crystallisation *(1 mark)*.
    b) +2 *(1 mark)*
    c) mass of water lost = 8.93 – 4.88 = 4.05 g
       moles of water lost = $4.05 \div (16 + (2 \times 1))$ = 0.225 mol
       (1 mark)
       M_r $FeSO_4$ = 55.8 + 32.1 + (16 × 4) = 151.9
       moles of anhydrous $FeSO_4$ = 4.88 ÷ 151.9 = 0.0321 mol
       (1 mark)
       ratio of H_2O : $FeSO_4$ = 0.225 : 0.0321
       (divide by 0.0321) = 7 : 1, so **x = 7**.
       So formula for hydrated iron(II) sulfate is **$FeSO_4 \bullet 7H_2O$**
       (1 mark)
7   a) (i) $HCl_{(aq)} + NaOH_{(aq)} \rightarrow NaCl_{(aq)} + H_2O_{(l)}$
              (1 mark for correct balanced equation, 1 mark for correct state symbols)

(ii) moles HCl = (concentration × volume) ÷ 1000 = $(0.6 \times 26) \div 1000$ = **0.0156 moles**.
     (2 marks for correct answer, otherwise 1 mark for correct method if answer incorrect)
(iii) From the equation you know that 1 mole of HCl reacts with 1 mole of NaOH. So 0.0156 moles of HCl must react with 0.0156 moles of NaOH. concentration of NaOH = (moles ÷ volume) × 1000 = $(0.0156 \div 20) \times 1000$ = **0.78 mol dm⁻³**
     (2 marks for correct answer, otherwise 1 mark for correct method if answer incorrect)
If you get a question like this where you need your answer to the previous part of a question to answer it, you'll get the marks if everything you've done is right, even if you don't get the right answer because you made an error in the earlier part of the question.
b) (i) +3 *(1 mark)*
   (ii) $AlCl_3$ *(1 mark)*
Cl forms Cl⁻ ions so has an oxidation number of –1. The overall oxidation number of aluminium chloride is 0 and aluminium has an oxidation number of +3, so there must be 3 Cl⁻ ions and the formula must be $AlCl_3$.
c) (i) The oxidation number of sodium increases from 0 to +1 *(1 mark)*.
   (ii) It is a reducing agent *(1 mark)*.
d) Assuming there was 100 g of hydrated calcium nitrate, 30.5 g would be water and 100 – 30.5 = 69.5 g would be calcium nitrate *(1 mark)*. moles water = mass ÷ M = 30.5 ÷ 18 = 1.694 mol *(1 mark)*.
   M of $Ca(NO_3)_2$ = 40.1 + [2 × (14 + (3 × 16))] = 164.1. moles $Ca(NO_3)_2$ = mass ÷ M = 69.5 ÷ 164.1 = 0.424 mol *(1 mark)*.
   $Ca(NO_3)_2$: H_2O = 0.424 : 1.694 = 1 : 4 so **x = 4** *(1 mark)*.
e) The student should have added dissolved calcium(II) nitrate to the volumetric flask, and then topped up the total volume to 250 cm³ *(1 mark)*. The student's solution will be too dilute *(1 mark)*.

Section 4 — Electrons, Bonding and Structure

1. Electronic Structure
Page 97 — Application Questions
Q1 a) $1s^2\ 2s^1$
   b) $1s^2\ 2s^2\ 2p^6\ 3s^2\ 3p^6\ 3d^2\ 4s^2$
   c) $1s^2\ 2s^2\ 2p^6\ 3s^2\ 3p^6\ 3d^{10}\ 4s^2\ 4p^1$
   d) $1s^2\ 2s^2\ 2p^3$
Q2 a) 1s   2s   2p   3s   3p   4s
       [↑↓] [↑↓] [↑↓|↑↓|↑↓] [↑↓] [↑↓|↑↓|↑↓] [↑↓]

   Remember — the 4s sub-shell has a lower energy level than the 3d sub-shell even though its principal quantum number is bigger. This means the 4s sub-shell fills up first.
   b) 1s   2s   2p   3s   3p
       [↑↓] [↑↓] [↑↓|↑↓|↑↓] [↑↓] [↑↓|↑↓|↑↓]
              3d   4s
       [↑↓|↑↓|↑↓|↑↓|↑]   [↑↓]

   c) 1s   2s   2p   3s
       [↑↓] [↑↓] [↑↓|↑↓|↑↓] [↑]

   d) 1s   2s   2p
       [↑↓] [↑↓] [↑↓|↑|↑]

Q3 a)

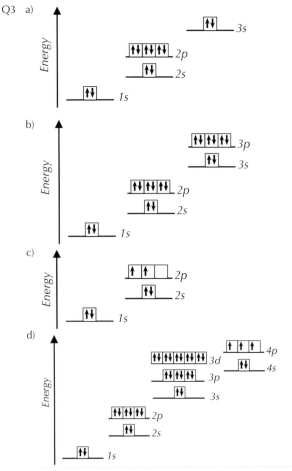

b)

c)

d)

Q4 a) $1s^2\ 2s^2\ 2p^6$
    b) $1s^2\ 2s^2\ 2p^6$
    c) $1s^2\ 2s^2\ 2p^6$
    d) $1s^2\ 2s^2\ 2p^6\ 3s^2\ 3p^6$
Q5 a) bromine
    b) phosphorus
    c) vanadium

Page 97 — Fact Recall Questions
Q1 3
Q2 6 (it can hold two electrons in each orbital)
Q3 18
Q4 a) spherical
    b) dumbbell-shaped
Q5 The number of electrons that an atom or ion has and
    how they are arranged.
Q6 The shells with the lowest energy (e.g. 1s then 2s then
    2p etc.).
Q7 Electrons fill orbitals singly before they start sharing, so
    the two electrons in the 2p sub-shell should be in separate
    orbitals.

2. Ionic Bonding
Page 100 — Application Questions
Q1 a) LiF

The lithium has a $+1$ charge and the fluoride ion has a -1
charge. To balance each other out and make a neutral ionic
compound, you only need one of each ion.

b) A lithium atom (Li) loses 1 electron to form a lithium ion
    (Li$^+$). The fluorine atom (F) gains 1 electron to form a
    fluoride ion (F$^-$). Electrostatic attraction holds the positive
    and negative ions together — this is an ionic bond.
c)

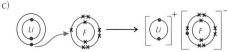

Q2 a) $+1$

The ionic formula is K_2O, and the charge on the oxide ion is
-2. So the two potassium ions must have a combined charge
of $+2$ to balance out the -2 charge and make the compound
neutral. This means each potassium ion will have a charge of
$+2 \div 2 = +1$.

b)

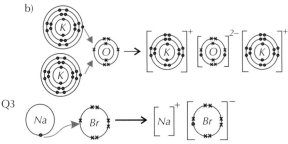

Q3

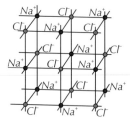

Page 100 — Fact Recall Questions
Q1 It holds positive and negative ions together.
Q2 A regular structure made up of ions.
Q3

Q4 The ions in a molten ionic compound are free to move (and
    they carry a charge).
Q5 It will have a high melting point and a high boiling point. It
    will dissolve in water.

3. Covalent Bonding
Page 103 — Application Questions
Q1

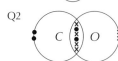

Q2

The overlapping region contains six electrons as it's a triple
bond. Two of the electrons come from carbon, one for each of
the normal covalent bonds, and four come from oxygen — one
for each of the two normal covalent bonds, and an extra two
for the dative covalent bond.

Page 103 — Fact Recall Questions

Q1 A covalent bond is the electrostatic attraction between a shared pair of electrons and the nuclei of the bonded atoms.

Q2

Q3 It is a covalent bond formed when two atoms share three pairs of electrons.

Q4 In a normal single covalent bond, one of the electrons in the shared pair of electrons comes from each atom. In a dative covalent bond, one of the atoms provides both of the shared electrons.

Q5

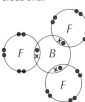

Q6 Average bond enthalpy tells you how strong a covalent bond is / how much energy is required to break a covalent bond.

4. Shapes of Molecules

Page 107 — Application Questions

Q1 a) Sulfur has 6 outer electrons and 2 hydrogen atoms donate one electron each. So there are 8 electrons on the S atom, which is **4** electron pairs.
b) 2 electron pairs are involved in bonding, so there are **2** lone pairs.
c)

non-linear
d) 104.5°

Q2

The shape is tetrahedral.
Carbon has 4 outer electrons and 2 chlorine and 2 fluorine atoms donate one electron each. So there are 8 electrons on the C atom, which is 4 electron pairs. All the electron pairs are involved in bonding and repel each other as much as possible, resulting in a tetrahedral shape.

Q3 Atom A: shape: trigonal pyramidal, bond angle: 120°
The carbon atom has 4 outer electrons. The two hydrogens donate one electron each and the adjacent carbon atom donates 2 electrons as it forms a double bond. So there are 8 electrons on the C atom, which is 4 electron pairs. All the electron pairs are involved in bonding. The double bond means that the shape is based on a molecule with three electron pairs surrounding the central atom, i.e. trigonal planar, where the bond angles are 120°.
Atom B: shape: tetrahedral, bond angle: 109.5°
The carbon atom has 4 outer electrons and each of the two hydrogen atoms and the oxygen and adjacent carbon atoms donate one electron. So there are 8 electrons on the C atom,

which is 4 electron pairs. All the electron pairs are involved in bonding so the shape is tetrahedral and the bond angles are 109.5°.
Atom C: shape: non-linear, bond angle: 104.5°
The oxygen atom has 6 outer electrons and the hydrogen and carbon atoms donate one electron each. So there are 8 electrons on the O atom, which is 4 electron pairs. Only two of the electron pairs are involved in bonding so there are two lone pairs. The shape is non-linear and the bond angle is 104.5°.

Page 107 — Fact Recall Questions

Q1 120°
Q2 octahedral

5. Polarisation

Page 110 — Application Questions

Q1 a) A C–O bond will have a permanent dipole.
b) An N–Cl bond will not have a permanent dipole.
c) A B–F bond will have a permanent dipole.

Q2 a)

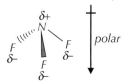

The molecule is polar.
b)

The polar C–Cl bonds point in opposite directions, so the molecule has no overall dipole and is non-polar.

Q3 a)

The polar B–Cl bonds cancel each other out, so the molecule has no overall dipole and is non-polar.
b)

The permanent dipoles on the two C–Cl bonds don't cancel each other out, so the molecule has an overall dipole and is polar.
c)

The permanent dipoles on the three P–F bonds don't cancel each other out, so the molecule has an overall dipole moment and is polar.

Page 110 — Fact Recall Questions

Q1 Electronegativity is the ability to attract the bonding electrons in a covalent bond. So a chlorine atom is better able to attract the electrons than a hydrogen atom.

Q2 Fluorine is more electronegative than hydrogen so attracts the electrons in the H—F covalent bond more than hydrogen. The bonding electrons are pulled towards the fluorine atom. This makes the bond polar.

Q3 A dipole is a difference in charge between two atoms caused by a shift in the electron density in the bond between them.

6. Intermolecular Forces

Page 115 — Application Questions

Q1 Induced dipole-dipole interactions

Q2

Q3 a) Oxygen is more electronegative than chlorine so it has a greater ability to pull the bonding electrons away from hydrogen atoms. So the bonds are more polarised in H_2O than in HCl, which means that hydrogen bonds form in H_2O but not in HCl.

b) H_2O molecules are able to form hydrogen bonds whilst HCl only forms induced dipole-dipole forces and permanent dipole-dipole forces. Hydrogen bonds are the strongest type of intermolecular force, and therefore require more energy to break, so water has a higher boiling point than hydrogen chloride.

c) fluorine/F

d) carbon/C

Q4 a) NH_3 has hydrogen bonds between molecules whereas PH_3 only has induced dipole-dipole interactions, as the electronegativity values of P and H are very similar. It takes less energy to break induced dipole-dipole interactions than hydrogen bonds so the boiling point of PH_3 is lower.

b) lower

Q5 CH_4, CH_3Cl, CH_3I, CH_3OH
CH_4 has the lowest boiling point because it is a non-polar molecule so the molecules are only held together by induced dipole-dipole interactions. It also has the smallest electron cloud, so its induced dipole-dipole interactions are the weakest. CH_3Cl is a polar molecule so is able to form permanent dipole-dipole interactions as well as induced dipole-dipole interactions. Although CH_3I is less polar than CH_3Cl, and so the permanent dipole-dipole interactions are weaker, it has a larger electron cloud and so the induced dipole-dipole interactions are stronger, and overall the boiling point is greater. CH_3OH contains an -OH group which is able to form strong hydrogen bonds, and so has the highest boiling point.

Page 115 — Fact Recall Questions

Q1 Induced dipole-dipole interactions / London (dispersion) forces, permanent dipole-dipole interactions and hydrogen bonds.

Q2 There are covalent bonds within iodine molecules and induced dipole-dipole interactions between iodine molecules. The intermolecular forces mean that iodine forms a simple molecular lattice.

Q3 Permanent dipole-dipole interactions are weak electrostatic forces of attraction between polar molecules.

Q4 a) hydrogen bonding

b)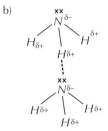

Q5 Ice has more hydrogen bonds than liquid water, and hydrogen bonds are relatively long. So the H_2O molecules in ice are further apart on average, making ice less dense than liquid water.

Q6 a) Water is a polar molecule so only tends to dissolve other polar substances well. Chlorine isn't polar so is only slightly soluble in water.

b) No — chlorine wouldn't conduct electricity because there are no free ions to carry the charge.

Exam-style Questions — pages 117–119

Q1 B *(1 mark)*

Q2 B *(1 mark)*

Q3 D *(1 mark)*

Q4 C *(1 mark)*

Q5 a) (i) Electronegativity is the ability of an atom to attract the bonding electrons in a covalent bond *(1 mark)*.

(ii) If there's a difference in the electronegativities of two covalently bonded atoms there's a shift in the electron density towards the more electronegative atom, making the bond polar *(1 mark)*. This creates a dipole and causes weak electrostatic forces of attraction between molecules *(1 mark)*.

b) (i) HCl: permanent dipole-dipole interactions and induced dipole-dipole interactions *(1 mark)*
CH_4: induced dipole interactions *(1 mark)*
HF: hydrogen bonds, permanent dipole-dipole interactions and induced dipole-dipole interactions *(1 mark)*

(ii)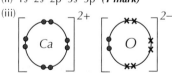

(3 marks — 1 mark for showing all lone pairs, 1 mark for showing the partial charges and 1 mark for showing the hydrogen bond going from a lone pair on an F atom to an H atom.)

(iii) The Cl atoms in Cl_2 have equal electronegativities so the covalent bond is non-polar *(1 mark)*.

Q6 a) (i) An ionic bond is an electrostatic attraction between two oppositely charged ions *(1 mark)*.

(ii) $1s^2\ 2s^2\ 2p^6\ 3s^2\ 3p^6$ *(1 mark)*

(iii)

$$\left[\begin{array}{c} Ca \end{array} \right]^{2+} \qquad \left[\begin{array}{c} O \end{array} \right]^{2-}$$

(2 marks — 1 mark for showing the correct number of outer electrons, 1 mark for showing the correct charges.)

b) Carbon dioxide is linear with a bond angle of 180° *(1 mark)*. The molecule has two double bonds and no lone pairs on the central atom *(1 mark)* and the bonding pairs repel each other as much as possible *(1 mark)*.

c) Calcium oxide will have a higher boiling point *(1 mark)*. The ionic bonds in calcium oxide are much stronger than the induced dipole-dipole interactions that form between the molecules in carbon dioxide, so will require more energy to break *(1 mark)*.

Q7 a) Going from PH_3 to SbH_3, the molecules have more electrons in them *(1 mark)* so the induced dipole-dipole interactions between the molecules increase in strength *(1 mark)*. It takes more energy to break stronger induced dipole-dipole interactions so the boiling points increase from PH_3 to SbH_3 *(1 mark)*. The boiling point of NH_3 doesn't follow this trend and is higher than expected because NH_3 is able to form strong hydrogen bonds between the molecules, which take more energy to break than induced dipole-dipole interactions *(1 mark)*.

b)

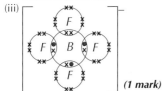

(2 marks — 1 mark for correct shape, 1 mark for correct bond angle.)

c) NH_3 is the only one of the Group 5 hydrides that can form hydrogen bonds with the water molecules *(1 mark)*. This allows for better mixing of the NH_3 molecules with water molecules than for the rest of the Group 5 hydrides *(1 mark)*.

Q8 a)

(1 mark)

The molecule has 6 bonding pairs of electrons on the central atom and these repel each other equally *(1 mark)*. This means that all the angles between the bonding pairs are 90° *(1 mark)* and the shape is octahedral *(1 mark)*.

b) (i) 120° *(1 mark)*

(ii) A covalent bond formed between two atoms where one of the atoms provides both of the shared electrons *(1 mark)*.

(iii)

(1 mark)

(iv) The shape will be tetrahedral *(1 mark)*. This is because the ion has four bonding pairs on its central atom which will repel each other equally, giving bond angles of 109.5° *(1 mark)*.

Module 3

Section 1 — The Periodic Table

1. The Periodic Table
Page 123 — Application Questions
Q1 a) 3   b) 4   c) 5
Q2 a) 6   b) 3   c) 1

Q3 a) $1s^2\,2s^2\,2p^6\,3s^1$
b) $1s^2\,2s^2\,2p^6\,3s^2\,3p^6\,4s^2$
c) $1s^2\,2s^2\,2p^6\,3s^2\,3p^5$
d) $1s^2\,2s^2\,2p^6\,3s^2\,3p^6\,3d^{10}\,4s^2\,4p^3$
e) $1s^2\,2s^2\,2p^6\,3s^2\,3p^6\,3d^3\,4s^2$
f) $1s^2\,2s^2\,2p^6\,3s^2\,3p^6\,3d^1\,4s^2$

Page 123 — Fact Recall Questions
Q1 a) Mendeleev arranged the elements by atomic mass but left gaps where the next element didn't seem to fit so that he could keep elements with similar chemical properties in the same group.
b) In the modern periodic table the elements are arranged by increasing atomic number.
Q2 a) A period is a row in the periodic table.
b) A group is a column in the periodic table.
c) Periodicity means the repeating trends in the physical and chemical properties of the elements as you go across a period.
Q3 Elements in a group have similar chemical properties because they all have the same number of electrons in their outer shell.

2. First Ionisation Energy
Page 127 — Application Questions
Q1 a) $Cl_{(g)} \rightarrow Cl^+_{(g)} + e^-$
b) $Si_{(g)} \rightarrow Si^+_{(g)} + e^-$

Q2 a) Aluminium and sulfur are both in Period 3, so they both have the same number of electron shells, and a similar amount of shielding of the nuclear charge by the inner electron shells. Aluminium has 13 protons and sulfur has 16 protons. So the positive charge of the nucleus of sulfur is greater. This means electrons are pulled closer to the nucleus, making the atomic radius of sulfur smaller than the atomic radius of aluminium.
b) sodium/magnesium
Q3 The outer electron being removed is in the same energy level and the shielding is identical in the two atoms. But the silicon atom has one more proton than the aluminium atom so its nuclear charge is greater. This means that the attraction between the outer electron and the nucleus is greater in silicon, and it takes more energy to remove it.
Q4 a) Strontium would have a smaller atomic radius than rubidium. Strontium has a higher nuclear charge so there's a greater attraction between the electrons and the nucleus and so the electrons are pulled closer to the nucleus.
b) Bromine would have a higher first ionisation energy than selenium. The outer electron being removed is in the same energy level and the shielding is very similar in the two atoms. But the bromine atom has one more proton than the selenium atom so its nuclear charge is greater. This means that the attraction between the outer electron and the nucleus is greater in bromine, and it takes more energy to remove it.
Q5 The electron being removed is in the same energy level and the shielding is identical in the two atoms. However, the first ionisation energy of oxygen is lower than for nitrogen, despite oxygen having a higher nuclear charge. This is because the electron being removed from oxygen is in an orbital where there are two electrons. The repulsion between these two electrons means that it's easier to remove the electron than it would be if it was unpaired (like in nitrogen), so the first ionisation energy of oxygen is lower than that of nitrogen.

Q6 Boron's outer electron is in a 2p orbital rather than a 2s (like beryllium's), which means it has a higher energy and is located further from the nucleus. The 2p orbital also has additional shielding provided by the 2s electrons. These two factors override the effect of the increased nuclear charge of the boron atom, and result in the first ionisation energy of beryllium being higher than the first ionisation energy of boron.

Page 127 — Fact Recall Questions
Q1 The first ionisation energy is the energy needed to remove 1 mole of electrons from 1 mole of gaseous atoms.
Q2 The more protons there are, the more positively charged the nucleus is, the stronger the attraction for the electrons and the higher the ionisation energy.
Q3 The atomic radius and the shielding effect of inner electrons.
Q4 As you go down a group the number of electron shells increases. This means that the atomic radius get larger and there are more inner electron shells shielding the outer electron from the nucleus. As a result, the attraction between the nucleus and the outer electron is reduced so the outer electron is easier to lose and the first ionisation energy is lower.
Q5 a) There's a general increase in the first ionisation energy as you go across a period.
   b) As you move across the period the amount of shielding remains roughly constant but the number of protons increases, so the strength of the nuclear attraction increases and the atomic radius decreases. As a result the electrons become more difficult to remove, increasing the first ionisation energy.

3. Successive Ionisation Energies
Page 129 — Application Questions
Q1 a) $B^+_{(g)} \rightarrow B^{2+}_{(g)} + e^-$
   b) $Cl^+_{(g)} \rightarrow Cl^{2+}_{(g)} + e^-$
   c) $Cl^{2+}_{(g)} \rightarrow Cl^{3+}_{(g)} + e^-$
Q2 Fifth ionisation energy
Q3 a) Group 6
   b) 2 electrons in the first shell and 6 electrons in the second shell.
   c) Oxygen
Q4 a)

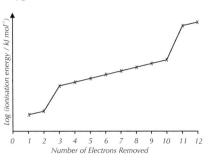

b) Within each shell, successive ionisation energies increase. This is because electrons are being removed from an increasingly positive ion — there's less repulsion amongst the remaining electrons, so they're held more strongly by the nucleus. The big jumps in ionisation energy happen when a new shell that's closer to the nucleus is broken into — the first shell has 2 electrons in it, the second shell has 8 electrons and the third shell has 2 electrons.

4. Giant Covalent Lattices
Page 131 — Fact Recall Questions
Q1 a) Diamond is a giant covalent lattice made up of carbon atoms. Each carbon atom is covalently bonded to four other carbon atoms and the atoms arrange themselves in a tetrahedral shape.
   b) All the outer electrons are held in localised bonds.
Q2 Graphite is a giant covalent lattice made up of carbon atoms. Each carbon atom is covalently bonded to three other carbon atoms and the atoms arrange themselves in sheets of flat hexagons. The fourth outer electron of each carbon atom is delocalised between the sheets of hexagons. The sheets are bonded together by weak induced dipole-dipole forces.
Q3 a) Graphene is a giant covalent lattice made up of carbon atoms. Each carbon atom is covalently bonded to three other carbon atoms and the atoms arrange themselves in a single sheet of flat hexagons. Each sheet is one atom thick. The fourth outer electron of each carbon atom is delocalised above and below the sheet of hexagons.
   b) The delocalised electrons in graphene are free to move quickly and freely above and below the sheet of carbon atoms, and so can carry an electric current.
   c) E.g. Graphene could be used in touchscreen technology/high-speed electronics/aircraft technology.

5. Metallic Bonding
Page 132 — Fact Recall Questions
Q1 Magnesium exists as a giant metallic lattice structure. The outermost electrons of magnesium atoms are delocalised — the electrons are free to move about the metal. This leaves positive metal ions, Mg^{2+}, which are attracted to the delocalised negative electrons. They form a lattice of closely packed positive ions in a sea of delocalised electrons.
Q2 metallic bonding
Q3 a) Copper shows metallic bonding. As there are no bonds holding specific ions together, the copper ions can slide over each other when the structure is pulled, so it can be drawn into a wire.
   b) Since copper shows metallic bonding, there are delocalised electrons which can pass kinetic energy to each other, making copper a good thermal conductor.

6. Periodic Trends in Melting and Boiling Points
Pages 134 — Application Questions
Q1 a) Lithium is a metal so it has strong metallic bonds holding all the atoms together. Nitrogen is a molecular substance with only induced dipole-dipole forces between the molecules. It takes much less energy to break induced dipole-dipole forces than metallic bonds, so the boiling point of lithium is much higher than the boiling point of nitrogen.
   b) Beryllium and lithium are both metals so both have strong metallic bonds holding the atoms together. But a beryllium ion has a charge of 2+ so there are 2 delocalised electrons per ion, while a lithium ion only has a charge of 1+ and 1 delocalised electron per ion. As a result, beryllium ions have a greater charge density so the metallic bonds in beryllium are stronger and it has a higher boiling point.

Q2 a) Magnesium forms 2+ ions so there are two delocalised electrons for each ion. Sodium only forms 1+ ions so there is only one delocalised electron for each ion. Because magnesium contains more delocalised electrons than sodium, magnesium has a higher charge density so the metallic bonds in magnesium are stronger than the metallic bonds in sodium. As a result, more energy is required to break the bonds and the melting temperature of magnesium is higher.

b) Sulfur forms S_8 molecules while phosphorus forms P_4 molecules. Because sulfur molecules are larger than phosphorus molecules, the induced dipole-dipole forces which hold the molecules together are stronger. This means more heat energy is required to break the induced dipole-dipole forces and the melting point of sulfur is higher.

Q3 a) Silicon has a giant covalent lattice structure so has strong covalent bonds linking all its atoms together. Phosphorus is a molecular substance with induced dipole-dipole forces between its molecules. It takes much less energy to break induced dipole-dipole forces than covalent bonds so the melting point of phosphorus is much lower than the melting point of silicon.

b) chlorine / argon

Q4 Calcium would have a higher boiling point than potassium. The boiling point of metals increases across a period and calcium is after potassium in Period 4.

Page 134 — Fact Recall Questions

Q1 The melting and boiling points generally increase from lithium to carbon, but then decrease from carbon to neon.

Q2 boron, carbon

Q3 argon

7. Group 2 — The Alkaline Earth Metals
Pages 137-138 — Application Questions

Q1 a) $Ca_{(s)} + 2H_2O_{(l)} \rightarrow Ca(OH)_{2(aq)} + H_{2(g)}$

b) The oxidation state of calcium increases from 0 to +2.

c) The solution would fizz as bubbles of hydrogen gas are given off.

d) The reaction would be more vigorous/happen faster.

You know the reaction would be faster/more vigorous because reactivity increases down the group.

Q2 a) $2Sr_{(s)} + O_{2(g)} \rightarrow 2SrO_{(s)}$

b) Strontium oxide is a white solid.

c) $SrO_{(s)} + H_2O_{(l)} \rightarrow Sr^{2+}_{(aq)} + 2OH^-_{(aq)}$

d) pH 12 – 13

The solution is strongly alkaline due to the OH⁻ ions that are released when the strontium hydroxide dissolves in the water.

Q3 a) $Ca + 2HCl \rightarrow CaCl_2 + H_2$

b) The oxidation state increases from 0 to +2.

c) The solution would fizz as bubbles of hydrogen gas are given off.

d) The reaction would be more vigorous if barium was used instead of calcium.

Page 138 — Fact Recall Questions

Q1 As you go down the group ionisation energy decreases. The lower the ionisation energy, the easier it is to lose electrons and the more reactive the element is. So reactivity increases down the group.

Q2 a) 2+

b) Group 2 elements have two electrons in their outer shell. When they lose these two electrons to form 2+ ions they end up with a full outer electron shell (the same as the noble gases). This is very stable so Group 2 elements usually form 2+ ions.

Q3 An increase in oxidation state from 0 to +2.

Q4 pH 12 – 13

Q5 Barium oxide

Q6 As you go down the group the reactivity of the elements with dilute acids increases.

Q7 E.g. calcium hydroxide is used in agriculture to neutralise acid soils. Magnesium hydroxide is used in some indigestion tablets as an antacid.

8. Group 7 — The Halogens
Page 143 — Application Questions

Q1 Bromine atoms have fewer electrons than iodine atoms. As a result the induced dipole-dipole forces in bromine are weaker than those in iodine. So less energy is required to break the intermolecular forces and the boiling point is lower.

Q2 a)
$$Cl_{2(aq)} + 2I^-_{(aq)} \rightarrow 2Cl^-_{(aq)} + I_{2(aq)}$$

Oxidation no. of Cl: 0 → −1
Oxidation no. of I: −1 → 0

b) The solution turns from brown to a violet/pink colour.

Q3 Atoms of the other halogens have a larger atomic radius than fluorine atoms. This means their outer electrons are further from the nucleus and there are more electron shells shielding the outer electrons from the nucleus. So the nuclear attraction is less and it is more difficult for the other halogens to gain an electron. So they are less reactive than fluorine.

Q4 a) There are iodide ions in the unknown solution.

b) $Br_{2(aq)} + 2I^-_{(aq)} \rightarrow 2Br^-_{(aq)} + I_{2(aq)}$

Q5 A: iodide ions   B: fluoride ions   C: bromide ions

Page 143 — Fact Recall Questions

Q1 A diatomic molecule is a molecule consisting of two atoms.

Q2 The boiling points of the halogens increase down the group. This is due to the increasing strength of the induced dipole-dipole interactions as the size and relative mass of the atoms increases.

Q3 As you go down the group, the atomic radius increases so the outer electrons are further from the nucleus. The outer electrons are also shielded more from the attraction of the positive nucleus, because there are more inner electrons. This makes it harder for larger atoms to attract the electron needed to form an ion (despite the increased charge on the nucleus), so larger atoms are less reactive.

Q4 Bromide ions and iodide ions.

Q5 a) Pale yellow / green
   b) Orange / red
   c) Violet / pink

Q6 The silver nitrate test. Add dilute nitric acid to remove any ions that might interfere with the reaction. Then add silver nitrate and a precipitate may form. The colour of the precipitate identifies the halide (chloride gives a white precipitate, bromide gives a cream precipitate and iodide gives a yellow precipitate). If no precipitate forms it must be fluoride ions.

9. Disproportionation and Water Treatment
Page 146 — Application Questions

Q1 a) $I_{2(s)} + 2KOH_{(aq)} \rightarrow KIO_{(aq)} + KI_{(aq)} + H_2O_{(l)}$

b) The oxidation number of iodine increases from 0 in I_2 to +1 in KIO and decreases from 0 to −1 in KI. So iodine is simultaneously oxidised and reduced and it is a disproportionation reaction.

Q2 The oxidation state of O in H_2O_2 is –1. When H_2O is formed, the oxidation state of O decreases from –1 to –2. This is a reduction reaction. When O_2 is formed the oxidation state of O increases from –1 to 0. This is an oxidation reaction. So O is being simultaneously oxidised and reduced and it is a disproportionation reaction.

Q3 a) $HClO_{(aq)} + H_2O_{(l)} \rightarrow ClO^-_{(aq)} + H_3O^+_{(aq)}$
b) Chlorate(I) ions kill bacteria so adding them to water can make it safe to drink or swim in.

Page 146 — Fact Recall Questions

Q1 Disproportionation is when a single element is simultaneously oxidised and reduced during a reaction.

Q2 a) sodium chlorate(I), sodium chloride, water
b) $2NaOH_{(aq)} + Cl_{2(g)} \rightarrow NaClO_{(aq)} + NaCl_{(aq)} + H_2O_{(l)}$

Q3 When you mix chlorine with water, it undergoes disproportionation. It makes a mixture of hydrochloric acid and chloric(I) acid. The aqueous chloric(I) acid then ionises to make chlorate(I) ions.

Q4 a) Chlorine kills disease-causing microorganisms. It also prevents the growth of algae, eliminating bad tastes and smells, and removes discolouration caused by organic compounds.
b) Chlorine gas is very harmful if it's breathed in — it irritates the respiratory system. Liquid chlorine on the skin or eyes causes severe chemical burns. Accidents involving chlorine could be really serious, or fatal. Water contains a variety of organic compounds, e.g. from the decomposition of plants. Chlorine reacts with these compounds to form chlorinated hydrocarbons, e.g. chloromethane (CH_3Cl) — and many of these chlorinated hydrocarbons are carcinogenic (cancer-causing).

Q5 a) Ozone is a strong oxidising agent, so it is very good at killing microorganisms.
b) It's expensive to produce, and its half-life is short so treatment isn't permanent.
c) ultraviolet light

10. Tests for Ions

Page 149 — Application Questions

Q1 sulfate ions

Q2 a) His test could have produced false positives. If there were any carbonate ions or sulfite ions present then they would react with the barium nitrate solution to form a white precipitate. He didn't add a dilute strong acid first to remove any of these ions, so they could be present and interfere with the test.
b) He should add a dilute strong acid such as HCl or HNO_3 to the unknown solution to get rid of any unwanted carbonate or sulfite ions before adding the barium nitrate solution.

Page 149 — Fact Recall Questions

Q1 Carbonates, then sulfates, then halides.

Q2 a) E.g. hydrochloric acid / nitric acid
b) E.g. hydrochloric acid / nitric acid
c) nitric acid

Q3 blue

Exam-style Questions — pages 151-153

1 B *(1 mark)*
2 A *(1 mark)*
3 B *(1 mark)*
4 a) (i) Arsenic, p-block *(1 mark)*
    (ii) $1s^2\ 2s^2\ 2p^6\ 3s^2\ 3p^6\ 3d^{10}\ 4s^2\ 4p^3$ *(1 mark)*

b) (i) $2Sr_{(s)} + O_{2(g)} \rightarrow 2SrO_{(s)}$ *(1 mark)*
    $2Ba_{(s)} + O_{2(g)} \rightarrow 2BaO_{(s)}$ *(1 mark)*
  (ii) Strontium and barium are in the same group of the periodic table so have similar electron configurations/have the same number of electrons in their outer shell *(1 mark)*. This means they have similar chemical properties so they react with oxygen in similar ways *(1 mark)*.
  (iii) Barium will react more vigorously with oxygen than strontium will *(1 mark)*. This is because barium has a lower ionisation energy *(1 mark)*.

5 a) (i) $Ca_{(s)} + 2H_2O_{(l)} \rightarrow Ca(OH)_{2\ (aq)} + H_{2\ (g)}$ *(1 mark)*.
  (ii) A calcium atom has the electron configuration $1s^2\ 2s^2\ 2p^6\ 3s^2\ 3p^6\ 4s^2$.
The calcium ion in calcium hydroxide has the electron configuration $1s^2\ 2s^2\ 2p^6\ 3s^2\ 3p^6$ *(1 mark — both electron configurations must be correct)*.
  (iii) The calcium would disappear/dissolve *(1 mark)* and the solution would fizz/bubbles would be produced *(1 mark)*.

Make sure you describe what you actually see here. If you just say hydrogen gas is given off you won't get the mark because you can't actually see the hydrogen gas. What you can see is the bubbles that are produced.

  (iv) pH 12-13 *(1 mark)*.
b) (i) E.g Calcium hydroxide is used in agriculture to neutralise acidic soils *(1 mark)*.
  (ii) $H^+_{(aq)} + OH^-_{(aq)} \rightarrow H_2O_{(l)}$ *(1 mark)*

6 a) (i) $Cl_{2(aq)} + 2Br^-_{(aq)} \rightarrow 2Cl^-_{(aq)} + Br_{2(aq)}$ *(1 mark)*
  (ii) Potassium bromide solution would give an orange/red colour *(1 mark)*, whereas potassium iodide solution would give a violet/pink colour *(1 mark)*.
b) (i) Add dilute nitric acid to the unknown solution, followed by silver nitrate *(1 mark)*. A cream precipitate of AgBr will form if Br^- ions are present *(1 mark)*.
  (ii) $Ag^+_{(aq)} + Br^-_{(aq)} \rightarrow AgBr_{(s)}$ *(1 mark)*

You know the AgBr has to be a solid because this is the precipitate that forms.

  (iii) He could add ammonia solution and look at the solubility of the precipitate *(1 mark)*. AgBr will dissolve in concentrated ammonia solution but not dilute ammonia solution *(1 mark)*.

7 a) (i) diamond, graphite, graphene *(1 mark)*
  (ii) diamond *(1 mark)*
  (iii) Silicon has a giant covalent lattice structure *(1 mark)*. Each silicon atom is covalently bonded to 4 other silicon atoms *(1 mark)*.
b) (i) Carbon has one less proton in its nucleus than nitrogen does, so it has a lower nuclear charge *(1 mark)* and the attraction of the outer electrons to the nucleus is weaker *(1 mark)*. This makes it less difficult to remove an electron so the ionisation energy of carbon is lower *(1 mark)*.
  (ii) **5-6 marks:**
The answer correctly describes how the melting points of Period 2 elements change across the period and gives a full explanation for the changes, in terms of the structure and the bonding of the ions/atoms of each element. Giant metallic, giant covalent and simple molecular structures, the bonding within these structures and the strength of the forces that need to be overcome to melt the element are all explained. The answer has a clear and logical structure. The information given is relevant and detailed.

3-4 marks:
The answer correctly describes how the melting points of Period 2 elements change across the period and gives some explanation for the changes, in terms of the structure and the bonding of the ions/atoms of each element. Some aspects of the structure of giant metallic, giant covalent and simple molecular substances, the bonding within these structures and the strength of the forces that need to be overcome to melt the element are explained but the explanation may be incomplete.

The answer has some structure. Most of the information given is relevant and there is some detail involved.

1-2 marks:
The answer describes some of the changes in the melting points of Period 2 elements across the period. Little or no explanation is given for the changes. The answer has no clear structure. The information given is basic and lacking in detail. It may not all be relevant.

0 marks:
No relevant information is given.

Here are some points your answer may include:
The melting points increase from lithium to carbon. The melting point decreases rapidly to nitrogen, oxygen, fluorine and neon (these have the lowest melting points of Period 2). The melting point increases from lithium to beryllium due to the increasing metallic bond strength from the increasing charge of the metal ions, the increasing number of delocalised electrons per ion and the decreasing ionic radius. These factors increase the strength of the metallic bonds in the giant metallic lattice. Boron and carbon have giant covalent lattice structures, so all of their atoms are bonded together by strong covalent bonds. A lot of energy is needed to break these bonds. Nitrogen, oxygen and fluorine have simple molecular structures. Only weak induced dipole-dipole forces between the molecules need to be overcome in order to melt the substance so they have low melting points.

Section 2 — Physical Chemistry

1. Enthalpy Changes

Page 155 — Fact Recall Questions

Q1 ΔH°

Q2   Standard enthalpy change of reaction, $\Delta_r H^\circ$, is the enthalpy change when a reaction occurs in the molar quantities shown in the chemical equation, under standard conditions with all reactants and products in their standard states.

Q3   Exothermic reactions give out energy, and endothermic reactions absorb energy. For exothermic reactions, the enthalpy change (ΔH) is negative. For endothermic reactions it is positive.

Q4   a)

b)   (See part a) for arrow.) The activation energy, E_a, is the minimum amount of energy needed to break reactant bonds and start a chemical reaction.

2. Bond Enthalpies

Page 158 — Application Questions

Q1   a)   Bonds broken = $(1 \times C=C) + (1 \times H-H)$
So total energy absorbed = 612 + 436
= 1048 kJ mol^{-1}.
Bonds formed = $(2 \times C-H) + (1 \times C-C)$
So total energy released = $(2 \times 413) + 347$
= 1173 kJ mol^{-1}.
Enthalpy change of reaction
= total energy absorbed – total energy released
= 1048 – 1173 = **–125 kJ mol^{-1}**.

You can ignore any bonds that don't change when you're calculating the enthalpy change of a reaction.

b)   Bonds broken = $(1 \times C-O) + (1 \times H-Cl)$
So total energy absorbed = 358 + 432
= 790 kJ mol^{-1}.
Bonds formed = $(1 \times C-Cl) + (1 \times O-H)$
So total energy released = 346 + 460
= 806 kJ mol^{-1}.
Enthalpy change of reaction
= total energy absorbed – total energy released
= 790 – 806 = **–16 kJ mol^{-1}**.

c)   Bonds broken =
$(2 \times C-C) + (8 \times C-H) + (5 \times O=O)$
So total energy absorbed =
$(2 \times 347) + (8 \times 413) + (5 \times 498) = 6488$ kJ mol^{-1}.
Bonds formed = $(6 \times C=O) + (8 \times O-H)$
So total energy released = $(6 \times 805) + (8 \times 460)$
= 8510 kJ mol^{-1}.
Enthalpy change of reaction/combustion
= total energy absorbed – total energy released
= 6488 – 8510 = **–2022 kJ mol^{-1}**.

It really helps if you draw out a sketch for this question.

d)   Bonds broken = $(1 \times C-Cl) + (1 \times N-H)$
So total energy absorbed = 346 + 391
= 737 kJ mol^{-1}.
Bonds formed = $(1 \times C-N) + (1 \times H-Cl)$
So total energy released = 286 + 432
= 718 kJ mol^{-1}.
Enthalpy change of reaction
= total energy absorbed – total energy released
= 737 – 718 = **+19 kJ mol^{-1}**.

Q2   The balanced equation for the combustion of ethene is:
$C_2H_4 + 3O_2 \rightarrow 2CO_2 + 2H_2O$.
Bonds broken =
$(1 \times C=C) + (4 \times C-H) + (3 \times O=O)$
So total energy absorbed =
$(1 \times 612) + (4 \times 413) + (3 \times 498) = 3758$ kJ mol^{-1}.
Bonds formed = $(4 \times C=O) + (4 \times O-H)$
So total energy released = $(4 \times 805) + (4 \times 460)$
= 5060 kJ mol^{-1}.
Enthalpy change of combustion
= total energy absorbed – total energy released
= 3758 – 5060 = **–1302 kJ mol^{-1}**.

Q3   The balanced equation for the formation of HCl is:
$H_2 + Cl_2 \rightarrow 2HCl$.
Bonds broken = $(1 \times H-H) + (1 \times Cl-Cl)$
So total energy absorbed = 436 + 243
= 679 kJ mol^{-1}.
Bonds formed = $2 \times H-Cl$
So total energy released = $2 \times 432 = 864$ kJ mol^{-1}.

Enthalpy change of reaction
= total energy absorbed – total energy released
= 679 – 864 = **–185 kJ mol⁻¹**.

Q4 Call the unknown bond enthalpy between N and O 'X'.
Bonds broken = $2 \times X$
So total energy absorbed = $2X$ kJ mol⁻¹.
Bonds formed = $(1 \times N\equiv N) + (1 \times O=O)$
So total energy released = 945 + 498
= 1443 kJ mol⁻¹.
Enthalpy change of reaction = –181 kJ mol⁻¹
= total energy absorbed – total energy released.
So: –181 = $2X$ – 1443
$2X$ = –181 + 1443 = 1262
X = 1262 ÷ 2 = **+631 kJ m⁻¹**

Page 158 — Fact Recall Questions
Q1 endothermic
Q2 The energy required to make bonds.
Q3 Average bond enthalpy is the energy needed to break one mole of bonds in the gas phase, averaged over many different compounds.
Q4 Enthalpy change of reaction =
Total energy absorbed – Total energy released

3. Measuring Enthalpy Changes
Page 161 — Application Questions
Q1 $q = mc\Delta T = 220 \times 4.18 \times (301 - 298) = 2758.8$ J
= 2.7588 kJ
$\Delta H = \dfrac{q}{n} = -\dfrac{2.7588 \text{ kJ}}{0.0500 \text{ mol}} = $ **–55.2 kJ mol⁻¹** (to 3 s.f.).

Don't forget — the enthalpy change must be negative because it's an exothermic reaction (you can tell because the temperature increased).

Q2 a) $q = mc\Delta T = 200 \times 4.18 \times 29.0 = 24\ 244$ J
= 24.244 kJ
$n = \dfrac{\text{mass}}{M} = \dfrac{0.500 \text{ g}}{72 \text{ g mol}^{-1}} = 0.00694$ moles of fuel

$\Delta H = \dfrac{q}{n} = -\dfrac{24.244 \text{ kJ}}{0.00694 \text{ mol}} = $ **–3490 kJ mol⁻¹** (to 3 s.f.).

b) E.g. some heat from the combustion will be transferred to the surroundings and not the water. / The combustion may not be complete combustion. / The combustion may not have taken place under standard conditions. / There could be inaccuracies due to the measuring equipment.

Q3 $q = mc\Delta T = 300 \times 4.18 \times 55.0 = 68\ 970$ J = 68.97 kJ

$\Delta_c H^\circ$ octane = –5512 kJ mol⁻¹ = $\dfrac{q}{n}$

$n = \dfrac{q}{\Delta H} = \dfrac{68.97 \text{ kJ}}{5512 \text{ kJ mol}^{-1}} = 0.0125...$ mol.

$n = \dfrac{\text{mass}}{M}$, so mass = $n \times M = 0.0125... \times 114$

= **1.43 g** of octane (to 3 s.f.).

Page 161 — Fact Recall Questions
Q1 The mass of reactant, the volume of the solution, and the initial and final temperature.

Q2 E.g.

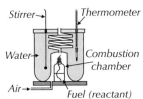

Q3 q is the heat lost or gained during a reaction. It's measured in joules (J).
Q4 The reaction needs to be performed at a constant pressure of 100 kPa, with all reactants and products in their standard states.
Q5 Find the number of moles of that reactant that reacts in the balanced chemical equation, then calculate $\Delta_r H^\circ$ using:

$\Delta_r H^\circ = \dfrac{q}{n} \times$ number of moles reacting in balanced chemical equation

4. Hess's Law
Page 164 — Application Questions
Q1 $\Delta_f H^\circ_{\text{(reactants)}} = \Delta_f H^\circ_{[\text{Mg}]} + (2 \times \Delta_f H^\circ_{[\text{H}_2\text{O}]})$
$\Delta_f H^\circ_{\text{(reactants)}} = 0 + (2 \times -286) = -572$ kJ mol⁻¹.
$\Delta_f H^\circ_{\text{(products)}} = \Delta_f H^\circ_{[\text{Mg(OH)}_2]} + \Delta_f H^\circ_{[\text{H}_2]}$
$\Delta_f H^\circ_{\text{(products)}} = -925 + 0 = -925$ kJ mol⁻¹.
Using Hess's Law: Route 1 = Route 2, so:
$\Delta_f H^\circ_{\text{(reactants)}} + \Delta_r H^\circ = \Delta_f H^\circ_{\text{(products)}}$
$-572 + \Delta_r H^\circ = -925$
$\Delta_r H^\circ = -925 + 572 = $ **–353 kJ mol⁻¹**.

Q2 a) First draw out a reaction scheme with an alternative reaction route that includes balanced equations for the formation of each compound:

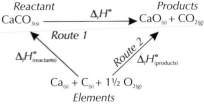

$\Delta_f H^\circ_{\text{(reactants)}} = \Delta_f H^\circ_{[\text{CaCO}_3]} = -1207$ kJ mol⁻¹.
$\Delta_f H^\circ_{\text{(products)}} = \Delta_f H^\circ_{[\text{CaO}]} + \Delta_f H^\circ_{[\text{CO}_2]}$
$\Delta_f H^\circ_{\text{(products)}} = -635 + -394 = -1029$ kJ mol⁻¹.

Using Hess's Law: Route 1 = Route 2, so:
$\Delta_f H^\circ_{\text{(reactants)}} + \Delta_r H^\circ = \Delta_f H^\circ_{\text{(products)}}$
$-1207 + \Delta_r H^\circ = -1029$
$\Delta_r H^\circ = -1029 + 1207 = $ **+178 kJ mol⁻¹**.

b)

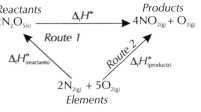

$\Delta_f H^\circ_{\text{(reactants)}} = 2 \times \Delta_f H^\circ_{[\text{N}_2\text{O}_5]}$
$\Delta_f H^\circ_{\text{(reactants)}} = 2 \times -41 = -82$ kJ mol⁻¹.
$\Delta_f H^\circ_{\text{(products)}} = (4 \times \Delta_f H^\circ_{[\text{NO}_2]}) + \Delta_f H^\circ_{[\text{O}_2]}$
$\Delta_f H^\circ_{\text{(products)}} = (4 \times 33) + 0 = 132$ kJ mol⁻¹.
Remember that the enthalpy change of formation of O_2 is zero because it's an element.

Using Hess's Law: Route 1 = Route 2, so:
$\Delta_f H^\circ_{\text{(reactants)}} + \Delta_r H^\circ = \Delta_f H^\circ_{\text{(products)}}$
$-82 + \Delta_r H^\circ = 132$
$\Delta_r H^\circ = 132 + 82 = \textbf{+214 kJ mol}^{-1}$.

Page 166 — Application Questions

Q1 a) First draw out balanced reactions for the formation of the compound, and the combustion of the reactants and product:

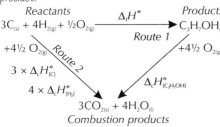

Using Hess's Law: Route 1 = Route 2, so:
$\Delta_f H^\circ + \Delta_c H^\circ_{[C_3H_7OH]} = (3 \times \Delta_c H^\circ_{[C]}) + (4 \times \Delta_c H^\circ_{[H_2]})$
$\Delta_f H^\circ + (-2021) = (3 \times -394) + (4 \times -286)$
$\Delta_f H^\circ = -1182 - 1144 + 2021 = \textbf{-305 kJ mol}^{-1}$.

b)

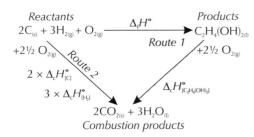

Using Hess's Law: Route 1 = Route 2, so:
$\Delta_f H^\circ + \Delta_c H^\circ_{[C_2H_4(OH)_2]} = (2 \times \Delta_c H^\circ_{[C]}) + (3 \times \Delta_c H^\circ_{[H_2]})$
$\Delta_f H^\circ + (-1180) = (2 \times -394) + (3 \times -286)$
$\Delta_f H^\circ = -788 - 858 + 1180 = \textbf{-466 kJ mol}^{-1}$.

c)

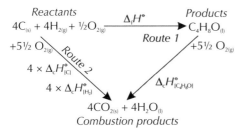

Using Hess's Law: Route 1 = Route 2, so:
$\Delta_f H^\circ + \Delta_c H^\circ_{[C_4H_8O]} = (4 \times \Delta_c H^\circ_{[C]}) + (4 \times \Delta_c H^\circ_{[H_2]})$
$\Delta_f H^\circ + (-2442) = (4 \times -394) + (4 \times -286)$
$\Delta_f H^\circ = -1576 - 1144 + 2442 = \textbf{-278 kJ mol}^{-1}$.

Q2 First label the reaction scheme with the known enthalpy changes, and the chosen routes:

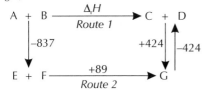

Using Hess's Law: Route 1 = Route 2, so:
$\Delta_r H = -837 + 89 + (-424) = \textbf{-1172 kJ mol}^{-1}$.

5. Reaction Rates
Page 169 — Application Questions
Q1

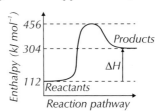

The reaction is endothermic (ΔH is positive) because the products have a higher enthalpy than the reactants.

Q2 B is the curve for the gas at a higher temperature because it is shifted over to the right, showing that more molecules have more energy.

Page 169 — Fact Recall Questions
Q1 The particles must collide in the right direction (facing each other the right way) and with at least a certain minimum amount of kinetic energy.

Q2 The minimum amount of kinetic energy that particles need to have in order to react when they collide.

Q3 A small increase in temperature gives all molecules more energy, so a greater number of them have at least the minimum amount of energy to react when they collide. They will also collide more often because they will be moving about faster.

Q4 If you increase the concentration of reactants in a solution, the particles will be closer together in a given volume and so collide more often, increasing the reaction rate.

6. Catalysts
Page 172 — Application Question
Q1 a) E.g.

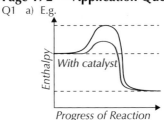

You can draw the line anywhere as long as the peak is lower than it was before and the shape of the graph stays the same.

b) Adding a catalyst would lower the activation energy for the reaction so that it would not need such a high temperature in order to take place. Being able to carry out the reaction at a lower temperature would save energy and money.

Page 172 — Fact Recall Questions
Q1 A substance that increases the rate of a reaction by providing an alternative reaction pathway with a lower activation energy. The catalyst is chemically unchanged at the end of the reaction.

Q2 Catalysts are used to speed up reactions in industrial processes that would be impossible or too slow to occur at practical temperatures and pressures. Using a catalyst means the temperature and pressure can be reduced, which saves energy and money.

Q3 A catalyst increases the rate of a reaction by providing an alternative reaction pathway with a lower activation energy. This means that more of the molecules collide with energies above the activation energy, and so can react.

Q4 A homogeneous catalyst is in the same physical state as the reactants. A heterogeneous catalyst is in a different physical state from the reactants.

7. Calculating Reaction Rates
Page 175 — Application Question
Q1 a)

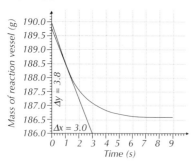

$$\text{gradient} = \frac{\Delta y}{\Delta x} = \frac{186.0 - 189.8}{3.0 - 0} = \frac{-3.8}{3.0} = -1.3$$

rate = 1.3 g s^{-1}

Drawing tangents accurately is tricky so there may be some variation between the answer you got and the 'official' answer. Don't worry though — in the exam, you'll usually be allowed a range of answers if you're asked to calculate a gradient. So for part a) allow yourself anything from 0.9 to 1.7.

b)

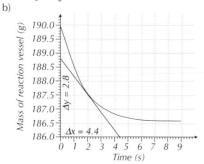

$$\text{gradient} = \frac{\Delta y}{\Delta x} = \frac{186.0 - 188.8}{4.4 - 0} = \frac{-2.8}{4.4} = -0.64$$

rate = 0.64 g s^{-1}

For part b) anything from 0.44 to 0.84 is OK.

c)

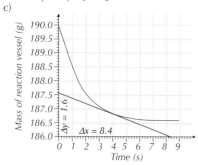

$$\text{gradient} = \frac{\Delta y}{\Delta x} = \frac{186.0 - 187.6}{8.4 - 0} = \frac{-1.6}{8.4} = -0.19$$

rate = 0.19 g s^{-1}

For part c) anything from 0.13 to 0.25 will do.

Q1 A reaction rate is the change in the amount of reactants or products per unit time.
Q2 E.g. g s^{-1} / cm^3 s^{-1}
Q3 E.g. by measuring the volume of gas produced / by measuring the change in mass.
Q4 a) Measure the mass of a reaction vessel at regular time points as a reaction progresses.
       Plot mass against time to produce a mass-time graph.
    b) Measure the gradient of the graph at that particular time. The gradient is the rate of reaction.

8. Reversible Reactions
Page 180 — Application Questions
Q1 a) Increasing the concentration of A will shift the equilibrium to the right (favouring the forwards reaction) in order to get rid of the excess A.
    b) There are 3 moles of gas on the left and only 2 moles of gas on the right. Increasing the pressure will shift the equilibrium to the right (favouring the forwards reaction) in order to reduce the number of moles of gas to reduce the pressure again.
    c) The forwards reaction is exothermic, so the backwards reaction must be endothermic. Increasing the temperature will shift the equilibrium to the left (favouring the endothermic backwards reaction) in order to remove the extra heat energy.
    d) The reaction should ideally be performed with a high concentration of A and B, at a high pressure and low temperature.
Q2 There are the same number of moles of gas on either side of the reaction. Increasing the pressure favours the reaction producing the fewest moles of gas, but since both reactions are equal in this respect, increasing the pressure will not shift the position of equilibrium.

Page 180 — Fact Recall Questions
Q1 The concentrations of reactants and products are constant, and the forwards reaction and the backwards reaction are going at the same rate.
Q2 If there's a change in concentration, pressure or temperature, the equilibrium will move to help counteract the change.
Q3 The addition of a catalyst has no effect on the position of equilibrium in a reversible reaction.
Q4 A low temperature would reduce the rate of reaction. This means that although you'd get a high yield it would take so long that it wouldn't be worth it.

9. The Equilibrium Constant
Page 182 — Application Questions

Q1 a) $K_c = \dfrac{[C_2H_5OH]}{[C_2H_4][H_2O]}$

Q2 a) $K_c = \dfrac{[SO_3]^2}{[SO_2]^2[O_2]}$

    b) $K_c = \dfrac{[SO_3]^2}{[SO_2]^5[O_2]} = \dfrac{0.360^2}{(0.250)^2(0.180)} = 11.5$

       $K_c = \dfrac{(\text{mol dm}^{-3})^2}{(\text{mol dm}^{-3})^2(\text{mol dm}^{-3})} = \dfrac{1}{(\text{mol dm}^{-3})}$

       $K_c = $ **11.5 mol^{-1} dm^3**

Page 182 — Fact Recall Questions

Q1 $K_c = \dfrac{[D]^d\,[E]^e}{[A]^a\,[B]^b}$

Q2 K_c changes with temperature. So a given value of K_c is only true at the temperature it was measured at.

Q3 As the temperature increases, the value of K_c increases, so the equilibrium must have shifted to the right.

Exam-style Questions — pages 185-189

1 a) B *(1 mark)*.
     Since the y-axis is 'number of molecules', the maximum of the distribution corresponds to the most likely energy of the molecules in the distribution.

   b) C *(1 mark)*.
     At higher temperatures, Boltzmann distributions are pushed over to the right, but keep the same area under the distribution.

2 A *(1 mark)*.
   The independent variable is the variable which you deliberately change during the experiment.

3 a) In a reversible reaction, dynamic equilibrium is reached when the concentrations of reactants and products are constant *(1 mark)*, and the forwards reaction and the backwards reaction are going at the same rate *(1 mark)*.

   b) The higher the pressure, the faster the reaction rate *(1 mark)*. A high pressure also favours the forwards reaction, which produces fewer moles of gas, so the higher the pressure, the greater the yield of ethanol *(1 mark)*. However, high pressures are very expensive / can produce side reactions / require strong and expensive equipment, so the pressure used is limited by these factors *(1 mark)*.

   c) Reducing the amount of H_2O will shift the position of equilibrium to the left *(1 mark)* in order to increase the amount of H_2O present *(1 mark)*. This shift will reduce the maximum yield of ethanol from the forwards reaction *(1 mark)*.

   d) $K_c = \dfrac{[C_2H_5OH]}{[C_2H_4]\,[H_2O]} = \dfrac{2.70}{0.400 \times 0.400}$
     $= 16.9 \text{ mol}^{-1} \text{ dm}^3$
     (2 marks for correct answer, otherwise 1 mark for correct equilibrium constant equation.)

4 a) (i) The minimum amount of kinetic energy *(1 mark)* that particles need to have in order to react when they collide *(1 mark)*.

      (ii)
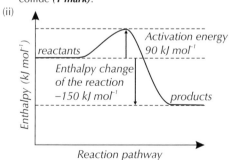

     (1 mark for correctly labelled axes, 1 mark for products lower than reactants, 1 mark for correctly labelled activation energy, 1 mark for correctly labelled enthalpy change of reaction.)

   b) Heating the reactants gives the molecules more energy *(1 mark)*. This means that more molecules will have an energy higher than the activation energy *(1 mark)*, so more collisions between molecules will result in

reaction, increasing the reaction rate *(1 mark)*.

   c) Lowering the pressure will reduce the rate of reaction *(1 mark)*. This is because there will be fewer gas molecules in a given volume/the concentration will be reduced/the molecules will be further apart *(1 mark)*, so there will be fewer collisions between molecules that result in reaction *(1 mark)*.

   d) (i) A catalyst is a substance that increases the rate of a reaction without being changed or used up by the reaction *(1 mark)*.

      (ii)
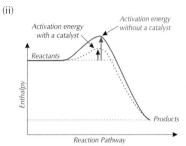

     (1 mark for diagram with correctly labelled activation energy)

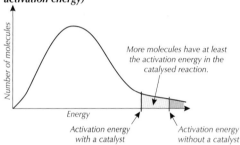

     (1 mark for diagram with correctly labelled axes)
     A catalyst increases the rate of a reaction by providing an alternative reaction pathway *(1 mark)* with a lower activation energy *(1 mark)*. With a catalyst present, the molecules still have the same amount of energy *(1 mark)*, so the Boltzmann distribution curve is unchanged. But because the catalyst lowers the activation energy, more of the molecules have energies above this threshold and are able to react *(1 mark)*.

5 a) $C_8H_{18(l)} + 12\tfrac{1}{2}O_{2(g)} \rightarrow 8CO_{2(g)} + 9H_2O_{(l)}$ *(1 mark)*

   b) (i)
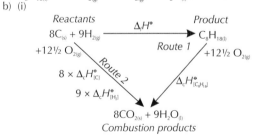

     Using Hess's Law: Route 1 = Route 2, so:
     $\Delta_f H^\circ + \Delta_c H^\circ_{[C_8H_{18}]} = (8 \times \Delta_c H^\circ_{[C]}) + (9 \times \Delta_c H^\circ_{[H_2]})$
     $\Delta_f H^\circ + (-5470) = (8 \times -394) + (9 \times -286)$
     $\Delta_f H^\circ = -3152 - 2574 + 5470 = \mathbf{-256 \text{ kJ mol}^{-1}}$.
     (3 marks for correct answer, otherwise 1 mark for correct equation using Hess's Law and 1 mark for correct molar quantities. Allow 1 mark only for an answer of +256 kJ mol^{-1}.)

      (ii) Exothermic *(1 mark)*. The enthalpy change for the formation of octane is negative *(1 mark)*.

c) (i) $q = mc\Delta T = 325 \times 4.18 \times 13.0 = 17\,660.5$ J
    $= 17.6605$ kJ

$n = \dfrac{\text{mass}}{M} = \dfrac{0.4503 \text{ g}}{114 \text{ g mol}^{-1}} = 0.00395$ moles of fuel

$\Delta H = \dfrac{q}{n} = -\dfrac{17.6605 \text{ kJ}}{0.00395 \text{ mol}} = -4470$ kJ mol^{-1} (3 s.f.).

(2 marks for correct answer, otherwise 1 mark for correct value of heat gained (q).)

(ii) Any two from e.g. some heat from the combustion will be transferred to the surroundings and not the water. / The combustion may not be complete combustion. / The combustion may not have taken place under standard conditions. / There could be inaccuracies due to the measuring equipment.
(1 mark each up to a maximum of 2 marks).

6 a) (i) Standard enthalpy of combustion, $\Delta_c H^{\circ}$, is the enthalpy change when 1 mole of a substance **(1 mark)** is completely burned in oxygen **(1 mark)** under standard conditions with all reactants and products in their standard states **(1 mark)**.

(ii) The balanced equation for the combustion of but-1-ene is: $C_4H_8 + 6O_2 \rightarrow 4CO_2 + 4H_2O$.
Bonds broken =
$(1 \times C=C) + (2 \times C–C) + (8 \times C–H) + (6 \times O=O)$
So total energy absorbed =
$(1 \times 612) + (2 \times 347) + (8 \times 413) + (6 \times 498)$
$= 7598$ kJ mol^{-1}.
Bonds formed = $(8 \times C=O) + (8 \times O–H)$
So total energy released = $(8 \times 805) + (8 \times 460)$
$= 10\,120$ kJ mol^{-1}.
Enthalpy change of combustion
= total energy absorbed – total energy released
$= 7598 – 10\,120 = \mathbf{-2522}$ **kJ mol**$^{-1}$.
(3 marks for correct answer, otherwise 1 mark for 'total energy absorbed – total energy released', and 1 mark for correct value for either energy released or energy absorbed. Allow 1 mark only for an answer of +2522 kJ mol^{-1}).

(iii) Some of the average bond enthalpies are average values for the bonds in many different compounds, so they are not accurate for the specific molecules involved in this combustion **(1 mark)**.

b) (i) $q = mc\Delta T = 200 \times 4.18 \times 32.8 = 27400$ J
    $= \mathbf{27.4}$ **kJ** (to 3 s.f.)
(2 marks for correct answer, otherwise 1 mark for correct working.)

(ii) $\Delta_c H^{\circ} = q \div n = 27.4 \div 0.0215$
    $= \mathbf{-1270}$ **kJ mol**$^{-1}$ (to 3 s.f.)
(1 marks for correct answer, 1 mark for minus sign)

(iii) When the reaction happens, reactant bonds are broken and product bonds are formed **(1 mark)**. The total energy needed to break the alkene bonds is less than the energy released when the product bonds are formed **(1 mark)** so the reaction is exothermic.

7 a) A gas syringe should be used to collect the hydrogen gas escaping from the reaction vessel **(1 mark)**. A stop clock or timer should be used to time the reaction so that measurements of gas volume can be taken at certain time intervals **(1 mark)**.

b)

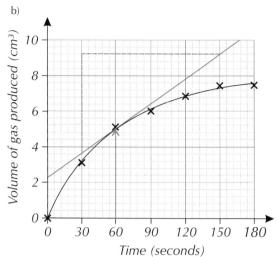

(1 mark for a correctly drawn tangent.)
Rate of reaction = gradient of tangent at 1 minute.
gradient = change in y ÷ change in x
e.g. $= (9.2 – 3.6) \div (150 – 30)$
      $= \mathbf{0.047}$ **cm**^{3} **s**$^{-1}$ (to 2 s.f.)
(1 mark for correct answer ±0.01 cm^3 s^{-1}.)
Different people will draw slightly different tangents and pick different spots on the tangent so there's a margin of error in this answer. 0.047 (± 0.01) cm^3 s^{-1} means any answer between 0.037 cm^3 s^{-1} and 0.057 cm^3 s^{-1} is worth the mark.

Module 4

Section 1 — Basic Concepts and Hydrocarbons

2. Formulas
Pages 193-194 — Application Questions
Q1

H Br H
| | |
H–C–C–C–H
| | |
H H H

It doesn't matter if you draw the bromine atom above or below the carbon atom — it means the same thing.
Q2 C_8H_{18}
Q3 a) CH_2
   b) C_4H_7Br
   c) $C_9H_{17}Cl_3$
Q4 a) C_4H_8
   b) Heptene contains 14 H atoms.
Q5 a) $C_3H_6Br_2$
   b) E.g.

H Br H
| | |
H–C–C–C–H
| | |
H H Br

   c) $C_3H_6Br_2$
For this molecule the empirical formula is the same as the molecular formula because you can't cancel the atoms down and still have whole numbers.
Q6 a) C_5H_{10}
   b) $CH_3CH_2CH_2CHCH_2$
   c) CH_2

Q7 a)

Skeletal formulas have a carbon atom at each end and at each junction.

b)

OH

c)

d)

Cl

Q8 a) $CH_3CH(CH_3)CH(CH_3)CH_2CH_2CH_3$
 b) $CH_3CH_2C(CH_3)CH_2CH_2CH_3$
 c) $CH_3CH_2CClCHCH_2CH_3$
 d) $CH_3CHBrCH(OH)CH_2CHCH_2$

Page 194 — Fact Recall Questions

Q1 A general formula is used to represent a homologous series.
Q2 A homologous series is a family of organic compounds which have the same general formula and similar chemical properties.
Q3 A displayed formula shows how all the atoms are arranged, and all the bonds between them.
Q4 The carbon and hydrogen atoms of the main carbon chain aren't shown.

3. Carbon Skeletons

Page 195 — Application Questions

Q1 C_3H_7
Q2 unsaturated

4. Structural Isomers

Page 198 — Application Questions

Q1 E.g.

You could draw the chlorine atom attached to any other carbon atom apart from the one it was on originally.

Q2 There are three chain isomers of C_5H_{12}.

E.g.

Q3

Q4 a) A and B
 b) chain isomerism

Page 198 — Fact Recall Questions

Q1 Isomers are molecules with the same molecular formula but a different arrangement of atoms.
Q2 Structural isomers have the same molecular formula but different structural formulas.

5. Alkanes and Nomenclature

Page 202 — Application Questions

Q1 a) butane
 b) ethane
 c) methane
 d) nonane
 e) heptane
 f) decane
Q2 a) 3-methylpentane
 b) 3-ethyl-3-methylpentane
 c) 3,3-diethylhexane
 d) 3,3-diethyl-2-methylhexane

Page 202 — Fact Recall Questions

Q1 An alkane is a saturated hydrocarbon containing only C–C and C–H bonds.
Q2 C_nH_{2n+2}
Q3 hex-
Q4 ethyl-
Q5 di-

6. Properties of Alkanes

Page 207 — Application Questions

Q1 a) Octane molecules are larger than propane molecules, so there is more surface contact between the octane molecules than the propane molecules. As a result the induced dipole-dipole interactions between octane molecules are stronger than those between propane molecules. So more energy is required to break the forces and the boiling point is higher.

In questions like this, make sure you give your answer as a comparison. If you just say octane molecules are big so it has a high boiling point you won't get the marks. You have to say that octane molecules are bigger than propane molecules so octane has a higher boiling point than propane.

 b) Complete combustion:
 $2C_8H_{18} + 25O_2 \rightarrow 16CO_2 + 18H_2O$ /
 $C_8H_{18} + 12\frac{1}{2}O_2 \rightarrow 8CO_2 + 9H_2O$
 Incomplete combustion:
 $2C_8H_{18} + 17O_2 \rightarrow 16CO + 18H_2O$ /
 $C_8H_{18} + 8\frac{1}{2}O_2 \rightarrow 8CO + 9H_2O$
Q2 2,2-dimethylpropane is branched, so the molecules don't pack together closely and there is less surface contact between molecules than in pentane, which is a straight-chain molecule. As a result there are more induced dipole-dipole interactions between molecules of pentane than between 2,2-dimethylpropane molecules and so more energy is required to break them. So pentane has the higher boiling point.

Q3 First write out the combustion equation using the values provided: $20X + 130O_2 \rightarrow 80CO_2 + ?H_2O$
Divide through by 20 so that there is only one mole of X on the left-hand side of the equation:
$X + 6\frac{1}{2}O_2 \rightarrow 4CO_2 + nH_2O$
It's OK to have ½ values in your reaction equation.
6½ moles of oxygen react to form 4 moles of carbon dioxide and n moles of water. So any oxygen atoms that don't end up in CO_2 must be in H_2O.
This means that $n = (6\frac{1}{2} \times 2) - (4 \times 2) = 5$
So the reaction equation is $X + 6\frac{1}{2}O_2 \rightarrow 4CO_2 + 5H_2O$.
All the carbon atoms from X end up in carbon dioxide, and all the hydrogen atoms from X end up in water, so the number of carbon atoms in X is 4 and the number of hydrogen atoms in X is 10.
The molecular formula of X is $\mathbf{C_4H_{10}}$.

Page 207 — Fact Recall Questions
Q1 The atoms or groups form tetrahedral shapes around each carbon.
Q2 σ-bonds form when atomic orbitals on neighbouring atoms overlap to form a new orbital directly between the bonded atoms.
Q3 E.g. the length of the carbon–carbon chain and the amount of branching in the molecule.
Q4 The products of complete combustion are carbon dioxide and water. The products of incomplete combustion are carbon monoxide and water (and sometimes particulate carbon and carbon dioxide).
Q5 Carbon monoxide binds to haemoglobin in the blood. This prevents the haemoglobin binding to oxygen. As a result, less oxygen can be transported around the body and symptoms of oxygen deprivation occur.

7. Bond Fission
Page 208 — Fact Recall Questions
Q1 The breaking of a covalent bond.
Q2 a) Heterolytic fission and homolytic fission.
b) In heterolytic fission the bond breaks unevenly, and one of the bonded atoms ends up with both of the bonding electrons. Two different substances are formed — a positively charged cation and a negatively charged anion. In homolytic fission, the bond breaks evenly, with each of the bonded atoms receiving one of the bonding electrons. Two electrically uncharged radicals are formed.
Q3 A radical is a particle with an unpaired electron.
Q4 You use a dot.
Q5 The movement of a pair of electrons.

8. Substitution Reactions
Page 210 — Application Questions
Q1 a) Initiation, propagation and termination.
b) Initiation: $Br_2 \rightarrow 2Br\cdot$
Propagation: $Br\cdot + CH_4 \rightarrow CH_3\cdot + HBr$
$CH_3\cdot + Br_2 \rightarrow CH_3Br + Br\cdot$
Termination: E.g. $CH_3\cdot + Br\cdot \rightarrow CH_3Br$ /
$CH_3\cdot + CH_3\cdot \rightarrow C_2H_6$
c) E.g. CH_2Br_2 / $CHBr_3$ / CBr_4
Q2 a) radical substitution
b) Initiation: UV light provides enough energy to split the Cl–Cl bond (homolytic fission), this produces two radicals.
$Cl_2 \rightarrow 2Cl\cdot$

Propagation: radicals are created and used up in a chain reaction.
E.g. $Cl\cdot + C_2H_6 \rightarrow C_2H_5\cdot + HCl$
E.g. $C_2H_5\cdot + Cl_2 \rightarrow C_2H_5Cl + Cl\cdot$
Termination: the radicals are mopped up — two radicals react together to form a stable molecule.
E.g. $C_2H_5\cdot + Cl\cdot \rightarrow C_2H_5Cl$ / $C_2H_5\cdot + C_2H_5\cdot \rightarrow C_4H_{10}$
c) Make sure the ethane is in excess.

Page 210 — Fact Recall Questions
Q1 $Cl_2 + CH_4 \rightarrow CH_3Cl + HCl$
Q2 homolytic fission
Q3 Some or all of the hydrogen atoms found on halogenoalkane molecules can be swapped for halogen atoms, creating multi-substituted products like CH_2Cl_2, $CHCl_3$ and CCl_4. For alkanes with longer carbon chains than methane, substitution can also happen at any point on a carbon chain, which can lead to a mixture of isomers such as 1-chloropropane and 2-chloropropane.

9. Alkenes and their Properties
Page 214 — Application Questions
Q1 a) propene
b) but-2-ene
c) hexa-1,3-diene / 1,3-hexadiene
d) methylpropene
Q2 Propene is an alkene so it contains a double bond. Because there are two electron pairs in the bond the C=C double bond has a really high electron density. Plus, the π bond sticks out above and below the rest of the molecule. These two factors mean that propene is susceptible to attack by electrophiles. Propane doesn't contain a double bond so isn't susceptible to attack by electrophiles. So propene is more reactive.
Q3 Double bonds are formed from a sigma bond and a pi bond. Single bonds are just sigma bonds. The pi bond is weaker than the sigma bond so the double bond is not twice as strong as a single bond.

Page 214 — Fact Recall Questions
Q1 C_nH_{2n}
Q2 a)

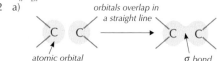

orbitals overlap in a straight line

atomic orbital   σ bond

This is how you need to draw your diagram in the exam (though it doesn't have to be coloured in). Make sure you label the atomic orbitals and the sigma bond and make sure you say how the orbitals are overlapping. Otherwise you might lose out on valuable marks.
b)

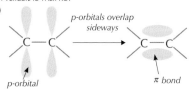

p-orbitals overlap sideways

p-orbital   π bond

Q3 electrophiles
Q4 a) Trigonal planar means that all of the atoms lie in the same plane and are at the corners of an imaginary equilateral triangle with bond angles of 120° between them, like the atoms attached to a double-bonded carbon atom.
b) The atoms attached to each carbon in the C=C double bond of alkenes have a trigonal planar shape.

10. Stereoisomers
Page 217 — Application Questions
Q1 a) (i) *Z*-isomer
        (ii) *E*-isomer
    b) (i) *cis*-isomer
        (ii) *trans*-isomer

Q2

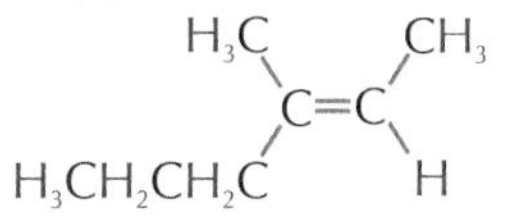

The highest priority group on carbon-2 is -CH$_3$, and on carbon-3 it's -CH$_2$CH$_2$CH$_3$.

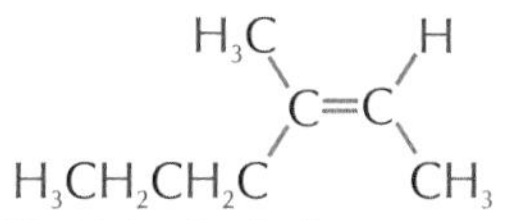

11. Reactions of Alkenes
Page 223 — Application Questions
Q1 pentane
Q2 a) $CH_3CHCH_2 + Br_2 \rightarrow CH_3CHBrCH_2Br$
    b) electrophilic addition

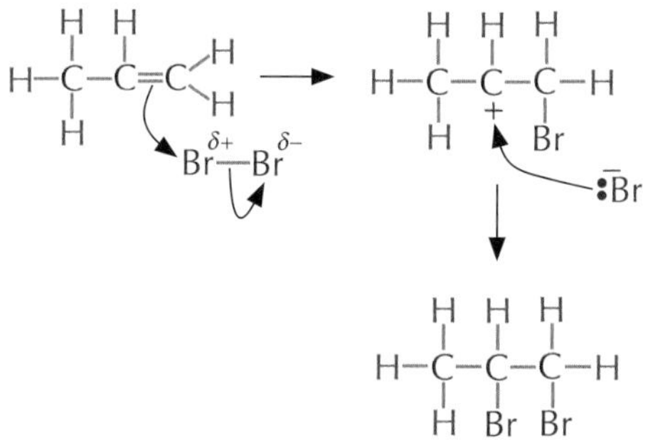

If you're asked to name and outline a mechanism, make sure you do just that. It's really easy to forget the name and dive straight in to the mechanism — but don't forget or you'll lose a valuable mark in the exam.

    c) It doesn't contain a C=C double bond / it is saturated.

Q3

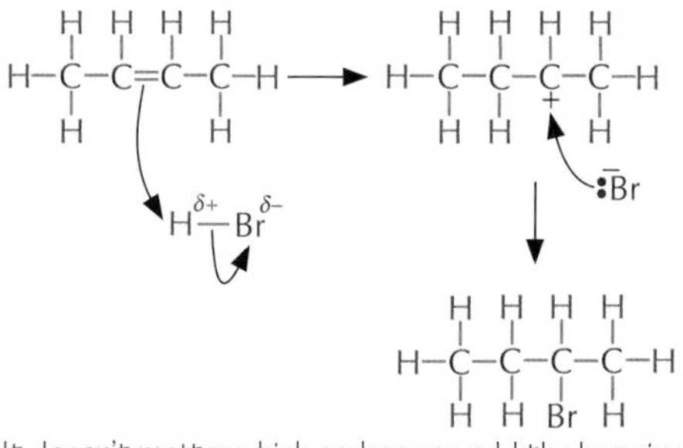

It doesn't matter which carbon you add the bromine to as you'll always end up with the same product (2-bromobutane).

Q4 a)

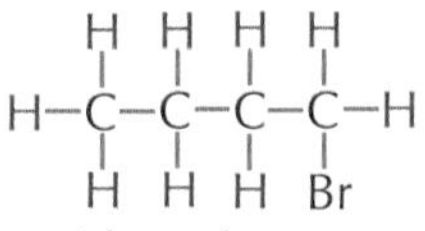

1-bromobutane 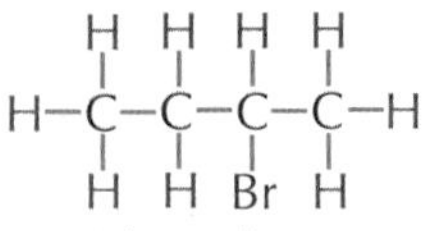   2-bromobutane

    b) The major product is 2-bromobutane. This is because it forms via the formation of a secondary carbocation, which is more stable and so more likely to form than the primary carbocation that is formed in the formation of 1-bromobutane.

Q5 If only one HBr adds onto the molecule you could get any of these products:

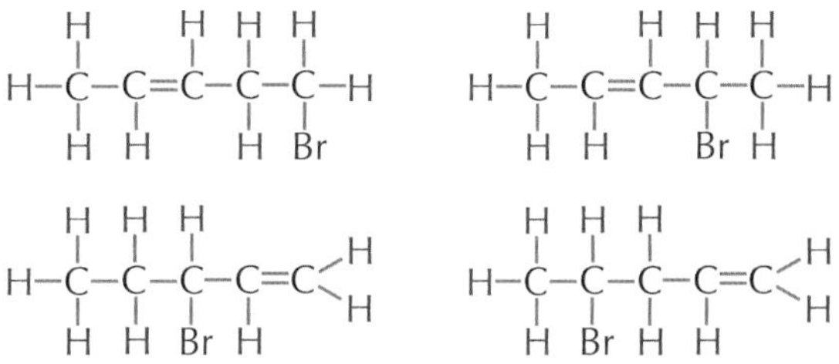

If two HBr add onto the molecule you could get any of these molecules:

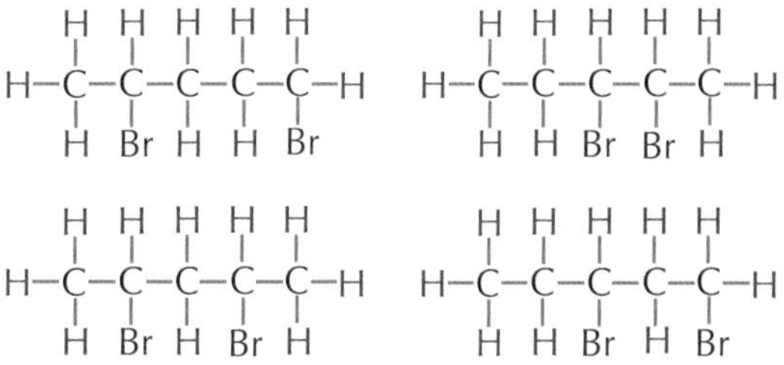

Give yourself a pat on the back if you managed to get all of these molecules.

Page 223 — Fact Recall Questions
Q1 An electrophile is an electron pair acceptor.
Q2 Any two from: e.g. NO_2^+ / H^+ / HBr / Br_2.
Q3 hydrogen bromide
Q4 carbon-carbon double bonds / unsaturation / alkenes
Q5

$$H_2C{=}CH_{2(g)} + H_2O_{(g)} \underset{\substack{300\ ^\circ C \\ 60\ atm}}{\overset{H_3PO_4}{\rightleftharpoons}} CH_3CH_2OH_{(g)}$$

Q6 That the major product from the addition of a hydrogen halide to an unsymmetrical alkene is the one where hydrogen adds to the carbon with the most hydrogens already attached / the one that forms as a result of the formation of the most stable carbocation in the reaction mechanism.

12. Addition Polymers
Page 225 — Application Questions
Q1 a)

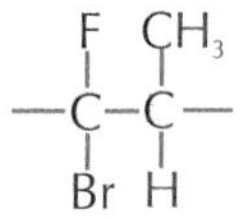

    b) 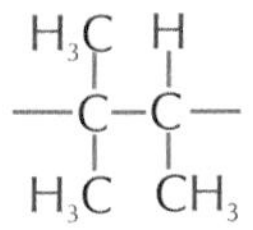   c)

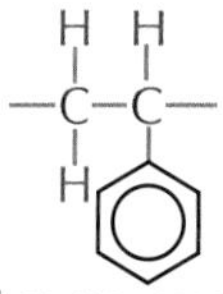

If you're asked to draw more than one repeating unit in the exam, make sure you draw them all linked together. You won't get the marks if you draw them separately.

Q2 a)

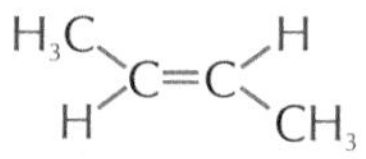

    b)

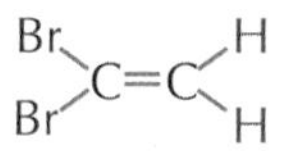

c)

$$H_3C\underset{H_3C}{>}C=C\underset{CH_3}{<}CH_3$$

Page 227 — Fact Recall Questions

Q1 addition polymers

Q2 The double bond of the alkene opens up and the alkenes join together to form a polymer.

Q3 a) It means they won't react when they are being used (e.g. food doesn't react with PTFE coating on pans, plastic windows don't rot etc.).

b) Because they are unreactive, most plastics are non-biodegradable, so disposing of them is a problem.

Q4 E.g. by melting and remoulding / by cracking into monomers which can be used as an organic feedstock to make more plastic or other chemicals.

Q5 a) HCl

b) By passing the waste gases through a scrubber which can neutralise the HCl by allowing it to react with a base.

Q6 E.g. renewable raw materials aren't going to run out like oil will / if the polymer is plant-based the CO_2 released as it decomposes is the same CO_2 absorbed by the plant when it grew, so it is more carbon-neutral than using non-renewable raw materials / over their lifetime some plant-based polymers save energy compared to oil-based plastics.

Q7 E.g. they require specific conditions to decompose so can't just be placed in a landfill — they still have to be separated from other waste / they are more expensive than oil-based equivalents.

Exam-Style Questions — pages 229-231

Q1 B *(1 mark)*

Q2 A *(1 mark)*

Q3 a) (i) Radicals are particles that have an unpaired electron *(1 mark)*.

(ii) homolytic fission *(1 mark)*

b) (i) $CH_3CH_3 + Br_2 \rightarrow CH_3CH_2Br + HBr$ *(1 mark)*

(ii) Initiation: $Br_2 \rightarrow 2Br\cdot$ *(1 mark)*
Propagation: $Br\cdot + CH_3CH_3 \rightarrow \cdot CH_2CH_3 + HBr$
$\cdot CH_2CH_3 + Br_2 \rightarrow CH_3CH_2Br + Br\cdot$ *(1 mark)*
Termination: $\cdot CH_2CH_3 + Br\cdot \rightarrow CH_3CH_2Br$
or $\cdot CH_2CH_3 + \cdot CH_2CH_3 \rightarrow C_4H_{10}$ *(1 mark)*

c) Any two from: e.g. CH_3CHBr_2 / CH_3CBr_3 / CH_2BrCBr_3 / $CHBr_2CBr_3$ / CBr_3CBr_3 / CH_2BrCH_2Br / $CHBr_2CHBr_2$ *(1 mark for each up to a maximum of 2 marks)*.

Q4 a) (i)

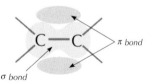

σ bond

(1 mark for diagram, 1 mark for labels)

Always make sure you label any diagram you draw in the exam. You could lose marks if you don't because it's the labels that show you really know what you're talking about.

(ii) The double bond contains two pairs of electrons, so has a really high electron density / the pi bond sticks out above and below the rest of the molecule *(1 mark)*. Electrophiles are attracted to these electron dense regions *(1 mark)*.

b) (i)

(1 mark for correct curly arrows in step 1, 1 mark for correct curly arrow in step 2, 1 one mark for correct dipole shown on Br_2, 1 mark for correct carbocation)

Make sure your curly arrows are all top-notch — they must be going from a pair of electrons/bond to the electron acceptor. Also make sure you've included the dipoles and all the charges. You'll lose marks if these are missing too.

(ii) The solution would go from orange to colourless *(1 mark)*.

c) E.g.

(1 mark)   *(1 mark)*

Q5 a) (i)

(1 mark)

(ii) Octane would have a higher boiling point *(1 mark)*. Octane is a straight-chain molecule. As a result there is more surface contact between octane molecules than between branched 2,2,4-trimethylpentane molecules *(1 mark)*. This means the induced dipole-dipole interactions between the octane molecules are stronger / there are more induced dipole-dipole interactions between the molecules *(1 mark)*. So more energy is required to overcome the induced dipole-dipole interactions and the boiling point is higher *(1 mark)*.

b) $2C_8H_{18} + 25O_2 \rightarrow 16CO_2 + 18H_2O$ /
$C_8H_{18} + 12\frac{1}{2}O_2 \rightarrow 8CO_2 + 9H_2O$ *(1 mark)*

c) With insufficient oxygen, incomplete combustion occurs *(1 mark)*. Incomplete combustion of alkanes produces carbon monoxide (CO) *(1 mark)*. Carbon monoxide binds to haemoglobin in the blood instead of oxygen, limiting the amount of oxygen that can be transported around the body and so leading to oxygen deficiency. This makes CO toxic to humans *(1 mark)*.

Q6 a) (i) Stereoisomerism occurs when molecules have the same structural formula but a different arrangement of atoms in space *(1 mark)*.

(ii) E.g.

(1 mark)

This is the E-isomer *(1 mark)*.

b) (i) An addition polymer *(1 mark)*.

(ii)

$$H_2C=CH\text{—}O\text{—}C(=O)CH_3$$

(1 mark)

c) Advantages: e.g. they won't permanently take up space in landfill / they avoid the need to burn plastics which produces toxic gases / they can be made from renewable materials which decreases our dependency on oil **(1 mark for each, maximum 2 marks)**.

Disadvantages: e.g. they need specific conditions to decompose so need to be sorted from other waste / they're more expensive than oil-based equivalents **(1 mark for each, maximum 2 marks)**.

If you're asked to discuss advantages and disadvantages, make sure you talk about both. If you only mention advantages or only talk about disadvantages you'll lose marks.

Section 2 — Alcohols and Haloalkanes

1. Properties of Alcohols

Page 234 — Application Questions

Q1 a) pentan-2-ol
   b) 2-methylbutan-2-ol
   c) 2,3-dimethylbutan-1-ol
   d) 3-ethyl-2-methylpentane-1,5-diol

That last one is a tricky one... Make sure you have the side chains in alphabetical order and that the name has the lowest possible numbers in it.

Q2 a) secondary
   b) tertiary
   c) primary

Q3 Propan-1-ol, as it has a shorter non-polar carbon chain, so there's more attraction to the polar water molecules (with which the alcohols can form hydrogen bonds).
Octan-1-ol has a larger non-polar carbon chain, so there will be less attraction for the polar water molecules, and it won't mix as easily with water molecules.

Q4 Butan-1-ol will have a higher boiling point than butane. Hydrogen bonding between the molecules in butan-1-ol means that the intermolecular forces between molecules of butan-1-ol are stronger than between the molecules in butane (which only has induced dipole-dipole interactions holding its molecules together). So it will take more energy to break the molecules apart in butan-1-ol.

Page 234 — Fact Recall Questions

Q1 -ol
Q2 A secondary alcohol is an alcohol with the -OH group attached to a carbon with two alkyl groups attached.
Q3

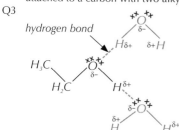

hydrogen bond

2. Reactions of Alcohols

Page 236 — Application Questions

Q1 E.g. 2-methylpropan-2-ol, sodium chloride (NaCl) and a concentrated sulfuric acid catalyst at room temperature.

Q2 *E*-4-methyl-hex-2-ene:

$$\underset{H_3C}{\overset{H}{>}}C=C\underset{H}{\overset{CH(CH_3)CH_2CH_3}{<}}$$

Z-4-methyl-hex-2-ene:

$$\underset{H_3C}{\overset{H}{>}}C=C\underset{CH(CH_3)CH_2CH_3}{\overset{H}{<}}$$

E-3-methyl-hex-3-ene:

$$\underset{H_3C}{\overset{H_3CH_2C}{>}}C=C\underset{CH_2CH_3}{\overset{H}{<}}$$

Z-3-methyl-hex-3-ene:

$$\underset{H_3C}{\overset{H_3CH_2C}{>}}C=C\underset{H}{\overset{CH_2CH_3}{<}}$$

To work out the products of the elimination reaction of an alcohol, first work out what alkenes are formed when the hydrogen atoms on either side of the hydroxyl group are eliminated. Then look to see whether either of these alkene products can form E/Z isomers.

Page 236 — Fact Recall Questions

Q1 a) $ROH + NaX \xrightarrow{\text{H}^+ \text{ (catalyst)}} RX + Na^+ + H_2O$
   b) nucleophilic substitution reaction
Q2 a) $CH_3CH_2OH \rightarrow CH_2CH_2 + H_2O$
   b) ethene and water
   c) E.g. concentrated sulfuric acid / concentrated phosphoric acid.
Q3 Often, two different alkene products can form depending on which side of the hydroxyl group the hydrogen atom is eliminated from. In addition, if the alkene product is able to form *E/Z* isomers, then a mixture of isomers will be formed.

3. Oxidising Alcohols

Page 240 — Application Questions

Q1 a) butanal
   b) methanoic acid
   c) pentan-3-one
   d) hexan-2-one
Q2 a)

$$H\text{—}\underset{H}{\overset{H}{C}}\text{—}\underset{H}{\overset{H}{C}}\text{—}\overset{O}{\overset{\|}{C}}\text{—}\underset{H}{\overset{H}{C}}\text{—}H$$

b)

$$H\text{—}\underset{H}{\overset{H}{C}}\text{—}\underset{H}{\overset{H}{C}}\text{—}\underset{H}{\overset{H}{C}}\text{—}\overset{O}{\overset{\|}{C}}\text{—}H$$

c)

$$H\text{—}\underset{H}{\overset{H}{C}}\text{—}\underset{H}{\overset{H}{C}}\text{—}\underset{H}{\overset{H}{C}}\text{—}\overset{O}{\overset{\|}{C}}\text{—}OH$$

You could also draw the skeletal structures of these molecules.

Page 240 — Fact Recall Questions

Q1 $C_2H_5OH_{(l)} + 3O_{2(g)} \rightarrow 2CO_{2(g)} + 3H_2O_{(g)}$
Q2 a) E.g. Aldehydes have the functional group C=O and have one hydrogen atom and one R group attached to the carbon atom.

b) E.g Ketones have the functional group C=O and have two R groups attached either side of the carbon atom.

c) E.g. Carboxylic acids have the functional group COOH. *As long as you've got the basic answer right, any way that you've chosen to describe the functional groups is fine — you might have written out their formulas, or even drawn them...*

Q3 $R-CH_2-OH + 2[O] \xrightarrow{reflux} R-\overset{\overset{\displaystyle O}{\|}}{C}-OH + H_2O$

4. Haloalkanes
Page 246 — Application Questions
Q1   a)

b)

c)

d)

Your skeletal diagrams may look slightly different, depending on the direction you've drawn the bonds going. It doesn't matter how you've drawn it, as long as you've got the right number of each atom, and they're all joined up in the right way.

Q2

Q3   Reactions A, B and C all involve breaking a carbon-halogen bond. Reaction C would happen the quickest because the C–I bond has the lowest bond enthalpy/is the weakest of all the carbon-halogen bonds. This means that the C–I bond is the easiest to break and therefore the reaction will happen the quickest.

Q4   a) A: bromine
       B: iodine
       C: chlorine
   b) The variables need to be kept the same so you can be sure that the only thing influencing the rate of reaction, and so the time taken for the X to disappear, is the identity of the haloalkane.

Page 246 — Fact Recall Questions
Q1   Haloalkanes contain a carbon atom which has a δ+ charge/is electron deficient, and can attract nucleophiles.
Q2   Nucleophilic substitution reactions are reactions in which a nucleophile attacks a polar molecule and replaces a functional group.
Q3   E.g. sodium hydroxide / potassium hydroxide / water.
Q4   For a hydrolysis reaction to occur the carbon-halogen bond needs to break. The C–F bond is the strongest carbon-halogen bond/is the hardest carbon-halogen bond to break — it has the highest bond enthalpy. So fluoroalkanes are hydrolysed more slowly than other haloalkanes.
Q5 $CH_3CH_2Br + OH^- \rightarrow CH_3CH_2OH + Br^-$
Q6   E.g. You could react the haloalkane with water in the presence of silver nitrate and ethanol in a 50 °C water bath. The colour of the precipitate formed will tell you what type of haloalkane the compound is — if the precipitate is white then the compound is a chloroalkane, if the precipitate is cream then the compound is a bromoalkane, and if the precipitate is yellow then the compound is an iodoalkane.

5. Chlorofluorocarbons
Page 248 — Fact Recall Questions
Q1   A haloalkane that contains only chlorine, fluorine and carbon atoms.
Q2   E.g. $CF_2Cl_2 + h\nu \rightarrow CF_2Cl\bullet + Cl\bullet$
         $Cl\bullet + O_3 \rightarrow ClO\bullet + O_2$
         $ClO\bullet + O \rightarrow Cl\bullet + O_2$
       The chlorine radical is regenerated and can go on to react again.
Q3   E.g. HCFCs / HFCs / hydrocarbons.

6. Global Warming
Page 251 — Fact Recall Questions
Q1   infrared radiation
Q2   E.g. Carbon dioxide (CO_2), water (H_2O) and methane (CH_4).
Q3   Human activities have caused a rise in greenhouse gas concentrations. This has enhanced the greenhouse effect, which means that more heat is being trapped by the Earth's atmosphere and the Earth is getting warmer. This is global warming.
Q4   Any from: e.g. Global warming may cause oceans to expand and ice sheets in polar regions to melt. This will cause sea levels to rise, leading to more flooding. / Global warming could influence ocean currents and wind speeds. This could lead to stormier and less predictable weather. / Global warming could cause a decrease in rainfall in some areas. This will lead to droughts and crop failures, causing famines. / Global warming could cause an increase in rainfall in some areas. This could lead to flooding, which would bring diseases like cholera.
Q5   E.g. creating international treaties such as the Kyoto protocol to limit greenhouse gas emissions / using more renewable energy resources such as by using wind turbines and solar panels / using less non-renewable energy resources such as coal power stations / encouraging the use of more energy-efficient electrical appliances such as energy-saving light bulbs and electric cars.

Exam-style Questions — pages 253-254
1   A *(1 mark)*
     If you draw the molecule out, you'll see there's only one hydrogen atom on the carbon atoms adjacent to the -OH carbon:
     This means only one alkene can form, and since this alkene can't form E/Z isomers, there's only one product.
2   B *(1 mark)*
3   C *(1 mark)*
4   a) (i) $CH_3CH_2Br + OH^- \rightarrow CH_3CH_2OH + Br^-$ *(1 mark)*
         You'd also get the mark if you included the Na+ ions in the equation, like this: $CH_3CH_2Br + NaOH \rightarrow CH_3CH_2OH + NaBr$
       (ii)

       (3 marks, 1 mark for each correct curly arrow and 1 mark for the C–Br dipole correctly shown.)

(iii) The reaction of sodium hydroxide with iodoethane would be quicker than the reaction of bromoethane with sodium hydroxide *(1 mark)*. This is because the C–I bond is weaker than the C–Br bond / the bond enthalpy of the C–I bond is lower than that of the C–Br bond, which means it is more easily broken *(1 mark)*.

b) (i) The hydroxyl groups can form hydrogen bonds with the water molecules *(1 mark)*.

(ii) In butan-1-ol, more of the molecule is a non-polar carbon chain, which doesn't mix easily with water molecules *(1 mark)*.

5 a) Molecule **A** is propan-1-ol *(1 mark)*:

$$H-\overset{\overset{\displaystyle H}{|}}{\underset{\underset{\displaystyle H}{|}}{C}}-\overset{\overset{\displaystyle H}{|}}{\underset{\underset{\displaystyle H}{|}}{C}}-\overset{\overset{\displaystyle H}{|}}{\underset{\underset{\displaystyle H}{|}}{C}}-O-H$$

(1 mark)

If you're asked to draw a displayed formula, remember that you've got to draw all the bonds — even the one between oxygen and hydrogen in the -OH group.

b) Acidified potassium dichromate(VI)/$K_2Cr_2O_7$ and H_2SO_4 *(1 mark)*. Heat under reflux *(1 mark)*.

6 a) Ozone in the atmosphere forms a layer which absorbs UV radiation and acts as a chemical sunscreen *(1 mark)*.

b) CFCs undergo homolytic fission with UV light to form chlorine radicals *(1 mark)*. These chlorine radicals act as catalysts in the breakdown of ozone *(1 mark)*.

c) E.g. $NO\bullet + O_3 \rightarrow NO_2 + O_2$ *(1 mark)*
$NO_2 + O \rightarrow NO\bullet + O_2$ *(1 mark)*
Overall: $O_3 + O \rightarrow 2O_2$ *(1 mark)*

Section 3 — Analysis and Organic Synthesis

1. Infrared Spectroscopy

Pages 258-259 — Application Questions

Q1 a) A (~3000 cm^{-1}, broad) — O–H (carboxylic acid)
B (~1700 cm^{-1}) — C=O

b)

$$H-\overset{\overset{\displaystyle H}{|}}{\underset{\underset{\displaystyle H}{|}}{C}}-\overset{\overset{\displaystyle H}{|}}{\underset{\underset{\displaystyle H}{|}}{C}}-\overset{\overset{\displaystyle O}{||}}{C}-O-H$$

The mass of the carboxylic acid group (COOH) is 45 (12 + 16 + 16 + 1). The M_r of the molecule is 74, so the rest of the molecule has a mass of 74 – 45 = 29. This corresponds to an ethyl group (CH_3CH_2), so the molecule must be propanoic acid.

Q2 E.g. There is a strong, sharp peak at about 1700 cm^{-1}. This indicates that a C=O bond is present in the molecule.

Q3 Spectrum A.
O–H bonds in an alcohol create a strong absorption at around 3200-3600 cm^{-1}. Spectrum A has this absorption and Spectrum B doesn't — so Spectrum A must be propan-2-ol.

Q4

Bond	Frequency / Wavenumber (cm^{-1})
C–C	750 – 1100
C=C	1620 – 1680
C=O	1630 – 1820
C–H	2850 – 3100

Page 259 — Fact Recall Questions

Q1 A beam of IR radiation is passed through a sample of a chemical. Some of the IR radiation is absorbed by the covalent bonds in the molecules, increasing their vibrational energy. Bonds between different atoms absorb different frequencies of IR radiation. Bonds in different places in a molecule absorb different frequencies too. The percentage of IR radiation transmitted at each frequency is plotted to give an IR spectrum.

Q2 E.g. If a person's suspected of drink-driving, they can be breathalysed by the roadside. If it says that the driver's over the limit, they're taken into a police station for a more accurate test using infrared spectroscopy. The amount of ethanol vapour in the driver's breath is found by measuring the intensity of the peak corresponding to the C–H bond in the IR spectrum. / Infrared spectroscopy can be used to monitor the levels of pollutant gases such as CO or NO. The intensity of the peaks corresponding to the C≡O or N=O bonds are used to monitor their levels.

2. Mass Spectrometry

Page 263 — Application Questions

Q1 E.g. CH_3^+ / $CH_3CH_2^+$ / CH_2^+ / $CH_3CH_2CH_2^+$ / OH^+.

Q2 The molecule is propene.

$$\underset{H}{\overset{H}{>}}C=\overset{\overset{\displaystyle H}{|}}{C}-\overset{\overset{\displaystyle H}{|}}{\underset{\underset{\displaystyle H}{|}}{C}}-H$$

This table shows some of the m/z peaks from the mass spectrum and the fragment ions they can be assigned to:

m/z	fragment ion
15	CH_3^+
27	CH_2CH^+
41	$CH_3CCH_2^+$
42	$CH_3CHCH_2^+$ (molecular ion)

Don't forget that you don't have to assign all of these peaks — just as long as you've done enough to be able to prove that it's propene...

Q3 E.g. $CH_3CH_2CHOH^+$ / CH_3CHOH^+.

Page 263 — Fact Recall Questions

Q1 The x-axis tells you the mass/charge ratio and the y-axis tells you the relative abundance of the molecular ion.

Q2 The molecular mass of the compound.

Q3 CH_3^+

3. Combined Techniques

Page 266 — Application Questions

Q1 B
The M peak on the mass spectrum appears at an m/z of 72, so the M_r of the compound will be 72. Both A and B have M_r = 72, but C has M_r = 58, so the compound is not C.
Looking at the IR spectrum, there is an intense peak at about 1700 cm^{-1}. This is the peak for a C=O bond, which shows that the molecule is B, since it has a ketone group (A has no carbonyl group).

Q2 First, work out the empirical formula from the percentage composition:

In 100 g of compound there will be 54.5 g of carbon, 9.01 g of hydrogen and 36.4 g of oxygen.

Use the formula moles = mass ÷ M_r to find the number of moles:

C: $\frac{54.5}{12}$ = 4.54 mol   H: $\frac{9.01}{1}$ = 9.01 mol

O: $\frac{36.4}{16}$ = 2.28 mol

Divide each number of moles by the smallest number (2.28)
C: 2   H: 4   O: 1

The ratio of C : H : O is 2 : 4 : 1, so the empirical formula is C_2H_4O, which has an M_r of [(2 × 12) + (4 × 1) + 16] = 44. Looking at the mass spectrum, the compound has a parent ion peak at m/z = 88, which is twice the mass of the empirical formula. So the molecular formula is $C_4H_8O_2$. The spectrum has a peak at an m/z of 45, which could be a $COOH^+$ fragment, so the compound is likely to be a carboxylic acid. The carboxylic acids with molecular formula of $C_4H_8O_2$ are butanoic acid and 2-methylpropanoic acid:

H H H O
H—C—C—C—C—OH
H H H

H CH₃ O
H—C—C—C—OH
H H

As well has the $COOH^+$ fragment, butanoic acid will have the fragment CH_2COOH^+ (59 m/z), and there is no fragment of equivalent mass formed by 2-methylpropanoic acid. Meanwhile 2-methylpropanoic acid will form the fragment $CHCOOH^+$ (58 m/z), and there is no fragment of equivalent mass formed by butanoic acid. The mass spectrum has a peak at 59 m/z, but no peak at 58 m/z.
This shows that the compound is **butanoic acid**.

4. Practical Techniques in Organic Synthesis
Page 269 — Application Questions
Q1 E.g. Redistil the mixture, as hexane will distil out of the mixture at a lower temperature than ethanol, so the two liquids can be collected separately. / Use a separating funnel to separate hexane (insoluble in water) from ethanol (soluble in water). You'll be left with an organic layer containing hexane and an aqueous layer containing water and ethanol. The ethanol can be separated from the water by redistillation (as ethanol has a lower boiling point than water) or can be dried using an anhydrous salt, e.g. $MgSO_4$ or $CaCl_2$, which can then be removed by filtration.
Q2 The student could carry out the reaction in a distillation apparatus, as the product would distil out of the reaction mixture as it formed, and so it wouldn't be over-oxidised.

Page 269 — Fact Recall Questions
Q1

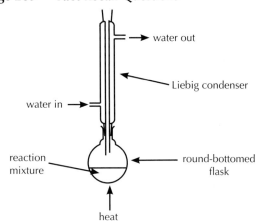

Q2 The different boiling points of the compounds.
Q3 E.g. anhydrous magnesium sulfate ($MgSO_4$) and anhydrous calcium chloride ($CaCl_2$).

5. Organic Synthesis
Page 272 — Application Questions
Q1 Carboxylic acid, alkene and a haloalkane.
Q2 a) Sodium chloride (NaCl) and a concentrated acid catalyst (e.g. H_2SO_4) at room temperature.
    b) Concentrated acid (e.g. H_2SO_4 or H_3PO_4) and heat.
    c)
    H Cl Cl H
    H—C—C—C—C—H
    H CH₃ H H

Q3 E.g.
    H H H H H
    H—C—C—C—C—C—Br
    H H H H H

    warm NaOH or
    KOH, H_2O
    reflux
    ↓

    H H H H H
    H—C—C—C—C—C—OH
    H H H H H

    $K_2Cr_2O_7$, H_2SO_4
    reflux
    ↓

    H H H H O
    H—C—C—C—C—C—OH
    H H H H H

Page 272 — Fact Recall Questions

Q1 a) an alkene
   b) an aldehyde
   c) a carboxylic acid
Q2 a) nucleophilic substitution
   b) radical substitution
   c) E.g. nucleophilic substitution / dehydration / elimination / oxidation
Q3 H_2, nickel catalyst, 150 °C.
Q4 It would be oxidised from to an aldehyde and then to a carboxylic acid.

Exam-style Questions — pages 274-276

Q1 D *(1 mark)*
Q2 B *(1 mark)*
Q3 B *(1 mark)*
Q4 a) hex-3-ene *(1 mark)*
   b) e.g. steam *(1 mark)*, H_3PO_4 catalyst, 300 °C, 60-70 atm *(1 mark)*
   c) E.g. the IR spectrum of hexan-3-ol would have a peak at about 3200-3600 cm^{-1} that is not in the spectrum of hex-3-ene, due to the presence of the -OH group / The IR spectrum of hex-3-ene would have a peak at about 1620-1680 cm^{-1} that is not in the spectrum of hexan-3-ol, due to the presence of the C=C bond *(1 mark)*.
   d) E.g.

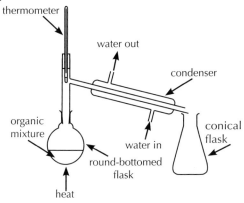

thermometer
water out
condenser
organic mixture
water in
conical flask
round-bottomed flask
heat

(3 marks — 1 mark for correct apparatus, 1 mark for a working system, e.g. open system, thermometer bulb level with outlet, correct direction of water flow, 1 mark for correct labels.)

   e) E.g. the mass spectrum shows that hexan-3-ol has been synthesised *(1 mark)*. The M peak is at $m/z = 102$, which is the same as the relative formula mass of hexan-2-ol *(1 mark)*. There is also a peak at $m/z = 73$ which matches the mass of a $CH_3CH_2CH_2CHOH^+$ fragment, and a peak at $m/z = 59$ which matches the mass of a $CH_3CH_2CHOH^+$ fragment *(1 mark)*.

Q5 a)

H-C-C-OH (structure)

conc. H_2SO_4 or H_3PO_4, heat

$C=C$ (structure)

Cl_2, 20 °C

Cl-C-C-Cl (structure)

(4 marks — 1 mark for correct synthetic route going via an alkene, 1 mark for correct reagents and conditions in step 1, 1 mark for correct reagents in step 2, 1 mark for correct intermediate.)

   b) E.g. redistillation *(1 mark)*.

Q6 a) If a person's suspected of drink-driving, they may be breathalysed using infrared spectroscopy *(1 mark)*. The amount of ethanol vapour in the driver's breath is found by measuring the intensity of the peak corresponding to the C–H bond in the IR spectrum *(1 mark)*.
   b) You can tell similar molecules apart using mass spectrometry because they won't produce exactly the same set of fragments *(1 mark)*.
   c) The molecular ion peak has an m/z of 58 and so the M_r of the compound is 58 *(1 mark)*.
   The peak at $m/z = 15$ could be caused by a CH_3^+ fragment ion. The peak at $m/z = 29$ could be caused by a $CH_3CH_2^+$ fragment ion. The peak at $m/z = 43$ could be caused by a $CH_3CH_2CH_2^+$ fragment ion. *(1 mark for each correctly assigned fragment up to a maximum of 2 marks)*
   The molecule is butane.

   H-C-C-C-C-H (butane structure)   *(1 mark)*

   There are only two hydrocarbons with an M_r of 58 — butane and 2-methylpropane. Molecule J has a strong mass spectrum peak at $m/z = 29$, so it can't be 2-methylpropane because that doesn't have a peak there.

   d) The infrared spectrum shows a strong broad peak at about 3300 cm^{-1}, which corresponds to an O–H group on an alcohol *(1 mark)*. Acidified potassium dichromate(VI) will oxidise secondary alcohols under reflux to ketones — so molecule **K** must be a secondary alcohol *(1 mark)*. The only secondary alcohol with an M_r of 74 is butan-2-ol *(1 mark)*.
   So molecule **K** is butan-2-ol.

   H-C-C-C-C-H (butan-2-ol structure)   *(1 mark)*

Glossary

A

Accurate result
A result that is close to the true answer.

Acid
A substance that releases hydrogen ions (H^+) in aqueous solution (a proton donor).

Activation energy
The minimum amount of kinetic energy that particles need to have in order to react when they collide.

Addition polymer
A long-chain molecule made by lots of small alkene molecules adding together.

Alcohol
A substance with the general formula $C_nH_{2n+1}OH$.

Aldehyde
A substance with the general formula $C_nH_{2n}O$ which has a hydrogen and one alkyl group attached to the carbonyl carbon atom.

Alicyclic compound
An organic compound that contains carbon and hydrogen joined together in a non-aromatic ring.

Aliphatic compound
An organic compound that contains carbon and hydrogen joined together in straight chains, branched chains or non-aromatic rings.

Alkali
A base that is soluble in water and releases hydroxide ions (OH^-) in aqueous solution.

Alkaline earth metal
An element in Group 2 of the periodic table.

Alkane
A hydrocarbon with the general formula C_nH_{2n+2}.

Alkene
A hydrocarbon with the general formula C_nH_{2n} and containing at least one carbon-carbon double bond.

Alkyl group
A hydrocarbon fragment with the general formula C_nH_{2n+1}.

Anhydrous salt
A salt that doesn't contain any water of crystallisation.

Anomalous result
A result that doesn't fit in with the pattern of the other results in a set of data.

Antacid
A substance which neutralises stomach acid.

Aromatic compound
An organic compound that contains a benzene ring.

Atom
A neutral particle made up of protons and neutrons in a central nucleus, and electrons orbiting the nucleus.

Atom economy
The proportion of reactant atoms that become part of the desired product, expressed as a percentage.

Atomic (proton) number
The number of protons in the nucleus of an atom.

Atomic radius
The distance between the nucleus of an atom and its outermost electrons.

Average bond enthalpy
The energy needed to break one mole of a bond in the gas phase, averaged over the different compounds that the bond is found in.

Avogadro constant
6.02×10^{23} — the number of particles in 1 mole of a substance.

B

Balanced equation
An equation that has the same number of each type of atom and the same overall charge on each side.

Base
A substance that removes hydrogen ions (H^+) from an aqueous solution (a proton acceptor).

Biodegradable
A substance that naturally decomposes because organisms can digest it.

Bohr model
A model for the structure of an atom proposed by Niels Bohr. He suggested that electrons only exist in fixed orbitals (shells) and not anywhere else.

Boltzmann distribution
A theoretical model that describes the distribution of kinetic energies of molecules in a gas.

Bond enthalpy
The energy required to break a bond between two atoms. Usually given as an 'average bond enthalpy' (an average value for the particular bond over the range of compounds it is found in).

Bond fission
The process of breaking a covalent bond.

C

Carbocation
An organic ion containing a positively charged carbon atom.

Carbon skeleton
The arrangement of all the carbon atoms in an organic compound.

Carbonyl compound
An organic compound that contains a carbon-oxygen double bond.

Carboxylic acid
A substance which has a COOH group attached to the end of a carbon chain.

Catalyst
A substance that increases the rate of a reaction by providing an alternative reaction pathway with a lower activation energy. The catalyst is chemically unchanged at the end of the reaction.

Catalytic converter
A device fitted to car exhausts to remove pollutant gases such as carbon monoxide, nitrogen monoxide and unburnt hydrocarbons.

Categoric data
Data that can be sorted into categories.

Causal link
The relationship between two variables where a change in one variable causes a change in the other.

Chain isomer
A molecule that contains the same atoms as another molecule but has a different arrangement of the carbon skeleton.

Charge density
The amount of charge in relation to the size of an ion.

Chlorofluorocarbon (CFC)
A haloalkane containing fluorine and chlorine and no hydrogen. CFCs contribute to ozone depletion.

Cis-trans isomerism
A special type of E/Z isomerism where two of the groups attached to the carbon atoms around the C=C double bond are the same.

Closed system
A system where nothing can get in or out.

Collision theory
The theory that a reaction will not take place between two particles unless they collide in the right direction and with at least a certain minimum amount of kinetic energy.

Complete combustion
Burning a substance completely in an excess of oxygen. Complete combustion of a hydrocarbon will produce carbon dioxide and water only.

Concentration
A measure of how many moles (or how many grams) of a substance are dissolved in a volume of solution.

Continuous data
Data that can have any value on a scale.

Coordinate (dative covalent) bond
A covalent bond formed when one atom provides both of the shared electrons. Also called a dative covalent bond.

Correlation
The relationship between two variables.

Covalent bond
The strong electrostatic attraction between a shared pair of electrons and the nuclei of the bonded atoms.

Curly arrow
An arrow used in a reaction mechanism to show the movement of a pair of electrons.

Cycloalkane
A type of alkane which has one or more non-aromatic carbon rings.

Dative covalent bond
A covalent bond formed when one atom provides both of the shared electrons. Also called a coordinate bond.

Dehydration reaction
A reaction in which water is eliminated from an organic molecule.

Delocalised electron
An electron that is not attached to a specific atom.

Dependent variable
The variable that you measure in an experiment.

Dipole
A difference in charge between two atoms caused by a shift in the electron density in a bond.

Discrete data
Data that can only take certain values.

Displacement reaction
A reaction where a more reactive element pushes out (displaces) a less reactive element from an ionic solution.

Displayed formula
A way of representing a molecule that shows how all the atoms are arranged, and all the bonds between them.

Disproportionation
When an element is both oxidised and reduced in a single chemical reaction.

Distillation
A technique used to separate liquids with different boiling points. A mixture is gently heated so that substances evaporate and can be collected in order of increasing boiling point.

Drying agent
An anhydrous salt used to remove small amounts of water from an organic mixture. Drying agents include anhydrous magnesium sulfate ($MgSO_4$) and anhydrous calcium chloride ($CaCl_2$).

Dynamic equilibrium
In a reversible reaction, dynamic equilibrium is reached when the concentrations of reactants and products are constant, and the forwards reaction and the backwards reaction are going at the same rate.

E/Z isomerism
A type of stereoisomerism that is caused by the restricted rotation about a carbon-carbon double bond. Each of the carbon atoms must be attached to two different groups.

Electron
A subatomic particle with a relative charge of 1− and a relative mass of 1/2000, located in orbitals around the nucleus.

Electron configuration
The number of electrons that an atom or ion has and how they are arranged.

Electron shell
A region of an atom with a fixed energy that contains electrons orbiting the nucleus.

Electron shell repulsion theory
The theory that in a molecule lone pair/lone pair bond angles are the biggest, lone pair/bonding pair bond angles are the second biggest and bonding pair/bonding pair bond angles are the smallest.

Electron shielding
When inner electrons effectively screen the outer electrons from the pull of the nucleus.

Electronegativity
The ability of an atom to attract the bonding electrons in a covalent bond.

Electrophile
An electron-pair acceptor.

Electrophilic addition
A reaction mechanism where a double bond in an alkene opens up and atoms are added to the carbon atoms.

Elimination reaction
A reaction in which a pair of atoms or groups of atoms are removed from an organic molecule.

Empirical formula
A formula giving the simplest whole number ratio of atoms of each element in a compound.

Endothermic reaction
A reaction that absorbs energy in the form of heat (ΔH is positive).

Enthalpy change
The heat energy transferred in a reaction at constant pressure (ΔH).

Enthalpy profile diagram
A graph showing how the enthalpy changes during a chemical reaction.

Equilibrium constant, K_c
A ratio worked out from the concentration of the products and reactants once a reversible reaction has reached equilibrium.

Exothermic reaction
A reaction that gives out energy in the form of heat (ΔH is negative).

False positive
A result that suggests the presence of something (e.g. ions) that isn't actually there.

First ionisation energy
The energy needed to remove 1 mole of electrons from 1 mole of gaseous atoms.

Functional group
The group of atoms that is responsible for the characteristic reactions of a molecule (e.g. –OH for alcohols, –COOH for carboxylic acids, C=C for alkenes).

Functional group isomer
A molecule that has the same molecular formula as another molecule, but with the atoms arranged into different functional groups.

General formula
An algebraic formula that can describe any member of a homologous series of compounds.

Giant covalent lattice
A structure consisting of a huge network of covalently bonded atoms. Also called a macromolecular structure.

Giant ionic lattice structure
A regular repeated structure made up of oppositely charged ions strongly attracted to each other in all directions.

Giant metallic lattice structure
A regular structure consisting of closely packed positive metal ions in a sea of delocalised electrons.

Global warming
The warming of the planet due to increased concentrations of greenhouse gases in the troposphere, which enhance the greenhouse effect.

Gradient
The steepness of a line.

Greenhouse effect
The absorption and re-emission of infrared radiation by greenhouse gases in the troposphere.

Greenhouse gas
A gas that absorbs and emits infrared radiation and so contributes to the greenhouse effect.

Group
A column in the periodic table.

Halide
A negative ion of a halogen.

Haloalkane
An alkane with at least one halogen atom in place of a hydrogen atom.

Halogen
An element in Group 7 of the periodic table.

Hess's Law
The total enthalpy change of a reaction is always the same, no matter which route is taken.

Heterogeneous catalyst
A catalyst which is in a different physical state from the reactants of the reaction it's catalysing.

Heterolytic fission
When a covalent bond breaks unevenly, with one of the bonding atoms receiving both of the electrons from the bonded pair, resulting in the formation of a positively charged cation and a negatively charged anion.

Homogeneous catalyst
A catalyst which is in the same physical state as the reactants of the reaction it's catalysing.

Homologous series
A family of organic compounds that have the same general formula and similar chemical properties.

Homolytic fission
When a covalent bond breaks evenly, with each bonding atom receiving one electron from the bonded pair, resulting in the formation of two electrically uncharged radicals.

Hydrated salt
A salt that contains water of crystallisation.

Hydrocarbon
A molecule that only contains hydrogen and carbon atoms.

Hydrogen bond
The strongest intermolecular force. It occurs when polarised covalent bonds cause hydrogen atoms to form weak bonds with lone pairs of electrons on the fluorine, nitrogen or oxygen atoms of other molecules.

Hydrolysis reaction
A reaction where molecules are split apart by water molecules. The water molecules are also split into hydrogen ions (H^+) and hydroxide ions (OH^-).

Incomplete combustion
Burning a substance in a poor supply of oxygen. Incomplete combustion of a hydrocarbon produces carbon monoxide, water and sometimes carbon and carbon dioxide.

Independent variable
The variable that you change in an experiment.

Indicator
A substance that changes colour at a certain pH.

Induced dipole-dipole interactions
A type of intermolecular force caused by temporary dipoles, which causes all atoms and molecules to be attracted to each other. Also called London (dispersion) forces.

Infrared (IR) spectroscopy
An analytical technique used to identify the functional groups present in a molecule, by measuring the infrared absorption frequencies of its bonds.

Intermolecular forces
Forces between molecules, e.g. induced dipole-dipole forces, permanent dipole-dipole forces and hydrogen bonding.

Ion
A charged particle formed when one or more electrons are lost or gained by an atom or molecule.

Ionic bond
An electrostatic attraction between positive and negative ions.

Ionic equation
An equation which only shows the reacting particles of a reaction involving ions.

Ionisation
The removal of one or more electrons from an atom or molecule, resulting in an ion forming.

Isotope
One of two or more forms of an element with the same number of protons but different numbers of neutrons and masses.

Isotopic abundance
The relative amount of a particular isotope occurring in a sample of an element.

Ketone
A substance with the general formula $C_nH_{2n}O$ which has two alkyl groups attached to the carbonyl carbon atom.

Lattice
A regular structure made up of atoms or ions.

Le Chatelier's principle
If there's a change in concentration, pressure or temperature, the equilibrium will move to help counteract the change.

Macromolecular structure
A structure consisting of a huge network of covalently bonded atoms. Also called a giant covalent lattice.

Mass number
The total number of protons and neutrons in the nucleus of an atom.

Mass spectrometry
An analytical technique used to find the structure of a molecule by measuring the masses of the ions it produces when it's bombarded with electrons.

Mass spectrum
A chart produced by a mass spectrometer.

Model
A simplified picture or representation of a real physical situation.

Molar mass
The mass of one mole of something.

Molar ratio
The ratio of the number of moles of each reactant and product in a balanced chemical equation.

Mole
The unit of amount of substance. One mole is roughly 6.02×10^{23} particles (the Avogadro constant).

Molecular formula
A way of representing molecules that shows the actual number of atoms of each element in a molecule.

Molecular ion
An ion made up of a group of atoms with an overall charge.

Monomer
A small molecule which is used to make a polymer.

Neutralisation reaction
A reaction between an acid and a base to produce a salt and water.

Neutron
A subatomic particle with a charge of 0 and a relative mass of 1, located in the nucleus of an atom.

Noble gas
An element in Group 0 of the periodic table. These elements are extremely stable because they have a full outer electron shell.

Nomenclature
A fancy word for naming organic compounds.

Nuclear model of the atom
A model for the structure of an atom proposed by Rutherford. He suggested that atoms consist of a small positively charged nucleus surrounded by a cloud of negatively charged electrons.

Nucleophile
An electron-pair donor.

Nucleophilic substitution reaction
A reaction where a nucleophile attacks a polar molecule and replaces a functional group in that molecule.

Nucleus
The central part of an atom or ion, made up of protons and neutrons.

Orbital
A region of a sub-shell that contains a maximum of 2 electrons with opposite spins.

Ordered / ordinal data
Categoric data where the categories can be put in order.

Oxidation
Loss of electrons.

Oxidation number
The total number of electrons an element has donated or accepted. Also called an oxidation state.

Oxidising agent
Something that accepts electrons and gets reduced.

Peer review
The evaluation of a scientific report by other scientists who are experts in the same area (peers). They go through it bit by bit, examining the methods and data, and checking it's all clear and logical.

Percentage yield
The amount of product that is actually obtained during a reaction expressed as a percentage of the amount of product that should form.

Period
A row in the periodic table.

Periodic table
A table of the elements arranged in order of increasing atomic number and organised into periods and groups.

Periodicity
The trends in physical and chemical properties of elements as you go across the periodic table.

Permanent dipole-dipole interactions
Intermolecular forces that exist because the difference in electronegativities in a polar bond causes weak electrostatic forces of attraction between molecules.

Pi (π-) bond
A type of bond formed when two p orbitals overlap sideways.

Plum pudding model
A model for the structure of an atom proposed by Thomson. He suggested that atoms consist of a positively charged sphere with negatively charged electrons embedded in them.

Polar bond
A covalent bond where a difference in electronegativity has caused a shift in electron density in the bond.

Polar molecule
A molecule containing polar bonds that are arranged so that the dipoles don't cancel each other out, causing an overall dipole to be created across the molecule.

Polymer
A long molecule formed from lots of smaller molecules (monomers) joined together.

Positional isomer
A molecule with the same molecular formula as another molecule but with the functional group in a different position.

Precise result
A result that can be consistently reproduced in independent experiments.

Proton
A subatomic particle with a relative charge of 1+ and a relative mass of 1, located in the nucleus of an atom.

Proton (atomic) number
The number of protons in the nucleus of an atom.

Q

Quantum model
The currently accepted model for the structure of an atom, where particles' positions are predicted by probabilities.

R

Radical
A particle with an unpaired electron, written like this — $Cl\bullet$ or $CH_3\bullet$.

Random error
The uncertainty in a measurement that results from random variations between repeated tests.

Reaction rate
The change in the amount of reactants or products per unit time.

Redistillation
A technique to purify a mixture of liquids that all have different boiling points. A mixture is gently heated so that substances evaporate and can be collected in order of increasing boiling point.

Redox reaction
A reaction where reduction and oxidation happen simultaneously.

Reducing agent
Something that donates electrons and gets oxidised.

Reduction
Gain of electrons.

Refluxing
Heating a reaction mixture in such a way that you boil it without losing volatile solvents, reactants or products. Any vaporised compounds cool, condense and drip back into the reaction mixture.

Relative atomic mass
The average mass of an atom of an element compared to 1/12 of the mass of an atom of carbon-12.

Relative formula mass
The average mass of a molecule or formula unit compared to 1/12 of the mass of an atom of carbon-12.

Relative isotopic mass
The mass of an atom of an isotope of an element compared to 1/12 of the mass of an atom of carbon-12.

Relative molecular mass
The average mass of a molecule compared to 1/12 of the mass of an atom of carbon-12.

S

Salt
A compound formed when the hydrogen in an acid molecule is replaced by a metal ion or ammonium ion.

Saturated hydrocarbon
A hydrocarbon where all the carbon-carbon bonds are single bonds.

Separation
A technique to separate the water-soluble impurities out of an organic mixture. The aqueous and organic solutions can be separated as they are immiscible, and separate out into two distinct layers due to their different densities.

Sigma (σ-) bond
A type of bond formed when two orbitals overlap directly between the bonded atoms.

Silver nitrate test
A test that uses silver nitrate to identify halide ions in a solution.

Simple molecular structure
A compound with strong covalent bonds within its molecules but weak forces between its molecules.

Skeletal formula
A simplified organic formula which only shows the carbon skeleton and associated functional groups.

Specific heat capacity
The amount of heat energy it takes to raise the temperature of 1 g of a given substance by 1 K.

Spin
A type of momentum possessed by an electron. Spin can either be 'down' or 'up'.

Standard conditions
100 kPa (about 1 atm) pressure and a temperature of 298 K.

Standard enthalpy change of combustion
The enthalpy change when 1 mole of a substance is completely burned in oxygen under standard conditions with all reactants and products in their standard states ($\Delta_c H^\circ$).

Standard enthalpy change of formation
The enthalpy change when 1 mole of a compound is formed from its elements in their standard states under standard conditions ($\Delta_f H^\ominus$).

Standard enthalpy change of neutralisation
The enthalpy change when an acid and an alkali react together to form 1 mole of water, under standard conditions ($\Delta_{neut} H^\ominus$).

Standard enthalpy change of reaction
The enthalpy change when a reaction occurs in the molar quantities shown in the chemical equation, under standard conditions ($\Delta_r H^\ominus$).

Standard solution
A solution with a precisely known concentration.

Standard state
A substance's physical state under standard conditions (100 kPa and 298 K).

State symbol
A symbol placed after a chemical in an equation that tells you what state of matter it is in.

Stereoisomer
A molecule that has the same structural formula as another molecule but its atoms are arranged differently in space.

Strong acid/base
An acid/base that almost completely ionises in an aqueous solution.

Structural formula
A way of representing molecules that shows the atoms carbon by carbon, with the attached hydrogens and functional groups.

Structural isomer
A molecule with the same molecular formula as another molecule, but with the atoms connected in a different way.

Sub-shell
A sub-division of an energy level (shell). Sub-shells may be s, p, d or f sub-shells.

Substitution reaction
A reaction where some atoms from one reactant are swapped with atoms from another reactant.

Successive ionisation energy
The energy needed to remove 1 mole of each subsequent electron from each ion in 1 mole of positively charged gaseous ions.

Synthetic route
A set of reactions showing how you can get from one compound to another, including the reagents, conditions and any intermediate products.

Systematic error
An error in a measurement that happens every time you repeat an experiment. It may be caused by the set-up or the piece of equipment that has been used.

Tangent
A line that just touches a curve and has the same gradient as the curve does at that point.

Theoretical yield
The mass of product that should be formed in a chemical reaction, if no reactant or product is 'lost'.

Titration
A type of experiment used to find the concentration of a solution. It involves gradually adding one solution to a known volume of another until the reaction between the two is complete.

Unsaturated hydrocarbon
A hydrocarbon with one or more carbon-carbon double bonds, carbon-carbon triple bonds or an aromatic group.

Valid result
A result which answers the question it was intended to answer.

Van der Waals forces
A term referring to both induced dipole-dipole interactions and permanent dipole-dipole interactions.

Variable
A quantity that has the potential to change.

Volatility
A substance's tendency to evaporate (turn into a gas).

Water of crystallisation
The water contained in an ionic lattice.

Weak acid/base
An acid/base that only slightly ionises in an aqueous solution.

Y

Yield
The amount of product you get from a reaction.

Acknowledgements

Photograph acknowledgements

Cover Photo **Laguna Design**/Science Photo Library, p 1 **Charles D. Winters**/Science Photo Library, p 2 (top) **Science Photo Library**, p 3 © **Nickos**/iStockphoto.com, p 4 (bottom) **Martin Bond**/Science Photo Library, p 7 **Andrew Lambert Photography**/Science Photo Library, p 8 © **Ximagination**/iStockphoto.com, p 9 **Dorling Kindersley/UIG**/Science Photo Library, p 10 (top) **Trevor Clifford Photography**/Science Photo Library, p 10 (bottom) **Andrew Lambert Photography**/Science Photo Library, p 12 (top) **Science Photo Library**, p 12 (bottom) **Martyn F. Chillmaid**/Science Photo Library, p 13 **Martyn F. Chillmaid**/Science Photo Library, p 22 **Gustoimages**/Science Photo Library, p 30 **Science Photo Library**, p 31 **Prof. Peter Fowler**/Science Photo Library, p 32 **Charles D. Winters**/Science Photo Library, p 34 **Food & Drug Administration**/Science Photo Library, p 37 **Andrew Lambert Photography**/Science Photo Library, p 39 **Science Photo Library**, p 42 **Andrew Lambert Photography**/Science Photo Library, p 48 **Science Photo Library**, p 49 **Science Photo Library**, p 51 © **TMMPhotography**/iStockphoto.com, p 53 **Charles D. Winters**/Science Photo Library, p 57 **Charles D. Winters**/Science Photo Library, p 60 **Andrew Lambert Photography**/Science Photo Library, p 66 **Andrew Lambert Photography**/Science Photo Library, p 67 **Martyn F. Chillmaid**/Science Photo Library, p 68 **Andrew Lambert Photography**/Science Photo Library, p 69 (top) **Andrew Lambert Photography**/Science Photo Library, p 69 (bottom) **Andrew Lambert Photography**/Science Photo Library, p 70 © **alexhstock**/iStockphoto.com, p 71 **Andrew Lambert Photography**/Science Photo Library, p 72 (top) © **sergio_p**/iStockphoto.com, p 72 (bottom) © **Tzsolt**/iStockphoto.com, p 74 **Andrew Lambert Photography**/Science Photo Library, p 77 **Martyn F. Chillmaid**/Science Photo Library, p 78 **Martyn F. Chillmaid**/Science Photo Library, p 80 © **dina2001**/iStockphoto.com, p 82 **Robert Brook**/Science Photo Library, p 83 **Charles D. Winters**/Science Photo Library, p 84 **Martyn F. Chillmaid**/Science Photo Library, p 88 **Charles D. Winters**/Science Photo Library, p 96 **Science Photo Library**, p 97 **Science Photo Library**, p 98 **Charles D. Winters**/Science Photo Library, p 99 **Bill Beatty, Visuals Unlimited**/Science Photo Library, p 100 (top) **GIPhotoStock**/Science Photo Library, p 100 (bottom) **GIPhotoStock**/Science Photo Library, p 103 © **JeffreyRasmussen**/iStockphoto.com, p 106 **Dr Tim Evans**/Science Photo Library, p 109 **Omikron**/Science Photo Library, p 112 © **Epsilon5th**/iStockphoto.com, p 114 **Andrew Lambert Photography**/Science Photo Library, p 121 **Ria Novosti**/Science Photo Library, p 122 (top left) **Charles D. Winters**/Science Photo Library, p 122 (top right) **Charles D. Winters**/Science Photo Library, p 122 (bottom) **E. R. Degginger**/Science Photo Library, p 125 © **cerae**/iStockphoto.com, p 131 © **ekinsdesigns**/iStockphoto.com, p 132 © **wertorer**/iStockphoto.com, p 134 © **Digiphoto**/iStockphoto.com, p 136 (top left) **Martyn F. Chillmaid**/Science Photo Library, p 136 (top right) **Andrew Lambert Photography**/Science Photo Library, p 136 (bottom) **Andrew Lambert Photography**/Science Photo Library, p 139 **Andrew Lambert Photography**/Science Photo Library, p 140 **Andrew Lambert Photography**/Science Photo Library, p 141 **Martyn F. Chillmaid**/Science Photo Library, p 142 (top) **Andrew Lambert Photography**/Science Photo Library, p 142 (bottom) **Andrew Lambert Photography**/Science Photo Library, p 147 **Science Photo Library**, p 148 **Charles D. Winters**/Science Photo Library, p 159 **Charles D. Winters**/Science Photo Library, p 160 **Martyn F. Chillmaid**/Science Photo Library, p 168 **Science Photo Library**, p 172 **Emmeline Watkins**/Science Photo Library, p 177 **Science Photo Library**, p 179 **Charles D. Winters**/Science Photo Library, p 180 **Andrew Lambert Photography**/Science Photo Library, p 190 **Laguna Design**/Science Photo Library, p 196 **Andrew Lambert Photography**/Science Photo Library, p 199 **Andrew Lambert Photography**/Science Photo Library, p 204 **Adam Hart-Davis**/Science Photo Library, p 205 **Martyn F. Chillmaid**/Science Photo Library, p 207 © **dehooks**/iStockphoto.com, p 211 **Martyn F. Chillmaid**/Science Photo Library, p 213 **Martyn F. Chillmaid**/Science Photo Library, p 216 **Science Photo Library**, p 219 **CC Studio**/Science Photo Library, p 220 **Andrew Lambert Photography**/Science Photo Library, p 221 **Ria Novosti**/Science Photo Library, p 227 **Sheila Terry**/Science Photo Library, p 233 **Science Photo Library**, p 238 © **ScantyNebula**/iStockphoto.com, p 239 (top) **Andrew Lambert Photography**/Science Photo Library, p 239 (bottom) **Martyn F. Chillmaid**/Science Photo Library, p 240 (top) **Andrew Lambert Photography**/Science Photo Library, p 240 (bottom) **Andrew Lambert Photography**/Science Photo Library, p 245 **Andrew Lambert Photography**/Science Photo Library, p 248 (top) **NASA**/Science Photo Library, p 248 (bottom) **NASA/Goddard Space Flight Center**/Science Photo Library, p 258 **Ria Novosti**/Science Photo Library, p 260 **Gustoimages**/Science Photo Library, p 267 **Andrew Lambert Photography**/Science Photo Library, p 269 **Science Photo Library**, p 282 **Jon Stokes**/Science Photo Library, p 286 **Science Photo Library**

Index